T0151990

Collected Works of Roger Sherman

ROGER SHERMAN

COLLECTED WORKS OF

Roger Sherman

Edited and with an Introduction by
Mark David Hall

Liberty Fund
INDIANAPOLIS

Introduction, compilation, and index © 2016 by Liberty Fund, Inc.

Frontispiece: Portrait of Roger Sherman by Ralph Earl (1751–1801). Yale University Art Gallery.

16 17 18 19 20 21 C 05 04 03 02 01
16 17 18 19 20 21 P 05 04 03 02 01

Library of Congress Cataloging-in-Publication Data
Names: Sherman, Roger, 1721–1793, author. | Hall, Mark David, 1966– editor.
Title: Collected works of Roger Sherman /
edited and with an introduction by Mark David Hall.
Description: Indianapolis : Liberty Fund, [2016] |
Includes bibliographical references and index.
Identifiers: LCCN 2015048805 |
ISBN 9780865978935 (hardcover : alk. paper) |
ISBN 9780865978942 (pbk. : alk. paper)
Subjects: LCSH: Sherman, Roger, 1721–1793—Correspondence. |
Statesmen—United States—Biography. |
United States. Declaration of Independence—Signers—Biography. |
United States. Continental Congress—Biography. |
Connecticut—Politics and government—1775–1865. |
United States—Politics and government—1775–1783.
Classification: LCC E302.6.S5 A4 2016 | DDC 973.3092—dc23
LC record available at http://lccn.loc.gov/2015048805

Liberty Fund, Inc.
8335 Allison Pointe Trail, Suite 300
Indianapolis, Indiana 46250-1684

To Anna Joy Hall, of whom I am very proud.

Contents

Introduction   xiii
Acknowledgments   xxi
A Note on the Texts   xxiii

Early Writings   1

Selections from Roger Sherman's Almanacs, 1750–1758, 1760–1761   3
"A Caveat against Injustice, by Philoeunomos," 1752   39
Letter to William Samuel Johnson, December 5, 1766   50
Letter to Rebecca Sherman, May 30, 1770   52

Connecticut Politics and Law   53

Susquehannah Controversy   59
    Article from *The Connecticut Journal,* April 8, 1774   60
    Unpublished Article, 1776   65
Revision of State Laws   69
    Letter to Richard Law, July 25, 1783   70
    Letter from Benjamin Huntington to Roger Sherman,
       February 11, 1784   73
    Selections from *Acts and Laws of the State of Connecticut,* 1784   74
Selected Judicial Opinions   131
    Arabas v. Ivers, 1784   132
    Symsbury Case, 1785   135
    Hinckley v. Willson, 1787   137

The War for Independence   139

Instructions from the Town of New Haven to Its Delegates
    Regarding the Stamp Act, 1765   143

Letter to Matthew Griswold, January 11, 1766   145
Letter to William Samuel Johnson, December 5, 1766 (excerpt)   147
Letter from Roger Sherman et al. to Merchants, 1770   148
Letter to Thomas Cushing, April 30, 1772   150
Excerpts from the Diary of John Adams, 1774 and 1775   152
Letter from Eliphalet Dyer, Roger Sherman, and Silas Deane to
    Governor Jonathan Trumbull Sr., October 10, 1774   154
Declaration and Resolves of the First Continental Congress,
    October 14, 1774   157
Articles of Association, October 20, 1774   162
Address to the People of Great Britain, October 21, 1774   167
Petition of Congress to the King, October 25, 1774   174
Letter to David Wooster, June 23, 1775   181
Letter to Jonathan Trumbull Sr., June 28, 1775   183
Letter to Joseph Trumbull, July 6, 1775   185
Letter to William Williams, July 28, 1775   187
Instructions Penned by John Adams, George Wythe, and
    Roger Sherman to a Congressional Commission to Canada,
    March 20, 1776   189
Declaration of Independence, July 4, 1776   193
Letter to Jonathan Trumbull Jr., August 16, 1776   198
Letter to Jonathan Trumbull Sr., March 4, 1777   200
Letter to Jonathan Trumbull Sr., April 9, 1777   203
Letter to Jonathan Trumbull Sr., May 14, 1777   205
Letter to Oliver Wolcott, May 21, 1777   207
Letter to Samuel Adams, July 11, 1777   208
Letter from Samuel Adams to Roger Sherman, August 11, 1777   209
Letter to Horatio Lloyd Gates, August 20, 1777   211
Letter to Samuel Adams, August 25, 1777   213
Letter to Richard Henry Lee, November 3, 1777   215
Report of the New Haven Convention, January 30, 1778   217
Congressional Resolution Recommending the Promotion of Morals,
    October 12, 1778   226
Letter to Benjamin Trumbull, October 20, 1778   229
Letter from Roger Sherman and Benjamin Huntington to Jonathan
    Trumbull Sr., July 22, 1780   231
Letter to Oliver Ellsworth, September 5, 1780   233
Letter from John Sullivan to George Washington, July 2, 1781   235
Letter from Roger Sherman and Richard Law to Jonathan Trumbull
    Sr., October 25, 1781   237

Call for Prayer and Fasting, October 26, 1781   238
Letter to Lyman Hall, January 20, 1784   240

The Continental and Confederation Congresses
and the Articles of Confederation   243

Letter to Volkert P. Douw, November 24, 1775   247
Letters to Zebulon Butler, 1776   248
Articles of Confederation, 1778   251
Letter to Benjamin Trumbull, August 18, 1778   259
Letter from Roger Sherman and Oliver Ellsworth to Jonathan
    Trumbull Sr., October 15, 1778   260
Letter to Elisha Payne, October 31, 1778   262
Letter to Jonathan Trumbull Sr., July 22, 1780   264
Letter from Roger Sherman and Benjamin Huntington to Jonathan
    Trumbull Sr., August 22, 1780   267
Letter to Josiah Bartlett, July 31, 1781   269
Sherman's Notes on Information Desired by François
    Barbé-Marbois, 1781   271
Draft Letter to François Barbé-Marbois, November 18, 1782   273
Pelatiah Webster, *A Dissertation on the Political Union and Constitution
    of the Thirteen United States, of North-America,* Published under the
    Pseudonym "A Citizen of Philadelphia," 1783   275
Roger Sherman, *Remarks on a Pamphlet Entitled "A Dissertation on the
    Political Union and Constitution of the Thirteen United States of North
    America by a Citizen of Philadelphia,"* 1784   296
Letter to Ezra Stiles, May 11, 1784   323

The Constitutional Convention   325

Excerpts from Debates at the Constitutional Convention of 1787   329
    May 1787   330
    June 1787   335
    July 1787   375
    August 1787   388
    September 1787   435
    Constitution of the United States   454
Sherman's Proposals   467

Ratification Debates   469

Roger Sherman and Oliver Ellsworth to Samuel Huntington,
    September 26, 1787   471
Letter to William Floyd, n.d.   473
Letter to Unknown Recipient, December 8, 1787   474
Draft of "Observations on the New Federal Constitution," 1787[?]   478
"Letters of a Countryman," November 14–December 20, 1787   482
"Observations on the New Federal Constitution," January 7, 1788   491
"Observations on the Alterations Proposed as Amendments to the
    New Federal Constitution," December 4, 1788   496

Roger Sherman as a Member of Congress   501

Letters   503
    Letter to Samuel Huntington, January 7, 1789   504
    Letter to Oliver Wolcott, May 14, 1789   505
    Letter to Simeon Baldwin, August 22, 1789   507
    Letter to Samuel Huntington, September 17, 1789   509
    Letter to Richard Law, October 3, 1789   511
    Letter to Samuel Huntington, March 6, 1790   512
    Letter to William Ellery, June 29, 1790   514
    Letter to Samuel Huntington, November 2, 1790   515
    Letter to William Williams, February 11, 1791   516
    Letter to Samuel Huntington, November 21, 1791   518
    Letter to Samuel Huntington, January 2, 1792   520
    Letter to Samuel Huntington, March 7, 1792   522
    Letter to Samuel Huntington, May 8, 1792   524
    Letter to Samuel Huntington, December 10, 1792   525
    Letter from George Washington to Roger Sherman, March 1, 1793   526
Debates in Congress   527
    Miscellaneous   527
        Congressional Chaplains   529
        Oaths   533
        John Adams   537
        National Capital   539
        Newspapers   543
        Appointment of Gouverneur Morris   549

National Power 553
    Excerpts from Congressional Debates over the Scope of
        National Power 553
    Note to James Madison, 1791 563
Finances 564
    Public Credit/State Debt 565
    Imposts 601
    Western Lands 621
Bill of Rights 624
    Correspondence between Henry Gibbs and Roger Sherman, 1789 625
    Excerpts from Congressional Debates over the Bill of Rights,
        June 8–July 21, 1789 629
    Draft House Committee Report in Sherman's Hand,
        July 21–28, 1789 643
    Final House Committee Report, July 28, 1789 645
    Excerpts from Congressional Debates over the Bill of Rights,
        August 13–22, 1789 649
    Conference Committee Report and House Resolution 671
    Amendments to the Constitution, September 28, 1789 673
    Call for Prayer, September 25, 1789 676
Executive Power 678
    Excerpts from Congressional Debates over the Executive's Power
        to Remove Appointed Officers 679
    Correspondence between John Adams and Roger Sherman, 1789 685
    Excerpts from Congressional Debates over Miscellaneous Issues
        Related to Executive Power 701
Militia Bill 707
    Excerpts from Congressional Debates over Militia Bill 707

Theological Writings and Final Days 723

Letter to Joseph Bellamy, July 23, 1772 727
White Haven Church Documents 731
Letter to John Witherspoon, July 10, 1788 738
Letter from John Witherspoon to Roger Sherman, July 25, 1788 740
Letter to Rebecca Sherman, June 29, 1789 741
Letter from Elizabeth Sherman to Roger Sherman, June 29, 1789 743
Letter to Simeon Baldwin, June 29, 1789 745

Letter to Rebecca Sherman, July 23, 1789   746

"A Short Sermon on the Duty of Self Examination, Preparatory to
    Receiving the Lord's Supper. Wherein the Qualifications for
    Communion Are Briefly Considered," 1789   747

Letter from Justus Mitchell to Roger Sherman, January 26, 1790   761

Letter to Justus Mitchell, February 8, 1790   764

Letter from Justus Mitchell to Roger Sherman, March 17, 1790   766

Letter to Simeon Baldwin, February 4, 1790   769

Letter to David Austin, March 1, 1790   771

Letter to Rebecca Sherman, March 6, 1790   774

Correspondence between Samuel Hopkins and Roger Sherman, 1790   776

Letter to Simeon Baldwin, January 4, 1791   799

Letter to Simeon Baldwin, January 21, 1791   800

Letter to Simeon Baldwin, November 26, 1791   801

Letter to Nathan Williams, December 17, 1791   802

Letter to Simeon Baldwin, December 22, 1791   806

Letter to Jedidiah Morse, February 14, 1792   807

Letter to Simeon Baldwin, December 22, 1792   809

Letter to Simeon Baldwin, January 25, 1793   811

Letter from Simeon Baldwin to Roger Sherman, January 28, 1793   812

Inventory of Pamphlets and Books, 1793   813

Selected Bibliography   817

Index   821

Introduction

Roger Sherman was the only founder to help draft and sign the Declaration and Resolves (1774), the Articles of Association (1774), the Declaration of Independence (1776), the Articles of Confederation (1777, 1778), and the Constitution (1787). He served longer in the Continental and Confederation Congresses than all but four men, and he was regularly appointed to key committees, including those charged with drafting the Declaration of Independence and the Articles of Confederation. At the Constitutional Convention, Sherman often outmaneuvered James Madison and, according to David Brian Robertson, the "political synergy between Madison and Sherman . . . may have been necessary for the Constitution's adoption."[1] He was also a representative and senator in the new republic, where, among other things, he played a significant role in drafting the Bill of Rights.

Even as he was helping create and run a nation, Sherman served in a variety of state and local offices. These included overlapping terms as a member of Connecticut's General Assembly, judge of the Superior Court, member of the Council of Safety, and mayor of New Haven. Of particular significance, he and Richard Law revised the entire legal code of Connecticut in 1783. Although not as prolific a writer as some founders, Sherman penned essays defending hard currency, supporting the Articles of Confederation, and urging the ratification of the U.S. Constitution. His letters and a sermon contain some of the most sophisticated theological commentary by an American founder.

Sherman was held in high esteem by his contemporaries. In September 1776, his Connecticut colleague William Williams observed to a friend:

> If our Assembly rechose their delegates, I hope they will be guided by wisdom and prudence. I must say that Mr. Sherman from his early acquaintance, his good

---

1. David Brian Robertson, "Madison's Opponents and Constitutional Design," *American Political Science Review* 99 (May 2005): 242; David Brian Robertson, *The Constitution and America's Destiny* (Cambridge: Cambridge University Press, 2005).

sense, judgment, steadiness, & inflexible integrity, has acquired much respect & is an exceedingly valuable member.[2]

In 1780, Richard Henry Lee wrote of the "very high sense that I entertain of your [Sherman's] sound and virtuous patriotism."[3]

John Adams agreed with Williams and Lee, as indicated by his 1777 description of Sherman as "an old Puritan, as honest as an angel and as firm in the cause of American Independence as Mount Atlas."[4] The following year Adams wrote to Sherman from Europe requesting his advice about a possible alliance with France, noting that "[f]rom the long series of arduous services, in which we have acted together, I have had experience enough of your accurate judgment, in cases of difficulty, to wish very often that I could have the benefit of it here."[5] Forty-four years later, Adams wrote to John Sanderson that Sherman was "one of the most cordial friends which I ever had in my life. Destitute of all literary and scientific education, but such as he acquired by his own exertions, he was one of the most sensible men in the world. The clearest head and steadiest heart. It is praise enough to say that the late Chief Justice Ellsworth told me that he had made Mr. Sherman his model in his youth. . . . [He] was one of the soundest and strongest pillars of the revolution."[6] Patrick Henry remarked that Sherman and George Mason were "the greatest statesmen he ever knew" and that George Washington, Lee, and Sherman were the "first men" in the Continental Congress.[7]

Thomas Jefferson, who was often at odds with both Adams and Henry, shared their admiration for Sherman, explaining to a visitor to the nation's temporary capital: "That is Mr. Sherman of Connecticut, a man who never

2. William Williams to Jabez Huntington, September 30, 1776, in *The Founders on the Founders: Word Portraits from the American Revolutionary Era*, ed. John Kaminski (Charlottesville: University of Virginia Press, 2008), 466.

3. Richard Henry Lee to Roger Sherman, January 22, 1780, Miscellaneous Bound Manuscripts, 1779–1784, Massachusetts Historical Society.

4. John Adams to Abigail Adams, March 16, 1777, in *Familiar Letters of John Adams and His Wife Abigail Adams, during the Revolution*, ed. Charles Francis Adams (New York: Hurd and Houghton, 1876), 251.

5. John Adams to Roger Sherman, December 6, 1778, in *The Adams Papers Digital Edition*, ed. C. James Taylor (Charlottesville: University of Virginia Press, Rotunda, 2008), http://rotunda.upress.virginia.edu/founders/ADMS-06-07-02-0174 (accessed August 3, 2010).

6. John Adams to John Sanderson, November 19, 1822, in *Biography of the Signers to the Declaration of Independence*, ed. Robert Waln and John Sanderson (Philadelphia: R. W. Pomeroy, 1822), 3: 298.

7. Henry Howe, *Historical Collections of Virginia* (Charleston, S.C.: WM. R. Babcock, 1852), 221.

said a foolish thing in his life."[8] Similarly, Nathanial Macon, a Democratic-Republican from North Carolina who served with Sherman in the House of Representatives, remarked to a friend that "Roger Sherman had more common sense than any man he ever knew."[9] Fisher Ames, a Federalist from Massachusetts in the same Congress, said that "if he happened to be out of his seat when a subject was discussed, and came in when the question was about to be taken, he always felt safe in voting as Mr. Sherman did; *for he always voted right.*"[10] Timothy Pickering, another New England Federalist, referred to him as "a very sagacious man."[11]

Although Sherman had many strengths, oratory was not one of them. In 1774, John Adams observed that both Sherman and Eliphalet Dyer "speak often and long, but very heavily and clumsily."[12] Similarly, William Pierce of Georgia noted in his famous sketches of the delegates to the Constitutional Convention that Sherman

> is awkward, un-meaning, and unaccountably strange in his manner. But in his train of thinking there is something regular, deep and comprehensive; yet the oddity of his address, the vulgarisms that accompany his public speaking, and that strange New England cant which runs through his public as well as private speaking make everything that is connected with him grotesque and laughable;—and yet he deserves infinite praise—no man has a better heart or a clearer head. If he cannot embellish he can furnish thoughts that are wise and useful.[13]

In an age that valued eloquence, Sherman stood out as a significant leader who was rhetorically handicapped. Yet his good heart, clear head, and common sense earned him the respect of friends and enemies alike.

Given this brief résumé and the high esteem in which he was held by his contemporaries, it is surprising that scholars have often neglected Sherman. He is mentioned only in passing in studies on the founding era, and American history and government texts often refer to him as an architect of the Con-

---

8. Waln and Sanderson, *Biography of the Signers,* 3: 296. See also Thomas Jefferson to Roger Sherman Baldwin, March 9, 1822, George Frisbie Hoar Papers, carton 189, folder 5, Massachusetts Historical Society.

9. Waln and Sanderson, *Biography of the Signers,* 3: 298.

10. Ibid.

11. Timothy Pickering to Obadiah Gore, February 2, 1791, in *The Susquehanna Company Papers,* ed. Robert J. Taylor (Ithaca, N.Y.: Cornell University Press, 1971), 10: 138.

12. Charles Francis Adams, ed., *The Works of John Adams* (Boston: Charles C. Little and James Brown, 1850), 2: 396.

13. Max Farrand, ed., *The Records of the Federal Convention of 1787* (New Haven, Conn.: Yale University Press, 1911), 3: 88–89.

necticut Compromise. With the exception of Christopher Collier's fine 1971 biography of Sherman and my 2013 book on his political theory, few academics have considered his thoughts and actions in much detail.[14] It is true that since the mid-1990s, students of the Constitutional Convention have come to recognize that Sherman was among the most effective delegates.[15] Even with this recent scholarship, law professor Scott Gerber's assessment that Sherman "is arguably the most under appreciated, not to mention the most under-studied, political leader of the American Founding" remains correct. Indeed, a 2008 survey of more than one hundred historians, political scientists, and law professors ranked Sherman among the most important forgotten founders.[16]

Perhaps one reason Sherman is not better known is that his writings have never been published in a systematic manner. Of course, it is possible to track down speeches he gave in the Constitutional Convention and the first federal Congress, laws he drafted, essays he wrote, and so forth. But doing so requires consulting dozens of different and sometimes obscure volumes. As well, a critical edition of his handwritten letters has never been published. Some of these letters are reproduced in two "life and letters" biographies, but in both cases only highly selective and heavily edited excerpts are included.[17]

Collected Works of Roger Sherman brings together for the first time Sherman's major writings and accounts of his speeches. Sherman left far fewer papers than the most famous founders, but even so, this collection is not comprehen-

14. Christopher Collier, *Roger Sherman's Connecticut: Yankee Politics and the American Revolution* (Middletown, Conn.: Wesleyan University Press, 1971); Mark David Hall, *Roger Sherman and the Creation of the American Republic* (New York: Oxford University Press, 2013).

15. Robertson, "Madison's Opponents and Constitutional Design"; Robertson, *The Constitution and America's Destiny*; Jack N. Rakove, *Original Meanings: Politics and Ideas in the Making of the Constitution* (New York: Knopf, 1996). Keith L. Dougherty and Jac C. Heckelman agree with Robertson and Rakove that "Sherman was an effective delegate that historians have traditionally overlooked" but suggest that his "influence at the Convention was partly the result of the voting scheme and partly his position relative to others." "A Pivotal Voter from a Pivotal State: Roger Sherman at the Constitutional Convention," *American Political Science Review* 100 (May 2006): 302.

16. Scott Gerber, "Roger Sherman and the Bill of Rights," *Polity* 28 (Summer 1996): 531. Sherman placed fifth in the survey, but there was negligible difference in the number of votes received by the third-, fourth-, and fifth-place finishers (Gouverneur Morris, John Jay, and Sherman). James Wilson and George Mason were ranked first and second among the forgotten founders. Gary L. Gregg and Mark David Hall, eds., *America's Forgotten Founders*, 2nd ed. (Wilmington, Del.: ISI Books, 2012), xv.

17. Lewis Boutell, *The Life of Roger Sherman* (Chicago: A. C. McClurg, 1896) and Roger Sherman Boardman, *Roger Sherman: Signer and Statesman* (Philadelphia: University of Pennsylvania Press, 1938).

sive.[18] A complete edition of his writings would fill approximately three volumes the size of this one, but many of the letters omitted from this collection contain political news readily available in other sources or business and legal correspondence that would be of interest only to a few academics. This collection includes every essay published by Sherman, his major speeches, and substantive correspondence. It also contains texts of major public documents that he helped draft.

A Life in Brief

Sherman was born in Massachusetts in 1721 to Mehetabel and William Sherman. William was a farmer and cobbler, and like many citizens in the region, he was a Congregationalist. Shortly after his father died in 1741, Roger moved to New Milford, Connecticut, where he worked as a cobbler, surveyor, and store owner. Sherman never went to college, but he was a voracious reader. He taught himself advanced mathematics, and in 1750 he began publishing a popular almanac that was issued annually or biannually until 1761. During this time Sherman studied law, and he was admitted to the Litchfield bar in 1754. Under the guidance of Roger and his older brother, the two younger Sherman brothers, Nathaniel and Josiah, attended the College of New Jersey (Princeton), from which they graduated in 1753 and 1754, respectively. They both became Congregational ministers.

As Sherman prospered professionally, he was selected for a variety of local offices, and in 1755 he was elected to several six-month terms in the lower house of Connecticut's General Assembly. In 1760, after the death of his first wife (with whom he had seven children), Sherman moved to New Haven. There he opened a store next to Yale College and sold general merchandise, provisions, and books. Sherman married Rebecca Prescott three years later, and the couple had eight children. Once again he was elected to local offices and to the lower house of the General Assembly. In 1766, Connecticut voters chose him as one of the twelve members of the upper house, or Council of Assistants. Traditionally, four assistants were selected by the General Assembly to serve with the deputy governor as judges on Connecticut's Superior Court. Sherman was appointed to this court in 1766, and he held both offices until

18. For instance, George Washington's papers are projected to reach ninety volumes, the Adams family papers more than one hundred, and Madison's and Franklin's papers approximately fifty each, while Hamilton's papers have been collected in thirty-two volumes.

1785, when he resigned as an assistant to retain his position as a judge in response to a 1784 law that prohibited individuals from holding both offices. He remained a Superior Court judge until he became a member of the U.S. House of Representatives in 1789.

Beginning in 1774, Sherman accepted multiple appointments to the Continental Congress. Altogether he served 1,543 days in that body, and he helped draft and signed virtually every significant document produced by it (the primary exception being the Northwest Ordinance).[19] He served on numerous committees, including those charged with drafting the Declaration of Independence and the Articles of Confederation. In 1783, Sherman and the aptly named Richard Law accepted the task of revising *all* of Connecticut's statutes.[20] Four years later he was appointed to the Federal Constitutional Convention. Despite being the second oldest delegate at 66, Sherman was an active member, speaking more often than all but three delegates and serving as the driving force behind the Connecticut Compromise. He was also a leader in Connecticut's ratification convention, and he wrote six letters for the *New Haven Gazette* responding to objections from anti-Federalists.

Under the new Constitution, Sherman was elected first to the House of Representatives (1789–91) and then appointed to the U.S. Senate to fill the unexpired term of William Samuel Johnson. In Congress, he played an important role in debates over the Bill of Rights, the assumption of state debts, and the creation of a national bank. Sherman served in the Senate until his death on July 23, 1793. His life is summed up well by Yale president Timothy Dwight:

> Mr. Sherman possessed a powerful mind; and habits of industry, which no difficulties could discourage, and no toil impair. In early life he began to apply himself, with inextinguishable zeal, to the acquisition of knowledge. In this pursuit, although he was always actively engaged in business, he spent more hours than most of those, who are professedly students. In his progress he became extensively acquainted with Mathematical science, with Natural philosophy, with Moral and Metaphysical philosophy, with History, Logic and Theology. As a lawyer, and a statesman, he was eminent. The late Judge Ingersoll, who has been already mentioned, once observed to me, that, in his opinion, the views which Mr. Sherman formed of political subjects, were more profound, just, and comprehensive, than

---

19. John G. Rommel, *Connecticut's Yankee Patriot: Roger Sherman* (Hartford: The American Revolution Bicentennial Commission of Connecticut, 1979), 28.

20. Sherman and Law had to revise, update, or reject previous statutes—and in some cases they composed entirely new laws. Sherman took the statutes beginning with the letters A–L, and Law took the rest. They consulted with each other before submitting the final draft to the legislature, where the proposed laws were amended and passed or, occasionally, rejected.

those of almost any other man, with whom he had been acquainted on this continent. His mind was remarkably clear and penetrating; and, more than almost
any other man, looked from the beginning of a subject to the end. Nothing
satisfied him but proof; or where that was impossible, the predominant probability
which equally controls the conduct of a wise man. He had no fashionable opinions,
and could never be persuaded to swim with the tide. Independent of every thing
but argument, he judged for himself; and rarely failed to convince others, that he
judged right.[21]

21. Timothy Dwight, *A Statistical Account of the City of New Haven* (New Haven: Connecticut
Academy of Arts and Sciences, 1811), 76–77.

Acknowledgments

Critical outside funding for writing this volume was provided by the Earhart Foundation. Over the years the Foundation has supported numerous academic projects that center on the American founding. It will be sorely missed. A small research grant from the American Political Science Association helped fund travel to key archives.

Hans Eicholz, senior fellow at Liberty Fund, was an important advocate of the project. I am grateful for his invitation to direct a Liberty Fund colloquium based on texts that later made their way into this collection. Working with Liberty Fund is always a joy.

Most of my academic projects involve collaborators, and this one is no exception. Vetta Berokoff of George Fox University, her assistants, and my teaching assistants—especially Sergio Cisneros, Austin Schaefer, and Chelsea McCombs—typed and checked numerous manuscripts. I am thankful for their hard and diligent work. As always, I am grateful for the support of George Fox University, the William Penn Honors Program, and the Institute for the Studies of Religion at Baylor University.

A Note on the Texts

Collected Works of Roger Sherman would not have been possible without the tremendous work of the many historians, editors, and archivists who have come before me. Because I do not believe it is necessary to reinvent the wheel, wherever possible I have taken texts from modern critical collections of papers. Particularly useful were Paul H. Smith et al., eds., *Letters of Delegates to Congress*, 26 vols. (Washington, D.C.: Government Printing Office, 1976–2000); Merrill Jensen, ed., *The Documentary History of the Ratification of the Constitution*, vol. 3: *Ratification of the Constitution by the States: Delaware, New Jersey, Georgia, Connecticut* (Madison: State Historical Society of Wisconsin, 1978); and Linda Grant de Pauw et al., eds., *The Documentary History of the First Federal Congress of the United States of America*, 20 vols. (Baltimore: Johns Hopkins University Press, 1972–2012).

Selecting texts from these and other fine collections was the easy part of this enterprise. Far more difficult was finding and transcribing letters and other documents that have never been published. Altogether I spent approximately two months in a wide variety of archives. The most important collections of Sherman's papers are found at the Library of Congress, Yale University's Manuscripts and Archives, and the Connecticut State Library. I am grateful to these institutions, as well as to the Connecticut Historical Society, Massachusetts Historical Society, New-York Historical Society, New York Public Library, and Historical Society of Pennsylvania, for granting me permission to publish manuscripts from their collections. Archivists in each institution made my job far easier than it might have otherwise been.

I reproduce texts taken from printed material exactly as they appear unless I note otherwise. Unless otherwise noted, brackets indicate material added by me.

As is the practice with Liberty Fund volumes, chapter introductions and headnotes are short and non-interpretive. I provide a very brief introduction to all but the most famous founders the first time they appear in the text. Portions of the introduction, chapter introductions, and headnotes are derived from material originally published in Mark David Hall, *Roger Sherman and the Creation of the American Republic* (New York: Oxford University Press, 2013).

Early Writings

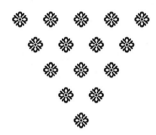

Little is known with certainty about Sherman's education. He was raised in Stoughton, Massachusetts, and his family attended a local Congregational church led by Samuel Dunbar (1704–83). Dunbar, a protégé of Cotton Mather and a 1723 graduate of Harvard, was fluent in Latin and Greek, and, like many ministers of that era, he likely supplemented his income by teaching. He arrived in Stoughton to pastor the Congregational church in 1727 and remained there until his death. Because the town's first school was not established until 1735, by which time Sherman was fourteen years old, it is probable that Sherman was educated, at least in part, by Dunbar.[1] This may help explain how the son of a cobbler and farmer who never attended college had the educational foundation to teach himself surveying, astronomy, law, and, eventually, politics.

Shortly after Sherman moved to New Milford, Connecticut, in 1743, he learned the art of surveying. In 1745 he was appointed county surveyor by the General Assembly. By 1749 his increasing knowledge of math had enabled him to do the calculations necessary to produce his own almanacs. These short books documented the moon's phases, predicted the weather, listed important meetings and other information, and offered a healthy dose of proverbs and literary excerpts. Sherman published these almanacs between 1750 and 1761.

Although Sherman was trained as a cobbler, he seemed to have spent little time in the trade. In addition to surveying and publishing, in the late 1740s and early 1750s he ran a general store with his brother. In the course of this business he was forced to confront the evils of paper money. Sherman undertook his first major literary endeavor in 1752 with his essay "A Caveat Against

---

1. Daniel T. V. Huntoon, *History of the Town of Canton* (Cambridge, Mass.: John Wilson and Son, 1893), 134–35.

Injustice," a passionate attack on such currency. Shortly thereafter, probably at the urging of William Samuel Johnson, Sherman turned to the study of law. He was admitted to the bar in 1754.

The documents in this chapter shine some light on an important period in Sherman's life as he transitioned from being a cobbler, farmer, and store owner to an attorney, politician, and statesman. Unfortunately, there are no diaries and few letters that reveal much about Sherman's private thoughts or domestic life. He married his first wife, Elizabeth, in 1749. She died in 1760 after bearing seven children, four of whom survived to adulthood. He moved to New Haven shortly thereafter and, in 1763, married Rebecca Prescott, with whom he had eight children. The chapter closes with a rare personal note from Sherman to his second wife.

Selections from Roger Sherman's Almanacs, 1750–1758, 1760–1761

Sherman published an almanac for every year from 1750 to 1761 (except, apparently, 1759). In some years he published two almanacs, with different calculations based on each city's meridian (the cities varied and included Boston, New York, New Haven, and New London). The almanacs were between 16 and 25 pages long and contained astronomical information, weather predictions, and other information. He would regularly insert moral, religious, and political sayings and poetry. These passages were often borrowed or paraphrased from other writers, but his choices give insight into his values and beliefs.

In his first almanac, the printer, Henry De Foreest, inserted material of which Sherman did not approve. He subsequently published a notice in the New York Gazette *distancing himself from it, especially "Observations upon the four Quarters of the Year."*[1] *After this experience it is likely that he took steps to make sure printers only included material he selected or at least approved. Of course, it is possible that printers inserted some quotations and passages without his consent. However, the vast majority of these texts contain ideas and sentiments consistent with Sherman's views.*

In this section I include a selection of excerpts and proverbs from Sherman's almanacs.[2] *When possible, I cite the work from which a quotation or passage is taken (although not necessarily the one to which Sherman had access).*

Almanacs are identified by the year for which they were published and the city of publication. They did not have page numbers, so the location of passages is identified by the month from which the quotation is taken (where possible).

1. Roger Sherman, notice published in the *New York Gazette,* January 22, 1749–50. One section of the objectionable "observations" and Sherman's response appear on pages 8 and 9.

2. A larger, but still not comprehensive, collection of material from these almanacs may be found in Victor Hugo Paltsits, ed., *The Almanacs of Roger Sherman, 1750–1761* (Worcester, Mass.: Davis Press, 1907).

An Astronomical Diary, Or,
an Almanack for the Year of Our Lord Christ,
1750 (Boston)

I have for several years past for my own amusement spent some of my leisure hours in the study of the *mathmaticks* not with any intent to appear in publick; but at the desire of my friends and acquaintances, I have been induced to calculate and publish the following ALMANACK for the year 1750. I have put in everything that I have thought would be useful that could be contained in such contracted limits. I have taken much care to perform calculations truly, not having the help of any *ephemeris,* and I would desire the reader not to condemn it if it should in something differ from other authors until observations have determined which is in the wrong. I need say nothing by the way of explanation of the following pages, they being placed in the same order that has been for many years predicted by the ingenious and celebrate Dr. *Ames,* with which you are well acquainted. If this shall find acceptance, perhaps it may encourage me to serve my country the way for time to come.

New Milford, August 1, 1749. R Sherman

JANUARY

In six Days space a wond'rous System stands,
Beaut'ous and large, made by eternal Hands;
In pleasant Harmony it's Glories shine,
And all bespeak their Architect Divine;
With daz'ling Light they strike our wond'ring Eyes,
And fill our Souls with Pleasure and Surprize.

FEBRUARY

This spacious Earth from empty Nothing sprung,
In wild Disorder, on her Centre hung,
Devoid of beauteous Form or proper Size;
While rolling Waters mingled with the Skies:
GOD soon a glorious Canopy provides,
And Waters from the Waters he divides.

MARCH

Yet Darkness still enfolds the Globe around,
And gloomy Horrors on the Deep are found:
Let there be Light, said the Almighty Lord,
And Light obsequious soon fulfil'd his Word:
Whose quick'ning Beams commence the glorious Day,
And chase the sullen Shades of Night away.

APRIL

Now radiant SOL comes blushing from the East
Like some fair Bride in nuptial Garments dress'd:
On lofty Hills he spreads his lucid Beams
And fertile Meads beside the purling Stream;
By whose prolifick Rays the Flowers arise,
And shoot their Branches to'ard the azure Skies.

MAY

Bright *Phoebus* still keeps on his destin'd Way,
Glides in an Arch, and marks the bounds of Day;
Or rather stable in the Centre stays,
While *Tellus* rolls beneath his splendid Rays:
At different times her diff'rent Parts she shews,
And he as oft his vital Heat renews.

JUNE

At his Retreat the beauteous Queen of Night
In Glory shines by his reflected Light:
Around the Earth her destin'd Orbit lies,
Beneath the higher Spheres along the Skies:
Beyond, a Planetary Chorus rolls,
And keep their steady Course around the Poles.

JULY

All Things prepar'd, in glorious Order stand,
Then soon arose the God-like Creature *Man*,
With Innocence array'd, and Glory crown'd,
Nor Spot nor Stain o'er all his Soul was found:
In noble Light his manly Virtues shine,
His Looks serene, his Temper all divine.

AUGUST

When deep in Sleep GOD from his op'ning side
Chose out a Rib, and form'd a charming Bride:
Before his Eyes a blushing Female stood,
Flesh of his Flesh, and Partner of his Blood.
To nuptial Rites their sweet Embraces move,
Held by the golden Chain of spotless Love.

SEPTEMBER

The happy Pair now plac'd in *Eden*'s Grove,
On mossy Banks to feed their mutual Love,
And Till the yielding Earth: A happy Life!
Secure from Danger, and remote from Strife,
Beneath the verdant Trees a pleasant Shade,
Where GOD himself some heavenly Visits made.

OCTOBER

But now a black and awful Scene appears,
While the old Serpent spreads delusive Snares:
And by his vile Deceits and cursed Plan,
Entic'd the Woman to beguile the Man:
And both seduc'd, perform the dreadful Fact,
And equally the awful Guilt contract.

NOVEMBER

Then the Almighty comes, with dreadful Awe,
To vindicate the Honour of his Law:
All Nature trembles, burning Thunders roll,
And forked Lightning flash from Pole to Pole:
With thund'ring Voice he bids the Wretches come
Before his Throne, and hear their awful Doom.

DECEMBER

Which must have been to dwell in endless Night,
Without one Spark of Hope or Gleam of Light:
But JESUS stands before the awful Throne,
To save their Lives, he offers up his own,
To pay the Price sustain'd the dreadful Load
Of all their Sins, and bore the Wrath of GOD.

An Almanack, for the Year of Our Lord Christ, 1750
(New York)

QUAKERS *General Meetings are kept.*

March 19 At Philadelphia,
April 23 At Salem,
    23 At Rie-Woods,
May 14 At Flushing,
    21 At West-River,
Jun. 11 At Providence,
    18 At New-port on
       Rhode Island,
    23 At New-town.

July 23 At Westchester,
Aug. 27 At Westbury,
Sept. 17 At Burlington,
Octo. 1 At Rie-Woods,
    8 At Choptank,
    15 At Shrewsbury,
    15 At Matiniconk,
Nov. 19 At Flushing,
Feb. 19 At Westbury,

FAIRS *are kept.*

April 8 At Noxonton,
    24 At Cohansie,
    28 At Wilmington,
May 1 At Salem,
    3 At New-Castle,
    5 At Chester,
    [?] At Bristol,
    [?] At Burlington,
    [?] At Providence,
    [?] At Philadelphia,
June 1 At Lancaster,

Octo. 5 At Chester,
    10 At Noxonton,
    16 At Cohansie,
    20 At Salem,
    20 At Germantown,
    24 At Wilmington,
    29 At Bristol,
Nov. 1 At Burlington,
    1 At Lancaster,
    3 At New-Castle,
    16 At Philadelphia.

Observations on Winter
(material added by De Foreest)

This being the last and worst Quarter of the four, like a Dish of chubs at the latter End of a Feast, brings up the Rear.

Now days are very short, and Nights premontriposterous long; consequently, now is the properest Time for the tearing of sheets, and begetting Bantlings; by reason lazy Lubbers have an Oppertunity to lie long in Bed, without the Disturbance of Day-light or hot Sun-shine.

This Quarter used to be welcome to poor People, when good Housekeeping was in fashion, because, it always brings Christmass along with it; but now Pride, Gaming, and Whoring, have turn'd good Housekeeping out of Doors.

Yet here and there remaineth some, that will,
Uphold good Orders, and keep Christmass still.

The Sun about the middle of this Quarter gliding through the Pitchers, signifies that many Persons, notwithstanding the cold Weather, will be very thirsty; so that whole Rivers of Beer and Ale will run down Gutter-Lane, even to the very exhausting of all their springs, were it not for the epidemical Disease, the want of Money: For most Hostesses are now turned Nullifidians, chusing rather to see white Money in their Purse, than white Chalk on a Post.

But to conclude (as the Parson says, and that sometimes perhaps before he hath half done) but to conclude, I say again during this season, good Fires, warm Cloths, a Pot of Ale and a Toast in the Morning, a shoulder of Mutton and a Capon for Dinner, and a good sack-posset for supper, are very excellent Things to keep out the cold. And so much for the four Quarters of the Year.

More might be said, but then more must be spoke,
Words are but Words, and Words but a mere Joke.

Sherman's Response to De Foreest's Additions

I the Subscriber, having, at the Desire of Mr. Henry De Foreest, of New-York, Printer, calculated an Almanack for the Year 1750, and sent it to him to print: Upon reading said Almanack after it was printed, was very much surprized to see what large Additions were made to it after it went from my Hands, and all in my Name; and also the Rising and Setting of the Moon was left out; all the Observations upon the 12 Months, inserted between the Title Page and the Eclipses; and also the Observations on the four Quarters of the Year, (towards the latter End of the Almanack) were added after it went from me, and without my Approbation or Knowledge. 'Tis true, I did desire the Printer to put in the Courts, Fairs, and Quaker's Meetings; for I had Opportunity to send the Copy before I had put them in; and the Person that carried it being in Haste, I sent it without inserting them: The last Thing in my Copy, was the Tide-Table. I think I gave the Printer Liberty in my Letter, to put in whatsoever else he should think proper; but did not expect that he would have added any Thing, but what is common in Almanacks; as the Discription of the Roads, &c. But since he was pleased to insert his aforesaid Prognostiferous Observations, which is such a rare and extraordinary Performance, that I thought I should not do Justice to the Gentleman's Character, if I did not let the Publick know who was the Author of it.

New-Milford, Jan. 16, 1749–50.

ROGER SHERMAN.

An Astronomical Diary, or an Almanack, for the Year of Our Lord Christ, 1751 (New York)

MARCH
Who is it willingly wold bear,
Eternal horror and despair,
Yet many love and live in sin,
which certainly will end therein.

SEPTEMBER
The mighty GOD from whom all Things proceed,
To his own Glory all Things hath decreed,
Those who refuse him praise in active way,
Must victims fall, his Justice to display.

An Astronomical Diary or, an Almanack for the Year of Our Lord Christ, 1751 (Boston)

February

A faithful Man in public Station.
is a Pillar in a Nation.

May

The Times wherein we live are very bad:
To see how Vice abounds, is very sad!
Let's every one mend our own Ways,
and we shall soon see better Days.

July

O' Seasons we predict by Nature's Laws,
but these are over-rul'd by God, the great First Cause.

August

The various Harmony in the Works of Nature:
Manifest the Wisdom of the Creator.

November

What is our Duty while we're here below,
Is our prime Wisdom carefully to know;
And diligently to perform the same
Is what should always be our End and Aim.

An Astronomical Diary, or, an Almanack for the Year of Our Lord Christ, 1752 (New York)

The Sun by Day rules with refulgent Light,
Thousands of lucid Globes appear by Night,
Five, like our World revolve about this Sun,
And doubtless are Inhabited each one,
Others far distant, Fix'd, with innate Light,
Are Sun's (no doubt) to Worlds beyond our Sight,
Numberless *Systems* through unbounded Space,
In fluid Aether keep their destin'd Place,
By Force projectile kept in swift Career,
And Gravitation guids each in his Sphere,
How great these Works? How great surpassing Thought,
Is GOD! who all from empty nothing brought?

July
Mahomet, Imposter died 631 but he hath many disciples
  yet alive deluded souls

October
"As Man perhaps the Moment of his Breath,
"Receives the lurking Principle of Death,
"The young Disease that must subdue at length,
"Grows with his Growth and strengthens with his strength,
Tho' from this *Victor* Death none can Exemption have,
We may thro' Christ obtain, a Hope beyond the Grave.[1]

November
The Farmer having gathere'd in his Store,
His Cares are not so anxious as before,

---

1. The first four lines are from Alexander Pope, *Essay on Man* (London: Millar & Tonson, 1763), 43. I include quotation marks only if they are in the original almanac. —Ed.

Hath GOD the fruitful year with goodness crown'd,
And made our Stores with Plenty to abound,
We shou'd with publick Praise his Name confess,
And not forget the Poor in their distress.

December

Those who have warm houses a good fire and
   provisions enough have cause of thankfulness
   and ought to be kind to such as want these things

Good Laws, and Courts that are for the Defence,
Of each Man's Right, and just Inheritence,
Can they be us'd to wrest out of our Hands,
And that unjustly too; our Goods or Lands?
Can Laws be ever constru'd to o'er throw
A Righteous Cause; that's evidently so?
Or some known Error rule to counter-act.
What evidently is the Truth in Fact?
Such Principles as these let ne'er obtain;
In Courts where Truth and Justice ought to reign.

An Astronomical Diary, or, an Almanack for the Year of Our Lord Christ, 1753 (New London)

MARCH
Two Principles in Human Nature Reign,
Self love to Urge, and Reason to Restrain,
Self love the spring of motion acts the Soul,
Reason's comparing Balance rules the Whole;
Man but for that no Action could attend,
And but for this were Active to no end.[1]

JULY
Britannia's free born Sons! How Happy they!
Under a GEORGE's mild and gentle sway,
A KING whose God like Mind is big with Joy,
To guard his Subjects, and their Foes destroy
Heav'n Bless him with a Long and Happy Reign,
Subdue his Foes, and make their Counsels Vain.

AUGUST
As English Subjects free born, brave;
Our Rights and Liberties we have:
Secur'd by good and Righteous Laws,
Which ought in Judging every cause
To be a Standing Rule; whereby
Each one may have his Property.

He who loves truth for its own sake,
  will not assent to any proposition farther
  than there's evidence to support it.

---

1. Ibid., 37–38 (with four lines removed between the first two and the last four lines quoted).
—Ed.

OCTOBER
Self Interest will turn some men's opinions
as certainly as the wind will a weathercock.

NOVEMBER
Behold the Child by Nature's kindly Law,
Pleas'd with a Rattle, tickled with a Straw.
Some livelier play Thing gives his youth Delight,
A little Louder, but as empty Quite.
Pleas'd with this Bauble still, as that before,
'Till tir'd he Sleeps, and Life's poor play is o'er.[2]

Profaness Intemperance & Injustice presage
Calamitious Times.

To fill up a vacant Page, I tho't it would not be amiss to offer some tho'ts upon the Loss & Damages which the Inhabitants of the Colony of *Connecticut* have sustain'd by the depreciation of the Bills of Credit of *R Island & N Hampshire*, since the year 1750. It appears by the reports of two Committees that were appointed by the Gen. Assembly of *R Island, viz* one in 1749, to enquire what sum in Bills made to supply the Treasury were then outstanding, & the other in 1750 to enquire what sum was outstanding upon Loan & both said sums amounted to £561,314 old tenor, & I suppose that almost or quite the whole of said sums is now out standing, & they have since emitted Bills to the value of £237037, old ten. And altho' I have not had any particular account of the amount of the outstanding Bills of the Province of *N Hampshire*, yet according to the best Observation that I have been able to make, there has been near or quite as many of the Bills of *N Hampsh.* as of the old emissions of *R Island* passing in *Connecticut.* And since the *Massachusetts Bay* has stopt the currency of those Bills in that Province, I suppose that near half,* of all the outstanding Bills aforesaid, (exclusive of the last emission of *R Island*) have generally been passing in said Colony. And in the year 1750, those Bills currently pass'd at the rate of 54 *s.* old tenor, for an ounce of Silver, but now 64 *s.* is the least sum that a *Spanish* Dollar can be purchased for, which weighs but about 17 *peny weight & an half,* at which rate an ounce would cost 73 *s.* so that the depreciation that has been since the year 1750, will amount to £176 000 old tenor, (at its present value) upon the whole of what has been in the hands of the

---

2. Ibid., 55. —Ed.
* Some under *good advantages* to know, say 2 thirds

Inhabitants of said Colony, allowing them to have had but about £500,000, which is less than one half of the outstanding Bills aforesaid, (upon supposition that *N Hampshire* has as many out standing as *R Island* has, exclusive of the new emission) and is not that a large Tribute! for the Inhabitants of said Colony to pay to those two Governments within about the space of two years? for which they have received no benefit. And the outstanding Bills of *Connecticut,* some of which may be in their hands, are not in a depreciating state, so what theirs depreciate in our hands is (as to us) wholly lost: And all this loss, (besides a great deal of injustice in *private dealings* would have been avoided, if the currency of those Bills had been stopt in that Colony at the time when they were stopt in the Province aforementioned: But such evils can't always be foreseen. And there seems to be a great probability that those Bills will sink in their value for the future as fast as ever they have in time past, if not faster; and what motive can there be to induce any of said Inhabitants to be desirous of having them pass among 'em any longer (especially as a standard in trade) at the expence of *justice, credit,* & *interest?* For what purpose is it to have other measures just & equal, if the Money which is the common measure to estimate the value of all things is uncertain & unequal? for it is evident that such an uncertain Medium of exchange puts an advantage into the hands of people to wrong one another many ways, without danger of being call'd to an account or punished by the Civil Authority; and 'tis to be fear'd that it has been a means of insensibly rooting principles of justice out of the minds of many people, occasioning them to think that what they gain of their ne'bour by keeping him out of his just due, & then taking *advantage* of the depreciation of the bills of Credit, to pay their debts with less than was the real value of them at the time of contract, is just & honest gain. And others by receiving in their debts in such depreciated bills, are necessitated either to be great sufferers in their estates, or else to make reprisals by taking advantage of the uncertainty of the medium of exchange to get an exorbitant price for the *wares & marchandizes* which they sell for the future to countervail their former loss. (But is suffering wrong, a sufficient excuse for doing wrong?) Besides, how many poor Orphans have been wronged out of great part of their estates by means of such an unstable medium? And who ever is the faulty cause of it, will find that they contract no small guilt. And how much so ever some may advance their present interest by the unjust methods aforesaid, & others may curry favour by conniving at such practices, yet all will be convinc'd sooner or later, that *Honesty is the best Policy.*

An Astronomical Diary. Or an Almanack, for the Year of Our Lord Christ, 1753 (New York)

MARCH

This is true Liberty when Free born Men
Having t'advise the Publick may speak free,
Which he who can, and will deserves his praise;
Who neither can nor will, may hold his Peace,
What can be juster in a State than this?

Milt. Eurip.[1]

MAY

Reason and passion answer one great aim. And
true self love and social are the same.

Count all the bliss that prosperous vice obtains
'Tis but what virtue flies from and disdains

JULY

Bias and grudge
Have made men mis-judge,

All men desire happiness but 'tis only the virtuous
that atain it.

---

1. This is the epigraph from John Milton's *Areopagitica* (London, 1644). Milton is quoting the Greek poet Euripides. —Ed.

An Astronomical Diary. Or an Almanack, for the Year of Our Lord Christ, 1754 (New York)

February

"This Magnanimity, great Things to scorn;
"Pompous Expences, and Parades August,
"And Courts; that insalubrious foil to Peace,
"True Happiness ne'er enter'd at an Eye;
"True Happiness resides in Things unseen.
"*Vertue*'s, future and eternal reward.[1]

April
Liberty and Property are dear to English men.

December
Some waste their precious time in gaming.
 Others in trifles not worth naming.

---

1. The first five lines are from Edward Young, *The Complaint: Or, Night Thoughts* (Paris, 1779), 2: 39. —Ed.

An Astronomical Diary, or, an Almanack for the Year of Our Lord Christ, 1754 (New London)

A Scene of Wonders to our view appears,
In the Gradation of the rolling Spheres:
Behold what Power and Wisdom are display'd!
World above World, with sure foundation laid!
And in the midst a radiant Globe of Light,
Tempers their Air; dispels their shades of Night;
Gives each it's Motion with Impetuous Force;
Confines their Limits, and marks out their Course
And in it's great and most stupendous Sphere,
Makes every Atom wisely to Cohere.

MARCH
Tis greater Honour to Retract an Error, than to Defend it.

APRIL
"Heav'n gives us Friends to bless the *present scene*;
"Resumes them, to prepare us for the *Next*.
All Evils *Natural* are *Moral* Goods;
All Discipline, *Indulgence*, on the whole
None are Unhappy; all have cause to smile
But such as to themselves that Cause deny.[1]

MAY
The Tyranny of OLD TENOR, that mystery of Iniquity,
source of Injustice, & disturber of the Peace,
is now Expiring; to the Joy of all Honest Men;

---

1. The first two lines are from Edward Young, "Night the Ninth and Last," in *The Poetical Works of the Rev. Dr. Young* (Philadelphia, 1805), 135–36. —Ed.

NOVEMBER
A Miser who loves money more than himself
will certainly rate it above Honesty.

An Astronomical Diary: Or, an Almanack, for the Year of Our Lord Christ, 1755 (Boston)

February

———————The Land wants such
As dare with Rigour execute her Laws;
Her festered Members must be lanc'd and tented:
He's a bad Surgeon that for Pity spares
The Part corrupted, 'till the Gangreen spread,
And all the Body perish: He that's merciful
Unto the Bad, is cruel to the Good.[1]

March

The Pillory must cure the Ears disease;
The Stocks the Foot's Offences; let the Sins
Of the Back, be purged at the Whipping Post;
And yet the secret and purse Punishment
Is held the wiser course; because at once
It helps the Virtuous, and corrects the Vicious.[2]

April

A poor Spirit's worse
Than a poor Purse.

If Virtue in a Court itself advance;
Vice there will soon grow out of countenance.

May

The Promises of Princes and Courts
   should not be by after arts evaded,
For who dares punish the breach of Oaths in Subjects
   and yet slight the Faith he has made them.

---

1. From Thomas Randolph, *The Muse's Looking Glass*, in *The Quintessence of English Poetry* (London, 1740), 3: 63. —Ed.
2. Ibid.

AUGUST

Plain down right Honesty, is the Beauty and Elegancy of life.

SEPTEMBER

Ignorance of the Law doth not excuse one.

Fortune always did approve: A present Wit, In War or Love.

OCTOBER

Oft Times we say some Things 'gainst Nature be,
Because such Things as those we seldom see:
But if we weigh'd with a religious Eye
The Power of doing, not the frequency;
All Things which God in the Creation wrought,
Would be alike in Strangeness to our Thought.[3]

Some Men study more how to seem judicious than to be so.

NOVEMBER

We must have Doves and Serpents in our Hearts;
But how they must be Marshall'd there's the Art:
They must agree, and not be far asunder;
The Dove must hold the wily Serpent under
Their Natures teach what Places they must keep;
The Dove can fly, the Serpent only creep.[4]

None pities him that's in the Snare;
And warn'd before, Would not beware.

DECEMBER

In Bodies Politick the World contains,
Princes for Arms and Counselors for Brains,
Lawyers for Tongues, Divines for Hearts, and more.
The Rich for Stomachs, and for Backs the Poor;

---

3. This is a paraphrase of [first name unknown] May, "Henry II," quoted in *Miscellaneous Prose Works by Edward Bulwer, Lord Lytton* (London: Richard Bentley, 1868), 3: 343. —Ed.

4. From Francis Quarles, *Divine Fancies* (1632), in *The Complete Works in Prose and Verse of Francis Quarles*, ed. Alexander Grosart (privately printed, 1882), 2: 238. —Ed.

The Officers for Hands, Merchants for Feet,
By which remote and distant Countries meet.[5]

The Health and Welfare of the People is the chiefest Law.

A POEM ON DRUNKENNESS

Drunkenness avoid, whose vile Incontinence,
Takes both away the Reason and the Sense:
Till with *Circean* Cups thy Mind's possest,
Leaves to be Man, and wholly turns a Beast.
Think while thou swallow'st the capacious Bowl,
Thou lett'st in Floods to wreck and drown thy Soul:
That Hell is open, to Remembrance call,
And think how subject Drunkards are to fall.
Consider how it soon destroys the Grace
Of human Shape, spoiling the beauteous Face:
Puffing the Cheeks, blaring the curious Eye,
Studding the Face with vicious Heraldry.
How does it nurse Disease, infect the Heart,
Drawing some Sickness into ev'ry Part?
The Stomach overcloy'd, wanting a Vent,
Doth up again resend her Excrement.
And then, O see what too much Wine can do,
The very Soul being drunk, spues Secrets too!
The Lungs corrupted, breathe contagious Air,
Belching up Fumes that unconcocted are.
The Brain o'er warm'd, losing her sweet Repose,
Doth purge her filthy Ordure through the Nose;
The Veins do boil, glutted with vicious Food.
And quickly fevers the distemper'd Blood.
The Belly swells, the Foot can hardly stand,
Lam'd with the Gout; the Palsy shakes the Hand;
And through the Flesh sick Waters sinking in,
Do, Bladder like, puft up the dropsy'd Skin.
It weaks the Brain, it spoils the Memory,
Hasting on Age, and wilful Poverty.

---

5. From John Donne, "A Funeral Elegy" (1633), in *The Poems of John Donne*, revised and edited by James Russell Lowell (New York: Grolier Club, 1895), 2: 90. The original poem does not contain the first three words: "In Bodies Politick." —Ed.

'Tis virtue's Poison, and the Bane of Trust,
The Match of Wrath, the Fuel unto Lust.
It drowns thy better Parts, making thy Name
To Foes a laughter, to thy Friends a Shame;
And if thou dost not from this Vice refrain
'Twill prove thy Ruin and eternal Bane.[6]

6. Excerpted from Thomas Randolph, "Necessary Observations: 35th Precept," in *Poetical and Dramatic Works of Thomas Randolph*, ed. W. Carew Hazlitt (London: Reeves and Turner, 1875), 2: 561–62. —Ed.

The Connecticut Diary: Or, Almanack for the Year of Our Lord Christ, 1756 (New Haven)

JANUARY

"The Miser's Gold, the painted Cloud
"Of Titles, that make vain Men proud;
"The Courtier's Pomp, or glorious Scar
"Got by the Soldier in the War,
Cannot equal his brave Mind,
That studies to preserve Mankind.[1]

FEBRUARY

Jealousy a Power o'er Judgment gains,
Although it only in the Fancy reigns;
Its Tyranny subverts ev'n Nature's Laws;
For oft it has Effects without a Cause:
And, which its Strength or Weakness doth detect,
It often has a Cause without Effect.

He that from Guilt is clear,
No Danger need to fear;

MARCH

Justice must be from Violence exempt,
But Fraud's her only Object of contempt:
Fraud in the Fox, Force in the Lion dwells;
But Justice both from human Hearts expels:
But he's the greatest Monster, without doubt,
Who is a Wolf within, a Sheep without.[2]

---

1. From Sir William Davenant, "The News from Plimouth," in *The Works of Sir William D'Avenant* (London, 1673), 24. —Ed.
2. From John Denham, "On Justice," in *The Works of the British Poets* (London, 1795), 5: 716. —Ed.

Love to our citadel resorts
thro' these deceitful sally-ports,
Our centinels betray our forts.

APRIL
The Plaintiffs and Defendants much mistake
Their Cure, and their Diseases lasting make:
For, to be reconcil'd, and to comply,
Would be their cheap and shortest Remedy.
The Length and Charge of Law vex all that sue;
Laws punish many, reconcile but few.

Peace-makers find
Content of Mind.

MAY
Against Diseases Temperance.
Will ever be the best Defence.

JUNE
A General sets his Army in Array
In vain, unless he fights, and wins the Day.

JULY
Who bears a man-like Soul, or valiant Breast,
Provokes not Dangers to disturb his Rest;
Nor yet will he on ev'ry trivial Cause,
Be free to spend his Strength: But when the Laws,
The true Religion, or his Country's Good,
Crave his Assistance, freely spills his Blood.

Look for ruin when a coward wins;
for fear and cruelty were ever twins.

AUGUST
"This World's a City full of straying Streets,
And Death's the Market-place where each one meets.
The World is a great Dance, in which we find
The Good and Bad have various Turns assign'd:

But when they've ended the great Masquerade,
One goes to Glory, th' other to a Shade.[3]

SEPTEMBER

A good Wife will be careful of her Fame;
Her Husband's Credit, and her own good Name.
A bad Wife will be spiteful, cross and madding;
Seldom at home, but always be a gadding.
Choose vertuous Wives, if Husbands you'd be blest,
Fair Wives are good, but vertuous Wives are best.[4]

Evil men occasion evil times.

Flattering Parasites are dangerous Persons.

DECEMBER

Those who stir up sedition among the People,
    are the worst enemies of the state.

3. The first two lines are from William Shakespeare, *Two Noble Kinsmen*, Act 1, Scene 4. The last four are from John Crowne, *Juliana; Or, The Princess of Poland*, in *The Dramatic Works of John Crowne* (Edinburgh, 1873), 1: 101. —Ed.

4. Excerpted from Joshua Cooke, *A Pleasant Conceited Comedie, wherein Is Shewed How a Man May Chuse a Good Wife from a Bad*, in *Old English Drama* (London, 1825), 99. —Ed.

The Connecticut Diary: Or, Almanack, for the Year of Our Lord Christ, 1757 (New Haven)

JANUARY

"It is some Justice to ascribe to Chance,
"The Wrongs you must expect from Ignorance;
"None can the Moulds of their Creation chuse,
"We therefore should Men's Ignorance excuse;
"When born too low, to reach at Things sublime,
" 'Tis rather their Misfortune than their Crime.[1]

FEBRUARY

Love is such a Wealth as must be gain'd by Consent;
    not Stealth.

MARCH

" 'Tis best Abroad with foreign Foes to fight,
"And not at Home to feel their hateful Spite;"
Where all our Friends of every Sex and Age,
Would be expos'd unto their cruel Rage;
"And for a Truth this ever hath been found,
"He speedeth best who fights on foreign Ground.

What's contrary to reason is against law.

APRIL

Money is the sinews of war.

MAY

Adam, receiv'd in full for Loss sustain'd,
When for one Rib, a better Self he gain'd;

---

1. From Sir William Davenant, "Poems on Several Occasions," in *The Works of Sir William D'Avenant* (London, 1673), 278. —Ed.

Who had he not that blest Creation seen,
An *Auchoret,* in *Paradise* had been;
Woman we see was made of noblest Birth,
For She of Man was made, Man but of Earth.

Publick good should be prefered to private Interest.

The law helps the watchful but not the negligent.

JUNE

One spade of Gold undermines faster than
    an hundred of steel.

Envious persons punish themselves.

JULY

The noblest Spur unto the Sons of Fame,
Is Thirst of Honour, and to have their Name
Inroll'd in faithful History: Thus Worth,
Was by a wise Ambition first brought forth;
Truth is the Historian's Crown, and Art
To it, doth only Comeliness impart.[2]

The drunkard or profane
no office should sustain.

Make your Hay
while you may.

AUGUST

The giddy Multitude, who never fear,
A threatning Danger till they see it near;
Do fondly from their own Protection fly,
And just Assistance to their King deny;
Oppos'd by Some, forsaken by the Rest,
All will be conquer'd, rather than opprest.[3]

---

2. John Hall on Charles Aleyn, quoted in *A Complete Dictionary of Poetical Quotations,* ed. Sarah Josepha Hale (Philadelphia: Lippincott, Grambo, & Co., 1850), 233. —Ed.

3. From John Crowne, "Charles the Eighth of France," in *The Dramatic Works of John Crowne,* 1: 141. —Ed.

A man had better die in a good cause, than
   live in a bad one.

September

Riches and Poverty should be no more,
'Twixt Man and Man, the only Difference deem'd;
True Worth should not be scorn'd for being poor,
Nor he that's Rich without it be esteem'd;
Honour, should be of Virtue the Reward,
And Those who most deserve, have most Regard.

A Right sometimes sleeps, but never dies.

The act of the law doth injury to none.

October

Strict adherence to rules of Law best secure
   Men's rights.

An Astronomical Diary: Or an Almanack, for the Year of Our Lord Christ, 1758 (New Haven)

I have been informed that some good People in the Country, dislike my *Almanack*, because the observable Days of the Church of *England* are inserted in it, from thence, concluding that I am a *Church-man*; but to remove this Prejudice I would take leave to inform them, that altho' I have a high Esteem of the Church of *England,* consider'd as a reform'd Protestant Church and as agreeing with other Protestant Churches in the most important Matters of Faith: Yet I never could see any Thing so necessary or elegible in those Rites and other Circumstantials, wherein it differs from other Protestants Churches, as to be a sufficient Inducement or Warrant for Separation from the *Presbyterian* or Congregational Churches in *New-England,* to join with the *Episcopal* Church; neither do I suppose the Observation of those Day necessary: But as I take Liberty in these Matters to judge for myself, so I think it reasonable that Others should have the same Liberty; and since my Design in this Performance is to serve the Publick, and the inserting those observable Days does not croud out any Thing that might be more serviceable, I hope none of my Readers will be displeased with it for the Future.

R. Sherman.

JANUARY
'Tis from the Ruler's Virtue, Subjects take,
Th' Ingredient which does public Virtue make;
At his bright Beam, they all their Tapers light,
And by his Dial set their Motions right;
Whose powerful examples are so strong,
They make the Times by them go right or wrong.

FEBRUARY
If ROME could pardon Sins as Romans hold,
And if such Pardons might be bought with Gold,
Then 'twould be easy to determine which
To choose; to be religious or be rich?

Nay, since ROME's Pardons are to Papists sold,
They'll search no Scriptures but the Mines for Gold.[1]

JULY

Consider all thy Actions, and take Heed,
On stolen Bread, though it is sweet, to feed;
Sin, like a Bee, unto thy Hive may bring
A little Honey, but expect the Sting:
Thou may'st conceal thy Sin by cunning Art,
But Conscience fits a Witness in thy Heart.[2]

AUGUST

How happy if All understood
That none are safe, unless They're good.

A timely Reformation,
Wo'd favour Land & Nation.

SEPTEMBER

'Tis never best that Councils be too full,
Number makes long Disputes, and Graveness dull:
Though their Advice be good, their Counsels wise,
Yet Length still loses Opportunities:
Debate destroys Dispatch; as Fruits we see
Rot, when they hang too long upon the Tree.[3]

NOVEMBER

Honour of Blood without the Ornament of Knowledge,
    is but a glorious Ignorance.

Mankind upon each other's Ruins rise, Cowards
    maintain the Brave, and Fools the Wise.

---

1. From Francis Quarles, *Divine Fancies* (1632), in Grosart, *Complete Works of Francis Quarles*, 2: 240–41. —Ed.

2. From Thomas Hayward, ed., *The British Muse* (London, 1738), 1: 143. —Ed.

3. From John Denham, "Of Prudence," in *The Works of the English Poets*, ed. Samuel Johnson (London, 1810), 7: 255. —Ed.

An Astronomical Diary, or, an Almanack for the Year of Our Lord Christ, 1760 (Boston)

Brave AMHERST, WOLFE, & SAUNDERS, all advance,
With dauntless Courage and collected Might;
To turn the War, and tell *Aggressing* France,
How *Britain*'s and *New-England*'s Sons can Fight.
On Conquest fix'd, behold them rushing on
Thro Woods, o'er Lakes, to meet the Gallic Hosts.
At their Approach the French and Indians run,
And seiz'd with Terror quit their destin'd Posts.
Their strongest Forts yield to these Sons of Thunder
Who take their Towns, and their rich Treasures plunder.

MARCH
George our most gracious King, both Great and Good,
His Fleets and Armies sends a-cross the Floods——
To guard his Subjects in these distant Lands,
And save us from the En'my's barb'rous Hands.
GOD prosper Britain's Forces, join'd with our's,
Quite to subdue the haughty Gallic Pow'rs.

In ev'ry Breast there glows an active Flame,
the Love of Glory and the dread of Shame.

APRIL
May Britain's Sons, with Prussian Pow'rs alli'd
Conquer the French, humble the Sons of Pride
Who are against the Prot'stant Cause combin'd;
A Scourge of Nations, Murd'rers of Mankind:
May universal Peace this Year obtain,
Fix'd on a Basis that shall long remain.

Oft private Faith and public Trust are sold,
and Traitors barter Liberty for Gold.

MAY
Thro' various Climes, and to each distant Pole,
In happy Tides, let active Commerce roll,
Let Britain's Ships export an annual Fleece;
Richer than *Argos,* brought to antient Greece:
Returning Loaden, with the shining Stores,
Which lie profuse, on both the India's Shores.

Gold raises Armies in a Nation's Aid,
but bribes a Senate and the Land's betray'd.

AUGUST
That now our Nation by kind Heav'n blest,
Enjoys rich Favours, ought to be confess'd;
Favours more great and num'rous, than are giv'n
To any other Nation, under Heav'n:
A wife and gracious KING, the best of LAWS,
JUDGES and STATESMEN, faithful in its Cause.

SEPTEMBER
Most brave Commanders both by Land and Sea,
Most valiant Soldiers, crown'd with Victory;
Good *Air,* rich *Soil,* much *Wealth,* extensive Trade,
By pure Religion, yet more happy made:
All these and more with Freedom we enjoy,
To praise the GIVER then, be our Employ.

OCTOBER
Let Reason judge which of these two is worse
Want with a full or with an empty Purse.

A Computation of the most remarkable Passages of the Times, from the Creation, to this present Year 1760.

The Creation of the World, according to Chronology, is	5709
Noah's Flood	4053
Sodom and *Gomorrah* destroyed by Fire	3661
The Destruction of *Troy*	2944
The Building of the Temple at *Jerusalem*	2777
Brute entered England	2867
The Building of *London*	2867
The Building of *Rome*	2811
The Building of *York*	2747
The Bible translated into *Greek* by the Seventy Interpreters, at the command of *Ptolemy Philadelphus*	2025
Clocks and Dials first set up in Churches	1147
London-Bridge, after thirty-three Years Labour, finished with Stone	551
The first Use of Guns	380
Printing first used in *England*	307
A great Plague whereof died in one Year, in *London*, 30,578 Persons	156
Gunpowder Treason, *Nov.* 5, 1605	155
The Long Parliament began *Nov.* 3, 1640	120
King *Charles* I. beheaded	111
King *Charles* II. arriv'd at *London*, May 29, 1660	100
Two Comets in *December* and *March*	96
The sad Mortality that followed, whereof died of the Plague, that were taken Notice of, besides many others, 98,596 Persons	95
The most dreadful Fire in *London*, *Sept.* 2,3,4,5,6	94
The Discovery of the Popish Plot	82
The great Comet, *December* and *January* 1680	80
A great thirteen Weeks Frost, with a Fair kept upon the frozen *Thames*	76
The glorious Revolution 1688	72
K. *William* conquer'd *Ireland*,	70
K. *James* II. (who abdicated his Km. *Dec.* 18, 1688) died at St. *Germans* in *France*, Sept. 5, 1701	59
The Uniting the two Kingdoms of *England* & *Scotland*, May 1, 1707	53
King *George* I. proclaimed to the Joy of true Protestants	46
A splendid Comet, *December, January* and *Feb.*	17
A Rebellion in *Scotland* and *England*	15
The Rebels defeated on *Culloden-More*, by the Duke of *Cumberland*, *April* 16, 1746	14

Remarkable Occurrences of later Date.

1749.	*Aug.* 11.	Governor SHIRLEY laid the first Stone for Rebuilding the KING's Chappel in *Boston*.
1750.	*Mar.* 20.	Frederick Prince of Wales died.
1751.	*Oct.* 11.	*Charles Henry Frizo,* Prince of Orange died. Princess *Louisa,* Queen of *Denmark,* died; youngest Daughter to his present Majesty.
1752.		—— Small Pox in *Boston*.
	Sept. 3.	New Style introduced.
1754.	*July* 3.	Major *Washington* with 300 Provincials, defeated by 900 French.
1755.	*June* 16.	*Beausejour* taken from the French by an Army of *New-England* Provincials; and the French Neutrals removed from *Nova-Scotia.*
	July 9.	General *Braddock* defeated.
	Sept. 8.	Major-General JOHNSON, with an Army of Provincials, defeated an Army of French Regulars, Canadians and Indians, near *Lake-George*; and took the French General, *Baron Deskeau,* Prisoner.
	Nov. 1.	The City of *Lisbon* destroy'd by an Earthquake.
	Nov. 18.	A terrible Earthquake in *New-England.*
1756.	*Apr* 18, 19.	The French landed 18000 Troops on the Island of *Minorca,* in Time of Peace.
	May 18.	War declared in *England,* against *France*; and in *Boston, August* 4th following.
	June 16.	The French King publishes his Declaration of War against *England.*
	—— 29.	*Minorca* taken by the French.
	Aug. 14.	*Oswego* taken by the French.
	Sept. 25.	Governor SHIRLEY sail'd from *Boston* for *London.*
1757.		The Rt. Hon. Sir WILLIAM PITT, to the inexpressible Joy of Great Britain and its American Settlements, placed at the Head of the British Ministry.
	Mar. 14.	Admiral *Byng* shot.
	Aug. 3.	Governor POWNALL arriv'd in *Boston.*
	—— 9.	Fort *William-Henry* taken by the French, after a vigorous Defence, and great Numbers of the *English* cruelly massacred, after the Capitulation.

	Nov. 5.	The King of Prussia gains a remarkable Victory over the French and Austrians.
	Dec. 5.	The heroick King of Prussia gains a compleat Victory over the Austrian Army, commanded by Prince *Charles* and Count *Daun*.
	—— 28.	Princess *Caroline* died at St. *James's, Aet.* 45.
1758.	*April* 11.	Treaty of mutual Defence between *England* and *Prussia*.
	May 7.	*Senegal* taken.
	June 1.	The Hon. THOMAS HUTCHINSON, Esq. sworn Lieut. Governor of the Province of the *Massachusetts-Bay*.
	July 8.	General *Abercrombie* repuls'd at *Ticonderoga*.
	—— 26.	*Louisbourg* taken by General AMHERST, and Admiral BOSCAWEN.
	Aug. 28.	Fort *Frontinack* taken by Col. *Bradstreet*, at the Head of a brave (tho small) Army of Provincials.
	Nov. 24.	Fort *Du Quesne* evacuated at the Approach of General FORBE'S Army.
	Dec. 29.	The Island of *Gorce* taken by the *English*.
1759.	*Jan.*	*Guadaloupe* besieged; and taken *April*, 29.
	—— 12.	Princess *Anne* died at the *Hague Aet.* 49.
	Apr. 9.	A Comet appear'd this Morning.
	June	General WOLFE, and Admiral SAUNDERS, with a respectable Army and large Fleet of Men of War, appear before *Quebeck*, and landed their Troops.
	June. 4.	George William, Prince of Wales, arriv'd at full Age.
	July 26.	*Niagara* taken by Sir WILLIAM JOHNSON, under the Direction of Gen. AMHERST; and an Army of 2500 French & Indians sent to its Relief, totally defeated.
	—— 27.	*Ticonderoga* taken by General AMHERST in Person.
	—— 31.	*Crown-Point* evacuated at the Approach of General AMHERST'S Army.
	Aug. 1.	Prince *Ferdinand* obtains a great Victory over the French, & so preserv'd *Hanover*.

An Almanack for the Year of Our Lord Christ, *1761*
(Boston)

How shall my Muse in proper Lines express
Our Northern Armies Valour and Success?
While I am writing, comes the joyful News,
Which chears my Heart; a-new inspires my Muse.
Our three brave Armies at *Montreal* meet,
A Conquest of *New-France,* they there compleat.
To GOD, we owe the Triumphs of the Day;
NEW-FRANCE submits to GEORGE's gentle Sway!
May *LEWIS,* that proud Tyrant, never more
Bear any Rule upon the Northern Shoar.

April
"Happy the Man, who, studying Nature's Laws,
"Thro' known Effects can trace the secret Cause;
"His Mind possessing, in a quiet State,
"Fearless of Fortune, and resign'd to Fate:
"Nor hopes the People's Praise, nor fears their Frown,
"Nor sets up one, nor pulls another down.[1]

The Nations seem inclin'd to Peace, and Wars and
    Fightings soon will cease.

September
The Rib he form'd, and fashion'd with his Hands:
Under his forming Hands, a Creature grew
Man-like; but diff'rent Sex: So lovely fair!
That what seem'd fair in all the World, seem'd now
Mean, or in her summ'd up, in her contain'd,
And in her Looks; which from that Time infus'd
Sweetness into my Heart, unfelt before.[2]   *Milton.*

---

1. Virgil, *Georgics,* trans. John Dryden, in Johnson, *Works of the English Poets,* 19: 313. —Ed.
2. John Milton, *Paradise Lost,* Book 8, lines 469–75. —Ed.

"A Caveat against Injustice, by Philoeunomos," 1752

Sherman, writing under the pseudonym Philoeunomos ("lover of good law"), published the following pamphlet in 1752. In it, he addresses problems resulting from each New England colony issuing its own bills of credit. All of these bills depreciated over time, but those from Rhode Island and New Hampshire lost value with alarming speed. To compound the difficulties created by this dynamic, some debtors argued that because merchants had traditionally accepted bills of credit from other colonies, there was now a common law requirement for them to do so.

A

CAVEAT Against INJUSTICE,

OR AN

ENQUIRY into the evil Consequences
of a Fluctuating

MEDIUM

OF

EXCHANGE,

WHEREIN is considered, whether the Bills of Credit on
the Neighbouring Governments, are a legal Tender in
Payments of Money,

In the COLONY

OF

CONNECTICUT,

FOR Debts due by Book, and otherwise, where the
Contract Mentions only *Old-Tenor* Money.

By PHILOEUNOMOS.

NEW YORK.

Printed by *Henry De Foreest in King-Street.* 1752.

Forasmuch, as there have been many Disputes arisen of late concerning the *Medium of Exchange* in this Colony, which have been occasioned chiefly by Reason of our having such large Quantities of Paper *Bills of Credit* on some of the Neighbouring Governments, passing in Payments among us, and some of those Governments having issued much larger Sums of such Bills than were necessary to supply themselves with a competent *Medium of Exchange,* and not having supplied their Treasuries with any Fund for the maintaining the Credit of such Bills; they have therefore been continually depreciating and growing less in their Value, and have been the principal Means of the Depreciation of the *Bills of Credit* emitted by this Colony, by their passing promiscuously with them; and so have been the Occasion of Much Embarrasment and Injustice, in the Trade and Commerce of this colony, and many People and especially Widows and Orphans have been great Sufferers thereby. But our Legislature having at length taken effectual Care to prevent a further Depreciation of the *Bills* of this Colony, and the other Governments not having taken the like prudent Care, their *Bills of Credit* are still sinking in their Value, and have in Fact sunk much below the Value of the *Bills* of this Colony. Yet some People among us, by long Custom, are so far prejudiced in Favour of a sinking Medium, and others not being really sensible of the true State of the Case, are inclined to think that *Bills of Credit* on the neighbouring Governments ought to be a legal Tender in Payments in this Colony for all Debts due by Book and otherwise where there is no special contract expressly mentioning some other Currency, and others being of a different Opinion, the Disputes have been carried on so far, as to occasion some Expence in the Law, and may be likely to occasion much more, unless prevented by those Prejudices being some way removed. And since it is a Cause wherein every one is more or less interested, I have ventured to shew my Opinion, with a sincere Desire to have Peace and Justice maintained and promoted in the Colony. Not desiring any Person to approve of my Observations any farther than he finds them agreeable to the Principles of Justice and right Reason.

The Case Stated.

Suppose a Man comes to a Trader's Shop in this Colony to buy Goods, and the Trader sells him a certain Quantity of Goods and tells him the Price is so many Pounds, Shillings and Pence, *(let it be more or less)* to be paid at the Expiration of one Year, from that Time, and the Man receives the Goods but their is nothing said either by Seller or Buyer, what Currency it is to be paid in, but the Goods are charged according to the Value of *Bills of Credit* Old Tenor on this Colony.

Now I Query what the Creditor has a Right to demand for a Debt so contracted; or what the Debtor can oblige him to accept in Payment?

The Creditor says, that the Debt being contracted in the Colony of *Connecticut,* he ought to have what is known by the Laws of said Colony to be Money: And that he has no Right to demand any thing else.

The Debtor says, That *Bills of Credit* on the neighbouring Governments have for many Years passed promiscuously with *Bills of Credit* on this Colony as Money in all Payments, *(except Special Contracts)* and that People in general where the Contracts ly at large have expected, and do still expect, that any of the *Bills of Credit* on any of the Governments in *New-England,* that have obtained a Currency in this Colony will answer in Payment, and in as much as the Creditor did not give him any Notice to the contrary, when he bought the Goods, therefore he thinks that such *Bills of Credit* ought to be accepted in Payment for the aforesaid Debt. And altho' there is no particular Statute in this Colony, that such *Bills of Credit* shall be a legal Tender in Payments of Money: Yet the Practice has been so universal for so long a Time, and the Creditor himself has both received and pass'd them as Money constantly without making Exceptions against them 'till this Debt was contracted, and for many Years all Demands on Book Debts have been for Old-Tenor Money indifferently, without Distinction of Colonies, and Judgments in all Courts have been given thereon accordingly: And any of the aforesaid *Bills of Credit* have pass'd in Payment to satisfy all Judgments, so obtain'd and this universal Custom, the Debtor saith, ought to be esteem'd as common Law and ought not without some Special Reason to be set aside, and that in this Case there is nothing Special; and therefore the Creditor ought not to make Demand or obtain Judgment different from the common Custom of the Colony.

In Answer to this the Creditor saith, that altho' *Bills of Credit* on the neighbouring Governments have for a Number of Years been pass'd and receiv'd in Payments: Yet it has been only by the voluntary Consent of the Persons receiving them, and not because they were under any Obligation to receive them; and that it is no Argument that a Person shall be obliged to receive any Species when it won't answer his End, because in Time past he has receiv'd it when it would answer. And the Creditor further saith, that such *Bills of Credit* are of no intrinsick Value, and their Extrinsical Value is fluctuating and very uncertain, and therefore it would be unjust that any Person should be obliged to receive them in Payment as Money in this Colony, (since neither the Colony nor any of the Inhabitants thereof are under any Obligation either to Refund said Bills or to maintain the Credit of them) for Money ought to be something of certain Value, it being that whereby other Things are to be valued. And I think it is a Principle that must be granted that no Government has a Right to impose on its Subjects any foreign Currency to be received in Payments as Money which is not of intrinsick Value; unless such Government will assume and undertake to secure and make Good to the Possessor of such Currency the full Value which they oblige him to receive it for. Because in so doing they would oblige Men to part with their Estates for that which is worth nothing in it self and which they don't know will ever procure him any Thing. And *Rhode-Island Bills of Credit* have been so far from being of certain Value and securing to the Possessor the Value that they were first stated at, that they have depreciated almost four seventh Parts in nine Years last past, as appears by their own Acts of Assembly. For in the Year 1743, it appears by the Face of the Bills then emitted that *Twenty-seven* Shillings Old-Tenor was equal to one Ounce of Silver. And by an Act of their General Assembly pass'd in *March* last, they stated *Fifty-four* Shillings Old-Tenor Bills equal to one Ounce of Silver, which sunk their Value one half. And by another Act in *June* last, (viz. 1751) they stated *Sixty-four* Shillings in their Old-Tenor Bills equal to one Ounce of Silver. And by another Act in *August* last they gave Order and Direction to the Courts in that Colony to make Allowance to the Creditors in making up Judgment from Time to Time as the Bills shall depreciate for the Future, which shews that they expect their *Bills of Credit* to depreciate for the Future. And since the Value of the *Bills of Credit* depend wholly on the Rate at which they are stated and on the Credit of the Government by whom they are emitted and that being the only Reason and Foundation upon which they obtained their first Currency and by which the same has been upheld ever since their first being current. and therefore when the Publick Faith and Credit of such Government is violated, then the Reason upon which such Bills obtained their Currency ceases and there remains no Reason why they should be any longer current.

And this I would lay down as a Principle that can't be denied that a Debtor ought not to pay any Debts with less Value than was contracted for, without the Consent or against the Will of the Creditor,

And the Creditor further saith, that his accepting *Rhode-Island Bills of Credit* when they stood stated equal to Silver at *Twenty-seven* Shillings an Ounce, can be no Reason that he should receive them at the same Value when they are stated equal to Silver at *Fifty-four* Shillings an Ounce, and still to receive them at the same Rate when they are so reduced down that *Sixty-four* Shillings is equal to but one Ounce of Silver, and whoever does receive them so must not only act without, but against Reason.

And the Debtor can't possibly plead without any Truth that he expected to pay in *Rhode-Island Bills of Credit* at their present Value and under their present Circumstances, (any Debts contracted before the aforesaid Acts of *Rhode-Island* were published) because there was no such Thing (as those Bills are under their present Circumstances) existing at the Time of Contract, for as was observ'd before, the Value of such *Bills of Credit* depend wholly upon the Rate at which they are stated and on the Credit of the Government by whom they are emitted, and a *Bill of Credit* for the same Sum that is stated equal to Silver at *Twenty-seven* Shillings an Ounce, must be of more than double the Value of one stated equal to Silver at *Sixty four* Shillings an Ounce if the Credit of the Emitter may be depended on: But if the Emitter's Credit can't be depended on then neither of the Bills aforesaid are of any Value, because it is evident that no *Bills of Credit* have any Value in themselves, but are given to secure something of intrinsick Value, to the Possessor.

So that the Arguments drawn from Custom are of no Force, because the Reasons upon which that Custom were grounded do now cease.

I grant that if any Thing whose Value is intrinsical and invariable the same should obtain a Currency as a *Medium of Exchange* for a great Number of Years in any Colony, it might with some Reason be urg'd that it ought to be accepted in Payments for Debts where there is no special Agreement for any other Species. But if what is us'd as a *Medium of Exchange* is fluctuating in its Value it is no better than unjust Weights and Measures, both which are condemn'd by the Laws of GOD and Man, and therefore the longest and most universal Custom could never make the Use of such a *Medium* either lawful or reasonable.

Now suppose that Gold or Silver Coines that pass current in Payments at a certain Rate by Tale should have a considerable Part of their Weight filed or clipp'd off will any reasonable Man judge that they ought to pass for the same Value as those of full Weight. But the State of *R----- I----d Bills of Credit* is much worse than that of Coins that are clipp'd, because what is left of those Coins is of intrinsick Value: But the General Assembly of *R----- I----d* having depreciated their *Bills of Credit* have thereby violated their Promise from Time to Time, and there is just Reason to suspect their Credit for the Future for the small Value which they now promise for said Bills, and they have not only violated their Promise as to the Value pretended to be secured to the Possessor by said Bills; but also as to the Time of calling them in and paying the same, they having lengthened out the Time Fifteen Years. So that if the Possessor must be kept out of the Use of his Money until that Term is expired (and the Bills secure nothing to him sooner.) One Ounce of Silver paid down now, would be worth more than *Seven* Pounds *Ten* Shillings in such *Bills of Credit* computing the Interest at 6 *per Cent per Annum*.

These Things considered can, any reasonable Man think that such *Bills of Credit* (or rather of no *Credit*) ought to be a legal Tender in Payment of Money in this Colony for Debts, for which the Debtor received Species of much more Value than those Bills provided the Creditor could get the full Value of them in Silver that they are now stated at. For it must be remembered that according to the State of the Case now in Question the Goods were charged according to the Value of Old-Tenor Bills of this Colony. Wherefore upon the whole it appears that it would be evidently unjust to impose *Rhode-Island Bills of Credit* in payment for such a Debt, or any other in this Colony, unless the Creditor obliged himself by a special Agreement to receive them in Payment.

And if he had agreed to receive them in Payment for Debts contracted any Time between last *March* and *June* it would be unjust to oblige him to take them without three Shillings on the Pound Allowance, for the General Assembly of *Rhode-Island* depreciated them so much in *June* below both their current and stated Value in *March* preceding. And to oblige People to receive them without such Allowance in this Colony; would be, to be more dishonest than they are in *Rhode-Island* Colony for they are obliged by Law to make Allowance for the Depreciation. But in as much as we are not under the Jurisdiction of *Rhode-Island* Government and therefore can take no Benefit by their equitable Acts, I suppose that according to the Rules of the Law, upon a Contract made in this Colony for the Payment of *Bills of Credit* on the Colony of *Rhode-Island* or any of the neighbouring Governments. If the Debtor could not procure such Bills under the same Circumstances that they were at the Time of Contract, the Courts would assess Damages for *Connecticut* Money, according to the Value of such Bills at the Time of Contract. And the Reason is, because if on the one Hand all such Bills should be called in and burnt between the Time of Contract and the Time of Payment it would be unreasonable to oblige the Debtor to an impossibility, and on the other Hand if there should between the Time of Contract and the Time of Payment be an Act pass'd that all such Bills should be brought into the Treasurer to be redeem'd by a certain Time or else be Outlawed and rendered of no Value and that Time should be expired before the Time of Payment, or if by an Act of Assembly they should be depreciated and sunk one half or two thirds in their Value, it would be unreasonable that the Creditor should be thereby defrauded of his just Due and lose so much of his Estate.

But to impose *Rhode-Island Bills of Credit* in Payments for Debts in this Colony when the Creditor never agreed to take them, and that without any Allowance for the Depreciation, would be to take away Men's Estates and wrong them of their just and righteous Dues without either Law or Reason.

And instead of having our Properties defended and secured to us by the

Protection of the Government under which we live; we should be always exposed to have them taken from us by Fraud at the Pleasure of other Governments, who have no Right of Jurisdiction over us. And according to this Argument, if *Rhode-Island* General Assembly had been pleased last *June* to have stated their Old-Tenor Bills equal to Silver at *Forty-eight* Pounds *Twelve* Shillings an Ounce, instead of *Sixty-four* Shillings, and to have cut off the Value of them *Eighteen* Shillings on the Pound, instead of *Three* Shillings, all Creditors in this Colony would thereby have been necessitated to lose *Ninety* Pounds out of every *Hundred* Pounds of their Debts which were then out standing, for if they could take away one Sixth Part of their Value and reduce them so much below the Old-Tenor Bills of this Colony and the Creditor be notwithstanding obliged to receive them without any Allowance, by the fame Rule they might have taken away three Quarters or Nine Tenths or indeed the whole, and the Creditor have had no more Remedy than he has now. And the Estates of poor Widows and Orphans must according to this Principle in the same unjust Manner be taken away from them and given to others that have no Right to them, (for what the Creditor loses in this way the Debtor gains because the more the *Bills of Credit* depreciate the less Value the Debtor can procure them for) and according to the Debtor's Argument the Executive Courts in this Colony must give Judgment in Favour of all this Fraud and Iniquity at least, 'till there is some special Act of Assembly to order them to the contrary; but I believe that every honest Man of common Sense, upon mature Consideration of the Circumstances of the Case, will think that this is an Iniquity not to be countenanced, but rather to be punished by the Judges.

But in Answer to what is said concerning Demands being made for Old-Tenor Money indifferently and the Courts giving Judgment accordingly. The Creditor saith that Phrase in all Demands made in this Colony ought to be understood to be the Old-Tenor Money of this Colony, and no other, for there never was any Law in this Colony that *Bills of Credit* on the neighbouring Governments should be a legal Tender in Payments of Money, and I have observed before that it would be unreasonable, that any such Foreign Currency should be imposed as Money, and the same Phrase is us'd in taxing Bills of Cost in the Executive Courts, but it is understood to be the Old-Tenor Money of this Colony only, for a *Thousand* Pounds in *Bills of Credit* on the neighbouring Governments would not be sufficient in the Law to satisfy a Bill of Cost of *Twenty* Shillings Old-Tenor.

☞ And the General Assembly of this Colony have sufficiently declared that they don't Esteem such *Bills of Credit* as Money, and that no Person ought to be obliged to receive them as such. In that, they themselves will not receive them for their Wages neither do they oblige any other Person whose Fees or

Wages are stated by Law to receive them, but have made Provision how they shall be paid exclusive of such Bills. And as to the Objection that they have been receiv'd in Payment to satisfy all Judgments given as aforesaid, the Creditor saith, that it was only by the voluntary Consent of the Receiver, but there is not the same Reasons that they should be received now at the same Value as *Bills of Credit* on this Colony that there was formerly because it is evident that there is now a real Difference in their Values. For by a Law of the Province of the *Massachusets-Bay*, their Bills of Old-Tenor are stated equal to Silver at *Fifty* Shillings an Ounce and *Seven* Shillings and *Six* Pence are equal to *One* Shilling Proclamation Money, and the Executive Courts in this Colony reckon *Eight* Shillings Old-Tenor Bills of this Colony equal to *One* Shilling Proclamation Money which is equal to Silver at *Fifty-four* Shillings Old-Tenor an Ounce. And by an Act of *Rhode-Island* General Assembly *Sixty-four* Shillings of their Old-Tenor Bills is stated equal to one Ounce of Silver, at which Rate *Nine* Shillings and *Six* Pence is equal to but *One* Shillings Proclamation Money, whereas three Years ago the Bills of Old-Tenor on all the three Governments aforesaid were of equal Value.

And since it appears, that there is such a Difference in the stated Value of the aforesaid *Bills of Credit,* no Man can with any Propriety be said to make them all without Distinction, a Standard to value Things by; for a Man could afford to sell any Goods or Merchandize for a less Sum in Old-Tenor Bills of the *Massachusets-Bay*, than for the Old-Tenor Bills of this Colony and he could afford to sell Goods for a less Sum by 15 *per Cent* for the Old-Tenor Bills of this Colony, than for the Old-Tenor Bills on *Rhode-Island* Colony.

And to say that an Accompt is charged in Old-Tenor Money indifferently of this and the neighbouring Governments, is to say that 7*s.*-6*d.* and 8*s.* and 9*s.*-6.*d* are one and the same Sum, or that there is no Difference between *Fifty* and *Fifty-four*, or between *Fifty-four* and *Sixty-four* Q. E. D.

And since it appears that it would be evidently absurd to make a Demand for Old-Tenor Money indifferently of this and the neighbouring Governments, it follows that all Demands made for Old-Tenor Money in this Colony must be for the Money of this Colony exclusive of the Old-Tenor of the neighbouring Governments, or else for the Old-Tenor Money of some one of the other Governments exclusive of the Old-Tenor of this and the rest.

And since nothing but a special Contract can intitle any Person to demand the Money of any other Government, for a Debt contracted and demanded in this Colony: It necessarily follows, that all Demands for Debts due by Book, where the Contract lyes at large must be for the Money of this Colony only.

What I would be understood to mean by Old-Tenor Money of the Colony of *Connecticut* is, whatsoever is established by Law in said Colony to pass as or in Lieu of Money, rated according to its Value in Old-Tenor Bills on said Colony, and I suppose that the Words (Old-Tenor) when us'd in Contracts are universally *understood* to be intended only to assertain the Value of the Sum to which they are affixed and they must be so understood when the Executive Courts tax Bills of Cost in Old-Tenor Money, for they have no Right neither do they mean to exclude Bills of the New-Tenor, or any of those Coins established by Law (to pass in Payment for Fees) from being a sufficient Tender in Payment of such Costs.

And now I have gone through with what I first proposed. But perhaps some, may be ready to say, *that we are sensible that it is of bad Consequence to have a fluctuating Medium of Exchange, but what can be done to Remedy it?*

I answer take away the Cause, and the Effect will necessarily cease.

But it may be further objected, that if it were not for the *Bills of Credit* on the neighbouring Governments, we should have no Money to Trade with, and what should we do for a *Medium of Exchange?* or how could we live without?

To this I answer, that if that were indeed the Case, we had better die in a good Cause than live in a bad one. But I apprehend that the Case in Fact is quite the reverse for we in this Colony are seated on a very fruitful Soil, the Product whereof, with our Labour and Industry, and the Divine Blessing thereon, would sufficiently furnish us with, and procure us all the Necessaries of Life and as good a *Medium of Exchange* as any People in the World have or can desire. But so long as we part with our most valuable Commodities for such *Bills of Credit* as are no Profit; but rather a Cheat, Vexation and Snare to us, and become a *Medium* whereby we are continually cheating and wronging one another in our Dealings and Commerce. And so long as we import so much more foreign Goods than are necessary, and keep so many Merchants and Traders employed to procure and deal them out to us: Great Part of which, we might as well make among ourselves; and another great Part of which, we had much better be without, especially the Spiritous Liquors of which vast Quantities are consumed in this Colony every Year, unnecessarily to the great Destruction of the Estates, Morals, Health and even the Lives of many of the Inhabitants.

I say so long as these Things are so we shall spend great Part of our Labour and Substance for that, which will not profit us. Whereas if these Things were reformed, the Provisions and other Commodities which we might have to export yearly, and which other Governments are dependant upon us for, would procure us Gold and Silver abundently sufficient for a *Medium* of Trade. And we might be as independent, flourishing and happy a Colony as any in the *British* Dominions.

And with Submission I would humbly beg Leave to propose it to the wise Consideration of the Honourable General Assembly of this Colony; whether it would not be conducive to the welfare of the Colony to pass some Act to prevent the Bills last emitted by *Rhode-Island* Colony from obtaining a Currency among us. And to appoint some reasonable Time (not exceeding the Term that our *Bills of Credit* are allowed to pass) after the Expiration of which none of the *Bills of Credit* on *New Hampshire* or *Rhode-Island,* shall be allowed to pass in this Colony, that so People having previous Notice thereof may order their Affairs so as to get rid of such bills to the best Advantage that they can before the Expiration of such Term.

And whether it would not be very much for the Publick Good to lay a large Excise upon all Rum imported into this Colony or distilled herein, thereby effectually to restrain the excessive use thereof, which is such a growing Evil among us and is leading to almost all other Vices. And I doubt not but that if those two great Evils that have been mentioned were restrained we should soon see better Times.

FINIS

Letter to William Samuel Johnson, December 5, 1766

NEW HAVEN

Although six years his senior, Sherman had studied law under William Samuel Johnson (1727–1819) in the early 1750s. In 1766, Johnson was serving as Connecticut's agent in London. This letter is particularly interesting because it shines some light on Sherman's legal education and because of his speculation regarding the limits of the colonists' obligation to obey the Crown.

Hawkins' Pleas of the Crown
— Abridgment of Coke on Lit.^{on}
Jacobs Law Dictionary
— Attorneys Practice
Ld. Raymond Reports
Law of Evidence
Hale's history of the Common Law
Attorneys pocket Companion
Prussian Laws 2 Vol.
Conductor Generalis

Sir,

The above is a list of the law books I now have. Please to get for me Bacon's Abridgment if compleat & such others on Law & Politicks as you shall think most beneficial to the amount of about £20. I could have sent the money, but as you have power to draw of the Governm. money in England which we want to have bro't into the Treasury—if I pay it on your return it may suit better than to send it. I have sent the Newspaper you spoke of by the Post. Since that paper was published this question hath been proposed to me, viz, Does not the King hold his Dominions in Great Brittain & America by the same Title, i.e. whether he is not King of America by virtue of his being King of Great Brittain, and if so, how are they distinct Dominions?

Source: William Samuel Johnson Papers, box 1, Connecticut Historical Society, Hartford, Connecticut.

There is no doubt but that the colonies are bound by the present Establishment of the Crown, as they have consented to it, sworn Allegiance &c.

But Query: If the succession according to the present Establishment should cease for want of an Heir, or if the Parliament should alter it & admit a Papist to the Crown, would not the colonies be at Liberty to Joyn with Brittain or not.

These questions may serve for speculation but it is not likely they will need to be Resolved in our Day, & I hope not till the time comes when the Nations shall learn War no more————[1]

I am, Sir, your Obedient Humble Sert

R. Sherman

1. A reference to Isaiah 2: 4, "And he shall judge among the nations, and shall rebuke many people: and they shall beat their swords into plowshares, and their spears into pruninghooks: nation shall not lift up sword against nation, neither shall they learn war any more." —Ed.

Letter to Rebecca Sherman, May 30, 1770

Sherman married his second wife, Rebecca Prescott, in 1763. He wrote this brief note to her on May 30, 1770.

This is your birth day. Mine was the 30th of last month. May we so number our days as to apply our Hearts to wisdom: that is, true Religion. Psalm 90: 12.
I remain affectionately yours,

ROGER SHERMAN.

Source: Lewis H. Boutell, *The Life of Roger Sherman* (Chicago: A. C. McClurg, 1896), 47.

Connecticut Politics and Law

The Fundamental Orders of Connecticut was the first constitution written to ensure popular self-government. Under it, inhabitants of towns governed themselves in most matters, and twice each year freemen in towns elected representatives to the General Court to address matters affecting the whole colony. This court met in May to elect a governor and other magistrates, and again in October to revise and pass legislation. As well, the General Court served as the highest judicial body in the colony. In 1662, King Charles II granted Connecticut a royal charter, one drafted by the General Court that retained civic institutions similar to those established in the Fundamental Orders. The colony remained almost completely self-governing, and the Crown exercised virtually no oversight over it. Over the next century, the number of towns in the colony increased rapidly, and in 1698 it adopted a bicameral legislature, but political and ecclesiastical structures remained stable. Upon independence, the legislature, now referred to as the General Assembly, simply removed all references to the Crown from its 1662 charter. This document functioned as the state's constitution for another forty-three years.[1]

When Sherman entered colonial politics in 1755, freemen in each town chose two representatives to serve in the lower house of the General Assembly. As well, each voter could nominate up to twenty men to serve in the upper house,

1. David M. Roth, *Connecticut: A Bicentennial History* (New York: W. W. Norton, 1979); Richard J. Purcell, *Connecticut in Transition: 1775–1818* (1918; reprint, Middletown, Conn.: Wesleyan University Press, 1963).

or Council of Assistants. The top nominees were placed on a list, with the current and ex-assistants listed first. Freemen then cast twelve votes for members of the council. This system had the effect of virtually guaranteeing the reelection of current assistants, for although they could theoretically be voted out of office in any given year, only a highly coordinated effort would succeed in doing so. The governor and deputy governor were elected at large, but if no candidate received a majority of the votes, the General Assembly filled the positions.

Although Connecticut had a bicameral legislature, separation of powers was minimal by modern standards. The chief executive was an ex officio member of the council and had little independent power. He possessed no veto, appointed only minor officials, and could not pardon criminals. Members of the General Assembly regularly accepted administrative and judicial responsibilities, and the legislature remained the final arbiter of judicial disputes until 1819. Throughout most of Sherman's life, Connecticut's highest judicial tribunal was the Superior Court, which consisted of a chief judge (after 1715 always the deputy governor) and four members appointed by the General Assembly. Although almost anyone could be appointed to this court, judges were always members of the upper house until 1785, when the legislature prohibited Superior Court judges from holding other high state or national offices. The General Assembly retained the power to review and overturn any judicial decision until 1819.

Sherman's Early Political Career

Sherman did not come from a prominent Connecticut family, but he gradually worked his way into the colony's political structure. In 1748, five years after moving to New Milford, he became a freeman. This status was granted to males "twenty-one years of age, in possession of a freehold estate of the value of forty shillings per annum, or of forty pounds personal estate in the general assessment lists of that year, and 'of a quiet and peaceable Behaviour, and Civil Conversation.' "[2] As a freeman, Sherman was eligible to vote and hold civic offices. In 1749 he became a grand juryman, then he received appointments as list-taker, leather sealer, society clerk, fence viewer, and surveyor. In 1753 he was elected selectman, and in 1755, one year after he was admitted to the Litchfield bar, he was chosen to represent New Milford in the lower house of

2. Quoted in Lawrence Henry Gipson, *American Loyalist: Jared Ingersoll* (1920; reprint, New Haven, Conn.: Yale University Press, 1971), 18.

the General Assembly. Representatives routinely served as local justices of the peace, and Sherman was accordingly appointed to this office.[3]

Sherman was not returned to the General Assembly for its 1756 sessions, but he was elected again in October 1758. Although he moved to New Haven in 1760, he continued to represent New Milford in the lower house until March 1761. In addition to the usual business of appointments and dealing with memorials and petitions, much of the legislature's work during those years involved the war with France and its Native American allies. The General Assembly passed legislation raising troops, required the quartering of His Majesty's soldiers, and, finally, called for a day of thanksgiving to return "gratitude to Almighty God" for the "termination of a bloody and expensive war."[4]

Susquehannah

One of the most significant issues running through Sherman's political career concerned Connecticut's claim to land in the Wyoming Valley along the Susquehannah River. The territory in question was physically separated from the rest of Connecticut by part of New York. Nevertheless, it was apparently granted to both Pennsylvania and Connecticut by charters issued by Charles II. For many years, the potential for conflict remained just that—potential. However, in 1753 the Susquehannah Company was founded in Connecticut to "Spread Christianity" and "to promote our own Temporal Interest."[5] The company purchased land in the Wyoming Valley from Native Americans and encouraged the settlement of Connecticut citizens in the region. Numerous towns were populated by these settlers in the mid to late 1750s. Pennsylvania proprietor Thomas Penn objected to the settlements and in 1763 was able to secure an order from the Crown requiring settlers to leave the Wyoming Valley. Connecticut citizens refused to leave and continued moving to the territory.[6]

Sherman's involvement with the issue began in 1769 when he was appointed

3. Details of Sherman's political career may be found in Collier, *Roger Sherman's Connecticut*, and Hall, *Roger Sherman and the Creation of the American Republic*.

4. Charles J. Hoadly, ed., *The Public Records of the Colony of Connecticut* (Hartford, Conn.: Press of the Case, Lockwood and Brainard Co., 1881), 12: 137.

5. Julian P. Boyd, ed., *The Susquehannah Company Papers* (Ithaca, N.Y.: Cornell University Press, 1936), 1: 25, 28.

6. On this controversy, see Julian P. Boyd, *The Susquehannah Company: Connecticut's Experiment in Expansion* (New Haven, Conn.: Yale University Press, 1935). See also Julian P. Boyd and Robert J. Taylor, eds., *The Susquehannah Company Papers*, 11 vols. (Ithaca, N.Y.: Cornell University Press, 1936–71).

as a representative for the council on a joint committee investigating the controversy. He quickly convinced himself of the justice of Connecticut's claim and became a steadfast advocate for the Susquehannah Company. In 1774, he voted with the General Assembly to grant a charter to the town of Westmoreland in the disputed territory. In the same year, Sherman wrote a private legal brief and published an essay in the *Connecticut Journal* arguing the colony's position based on prior charter rights, the legality of purchases from Native Americans, and settlement. During the War for Independence, the Susquehannah Company ceased planting new settlements, although controversies about existing ones continued. In 1782, a court of commissioners established under Article IX of the Articles of Confederation resolved the dispute in Pennsylvania's favor. Still, cases concerning specific property claims were heard into the nineteenth century, and Connecticut did not give up all of its western land claims until it was compensated with approximately 3.5 million acres in Ohio— land that was eventually sold to support public education in the state.[7]

Revision of Laws

After the war, one of Sherman's most significant accomplishments at the state level was his revision of Connecticut's statutes. He had been involved in a similar project in 1768, but since that time many new statutes had been passed, some had been repealed, and independence had made others obsolete. The legislature asked Sherman and Richard Law to revise existing statutes "and make such Alterations Additions exclusions and Amendments as they shall Judge Proper and expedient."[8] It was an enormous task. To divide it, Sherman took statutes beginning with the letters A–L, and Law took the rest. Sherman and Law worked on their project throughout the summer and fall of 1783. The two men corresponded about changes in each other's sections. Sherman participated in debates over them as an assistant when the General Assembly reviewed their work, accepting, rejecting, or amending their proposals, and approving the new one-volume state code (still organized alphabetically) in January 1784.[9]

---

7. Robert J. Taylor, ed., *The Susquehannah Company Papers* (Ithaca, N.Y.: Cornell University Press, 1969), 7: 245–46.

8. Leonard Woods Labaree, ed., *The Public Records of the State of Connecticut* (Hartford, Conn.: State of Connecticut, 1943), 5: 122, 281.

9. Roger Sherman to Richard Law, July 25, 1783, Ernest Law Papers, Connecticut Historical

Judge Sherman

Sherman served on Connecticut's Superior Court from 1766 until 1789. Unfortunately, judicial decisions were not formally reported until the end of Sherman's career. From the records and unofficial accounts that are available, it appears that most cases adjudicated by Sherman and his colleagues involved mundane criminal, civil, and procedural issues.[10] Some of these reflect the political culture of late eighteenth-century Connecticut. For instance, divorces were granted only for causes like desertion and cruelty, and an ecclesiastical society was denied the ability to fire a minister who had not violated the "covenant" between him and the society. One case involved "a Presentment of Grandjury against Drake for Defaming Mr. P. a Clergyman viz. for charging him for being an Arminian, unfit to be a Minister of the Gospel." None of the judges who heard the case denied that such an accusation was slander, but the lower court decision was overturned on a procedural issue.[11]

At the very end of Sherman's judicial service, a few of his votes and a handful of individual opinions were reported by "the first full-fledged official law report in the country," Ephraim Kirby's *Reports of Cases Adjudged in the Superior Court of the State of Connecticut, from the Year 1785, to May, 1788.*[12] As a matter of legal trivia, it is worth noting that Sherman wrote the first dissenting opinion published in an American law report.[13] Similarly, he was on the court that

---

Society. Sherman and Law's draft, with alterations by the General Assembly, was bound and is available in the Connecticut State Library. The final version of the code was printed in 1784 and is reprinted in John D. Cushing, ed., *The First Laws of the State of Connecticut* (Wilmington, Del.: Michael Glazier, 1982).

10. Relatively early in his service on the Superior Court, Sherman was joined by William Samuel Johnson. Johnson kept notes on the 130 cases the two heard together between December 1772 and March 1773. In many instances, Johnson did little more than note the decision of the court, but in twenty-two cases he specifically stated that Sherman dissented or joined a fractured majority. In 1785 the General Assembly required Superior Court judges to issue written opinions, many of which are available in the Connecticut State Library. However, many of these manuscript opinions merely state the decision of the court. Some of these were later published in Kirby's *Reports* (1789). John T. Farrell, ed., *The Superior Court Diary of William Samuel Johnson, 1772–1773* (Washington, D.C.: American Historical Association, 1942), 60–61, 105, 231; Ephraim Kirby, ed., *Reports of Cases Adjudged in the Superior Court of the State of Connecticut, from the Year 1785, to May, 1788, with Some Determinations in the Supreme Court of Errors* (Litchfield, 1789).

11. *Ecclesiastical Society v. Beckwith* (1786); 1 Kirby 91 (1786). The handwritten opinion for the last case is available in the Connecticut State Library.

12. Farrell, *Superior Court Diary of William Samuel Johnson*, vii.

13. *Whiting and Frisbie v. Jewel*, 1 Kirby 1 (1786).

issued the first reported search and seizure case. In the decision, he joined his colleagues in declaring a general warrant "to search all places, and arrest all persons" to be "clearly illegal."[14] This chapter concludes with a few of the more interesting judicial opinions penned by Sherman.

14. *Frisbie v. Butler,* 1 Kirby 213 (1787).

Susquehannah Controversy

Article from *The Connecticut Journal,* April 8, 1774

This article concerns the controversy between Connecticut and Pennsylvania over the Wyoming Valley.

Messi'rs Greens,

Please to insert the following in your paper for information of the freemen of this colony.

There has been much altercation of late concerning the doings of the Hon. General Assembly, relative to the western lands contained in our charter, and many false insinuations have been industriously circulated by some men, to prejudice the minds of the people against the Assembly; from what motives I shall not undertake to determine. It is hard to suppose that the good of the colony has been the motive, when the measures taken have the most direct tendency to its destruction; for every *kingdom divided against itself is brought to desolation.* I am sensible that the good people of the towns concerned in the late Middletown convention, have been greatly deceived and misled; but I can't but wonder at their credulity in giving credit to an anonymous writer in a News Paper, whose character they knew nothing of, who, in an audacious, as well as false manner, has undertaken to impeach the integrity of the General Assembly of the colony. But as Luther once said, when he was condemned by the pope, he would appeal from the pope uninformed, to the pope rightly informed, so I would take leave to inform the people of some facts which I know to be true, as to the doings of the General Assembly relative to the matters in question, and then appeal to the people, whether the Assembly hath not acted a wise and prudent part therein.

In May, 1770, in consequence of a memorial preferred by more than four thousand of the freemen of the colony, (none of them interested in Susquehannah purchase,) praying the Assembly to assert and support the claim of this colony to the lands contained in our charter, lying west of Delaware River,

Source: Robert Taylor, ed., *The Susquehannah Company Papers* (Ithaca, N.Y.: Cornell University Press, 1968), 6: 179–83. Used by permission of the Luzerne County Historical Society.

as they esteemed it to be a valuable interest which the Governor and Company held in trust for the freemen of the colony; The Assembly, after mature deliberation, ordered a true and full state of the case to be laid before council learned in the law in England; accordingly the case was stated, and laid before four of the principal lawyers in the kingdom, who unanimously gave their opinion in favor of the title of the Colony. And this measure was not taken by influence of the Susquehannah company, for the principal proprietors thought it a needless precaution, they having no doubt about the validity of the colony's claim.

After the opinion of council was obtained, the Assembly in October last, by a very full vote, resolved to assert, and in some proper way, support the colony's claims to said lands, and then appointed a committee to consider of proper measures to be taken by the Assembly, (the exercising of jurisdiction over the people settled there, not excepted,) which report was accepted in full Assembly. A great clamour has been made about the Assembly's suffering the members interested in the Susquehannah purchase to sit and vote in those matters; but that complaint, I conceive, is without any just foundation. I was in the lower house in the year 1755, when the assembly acted on the memorial of the Susquehannah Company, and then all that were of the company were excluded; and I understand that the same method has been taken by the house, at all times since, when any matter has been debated, or vote taken, that concerned the peculiar interest of that company. But I don't remember any vote taken by the assembly in October or January last, wherein they were particularly interested.

The acts then passed, relative to the western lands, were such as concerned the colony in general and they could not by any rule or principle of law or equity, have been excluded.

The assembly consider the Governor and Company to be vested with the legal title to all the lands contained in our charter, lying between the river *Delaware* and *Mississippi*, except what the Indians are possessed of; and no persons can acquire a title to any part of them by purchase from the Indians, without a grant of the assembly; and the Susquehannah purchasers don't pretend they have any legal title to any part of said lands. But if the government avail themselves of their purchase of the native right, the purchasers will expect to be quieted in such a part of the land as will be an equitable compensation for their expence therein; which must be determined by the assembly; in which determination none of the company will be allowed to vote. If the idea here suggested is just, it will obviate the principal difficulty suggested in the petition drawn up and published by the convention at Middletown.

They seem to make some further difficulty about exercising jurisdiction over the people of the town of Westmoreland, because they say the colony's title to those lands is contested. In answer to which I would say, that it is not contested but acknowledged by the proprietaries of Pennsylvania, that the lands are contained within the original boundaries of our charter as may appear by a petition presented by them to the king in council a few years ago: If it once belonged to the colony and we have never yielded it up, nor have been divested of it by any judicial determination, what can be the mighty danger of exercising government over the people who claim the privilege of being under the jurisdiction of the colony claim a title to the lands as being within their charter, I don't see how they could excuse themselves in neglecting to govern the people settled on the lands, for their right of soil and of jurisdiction by the charter are commensurate. But it is further said that the doings of the assembly will tempt great numbers of the people to settle on those lands, and if they should be evicted they will be reduced to poverty, &c. But this is a groundless surmise; for the assembly have caused a proclamation to be issued expressly forbidding any more persons settling on said lands without leave first obtained from the assembly. As to their fears of what bloody tragedies may ensue from clashing jurisdictions, &c. Exercising jurisdiction was judged by the assembly the most likely measure to prevent all mischiefs of that kind, and to preserve peace and good order among the people.

As to what the convention say concerning the title of the colony to the lands in question, that it is a matter of which they are not so competent judges, nor furnished with facts and documents by which a judgment might be made, and so are willing and desirous that the right of the colony to them, and the prudence and policy of asserting that right should be judged of and determining by a disinterested assembly; if this had gone to the whole of their proceedings they would have done justice to the cause, and they would have merited the applause of their constituents. It is a little extraordinary that when the colony has a cause to be tried, which all parties seem to think best should be tried, and yet those who profess to be so very zealous for the public good should use every method in their power to defeat its success: Much has been said to alarm the people about the expence of a trial before the king and council. Governor Penn in his late conference with our commissioners, says that an adversary suit can't occasion much delay or expence. I presume it would not cost more than one farthing on the pound in the list of this colony, to decide the question whether this colony joins to Pennsylvania or not; and if that is determined against us there would be an end of the controversy; but if in our favour, a further expence would be incurred in fixing our south boundary which could not amount to any great sum; great part of the expence in the Mason cause was occasioned by the delay, because Mason was not able to carry it on. But the final decision of that cause in our favour, furnished us with an evidence of the safety of confiding in the integrity of that High Court when acting as a court of law. Mr. Ingersol, in a piece lately published in the News papers, speaking of this affair says, 'a defeat will be very detrimental; but a victory must be absolute ruin; at least I think so.' But he gives no reason for his opinion; and can his bare assertion make the people of this colony, who are a company of farmers, believe that to be quieted in their claim to a large tract of valuable land would ruin them? I know some gentlemen who love to monopolize wealth and power, think it is best for lands to be in a few hands, and that the common people should be their tenants; but it will not be easy to persuade the people of this colony, who know the value of freedom, and of enjoying fee-simple estates, that it would be best for them to give up the lands acquired for them by their ancestors, for the privilege of enjoying the same lands as tenants under the proprietaries of Pennsylvania.

The lands in question are situated about the centure, as to latitude, of the English territories in North America, in a healthy climate; and the soil is said to be generally very good; and there is enough purchased of the Indians to supply the inhabitants of this colony, that may want land to settle on, perhaps for half a century to come. They will be connected with us, and by sharing in our civil and religious privileges, will be under the best advantages to be virtuous and happy; and those who continue in this part of the colony, may be greatly benefitted by monies that may be raised by the sale of those lands and yet the purchasers have them on better terms than they can procure lands elsewhere; and if in time to come that part of the colony should be so populous as to render it inconvenient to be connected with this part of the colony in government, the crown would doubtless be ready, upon application, to constitute them a distinct colony.

Thus I have given a short account of the doings of the assembly, and endeavoured to obviate the difficulties and misapprehensions which some people have laboured under, relative to the affair, and also to mention some of the advantages which may accrue to the colony by supporting their claim to the lands. And as I have no interest in the affair but in common with every other freeman in the colony, nor any party views to serve, I am quite willing the freemen should shew their minds and determine it as they shall think best. About half the freemen have already manifested their desire to have the colony's claim supported, viz. the 4000 memorialists afore-mentioned, and the Susquehannah and Delaware companies which I suppose will amount to about 1000 more; and I hope the other freemen will not relinquish the colony's claim, without full information and mature deliberation, least they injure themselves, their brethren and posterity. I think no more need be done than to chuse gentlemen of known virtue, integrity, and prudence to be members of the next

General Assembly, who have approved themselves firm friends to our civil and religious liberties, and not embarrass them with petitions or instructions; they will be under a solemn oath to act as in their consciences, they shall judge most for the good of the colony, and that must be the only rule of their conduct. But I must conclude, and can with sincerity subscribe myself a cordial well-wisher to the peace and welfare of the colony.

R. Sherman

Unpublished Article, 1776

Sherman penned this account of the Susquehannah controversy for his own use. It was not published in his lifetime.

As the late disturbances among the people inhabiting the lands on the sus-quehannah River, in controversy between the Proprietor of Pennsylvania and the Colony of Connecticut, have drawn the attention of the Public, it may not be amiss to give a Short and impartial State of the Facts relative to that affair, to prevent Misapprehension and unjust censure of any of the persons concerned on either side. There is a real Claim of Title and Jurisdiction by both parties over a tract of territory about Seventy Miles wide North and South and about two hundred and fifty miles long East and West bounded East by the River Delaware and South by 41 degrees North Latitude. The Colony of Connecticut claims by a Charter Granted by King Charles II. Dated the 23ᵈ day of April 1662.

The Proprietors of Pennsylvania claims Land by a Charter granted by the Same King, bearing date 1681.

Said Proprietors acknowlege Said lands to be included in said Charter to Connecticut, as appears by their late Petition to the King in Council, and there is no dispute but that it is also contained in the Charter to Said Proprietors. A Number of the Inhabitants of Connecticut in the year 1754 purchased the Native right to that part of Said land which is now inhabited on the East and West branches of Susquehannah River of the Sachems of the Six Nations of Indians in a Grand Congress at Albany. Which purchase was approved by Act of the General Assembly of Connecticut in may 1755. and sᵈ purchasers begun a Settlement thereon about the year 1762, but it being represented to the Sec-retary of State that continuing the Settlement would likely bring on an Indian war a requisition was made to the Govʳ of Connecticut to recall the Settlers until proper measures should be taken by the Crown to prevent any fresh

Source: Robert Taylor, ed., *The Susquehannah Company Papers* (Ithaca, N.Y.: Cornell University Press, 1968), 7: 28–32. Used by permission of the Luzerne County Historical Society.

troubles with the Indians. upon which Said Settlers removed off from Said lands, and in 1768 a line was Settled by the order between the English and Indians upon which the Proprietors of Pennsylvania made a purchase of part of the Same lands of Said Indians. this Settlement of the line was in the fall of 1768, and in February 1769 the Connecticut people returned to their former possessions on Said Lands Since which time great part of Said lands have been by Said Proprietors Granted and Surveyed to particular persons in Pennsylvania, and the Assembly of Said Province has extended Jurisdiction over the whole of the lands purchased of the Indians as aforesaid, by including them within the Counties of *Northampton* and *Northumberland.* The Colony of Connecticut also incorporated a Town called *Westmoreland* including all the Inhabited part of Said Lands and annexed it to the County of *Litchfield.* The Settlers under the claim of Connecticut are on the Lands near the East branch of the River Susquehannah; And the Settlers under the Claim of Pennsylvania Proprietors on or near the West branch of Said River. The Proprietors of Pennsylvania about two years ago presented a Petition to the King in Council Praying for a decision of Said Controversy, which was then depending & undetermined.

The Assembly of Connecticut about the same time Authorized the Governor with the Assistance of a Committee to take advice of Counsel in England, and prefer a Petition to the King in Council to Commissioners to hear and decide the Controversy, and the Necessary preparations were made, and Counsel engaged, but before the Petition was preferred, Hostilities were commenced by the British Troops in Massachusets bay—which prevented any further proceedings therein: Last Summer a Petition was preferred to the Continental Congress by some of the Claimants under Pennsyvania expressing their apprehensions of being disturbed in their settlements & dispossessed by the Settlers under *Connecticut* Occasioned as tis Said by a letter wrote by one Pierce who had a brother in Goal at Sunsbury.

The Congress recommended to the Delegates of Pennsylvania and Connecticut to take proper measures to quiet the minds of the people and prevent any disturbance among them whereupon a letter was wrote by the Delegates of each of Said Colonies to the Inhabitants on Said Lands exhorting them to Peace and good order, and by no means to give the least disturbance or molestation to the persons properties or possessions of any persons Settled under either of the Claims aforesaid. All that is Said in s^d Letter concerning making new settlements is expressed in these words viz, "You are desired to make no settlements by force, nor use any threats for that purpose."

Some of the Connecticut people having before that time Surveyed some of the uncultivated lands near the west branch of S^d River susquehanna and made preparation for settling thereon, Judged that it would not be contrary to the advice given in Said letter for them to proceed in making said Settlement provided they did it in a peaceable manner without force or threats; Whereupon about 80 persons Set out from Wyoming and went over to view the lands toward Said West branch. Some of them intending to settle on the vacant Lands there if it would give no offence to the people Settled under Pennsylvania. they had their Guns with them as is usual when they travel in the Woods. they visited the Inhabitants at Warriours run, where they met with kind treatment, and to prevent any of the people being alarmed they sent the following letters to the Magistrates at Sunsbury, viz

To which they received for answer that they must Surrender themselves prisoners of War with all their effects—to which they replied, that they came not for war, and would return home peaceably, if their Settling on Said lands would give offence; but they were not suffered to return but were fired on and one of them killed and two others wounded, but they did not return the fire or attempt any resistance but suffered themselves to be taken prisoners rather than Use any Violence for they had entered into an Engagement in writing signed by each before they set out from home, Strictly to adhere to the recommendations of the Congress, and not molest or disturb any persons settled under the claim of the proprietors of Pennsylvania, nor use any violence or threatning language, but to behave themselves orderly and peaceably, which the Majistrates who went took as an additional Security for their peacable behaviour. Some of them were imprisoned; others were released on bonds and their effects detained, about 70 or 80 small Arms & Near thirty of their horses, forceably taken from them & sold and distributed to the enraged Multitude without law or legal process. These matters were represented to Congress, and Some resolutions passed by the Congress thereon recommending to both parties proper measures to be observed for preserving peace and good order among s^d Inhabitants which resolutions together with an Act of the General Assembly of the Colony of Connecticut were published in the Pennsylvania Journal No. 1726. The Assembly of Pennsylvania also passed an order relative to the Affair which is as follows viz. Pensylv^a ss^t In Assembly Novr 25th 1775, The House taking into Consideration the letter from Northumberland respecting the Connecticutt Setlers at Wyoming Ordered that Mr Polls and Mr Brown wait on the Govr with Said letter & request his Honor will be pleased to Give Orders for a due Execution of the Laws of this Province in the counties of Northumberland & Northampton. What orders were given in Consequence of Said resolve, May be known from the Majistrates of those Counties. As a number of Armed Men belonging to the Colony of Pennsylvania were raised

& supplyd with Amunition & other warlike furniture & marched in marshall array to or near Wyoming to attack the people Settled under the claim of Connecticut & drive them from their settlements, there in that Inclement Season of Y^e year which if Accomplishd many especially Women & Children must have perishd in the Wilderness which obliged the Connecticutt people to give them that resistance which Caused them to retreat & Unhappily with Some loss. By what authority they proceeded and all the circumstances that attended their attack are not yet known here or how far the Magistrates & people in the Counties of *Northampton* and *Northumberland* had been informed of Said orders or Resolves of Congress is not at present known, tho it is certain an express was Immediately dispatched with Copys to be delivered to them. however that may be, it is hoped that the Several resolutions of the Congress and of the Said Assemblies being now duly published will effectually preserve peace and good order among the people Inhabiting said disputed territory until there can be a legal decision of the Controversy.

N : B the publick may be Assured (notwithstanding many false Suggestions made to the Contrary) that no other letter was sent by the Connecticut Delegates about or either of them about or after the time of ye letter above referr^d [illegible] by desire of Congress. & what letters were sent before strongly remonstrated against every act of force or Violence upon the pensylvania setlers their property or possession, and Inculcated the same quiet & peacable Conduct as expressd in the letter referred to & every Method has taken by them both in Congress & out have been taken by them to prevent every appearance of Hostility on either side.

Endorsed: Narrative of Wyoming Affairs.

Also: State of Controversy Connecticut & Pensylvania

Revision of State Laws

Letter to Richard Law, July 25, 1783

NEW HAVEN

In 1783, Sherman and Richard Law (1733–1806) were given the assignment of revising Connecticut's laws. Sherman took the statutes beginning with the letters A–L, and Law took the rest. They corresponded with each other about the changes, as demonstrated by this letter from Sherman to Law.

Dear Sir

I received your letter with the last laws enclosed. I have now taken the whole of the Act in page 235 into my Code, the first and last paragraphs under Civil Actions and the residue with Some Additions under the head of Bail [?] which I have endeavoured to regulate both in civil and criminal causes.

I insert the Act page 608, next after the Law for Settling Testate and Intestate estates, omitting the words that respect future confiscations. The maintaining the Light house I have left for you perhaps it may come under the Head of Ships or Shipping. I have now compleated my part of the Laws except a few blanks left for your opinion. I sent you a list of those I had then determined to take in, I don't know but I have included some others since.

I have taken in under the head of Foreigners, four Acts, viz., To prevent Mischief—Infractions of the Laws of Nations—Rendering Speedy Justice to those in Alliance—and to prevent their holding Lands.

I have taken the Seale Act, and what ever concerns depreciation—and every thing relating to Dissenters. I think it would be well to make some addition to the Law respecting Societies, for regulating several Societies within the same bounds, of which I send a sketch. I dont hear of the arrival of the Definitive Treaty. I should not think it best to call the Assembly till that is received with the recommendation of Congress upon it.

I have looked over the remaining Laws and arranged them as follows that you may see which I have not taken. Mine contains 98 Laws, reckoning those under the Title lands but one, though containing several Acts. When you have

Source: Ernest Law Papers, Connecticut Historical Society, Hartford, Connecticut.

arranged and revised your part it will be best for us to meet and Inspect the whole.

The several Crimes mentioned in the Law for making New Gate a Prison are now arranged under their proper heads in the Alphabet. So that what remains is only to regulate the place. Would it not be best to have it subject to the orders of the Superior Courts as to Government and repairs & have only one keeper or over seer appointed by said Court, with power to appoint a Deputy under him, for whose conduct he shall be accountable?

R.S.

That where two or more Societies constituted by act of the General Assembly of this State have the same limits and boundaries, the members belonging to each shall be designated by enrolling their Names with the Clerk of the Society to which they respectively belong.

And all persons who shall arrive at the age of twenty one years; or women who shall become Widows, dwelling within the limits of such Societies, shall have liberty at any time within twelve months after said times, respectively, to Elect which Society they will belong to; and all persons coming from any other place, to dwell within the limits of such Societies may at any time Elect which Society they will belong to; which election shall be Manifested by causing their names to be enrolled with the Clerk of the Society to which they join; and in case of non Election, as aforesaid, the persons so arriving at twenty one years of age shall belong to that Society to which their parents belonged (if they dwelt there), otherwise to the Society to which the head of the family in which they dwelt belonged; and widows to that Society to which their Husbands did belong.

And persons who come from another place to dwell there shall be liable to be taxed by the Society that is lowest in the List of Polls and rateable Estate (that support their ministry by taxing) until they make and manifest their Election as aforesaid.

And any persons having become legal members of any such Society shall continue members of the same during their continuance within the limits thereof, unless released by a vote of said Society and joining to another within the same limits: which release such Society is hereby authorized to grant if they think fit, on application of any person desiring the same, and it shall be the duty of the Clerks of such Societies to enroll the names of all the members of such Societies respectively in the Society records. Provided that nothing in this Act shall affect the privileges granted by law to any dissenters from the Worship and Ministry established by the laws of this State.

[Following this proposed law there is a list of titles of laws from "Man-slaughter" to "Wrecks." The letter ends:]

I am Sir with Esteem and respect
Your humble servant
Roger Sherman

P.S. I have added a clause in the Act for regulating civil Actions concerning joint contracts, that serving the process on those who belong to this State shall be sufficient notice to obtain judgment against all.

Letter from Benjamin Huntington to Roger Sherman, February 11, 1784

NEW HAVEN

In this letter, Governor Benjamin Huntington (1736–1800) reveals something about the process by which the General Assembly altered, approved, or rejected the revisions proposed by Sherman and Law. He also notes that New Haven was granted a charter and that Sherman was elected its first mayor, a position he held until his death.

Honored Sir,—I have been so happy as to board at your house since the session of assembly which rises this day having finished the revisal of the Laws with some alteration from the draughts made by the committee. Where the committee's alterations were not agreed to, the old Statutes are to stand as in time passed. The pay of the Supreme Court is not raised nor any alteration in Court or Counties excepting Colchester which is annexed [to] New London County. The impost not yet granted but much nearer to it than in October. The people at large begin to see their interest in the measure and I hope that by the May next they will be undeceived; about one third of the lower house are in favor of it now.

The New Haven and New London City bills are passed and the freemen of the city of New Haven are now in the upper house of the State house choosing their City magistrates and have made choice of a member of Congress for the Mayor and Deacon Howell, Deacon Bishop, Deacon Austin and Mr Isaac Beers are chosen Aldermen. Your little son, Oliver, hearing that his Papa was chosen Mayor was concerned and inquired who was to ride the Mare?

Mrs Sherman received some addresses on the subject of the election and by way of answer has fed some hungry bellies whilst others wanted money to buy powder to fire in honor of the Lord Mayor elect. Thus the emoluments of office are felt by her in your absence. The cannon are this moment firing in a most tremendous manner on the subject. I wish you could hear it. I am with esteem and respect

Your most humble servant,

BENJ. HUNTINGTON.

Source: Lewis H. Boutell, *The Life of Roger Sherman* (Chicago: A. C. McClurg, 1896), 120–21.

Selections from *Acts and Laws of the State of Connecticut*, 1784

When Roger Sherman and Richard Law revised Connecticut's statutes in 1783, in some instances they penned new laws, but in many cases they altered or combined previous statutes. The General Assembly then approved, rejected, or altered their proposals. The following selections shine light on the governing and ecclesiastical structures and the social and political culture of the time. Of particular note are the following: (1) the first statute, which is sometimes called Connecticut's Bill of Rights. Although it lists certain rights, it is clearly statutory law. (2) Sherman's "Act for securing the Rights of Conscience in Matters of Religion," which offered important protection to religious minorities in Connecticut. However, Congregationalism remained the favored denomination, and the state retained a system of plural or multiple establishment until 1819. (3) "An Act for the Encouragement of Literature and Genius," the first copyright law in the nation (a result of a campaign spearheaded by Noah Webster). (4) "An Act concerning Indian, Molatto, and Negro Servants and Slaves," which required that slaves born in the state after March 1, 1784, be freed when they turned twenty-five.

All selections are from Acts and Laws of the State of Connecticut, in America *(New London, Conn.: Timothy Green, 1784), hereafter cited as* Acts and Laws.

An Act containing an Abstract and Declaration of the Rights and Privileges of the People of this State, and securing the same.

The People of this State, being by the Providence of God, free and independent, have the sole and exclusive Right of governing themselves as a free, sovereign, and independent State; and having from their Ancestors derived a free and excellent Constitution of Government, whereby the Legislature depends on the free and annual Election of the People, they have the best Security for the Preservation of their civil and religious Rights and Liberties. And forasmuch as the free Fruition of such Liberties and Privileges as Humanity, Civility and Christianity call for, as is due to every Man in his Place and Proportion, without Impeachment and Infringement, hath ever been, and will be the Tranquility and Stability of Churches and Commonwealths; and the denial thereof, the Disturbance, if not the Ruin of both. — Preamble.

Be it Enacted and Declared by the Governor, Council and Representatives, in General Court assembled, and by the Authority of the same, That the ancient Form of Civil Government, contained in the Charter from *Charles* the Second, King of *England,* and adopted by the People of this State, shall be and remain the Civil Constitution of this State, under the sole Authority of the People thereof, independent of any King or Prince whatever. And that this Republic is, and shall forever be and remain, a free, sovereign and independent State, by the Name of the STATE OF CONNECTICUT. — Constitution and name of the State.

And be it further Enabled and Declared by the Authority aforesaid, That no Man's Life shall be taken away: No Man's Honor or good Name shall be stained: No Man's Person shall be arrested, restrained, banished, dismembered, nor any ways punished: No Man shall be deprived of his Wife or Children: No Man's Goods or Estate shall be taken away from him, nor any ways indamaged under the colour of Law, or countenance of Authority; unless clearly warranted by the Laws of this State. — General security of the rights of the people.

Source: *Acts and Laws,* 1–2.

Equal justice to be administered.

That all the free Inhabitants of this or any other of the United States of *America*, and Foreigners in Amity with this State, shall enjoy the same Justice and Law within this State, which is general for the State, in all Cases proper for the Cognizance of the Civil Authority and Courts of Judicature within the same, and that without Partiality or Delay.

No person to be imprisoned without law—and bailable in all cases, except, &c.

And that no Man's Person shall be restrained, or imprisoned, by any Authority whatsoever, before the Law hath sentenced him thereunto, if he can and will give sufficient Security, Bail, or Mainprize for his Appearance and good Behaviour in the mean Time, unless it be for Capital Crimes, Contempt in open Court, or in such Cases wherein some express Law doth allow of, or order the same.

An Act against, and for the punishment of Adultery.

Adultery how punished.

Be it enacted by the Governor, Council and Representatives, in General Court assembled, and by the Authority of the same, That whosoever shall commit Adultery with a married Woman, and be thereof convicted before the Superior Court, both of them shall be severely punished, by Whipping on the naked Body, and stigmatized, or burnt on the Forehead with the Letter *A,* on a hot Iron: And each of them shall wear a Halter about their Necks, on the outside of their Garments, during their abode in this State, so as it may be visible: And as often as either of them shall be found without their Halters, worn as aforesaid, they shall, upon Information and Proof of the same, made before an Assistant or Justice of the Peace, be by him ordered to be whipt, not exceeding thirty Stripes.

Source: *Acts and Laws,* 8.

An Act for educating and governing of Children.

Preamble. *Forasmuch as the Education and well Governing of Children is of singular Benefit to a People: And whereas many Parents and Masters are too negligent of their Duty in the Matter:*

Children to be instructed, &c. *Be it enacted by the Governor, Council and Representatives, in General Court assembled, and by the Authority of the same,* That all Parents and Masters of Children shall, by themselves or others, teach and instruct, or cause to be taught and instructed, all such Children as are under their Care and Government, according to their Ability, to read the English Tongue well, and to know the Laws against Capital Offences: And if unable to do so much, then at least to learn some short orthodox Catechism without Book, so as to be able to answer to the Questions that shall be propounded to them out of such Catechism, by their Parents, Masters, or Ministers, when they shall call them to an Account of what they have learned of that Kind.

Penalty on parents, &c. for neglect of duty. And if any Parent or Master shall neglect the performing what is by this Act required of them, every such Parent, or Master being thereof legally convicted before any one Assistant or Justice of the Peace, shall forfeit and pay the Sum of *twenty Shillings,* to and for the Use of the Poor of the Town whereto they belong.

Select-men to inspect, &c. And that the Select-men of every Town in this State, in their several Precincts, and Quarters, shall have a vigilant Eye and Inspection over their Brethren and Neighbours; and see that none of them suffer so much Barbarism in any of their Families, as to want such Learning and Instruction; and to take Care that due Prosecutions be made for the Breach of this Act.

Grand-jury to present, &c. And the Grand-jury-men in each Town, are hereby required to take Care, and see that what is by this Act required for the Education of Children, be duly performed, and to make Presentment of all Breaches of this Act which shall come to their Knowledge.

Source: *Acts and Laws,* 20.

And be it further enacted by the Authority aforesaid, That all Parents and Masters, shall employ and bring up their Children and Apprentices in some honest and lawful Calling, Labour or Employment, profitable for themselves and the State.

And if the Select-men of the Town where such Parents or Masters live, after Admonition by them given to such Parents or Masters, shall find them still negligent of their Duty, in the Particulars aforementioned in this Act; whereby such Children grow rude, stubborn and unruly, such Select-men (with the Advice of the next Assistant or Justice of the Peace), shall take, and they are hereby fully authorized and impowered, to take such Children and Apprentices from their Parents or Masters, and place them with, and bind them to some Master or Masters; Males till they are Twenty-one Years of Age, and Females till they are Eighteen Years of Age; to the End they may be suitably instructed, employed and governed: Which binding shall be good and effectual, for the holding and governing such Children, the Terms aforesaid.

And that whatsoever Child or Servant, upon Complaint made, shall be convicted of any stubborn or rebellious Carriage, against their Parents or Governors, before any two Assistants or Justices of the Peace, such Assistants or Justices are hereby authorized and impowered, upon such Conviction, to commit such Child or Servant to a House of Correction; there to remain under hard Labour and severe Punishment, so long as said Authority shall judge meet; who, on the Reformation of such Children and Servants, may order their Release, and Return to their Parents or Masters aforesaid.

[Marginal notes:]

Children to be bro't up to some honest calling, &c.

Stubborn children to be bound out, &c.

Stubborn rebellious children to be sent to a house of correction.

An Act for securing the Rights of Conscience in Matters of Religion, to Christians of every Denomination in this State.

Preamble. *As the happiness of a People, and the good Order of Civil Society, essentially depend upon Piety, Religion and Morality, it is the Duty of the Civil Authority to provide for the Support and Encouragement thereof; so as that Christians of every Denomination, demeaning themselves peaceably, and as good Subjects of the State, may be equally under the Protection of the Laws: And as the People of this State have in general, been of one Profession in Matters of Faith, religious Worship, and the mode of settling and supporting the Ministers of the Gospel, they have by Law been formed into Ecclesiastical Societies, for the more convenient Support of their Worship and Ministry: And to the End that other Denominations of Christians who dissent from the Worship and Ministry so established and supported, may enjoy free Liberty of Conscience in the Matters aforesaid:*

Dissenters not to incur any penalty for not attending, &c.

Be it enacted by the Governor, Council and Representatives, in General Court assembled, and by the Authority of the same, That no Persons in this State, professing the Christian Religion, who soberly and conscientiously dissent from the Worship and Ministry by Law established in the Society wherein they dwell, and attend public Worship by themselves, shall incur any Penalty for not attending the Worship and Ministry so established, on the Lord's-Day, or on account of their meeting together by themselves on said Day, for public Worship in a Way agreeable to their Consciences.

When exempted from taxes, &c.

And be it further enacted by the Authority aforesaid, That all denominations of Christians differing in their religious Sentiments from the People of the established Societies in this State, whether of the Episcopal Church, or those Congregationalists called Separates, or of the People called Baptists, or Quakers, or any other Denomination who shall have formed themselves into distinct Churches or Congregations, and attend public Worship, and support the gospel Ministry in a Way agreeable to their Consciences and

Source: *Acts and Laws,* 21–22.

respective Professions; and all Persons who adhere to any of them, and dwell so near to any Place of their Worship that they can and do ordinarily attend the same on the Sabbath, and contribute their due Proportion to the support of the Worship and Ministry where they so attend, whether such Place of Worship be within this, or any adjoining State, and produce a Certificate thereof from such Church or Congregation, signed by their Order, by the Minister or other Officer thereof, and lodge the same with the Clerk of the Society wherein such Person or Persons dwell, every such Person shall be exempted from being taxed for the support of the Worship and Ministry of said Society, so long as he or they shall continue so to attend and support public Worship with a different Church or Congregation as aforesaid.

And be it further enacted by the Authority aforesaid, That all such Protestant Churches and Congregations as dissent from the Worship and Ministry established as aforesaid, and who maintain and attend public Worship by themselves, shall have Liberty and Authority to use and exercise the same Powers and Privileges for maintaining and supporting their respective Ministers, and building and repairing their Meeting-Houses for the public Worship of God, as the Ecclesiastical Societies, constituted by Act of the General Assembly of this State by Law have and do exercise and enjoy; and in the same Manner may commence and hold their Meetings, and transact their Affairs, as Occasion may require for the Purpose aforesaid. *[All dissenters the same powers, &c.]*

And all Persons shall be taxed for the support of the Ministry and other Charges of the Society wherein they dwell, who do not attend and help Support, any other public Worship; any thing in this Act notwithstanding. *[To pay taxes for the support of public worship.]*

And every Person claiming the benefit of this Act, shall be disqualified to vote in any Society Meeting, save only for granting Taxes for the support of Schools, and for the Establishment of Rules and Regulations for Schools, and the Education of Children in them. *[Disqualified from voting in society meetings.]*

An Act for constituting and regulating Courts; and appointing the Times and Places for holding the same.

Two General Courts yearly. *Be it enacted by the Governor, Council and Representatives, in General Court assembled, and by the Authority of the same,* That there shall be yearly, two General Courts, or Assemblies, held in this State; the one at *Hartford,* on the second Thursday in *May,* and the other at *New-Haven,* on the second Thursday in *October,* (unless necessitated by infectious or epidemical Diseases or otherways, occasionally to remove to some other Place): And the first shall be called the Court of Election; wherein shall be chosen from Time to Time, one Governor, who shall be the Chief Magistrate of this State, and be stiled, *His Excellency*; and one Lieutenant-Governor, whose Title shall be, *His Honor*; and twelve Assistants or Counsellors; a Treasurer, and Secretary for this State.

Of whom to consist. And the said General Court shall be composed of two Branches; the Governor and Council, and the House of Representatives; who shall convene in different Apartments to transact the public Business: And any Act may be originated by either Branch, but not be valid without the Concurrence of both. The Governor, or in his Absence the Lieutenant-Governor shall preside in Council: And when the Governor is present to preside, the Lieutenant-Governor shall have a Voice in Council; and the Governor, or Lieutenant-Governor and six Counsellors, shall be necessary to make a Quorum for doing Business. That if at any Time, by Death or otherwise, the Offices of Governor and Lieutenant-Governor shall be vacant, or if the Governor and Lieutenant-Governor shall be Absent out of the State, or be unable to attend the General Court, the senior Member of the Council present, shall preside in Council; who, together with six other Members, shall have Power to transact the Business of the Council. And not less than forty of the Deputies or Representatives from the several Towns in this State, that shall be present to attend the said Court, shall make a House of Representatives for transacting Business.

Their power. In which General Court, shall consist the Supreme Power and Authority

Source: *Acts and Laws,* 27–29.

82

of this State; and they only shall have Power to make Laws and repeal them; to grant Levies, to dispose of Lands undisposed of, to Towns, or particular Persons: And also to institute and stile Judicatories and Officers as they shall see necessary for the good Government of this State.

Also to call any Court, or Magistrate, or any other Officer or Person whatever to an Account, for any Misdemeanor or Male-Administration; and for just Cause, may fine, displace or remove them, or deal otherwise as the Nature of the Cause shall require; and also may deal and act in any other Matter that concerns the good of this State; except the Election of Governor, Lieutenant-Governor, Assistants or Counsellors, which shall be done by the Votes of the Freemen, at the yearly Court of Election. *To call any officer to account.*

Provided, That if there be any want of any of the said Officers, be reason of Death or otherways, after the Election, such Want shall or may be supplied and made up by the General Court's Election, or appointing some suitable Person or Persons to supply such Vacancy. *Proviso.*

That the General Court only, shall have Power, upon Grounds to them satisfying, to grant Pardons, Suspensions and Gaol-Delivery upon Reprieve in capital and criminal Cases, unto any Person or Persons that have been sentenced in any other Court whatever in this State. *To grant reprieve.*

That none of our General Courts shall be dissolved or prorogued without the consent of the major Part thereof. *Not to be dissolv'd without, &c.*

That the Governor, or in his Absence the Lieutenant-Governor, by himself, or the Secretary, shall upon any emergent or special Occasion, call a General Court upon fourteen Days Warning, or less, if he see it needful; *provided,* he give an Account thereof to the Assembly when they shall be met together. *Power to call special assembly.*

That if any Member of the General Court, shall reveal or disclose any Matter which the Court enjoins to be kept secret; or shall make known to any Person what any one Member of the Court speaks concerning any Person, or Business that may come in Agitation in the Court, he shall for every such Offence, forfeit *ten Pounds* to the public Treasury. *Penalty for revealing secrets, 10l.*

That no Member of the General Court shall appear as an Attorney at the Bar of the said Court; unless it be in his own Cause, or in behalf of the Town he represents; or such Cases wherein the Law will not allow him to sit as Judge. *No member to appear as attorney.*

Nor shall any Member of the said Court, during the Sessions thereof, or in going to, or from the said Court, be arrested, sued or imprisoned, or any ways molested or troubled, or compelled to answer to any Suit, Bill, Plaint, Declaration or otherwise, before any other Court, Judge or Justice; Cases of High-Treason and Felony excepted. *Free from arrests, &c.*

Towns liberty to send one or two deputies.

And that the Freemen in every Town in this State, shall have Liberty to send one, or two Deputies to every Session of the General Assembly; which Deputies shall have the Power and Voices of all the Freemen deputing them in any Matter proper for said Assembly to act in.

Deputies to meet on election day at 8 o'clock, and chuse speaker and clerk.

That the Deputies or Representatives, who are returned from the respective Towns to serve in the General Assembly in *May*, annually, shall meet at their Chamber in the State-House, at eight of the Clock in the Morning on the said Day of Election; when and where they shall choose a Speaker and Clerk for their House, for that Session; and do any other Matter proper and meet for them to act, before the public Service, and Election on said Day. And that the said Deputies returned to serve in the

In October at 9 o'clock.

General Assembly in *October*, annually, shall meet at the State-House in *New-Haven*, at nine of the Clock in the Morning, on the second Thursday of *October*, and proceed to form the House, as abovesaid.

Right to determine the election of their own members.

And when the said Deputies or Representatives are met together at any General Assembly, it shall be lawful for them, or the major Part present, to examine, hear, and determine any Difference that may arise about the Election of any of their Members.

Deputy must be a freeman, & regularly chosen.

And that no Person shall be accepted a Deputy in the General Court, that is not known to be a Freeman of this State, and regularly chosen thereunto by the Freemen of that Town for whom he serves; nor before he takes the Deputy's Oath by Law provided to be administred to them.

Absence to be daily noted.

That at the opening of every General Assembly, the Clerk of the House of Representatives, then, and every Morning, from Day to Day during the whole Sessions, shall in the Lower-House, call over the Names of the several Deputies or Representatives of the respective Towns in this State, returned to serve as aforesaid, and note those that are absent when called.

Governor & speaker to have casting voice, &c.

And the Governor, or in his Absence the Lieutenant-Governor, shall have a casting Voice, whenever an equi-vote shall happen in the Upper-House: And the Speaker shall have a casting Voice whenever an equi-vote shall happen in the Lower-House.

Powers of superior court.

Be it further enacted by the Authority aforesaid, That there shall be a Superior Court of Judicature over this State, held and kept annually, at the respective Times and Places hereafter in this Act mentioned, by one Chief Judge, and four other Judges; to be appointed and commissioned for that Purpose: Any Three of whom shall have Power to hold said Court: Which Court shall have Cognizance of all Pleas of a criminal Nature, that relate to Life, Limb or Banishment, and other high Crimes and Misdemeanors, and of Divorce, and of Adultery; and also shall have Cognizance of all Pleas, real, personal or mixt, in civil Causes or Actions, between Party and Party, whether the same do concern the Reality, and relate to any right of Freehold or Inheritance; or whether the same do concern the Personality, and relate to matters of Debt, Contract, Damage or any other personal Right or Injury; or whether the same do concern and relate both to the Reality and Personality, and are of a mixt Nature, brought before them by Appeal, Writ of Error, *Scire Facias*, Complaint or otherwise as the Law directs; and the same to try by a Jury or otherwise, according to Law; and therein to proceed to Judgment, and award Execution thereon accordingly.

And also shall have Jurisdiction of all Suits for Relief in Equity, wherein the Value of the Matter or Thing in Demand, exceeds the Sum of *One Hundred Pounds*; and to enquire into the same by themselves or a Committe; and proceed therein to final Sentence and Decree, and enforce the same according to the Rules of Equity.

Jurisdiction of matters of equity.

An Act relating to Bills of Divorce.

In what cases bills of divorce are obtainable. *Be it enacted by the Governor, Council, and Representatives, in General Court assembled, and by the Authority of the same,* That no Bill of Divorce shall be granted to any Man or Woman, lawfully married, but in Case of Adultery, or fraudulent Contract, or wilful Desertion for three Years with total neglect of Duty; or in Case of seven Years absence of one Party not heard of: After due Enquiry is made, and the Matter certified to the Superior Court, in which Case the other Party may be deemed and accounted single and un-married. And in that Case, and in all other Cases aforementioned, a Bill of Divorce may be granted by the Superior Court to the aggrieved Party; who may then lawfully marry or be married again.

Source: *Acts and Laws,* 41.

An Act for regulating the Election of the Governor, Lieutenant-Governor, Assistants, &c.

Be it enacted by the Governor, Council and Representatives, in General Court assembled, and by the Authority of the same, That all Constables in the several Towns in this State, without further order, shall warn all the Freemen in their respective Towns, to meet together yearly; *That is to say:*

In the Counties of *Hartford, New-Haven, Fairfield,* and *Litchfield,* on the third *Tuesday* of *September.*

And in the Counties of *New-London* and *Windham,* on the second *Tuesday* of *September,* about nine of the Clock in the Morning, at some convenient Place where they have usually been held, when and where they shall first choose Deputies or Representatives to attend the General Court in *October* then next ensuing: And then every Freeman in each Town there present, shall give in his Vote or Suffrage for twenty Persons (their Names being fairly written on a Piece of Paper) whom he judgeth qualified to stand in Nomination for Election in the Month of *May* next following: Which Votes or Suffrages shall be delivered to an Assistant or Justice of the Peace, (if any be present) otherwise, to such Constable as shall inhabit in the Town where such Votes are given in; which Assistant, Justice, or Constable, shall make Entry of the Names of all such Persons as the Freemen do vote for; with the Number of Votes that each Person hath: A Copy whereof the said Assistant, Justice, or Constable in each Town, shall send sealed up, to the General Assembly in *October* next following, by the Deputy or Representatives of such Town.

At which Assembly all the Votes of the Freemen of this State shall be compared, and those twenty Persons who shall have the greatest Number of Votes, shall be the Persons whose Names shall be returned to the several Towns to be the Persons nominated to stand for Election in *May* next following: Out of which Number the twelve Assistants shall be chosen. But the Freemen shall have Liberty to choose the Governor and Lieutenant-Governor, where they see Cause, of all or any Freemen within this State.

Marginal notes:
Constables to warn the freemen to meet yearly, &c.

When and where to choose representatives, and twenty to stand in nomination.

Votes compar'd at the assembly.

Source: *Acts and Laws,* 44–46.

Penalty on constables for neglect.

And all and every Constable shall attend this Order annually, on Penalty of forfeiting the Sum of *four Pounds*, to the public Treasury of the State, for every Neglect thereof.

Election to be consummated at the assembly in May.

And be it further enacted by the Authority aforesaid, That the election of Governor, Lieutenant-Governor, Assistants, and such other public Officers as shall be appointed to be chosen, shall by Proxy of the Freemen be attended and consummated in the General Assembly to be holden at *Hartford*, upon the second Thursday of *May*, annually.

And that the election by Proxies may be so regulated and managed, as to prevent the using any Fraud or Deceit therein:

Secretary to send the nomination to the printer, &c.

It is further Enacted, That the Secretary of the State, for the Time being, shall with the Acts and Orders of the General Court in *October*, yearly, send a Copy of the Names of all those Persons who are nominated as aforesaid, to stand for Election as aforesaid, to the Printer, in order that the said Persons Names may, with the said Acts, be distributed to the several Towns in this State.

Constables duty to warn the freemen to meet on Monday next after the first Tuesday in April annually, to choose representatives for May sessions.

And the several Constables in the respective Towns throughout this State, without further Order, on the Penalty aforesaid, shall by themselves, or some deputed by them, warn all the Freemen in their respective Towns, to convene at the Place where such Meetings are usually held, on the Monday next following the first Tuesday in *April*, annually, at nine of the Clock in the Morning; when and where they shall first choose Deputies to attend the General Court in *May* next following; where also shall be read to them the Freeman's Oath; the three last Paragraphs of this Act, and the Names of those Persons nominated to stand for Election: And then the Freemen shall proceed to bring in to the Civil Authority, (or if none be present) to

Mode of voting for governor, &c.

the Constable or Constables present, the Name of him whom they would have for Governor for the Year ensuing, fairly written upon a piece of Paper; which the said Authority, or Constable or Constables shall receive, and in the presence of the Freemen seal up the same in a piece of Paper, and write on the out-side of the Paper so sealed, the Name of the Town; and then add these Words, viz. *Votes for the Governor*. In like Manner they shall proceed in bringing in, sealing up, and writing upon their Votes for the

Treasurer.

Secretary.

Lieutenant-Governor, Treasurer and Secretary. But before the Treasurer and Secretary are voted for, the Freemen shall bring in their Votes for those nominated to stand for Election; beginning with him that stands first in the Nomination, and bring in their Votes for him; which by the said Authority, or Constable or Constables, shall be received, sealed up, and written upon, as aforesaid; inserting the Name of the Person voted for; and so shall they proceed till they have passed through the whole Nomination. But no one Freeman to vote for more than twelve of the Number in Nomination to be Assistants.

And the Votes for election of Assistants shall be a written piece of Paper, (and no unwritten piece of Paper shall be given in): And the Civil Authority or Constables who receive the Votes and seal them up as aforesaid, shall by themselves, or one of the Deputies of the Court, convey the said Proxies to *Hartford,* and deliver them at the Election, as they shall be ordered, to those Persons who are appointed to receive, sort, and count the said Votes. _Assistants._

And at the Time of the Election (the Governor and Lieutenant-Governor being first chosen and declared) those standing in Nomination shall be put to Election in the same Order as they are propounded; after which those twelve Persons who shall have the greatest Number of Votes, shall be the Assistants of this State for the Year then ensuing; and shall be so declared accordingly. And also Declaration shall be made of the choice of the Treasurer and Secretary. _Gov. & Lt. Governor to be first chosen & declared, & then the assistants._

And if any Person that is not a Freeman of this State, admitted and sworn according to Law, shall presume to vote or give in his Proxy in the Election of any of the Members of the General Assembly; or if any Freeman shall put in above one Vote or Proxy for one Person at the same Election to one Office, he shall pay a fine of *five Pounds,* to the public Treasury of this State. _Penalty on such as vote who are not qualified, &c._

And whereas undue Influence, Bribery, and Corruption in Elections, are of pernicious Tendency in a State:

Be it further enacted by the Authority aforesaid, That if any Person shall endeavour unduly to persuade or influence any other Person or Persons, in giving their Vote or Suffrage for any Member of the Legislature, by offering to any Person or Persons any written Vote or Votes for that Purpose, without being first thereto requested, such Person so offending, shall pay a Fine of *forty Shillings,* for the Use of the Town Treasury. _Penalty on such as unduly influence others in their votes._

And be it further Enacted, That no Person or Persons shall offer, accept, or receive any Sum or Sums of Money, or other Matter or Thing, by way of Gift, Fee or Reward, for giving or refusing to give any Vote or Suffrage for electing any Member of the General Assembly of this State, nor promise, procure, or any ways confer any Gratuity, Reward, or Preferment for, or on account of any Vote or Suffrage given, or to be given in any Election: And every Person so giving, offering, accepting or receiving as aforesaid, shall in every such Case, forfeit and pay the Sum of *five Pounds*; one Half to him or them that shall sue for and prosecute the same to Effect, and the other Half to the Treasury of the Town where the Offence is committed. And _and on such as accept a fee for giving or refusing to give any vote._

any Person who shall be convicted a second Time of the like Offence, shall be disfranchised.

Members un-
duly elected,
incapable to
serve. And that every Person who shall be elected by Means of such evil and illegal Practice as aforesaid, shall be and hereby is declared to be incapable to serve as a Member in such Assembly; unless such Person shall be able to satisfy said Assembly, that the same was done altogether without his Privity, and that he was not directly or indirectly concerned therein.

Who to make
presentment. *And be it further enacted by the Authority aforesaid,* That it shall be the Duty of every Constable and Grand-jury-man, to enquire after, and make Presentment of all Breaches of this Act.

An Act for the Punishment of divers capital and other Felonies.

Be it enacted by the Governor, Council and Representatives, in General Court Beastiality.
assembled, and by the Authority of the same, That if any Man or Woman shall
lie with any Beast or Brute Creature, by carnal Copulation, such Person
shall be put to death; and the Beast shall be slain and buried.

That if any Man shall lie with Mankind, as he lieth with Womankind, Sodomy.
both of them have committed Abomination, they both shall be put to
Death; except it shall appear that one of the Parties was forced, or under
fifteen Years of Age; in which Case the Party forced, or under the Age
aforesaid, shall not be liable to suffer the said Punishment.

That if any Person rise up by false Witness, wilfully, and of Purpose to False witness.
take away any Man's Life, such Offender shall be put to Death.

That if any Person of the Age of sixteen Years, or more, shall wilfully, Arson.
and of Purpose, burn any Dwelling-house, Barn, or Out-house, he shall be
put to Death: Or if no Prejudice or Hazard to the Life of any Person happen
thereby, shall suffer such other severe Punishment as the Superior Court
shall determine, and also satisfy all Damage to the injured or aggrieved
Party.

That if any Person or Persons shall wilfully and maliciously burn or Burning mag-
destroy, or attempt or conspire to burn or destroy any Magazine of Provi- azines, vessels,
sions, or of military or naval Stores, belonging to the United States of &c.
America, or to this State; or if any Master, Officer, Seaman, Mariner, or
other Person intrusted with the Navigation or Care of any Vessel belonging
to the said United States, or Vessel belonging to this State, shall wilfully
and maliciously burn or destroy, or attempt or conspire to burn or destroy
such Vessel, or in Time of War, shall wilfully betray, or voluntarily yield or
deliver any such Vessel to the Enemies of the United States of *America;*
every such Person, and their Aiders or Abettors, on legal Conviction of
either of the Offences aforesaid, shall suffer Death; or if any of the said
Offences, when committed in Time of Peace, shall be attended with such

Source: *Acts and Laws,* 66–67.

alleviating Circumstances as in the Judgment of the Superior Court may render it reasonable to inflict a lower Punishment, such person may be punished by whipping on his naked Body, not exceeding forty Stripes, and by Banishment, or Imprisonment in any Work-house, or House of Correction, not exceeding ten Years, and a Forfeiture of all the Estate of such Offender, to the Use of this State, at the Discretion of the said Court.

Cutting off members. That if any Person on Purpose, and of Malice, Fore-thought, and by laying in wait, shall cut out or disable the Tongue; or put out an Eye or Eyes, so that the Person is thereby made blind; or shall cut off all, or any of the privy Members of any Person; or shall be aiding or assisting therein, such Offender, or Offenders shall be put to Death.

Blasphemy. That if any Person within this State, shall presume wilfully to blaspheme the Name of God the Father, Son, or Holy Ghost, either by denying, cursing, or reproaching the true God or his Government of the World; every Person so offending, shall be punished by whipping on the naked Body, not exceeding forty Stripes, and sitting in the Pillory one Hour; and may also be bound to his good Behaviour, at the Discretion of the Superior Court who shall have Cognizance of the Offence.

Deism. *And be it further enacted by the Authority aforesaid,* That if any Person within this State, having been educated in, or having made Profession of the Christian Religion, shall by writing, printing, teaching, or advised speaking, deny the Being of a God; or any One of the Persons in the Holy Trinity to be God; or shall assert and maintain that there are more Gods than One; or shall deny the *Christian* Religion to be true, or the Holy Scriptures of the Old and New-Testament to be of Divine Authority, and be thereof lawfully convicted before any of the Superior Courts of this State, shall for the first Offence, be incapable to have or enjoy any Offices or Employments, ecclesiastical, civil or military, or any Part in them, or Profit by them: And the Offices, Places and Employments enjoyed by such Persons at their Conviction, shall be void.

2d. Offence. And such Person being a second Time convicted of any of the aforesaid Crimes, shall be disabled to sue, prosecute, plead, or maintain any Action or Information in Law or Equity; or be Guardian of any Child, or Executor of any Will, or Administrator of any Estate.

Proviso. *Provided nevertheless,* That no Person shall be prosecuted by Virtue of this Act, for Words spoken contrary to this Paragraph thereof, unless Information thereof be given within six months after the Offence committed.

Proviso. *Provided also,* That any Persons convicted of any of the said Crimes, shall for the first Offence, upon renouncing such erroneous Opinions in the Court where convicted, within twelve Months after Conviction, from the

Time of such renouncing, be discharged from all Disabilities incurred by such Conviction.

And be it further enacted and provided by the Authority aforesaid, That the Governor, or Lieutenant-Governor of this State, for the Time being, or any three Assistants concurring, shall have Power to reprieve a condemned Malefactor to the next General Court.

Governor, or, &c. may reprieve.

That any Person arraigned before the Superior Court, for Trial, on an Indictment for any capital Offence, by Law punishable with Death, shall have Liberty peremptorily, without giving any Reason, to challenge twenty of the Jurors, summoned and impannelled for said trial, and no more, without shewing sufficient Reasons.

Jury may be challenged.

An Act for enjoining an Oath of Fidelity to this State.

All officers, &c. to take the oath.

Be it enacted by the Governor, Council and Representatives, in General Court assembled, and by the Authority of the same, That all Members of the General Assembly, and all Officers, Civil and Military, and Freemen of this State, shall take the Oath of Fidelity to this State prescribed by Law,

Not taking the oath, a disqualification, &c.

And be it further enacted by the Authority aforesaid, That no Person shall execute any Office, Civil or Military, nor vote in any Town, Society, or other public Meeting appointed by Law, nor plead in any Court (except in his own Case) nor any Male Person act as Executor or Administrator, or Guardian to any Minor, until he shall have taken the Oath aforesaid.

Certificate to be given.

And it shall be the Duty of the Authority administring said Oath, to give a Certificate thereof, if requested.

Source: *Acts and Laws,* 77.

An Act against Gaming.

Be it enacted by the Governor, Council and Representatives, in General Court assembled, and by the Authority of the same, That if any Person or Persons in this State, of what Rank or Quality soever, shall play at Cards, Dice or Tables; every such Person shall pay a Fine of *Twenty Shillings*, for every such Offence he or they shall be convicted of.

And the Head of every Family where any such Game is used, with his or her Privity or Consent, shall pay in like Manner the Sum of *Twenty Shillings* for each Time any such Game is used in his or her House.

And whosoever shall sell any Playing-Cards in this State, or have any for Sale in his Possession, or offer to sell any; every such Person shall pay a fine of *Forty Shillings*, for every Pack of Cards by him sold, offered to Sale, or found in his Possession.

And no Taverner, Inn-keeper, Ale-house-keeper or Victualler, shall have, or keep in or about their Houses, or any of the Dependencies thereof, any Dice, Cards, Tables, Bowls, Shuffle-board, Billiards, Coytes, Keils, Loggets or any other Implement used in Gaming; nor shall suffer any Person or Persons resorting unto any of their Houses, to use or exercise any of the said Games, or any other unlawful Game within their said Houses, or any of the Dependencies as aforesaid, or Places to them belonging, on pain of forfeiting the Sum of *Forty Shillings* for every such Offence, upon the Conviction thereof.

And every Person who shall be convicted of playing Cards, Dice or Tables in any such House, or the Dependencies thereof, shall incur the same Penalty as is before in this Act provided for playing at said Games; and for playing at any of the other Games aforesaid, in any such House or Dependencies, shall pay a fine of *Ten Shillings*; one half of the Fines that shall be recovered by virtue of this Act, shall belong to any Person or Persons who shall discover and give Information of the Offence; and the other half to the Treasury of the Town where the Offence is committed. And it shall be the Duty of every Informing Officer, to enquire after, and present all Breaches of this Act that shall come to their Knowledge.

Source: *Acts and Laws,* 88–89.

An Act for the Encouragement of Literature and Genius.

Preamble. *Whereas it is perfectly agreeable to the Principles of natural Equity and Justice, that every Author should be secured in receiving the Profits that may arise from the Sale of his Works, and such Security may encourage Men of Learning and Genius to publish their Writings; which may do Honor to their Country, and Service to Mankind.*

Authors of books, &c. have the sole right of publishing, &c. for the term of 14 years.

Be it enacted by the Governor, Council and Representatives, in General Court assembled, and by the Authority of the same, That the Author of any Book or Pamphlet not yet printed, or of any Map or Chart, being an Inhabitant or Resident in these United States, and his Heirs and Assigns, shall have the sole Liberty of printing, publishing and vending the same within this State, for the Term of fourteen Years, to commence from the Day of its first Publication in this State. And if any Person or Persons within said Term of fourteen Years as aforesaid, shall presume to print or re-print any such Book, Pamphlet, Map or Chart within this State, or to import or introduce into this State for Sale, any Copies thereof, re-printed beyond the Limits of this State, or shall knowingly publish, vend and utter, or distribute the same without the Consent of the Proprietor thereof in Writing, signed in the Presence of two credible Witnesses, every such Person or Persons shall forfeit and pay to the Proprietor of such Book, Pamphlet, Map or Chart double the Value of all the Copies thereof, so printed, imported, distributed, vended, or exposed for Sale; to be recovered by such Proprietor in any Court of Law in this State, proper to try the same.

Penalty for publishing, &c. without the proprietor's consent.

Proviso.

Provided nevertheless. That no Author, Assignee or Proprietor of any such Book, Pamphlet, Map or Chart shall be entitled to take the Benefit of this Statute, until he shall duly register his Name as Author, Assignee, or Proprietor, with the Title thereof, in the Office of the Secretary of this State, who is hereby impowered and directed to enter the same on Record.

Source: *Acts and Laws,* 133–34.

And be it further enacted by the Authority aforesaid, That at the Expiration of said Term of fourteen Years, in the Cases above mentioned, the sole Right of printing and disposing of any such Book, Pamphlet, Map or Chart in this State, shall return to the Author thereof, if then living, and his Heirs and Assigns, for the Term of fourteen Years more, to commence at the End of said first Term; and that all and every Person or Persons, who shall re-print, import, vend, utter or distribute in this State, any Copies thereof without the Consent of such Proprietor, obtained as aforesaid, during said second Term of fourteen Years, shall be liable to the same Penalties, recoverable in the same Manner as is herein before enacted and provided.

And whereas it is equally necessary, for the Encouragement of Learning, that the Inhabitants of this State be furnished with useful Books, &c. at reasonable Prices.

Be it further enacted, That when ever any such Author or Proprietor of such Book, Pamphlet, Map or Chart, shall neglect to furnish the Public with sufficient Editions thereof, or shall sell the same at a Price unreasonable, and beyond what may be adjudged a sufficient Compensation for his Labour, Time, Expence and Risque of Sale, the Judge of the Superior Court in this State, on Complaint thereof made to him in Writing, is hereby authorized and impowered to summon such Author or Proprietor to appear before the next Superior Court, to be holden in that County where such Author or Proprietor dwells, if a Resident in this State, if not, in that County where such Complainant dwells; and said Court are hereby authorized and impowered to enquire into the Justice of said Complaint, and if the same be found true, to take sufficient Recognizance and Security of such Author or Proprietor, conditioned that he shall within such reasonable Time, as said Court shall direct, publish and offer for Sale in this State, a sufficient Number of Copies of such Book, Pamphlet, Map or Chart, at such reasonable Price as said Court shall, on due Consideration affix: And if such Author or Proprietor shall, before said Court, neglect or refuse to give such Security as aforesaid, the said Court are hereby authorized and impowered to give to such Complainant, a full and ample Licence to reprint and publish such Book, Pamphlet, Map or Chart, in such Numbers and for such Term as said Court shall judge just and reasonable: Provided said Complainant shall give sufficient Security before said Court, to afford said reprinted Edition at such reasonable Price as said Court shall thereto affix.

Further term.

Proprietor neglecting to furnish the public with sufficient editions, &c.

Penalty on such as procure & print unpublished manuscript, without consent of the author.

And be it further enacted, That any Person or Persons who shall procure and print any unpublished Manuscript, without the Consent and Approbation of the Author or Proprietor thereof, first had and obtained, (if such Author or Proprietor be living, and resident in, or Inhabitant of these United States) shall be liable to suffer and pay to the said Author or Proprietor his just Damages for such Injury; to be recovered by Action brought on this Statute, in any Court of Law in this State, proper to try the same.

Provided always, That nothing in this Act shall extend to affect, prejudice or confirm the Rights which any Person may have to the printing or publishing of any Book, Pamphlet, Map or Chart, at Common Law, in Cases not mentioned in this Act, or to screen from legal Punishment any Person or Persons who may be guilty of printing or publishing any Book, Pamphlet or Paper that may be prophane, treasonable, defamatory, or injurious to Government, Morals or Religion.

Proviso.

Provided also, That this Act shall not extend, or be construed to extend in Favour, or for the Benefit of any Author or Persons residing in, or Inhabitants of any other of the United States, until the State or States, in which such Person or Persons reside or dwell, shall have passed similar Laws in Favour of the Authors of new Publications, and their Heirs and Assigns.

An Act for forming, regulating, and conducting the military Force of this State.

Whereas the Defence and Security of all free States depends (under God) upon the Exertions of a well regulated and disciplined Militia.
Wherefore,

Be it Enacted by the Governor, Council and Representatives, in General Court assembled, and by the Authority of the same, That all male Persons, from sixteen Years of Age to Forty-five, shall constitute the military Force of this State, except Members of the Council, of the House of Representatives, and of the Congress of the United States for the Time being, the State Treasurer, and Secretary, Justices of the Peace, field, commissioned, and staff Officers, honourably discharged, Ministers of the Gospel, the President, Tutors and Students of College, Physicians and Surgeons, Select-men, constant School-masters, one Miller to each Grist-mill, being approved by the Select-men, and having a Certificate thereof, constant Mariners who make it their constant Business to go to Sea, Sheriffs and Constables, constant Ferrymen, Persons disabled through Lameness or other bodily Infirmity, during the Continuance of such Disability, producing a Certificate thereof from two able Physicians, to the Acceptance of his or their commissioned Officers, non-commissioned Officers and Privates who have inlisted or shall hereafter inlist into the *Connecticut* Line of the Army of the United States, for the Term of the present War, and have faithfully served for said Term, or obtained an honourable Discharge, and Indians, Negroes and Molattoes.

Provided nevertheless, That such military Officers, and all Housholders and others not fifty-five Years of Age, shall give their Attendance on Days appointed for viewing of Arms, as hereafter directed; and such Officers shall be subject to do their Proportion of military Duty, when called by a superior Officer, in the Office they have respectively sustained.

And whereas sundry Persons have heretofore obtained Discharges from military Duty, on Account of temporary Disorders and Infirmities of Body, which in

> **Preamble.**

> **Who obliged to bear arms, and who exempt.**

> **Proviso.**

Source: *Acts and Laws,* 144–45.

many Instances are removed, and others have obtained such Discharges from an Abuse of the Provisions of the Law heretofore in force for that Purpose.
Therefore,

When discharges shall not avail to exempt from military duty.

Be it enacted by the Authority aforesaid, That no able-bodied and effective Man, in the Judgment of the commissioned Officers of the Company, within the Limits of which he may belong, shall, on Account of such Discharges, be exempted from military Duty, but shall be enrolled in their respective Companies, agreeable to the Provisions of this Act, and be liable to do Duty in such Companies as others by Law are, such Discharges notwithstanding.

Companies to remain the same, &c.

Be it further enacted, That the military Companies shall continue and remain as they now are, in respect to the Lines of Division and Boundaries and Order of Dignification.

Divided into regts. & brigades, &c.

And that the several military Companies aforesaid, shall be divided into Regiments, Brigades and Divisions, in Manner following, viz.

1st. Regt.

Those in the Towns of *Hartford, Windsor, Suffield,* and that Part of the Town of *Farmington* lying in the Parish of *Wintonbury,* shall constitute the first Regiment.

2d. Regt.

Those in the Towns of *New-Haven, Milford, Derby* and *Woodbridge,* shall constitute the second Regiment.

An Act for the Settlement, Support, and Encouragement of Ministers; and for the well-ordering Estates given for the Support of the Ministry.

Be it enacted by the Governor, Council and Representatives, in General Court assembled, and by the Authority of the same, That the Inhabitants of any Town or Society, constituted by this Assembly, who are or shall be present at a Town or Society Meeting, legally warned, shall have Power by the major Vote of those so met, to call, and settle a Minister or Ministers among them, and to provide for his or their Support and Maintenance. Power to call and settle a minister.

Provided, That no Person be allowed to Vote in any such Affairs, unless such Person or Persons have a Freehold in the same Town or Society, rated at *Fifty Shillings,* or *Forty Pounds* in the common List, or are Persons of full Age, and in full Communion with the Church in the said Town or Society. Proviso.

That the Minister or Ministers which have been, or shall be so called and settled, shall be the Minister or Ministers of such Town or Society. Such called and settled to be the minister.

And all Agreements which have been, or shall be made by the major Part of the Inhabitants of such Town or Society, qualified and met as aforesaid, with such Minister or Ministers, respecting his or their Settlement and Maintenance, shall be Binding and Obligatory on all the Inhabitants of such Town or Society so agreeing, and on their Successors, according to the true Intents and Purposes thereof. Agreements made by the major part binding on the whole.

That the several Towns wherein there is but one ecclesiastical Society, and the several Societies aforesaid within this State, shall pay unto their respective Ministers for the Time being, who dispense the Gospel therein, and are, or shall be according to the Laws of this State, settled or called to preach among them, annually, the several Sums or Payments agreed upon between them, as aforesaid, according to the true Intent and Meaning of such Agreements, both for the Specie, and Valuation thereof. Regard to be had to the specie and valuation.

And that all such Towns and Societies, by their proper Votes or Acts, shall annually take care to grant a Tax for the Purpose aforesaid, to be levied on their several Inhabitants according to their respective List, in the com- Annual tax to be granted

Source: *Acts and Laws,* 157–60.

mon List or Lists of the Persons and Estates of said Inhabitants; which shall be collected by such Person or Persons as such Towns or Societies shall annually choose and appoint for that End.

Selectmen & committees to take care, &c.

And the Select-men of such Towns, and the Committee of such Societies are hereby required to take all proper Care in their respective Precincts, that such Rates or Taxes be granted and collected, as aforesaid, for the Support of their Minister.

To apply to an assistant or justice, &c.

And when any such Rate or Tax is granted and made, as aforesaid, the said Select-men or Committee shall apply to some Assistant or Justice of the Peace in the same County, for a Writ or Warrant, directed to the Collector or Collectors chosen and appointed to collect such Rate or Tax, enabling and requiring him or them to levy and collect the same: Which Assistant or Justice shall forthwith proceed to grant out said Writ.

Collectors duty to be speedy, &c.

And every such Collector or Collectors shall with convenient Speed, levy and collect every such Rate committed to him or them: The whole of which they shall do, and pay unto the said Minister or Ministers within two Months after the yearly Salary is become due, for the payment of which such Rate or Tax is or shall be granted.

Proviso.

Always provided, That if any Person or Persons shall be assessed wrongfully, or more than his or their Proportion, they shall have Remedy by the County Court of the same County whereto he or they belong, upon Proof made thereof.

Distress against negligent collectors to be taken out by select-men, &c.

And if at any Time the said two Months shall be expired, and run out, and such Minister hath not received his Salary for the Year then past; the Select-men of such Town and the Committees of such Societies where such Neglects or Delays shall happen, shall forthwith take out a Distress upon such negligent Collector or Collectors who should have collected such Rate, directed to the Sheriff of the County, or Constable of the Town, signed by an Assistant or Justice of the Peace; who are impowered to grant the same, to levy such Part of such Rate as then remains unpaid, to such Minister, out of the Estate of such Collector or Collectors; which the said Sheriff or Constable shall forthwith proceed to do, and pay the same unto such Minister.

On neglect of selectmen, &c they to pay the arrearages, and a fine.

That if any of the Select-men or Committees aforesaid, shall neglect their Duty in not taking out a Distress as aforesaid, upon the Collector or Collectors as aforesaid, such Part of the said Rate remaining unpaid, shall be paid by such Select-men or Committee so neglecting, together with a Fine of *Three Pounds* to the County Treasury for every such Neglect.

How recovered.

All which shall be recovered by Action brought by the State's Attorney, to the County Court in the same County; and no Appeal shall be granted in such Case.

And in case any such Town or Society shall neglect to choose and appoint a Collector or Collectors, as aforesaid, any one Assistant or Justice of the Peace, next residing to such Town or Society shall, and he is hereby authorized to appoint and impower by his Warrant, such Collector or Collectors for the Purpose aforesaid.

And where any Town or Society within this State, shall have made no Agreement with their Minister or Ministers for the Sum of their yearly Maintenance, and such Minister or Ministers do find him or themselves aggrieved by too scanty Allowance, every such Minister making Application to the General Assembly, shall by said Assembly have ordered unto him or then: a suitable and sufficient Maintenance to be given him or them by the Inhabitants of the Town or Society whereto he or they belong.

And that if any Town or Society shall be for any Year or Years without a Minister preaching the Gospel to them, such Town or Society shall in the said Year or Years pay such Sum or Payment as the General Court shall appoint, of which Payment or Payments the Collector or Collectors who shall collect the same shall make Certificate to the next County Court of that County, which Court shall dispose of and improve the said Sums for the Use of the Ministry in the Town or Society where it is collected as soon as Opportunity may be had for it according to the Discretion of the Court.

And whereas there have been divers Grants, Donations, or Sequestrations of Lands, Monies, or other Estates or Interests, made for the Use and Support of the Ministry, settled and established by the Laws of this State; by Means whereof, in sundry of the Towns and Societies in this State, there are considerable Estates belonging to such Towns or Societies, for the Use and Support of the Ministry therein settled, or that shall be settled as aforesaid.

And whereas it is convenient that suitable Provision be made for the taking Care of, and improving such Estates for the End designed in granting, giving or sequestring the same:

Therefore,

Be it further Enacted, by the Authority aforesaid, That where there are any Lands, Monies, or other Estates granted, given, or sequestred according to antient Custom, Usage or Practice, or shall hereafter be given, granted, or squestred for the Use and Support of such Ministry in any Town or Society in this State, then and in every such Case, the Select-men for the Time being, of such Town where there is but one ecclesiastical Society; and the Committees for the Time being, of such eclesiastical Societies as have been, or shall be Constituted by this Assembly; or a Committee appointed by such Town or Society, (which Committee they are hereby respectively impowered to that End to appoint) shall have full Power and Authority to

Marginalia:

Societies neglecting to choose a collector, an assistant or justice to appoint &c

Where no agreement is made, general assembly to order, &c.

Town or society being without a minister for a year, &c. to pay, &c.

Estates given for the support of ministry how to be improved, &c.

demand, recover, receive, take care of, and improve all such Lands, Monies, or other Estates, to, and for the Use and Support of such Ministry settled in such Town or Society which they respectively represent, according to the true Meaning, Intent and Design in such Grants, Donations, or Sequestrations contained; and for their Improvement thereof, and of the Increase, Profits and Interests thereof to be accountable from Time to Time to such Town or Society as they respectively represent.

And that such Select-men and Committee may be enabled the better to do said Service;

Selectmen & Committees to make contracts, &c.

Be it further enacted by the Authority aforesaid, That the Select-men and Committee aforesaid, or the major Part of them, shall and may make all proper and necessary Contracts, and commence, prosecute and pursue all needful Suits, Actions and Causes in the Law, for the Purpose and End aforesaid.

Successors enabled to sue, &c.

And that such Select-men and Committees as shall from Time to Time succeed, and come in the Room and Stead of others removed by Death or otherwise, shall have the same Power in their own Names to act, appear, prosecute and pursue, in and upon any Contract, Suit, Action or Cause, for or concerning the Matters aforesaid, as fully as those whom they succeed in the Office aforesaid, might or could do if they had not been removed, as aforesaid.

And whereas divers of the Societies aforesaid, are made, or such Societies may be hereafter made and constituted of two or more adjoining Towns, so that part of the Inhabitants of the Society live in one Town, and part in another.

And whereas by Virtue of the Grants, Donations, or Sequestrations aforesaid, such Part of a Society that live in one of the said adjoining Towns, have or may have Lands, Monies, or other Estates, belonging to that Part distinct from the rest of the Society, for the Use aforesaid.

Such parts of societies as have distinct interest, to meet, &c.

Be it therefore further Enacted, by the Authority aforesaid, That such parts of Societies having such distinct Interests, shall, and may meet among themselves, and from Time to Time act, order, and direct, respecting such their distinct Interests, for the Use aforesaid, according to the Provision before in this Act made for Societies in regard to such Interests.

And to form themselves agreeable to Law.

And where any such Parts of a Society have not already had any Meeting, or formed themselves, they may, and hereby are directed to take the same Method in forming themselves as Societies by Law are directed to take, in their first forming themselves to act: And being formed, may choose a Clerk, who shall be sworn to a faithful Discharge of his Trust; and also may choose a Committee to take care of and improve the Interests aforesaid, for the Use aforesaid; who shall have the same Power and Authority, and be under the same Regulation in their said Trust, as is given and provided by this Act, to, and concerning the Committees of Societies respecting such Interests.

And the said Committee of such Part of a Society may warn Meetings of the Inhabitants of such Parts, and appoint Time and Place for that Purpose, or on their Neglect or Refusal, the Clerk of such Part of a Society, on Application of any five Inhabitants, may warn the same by setting up a Warning for that Purpose, in some proper Place or Places within the limits of such part of a Society. In which Meetings the Inhabitants may proceed to act in any Matters proper for them to act in. *To warn meetings, &c.*

Provided always, That no Meeting mentioned in this Act, be held within less than five Days after Warning given, or set up, as aforesaid; and that no Person be allowed to vote or act in any Meeting of any Town, Society, or part of a Society, in the Matters aforesaid, not qualified as before in this Act is provided, or that doth not belong to, or pay towards the maintenance of that Ministry for the Support whereof such Interests have been, or shall be granted, given, or sequestred, as aforesaid; any Thing before in this Act to the contrary in any wise notwithstanding. *Proviso.*

An Act for prescribing and establishing Forms of Oaths in this State.

Forms of oaths.   *Be it Enacted by the Governor, Council and Representatives, in General Court assembled, and by the Authority of the same,* That the several Forms of Oaths here following, be, and they are hereby established, to be taken by, and administred unto the several and respective Officers and Persons for whom they are appointed, as followeth.

Oath of Fidelity.

Oath of fidelity.   You *A. B.* do swear by the Name of the Everliving GOD, that you will be true and faithful to the State of *Connecticut,* as a free and independent State, and in all Things do your Duty as a good and faithful Subject of the said State, in supporting the Rights, Liberties and Privileges of the same.

So help you GOD.

For the Freemen, viz.

Freemen.   You *A. B.* being by the Providence of God, an Inhabitant of this State of *Connecticut,* and now to be made Free of the same, do swear by the Name of the Everliving GOD, that you will be true and faithful to said State, and the Constitution and Government thereof, as a free and independent State, and whensoever you shall be called to give your Vote or Suffrage touching any Matter which concerns this State, you shall give it as in your Conscience you shall judge will conduce to the best Good of the same, without respect of Persons or favour of any Man.   *So help you GOD.*

For the Governor, viz.

Governor.   You *J. T.* now chosen to be Governor over this State of *Connecticut,* for this Year ensuing, and until a new be chosen and sworn, Do swear by the Everliving God, to promote the public Good and Peace of the same, according to the best of your Skill; and that you will maintain the lawful Rights and Privileges thereof as a sovereign, free, and independent State; as also, that all wholesome Laws and Orders that are or shall be made by lawful Authority here established, be duly executed; and will further the Execution of Justice, for the Time aforesaid, according to the Rules of God's Word, and the Laws of this State.   *So help you GOD.*

Source: *Acts and Laws,* 182–83.

For the Lieutenant Governor, viz.

You *M. G.* now chosen to be Lieutenant-Governor over this State of *Con-* Lt. Governor
necticut, for this Year ensuing, and until a new be chosen and sworn, Do
swear, &c.—as in the Oath for the Governor, *mutatis mutandis.*

For the Assistants, viz.

You *J. H.* being chosen an Assistant over this State for the Year ensuing. Assistants.
Do swear by the Everliving God, to promote the public Good and Peace
of the same, according to the best of your Skill; and that you will maintain
the lawful Privileges thereof, according to your Understanding; and also
assist in the Execution of all such wholesome Laws and Orders as are or
shall be made by lawful Authority here established; and will further the
Execution of Justice for the Time aforesaid, according to the righteous
Rules of God's Word and the Laws of this State.   *So help you GOD.*

For the Judges of the Superior, and County Courts, mutatis mutandis, viz.

You   being appointed Judges of the Superior Court over this State, for Judges of
the Year ensuing, Do swear by the Name of the Everliving GOD, that as superior and
Judges of the said Court, you will faithfully and impartially administer Justice county courts
according to Law, take no Bribe, give no Counsel in any Matter that shall
come before you, nor deny Right to any; but well and truly perform your
Office of Judges, as aforesaid, according to your best Skill and Judgment.

So help you GOD.

For Justices of the Peace, viz.

You   swear by the Name of the Everliving GOD, that as Justice of the Justices.
Peace in the County of *H.* according to the Commission given you, you
will administer Justice equally and impartially in all Cases, and do equal
Right to the Poor and to the Rich, after your best Skill and Power and
according to Law: And you shall not be of Counsel in any Quarrel that
shall come before you, nor let for Gift or other Cause; but well and truly
do your Office of Justice of the Peace, taking only your lawful Fees. And
you shall not direct or cause to be directed, any Warrant by you made, to
the Parties, but you shall direct your Warrant to the Sheriff, his Deputy or
Constable, or other Officer proper for the Execution of the same, in the
County, or to some indifferent Person; and this you shall do without favour
or respect of Persons.   *So help you GOD.*

An Act relative to the People commonly called Quakers.

Preamble. *Whereas the People commonly called Quakers, decline and refuse to take an Oath in the usual Form, by Reason of Scruples of Conscience.*
Wherefore, in Easement thereto:

Quakers admitted to take the affirmation. *Be it enacted by the Governor, Council and Representatives, in General Court assembled, and by the Authority of the same,* That every Quaker within this State, who shall be required upon any lawful Occasion to take the Witnesses Oath, shall instead of the usual Form, be permitted to make his or her solemn Affirmation; and the same shall be administred to him or her in the Words following, viz.

Form. *You A. B. do solemnly and sincerely affirm and declare, that the Evidence you shall give to this Court concerning the Case now in Question, shall be the Truth, the whole Truth, and nothing but the Truth; upon the Pains and Penalties of Perjury.*

Affirmation how and when admitted. And that in every other Case, where an Oath by Law is enjoined, the same shall and may be administred to them in the usual Form in such Case by Law prescribed, excepting instead of the Words, "*swear by the Name of the everliving God,*" these Words, viz. "*solemnly, sincerely and truly affirm and declare,*" shall be made Use of in the Room thereof; and omitting the usual close of these Words in the Form, viz. "*So help you God.*"

Authority given to administer the affirmation. And all Persons authorized or required by Law to administer any Oath, are hereby authorized and directed to administer and tender the same, when thereto by Law required, to the People called Quakers, in the Form in this Act prescribed.

Affirmation of the same validity of an oath. *And be it further enacted by the Authority aforesaid,* That the aforesaid solemn Affirmation or Declaration, when made as aforesaid, shall be adjudged and taken to be of the same Force and Effect, to all Intents and Purposes in all Courts of Justice and other Places, where by Law an Oath is required, within this State, as if such Quaker had taken an Oath in the usual Form.

Source: *Acts and Laws,* 196–97.

And if any Quaker making such solemn Affirmation or Declaration, shall be lawfully convicted of having wilfully, falsly, and corruptly affirmed or declared any Matter or Thing, which if the same had been in the usual Form, would have amounted to wilful and corrupt Perjury; every such Quaker so offending, shall incur the same Penalties and Forfeitures as by the Laws of this State are enacted against wilful and corrupt Perjury.

Punishment for false affirmation, &c. as for perjury.

An Act for the due Observation of the Sabbath or Lord's-Day.

Be it enacted by the Governor, Council and Representatives, in General Court assembled, and by the Authority of the same, That all and every Person and Persons in this State shall, and they are hereby required, on the Lord's-Day carefully to apply themselves to duties of Religion and Piety, publicly and privately: And whatsoever Person shall not duly attend the public Worship of God on the Lord's-Day in some Congregation allowed by Law, provided there be any on which he can conscientiously and conveniently attend, un-

less hindred by Sickness, or otherwise necessarily prevented, shall for every such Offence, pay a Fine of *Three Shillings,* and being presented to Authority shall be deemed guilty thereof, if such Person shall not be able to prove to the satisfaction of such Authority, that he or she has attended the said Worship.

That no Person or Persons whatever shall keep open his or her Shop, Ware-house or Work-house; nor shall upon Land or Water, do any Manner of secular Business, Work or Labour, (works of Necessity and Mercy excepted) nor be present at any Concert of Music, Dancing, or any public Diversion, Shew, or Entertainment, nor use any Sport, Game, Play or

Recreation on the Lord's-Day, or any Part thereof, upon Penalty that every Person so offending shall pay a Fine not exceeding *Twenty Shillings,* nor less than *Ten Shillings.*

That no Traveller, Drover, Waggoner, Teamster or any of their Servants shall travel on the Lord's-Day, (except from Necessity or Charity) on Penalty of forfeiting a Sum, not exceeding *Twenty Shillings,* nor less than *Ten Shillings.*

And that no Persons shall convene and meet together in Company or Companies in the Streets or elsewhere, nor go from his or her Place of Abode on the Lord's-Day, unless to attend upon the public Worship of God, or some work of Necessity or Mercy, on Penalty of *Five Shillings.*

Source: *Acts and Laws,* 213–15.

That no Innholder or other Person keeping any public House of Entertainment, shall entertain, or suffer any of the Inhabitants of the respective Towns where they dwell, or others, not being Strangers or Lodgers in such Houses, to abide or remain in their Houses, or any of the Dependencies thereof, drinking or idly spending their Time on Saturday Night after sunset, or on the Lord's-Day, or on the Evening following, upon the Penalty of *Five Shillings*; and also every Person that shall be found there so spending his Time or Drinking, shall forfeit the Sum of *Five Shillings*. Not to frequent taverns &c.

Provided, That all Presentments or Informations against any Person or Persons for any of the forementioned Offences, be made within one Month after the Commission thereof. Proviso.

That no Warning or Notification of any Meeting or Business of a secular Nature, shall be set up or fixed on the Door or other Part of any Meeting-House for public Worship, so as to remain there on the Lord's-Day, or any Fast or Thanksgiving-Day, on Penalty of *Five Shillings,* to be paid by the Person who shall have set up the same, or ordered it to be set up. Notifications of secular officers not to be set up on meeting-house doors, &c.

And it shall be the Duty of the Grand-jurors, Constables and Tithing-men in such Town, to pull down and destroy the same. Duty of grand-jury-men, &c.

That no Vessel shall unnecessarily depart out of any Harbour or Port, Creek or River, within this State, on the Lord's-Day, or sail or pass by any Town or Society on *Connecticut*-River, where the public Worship of God is maintained, nor weigh Anchor within two Miles of such Place, unless to get nearer thereto, on the Lord's-Day, any Time between the Morning-light and the Setting-sun, on Penalty that the Master of every such Vessel shall, for every such Offence, forfeit *Thirty Shillings*. No vessel to sail, &c. unless, &c.

That if any Person or Persons, either on the Lord's-Day, or any other Time, shall wilfully interrupt or disturb any Assembly of People met for the public Worship of God, within the Place of their assembling, or out of it; each Person so offending shall pay a Fine not exceeding *Ten Pounds,* nor less than *Twenty Shillings*. Penalty for disturbing public worship.

And any Person who shall behave rudely or indecently, within the House where any Congregation are met for public Worship, shall pay a Fine not exceeding *Forty Shillings,* nor less than *Five Shillings*. Indecent behavior how punished.

And if any civil Process shall be issued or served on the Lord's-Day, it shall be void and of no Effect: And the Officer who shall serve the same on said Day, shall pay a Fine of *Ten Shillings,* and all Damage that shall accrue to any Person thereby. No civil process allowed.

And be it further enacted by the Authority aforesaid, That each Town in this State, at their annual Meeting in *December,* shall chuse two or more Tithing- Tything-men.

men, in each Society for Divine Worship in such Town, who shall be sworn to a faithful Discharge of the Office.

Grand-jurors   That the Grand-jury-men, Constables and Tithing-men of each Town, shall carefully inspect the Behaviour of all Persons on the Sabbath or Lord's-Day; and especially between the Meetings for divine Worship on said Day, whether in the Place of such public Worship or elsewhere; and due Presentment make of any profanation of the worship of God on the Lord's-day, or any Day of public Fast or Thanksgiving; and of every Breach of Sabbath which they, or any of them shall see or discover any Person to be guilty of, to the next Assistant or Justice of the Peace, who is hereby impowered to proceed therein as the nature of the Offence requires.

Their allowance.   That every Grand-jury-man, Tithing-man, or Constable shall be allowed *Two Shillings per Diem,* for each Day he spends in prosecuting such Offenders, to be paid by the Person offending, or the Parent, Guardian, or Master of such Person when under Age: And all Fines imposed for the Breach of this Act on Minors, shall be paid by their Parents, Guardians, or Masters, if any be, otherwise such Minor to be disposed of in Service to answer the same. And upon refusal or neglect of paying such Fines and Costs, the Offender may be committed; unless he be a Minor, in which Case Execution for the Fine and Cost shall be issued against his Parent, Guardian or Master, after the Expiration of one Month next after the Conviction of such Minor, and not sooner.

Persons refusing to pay charge to be committed.

Proviso.   Provided, No Person prosecuted on this Act, shall be charged with more than for one Person prosecuting him for such Offence.

Neglecting to pay fine to be whipt.   That whatsoever Person shall be convicted of any Profanation of the Lord's-Day, or of any Disturbance of any Congregation allowed for the Worship of God, during the Time of their assembling for, or attending on such Worship, and shall, being fined for such Offence, neglect or refuse to pay the same, or to present Estate for that Purpose; the Court, Assistant or Justice before whom Conviction is had, may Sentence such Offender to be whipt, not exceeding twenty Stripes; respect being had to the Nature and Aggravation of the Offence.

No appeal.   That no Person convicted of any Offence mentioned in this Act, shall be allowed any Appeal.

Children, &c to be corrected by their parents, &c. or.   But if any Children or Servants under the Age of fourteen Years, shall be convicted of such Profanation or Disturbance, they shall be punished therefor by their Parents, Guardians or Masters giving them due Correction in the Presence of some Officer, if the Authority so appoint, and in no other way; and if such Parent, Guardian or Master shall refuse or neglect to give such due Correction, that every such Parent, Guardian or Master shall incur the Penalty of *three Shillings.*

And be it further enacted by the Authority aforesaid, That every Assistant in this State, and every Justice of the Peace, within the Limits of their Authority, are hereby impowered and directed, when they shall have plain View, or personal Knowledge thereof, either with or without a written Warrant, to cause all Persons unnecessarily travelling on the Sabbath or Lord's-Day to be apprehended, and to examine them, and if need be to command any Person or Persons to seize, arrest, and secure any such Person unnecessarily travelling on the Lord's-Day, as aforesaid, and them to hold till Judgment may be had thereon. _{Assistant and Justices upon view to apprehend, &c.}

And every Sheriff, Constable, Grand-jury-man, and Tything-man, are hereby impowered and directed, without Warrant, to apprehend and carry before the next Assistant or Justice of the Peace, all Persons transgressing said Law, as aforesaid. Provided they be taken upon Sight, or present Information of others, and to command all necessary Assistance therefor. _{Constables, &c. Proviso.}

And it is further enacted by the Authority aforesaid, That every Person or Persons that shall refuse to obey the command of any Assistant, Justice of the Peace, Sheriff, Constable, Grand-jury-man or Tithing-man, or neglecting to afford his utmost Assistance to apprehend and secure any Person transgressing said Act as aforesaid, shall be, and hereby are subjected to the same Pains and Penalties as by Law Persons are subjected to for refusing to assist Sheriffs and Constables in the Execution of their Office. _{Penalty for such as disobey to assist, &c.}

And it is further enacted by the Authority aforesaid, That when any Sheriff, Constable, or indifferent Person shall receive any Warrant from lawful Authority to apprehend any Person for transgressing said Law, as aforesaid, they are hereby impowered and directed to pursue and apprehend such Person or Persons, any where within the limits of the Authority of the Officer granting such Warrant: Any Law, Usage, or Custom to the contrary notwithstanding. _{Sheriff, &c. to pursue, &c.}

An Act for appointing, encouraging, and supporting Schools.

Every society of 70 families to keep school 11 months in a year at least.

Be it enacted by the Governor, Council and Representatives, in General Court assembled, and by the Authority of the same, That every Town within this State, wherein there is but one Ecclesiastical Society, and wherein there are seventy Housholders, or Families, or upwards; and every Ecclesiastical Society constituted, or that shall be constituted by the General Assembly of this State, wherein there are the Number of seventy Housholders or Families, or upwards, shall be at least eleven Months in each Year constantly provided with, and shall keep and maintain one good and sufficient School for the teaching and instructing of Youth and Children to read and write; which School shall be steadily supplied with and kept by a Master sufficiently and suitably qualified for that Service.

Under that number half a year.

And every such Town and Society wherein there is not the said Number of seventy Housholders or Families, shall be provided with, and maintain a School, and a School-Master, as aforesaid, for the Purpose aforesaid, at least one Half of the year annually.

Grammar school to be kept in each town.

And also there shall be a Grammar School set up, kept and constantly maintained in every head or County Town of the several Counties that are, or shall be made in this State; which shall be steadily kept by some discreet Person of good Conversation, and well skilled in and acquainted with the learned Languages, especially Greek and Latin.

Committees appointed.

And every such Town and Society and hereby impowered to appoint Committees for such Schools respectively, to take Care and see the same kept accordingly.

And for the Encouragement and Maintenance of such Schools and School-Masters.

School masters how maintained.

Be it further enacted by the Authority aforesaid, That the Treasurer of this State shall annually deliver the Sum of *forty Shillings* upon every *thousand Pounds* in the Lists of the respective Towns in this State, and proportionably for lesser Sums, out of the Rate of each Town, as the same shall be brought

Source: *Acts and Laws,* 215–18.

in to the public Treasury by the several Constables, in such Money, or Bills of Public Credit, as the Rate shall be paid in; out of which the same is to be taken, unto the School Committees; or for Want of such Committees, to the Select-men of said Towns respectively, to be by them distributed to the several Societies in each Town for the Benefit of their respective Schools, in Proportion to the Lists in said Society.

Provided, The said School Committees or Select-men shall deliver their Certificates, that there hath been a School kept in each of the Towns and Societies they desire to take the Money out for, in the preceding Year, according to this Act.

Proviso.

And Whereas the several Towns and Societies in this State, which made and computed Lists of their Polls and rateable Estate in the Year of Our Lord *One Thousand Seven Hundred and Thirty-two;* by Virtue of an Act of this Court, made in *May, One Thousand Seven Hundred and Thirty-three,* received by their Committees respectively, for that Purpose appointed, considerable Monies, or Bills of public Credit, raised by the Sale of certain Townships laid out in the western Lands, then so called, (for which Receipts were given and lodged in the Secretaries Office) to be let out, and the Interest thereof used for the support of the respective Schools aforesaid, for ever, and to no other Use.

Preamble.

And Whereas certain Sums of Money have likewise been received by the several Towns and Societies in this State, by Virtue of an Act of this Court, made in *October, One Thousand Seven Hundred and Seventy-four,* directing the Treasurer to pay out of the public Treasury to the several Towns, the principal Sums paid in by them as Excise Money, together with the Interest due at the Time of Payment, taking a Receipt therefor, appropriating the same, solely to the Use of the respective Schools.

Preamble.

Be it therefore enacted by the Authority aforesaid, That if at any Time after the Receipt of said Monies aforesaid, or if at any Time hereafter, the said Monies, or Interest thereof, hath been or shall be, by order of such Town or Society, or the Committees chosen by them, put to, or imployed for any other Use than for the support of a School, as aforesaid, such Sum of Money received as aforesaid, shall be returned into the State Treasury; and the Treasurer of this State, upon Refusal thereof, shall recover the same Sum or Sums of such Town or Society, for the Use of the State.

School money misapplied forfeited.

And such Town or Society that misapplies such Money, shall forever lose the Benefit thereof.

That where, in any Town or Society, there is not a sufficiency of Money or Interest provided, in the Manner aforesaid, or by charitable Donations,

Further provision made.

or Sequestrations, or any other Ways procured for the maintenance of a School as aforesaid, therein, and a suitable School-Master to keep the same, a sufficient Maintenance shall be made up, the one Half by the Inhabitants of such Town or Society, and the other Half thereof by the Parents or Masters of the Youth or Children that go to such School; unless any Town or Society shall agree otherwise; which they are hereby impowered to do.

Towns & societies may tax, &c.

And every such Town and Society by their Vote, shall have full Power to grant Rates for the support of such School, and choose a Collector to gather and collect such Rates. And what such Town or Society shall agree upon and enact respecting the Encouragement and Support of the School aforesaid, among themselves, shall be obligatory upon the whole Town or Society, and every Member therein.

To divide into districts.

And be it further enacted and provided, That each Town and Society, shall have full Power and Authority to divide themselves into proper and necessary Districts for keeping their Schools, and to alter and regulate the same, from Time to Time, as they shall have Occasion; which Districts so made, shall draw their equal Proportion of all the public Monies appropriated for the support of Schools, belonging to such respective Towns or Societies, according to the List of each respective District therein.

And that the good Ends proposed in erecting and keeping Schools, may not be defeated;

Civil authority & select-men inspectors.

Be it further enacted by the Authority aforesaid, That the Civil Authority, together with the Select-men in every Town, or the major Part of them, shall inspect, and they are hereby impowered and directed, as Visitors, to visit and inspect the state of all such Schools as are by this Act appointed to be kept within said Towns, from Time to Time, and particularly once each quarter of a Year, at such Time as they shall think proper, and enquire concerning the Time such Schools are kept, and into the Qualifications of the Masters of such Schools, together with the Proficiency of the Children under their Care: And they are to give such Directions as they shall find needful, to render such Schools most serviceable for the increase of Knowledge, Religion and good Manners: And if the said Inspectors or Visitors observe any such Disorders or Misapplication of public Money, allowed for the support of such Schools, as will be likely to defeat the good Ends proposed, they shall lay the same before this Assembly, that proper Orders therein may be given.

And that all Estates and Interests, granted and sequestered for the Support of the Schools in this State, may be truly and properly improved for that Purpose;

Be it further enacted by the Authority aforesaid, That the Select-men of such Towns wherein there is but one Ecclesiastical Society, and the Society Committee of such Societies where there are more than One in any Town, (for the Time being) or a Committee by such Town or Society for that Purpose appointed, (which Committee such Town and Society are hereby impowered to appoint) shall be, and they are hereby impowered and directed to take Care of, and improve such Bonds and Monies as have been divided and set out to such Town or Society, out of the Monies raised by the Sale of the said Townships, or otherways, and to receive such as shall hereafter be divided to them, for the Purpose aforesaid, giving Receipts therefor, to be lodged in the Secretary's Office; and of their Improvement thereof, shall from Time to Time be accountable to the Town or Society, by whom they are or shall be appointed: And such Town and Society shall be accountable for the same before this Assembly, when thereto required, and be liable to be dealt with for their Misuse of the same, according to the Declaration before in this Act made.

Select-men or committees to take care of the school monies.

And such Select-men, and Committee or Committees, are hereby authorized and impowered to take and receive into their Care and Custody, all other Estates, Lands, and Interests that have been given, granted, sequestered or do belong to such Schools, or that shall hereafter belong thereto, for the Support thereof; and shall use, improve, and dispose of the Interest, Increase, Profit or Rent arising or coming upon any such Monies, Lands or Interests, according to the true Intent of such Gift, Grant or Sequestration, for the Purpose aforesaid; which shall be disposed of either to the School-Master, or to a Committee of the School, to be by them improved for the support of the School.

Also real estates, &c. To lease, &c.

And that the said Select-men, Committee or Committees may be the better enabled to do said Service;

It is further enacted by the Authority aforesaid, That they, the said Select-men, Committee or Committees, or the major Part of them, shall be, and they are hereby authorized and impowered to lease all such Lands and real Estates, and loan such Monies as do or shall appertain to such Schools, and is or shall be given for the Use aforesaid; and to commence and prosecute such Suit or Suits as may be necessary for the Recovery and obtaining such Lands, Monies and other Estates; and to take Leases, Bonds, or other Securities to themselves and their Successors, for the use of such Schools: Which Leases, Bonds, or other Securities the said Select-men, Committee, or Committees who take the same, shall have Power to sue and recover therein: And in case of the Removal of them, or any of them, by Death or

On removal of committee others to be chosen.

otherwise, their Successors in that Office or Offices, shall have as full Power in the Matters aforesaid, to prosecute in their own Names, as those whom they succeed as aforesaid, might or could do, if they had not been removed as aforesaid; which Bonds, Leases and Securities shall, by said Select-men and Committee be lodged with the Clerk of such Town or Society, who is directed and required to keep an Account thereof, and hold the same under the Direction of the said Select-men and Committees, for the Purpose aforesaid; and such Select-men and Committees shall render their Accounts of their Use and Improvements of such Estate and Interest, unto such Town and Society by whom they are appointed, when thereunto required.

Proviso.   *Provided nevertheless,* That this Act shall not extend to any Estate formerly granted by any particular Person for the Benefit of any School or Schools in any particular Town or Society; nor to Grants of any Interests formerly made by any Person to any Town or Society for the support of Schools wherein the Grantor hath committed the Care and Improvement of such Estate by him given, to particular Persons, with particular Directions for a continual Succession in said Trust; or where the General Assembly hath formerly interposed and committed the disposition of the Profits of such Estates to a Committee in continual Succession; any Thing contained in this Act to the contrary notwithstanding.

An Act concerning Indian, Molatto, and Negro Servants and Slaves.

Be it enacted by the Governor, Council and Representatives, in General Court assembled, and by the Authority of the same, That whatsoever Negro, Molatto or Indian Servant or Servants shall be found wandering out of the Bounds of the Town or Place to which they belong, without a Ticket or Pass in Writing under the Hand of some Assistant, or Justice of the Peace, or under the Hand of the Master or Owner of such Negro, Molatto or Indian Servants, shall be deemed and accounted to be Run-aways, and may be treated as such: And every Person inhabiting in this State, finding or meeting with any such Negro, Molatto or Indian Servant or Servants not having a Ticket, as aforesaid, is hereby impowered to seize and secure him or them, and bring him or them before the next Authority to be examined and returned to his or their Master or Owner, who shall satisfy the Charge accruing thereby. *[Negro, molatto, or indian servants not to travel without a pass, &c.]*

And all Ferry-men within this State, are hereby required not to suffer any Indian, Molatto or Negro Servant, without Certificate, as aforesaid, to pass over their respective Ferries, by assisting them therein, directly or indirectly, on the Penalty of paying a Fine of *Twenty Shillings,* for every such Offence, to the Owner of such Servants. *[Ferrymen not to transport such on penalty of 20s.]*

And all Vagrants or suspected Persons may be used in the like Manner, when found Wandering from Town to Town having no Certificate or Pass, as aforesaid; who shall be seized and conveyed before the next Authority, to be examined and disposed of according to Law. *[Vagrants, &c. to be taken up, &c.]*

And if any free Negroes shall travel without such Certificate or Pass, and be stopped, seized or taken up as aforesaid, they shall pay all Charges arising thereby. *[Free negroes not to travel without pass.]*

And for the preventing such Servants from Stealing from their Masters and others, and for the better governing them;

Be it further enacted by the Authority aforesaid, That every free Person which shall presume, either openly or privately, to buy or receive of or from any Indian, Molatto or Negro Servant or Slave, any Money, Goods, Mer- *[Persons prohibited from trading with servants.]*

Source: *Acts and Laws,* 233–35.

chandizes, Wares or Provisions, without Order from the Master or Mistress of such Servant or Slave; every Person so offending, and being thereof convicted, shall be sentenced to restore all such Monies, Goods, Wares and Provisions unto the Party injured, in the specific Articles, (if not altered) and also forfeit to the Party double the Value thereof, over and above, or treble the Value where the same are disposed of, or not to be obtained: And if the Person so offending be unable to, or shall not make Restitution as awarded, then to be publicly whipt with so many Stripes (not exceeding Twenty) as the Court or Justice that hath Cognizance of such Offence, shall order; or make Satisfaction by Service: To be assigned therein by such Court or Justice.

On penalty, &c.

And every Indian, Negro or Molatto Servant or Slave, of, or from whom such Money, Goods, Merchandizes, Wares or Provisions shall be received or bought, if it appear they were stolen, or that shall steal any Money, Goods, Merchandizes, Wares or Provisions, and be thereof convicted, (although the Buyer or Receiver be not found) shall be punished by Whipping, not exceeding thirty Stripes, and the Things stolen to be restored to the Party injured, if found, or the Value thereof if not found: To be determined as aforesaid.

Indian servants, &c. stealing to be whipped.

That if any Negro, Molatto or Indian Servant or Slave, shall be found abroad from Home in the Night-season, after nine of the Clock, without special Order from his or their Master, or Mistress, it shall be lawful for any Person or Persons, to apprehend and secure such Negro, Molatto, or Indian Servant or Slave, so offending, and him, her, or them, bring before the next Assistant or Justice of the Peace; which Authority shall have full Power to pass Sentence upon such Servant or Slave, and order him, her, or them, to be publicly whipped on the naked Body, not exceeding ten Stripes, and to pay Cost of Court; except his or their Master or Mistress shall redeem them, by paying a Fine not exceeding *ten Shillings.*

Servants, &c. not to go abroad after 9 o'clock at night, unless, &c.

And if such Servant, or Slaves, shall have Entertainment in any House after nine of the Clock, as aforesaid, (except to do any Business they may be sent upon) the Head of the Family that entertains, or tolerates them in his or her House, or any the Dependences thereof, shall forfeit and pay the Sum of *ten Shillings*: One Half to the Complainer, and the other Half to the Treasurer of the Town where the Offence is committed.

Penalty for entertaining servants, &c.

And whereas the increase of Slaves in this State is injurious to the Poor, and inconvenient:

Be it further enacted by the Authority aforesaid, That no Indian, Negro or Molatto Slave, shall at any Time hereafter, be brought or imported into this State, by Sea or Land, from any Place or Places whatsoever, to be disposed of, left or sold within this State.

No slaves to be bro't into this state.

Be it further enacted by the Authority aforesaid, That any Person or Persons who shall hereafter, contrary to the true Intent of this Act, import or bring any Indian, Negro, or Molatto Slave or Slaves into this State, to be disposed of, left or sold within the same, or who knowing such Slave or Slaves to be so imported and brought into this State, shall receive and purchase them, or any of them, shall forfeit and pay to the Treasurer of this State, the Sum of *One hundred Pound* lawful Money, for every Slave so imported, brought into this State, received or purchased, to be recovered by Bill, Plaint, or Information, in any Court of Record proper to try the same. And that it be the Duty of all Constables and Grand jurors, to enquire after, and make Presentment of all Breaches of this Act. Penalty on importers or purchasers of slaves.

And that all Slaves set at Liberty by their Owners, and all Negro, Molatto, and Spanish Indians who are Servants to Masters for Time, in Case they come to Want, after they shall be set at Liberty, or the Time of their said Service be expired, shall be relieved by such Owners or Masters respectively, their Heirs, Executors, or Administrators; and upon their, or either of their Refusal so to do, the said Slaves and Servants shall be relieved by the Select-men of the Towns to which they belong; and the said Select-men shall recover of the said Owners or Masters, their Heirs, Executors, or Administrators, all the Charge and Cost they are at for such relief, in the usual Manner, as in Case of any other Debts. Slaves set free to be maintained by their late owners in case they come to want.

Provided nevertheless, That if any Master or Owner of any Servant or Slave, shall apply to the Select-men of the Town to which he belongs, for Liberty or Licence to emancipate or make free any such Servant or Slave, it shall be the Duty of such Select-men to enquire into the Age, Abilities, Circumstances and Character of such Servant or Slave, and if they or the major Part of them, shall be of Opinion that it is likely to be consistent with the real Advantage of such Servant or Slave, and that it is probable that the Servant or Slave will be able to support his or her own Person, and he or she is of good and peaceable Life and Conversation; such Select-men or the major Part of them, shall give to the Owner or Master of such Servant or Slave, Certificate under their Hands, of their Opinion in the Premises, and that the Master or Owner of such Servant or Slave, hath Liberty to emancipate and set at Liberty such Servant or Slave. And if the Master or Owner of any Servant or Slave, shall, on receiving such Certificate, emancipate and set at Liberty such Servant or Slave, he, his Heirs, Executors and Administrators, shall be forever discharged from any Charge or Cost, which may be occasioned by maintaining or supporting the Servant or Slave, made free as aforesaid; any Law, Usage or Custom, to the contrary notwithstanding. Proviso. Owners of emancipated slaves freed from charge, on certificate being procured, &c.

And whereas sound Policy requires that the Abolition of Slavery should be effected as soon as may be, consistant with the Rights of Individuals, and the public Safety and Welfare.   Therefore,

All born after   *Be it enacted by the Authority aforesaid,* That no Negro or Molatto Child,
1st Mar. 1784,   that shall, after the first Day of *March, One thousand seven hundred and*
to be free at
the age of 25.   *eighty-four,* be born within this State, shall be held in Servitude, longer than
until they arrive to the Age of twenty-five Years, notwithstanding the
Mother or Parent of such Child was held in Servitude at the Time of its
Birth; but such Child, at the Age aforesaid, shall be free; any Law, Usage
or Custom to the contrary notwithstanding.

An Act for forming, ordering, and regulating Societies.

Be it Enacted by the Governor, Council and Representatives, in General Court assembled, and by the Authority of the same, That the settled and approved Inhabitants, qualified as is hereafter in this Act provided, in each respective Society made, or that shall be made, and constituted by this Assembly, shall meet and assemble together, annually, some time in the Month of *December,* or in any other Month in the Year, as they shall judge most convenient, at some Place in such Society, according to the Notice thereof, to be given them at least five Days before such Meeting, by the Committee for ordering the Affairs of the Society, or for want of such Committee, by the Clerk of the Society.

Inhabitants to meet annually, &c. on five days notice.

And the Inhabitants being legally assembled, are impowered by the Vote of the major Part of them present, to choose a Moderator, a Society Clerk, and three or more discreet, able Inhabitants, to be a Committee to order the Affairs of the Society for the Year ensuing; which Clerk shall take the Oath by Law provided for Society Clerks; and being so qualified, shall have the same Powers and Authorities, as to the Business of the said Society, as the Town Clerks have in the respective Towns; and his Doings shall be as effectual in Law: And the said Society Clerk, being chosen and sworn, shall continue in his Office until another be chosen and sworn in his Room.

To choose moderator, clerk and committee.

Clerk to be sworn.

And also to choose a Society Treasurer, who shall be under the same Regulation, and have the same Power and Authority in said Societies, as Town Treasurers have in their respective Towns.

Also society treasurer.

And also the said Inhabitants in their lawful Meetings, by their major Vote, as aforesaid, shall have Power to grant, and lay such Rates and Taxes, on the Inhabitants of such Society, and others by Law rateable by such Society, for the raising such Sum or Sums of Money, as may be needed for the Support of the Ministry, and School there, and other Matters necessary for them to do; and to appoint Committees for such Purposes as their

To grant rates and levy taxes.

Source: *Acts and Laws,* 235–37.

Occasions call for, as the Law directs: And to choose and appoint a Collector or Collectors for the gathering such Rates and Taxes. And every Collector so chosen that shall refuse to serve, shall suffer the same Penalty as is provided by Law in Case of Town Officers refusing to serve in the Offices to which they are chosen.

New societies how warned to meet the first time.

That when any Society or Societies are legally set off in any Town or Towns in this State, whereby such Town or Towns are divided into separate Societies, such new Society so set off, and also the remaining Part or first Society in any Town may, in order to their being formed and furnished with proper Officers, warn their first Meeting in the following Manner, viz. An Assistant or Justice of the Peace, together with three principal Inhabitants in any such first Society, or in any such other Society set off as aforesaid, shall grant a Warrant under their Hands, to some proper Person by them deputed, to warn all the Inhabitants in the Limits of such first or other Society, to meet together at such Time and Place as they shall appoint: The said Warning to be given five Days before such Meeting; and being so met, shall and may act and do all and every Thing lawful and proper for a Society to do as before in this Act is provided.

Such inhabitants as have the gospel preached for certain months, &c.

That such Inhabitants of Towns and Societies as have obtained or hereafter shall obtain Liberty of the General Assembly to procure, and have the preaching of the Gospel among themselves for certain Months in the Year, distinct and separate from the established Place of Worship in such Town or Society to which they belong, shall and may, when and so often as there may be Occasion, meet together at such Time and Place as shall be appointed, and according to the Notice thereof to be given them at least five Days before such Meeting, by their Committee, or for want of Committee, by one of the said principal Inhabitants; and being so assembled, may choose a Clerk to enter their Votes, and also a Committee of three or more able,

Their privileges and power.

discreet Men, of the Inhabitants aforesaid, to order the prudential Affairs of such Precincts, for the End aforesaid; and may by their major Vote in such their Meetings, grant and lay such Rates and Taxes on the said Inhabitants as shall be needful for the support of the Minister whom they shall procure to preach with them for such Time, and for other necessary Charges arising among them; and to appoint a Collector or Collectors for the gathering such Rates: Who shall have the same Power to proceed in Collecting the same as Collectors of Societies have, and shall be accountable therefor in the same Manner as Collectors of Society Rates by Law are.

And for the preventing Disputes about the Votes made in Society Meetings, and for the determining the Qualification of Voters therein.

Be it further enacted by the Authority aforesaid, That no Person shall presume to vote in any Society Meeting, aforesaid, unless such Person hath a Freehold in the same Town or Society, rated at *fifty Shillings,* or *forty Pounds* in the common List, or is a Person of full Age, and in full Communion with the Church; nor shall any Person who is or shall be by the Laws of this State, freed or exempted from the Payment of those Taxes, granted by any Town or Society, for the Support of the Worship, and Ministry of the presbyterian, congregational or consociated Churches, in this State, and for the building and maintaining Meeting-Houses for such Worship, on Account or by Reason of his dissenting from the Way of Worship and Ministry, aforesaid, be allowed or admitted to act or vote in any Town or Society Meeting, in those Votes which respect or relate to the Support of the Worship and Ministry, aforesaid, and the building and maintaining of the Meeting-Houses aforesaid.

And the Acts and Votes of such Town and Society Meetings, passed without computing Persons not qualified as above is expressed, and the Acts and Votes respecting the Support of the Worship and Ministry, and Meeting-Houses aforesaid, made and passed without computing the Votes of such exempt Persons, shall be deemed and accounted the Acts and Votes of such Town and Society; any Law, Usage or Custom, to the contrary in any wise notwithstanding.

And be it further Enacted, That upon the Refusal, Death or Removal, of any Society Clerk or other ordinary Society Officer in any Society in this State, such Society may assemble together, and choose a New to fill up such vacant Place.

And be it further enacted by the Authority aforesaid, That the Fines by Law inflicted on Persons chosen to any Society Office, and who do not accept or execute such Office, shall be paid to the Treasury of such Society; and shall be recovered by Action brought in the Name of the Committee of such Society; any Law, Usage, or Custom to the contrary notwithstanding.

And be it further enacted by the Authority aforesaid, That if any Person, who is not duly qualified according to this Act, to vote in any Society Meeting, shall adventure to act, deal or intermeddle, or presume to vote in any Society Meeting, for the choice of Officers, granting of Rates, or any other Affairs whatsoever, such Offender shall forfeit the Sum of *fifteen Shillings,* for every such Offence; to be levied by Distress and Sale of the Offender's Goods; one Half thereof to the Complainer, who shall prosecute to Effect, the other Half to the Treasurer of such Society wherein said Offence is committed.

[Margin notes:] Who have right to vote. · Acts valid without, &c. · Society clerks, &c. refusing, others to be chosen. · Penalty on unqualified voters, &c.

Where socie-
ties are not
distinguished
by local limits,
to be desig-
nated by
enrollment.

And be it further enacted by the Authority aforesaid, That where two or more Societies, constituted by Act of the General Assembly, have the same Limits and Boundaries, the Members belonging to each shall be designated by inrolling their Names with the Clerk of the Society to which they respectively belong; and it shall be the Duty of the said Clerks to inrol the same accordingly.

In case they make no election, how to be considered &c.

And all Persons who shall arrive at the Age of Twenty-one Years, or Women who shall become Widows, dwelling within the Limits of such Societies, shall have Liberty at any Time within twelve Months after said Times respectively, to elect which Society they will belong to: And all Persons that shall come from any other Place, to dwell within the Limits of such Societies, may at any Time elect which Society he or they will belong to; which Election shall be manifested by causing his or their Name or Names to be inrolled with the Clerk of the Society to which they join: And in case of Non-election within the Time limited by this Act, the Persons brought up within said Limits shall belong to that Society to which their Parents belonged, (if they dwelt there) otherwise to the Society to which the Head of the Family in which they were brought up, belonged; and Widows, to the Society to which their Husbands did belong: And Persons who come from any other Place to dwell there, shall be taxed by the Society lowest in the List within such Limits, which support the Ministry by taxing, until they make their Election, as aforesaid.

To continue to that society whereof they are legal members, unless, &c.

And all Persons who have or shall become legal Members of any such Society, shall continue Members of the same, during their Continuance within the Limits thereof, unless released by Act of the General Assembly, or Vote of such Society, and joining to another Society within the same Limits; which Release such Society is hereby authorized to grant, by a legal Vote in their Meeting, if they think fit, on Application of any Person desiring the same.

Proviso.

Provided, That nothing in this Act shall affect the Privileges allowed by Law to any Persons who soberly dissent from the Worship and Ministry established by the Laws of this State.

An Act against profane Swearing and Cursing.

Be it enacted by the Governor, Council and Representatives, in General Court assembled, and by the Authority of the same, That if any Person within this State shall swear rashly, vainly or profanely, either by the holy Name of God, or any other Oath: Or shall sinfully and wickedly curse any Person or Persons, such Person so offending, shall upon Conviction thereof before any one Assistant or Justice of the Peace, forfeit and pay for every such Offence the Sum of *six Shillings.* Penalty for swearing, &c. 6s.

And if such Person or Persons so convict, shall not be able, or shall refuse to pay the aforesaid Fine, he or they shall be set in the Stocks, not exceeding three Hours, and not less than one Hour for one Offence, and pay Cost of Prosecution. If unable to pay, &c. to be set in the stocks.

Source: *Acts and Laws,* 240.

An Act for the more effectual putting in Execution the Laws against Vice, Immorality and Profaneness, and for promoting Christian Knowledge.

Preamble.   *Whereas putting in Execution the good and wholesome Laws, made for restrain-ing, punishing and suppressing profane, immoral and irreligious Practices in this State, and promoting Christian Knowledge, will greatly tend to the honor of Religion, the Peace and good Order of human Society, and to suppress Vice and Wickedness:*

Therefore, that the same may be more generally and effectually done;

Duty of the civil authority herein.   *Be it enacted by the Governor, Council and Representatives, in General Court assembled, and by the Authority of the same,* That all Judges and Justices of the Peace in the respective Counties in this State, be, and they are hereby required to be diligent and careful in putting in Execution all such Laws and Acts as are or shall be made in this State, for the punishing, restraining or suppressing any Profaneness, Immorality, or irreligious Practices or Dis-orders, that thereby the good Ends proposed in such Acts and Laws may be attained.

Of the selectmen.   That the Select-men from Time to Time, shall make diligent Enquiry of all Housholders within their respective Towns, how they are furnished with Bibles; and if upon such Enquiry any Housholder be found without

Housholders to have bibles in their families;   one Bible at least, then the Select-men shall warn the said Housholder forthwith to procure one Bible at least, for the Use and Benefit of their Families respectively: And if the same be neglected, then the said Select-

for neglect, how dealt with, &c.   men shall make Return thereof to the next Authority, who may deal with such Housholder's Family according to the directions of the Law relating to the educating and governing of Children.

And with cat-echisms, &c.   And all such Families as are numerous, and whose Circumstances will allow thereof, shall be supplied with Bibles according to the Number of Persons of Capacity to use the same in such Families; and with a suitable Number of Orthodox Catechisms, and other good Books of practical God-liness, and the like.

Source: *Acts and Laws,* 258–59.

That the Constables, Grand-jury-men and Tithing-men in the respective Towns in this State, shall, and they are hereby required to make diligent Search after, and Presentment make of all the Breaches of the Laws which relate to their Office or Offices respectively. Constables, &c. to make Presentment, &c.

And the Constables and Grand-jury-men in the respective Towns shall, on the Evenings after the Lord's-Day, and other public Days of religious Solemnity, walk the Street, and duly search all Places suspected for harbouring or entertaining any People or Persons assembled contrary to Law. Constables & grand-jury-men.

Be it further enacted by the Authority aforesaid, That the Justices of the Peace, Grand-jurors, Constables and Tithing-men in the respective Towns in this State, shall annually meet in the respective Towns to which they belong, on the first Monday of *January,* and on the third Monday in *June,* at the Place where their annual Town-Meetings are held, or at some other Place by them appointed, there to advise, consider, and use their joint Interest in suppressing Profaneness, Vice, and Immorality; and for the due Execution of all the Laws of this State, to which their respective Offices have Relation. Civil authority, &c. to meet annually on the first Monday of January, and third Monday of April, to advise, &c.

And be it further enacted by the Authority aforesaid, That the Town-Clerk of each respective Town in this State, at the opening of the public Town-Meeting for electing Town-Officers in *December* annually, if present, and in his Absence the Select-men for the Time being, who shall be present, shall read, or cause to be read this Act, and every Paragraph thereof publicly in this Meeting. This act to be read annually in town-meeting in December.

And if such Clerk, being present, or such Select-men present in the Clerk's Absence, shall neglect or refuse publicly to read, or cause to be read this Act; then the said Clerk or Select-men in refusing or neglecting, shall forfeit and pay the Sum of *Twenty Shillings*; one Half to the Complainer, who shall prosecute to Effect, and the other Half to the Town-Treasury.

And the Constables and Grand-jury-men are directed to inquire after, and due Presentment make of all Breaches of this Act, to some Assistant or Justice of the Peace; who are hereby impowered to hear and determine the same. Constables & grand-jury to make presentment.

Selected Judicial Opinions

Arabas v. Ivers, 1784

This case involved a slave, Jack Arabas, who had enlisted in the Continental army in 1777 as a substitute for his owner's son. After Arabas was honorably discharged, his owner, Thomas Ivers of New York, sought to reclaim his property. Arabas was jailed in New Haven, where he appealed to the Superior Court for a writ of habeas corpus. Jesse Root included the case in his famous Reports, *but he did not indicate which Superior Court justices participated in the ruling or why, exactly, Arabas was declared to be free. The original manuscript record of the case shows that the decision was by Samuel Huntington, Eliphalet Dyer, Roger Sherman, and William Pitkin and, significantly, clarifies the court's reasoning.*

Published Opinion

The case was—Jack was a slave to Ivers, and enlisted into the continental army with his master's consent—served during the war, and was discharged. Ivers claimed him as his servant; Jack fled from him to the eastward, Ivers pursued him, and took him and brought him to New Haven on his return to New York, where he belonged, and for safe-keeping while he stayed at New Haven, he got the gaoler to commit Jack to prison; and upon Jack's application to the court, complaining of his being unlawfully and unjustly holden in prison, the court issued a habeas corpus, to bring Jack before the court; also ordering the gaoler to certify wherefore he held Jack in prison; which being done, Ivers was cited before the court; and upon a summary hearing, Jack was discharged from his imprisonment, upon the ground that he was a freeman, absolutely manumitted from his master by enlisting and serving in the army as aforesaid.

Source: 1 Root 92 (1784).

Original Manuscript Opinion

A Superior Court holden at New Haven in the County of New Haven in the State of Connecticut by adjounment on the Fifth Tuesday of December being the 7ᵗʰ Day, Anno Domini 1784

One Jack Arabass[1] a Negro Man Confined in the Gaol in this place being brot Before this Court by Writ of Habeas Corpuss Directed to the Sheriff of Said County Commanding him to bring his Said Prisoner together with the Time, Cause and Reason of his Commitment And the Sheriff having Returned that said Jack was Commited by Thomas Ivers of the City and State of New York as a Runaway Slave and by said Ivers Claimed as a Slave for life. Whereupon this Court having fully Examined into the State of the facts Relative hereto and fully heared the Said parties with their proofs, pleas and allegations therein And it Appearing to this Court that Said Negro Jack Sometime in the Year 1777 being then a slave for life of the Said Ivers was by his Said Masters Leave and Consent Duly Enlisted as a Soldier into the Continental Army for and during the War—And that at said time of Enlistment his said Master Received the Bounty for Said Enlistment and that he the Said Jack faithfully performed the Duties of a Soldier during the Warr. and at the Close thereof was Honourably discharged. . . . Upon which facts this Court Are of Opinion that as none but freeman Could by the Regulations of Congress be Enlisted into the Continental Army, the Consent of Said Master to such Enlistment in judgment of Law Amounts to a Manumission and that Said Negro Jack cannot be any longer held as a Slave for life and therefore Order and Decree that he be no longer held in Custody but Set at Liberty. past and Allow'd in Court Test. Geo. Pitkin Clerk—

Source: Connecticut Superior Court Records, Connecticut State Library, 24: 11–12.

1. In the original manuscript "Arabas" appears as "Arabass," and in his company's rolls it is spelled "Arabus." *Collections of the Connecticut Historical Society* (Hartford: Connecticut Historical Society, 1909), 12: 58, 338. —Ed.

Symsbury Case, 1785

This case involved two competing land grants by the General Assembly. The Superior Court, then consisting of Richard Law, Eliphalet Dyer, Oliver Ellsworth, William Pitkin, and Roger Sherman, declared the second grant by the legislature to be void. Symsbury Case *is regularly considered to be an early example of judicial review at the state level.*[1]

By the COURT. It is conceded by the pleadings, that the land demanded lies within ten miles of the west line of Windsor, and the original grant and patent to Symsbury is bounded south on Farmington, and extending from thence ten miles north, and east on Windsor, extending from thence ten miles west; and the north line of Farmington, and the west line of Windsor, form an obtuse angle of about one hundred and thirteen degrees:—We are, therefore, of opinion, that the form of the township of Symsbury, according to the true construction of the original grant and patent, is a regular four sided figure, called a rhombus, the opposite sides being parallel, and ten miles distant from each other; the outside lines are consequently of equal length, and something more than ten miles, and include the lands demanded. The title is, therefore, in the plaintiffs, if they have not been divested by some act subsequent to the original grant.

This leads us to consider the several surveys and proceedings, in order to ascertain the limits and boundaries of the grants, as they are set up in the pleadings. . . .

I think it ought to be admitted in the case before us, that the proprietors of Symsbury could not have their grant taken from them, or curtailed, even by

Source: 1 Kirby 444, at 446–53 (1785).

1. For an excellent discussion of the background of the case and how scholars have treated it, see "Symsbury Case," *Connecticut Supreme Court Historical Society* 1 (2006): 27–48. William Winslow Crosskey and William Jeffrey deny that *Symsbury* is properly categorized as a case of judicial review because the General Assembly could have overturned the Superior Court decision. Crosskey and Jeffrey, *Politics and the Constitution in the History of the United States* (Chicago: University of Chicago Press, 1980), 3: 961.

the General Assembly, without their consent; and when the survey was made by Kimberly, etc. and approved by the assembly, the proprietors had their election, either to rely upon the construction of the words of the patent for their title, or to accept of the location, and thereby reduce it to a legal and practical certainty; they wisely chose the latter, it being material in their favor, and substantially fulfilling the original intention of all parties, by enlarging the patent to the contents of ten miles square; and though it could not be laid in a square form, by means of the two given lines before mentioned, yet the form and quality is equally good; for I do not find it suggested in any of the pleadings, that the proprietors are injured by the form or quality of the lands circumscribed in the location.

If we take up this case upon the facts stated in the pleadings, in a summary manner, and without any refined subtilties, consider it on the principles of substantial right, it appears in this light, viz.—That the defendant's grant, and all mean conveyances, confessedly cover the lands demanded: That the grant and patent to Symsbury, at the times they were made, were intended to include a tract of territory ten miles square, but did actually include all the lands within four lines, each ten miles long, and no more, in form of a rhombus, or diamond figure:—This being less than ten miles square, occasioned disputes and uneasiness when the mistake was discovered, and various constructions of the patent, which it will not bear, in order to help out this mistake: That finally, when the matter came before the assembly, in 1727, they took up the mistake where it was obviously found, and upon principles consonant to law and equity; by a location, rectified substantially this mistake, by making the survey in good form, and as large as the contents of ten miles square; which the patentees accepted, and thereby obtained an indisputable title to the same, which they still quietly enjoy.

Now, shall we still extend the west line of Symsbury about two miles further west, and take upwards of four thousand acres in addition, as is earnestly contended by the counsel for the plaintiffs? Take it from the present possessors, who have honestly purchased the same? And for what purpose, or on what principle, shall we give it to the adverse party, who have, by mensuration, the full contents of their patent without it?

I am, therefore, of opinion, that these ancient transactions of the survey and settlement of Kimberly's line, are too sacred to be set aside; and that judgment in this case ought to be for the defendant.

Hinckley v. Willson, 1787

In seventeenth- and eighteenth-century Connecticut, Native Americans captured in war or in a few other circumstances could be enslaved. In the Superior Court case of Hinckley v. Willson *(1787), judges Sherman, Pitkin, Ellsworth, Law, and Dyer, in an opinion written in Sherman's hand, addressed a case involving the widow of a Native American who had been held as a "servant and slave" to Joseph Hovey. The judges ruled that because Timothy Caesar was "born of a free woman, a native of the land," he was not a slave and thus was able to establish residency in the town of Coventry (which made the town liable for the support of his widow and children). This case played an important role in establishing the principle that anyone born to a free person is free.*[1]

County of Tolland
1787
Hinckley v. Willson
    Error from a Justice of the Peace—Judgment affirmed.
    With regard to the Plea in abatement—A Justice of the Peace is bound by his oath not to be "of counsel in any in any quarrel that shall come before him"; & he ought also to be cautious in declaring extrajudicial opinions lest an undue use should be made of them. Yet is he not, merely by having manifested his opinion on a question of law legally disqualified from judging in a cause in which that question comes up; which is the amount of the exception in the present case.—Nor is it material to his jurisdiction of what description the parties are or what the cause is, if the title of land is not concerned & the demand does not exceed four pounds. The decision of the Justice in this Case is limited in its operation merely to the sum demanded in the writ, & does

---

Source: Connecticut Superior Court Records, Connecticut State Library.

    1. Kirby reports the case as *Wilson v. Hinkley*, 1 Kirby 199 (1787). He notes that the opinion was by "the whole Court," without mentioning specific justices. The manuscript of the opinion in the Connecticut State Library lists the case as *Hinckley v. Willson* and contains the signatures of the five judges.

not determine the settlement of the paupers as it may respect demand for their future support.

As to the merits—The said Caesar, being born of a free woman, a native of the land, was not a slave; nor was he within the meaning of the statute, "a servant bought for time"; nor does it appear that he was an apprentice under-age; or that he was under any disability to gain a settlement by commorancy;— And having resided more than one whole year in the town of Conventry with his Wife the said Amy, he there gained a settlement for himself & her as also for her children. Nor was Edgerton, her former master, holden for her support for she had never been his slave or servant bought for time, but the burthen of her support devolved on the town of Coventry, from whence having been removed to the town of Tolland & there become chargeable, a right of recovery for the expense in favour of the town of Tolland against the town of Coventry accrued.

R Sherman
Pitkin
Richard Law
Ellsworth
Dyer

The War for
Independence

Following the conclusion of the Seven Years' War (1754–63), Parliament for the first time attempted to raise money by directly taxing American colonists. Although the taxes were not high, in the minds of many Americans they were clearly unconstitutional and to pay them would encourage arbitrary government. Of all the direct taxes passed by Parliament, particularly imprudent was the Stamp Act of 1765, which "fell particularly hard on two categories of men skilled in circulating grievances—publicans (who had to pay a registration fee of £1 a year) and newspapers (who had to print on stamped paper)."[1] Sherman, like many patriots, objected to the statute because he believed Parliament had no power to tax the colonists. He led a New Haven town meeting that instructed the city's delegates, himself and Samuel Bishop, to oppose the act. In the General Assembly, Sherman served on a committee that drew up a petition to the king and instructions for Connecticut's agent in Great Britain that insisted that the colonists had not forfeited the "sacred and inviolable" rights of Englishmen, so they could not be taxed without their consent.[2]

Parliament repealed the Stamp Act in March 1766, but it immediately passed the Declaratory Act, which asserted that it had the authority to make laws binding colonists "in all cases whatsoever," a claim Americans found to be both

---

1. Paul Johnson, *A History of the American People* (New York: HarperCollins, 1997), 133.

2. Hoadly, *Public Records of the Colony of Connecticut*, 12: 422, 425. See generally Edmund S. Morgan and Helen M. Morgan, *The Stamp Act Crisis: Prologue to Revolution* (Chapel Hill: University of North Carolina Press, 1953).

remarkable and dangerous. As if to further provoke the colonists, Parliament also passed the Quartering Act and, in 1767, the Townshend Acts. Sherman again helped craft a petition to the king challenging the legality of the legislation. After the colonial boycott of British goods forced Parliament to largely repeal the Townshend Acts in 1770, some merchants began to waver in their commitment to the boycott. Sherman remained adamant in his support because of his commitment to the principle that Parliament had no power to tax or regulate the internal affairs of the colonists. Also of serious concern to him and his fellow Calvinists were the Quebec Act of 1774 and the threat that an Anglican bishop would be sent to the colonies.

In 1774, the General Assembly appointed Sherman as one of Connecticut's delegates to the Continental Congress. He arrived in Philadelphia on September 1 with his fellow representatives Eliphalet Dyer and Silas Deane. Inspired in part by the Suffolk Resolves, Congress agreed on a forceful statement of colonial rights (although not as strong as Sherman would have preferred). Congress also produced the Articles of Association, an appeal to the people of Great Britain, and a petition to the king. Sherman was returned to Congress in May 1775, and he continued to advocate American independence. Notably, he voted for and signed Congress's Declaration of the Causes and Necessity of Taking Up Arms. These documents are often neglected by students of the American founding, but they are worthy of careful study as they reflect some concerns only hinted at by the Declaration of Independence.

Since at least 1766, Sherman had steadfastly denied that Parliament had any authority whatsoever over the colonies. Their only allegiance was to the Crown, and in his mind the king had clearly removed the colonists from his protection. When it came time to appoint a committee to write a declaration of independence, Sherman was a logical candidate. On June 11, 1776, Congress appointed Benjamin Franklin, John Adams, Thomas Jefferson, Robert Livingston, and Robert Sherman to this committee. The very next day Sherman was also appointed to a committee to draft what became the Articles of Confederation (Livingston was the only other delegate to serve on both committees). Two days later, he was appointed to the Board of War. He was the only member of Congress to serve on all three of these committees.[3]

According to John Adams, the committee on the declaration "had several meetings, in which were proposed the articles of which the declaration was to consist and minutes made of them. The committee then appointed Mr. Jefferson and me to draw them into form, and clothe them in a proper dress."

3. Worthington C. Ford et al., eds., *Journals of the Continental Congress, 1774–1789* (Washington, D.C.: Government Printing Office, 1904–37), 1: 33–35; 5: 431, 433, 438 (hereafter cited as *JCC*).

As Adams recalled the story, he insisted Jefferson write the draft, the committee met to discuss it, and Franklin and Sherman were too pressed for time to criticize anything.[4] Jefferson's account varies slightly from Adams's, but not significantly with respect to Sherman's participation.[5] Nevertheless, although many of the changes in the draft declarations are in Jefferson's hand, Julian P. Boyd reasonably asks how we can be "certain whether some of these corrections and changes . . . were not suggested by Adams or Franklin—or even by Roger Sherman, a very wise man, or by Robert R. Livingston, an intelligent youngster."[6]

This chapter includes a variety of texts that shine light on Sherman's position on, and contributions to, America's War for Independence. It contains the final texts of several key public documents that he helped craft, voted for, and signed.

4. John Adams, *Autobiography*, and John Adams to Timothy Pickering, August 6, 1822, both in *The Works of John Adams*, ed. Charles Francis Adams (Boston: Charles C. Little and James Brown, 1850), 2: 512–14.

5. Thomas Jefferson to James Madison, August 30, 1823, in *The Writings of Thomas Jefferson*, ed. Paul L. Ford (New York: G. P. Putnam's Sons, 1892), 10: 266–69.

6. Julian P. Boyd and Gerard W. Gawalt, eds., *The Declaration of Independence: The Evolution of the Text*, rev. ed. (Hanover, N.H.: University Press of New England, 1999), 30.

Instructions from the Town of New Haven to Its Delegates Regarding the Stamp Act, 1765

Sherman led the committee that penned the following instructions for New Haven's delegates to the General Assembly (Sherman and Samuel Bishop).

To Gentlemen,

The Freemen of the Town of New Haven by Electing you to Represent them in the General Assembly of this colony have Delegated to you the Power of acting in their publick affairs in general as you shall think prudent yet as your constituents have Right to express our Minds and give Instruction to our Representatives in any particular matters. We think it expedient at this time to recommend to your consideration some important matters which very nearly affect the Interests and Liberties of the people of this colony & all other his Majestys Subjects in America. As the Parliament of Great Brittain have lately passed an Act for imposing and collecting certain Stamp Duties in this & the other American colonies which if carried into Execution will be very Grievous to his majesties Loyal Subjects in said colonies,

1 In that it will impose a Tax upon them without their consent by themselves or Representatives

2 That it will occasion much trouble & Embarrassment in transacting their affairs

3 That it is not so equitable a way of raising money as their ordinary way of Taxing

4 That it extends the Jurisdiction of the Court of Admiralty in the colonies in that it subjects them to prosecutions in that Court for any supposed breaches of the Stamp Act or any other Revenue Act & so deprives them of the privilege of Tryal by a Jury, and that herein the colonists are distinguished from their fellow subjects in great Brittain.

And what necessity can there be for these extraordinary measures?

Are not the Americans as Loyal [as] any of the Kings Subjects?

Source: William Samuel Johnson Papers, box 1, folder 3, Connecticut Historical Society, Hartford, Connecticut.

Did not this colony & the other Northern colonies whose Forces acted in conjunction in the late war readily & chearfully exert themselves in raising men & money for his majesties service Pursuant to his Majesty's Requisitions?

And will not a principle of Self Preservation, and a Sense of Duty and Allegiance to their King who is the safe Guardian of their Liberties always be a sufficient Inducement to a Loyal & Free People chearfully to Tax themselves when ever it appears necessary for their own Defence or for the support of Government?

We would therefore earnestly recommend it to you to use your utmost endeavours that these important matters which so greatly concern the Interests & Liberties of this people may be taken into consideration by the General Assembly in the ensuing session and such measures resolved on as shall be Judged most likely to obtain a Repeal of the Stamp Act & relief in other matters of grievance, and we are of opinion that it will be best that commissioners be appointed to meet the commissioners of the other colonies in order to unite in a Suitable Petition to the King.

And we humbly hope that our most gracious Sovereign when he shall be informed how very grievous and disquieting the aforesaid measures are to so great a number of his Dutiful Subjects; He will hear & regard their united cries and be graciously pleased to Interpose for their Relief, and that repeal of the aforesaid grievous measures will be obtained, and such other measures agreed upon as may answer the ends of government, quiet the people in America, Secure their Rights, and lay a Foundation for a cordial, happy, & lasting union between the mother country and her colonies.

Letter to Matthew Griswold, January 11, 1766

NEW HAVEN

Matthew Griswold (1714–99) was a member of Connecticut's Council of Assistants (the upper house of the General Assembly) when Sherman wrote this letter to him. Griswold later served as governor of the state from 1784 to 1786.

Sir,

I hope you will excuse the freedom which I take of mentioning, for your consideration, some things which appear to me a little extraordinary, and which I fear (if persisted in) may be prejudicial to the Interests of the Colony—more especially the late practice of great numbers of people Assembling and Assuming a kind of Legislative Authority, passing & publishing resolves &c.—will not the frequent Assembling such large Bodies of people, without any Laws to regulate or Govern their proceedings, tend to weaken the Authority of the Government, and naturally possess the minds of the people with such lax notions of Civil Authority as may lead to such disorders & confusions as will not be easily suppress'd or reformed? especially in such a popular Government as ours, for the well ordering of which good rules, and a wise, Steady Administration are necessary.—I esteem our present form of Government to be one of the happiest & best in the world: it secures the civil & religious rights and privileges of the people, and by a due administration has the best tendency to preserve and promote publick virtue, which is absolutely necessary to publick happiness. . . . There are doubtless some who envy us the enjoyment of these . . . privileges, and would be glad of any plausible excuse to deprive. . . . therefore behoove . . . to conduct with prudence and caution at this critical juncture, when Arbitrary principles & measures, with regard to the colonies, are so much in vogue; and is it not of great importance that peace & harmony be preserved & promoted among ourselves; and that everything which may tend to weaken publick Government, or give the enemies of our happy constitution any advantage against us, be carefully avoided? I have no doubt of the upright intentions of those gentlemen who have promoted the late meetings in several parts

Source: *Magazine of American History* (March 1884), 11: 220–21.

of Colony, which I suppose were principally Intended to concert measures to prevent the Introduction of the Stampt papers, and not in the least to oppose the Laws or authority of the Government; but is there not danger of proceeding too far, in such measures, so as to involve the people in divisions and animosities among themselves, and . . . endanger our Charter-privileges? May not . . . being informed of these things view them in such a light . . . our present Democratical State of Government will not be Sufficient to Secure the people from falling into a State of Anarchy, and therefore determine a change to be necessary for that end, especially if they should have a previous Disposition for such a change?—Perhaps the continuing Such Assemblies will now be thought needless, as Mr Ingersoll has this week declared under Oath that he will not execute the office of Distributor of Stamps in this Colony, which declaration is published in the New Haven Gazette. I hope we shall now have his influence & Assistance in endeavoring to get rid of the Stamp Duties. . . .

I hear one piece of News from the East which a little Surprizes me, that is, the publication of some exceptionable passages extracted from Mr Ingersoll's letters, after all the pains taken by the Sons of Liberty to prevent their being sent home to England. I was glad when those letters were recalled, and that Mr. Ingersoll was free to retrench all those passages which were thought likely to be of disservice to the Government, and to agree for the future, during the present critical situation of affairs, not to write home anything but what should be inspected & approved by persons that the people of the Government would confide in; but by means of the publication of those passages in the Newspapers they will likely arrive in England near as soon as if the original Letters had been sent, and perhaps will not appear in a more favourable point of light.—

Sir, I hint these things for your consideration, being sensible that, from your situation, known abilities and interest in the Affections and esteem of the people, you will be under the best advantage to advise & influence them to such a conduct as shall be most likely to conduce to the publick Good of the Colony. I am, Sir, with great esteem, your Obedient, Humble Servt

Roger Sherman.

Letter to William Samuel Johnson, December 5, 1766 (excerpt)

NEW HAVEN

This letter is printed in full on pages 50–51. It is reprinted in part here because it shines important light on the views and concerns that informed Sherman's opposition to Parliament and, later, the Crown.

Sir,

. . .

I have sent the Newspaper you spoke of by the Post. Since that paper was published this question hath been proposed to me, viz, Does not the King hold his Dominions in Great Brittain & America by the same Title, i.e. whether he is not King of America by virtue of his being King of Great Brittain, and if so, how are they distinct Dominions?

There is no doubt but that the colonies are bound by the present Establishment of the Crown, as they have consented to it, sworn Allegiance &c.

But Query: If the succession according to the present Establishment should cease for want of an Heir, or if the Parliament should alter it & admit a Papist to the Crown, would not the colonies be at Liberty to Joyn with Brittain or not.

These questions may serve for speculation but it is not likely they will need to be resolved in our Day, & I hope not till the time comes when the Nations shall learn War no more————[1]

I am, Sir, your Obedient Humble Servt
R. Sherman

Source: William Samuel Johnson Papers, box 1, Connecticut Historical Society, Hartford, Connecticut.

1. A reference to Isaiah 2: 4, "And he shall judge among the nations, and shall rebuke many people: and they shall beat their swords into plowshares, and their spears into pruninghooks: nation shall not lift up sword against nation, neither shall they learn war any more." —Ed.

Letter from Roger Sherman et al. to Merchants, 1770

NEW HAVEN

After the colonial boycott of British goods forced Parliament to largely repeal the Townshend Acts in 1770, some merchants began to waver in their commitment to the boycott. In towns throughout America, meetings were held to encourage the colonists to persevere. A New Haven committee consisting of Sherman and five colleagues sent a letter to merchants in Weatherfield and Hartford urging them not to forsake the cause of liberty.

Gentlemen,

The time is now come for us to determine whether we will be FREEMEN or SLAVES, or in other words, whether we will tamely coalesce with the measures of our backsliding Brethren of New York who by resolving on importation at this juncture have meanly prostituted the Common Cause to the present sordid prospect of a little Pelf; or by a virtuous & manly Effort endeavour to heal this Breach in the Common Union by adhering more firmly than ever to our first Agreement. There is no time to lose—and can we hesitate a moment in choosing whether we will continue our Connection with those degenerate Importers, and with the prospect of a little temporary Wealth bequeath Infamy, Poverty, & Slavery to our Posterity; or by discarding them entirely until they shall return to their Agreement evince to future Ages, God, and ourselves that we are still uncontaminated & free? Let not our present Connection with any of them deter us: it is the Cause of our Country, it is the Cause of Liberty, it is the Cause of All; and our Country betrayed, & our Liberty sold, and ourselves enslaved, what have we left? With what can New York supply us that can't be had on equal Advantage and perhaps on a more generous Footing from our *Natural* Friends and Neighbors of Boston, whose manly fortitude and persevering measures justly claim our preference.

It is with peculiar satisfaction we have the pleasure to inform you of the determinate Resolution & spirited Behavior of all Ranks and Denominations

Source: Thomas Addis Emmet Collection, reel 1, 357, Manuscripts and Archives Division, New York Public Library. Astor, Lenox, and Tilden Foundations.

among us who with one Voice determine upon the Expediency of abiding by the general non-Importation Agreements and breaking off all Connexion with any of our Neighbors who have or shall infringe the same as you'll see by the copies of the inclos'd letters and Resolves passed in a fuller meeting than has ever been known on the like Occasion. We have full Confidence that our Brethren among you will now manifest their sense of the Defection of the majority of the Merchants of New York in a manner proper and consistent with ourselves for which purpose we have transmitted the same Intelligence to our Brethren throughout the Colony not doubting they have even gone before us on these our virtuous Endeavors—

and are, with Esteem & Regard

Gent, your most obedt.

humble Servts.

Roger Sherman

Thomas Howell

Jesse Leavenworth

Joseph Munson   Committee

David Austin

Adam Babcok

To the merchants at Weatherfield & Hartford.

Letter to Thomas Cushing, April 30, 1772

NEW HAVEN

The legal business in the first two paragraphs is not particularly significant, but I include it to remind readers that Sherman wore many hats—store owner, attorney, judge, and elected official at the city, state, and national levels.

Sir

I have sent by Capt. Daniel Olds the balance due for your 95 acre Lot sold to Buck & Plat which is £9:10 as per account transmitted to you last year. I received your favour of the 20th January last but had no opportunity to answer it till now.

As to the Land your sister sold to Mr. Nichols, I was Instructed to take a mortgage of it for security which I did and took no other security. I understand he has entered upon the Land, fenced, cleared, & plowed some of it and is willing to perform the Bargain if he can be quieted in the possession of the whole of it, or have a reasonable deduction from the price for what may be with held from him by a prior title. I saw Mr. Canfield this week who says designs to look into the matter & inform you how it is.

The Land your sister sold to Abijah Ruggles was 8 acres, part of a 32 acre Lot, the residue of which belongs to your children, which he intends to purchase if he can—as to the undivided Right, I believe there will be no more Divisions upon it.

The observations you make relative to the measures proper to be taken to preserve the Rights of the colonies I Esteem Just, but in order to do any thing Effectual it will be needful for the people of the several colonies to be agreed in sentiment as to the extent of their Rights.

It is a Fundamental principle in the British Constitution and I think must be in every free State, That no Laws bind the people but such as they consent to be governed by, therefore so far as the people of the colonies are Bound by Laws made without their consent, they must be in a state of Slavery or absolute

Source: Historical Society of Pennsylvania autograph collection, collection no. 0022A, Historical Society of Pennsylvania.

Subjection to the Will of others, if this Right belongs to the people of the colonies why should they not claim & Enjoy it? If it does not belong to them as well as to their fellow subjects in great Britain how came they to be deprived of it? are great Britain & the colonies at all connected in their Legislative Powers? have not each colony distinct and compleat Powers of Legislation for all the purposes of public government, and are they in any proper sense Subordinate to the Legislature of Gr. Br—tho subject to the same King—and tho' some general Regulations of Trade etc. may be necessary for the General Interest of the nation is there any constitutional way to Establish such Regulations so as to be legally binding upon the people of the several distinct Dominions which comprise the British Empire but by consent of the Legislature of Each governt?

These are points which appear to me Important to be agreed in and settled right, and any concessions made by [any?] of the Assemblies disclaiming any privileges essential to Civil Liberty which the colonies are Justly entitled to, must greatly disserve the common cause—if they think it not prudent at present to assert every Right in the most explicit manner yet all concessions which may be construed as a disclaimer; ought to be carefully avoided.

I am Sir Your
Humble Servant
Roger Sherman

Excerpts from the Diary of John Adams, 1774 and 1775

The following entries from John Adams's diary shine some light on Sherman's political views and speaking ability. The first, from August 1774, records Adams's first impression of Sherman. The second and third excerpts are from September 8, 1774, and September 15, 1775, respectively.

From August 1774

17. Wednesday. At New Haven. We are told here that New York is now well united and very firm. This morning, Roger Sherman, Esquire, one of the delegates for Connecticut, came to see us at the tavern, Isaac Bears's. He is between fifty and sixty, a solid, sensible man. He said he read Mr. Otis's Rights, &c. in 1764, and thought that he had conceded away the rights of America. He thought the reverse of the declaratory act was true, namely, that the Parliament of Great Britain had authority to make laws for America in no case whatever. He would have been very willing that Massachusetts should have rescinded that part of their Circular Letter where they allow Parliament to be the supreme Legislative over the Colonies in any case.

From September 8, 1774

Mr. Sherman. The ministry contend that the Colonies are only like corporations in England, and therefore subordinate to the legislature of the kingdom. The Colonies not bound to the King or Crown by the act of settlement, but by their consent to it. There is no other legislative over the Colonies but their respective assemblies.

The Colonies adopt the common law, not as the common law, but as the highest reason.

Source: Charles Francis Adams, ed., *The Works of John Adams* (Boston: Charles C. Little and James Brown, 1850), 2: 343, 371, 423.

From September 15, 1775

... Sherman's air is the reverse of grace; there cannot be a more striking contrast to beautiful action, than the motions of his hands; generally he stands upright, with his hands before him, the fingers of his left hand clenched into a fist, and the wrist of it grasped with his right. But he has a clear head and sound judgment; but when he moves a hand in any thing like action, Hogarth's genius could not have invented a motion more opposite to grace;—it is stiffness and awkwardness itself, rigid as starched linen or buckram; awkward as a junior bachelor or a sophomore.

Letter from Eliphalet Dyer, Roger Sherman, and Silas Deane to Governor Jonathan Trumbull Sr., October 10, 1774

PHILADELPHIA

Connecticut's delegates regularly wrote to the state's governor to apprise him of Congress's actions as well as political and military news. Many of these letters contain factual information readily available elsewhere, so I include them only if they seem particularly significant or if they reveal something about Sherman's personal opinions. This letter was penned by Silas Deane but signed by all three delegates.

Jonathan Trumbull (1701–85) was governor of Connecticut from 1769 to 1784. One of his sons, Jonathan Trumbull Jr. (1740–1809), was governor of Connecticut from 1798 to 1809. Another son, John Trumbull (1756–1843), is widely considered to be the "Painter of the American Revolution."

Sir,

We arrived in this City the 1st of Septr. last, and the Delegates from Virginia, North Carolina, and New York not being come, The Congress was not formed untill the 5th when the Honle. Peyton Randolph Esqr. was unanimously chosen President, and Charles Thompson Esqr. Secretary, a List of the Members We inclose. The mode of Voting in this Congress was First resolved upon, which was that each Colony should have one Voice, but as this was objected To as unequall, an Entry was made on the Journals To prevent its being drawn into precedent in future. Committees were then appointed to state American Rights, and greivances; And of the various Acts of the British Parliament which affect the Trade and Manufactures of these Colonies, on these Subjects The Committees Spent several Days, when The Congress judg'd it necessary, previous to compleating & resolving on these Subjects, to take under Consideration, That of Ways and Means for redress. On the 16th arrived an Express from Boston with Letters to The Delegates and the Suffolk Resolves. These were laid before the Congress and were highly approved of & applauded, as

Source: Paul H. Smith et al., eds., *Letters of Delegates to Congress* (Washington, D.C.: Government Printing Office, 1976), 1: 168–70.

You will see, by the inclosed Paper of the 19th, in which the proceedings of the Congress, thereon, is published at large, by their Order. A general Non-importation of British Goods & Manufactures or of any Goods from thence, appearing to the Congress one of the means of redress in our power, and which might probably be adopted, to prevent future difficulties and altercations on this Subject among those who might Now, or for sometime past, had been sending Orders for Goods, The Congress Unanimously came into the inclosed Resolution on the 22d and the same was ordered to be published immediately. Since this a Nonimportation and Non Consumption of Goods, &c from Great Brittain & Ireland from & after the first of December next, has been Unanimously resolved on, but to carry so important a resolution into effect, it is necessary, that every possible precaution should Now be taken, on the one hand to prevent wicked, & desperate Men, from breaking through, & defeating it, either by Fraud, or Force, and on the other to remove as farr as possible every Temptation to, or Necessity for the Violation thereof. For this a Committee, are appointed, who not having as yet compleated their Report, nothing is published particularly on this Subject, more than what, We now are at Liberty, in general to relate.

We have the pleasure of finding the whole Congress, & through them the whole Continent of the same Sentiment, & opinion, of the late proceedings & Acts of the British Parliament, but at the same time confess Our anxiety for greater dispatch of the Business before Us, than it is in Our power, or perhaps in the Nature of the Subject, to effect. An Assembly like this, though it consists, of less than Sixty Members, yet coming from remote Colonies, each of which, has some modes, of transacting public Business, peculiar to itself some particular provincial rights and Interests to guard, & secure, must take some Time, to become so acquainted with each ones situations & connections, as to be able to give an united assent, to the ways & means proposed for effecting, what all are ardently desirous of. In this View Our president, Though a Gentleman of great Worth, & one who fills & supports the Dignity of his Station to Universal acceptance, yet cannot urge Forward matters to an issue with that dispatch, which he might in a different Assembly. Nor considering the great importance of something more than a Majority, an Unanimity would it be safe and prudent—Unanimity being in Our View of the last importance, every one must be heard, even on those points, or Subjects which are in themselves not of the last importance And indeed it often happens that what is of little or No Consequence to one Colony, is of the last To another. We have thus hinted to Your Honor Our general Situation, which hope will Acct. For Our being delayed here beyond the Time which either the Colony or We ourselves expected.

Though Our private Concerns, & Connections, as well as the public expectation, & Interest of the Colony urge Us, to make all possible dispatch, Yet as we find it would not only be of dangerous Consequence, but perhaps impracticable, to attempt pushing Matters, to a decision Faster, than they now come to it in the Course they are, We Find it most prudent patiently to wait the issue. We shall be able to write You more particularly, in a few Days but could not omit this Opportunity of writing Thus farr, on the subject of Our delegation here.

We take Liberty to inclose the Copy of Lord Dunmore's proclamation on which shall only say it appears in some parts of it very extraordinary, and would occasion much greater Speculations here than it does were it not that few or None save the Proprietors consider themselves interested in the Controversy, & the whole Attention of the public is taken up on more important Subjects. Laurel Hill is about Forty Miles on this Side *Fort Duquesne* alias Fort Pitt and is a range of Mountains running Northerly nearly in a Line with the West Boundary of the province of Maryland, and Cuts off from that province, one whole County, lately erected by the Name of Westmoreland. His Lordship is now in those parts near the Ohio with an Army of Fifteen Hundred Virginians, reducing the Indian Tribes to Subjection or driving them off the Land. We cannot be positive as To The Time of Our Return, but hope to be at New Haven before the rising of the Assembly, and may probably be able to write with greater certainty in Our Next. We are with the greatest respect Your Honors most Obedt. & most Humle. Servts.

> Elipht Dyer
> Roger Sherman
> Silas Deane

[*P.S.*] Since Writing the above We see the Resolutions of the Congress respecting Suffolk County &c are printed in the Connct. papers therefore judge it Unnecessary to inclose them.

Declaration and Resolves of the First Continental Congress, October 14, 1774

Representatives from every colony except Georgia met in Philadelphia from September 5 to October 26, 1774, to discuss possible responses to the Intolerable Acts. Among the most important products of this meeting is the following Declaration and Resolves, sometimes called a Declaration of Rights.[1]

The Congress met according to adjournment, & resuming the consideration of the subject under debate—came into the following Resolutions:[2]

Whereas, since the close of the last war, the British parliament, claiming a power of right to bind the people of America, by statute in all cases whatsoever, hath in some acts expressly imposed taxes on them, and in others, under various pretences, but in fact for the purpose of raising a revenue, hath imposed rates and duties payable in these colonies, established a board of commissioners, with unconstitutional powers, and extended the jurisdiction of courts of Admiralty, not only for collecting the said duties, but for the trial of causes merely arising within the body of a county.

And whereas, in consequence of other statutes, judges, who before held only estates at will in their offices, have been made dependant on the Crown alone for their salaries, and standing armies kept in times of peace:

And it has lately been resolved in Parliament, that by force of a statute, made in the thirty-fifth year of the reign of king Henry the eighth, colonists may be transported to England, and tried there upon accusations for treasons,

Source: *JCC,* 1: 63–73.

1. All footnotes in documents taken from the *Journals of the Continental Congress* are by the original editors.

2. The first draft of the sub-committee's report on violations of rights was prepared by John Sullivan. Among the Adams' Papers is a paper in a script "somewhat resembling that of Major Sullivan," which is believed to be the report as first submitted. It is printed in Adams' *Works,* II, 535.

The fourth article as adopted (p. 68) was prepared by John Adams, and caused much debate in committee and in Congress. Galloway, and his followers, thought it aimed at independence, and sought to have it amended. It was left unaltered in its essentials, and the final form of the report was the work of John Adams. See his letter to Edward Biddle, 12 December, 1774.

and misprisions, or concealments of treasons committed in the colonies; and by a late statute, such trials have been directed in cases therein mentioned.

And whereas, in the last session of parliament, three statutes were made; one, intituled "An act to discontinue, in such manner and for such time as are therein mentioned, the landing and discharging, lading, or shipping of goods, wares & merchandise, at the town, and within the harbour of Boston, in the province of Massachusetts-bay, in North-America;" another, intituled "An act for the better regulating the government of the province of the Massachusetts-bay in New-England;" and another, intituled "An act for the impartial administration of justice, in the cases of persons questioned for any act done by them in the execution of the law, or for the suppression of riots and tumults, in the province of the Massachusetts-bay, in New-England." And another statute was then made, "for making more effectual provision for the government of the province of Quebec, &c." All which statutes are impolitic, unjust, and cruel, as well as unconstitutional, and most dangerous and destructive of American rights.

And whereas, Assemblies have been frequently dissolved, contrary to the rights of the people, when they attempted to deliberate on grievances; and their dutiful, humble, loyal, & reasonable petitions to the crown for redress, have been repeatedly treated with contempt, by his majesty's ministers of state:

The good people of the several Colonies of New-hampshire, Massachusetts-bay, Rhode-island and Providence plantations, Connecticut, New-York, New-Jersey, Pennsylvania, Newcastle, Kent and Sussex on Delaware, Maryland, Virginia, North Carolina, and South Carolina, justly alarmed at these arbitrary proceedings of parliament and administration, have severally elected, constituted, and appointed deputies to meet and sit in general congress, in the city of Philadelphia, in order to obtain such establishment, as that their religion, laws, and liberties may not be subverted:

Whereupon the deputies so appointed being now assembled, in a full and free representation of these Colonies, taking into their most serious consideration, the best means of attaining the ends aforesaid, do, in the first place, as Englishmen, their ancestors in like cases have usually done, for asserting and vindicating their rights and liberties, declare,

That the inhabitants of the English Colonies in North America, by the immutable laws of nature, the principles of the English constitution, and the several charters or compacts, have the following Rights:

Resolved, N. C. D. 1. That they are entitled to life, liberty, & property, and they have never ceded to any sovereign power whatever, a right to dispose of either without their consent.

Resolved, N. C. D. 2. That our ancestors, who first settled these colonies, were at the time of their emigration from the mother country, entitled to all the rights, liberties, and immunities of free and natural-born subjects, within the realm of England.

Resolved, N. C. D. 3. That by such emigration they by no means forfeited, surrendered, or lost any of those rights, but that they were, and their descendants now are, entitled to the exercise and enjoyment of all such of them, as their local and other circumstances enable them to exercise and enjoy.

Resolved, 4. That the foundation of English liberty, and of all free government, is a right in the people to participate in their legislative council: and as the English colonists are not represented, and from their local and other circumstances, cannot properly be represented in the British parliament, they are entitled to a free and exclusive power of legislation in their several provincial legislatures, where their right of representation can alone be preserved, in all cases of taxation and internal polity, subject only to the negative of their sovereign, in such manner as has been heretofore used and accustomed. But, from the necessity of the case, and a regard to the mutual interest of both countries, we cheerfully consent to the operation of such acts of the British parliament, as are bona fide, restrained to the regulation of our external commerce, for the purpose of securing the commercial advantages of the whole empire to the mother country, and the commercial benefits of its respective members; excluding every idea of taxation, internal or external, for raising a revenue on the subjects in America, without their consent.

Resolved, N. C. D. 5. That the respective colonies are entitled to the common law of England, and more especially to the great and inestimable privilege of being tried by their peers of the vicinage, according to the course of that law.

Resolved, 6. That they are entituled to the benefit of such of the English statutes as existed at the time of their colonization; and which they have, by experience, respectively found to be applicable to their several local and other circumstances.

Resolved, N. C. D. 7. That these, his majesty's colonies, are likewise entitled to all the immunities and privileges granted & confirmed to them by royal charters, or secured by their several codes of provincial laws.

Resolved, N. C. D. 8. That they have a right peaceably to assemble, consider of their grievances, and petition the King; and that all prosecutions, prohibitory proclamations, and commitments for the same, are illegal.

Resolved, N. C. D. 9. That the keeping a Standing army in these colonies, in times of peace, without the consent of the legislature of that colony, in which such army is kept, is against law.

Resolved, N. C. D. 10. It is indispensably necessary to good government, and rendered essential by the English constitution, that the constituent branches of the legislature be independent of each other; that, therefore, the exercise of legislative power in several colonies, by a council appointed, during pleasure, by the crown, is unconstitutional, dangerous, and destructive to the freedom of American legislation.

All and each of which the aforesaid deputies, in behalf of themselves and their constituents, do claim, demand, and insist on, as their indubitable rights and liberties; which cannot be legally taken from them, altered or abridged by any power whatever, without their own consent, by their representatives in their several provincial legislatures.

In the course of our inquiry, we find many infringements and violations of the foregoing rights, which, from an ardent desire, that harmony and mutual intercourse of affection and interest may be restored, we pass over for the present, and proceed to state such acts and measures as have been adopted since the last war, which demonstrate a system formed to enslave America.

Resolved, N. C. D. That the following acts of Parliament are infringements and violations of the rights of the colonists; and that the repeal of them is essentially necessary in order to restore harmony between Great-Britain and the American colonies, viz:

The several acts of 4 Geo. 3. ch. 15, & ch. 34.—5 Geo. 3. ch. 25.—6 Geo. 3. ch. 52.—7 Geo. 3. ch. 41, & ch. 46.—8 Geo. 3. ch. 22, which impose duties for the purpose of raising a revenue in America, extend the powers of the admiralty courts beyond their ancient limits, deprive the American subject of trial by jury, authorize the judges' certificate to indemnify the prosecutor from damages, that he might otherwise be liable to, requiring oppressive security from a claimant of ships and goods seized, before he shall be allowed to defend his property, and are subversive of American rights.

Also the 12 Geo. 3. ch. 24, entitled "An act for the better securing his Majesty's dock-yards, magazines, ships, ammunition, and stores," which declares a new offence in America, and deprives the American subject of a constitutional trial by a jury of the vicinage, by authorizing the trial of any person, charged with the committing any offence described in the said act, out of the realm, to be indicted and tried for the same in any shire or county within the realm.

Also the three acts passed in the last session of parliament, for stopping the port and blocking up the harbour of Boston, for altering the charter & government of the Massachusetts-bay, and that which is entituled "An act for the better administration of Justice," &c.

Also the act passed in the same session for establishing the Roman Catholick Religion in the province of Quebec, abolishing the equitable system of English laws, and erecting a tyranny there, to the great danger, from so total a dissimilarity of Religion, law, and government of the neighbouring British colonies, by the assistance of whose blood and treasure the said country was conquered from France.

Also the act passed in the same session for the better providing suitable quarters for officers and soldiers in his Majesty's service in North-America.

Also, that the keeping a standing army in several of these colonies, in time of peace, without the consent of the legislature of that colony in which such army is kept, is against law.

To these grievous acts and measures, Americans cannot submit, but in hopes that their fellow subjects in Great-Britain will, on a revision of them, restore us to that state in which both countries found happiness and prosperity, we have for the present only resolved to pursue the following peaceable measures:
. . .

1st. To enter into a non-importation, non-consumption, and non-exportation agreement or association.

2. To prepare an address to the people of Great-Britain, and a memorial to the inhabitants of British America, &

3. To prepare a loyal address to his Majesty; agreeable to Resolutions already entered into.

Articles of Association, October 20, 1774

This agreement was intended to pressure the British government into repealing the Intolerable Acts by having the colonists boycott British goods.

The Congress met.

The association being copied, was read and signed at the table, and is as follows:—

Here insert the Association.

We, his majesty's most loyal subjects, the delegates of the several colonies of New-Hampshire, Massachusetts-Bay, Rhode-Island, Connecticut, New-York, New-Jersey, Pennsylvania, the three lower counties of New-Castle, Kent and Sussex, on Delaware, Maryland, Virginia, North-Carolina, and South-Carolina, deputed to represent them in a continental Congress, held in the city of Philadelphia, on the 5th day of September, 1774, avowing our allegiance to his majesty, our affection and regard for our fellow-subjects in Great-Britain and elsewhere, affected with the deepest anxiety, and most alarming apprehensions, at those grievances and distresses, with which his Majesty's American subjects are oppressed; and having taken under our most serious deliberation, the state of the whole continent, find, that the present unhappy situation of our affairs is occasioned by a ruinous system of colony administration, adopted by the British ministry about the year 1763, evidently calculated for inslaving these colonies, and, with them, the British empire. In prosecution of which system, various acts of parliament have been passed, for raising a revenue in America, for depriving the American subjects, in many instances, of the constitutional trial by jury, exposing their lives to danger, by directing a new and illegal trial beyond the seas, for crimes alleged to have been committed in America: and in prosecution of the same system, several late, cruel, and oppressive acts have been passed, respecting the town of Boston and the Massachusetts-Bay, and also an act for extending the province of Quebec, so as to border on the western frontiers of these colonies, establishing an arbitrary government therein, and discouraging the settlement of British subjects in that wide extended country; thus, by the influence of civil principles and

Source: *JCC,* 1: 75–81.

ancient prejudices, to dispose the inhabitants to act with hostility against the free Protestant colonies, whenever a wicked ministry shall chuse so to direct them.

To obtain redress of these grievances, which threaten destruction to the lives, liberty, and property of his majesty's subjects, in North America, we are of opinion, that a non-importation, non-consumption, and non-exportation agreement, faithfully adhered to, will prove the most speedy, effectual, and peaceable measure: and, therefore, we do, for ourselves, and the inhabitants of the several colonies, whom we represent, firmly agree and associate, under the sacred ties of virtue, honour and love of our country, as follows:

1. That from and after the first day of December next, we will not import, into British America, from Great-Britain or Ireland, any goods, wares, or merchandise whatsoever, or from any other place, any such goods, wares, or merchandise, as shall have been exported from Great-Britain or Ireland; nor will we, after that day, import any East-India tea from any part of the world; nor any molasses, syrups, paneles,[1] coffee, or pimento, from the British plantations or from Dominica; nor wines from Madeira, or the Western Islands; nor foreign indigo.

2. We will neither import nor purchase, any slave imported after the first day of December next;[2] after which time, we will wholly discontinue the slave trade, and will neither be concerned in it ourselves, nor will we hire our vessels, nor sell our commodities or manufactures to those who are concerned in it.

3. As a non-consumption agreement, strictly adhered to, will be an effectual security for the observation of the non-importation, we, as above, solemnly agree and associate, that, from this day, we will not purchase or use any tea, imported on account of the East-India company, or any on which a duty hath been or shall be paid; and from and after the first day of March next, we will not purchase or use any East-India tea whatever; nor will we, nor shall any person for or under us, purchase or use any of those goods, wares, or merchandise, we have agreed not to import, which we shall know, or have cause to suspect, were imported after the first day of December, except such as come under the rules and directions of the tenth article hereafter mentioned.

4. The earnest desire we have, not to injure our fellow-subjects in Great-Britain, Ireland, or the West-Indies, induces us to suspend a non-exportation, until the tenth day of September, 1775; at which time, if the said acts and parts of acts of the British parliament herein after mentioned are not repealed, we will not, directly or indirectly, export any merchandise or commodity whatsoever to Great-Britain, Ireland, or the West-Indies, except rice to Europe.[3]

5. Such as are merchants, and use the British and Irish trade, will give orders, as soon as possible, to their factors, agents and correspondents, in Great-Britain

---

1. Brown unpurified sugar.

2. In the pamphlet edition this sentence reads: "That we will neither import, nor purchase any slave imported, after the first day of December next."

3. See *Journals of Congress*, 1 August 1775, *post*.

and Ireland, not to ship any goods to them, on any pretence whatsoever, as they cannot be received in America; and if any merchant, residing in Great-Britain or Ireland, shall directly or indirectly ship any goods, wares or merchandise, for America, in order to break the said non-importation agreement, or in any manner contravene the same, on such unworthy conduct being well attested, it ought to be made public; and, on the same being so done, we will not, from thenceforth, have any commercial connexion with such merchant.

6. That such as are owners of vessels will give positive orders to their captains, or masters, not to receive on board their vessels any goods prohibited by the said non-importation agreement, on pain of immediate dismission from their service.

7. We will use our utmost endeavours to improve the breed of sheep, and increase their number to the greatest extent; and to that end, we will kill them as seldom[4] as may be, especially those of the most profitable kind; nor will we export any to the West-Indies or elsewhere; and those of us, who are or may become overstocked with, or can conveniently spare any sheep, will dispose of them to our neighbours, especially to the poorer sort, on moderate terms.

8. We will, in our several stations, encourage frugality, economy, and industry, and promote agriculture, arts and the manufactures of this country, especially that of wool; and will discountenance and discourage every species of extravagance and dissipation, especially all horse-racing, and all kinds of gaming, cock-fighting, exhibitions of shews, plays, and other expensive diversions and entertainments; and on the death of any relation or friend, none of us, or any of our families, will go into any further mourning-dress, than a black crape or ribbon on the arm or hat, for gentlemen, and a black ribbon and necklace for ladies, and we will discontinue the giving of gloves and scarves at funerals.

9. Such as are venders of goods or merchandise will not take advantage of the scarcity of goods, that may be occasioned by this association, but will sell the same at the rates we have been respectively accustomed to do, for twelve months last past.—And if any vender of goods or merchandise shall sell any such goods on higher terms, or shall, in any manner, or by any device whatsoever violate or depart from this agreement, no person ought, nor will any of us deal with any such person, or his or her factor or agent, at any time thereafter, for any commodity whatever.

10. In case any merchant, trader, or other person,[5] shall import any goods or merchandise, after the first day of December, and before the first day of February next, the same ought forthwith, at the election of the owner, to be either re-shipped or delivered up to the committee of the county or town, wherein they shall be imported, to be stored at the risque of the importer, until the non-importation agreement shall cease, or be sold under the direction of the committee aforesaid; and in the last-mentioned case, the owner or owners of such goods shall be reimbursed out of the sales, the first cost and charges, the profit, if any, to be

4. The pamphlet says *sparingly*.
5. Persons is used in the pamphlet.

applied towards relieving and employing such poor inhabitants of the town of Boston, as are immediate sufferers by the Boston port-bill; and a particular account of all goods so returned, stored, or sold, to be inserted in the public papers; and if any goods or merchandises shall be imported after the said first day of February, the same ought forthwith to be sent back again, without breaking any of the packages thereof.

11. That a committee be chosen in every county, city, and town, by those who are qualified to vote for representatives in the legislature, whose business it shall be attentively to observe the conduct of all persons touching this association; and when it shall be made to appear, to the satisfaction of a majority of any such committee, that any person within the limits of their appointment has violated this association, that such majority do forthwith cause the truth of the case to be published in the gazette; to the end, that all such foes to the rights of British-America may be publicly known, and universally contemned as the enemies of American liberty; and thenceforth we respectively will break off all dealings with him or her.

12. That the committee of correspondence, in the respective colonies, do frequently inspect the entries of their custom-houses, and inform each other, from time to time, of the true state thereof, and of every other material circumstance that may occur relative to this association.

13. That all manufactures of this country be sold at reasonable prices, so that no undue advantage be taken of a future scarcity of goods.

14. And we do further agree and resolve, that we will have no trade, commerce, dealings or intercourse whatsoever, with any colony or province, in North-America, which shall not accede to, or which shall hereafter violate this association, but will hold them as unworthy of the rights of freemen, and as inimical to the liberties of their country.

And we do solemnly bind ourselves and our constituents, under the ties aforesaid, to adhere to this association, until such parts of the several acts of parliament passed since the close of the last war, as impose or continue duties on tea, wine, molasses, syrups, paneles, coffee, sugar, pimento, indigo, foreign paper, glass, and painters' colours, imported into America, and extend the powers of the admiralty courts beyond their ancient limits, deprive the American subject of trial by jury, authorize the judge's certificate to indemnify the prosecutor from damages, that he might otherwise be liable to from a trial by his peers, require oppressive security from a claimant of ships or goods seized, before he shall be allowed to defend his property, are repealed.—And until that part of the act of the 12 G. 3. ch. 24, entitled "An act for the better securing his majesty's dock-yards, magazines, ships, ammunition, and stores," by which any persons charged with committing any of the offences therein described, in America, may be tried in any shire or county within the realm, is repealed—and until the four acts, passed the last session of parliament, viz. that for stopping the port and blocking up the harbour of Boston—that for altering the charter and government of the Massachusetts-Bay—and that which is entitled "An act for the better administration of justice, &c."—

and that "for extending the limits of Quebec, &c." are repealed. And we recommend it to the provincial conventions, and to the committees in the respective colonies, to establish such farther regulations as they may think proper, for carrying into execution this association.

The foregoing association being determined upon by the Congress, was ordered to be subscribed by the several members thereof; and thereupon, we have hereunto set our respective names accordingly.

IN CONGRESS, PHILADELPHIA, *October 20, 1774.*

Signed,   PEYTON RANDOLPH, *President.*

New Hampshire	Jnᵒ Sullivan Nathᵉˡ Folsom
Massachusetts-Bay	Thomas Cushing Samˡ Adams John Adams Robᵗ Treat Paine
Rhode Island	Step. Hopkins Sam: Ward
Connecticut	Elipht Dyer Roger Sherman Silas Deane
New York	Isaac Low John Alsop John Jay Jaˢ Duane Phil. Livingston Wᵐ Floyd Henry Wisner S: Boerum
New Jersey	J. Kinsey Wil: Livingston Stepⁿ Crane Richᵈ Smith John De Hart
Pennsylvania	Jos. Galloway John Dickinson Cha Humphreys Thomas Mifflin E. Biddle John Morton Geo: Ross

The Lower Counties New Castle	Caesar Rodney Tho. M: Kean Geo: Read
Maryland	Mat Tilghman Thˢ Johnson Junʳ Wᵐ Paca Samuel Chase
Virginia	Richard Henry Lee Gᵒ Washington P. Henry Jʳ Richard Bland Benjᵃ Harrison Edmᵈ Pendleton
North Carolina	Will Hooper Joseph Hewes Rᵈ Caswell
South Carolina	Henry Middleton Tho Lynch Christ Gadsden J Rutledge Edward Rutledge

Ordered, that this association be committed to the press, and that one hundred & twenty copies be struck off.

The Congress then resumed the consideration of the Address to the Inhabitants of these colonies, & after debate thereon, adjourned till to-morrow.

Address to the People of Great Britain, October 21, 1774

Drafted by future chief justice of the U.S. Supreme Court John Jay (1745–1829), this appeal to the people of Great Britain was approved by the Continental Congress on October 21, 1774.

The address to the people of Great-Britain being brought in, and the amendments directed being made, the same was approved, and is as follows:
Here insert the address to the people of Great-Britain.

To the people of Great-Britain, from the delegates appointed by the several English colonies of New-Hampshire, Massachusetts-Bay, Rhode-Island and Providence Plantations, Connecticut, New-York, New-Jersey, Pennsylvania, the lower counties on Delaware, Maryland, Virginia, North-Carolina, and South-Carolina, to consider of their grievances in general Congress, at Philadelphia, September 5th, 1774.

FRIENDS AND FELLOW SUBJECTS,

When a Nation, led to greatness by the hand of Liberty, and possessed of all the glory that heroism, munificence, and humanity can bestow, descends to the ungrateful task of forging chains for her Friends and Children, and instead of giving support to Freedom, turns advocate for Slavery and Oppression, there is reason to suspect she has either ceased to be virtuous, or been extremely negligent in the appointment of her rulers.

In almost every age, in repeated conflicts, in long and bloody wars, as well civil as foreign, against many and powerful nations, against the open assaults of enemies, and the more dangerous treachery of friends, have the inhabitants of your island, your great and glorious ancestors, maintained their independence and transmitted the rights of men, and the blessings of liberty to you their posterity.

Be not surprized therefore, that we, who are descended from the same common ancestors; that we, whose forefathers participated in all the rights, the liberties, and the constitution, you so justly boast [of], and who have carefully conveyed the same fair inheritance to us, guarantied by the plighted faith of government and the most solemn compacts with British Sovereigns, should refuse to surrender

Source: *JCC,* 1: 81–90.

them to men, who found their claims on no principles of reason, and who prosecute them with a design, that by having our lives and property in their power, they may with the greater facility enslave you.

The cause of America is now the object of universal attention: it has at length become very serious. This unhappy country has not only been oppressed, but abused and misrepresented; and the duty we owe to ourselves and posterity, to your interest, and the general welfare of the British empire, leads us to address you on this very important subject.

Know then, That we consider ourselves, and do insist, that we are and ought to be, as free as our fellow-subjects in Britain, and that no power on earth has a right to take our property from us without our consent.

That we claim all the benefits secured to the subject by the English constitution, and particularly that inestimable one of trial by jury.

That we hold it essential to English Liberty, that no man be condemned unheard, or punished for supposed offences, without having an opportunity of making his defence.

That we think the Legislature of Great-Britain is not authorized by the constitution[1] to establish a religion, fraught with sanguinary and impious tenets, or, to erect an arbitrary form of government, in any quarter of the globe. These rights, we, as well as you, deem sacred. And yet sacred as they are, they have, with many others, been repeatedly and flagrantly violated.

Are not the Proprietors of the soil of Great-Britain Lords of their own property? can it be taken from them without their consent? will they yield it to the arbitrary disposal of any man, or number of men whatever?—You know they will not.

Why then are the Proprietors of the soil of America less Lords of their property than you are of yours, or why should they submit it to the disposal of your Parliament, or any other Parliament, or Council in the world, not of their election? Can the intervention of the sea that divides us, cause disparity in rights, or can any reason be given, why English subjects, who live three thousand miles from the royal palace, should enjoy less liberty than those who are three hundred miles distant from it?

Reason looks with indignation on such distinctions, and freemen can never perceive their propriety. And yet, however chimerical and unjust such discriminations are, the Parliament assert, that they have a right to bind us in all cases without exception, whether we consent or not; that they may take and use our property when and in what manner they please; that we are pensioners on their bounty for all that we possess, and can hold it no longer than they vouchsafe to permit. Such declarations we consider as heresies in English politics, and which can no more operate to deprive us of our property, than the interdicts of the Pope can divest Kings of sceptres which the laws of the land and the voice of the people have placed in their hands.

---

1. In the 1774 edition of the Journal, this word is printed *condition.*

At the conclusion of the late war—a war rendered glorious by the abilities and integrity of a Minister, to whose efforts the British empire owes its safety and its fame: At the conclusion of this war, which was succeeded by an inglorious peace, formed under the auspices of a Minister of principles, and of a family unfriendly to the protestant cause, and inimical to liberty.—We say at this period, and under the influence of that man, a plan for enslaving your fellow subjects in America was concerted, and has ever since been pertinaciously carrying into execution.

Prior to this aera you were content with drawing from us the wealth produced by our commerce. You restrained our trade in every way that could conduce to your emolument. You exercised unbounded sovereignty over the sea. You named the ports and nations to which alone our merchandise should be carried, and with whom alone we should trade; and though some of these restrictions were grievous, we nevertheless did not complain; we looked up to you as to our parent state, to which we were bound by the strongest ties: And were happy in being instrumental to your prosperity and your grandeur.

We call upon you yourselves, to witness our loyalty and attachment to the common interest of the whole empire: Did we not, in the last war, add all the strength of this vast continent to the force which repelled our common enemy? Did we not leave our native shores, and meet disease and death, to promote the success of British-arms in foreign climates? Did you not thank us for our zeal, and even reimburse us large sums of money, which, you confessed, we had advanced beyond our proportion and far beyond our abilities? You did.

To what causes, then, are we to attribute the sudden change of treatment, and that system of slavery which was prepared for us at the restoration of peace?

Before we had recovered from the distresses which ever attend war, an attempt was made to drain this country of all its money, by the oppressive Stamp-Act. Paint, Glass, and other commodities, which you would not permit us to purchase of other nations, were taxed; nay, although no wine is made in any country, subject to the British state, you prohibited our procuring it of foreigners, without paying a tax, imposed by your parliament, on all we imported. These and many other impositions were laid upon us most unjustly and unconstitutionally, for the express purpose of raising a Revenue.—In order to silence complaint, it was, indeed, provided, that this revenue should be expended in America for its protection and defence.—These exactions, however, can receive no justification from a pretended necessity of protecting and defending us. They are lavishly squandered on court favourites and ministerial dependents, generally avowed enemies to America and employing themselves, by partial representations, to traduce and embroil the Colonies. For the necessary support of government here, we ever were and ever shall be ready to provide. And whenever the exigencies of the state may require it, we shall, as we have heretofore done, chearfully contribute our full proportion of men and money. To enforce this unconstitutional and unjust scheme of taxation, every fence that the wisdom of our British ancestors had carefully erected against arbitrary power, has been violently thrown down in America, and the inestimable right of trial by jury taken away in cases that touch both life and property.—It was ordained, that whenever offences should be committed in the colonies against particular Acts imposing various duties and restrictions upon trade, the prosecutor might bring his action for the penalties in the Courts of Admiralty; by which means the subject lost the advantage of being tried by an honest uninfluenced jury of the vicinage, and was subjected to the sad necessity of being judged by a single man, a creature of the Crown, and according to the course of a law which exempts the prosecutor from the trouble of proving his accusation, and obliges the defendant either to evince his innocence or to suffer. To give this new judicatory[2] the greater importance, and as, if with design to protect false accusers, it is further provided, that the Judge's certificate of there having been probable causes of seizure and prosecution, shall protect the prosecutor from actions at common law for recovery of damages.

By the course of our law, offences committed in such of the British dominions in which courts are established and justice duely and regularly administred, shall be there tried by a jury of the vicinage. There the offenders and the witnesses are known, and the degree of credibility to be given to their testimony, can be ascertained.

In all these Colonies, justice is regularly and impartially administered, and yet by the construction of some, and the direction of other Acts of Parliament, offenders are to be taken by force, together with all such persons as may be pointed out as witnesses, and carried to England, there to be tried in a distant land, by a *jury* of strangers, and subject to all the disadvantages that result from want of friends, want of witnesses, and want of money.

When the design of raising a revenue from the duties imposed on the importation of tea into America had in great measure been rendered abortive by our ceasing to import that commodity, a scheme was concerted by the Ministry with the East-India Company, and an Act passed enabling and encouraging them to transport and vend it in the colonies. Aware of the danger of giving success to this insidious manoeuvre, and of permitting a precedent of taxation thus to be established among us, various methods were adopted to elude the stroke. The people of Boston, then ruled by a Governor, whom, as well as his predecessor Sir Francis Bernard, all America considers as her enemy, were exceedingly embarrassed. The ships which had arrived with the tea were by his management prevented from returning.—The duties would have been paid; the cargoes landed and exposed to sale; a Governor's influence would have procured and protected many purchasers. While the town was suspended by deliberations on this important subject, the tea was destroyed. Even supposing a trespass was thereby committed, and the Proprietors of the tea entitled to damages.—The Courts of Law were open, and Judges appointed by the Crown presided in them.—The East India Company however did not think proper to commence any suits, nor did they even demand satisfaction, either from individuals or from the community in

2. In the original pamphlet this word is printed *indicatory.*

general. The Ministry, it seems, officiously made the case their own, and the great Council of the nation descended to intermeddle with a dispute about private property.—Divers papers, letters, and other unauthenticated ex parte evidence were laid before them; neither the persons who destroyed the Tea, or the people of Boston, were called upon to answer the complaint. The Ministry, incensed by being disappointed in a favourite scheme, were determined to recur from the little arts of finesse, to open force and unmanly violence. The port of Boston was blocked up by a fleet, and an army placed in the town. Their trade was to be suspended, and thousands reduced to the necessity of gaining subsistance from charity, till they should submit to pass under the yoke, and consent to become slaves, by confessing the omnipotence of Parliament, and acquiescing in whatever disposition they might think proper to make of their lives and property.

Let justice and humanity cease to be the boast of your nation! consult your history, examine your records of former transactions, nay turn to the annals of the many arbitrary states and kingdoms that surround you, and shew us a single instance of men being condemned to suffer for imputed crimes, unheard, unquestioned, and without even the specious formality of a trial; and that too by laws made expres[s]ly for the purpose, and which had no existence at the time of the fact committed. If it be difficult to reconcile these proceedings to the genius and temper of your laws and constitution, the task will become more arduous when we call upon our ministerial enemies to justify, not only condemning men untried and by hearsay, but involving the innocent in one common punishment with the guilty, and for the act of thirty or forty, to bring poverty, distress and calamity on thirty thousand souls, and those not your enemies, but your friends, brethren, and fellow subjects.

It would be some consolation to us, if the catalogue of American oppressions ended here. It gives us pain to be reduced to the necessity of reminding you, that under the confidence reposed in the faith of government, pledged in a royal charter from a British Sovereign, the fore-fathers of the present inhabitants of the Massachusetts-Bay left their former habitations, and established that great, flourishing, and loyal Colony. Without incurring or being charged with a forfeiture of their rights, without being heard, without being tried, without law, and without justice, by an Act of Parliament, their charter is destroyed, their liberties violated, their constitution and form of government changed: And all this upon no better pretence, than because in one of their towns a trespass was committed on some merchandize, said to belong to one of the Companies, and because the Ministry were of opinion, that such high political regulations were necessary to compel due subordination and obedience to their mandates.

Nor are these the only capital grievances under which we labor. We might tell of dissolute, weak and wicked Governors having been set over us; of Legislatures being suspended for asserting the rights of British subjects—of needy and ignorant dependents on great men, advanced to the seats of justice and to other places of trust and importance;—of hard restrictions on commerce, and a great variety of lesser evils, the recollection of which is almost lost under the weight and pressure of greater and more poignant calamities.

Now mark the progression of the ministerial plan for inslaving us.

Well aware that such hardy attempts to take our property from us; to deprive us of that valuable right of trial by jury; to seize our persons, and carry us for trial to Great-Britain; to blockade our ports; to destroy our Charters, and change our forms of government, would occasion, and had already occasioned, great discontent in all the Colonies, which might produce opposition to these measures: An Act was passed to protect, indemnify, and screen from punishment such as might be guilty even of murder, in endeavouring to carry their oppressive edicts into execution; And by another Act the dominion of Canada is to be so extended, modelled, and governed, as that by being disunited from us, detached from our interests, by civil as well as religious prejudices, that by their numbers daily swelling with Catholic emigrants from Europe, and by their devotion to Administration, so friendly to their religion, they might become formidable to us, and on occasion, be fit instruments in the hands of power, to reduce the ancient free Protestant Colonies to the same state of slavery with themselves.

This was evidently the object of the Act:—And in this view, being extremely dangerous to our liberty and quiet, we cannot forebear complaining of it, as hostile to British America.—Superadded to these considerations, we cannot help deploring the unhappy condition to which it has reduced the many English settlers, who, encouraged by the Royal Proclamation, promising the enjoyment of all their rights, have purchased estates in that country.—They are now the subjects of an arbitrary government, deprived of trial by jury, and when imprisoned cannot claim the benefit of the habeas corpus Act, that great bulwark and palladium of English liberty:—Nor can we suppress our astonishment, that a British Parliament should ever consent to establish in that country a religion that has deluged your island in blood, and dispersed impiety, bigotry, persecution, murder and rebellion through every part of the world.

This being a true state of facts, let us beseech you to consider to what end they lead.

Admit that the Ministry, by the powers of Britain, and the aid of our Roman Catholic neighbours, should be able to carry the point of taxation, and reduce us to a state of perfect humiliation and slavery. Such an enterprize would doubtless make some addition to your national debt, which already presses down your liberties, and fills you with Pensioners and Placemen.—We presume, also, that your commerce will somewhat be diminished. However, suppose you should prove victorious—in what condition will you then be? What advantages or what laurels will you reap from such a conquest?

May not a Ministry with the same armies inslave you—It may be said, you will cease to pay them—but remember the taxes from America, the wealth, and we may add, the men, and particularly the Roman Catholics of this vast continent will then be in the power of your enemies—nor will you have any reason to expect, that after making slaves of us, many among us should refuse to assist in reducing you to the same abject state.

Do not treat this as chimerical—Know that in less than half a century, the quit-rents reserved to the Crown, from the numberless grants of this vast continent, will pour large streams of wealth into the royal coffers, and if to this be added the power of taxing America at pleasure, the Crown will be rendered independent on [of] you for supplies, and will possess more treasure than may be necessary to purchase the *remains of* Liberty in your Island.—In a word, take care that you do not fall into the pit that is preparing for us.

We believe there is yet much virtue, much justice, and much public spirit in the English nation—To that justice we now appeal. You have been told that we are seditious, impatient of government and desirous of independency. Be assured that these are not facts, but calumnies.—Permit us to be as free as yourselves, and we shall ever esteem a union with you to be our greatest glory and our greatest happiness, we shall ever be ready to contribute all in our power to the welfare of the Empire—we shall consider your enemies as our enemies, and your interest as our own.

But if you are determined that your Ministers shall wantonly sport with the rights of Mankind—If neither the voice of justice, the dictates of the law, the principles of the constitution, or the suggestions of humanity can restrain your hands from shedding human blood in such an impious cause, we must then tell you, that we will never submit to be hewers of wood or drawers of water for any ministry or nation in the world.

Place us in the same situation that we were at the close of the last war, and our former harmony will be restored.

But lest the same supineness and the same inattention to our common interest, which you have for several years shewn, should continue, we think it prudent to anticipate the consequences.

By the destruction of the trade of Boston, the Ministry have endeavoured to induce submission to their measures.—The like fate may befal us all, we will endeavour therefore to live without trade, and recur for subsistence to the fertility and bounty of our native soil, which will afford us all the necessaries and some of the conveniences of life.—We have suspended our importation from Great Britain and Ireland; and in less than a year's time, unless our grievances should be redressed, shall discontinue our exports to those kingdoms and the West-Indies.

It is with the utmost regret however, that we find ourselves compelled by the overruling principles of self-preservation, to adopt measures detrimental in their consequences to numbers of our fellow subjects in Great Britain and Ireland. But we hope, that the magnanimity and justice of the British Nation will furnish a Parliament of such wisdom, independance and public spirit, as may save the violated rights of the whole empire from the devices of wicked Ministers and evil Counsellors whether in or out of office, and thereby restore that harmony, friendship and fraternal affection between all the Inhabitants of his Majesty's kingdoms and territories, so ardently wished for by every true and honest American.

Petition of Congress to the King, October 25, 1774

John Dickinson (1732–1808), known as the "Penman of the Revolution," drafted this petition, which was approved by the Continental Congress and signed by its members, including Sherman.

To the Kings most excellent majesty

Most gracious Sovereign

We your majestys faithful subjects of the colonies of Newhampshire, Massachusetts-bay, Rhode-island and Providence Plantations, Connecticut, New-York, New-Jersey, Pennsylvania, the counties of New-Castle Kent and Sussex on Delaware, Maryland, Virginia, North-Carolina, and South Carolina, in behalf of ourselves and the inhabitants of these colonies who have deputed us to represent them in General Congress, by this our humble petition, beg leave to lay our grievances before the throne.

A standing army has been kept in these colonies, ever since the conclusion of the late war, without the consent of our assemblies; and this army with a considerable naval armament has been employed to enforce the collection of taxes.

The Authority of the commander in chief, and, under him, of the brigadiers general has in time of peace, been rendered supreme in all the civil governments in America.

The commander in chief of all your majesty's forces in North-America has, in time of peace, been appointed governor of a colony.

The charges of usual offices have been greatly increased; and, new, expensive and oppressive offices have been multiplied.

The judges of admiralty and vice-admiralty courts are empowered to receive their salaries and fees from the effects condemned by themselves. The officers of the customs are empowered to break open and enter houses without the authority of any civil magistrate founded on legal information.

Source: *JCC,* 1: 115–22.

The judges of courts of common law have been made entirely dependant on one part of the legislature for their salaries, as well as for the duration of their commissions.

Councellors holding their commissions, during pleasure, exercise legislative authority.

Humble and reasonable petitions from the representatives of the people have been fruitless.

The agents of the people have been discountenanced and governors have been instructed to prevent the payment of their salaries.

Assemblies have been repeatedly and injuriously dissolved.

Commerce has been burthened with many useless and oppressive restrictions.

By several acts of parliament made in the fourth, fifth, sixth, seventh, and eighth years of your majestys reign, duties are imposed on us, for the purpose of raising a revenue, and the powers of admiralty and vice-admiralty courts are extended beyond their ancient limits, whereby our property is taken from us without our consent, the trial by jury in many civil cases is abolished, enormous forfeitures are incurred for slight offences, vexatious informers are exempted from paying damages, to which they are justly liable, and oppressive security is required from owners before they are allowed to defend their right.

Both houses of parliament have resolved that colonists may be tried in England, for offences alledged to have been committed in America, by virtue of a statute passed in the thirty fifth year of Henry the eighth; and in consequence thereof, attempts have been made to enforce that statute. A statute was passed in the twelfth year of your majesty's reign, directing, that persons charged with committing any offence therein described, in any place out of the realm, may be indicted and tried for the same, in any shire or county within the realm, whereby inhabitants of these colonies may, in sundry cases by that statute made capital, be deprived of a trial by their peers of the vicinage.

In the last sessions of parliament, an act was passed for blocking up the harbour of Boston; another, empowering the governor of the Massachusetts-bay to send persons indicted for murder in that province to another colony or even to Great Britain for trial whereby such offenders may escape legal punishment; a third, for altering the chartered constitution of government in that province; and a fourth for extending the limits of Quebec, abolishing the English and restoring the French laws, whereby great numbers of British freemen are subjected to the latter and establishing an absolute government and the Roman Catholick religion throughout those vast regions, that border on the westerly and northerly boundaries of the free protestant English settlements; and a fifth for the better providing suitable quarters for officers and soldiers in his majesty's service in North-America.

To a sovereign, who "glories in the name of Briton" the bare recital of these acts must we presume, justify the loyal subjects, who fly to the foot of his throne and implore his clemency for protection against them.

From this destructive system of colony administration adopted since the conclusion of the last war, have flowed those distresses, dangers, fears and jealousies, that overwhelm your majesty's dutiful colonists with affliction; and we defy our most subtle and inveterate enemies, to trace the unhappy differences between Great-Britain and these colonies, from an earlier period or from other causes than we have assigned. Had they proceeded on our part from a restless levity of temper, unjust impulses of ambition, or artful suggestions of seditious persons, we should merit the opprobrious terms frequently bestowed upon us, by those we revere. But so far from promoting innovations, we have only opposed them; and can be charged with no offence, unless it be one, to receive injuries and be sensible of them.

Had our creator been pleased to give us existence in a land of slavery, the sense of our condition might have been mitigated by ignorance and habit. But thanks be to his adoreable goodness, we were born the heirs of freedom, and ever enjoyed our right under the auspices of your royal ancestors, whose family was seated on the British throne, to rescue and secure a pious and gallant nation from the popery and despotism of a superstitious and inexorable tyrant. Your majesty, we are confident, justly rejoices, that your title to the crown is thus founded on the title of your people to liberty; and therefore we doubt not, but your royal wisdom must approve the sensibility, that teaches your subjects anxiously to guard the blessings, they received from divine providence, and thereby to prove the performance of that compact, which elevated the illustrious house of Brunswick to the imperial dignity it now possesses.

The apprehension of being degraded into a state of servitude from the preeminent rank of English freemen, while our minds retain the strongest love of liberty, and clearly foresee the miseries preparing for us and our posterity, excites emotions in our breasts, which though we cannot describe, we should not wish to conceal. Feeling as men, and thinking as subjects, in the manner we do, silence would be disloyalty. By giving this faithful information, we do all in our power, to promote the great objects of your royal cares, the tranquility of your government, and the welfare of your people.

Duty to your majesty and regard for the preservation of ourselves and our posterity, the primary obligations of nature and society command us to entreat your royal attention; and as your majesty enjoys the signal distinction of reigning over freemen, we apprehend the language of freemen can not be displeasing. Your royal indignation, we hope, will rather fall on those designing and dangerous men, who daringly interposing themselves between your royal person and your faithful subjects, and for several years past incessantly employed to dissolve the bonds of society, by abusing your majesty's authority, misrepresenting your American subjects and prosecuting the most desperate and irritating projects of oppression, have at length compelled us, by the force of accumulated injuries too severe to be any longer tolerable, to disturb your majesty's repose by our complaints.

These sentiments are extorted from hearts, that much more willingly would bleed in your majesty's service. Yet so greatly have we been misrepresented, that a necessity has been alledged of taking our property from us without our consent "to defray the charge of the administration of justice, the support of civil government, and the defence protection and security of the colonies." But we beg leave to assure your majesty, that such provision has been and will be made for defraying the two first articles, as has been and shall be judged, by the legislatures of the several colonies, just and suitable to their respective circumstances: And for the defence protection and security of the colonies, their militias, if properly regulated, as they earnestly desire may immediately be done, would be fully sufficient, at least in times of peace; and in case of war, your faithful colonists will be ready and willing, as they ever have been when constitutionally required, to demonstrate their loyalty to your majesty, by exerting their most strenuous efforts in granting supplies and raising forces. Yielding to no British subjects, in affectionate attachment to your majesty's person, family and government, we too dearly prize the privilege of expressing that attachment by those proofs, that are honourable to the prince who receives them, and to the people who give them, ever to resign it to any body of men upon earth.

Had we been permitted to enjoy in quiet the inheritance left us by our forefathers, we should at this time have been peaceably, cheerfully and usefully employed in recommending ourselves by every testimony of devotion to your majesty, and of veneration to the state, from which we derive our origin. But though now exposed to unexpected and unnatural scenes of distress by a contention with that nation, in whose parental guidance on all important affairs we have hitherto with filial reverence constantly trusted, and therefore can derive no instruction in our present unhappy and perplexing circumstances from any former experience, yet we doubt not, the purity of our intention and the integrity of our conduct will justify us at that grand tribunal, before which all mankind must submit to judgment.

We ask but for peace, liberty, and safety. We wish not a diminution of the prerogative, nor do we solicit the grant of any new right in our favour. Your royal authority over us and our connexion with Great-Britain, we shall always carefully and zealously endeavour to support and maintain.

Filled with sentiments of duty to your majesty, and of affection to our parent state, deeply impressed by our education and strongly confirmed by our reason, and anxious to evince the sincerity of these dispositions, we present this petition only to obtain redress of grievances and relief from fears and jealousies occasioned by the system of statutes and regulations adopted since the close of the late war, for raising a revenue in America—extending the powers of courts of admiralty and vice-admiralty—trying persons in Great Britain for offences alledged to be committed in America—affecting the province of Massachusetts-bay, and altering the government and extending the limits of Quebec; by the abolition of which system, the harmony between Great-Britain and these colonies so necessary to the happiness of both and so ardently desired by the latter, and the usual intercourses will be immediately restored. In the magnanimity and justice of your majesty and parliament we confide, for a redress of our other grievances, trusting, that when the causes of our apprehensions are removed, our future conduct will prove us not unworthy of the regard, we have been accustomed, in our happier days, to enjoy. For appealing to that being who searches thoroughly the hearts of his creatures, we solemnly profess, that our councils have been influenced by no other motive, than a dread of impending destruction.

Permit us then, most gracious sovereign, in the name of all your faithful people in America, with the utmost humility to implore you, for the honour of Almighty God, whose pure religion our enemies are undermining; for your glory, which can be advanced only by rendering your subjects happy and keeping them united; for the interests of your family depending on an adherence to the principles that enthroned it; for the safety and welfare of your kingdoms and dominions threatened with almost unavoidable dangers and distresses; that your majesty, as the loving father of your whole people, connected by the same bands of law, loyalty, faith and blood, though dwelling in various countries, will not suffer the transcendant relation formed by these ties to be farther violated, in uncertain expectation of effects, that, if attained, never can compensate for the calamities, through which they must be gained.

We therefore most earnestly beseech your majesty, that your royal authority and interposition may be used for our relief; and that a gracious answer may be given to this petition.

That your majesty may enjoy every felicity through a long and glorious reign over loyal and happy subjects, and that your descendants may inherit your prosperity and dominions 'til time shall be no more, is and always will be our sincere and fervent prayer.

Henry Middleton
Jn° Sullivan
Nath! Folsom
Thomas Cushing
Samuel Adams
John Adams
Rob! Treat Paine
Step Hopkins
Sam: Ward
Elipht Dyer
Roger Sherman
Silas Deane
Phil. Livingston
John Alsop
Isaac Low
Jas. Duane
John Jay
W ͫ Floyd
Henry Wisner
S: Boerum
Wil: Livingston
John De Hart
Step ͩ Crane
Rich ͩ Smith
E Biddle
J: Galloway

John Dickinson
John Morton
Thomas Mifflin
George Ross
Cha ˢ Humphreys
Caesar Rodney
Tho ˢ M: Kean
Geo: Read
Mat. Tilghman
Th ˢ Johnson Jun ͬ
W ͫ Paca
Samuel Chase
Richard Henry Lee
Patrick Henry
G ͦ Washington
Edmund Pendleton
Rich ͩ Bland
Benj ⁿ Harrison
Will Hooper
Joseph Hewes
R ͩ Caswell
Tho Lynch
Chris ͭ Gadsden
J. Rutledge
Edward Rutledge

Agents to whom the Address to King is to be sent for New Hampshire, Paul Wentworth Esq ͬ

Massachusetts bay, { William Bollan Esq ͬ, Doct ͬ Benj: Franklin Doct ͬ Arthur Lee.

Rhode Island, none
Connecticut, Thomas Life, Esq ͬ
New Jersey, Doct ͬ Benj. Franklin
Pensylvania,   ditto
New York, Edmund Burke
Delaware, Maryland } none
Virginia, N. Carolina
South Carolina, Charles Garth, Esq ͬ

Wednesday sent an Address to the King & under cover to Doct: Franklin directed to the above Agents.

27. Thursday. Sent p: M: H. Middleton 2 letters to Georgia, one directed to Glen the other to Lyman Hall & others.

Also one to East Florida & one to West Florida.

Same day sent p: M: S. Adams a Letter to Nova Scotia & one to S: Johns.

6 Nov: sent the 2^d copy of Address to his Majesty by Capt: Falconer.

The Address to the people of Quebec being translated by M: Simiteir, 2000 copies were struck off, of which 300 were sent to Boston by Capt: Wier 16th Nov:

Letter to David Wooster, June 23, 1775

PHILADELPHIA

David Wooster (1711–77), a native of Connecticut, did not receive the military appointment he thought he deserved, but he served his country anyway. He died from wounds sustained in the Battle of Ridgefield.

Dear Sir

The Congress having determined it necessary to keep up an Army for the Defence of America at the Charge of the United Colonies have Appointed the following General Officers: George Washington Esqr. Commander in Chief Majr. Generals Ward, Lee, Schuyler and Putnam; Brigadier Generals Pomroy, Montgomery, your Self—Heath, Spencer, Thomas, Majr. Sullivan, of New Hampshire, & one Green of Rhode Island. I am sensible that according to your former Rank you were intitled to the place of a Major General, and as one was to be appointed in Connecticut I heartily recommended you to the Congress. I informed them of the Arrangement made by our Assembly, which I thought would be Satisfactory to have them continue in the Same Order, but as General Putnam's fame was Spread Abroad and especially his successful enterprise at Noddles Island the account of which had Just arrived, it gave him a preference in the opinion of the Delegates in General So that his appoint[ment] was Unanimous among the Colonies. But from your known Abilities and firm attachment to the American cause we were very desirous of your continuance in the Army, and hope You will accept of the appointment made by the Congress, I think the pay of a Brigadier is about 125 Dollars per Month. I Suppose a Commission is Sent to you by General Washington. We received Intelligence yesterday of an Engagement at Charlestown but have not had the particulars.

All the Connecticut Troops are now taken into the Continental Army. I hope proper care will be taken to Secure the Colony against any Sudden Invasion, which must be at their own expense. I have nothing further that I am

Source: Paul H. Smith et al., eds., *Letters of Delegates to Congress* (Washington, D.C.: Government Printing Office, 1976), 1: 539–40.

at Liberty to acquaint you with of the doings of the Congress but what have been made public. I would not have any thing published in the Papers that I write lest Something may inadvertantly escape me which ought not to be published. I Should be Glad if you would write to me every convenient opportunity & inform me of Such Occurrences, and other matters as you may think proper and useful for me to be acquainted with. I am with great esteem Your humble Servant

Roger Sherman

P.S. The General Officers were Elected in the Congress not by Nomination but by Ballot.

Letter to Jonathan Trumbull Sr., June 28, 1775

PHILADELPHIA

A constant concern for Sherman and other political leaders was ensuring that the Continental army as well as state militias had necessary supplies.

Hond. Sir

Yesterday the Congress ordered Major Skeen (who has some time been Confined here within certain limits) to be sent to Hartford and confined to the limits of that Town on his parole of honor, not to depart nor hold correspondence with our Enemies, or Meddle in political Affairs. Also a resolve was passed to request your Honor on behalf of the Colony to Supply General Schuyler with such sums of Money, and Quantities of Ammunition as he may apply for, and can be furnished by the Colony. It is supposed that he wont have occasion for more than £20,000 in Bills of Credit of our Colony, if so much, to be repaid by the Continent. We were not able to Inform what some of Money was in our Treasury but thought it probable he might be furnished with what is necessary. I am most of all concerned about a Supply of Gun Powder our Colony have taken Such an Active part, that I should not think it strange if Some Attack should be made upon it, and it wont be safe to be destitute of Ammunition. I am affraid that our stores are two much exhausted already. Care has been taken by our Enemies to prevent our being supplyed [*by*] the Dutch or Danes, in the West Indies. It is probable General Schuyler may indertake some important enterprise which I wish to have the Colony afford him all possable Assistance.

I wish to be informed of the arrival of any Supplies of Powder in any of the New England Governments. I dont know whither your Honr has been informed who are appointed General Officers in the Continental Army. All Officers below the rank of a Brigadier are left to the appointment of the Several Colonies but their Commissions to be signed by the President of this Congress. The Congress have appointed four Major Generals viz, Artemus Ward, Charles

Source: Paul H. Smith et al., eds., *Letters of Delegates to Congress* (Washington, D.C.: Government Printing Office, 1976), 1: 555–56.

Lee, Philip Schuyler and Israel Putnam; and Eight Brigadiers viz Colo Pomroy Colo Montgomery of New York, General Wooster, Colo Heath, Colo Spencer, Colo Thomas of Massachusetts, Major Sullivan of New Hampshire, Mr Green Rhode Island. They were Elected by Ballot in the order above.

We informed who were appointed in Connecticut and in what Order, and the Rank they had before Sustained in the Army, but General Putnam had rendred himself famous by his Intrepidity and especially in the late Action at Noddle's Island so that the Election was unanimous. An Ajutant General is appointed from Virginia. I forget his Name. The Chief General is allowed 3 Aid De Camps and each Major General 2. Their pay is 33 Dollars per Month, the Persons to be appointed by the Generals respectively. I have not seen all the Letters wrote by Colo Dyer & Mr Dean to your Honour. As I lodge at some Distance from them we have but little leisure to confer togather. The Congress sits from 9 in the Morning to 4 or 5 and sometimes 6 in the Afternoon. I have not been absent when the Congress were on Business So much as ten Minutes during the Session. The controversy between Great Britain and the Colonies has been carried to greater extremity than I expected but I have now no expectation that the Ministry will relax their Measures unless they are convinced that they cannot carry them into Execution. The Salvation of the Colonies under Divine Providence depends upon their united and Vigorous application to Arms, that is the only conciliatory Plan that appears to me likely to prove Successful, or at least without which no other will have any effect. I am Your Honors Most Obedient humble Servant

Roger Sherman

Letter to Joseph Trumbull, July 6, 1775

PHILADELPHIA

Joseph Trumbull (1737–78), a son of Governor Jonathan Trumbull Sr., was the first commissary general of the Continental army.

Dear Sir

I am obliged to you for the kind notice You took of my Son in mentioning to Colo. Dyer that he was well. I have not heard from him Since the Battle at Charles town. When You write again Should be glad You would inform whether he was in that Battle and what Place he Sustains in the Army. I did not know that he was there till You mentioned it. The Congress are very diligent in making every needful provision in their power for the Support of the American Cause at the Same time do not Neglect any probable means for a reconciliation with Great Britain, tho' I have no expectation that administration will be reconciled unless the Colonies submit to their Arbitrary System, or convince them that it is not in their power to carry it into execution. The latter, I hope will soon be done. You have had a bloody Battle, but I think in every encounter through the merciful Interposition of Divine Providence the advantage has been much in our favour. The people here Seem as Spirited in the Cause as in New England. Many of the Quakers as well as others have armed themselves and are Training every Day. Majr. Mifflin of this City who was a very Useful member of this Congress has before now Joyned Your Army as Aid de Camp to General Washington, whom I would recommend to your Notice as an upright, firm, Spirited and Active Friend in the Cause of Liberty. The Congress has agreed on articles for regulating the Army not much differing from those Established by the New England Colonies except the addition of a few, and a more particular limitation of the discretionary powers given to Courts Martial. Ships are frequently arriving here from London but bring no important News. I want to know what measures the ministry will take after hearing of the Battle at Concord & Lexington; if they dont relax,

Source: Paul H. Smith et al., eds., *Letters of Delegates to Congress* (Washington, D.C.: Government Printing Office, 1976), 1: 599–600.

but order reinforcements, I hope every Colony will take Government fully into their own hands until matters are Settled. I have nothing to acquaint you with of the doings of the Congress but what you will hear of before this comes to hand. I Should be glad if you would write to me when you have leisure. We want as circumstantial an account as may be of occurrences there. When we hear of numbers wounded we want to know whether dangerously, or Slightly &c. Your accounts have been the most particular that I have seen. I Should be glad if you would mention my sons State of health when you write to me or Colo. Dyer. I wish this Congress would adjourn nearer the great Scene of action and am not without Expectations that it will. I am Sir Your Friend & humble Servant.

Roger Sherman

Letter to William Williams, July 28, 1775

PHILADELPHIA

William Williams (1731–1811), a major political leader in Connecticut, later joined Sherman in signing the Declaration of Independence. He initially opposed the Constitution in Connecticut's ratifying convention but eventually voted to ratify it.

Dear Sir

I this Day received Your favour of the 22d Instant. We Should have wrote to You oftener but had not much Intelligence of importance to communicate but what was by order of Congress Transmitted to the his Honr. the Govr. which we Supposed you would be acquainted with, besides we have had but little leisure being obliged to attend Congress from 8 or 9 in the morning to 4 or 5 in afternoon. We have lately received Six Tuns of Powder which is Sent to the army near Boston, also 5000 lb Sent to General Schuyler this Day. A Ship arrived here from Bristol Yesterday which Sailed the 4th of June & brings intelligence that the account of the Battle of Lexington Sent by the province with the affidavits had arrived in London, that it occasioned the Stocks to fall one & half per cent, that Lord North was greatly Astonished &c but there had not been time to know what effect it would have on the people.

The Congress have recommended the making Salt Petre & gun Powder and offer half a Dollar per pound for all the Salt Petre that Shall be made in any of the United Colonies within fifteen months from this Day. I am Sorry for the Uneasiness occasioned by the appointment of General officers; General Wooster is dissatisfied as well as General Spencer. I feared that would be the Case. We had just heard of the Engagement at Noddles Island before we proceeded to the appointment of General officers, which engagement being conducted by General Putnam occasioned him to be highly esteemed for his Bravery by the Congress. The officers were chosen by Ballot—but previous to giving in the votes I informed the Congress of the Choice and Arrangement made by our Gen. Assembly and that I supposed if the Same order Should be

Source: Paul H. Smith et al., eds., *Letters of Delegates to Congress* (Washington, D.C.: Government Printing Office, 1976), 1: 674–75.

preserved by the Congress it would best Satisfy the officers & the Colony. Colo. Dyer was not then in the Room but came in immediately afterward and made the same representation without knowing what I had said, but the votes turned as you have heard. There was likewise an uneasiness in the Massachusetts Bay on a like occasion which General Washington being made acquainted with before he delivered the Commissions represented it to the Congress and it was rectified, but he had delivered General Putnam his Commission before he heard of the uneasiness, so that I dont know how the difficulty can be remedied at present. I hope Generals Wooster & Spencer will consider the Grand Cause we are Engaged in of So much Importance as not to let it suffer any disadvantage on account of this disagreable circumstance which was not occasioned by any disregard in the Congress toward those Gentlemen but for want of a more mature consideration of the ill consequences that might attend Such a transposition.

The Congress has Set much longer than I at first expected it would, but I believe not longer than was needful. I hope it will adjourn the beginning of next week & have a recess of a few weeks. It is very tedious Sitting here this hot Season: I have herewith Enclosed a Declaration and an address to the people of England. The whole proceedings will be published within a few Days—which will make a considerable volume. The reason why I dont Sign more of the Letters is not because our Lodgings are very far distant but because expresses are often Sent off in haste, and Colo Dyer and Mr Dean being together have the Custody of the Papers. I sometimes Sign with them, sometimes they Sign my name, others they Sign only with their own names it not being very material and in Congress hours it is needful Some Should attend while others are writing. I have not been absent at any time while the Congress has been sitting. Mr. Jonathan Trumbull Junr. was this Day appointed Paymaster for the New York Department. The pay is 50 Dollars per month. I am Sir Your Sincere Friend & humble Servant

Roger Sherman

Instructions Penned by John Adams, George Wythe, and Roger Sherman to a Congressional Commission to Canada, March 20, 1776

On February 17, 1775, John Adams, George Wythe, and Sherman were appointed to a committee charged with penning instructions for commissioners being sent to Canada to convince colonists there (particularly French Roman Catholics) to join the fight for independence. The following instructions were adopted by Congress on March 20, 1776, and this and other messages were duly relayed to Canada.

The Congress resumed the consideration of the instructions and commission to the commissioners appointed to go to Canada, which being debated by paragraphs, were agreed to, as follows:

INSTRUCTIONS, &c.

Gentlemen,

You are, with all convenient despatch, to repair to Canada, and make known to the people of that country, the wishes and intentions of the Congress with respect to them.

Represent to them, that the arms of the United Colonies, having been carried into that province for the purpose of frustrating the designs of the British court against our common liberties, we expect not only to defeat the hostile machinations of Governor Carleton against us, but that we shall put it into the power of our Canadian brethren, to pursue such measures for securing their own freedom and happiness, as a generous love of liberty and sound policy shall dictate to them.

Inform them, that in our judgment, their interests and ours are inseparably united; That it is impossible we can be reduced to a servile submission to Great Britain without their sharing our fate: And, on the other hand, if we shall obtain, as we doubt not we shall, a full establishment of our rights, it depends wholly on their choice, whether they will participate with us in those blessings, or still remain subject to every act of tyranny, which British ministers shall please to exercise over them. Urge all such arguments as your prudence shall suggest, to enforce our opinion concerning the mutual interest of the two countries, and to convince them of the impossibility of the war being concluded to the disadvantage of these colonies, if we wisely and vigorously co-operate with each other.

Source: *JCC,* 4: 159, 215–19.

To convince them of the uprightness of our intentions towards them, you are to declare, that it is our inclination, that the people of Canada may set up such a form of government, as will be most likely, in their judgment, to produce their happiness: And you are, in the strongest terms, to assure them, that it is our earnest desire to adopt them into our union, as a sister colony, and to secure the same general system of mild and equal laws for them and for ourselves, with only such local differences as may be agreeable to each colony respectively.

Assure the people of Canada, that we have no apprehension that the French will take any part with Great Britain; but, that it is their interest, and we have reason to believe their inclination, to cultivate a friendly intercourse with these colonies.

You are from this, and such other reasons as may appear most proper, to urge the necessity the people are under of immediately taking some decisive step, to put themselves under the protection of the United Colonies. For expediting such a measure, you are to explain to them our method of collecting the sense of the people, and conducting our affairs regularly by committees of observation and inspection in the several districts, and by conventions and committees of safety in the several colonies. Recommend these modes to them. Explain to them the nature and principles of government among freemen; developing, in contrast to those, the base, cruel, and insidious designs involved in the late act of parliament, for making a more effectual provision for the government of the province of Quebec. Endeavour to stimulate them by motives of glory, as well as interest, to assume a part in a contest, by which they must be deeply affected; And to aspire to a portion of that power, by which they are ruled; and not to remain the mere spoils and prey of conquerors and lords.

You are further to declare, that we hold sacred the rights of conscience, and may promise to the whole people, solemnly in our name, the free and undisturbed exercise of their religion; and, to the clergy, the full, perfect, and peaceable possession and enjoyment of all their estates; that the government of every thing relating to their religion and clergy, shall be left entirely in the hands of the good people of that province, and such legislature as they shall constitute; Provided, however, that all other denominations of Christians be equally entitled to hold offices, and enjoy civil privileges, and the free exercise of their religion, and be totally exempt from the payment of any tythes or taxes for the support of any religion.

Inform them, that you are vested, by this Congress, with full powers to effect these purposes; and, therefore, press them to have a complete representation of the people assembled in convention, with all possible expedition, to deliberate concerning the establishment of a form of government, and a union with the United Colonies. As to the terms of the union, insist on the propriety of their being similar to those on which the other colonies unite. Should they object to this, report to this Congress those objections, and the terms on which alone they will come into our Union. Should they agree to our terms, you are to promise in the names of the United Colonies, that we will defend and protect the people of Canada against all enemies, in the same manner as we will defend and protect any of the United Colonies.

You are to establish a free press, and to give directions for the frequent publication of such pieces as may be of service to the cause of the United Colonies.

You are to settle all disputes between the Canadians and the continental troops, and to make such regulations relating thereto, as you shall judge proper.

You are to make a strict and impartial enquiry into the cause of the imprisonment of Colonel Du Fee, Lieutenant Colonel Nefeu, Major St. George Du Pres, and Major Gray, officers of the militia, and of John Frazer, Esq: late a judge of the police at Montreal, and take such orders concerning them as you shall judge most proper.

In reforming any abuses you may observe in Canada, establishing and enforcing regulations for preservation of peace and good order there, and composing differences between the troops of the United Colonies and the Canadians, all officers and soldiers are required to yield obedience to you; and, to enforce the decisions that you or any two of you may make, you are empowered to suspend any military officer from the exercise of his commission, till the pleasure of the Congress shall be known, if you, or any two of you, shall think it expedient.

You are also empowered to sit and vote as members of councils of war, in directing fortifications and defences to be made, or to be demolished, by land or water; and to draw orders upon the president for any sums of money, not exceeding one hundred thousand dollars in the whole, to defray the expence of the works.

Lastly, you are by all the means you can use, to promote the execution of the resolutions now made, or hereafter to be made, in Congress.[1]

On motion made, *Resolved,* That the following additional Instructions be given to the commissioners aforesaid:

You are empowered and directed to promote and encourage the trade of Canada with the Indian Nations, and to grant passports for carrying it on as far as it may consist with the safety of the troops, and the public good.

You are also directed and authorized to assure the inhabitants of Canada, that their commerce with foreign nations shall, in all respects, be put on an equal footing with, and encouraged and protected in the same manner, as the trade of the United Colonies.

You are also directed to use every wise and prudent measure to introduce and give credit and circulation to the continental money in Canada.

---

1. "It will readily be supposed that a great part of these instructions were opposed by our antagonists with great zeal; but they were supported on our side with equal ardor, and the acceptance of them afforded a strong proof of the real determination of a majority of Congress to go with us to the final consummation of our wishes." John Adams, "Autobiography," *Writings,* III, 36.

In case the former resolution of Congress respecting the English American troops in Canada, has not been carried into effect, you are directed to use your best endeavours to form a batallion of the New York troops in that country, and to appoint the field and other officers out of the gentlemen who have continued there during the campaign, according to their respective ranks and merit. And, if it should be found impracticable, you are to direct such of them as are provided for in the four batallions now raising in New York, to repair to their respective corps. To enable you to carry this resolution into effect, you are furnished with blank commissions, signed by the president.

Declaration of Independence, July 4, 1776

On July 2, 1776, the Continental Congress approved Richard Henry Lee's resolution "[t]hat these United Colonies are, and of right ought to be, free and independent States, that they are absolved from all allegiance to the British Crown, and that all political connection between them and the State of Great Britain is, and ought to be, totally dissolved." Congress had appointed a committee consisting of Thomas Jefferson, John Adams, Benjamin Franklin, Roger Sherman, and Robert Livingston to write a declaration of independence. Jefferson wrote the first draft, which was revised by committee members. Congress then debated, amended, and passed the declaration on July 4, 1776.

The unanimous Declaration of the thirteen United States of America.

When, in the Course of human events, it becomes necessary for one people to dissolve the political bands which have connected them with another, and to assume, among the Powers of the earth, the separate and equal station to which the Laws of Nature and of Nature's God entitle them, a decent respect to the opinions of mankind requires that they should declare the causes which impel them to the separation.

We hold these truths to be self-evident, that all men are created equal, that they are endowed by their Creator with certain unalienable Rights, that among these, are Life, Liberty, and the pursuit of Happiness. That, to secure these rights, Governments are instituted among Men, deriving their just Powers from the consent of the governed. That, whenever any form of Government becomes destructive of these ends, it is the Right of the People to alter or to abolish it, and to institute new Government, laying its foundation on such Principles, and organizing its Powers in such form, as to them shall seem most likely to effect their Safety and Happiness. Prudence, indeed, will dictate that

Source: JCC, 5: 431, 510–15.

Governments long established should not be changed for light and transient causes; and, accordingly, all experience hath shewn, that mankind are more disposed to suffer, while evils are sufferable, than to right themselves by abolishing the forms to which they are accustomed. But, when a long train of abuses and usurpations, pursuing invariably the same Object, evinces a design to reduce them under absolute Despotism, it is their right, it is their duty, to throw off such Government, and to provide new Guards for their future Security. Such has been the patient sufferance of these Colonies; and such is now the necessity which constrains them to alter their former Systems of Government. The history of the present King of Great Britain is a history of repeated injuries and usurpations, all having in direct object the establishment of an absolute Tyranny over these States. To prove this, let Facts be submitted to a candid world.

He has refused his Assent to Laws the most wholesome and necessary for the public good.

He has forbidden his Governors to pass Laws of immediate and pressing importance, unless suspended in their operation till his Assent should be obtained; and when so suspended, he has utterly neglected to attend to them.

He has refused to pass other Laws for the accommodation of large districts of People, unless those People would relinquish the right of Representation in the legislature; a right inestimable to them and formidable to tyrants only.

He has called together legislative bodies at places unusual, uncomfortable, and distant from the depository of their Public Records, for the sole Purpose of fatiguing them into compliance with his measures.

He has dissolved Representative Houses repeatedly, for opposing, with manly firmness, his invasions on the rights of the People.

He has refused for a long time, after such dissolutions, to cause others to be elected; whereby the Legislative Powers, incapable of Annihilation, have returned to the People at large for their exercise; the State remaining in the mean time exposed to all the dangers of invasion from without, and convulsions within.

He has endeavoured to prevent the Population of these States; for that purpose obstructing the Laws for Naturalization of Foreigners; refusing to pass others to encourage their migrations hither, and raising the conditions of new Appropriations of Lands.

He has obstructed the Administration of Justice, by refusing his Assent to Laws for establishing Judiciary Powers.

He has made Judges dependent on his Will alone, for the tenure of their offices, and the amount and payment of their salaries.

He has erected a multitude of New Offices, and sent hither swarms of Officers to harrass our People, and eat out their substance.

He has kept among us, in times of Peace, Standing Armies, without the Consent of our legislatures.

He has affected to render the Military independent of and superior to the Civil Power.

He has combined with others to subject us to a jurisdiction foreign to our constitution, and unacknowledged by our laws; giving his Assent to their Acts of pretended Legislation:

For quartering large bodies of armed troops among us:

For protecting them, by a mock Trial, from Punishment for any Murders which they should commit on the Inhabitants of these States:

For cutting off our Trade with all parts of the world:

For imposing Taxes on us without our Consent:

For depriving us, in many cases, of the benefits of Trial by Jury:

For transporting us beyond Seas to be tried for pretended offences:

For abolishing the free System of English Laws in a neighbouring province, establishing therein an Arbitrary government, and enlarging its Boundaries, so as to render it at once an example and fit instrument for introducing the same absolute rule into these Colonies:

For taking away our Charters, abolishing our most valuable Laws, and altering fundamentally the Forms of our Governments:

For suspending our own Legislatures, and declaring themselves invested with Power to legislate for us in all cases whatsoever.

He has abdicated Government here, by declaring us out of his protection, and waging War against us.

He has plundered our seas, ravaged our Coasts, burnt our towns, and destroyed the Lives of our People.

He is at this time transporting large Armies of foreign Mercenaries to compleat the works of death, desolation and tyranny, already begun with circumstances of Cruelty and perfidy scarcely paralleled in the most barbarous ages, and totally unworthy the Head of a civilized nation.

He has constrained our fellow Citizens, taken Captive on the high Seas, to bear Arms against their Country, to become the executioners of their friends and Brethren, or to fall themselves by their Hands.

He has excited domestic insurrections amongst us, and has endeavoured to bring on the inhabitants of our frontiers, the merciless Indian Savages, whose known rule of warfare, is an undistinguished destruction of all ages, sexes and conditions.

In every stage of these Oppressions, We have Petitioned for Redress, in the most humble terms: Our repeated Petitions, have been answered only by repeated injury. A Prince, whose character is thus marked by every act which may define a Tyrant, is unfit to be the ruler of a free People.

Nor have We been wanting in attentions to our Brittish brethren. We have warned them from time to time of attempts by their legislature to extend an unwarrantable jurisdiction over us. We have reminded them of the circumstances of our emigration and settlement here. We have appealed to their native justice and magnanimity, and we have conjured them by the ties of our common kindred, to disavow these usurpations, which, would inevitably interrupt our connexions and correspondence. They too have been deaf to the voice of justice and of consanguinity. We must, therefore, acquiesce in the necessity, which denounces our Separation, and hold them, as we hold the rest of mankind, Enemies in War, in Peace Friends.

We, therefore, the Representatives of the united States of America, in GENERAL CONGRESS assembled, appealing to the Supreme Judge of the World for the rectitude of our intentions, DO, in the Name, and by Authority of the good People of these Colonies, solemnly PUBLISH and DECLARE, That these United Colonies are, and of Right, ought to be Free and Independent States; that they are Absolved from all Allegiance to the British Crown, and that all political connexion between them and the State of Great Britain, is and ought to be totally dissolved; and that, as FREE and INDEPENDENT STATES, they have full Power to levy War, conclude Peace, contract Alliances, establish Commerce, and to do all other Acts and Things which INDEPENDENT STATES may of right do. AND for the support of this Declaration, with a firm reliance on the protection of divine Providence, we mutually pledge to each other our Lives, our Fortunes, and our sacred Honour.

The foregoing declaration was, by order of Congress, engrossed, and signed by the following members:

JOHN HANCOCK.

JOSIAH BARTLETT.	GEO. TAYLOR.
W^M WHIPPLE.	JAMES WILSON.
SAM^L ADAMS.	GEO. ROSS.
JOHN ADAMS.	CAESAR RODNEY.
ROB^T TREAT PAINE.	GEO READ.
ELBRIDGE GERRY.	THOS M:KEAN.
STEPH. HOPKINS.	SAMUEL CHASE.
WILLIAM ELLERY.	W^M PACA.
ROGER SHERMAN.	THO^S STONE.
SAM^{EL} HUNTINGTON.	CHARLES CARROLL OF CARROLLTON.

W^M Williams.

Oliver Wolcott.

Matthew Thornton.

W^M Floyd.

Phil Livingston.

Fran^S Lewis.

Lewis Morris.

Rich^D Stockton.

Jno Witherspoon.

Fra^S Hopkinson.

John Hart.

Abra Clark.

Rob^T Morris.

Benjamin Rush.

Benj^A Franklin.

John Morton.

Geo Clymer.

Ja^S Smith.

George Wythe.

Richard Henry Lee.

Th. Jefferson.

Benj^A Harrison.

Tho^S Nelson, Jr.

Francis Lightfoot Lee.

Carter Braxton.

W^M Hooper.

Joseph Hewes.

John Penn.

Edward Rutledge.

Tho^S Heyward, Jun^R.

Thomas Lynch, Jun^R.

Arthur Middleton.

Button Gwinnett.

Lyman Hall.

Geo Walton.

Letter to Jonathan Trumbull Jr., August 16, 1776

PHILADELPHIA

Jonathan Trumbull Jr. served as paymaster general of the Northern Department (New York) from July 1775 to July 1778. Among other things, this letter illustrates the importance Sherman placed on regular correspondence to keep abreast of current events.

Dear Sir

I have not been favoured with a letter from You Since You was appointed to the office You now Sustain. I now take the liberty to begin a correspondence with You, which I wish may be continued for the future. There have been great complaints for want of money in the Northern department. That want has been partly owing to a neglect of making application to Congress for it, as Paper currency might have been Sent at any time, but a Sufficient Supply of Specie could not be obtained to Support the Army in Canada, therefore Supplies of provisions &c ought to have been Sent from the Colonies. Who is most blameworthy for the neglect I shall not undertake to Say.

500,000 Dollars were Sent forward to You about a fortnight ago which I hope are Safe arrived. As Many more were ordered yesterday, to be forwarded immediately, So that I hope You will in future have Sufficient Supplies of that article, especially as Congress has directed the Paymasters to make returns weekly of the State of their Military Chests, which returns 'tis expected will be Sent by the Post.

I should take it as a favour if You would as often as may be conveniente, write to me the State of Affairs in that department & the remarkable occurrences. The Enemy have now a very formidable force at Staten Island, and a Battle may soon be expected at New York which will probably be attended with very important consequences to the United States. Hitherto the Lord hath helped Us, On him may we Still depend, and find Him a present help in every time of trouble & danger. The enemy have now collected their whole

Source: Paul H. Smith et al., eds., *Letters of Delegates to Congress* (Washington, D.C.: Government Printing Office, 1979), 5: 8–9.

force at New York & Canada, with intention, no doubt to open a communication between their two Armies by the way of Hudson's River. A vessel Arrived here this week with 100 Barrels of Powder & 50 Tons of Lead and a
large quantity of Duck for the Use of the United States. Ammunition hath
also been lately brought in at Several other Ports so that we have a good Supply
at present.

My son William, to whom the enclosed letter is directed, is appointed Paymaster to Colo. Warner's Regiment. I dont know where he resides, but request
You to forward the Letter to him as soon as may be. I wish to know what
progress Colo. Warner has made in raising a Regiment. I am Sir, with due
regards, Your humble Servant,

Roger Sherman

Letter to Jonathan Trumbull Sr., March 4, 1777

PHILADELPHIA

Sherman's letters to Governor Trumbull often simply relayed information, but occasionally Sherman made observations or suggestions that shed light on his thoughts.

Honored Sir

The Congress adjourned from Baltimore last Thursday to meet in this City yesterday but a Sufficient Number of Members did not come in to proceed to business. It was found very inconvenient to set at so great a distance from the Seat of War especially at a time when a new army is forming. Orders have been lately Issued to reinforce the Army in New Jersy by calling in all the new recruits, and the neighbouring Militia. The reason given in the resolution is "The Congress being earnestly desirous to Strengthen the Army under General Washington's immediate Command So as to enable him not only to curb the Enemy & prevent their ravaging the Country & obtaining any supplies or provisions or forage, but by the Divine blessing totally to Subdue them before they can be reinforced."

It appears to me that a vigorous exertion at this time might be attended with very happy consequences, if not totally put an end to the war, for by the best accounts the enemy are in great want of many necessaries, and much dispirited, and tis thought if they were closely pursued with Superior or equal numbers they would be obliged to Submit. Congress never gave any orders at any time not to risque a general Battel as was reported last Fall, but always left that matter to the discretion of the Commanding Officers. Congress has considered the resolutions of the Committees of the four New England States, approves of the measures for the Defence of Rhode Island, and those recommended for the Support of their paper currencies, but do not think it advisable to Issue Bills on Interest. I think that would have no good effect, it might Interfere with the continental loans & would in my opinion burthen the particular States with a useless expence. The evils occasioned by the fluctuating

Source: Paul H. Smith et al., eds., *Letters of Delegates to Congress* (Washington, D.C.: Government Printing Office, 1980), 6: 403–5.

and exorbitant prices of things is very sensibly felt here. Congress has referred the considering of the doings of the New England Governments as to fixing the prices of articles, to the consideration of the other States, recommending to them to appoint Commissioners to meet for that purpose & to adopt Some plan to remedy the evils aforesaid. The middle States from New York to Virginia inclusive are to meet the third Tuesday in this month. Congress has Agreed to allow 6 per cent per annum on any monies borrowed or to be borrowed on loan office Certificates being informed from Massachusetts and Philadelphia that money could not be obtained on a lower Interest, moneyed men being unwilling to lower their incomes when the prices of all necessaries are greatly increased. The best way to preserve the Credit of the currency & render the price of articles Stable is to raise the Supplies for carrying on the war by Taxes as far as possible, & the rest by loans. It Seems to be the present opinion of the Congress that there be no further Emission of Bills than what is already ordered if it can possibly be avoided, and that the most effectual measures be taken to Support the Credit of those already emited. Accordingly a Tax is recommended to the Several States, and as the rule to determine the Quotas is not yet Established by the legislatures of the Several States (which is to be done by the Confederation) each State is called upon to raise as large a Sum as circumstances will admit, with an Engagement to allow Interest at 6 per cent for what any State may raise more than its Just Quota of the whole Sum that Shall be raised.

I suppose the expences of the current year will not be less than twenty million dollars, but perhaps more unless the enemy's Army Should be subdued before they can be reinforced or a diversion given to the British Arms by a war with France. I wish that I could furnish your Honr with printed copies of the Journals of Congress to this time; but notwithstanding the utmost endeavours of Congress to have them printed here, they have by one excuse or other been delayed, sometimes the printers complain of the want of paper, at other times their workmen are obliged to go with the Militia into the Field. Orders have lately been given to the Committee to agree with some printer who will perform the work.

Your Honr has doubtless been informed of the promotions lately made of General Officers in the army. Previous to the choice the Congress resolved, "That in the appointment of General officers due regard shall be had to the line of Succession, personal merit, and the number of troops raised or to be raised by the several States." We mentioned Brigadiers Wooster and Arnold as candidates for Major generals on the two first principles, & Brigadier Wadsworth and Colo Huntington, who were both recommended by General Washington, as fit persons for Brigadiers; but the last principle prevailed to pass them all by—viz, That Connecticut had more General Officers than in proportion to the number of Troops furnished by that State.

By a letter from Mr Dean dated Octr 25th, no authenticated account of these States having declared themselves independent had been received by him, so that nothing material had been transacted by him, except Some contracts for Goods. We have accounts in the newspapers that Doctr Franklin arrived in France the 7th of December last, but Congress has not received any Letters from him since his arrival. By the best accounts from France & Spain they are disposed to favour our cause.

I wish to know your Honrs opinion what would be most agreable to our State as to providing for the Sick in the army, whether to have it done by Congress or each State to provide for their own troops, & whether Doctr. Turner would not be a Suitable person to be recommended as Director of a Hospital on the East side of Hudson's River, or where ever else the N.E. Troops may be stationed, or whether any other person in either of the N.E. States would be more Suitable or acceptable for Such an appointment. We were Honored with the receipt of one of your Honor's letters at Baltimore, but my papers not being here I cant refer to the date wherein your Honr mentions that it will be most Agreable to the other Gentlemen Delegates for two of them to come together. I think it would be well to have a fuller representation at this time, and as but two, & part of the time but one has attended for a considerable time past, if four Should attend for Some time, the expence would not be more than if three had attended the whole time.

Doctr. Jackson, one of the Managers of the Lottery of the united States by whom I expect to send this, is on a Journey through New England to dispose of the lottery tickets. He requested me to recommend to him Suitable persons in Connecticut to receive a number of them for Sale. I accordingly recommended Thaddeus Burr Esqr. in Fairfield County, Samll. Bishop Esqr. in New Haven & John Lawrence Esqr. in Hartford and took the Liberty to refer him to your Honr to advise him to Suitable persons in the Eastern counties. I me[ntioned] Doctr. Smith for Litchfield County.

I am, very respectfully, your Honrs Obedient, humble Servant,

Roger Sherman

P.S. General Wolcott is well.

Letter to Jonathan Trumbull Sr., April 9, 1777

PHILADELPHIA

In addition to relating political news about a variety of topics, this letter reveals Sherman's view on oaths of fidelity.

Sir,

Capt. Niles of the Spy was here last Saturday. He Said That there were a number of the Enemy's Ships of War in Chesepeak Bay So that he could not go to Virginia, That he wanted 750 Dollars toward paying for a Cargo of Flour which he had purchased upon which I moved Congress to Advance to the State of Connecticut one thousand Dollars which was Granted, and I delivered 750 of them to Captain Niles and he drew a Bill on your Honr. for payment. The whole is Charged to the State and I must acct for it when I return home. Nothing very material has occurred here Since my last. Congress has passed Some Resolutions for regulating a Hospital in the army which will be published in the News Papers. All the States are now Represented, and next Monday is assigned for considering the Articles of Confederation. I wish there was a more full representation from our State. Congress received a Letter from Dr. Franklin, Arthur Lee & Silas Dean dated about the 27th of January. It does not contain any thing material more than what has been published in the News Papers. They have been offered a loan of Two million Livres without Interest payable after the United States are settled in Peace and Safety which they Gratefully accepted for the use of the States & 500,000 Livres has been received. All ranks favour our cause. It was not certainly known to them whether a war between Gr Britain & France would be Soon Declared. I am informed by Mr. Duer a Delegate from the State of New York that Governor Franklin is very busy with the Tories and has delivered out a number of Protections from General How and that any person can obtain a Protection in Connecticut, that this is publickly known there and no measures taken to prevent it. I received a Letter from a Friend Yesterday informing me that the Assembly has

Source: Paul H. Smith et al., eds., *Letters of Delegates to Congress* (Washington, D.C.: Government Printing Office, 1980), 6: 560–61.

repealed the Law prescribing an Oath of Fidelity which I was very Sorry to hear. I expect a recommendation will soon be made by Congress to all the States to administer an Oath not only to the officers & Electors, but to all Suspected persons as a Test to discriminate between Friends & foes. I esteem our internal enemies much the most dangerous. The people on the New Hamshire Grants have Petitioned Congress to be acknowledged an Independent State, and admited to Send Delegates to Congress. The Convention of New York has also remonstrated against their proceedings, requesting Congress to interpose for preventing the defection of the people on the Grants from that State. Nothing has been yet acted on the affair. The recruiting Service does not go on here so fast as could be wished. In Virginia I understand their Battalions are about two thirds full, in the Carolinas near full. It is Strange that we can't muster an army of fifteen thousand from all the States. I Suppose that number would now be Sufficient to Subdue the Enemy's force in New Jersey.

It Seems to me the Spirit of true Patriotism declines, a Spirit of Selfishness & Oppression prevails.

The Convention of Committees for the Middle States is broke up without doing any thing to remedy the evils attending the high & fluctuating prices of articles.

A Vessel has lately arrived here from Sweden with Arms & Ammunition. I hope two of the Connecticut Delegates are on their way for this place before now. I should have wrote to them, but have long expected that they were coming here, & So would probably miss of receiving my letters. I Should be Glad to return home for a Short time, but cant, before more Members arrive.

I am with the greatest respect Your Honor's Obedient humble Servant,

Roger Sherman

Letter to Jonathan Trumbull Sr., May 14, 1777

PHILADELPHIA

This letter to Governor Trumbull provides insight into Sherman's views on a number of different political issues.

Honored Sir

Your letter to Congress was received and read, and then committed to the Board of War. I am Sorry to hear that the Militia are no better Armed in this time of danger. I believe there are no Continental Arms to Spare at present, more are daily expected. If any are due to the State of Connecticut, it would be best to Send a particular account of the Number and request Congress that they be replaced as Soon as any Shall arrive. Congress has lately been employed in regulating the Several departments of the Army that the business may be properly conducted and frauds and abuse prevented. The Articles of Confederation have Several times come Under consideration but not much progress made therein. Rhode Island is not represented. Mr Ellery's time expired last week & he has no information of being reappointed. Letters as late as the 15th of April received from our Agent in Martineco Inform that our Trade receives all the protection that could be desired from the Govt of the French Islands, but no certain accounts whether a war will Soon take place between France & Britain.

Your Honr has probably Seen the late Act of Parliament for Sending the Americans to England & detaining them in prison without Bail or mainprize till the first of Jany. 1778. The best way to relieve our people who may fall into their hands, is by a vigorous exertion to get as many of theirs as possible into our custody, as nothing but the fear of retaliation will induce them to regard the laws of humanity.

The Gentleman who gave information of Governor Franklin's misbehaviour and the inattention of our Government to prevent it seemed displeased that any part of the information was contradicted by your Honrs letter. I have no

Source: Paul H. Smith et al., eds., *Letters of Delegates to Congress* (Washington, D.C.: Government Printing Office, 1981), 7: 81–83.

doubt but his information was good as to Govr Franklin's Misconduct. As to our Government being informed of it he says that he told Genll Parsons of it and Mr Burr of Fairfield was also informed of it. Mr Duer is Zealously engaged to Suppress Tories.

The Congress promoted Colonels Huntington and Read to the rank of Brigadiers General on the 12th instant, the first on General Washington's request. I wish for leave to return home for a Short time at least, but it wont do to leave the State of Connecticut unrepresented. I hope other Delegates will Soon arrive.

I am with great Esteem [and] regard Your Honrs. Obedient humble Servant,

Roger Sherman

Letter to Oliver Wolcott, May 21, 1777

PHILADELPHIA

Oliver Wolcott (1726–97) came from a prominent Connecticut family. He joined Sherman in signing the Declaration of Independence and Articles of Confederation and served as governor of Connecticut from 1796 until his death the following year.

Sir

The enclosed Letters came to hand yesterday by the Post. I was in doubt Whether it was best to Send them back, or keep them till you return here. I hope it will not be long before a Delegation arives, that I may have leave of absence. I understand that an Inhabitant of Connecticut has been lately executed by a Sentence of a General Court Martial. I think it dangerous to admit Citizens not connected with the army to be tried by a Court Martial. The resolution of Congress concerning Spies does not warrant it—that respects only Such as are not Subjects of any of the States. It is easy to accuse any person with being a Spy & to put his life into the power of a Court Martial. I have no doubt but that the person executed was an attrocious offender & deserved Death but if he was an Inhabitant of the State he ought to have been tryed before the Supr. Court. We have nothing new here since my last. General Arnold is here. Congress has ordered the Quarter Master General to procure and present to him a Horse properly caparisoned for his Bravery in attacking the enemy who m[arched] to Danbury, in which action he had one horse killed under him and another wounded. A Committee is appointed to consider what Honors are due to the Memory of Genll. Wooster. There are different accounts of the day of his death. Some say Thursday, others Friday and others Saturday. I wish that could be ascertained, & that I could be informed of his age. I have had an account of the Election in the Hartford paper. A few lines from you with Some account of the proceedings of the Assembly, will oblige your humble Servant

Source: Paul H. Smith et al., eds., *Letters of Delegates to Congress* (Washington, D.C.: Government Printing Office, 1981), 7: 101–2.

Letter to Samuel Adams, July 11, 1777

NEW HAVEN

Samuel Adams (1722–1803) was a very influential political leader in Massachusetts and a key advocate of American independence. This letter and Adams's response are primarily concerned with the loss of Fort Ticonderoga by General Philip Schuyler.

Sir,

I arrived here last evening and found my family in health. I don't hear of any movement of the Enemy from New York or Staten Island, nor can I learn which way they intend to steer next. We hear that Ticonderoga is taken by the Enemy, that General Schuyler wrote from Still Water to Gen. Wolcott requesting him to come with the militia under his command. I don't hear any particulars attending the affair or whether there has been any Battle fought, nor why General Schuyler was not present with the army. You will doubtless have a particular account before this reaches you. General Nixon's Brigade was to embark last Sunday morning at Peeks Kill to join on the Northern Army, General Sullivan with his Division, and General Parsons with his Brigade were on their March from Morristown to Peeks Kill when I came through New Jersey last week. I understand that the removal of General Gates from the command of the Northern Army has occasioned general uneasiness in the Country, and it is my opinion that part of the country will not be defended unless he returns, but Congress is wise [sic] who have the conduct of that affair. We have no news here remarkable. I am Sir with great esteem and regard your humble servant,

Roger Sherman

Source: Samuel Adams Papers, reel 2, Manuscripts and Archives Division, New York Public Library. Astor, Lenox, and Tilden Foundations.

Letter from Samuel Adams to Roger Sherman, August 11, 1777

PHILADELPHIA

Dᴇᴀʀ Sɪʀ/

I duly receivd your obliging Letter of the 11ᵗʰ of July. I thank you for the favor, and beg you to continue to write to me as often as your Leisure will admit of it. The Rumour you mention'd has since appeard to be a serious Fact. We have lost Ti[c]onderoga, and as far as I can yet judge, shamefully: I was going to add, vilainously; for indeed I cannot account for it, but upon the worst of Principles. The whole appears to me to carry the evident Marks of Design. But I hope & believe it will undergo the strictest Scrutiny. The People at large ought not, they will not be satisfied, until a thorough Inquiry is made into the Causes of an Event in which their Honor and Safety is so deeply interested. The only Letter receivd by Congress from Sᵗ Clair, you have seen publishd under their Sanction. Schuyler has written a Series of weak & contemptible *Things* in a Stile of Despondence which alone, I think, is sufficient for the Removal of him from that Command; for if his Pen expresses the true Feelings of his Heart, it cannot be expected that the bravest Veterans would fight under such a General, admitting they had no Suspicion of Treachery. In a Letter dated the 4ᵗʰ Instant at Still Water, he writes in a Tone of perfect Despair. He seems to have no Confidence in his Troops, nor the States from whence Reinforcements are to be drawn. A third Part of his Continental Troops, he tells us, consists "of Boys Negroes & aged Men not fit for the Field or any other Service." "A very great Part of the Army naked—without Blanketts—ill armed and very deficient in Accoutrements: without a Prospect of Reliefe." "Many, too Many of the Officers woᵈ be a Disgrace to the most contemptible Troops that ever was collected." The Exertions of others of them of a different Character "counteracted by the worthless." "Genˡ Burgoyne is bending his Course this Way. He will probably be here in Eight Days, and unless we are well reinforced" (which he does not expect) "as much farther as he pleases to go."——Was ever any poor General more mortified! But he has by this Time receivd his Quietus. Gates takes the Command there, agreeably to what you

Source: *The Writings of Samuel Adams: 1773–1777* (New York: G. P. Putnam's Sons, 1907), 3: 404–6.

tell me is the Wish of the People; and I trust our Affairs in that Quarter will soon wear a more promising Aspect.

The Enemies Ships, upwards of 200 sail, after having been out of Sight six Days, were discoverd on Thursday last, off Sinapuxint 15 Leagues from the Capes of Delaware Steering towards Chesapeake Bay.

Your Friends here are well, except Col° Williams, who has been confined a few days, but is growing better. I have a thousand things to say to you, but must defer it to other Opportunities, & conclude in Haste, with friendly Regards to your Family, very affectionately yours,

Letter to Horatio Lloyd Gates, August 20, 1777

Horatio Lloyd Gates (1727–1806), a former British soldier, was appointed brigadier general and adjutant general of the Continental army in 1775. He was given command of the Northern Department on August 5, 1777, and he led the American army to victory over the British at the Battles of Saratoga, a key turning point in the war.

Sir,

Your reappointment to the chief command in the northern gives great pleasure to the friends of American freedom in this part of the country. The abandoning the forts at Ticonderoga and Independence occasioned great and general uneasiness and concern to the people in the eastern states, and tho' they wished to turn out and repulse the enemy, their want of confidence in the late commanders prevented, not from any personal disaffection to them, but from an apprehension that they could do no good while those gentlemen continued in command.

On intelligence of the late action near Bennington a considerable number of militia from this state mustered and are on their march to the assistance of that party. I congratulate you on the successes of our people in that engagement and at Fort Stanwix. I doubt not but that you will soon be joined by the militia of this and the other states in as great numbers, as can be defined, but if they are not kept in action, fighting the enemy they will soon be homesick. I hope by an immediate vigorous exertion you will be able to prevent the retreat of Burgoyne's Army over the Lakes and make a complete conquest of them.

Governor Trumbull received your letter requesting 750 militia from this state, previous to that, the Assembly had ordered a greater number, to continue in service two months, from the time they join the army—the Gov. will write to you fully on that subject.

Tho' our affairs at the northward afforded us a gloomy prospect I hope they will be mercifully over ruled by Divine Providence for the good of those states.

Source: Horatio Gates Papers, reel 5, 117–18, courtesy of the New-York Historical Society.

I hope it will be a means of killing or curing great part of the Tories in that quarter, and of giving warmth & vigour to the cool & timid Whigs—It will give our army an opportunity, lay them under a necessity of fighting the enemy, and I hope of gaining a complete victory. It may discover and remove from public confidence some men, who would sacrifice the public good, to their own private interest, or party views.

My son who was Pay Master in Col. Warner's Regiment writes to me that he has been cashiered by a court martial for inoculating a man not belonging to the army, who brought the infectious matter to him and promised immediately to go to a place about 30 miles distant from the army where inoculation was allowed under the inspection of a committee . . . that he did it inadvertently without any ill design—as he has always been a friend to the American cause he seems much grieved to leave the Service under a censure, and tho' the emoluments of that office are not worth seeking for, yet for the sake of his reputation he wishes to be restored, I never heard but that he has been faithful in his public truth—he served some time as an Assistant Paymaster in Canada where he went as a volunteer—I understand that application has been made to Congress by him & some officers in his behalf but Col. Dyer writes me that it was said in Congress that the application ought to be made to the officer who dismissed him, or the state who appointed him, so they did not enter into the consideration of the matter—as the officers of that regiment were appointed by Congress being from different states, he has no where to apply but to the Commander of the Department. If you on consideration of the case shall think fit afford him relief it will oblige him, and be gratefully acknowledged by

Your obedient humble servant,
Roger Sherman

Letter to Samuel Adams, August 25, 1777

NEW HAVEN

Sherman responds to Adams's letter of August 11 with the following missive.

Dear Sir,

Your favour of the 11th Instant is just come to hand. I fully agree in opinion with you that the Fortresses at the Northward were shamefully abandoned, the public have right to expect a full and impartial inquiry into the causes.

Some fear that proper care will not be taken on the part of the public to procure the best and fullest proof of the Facts, but that it will be determined on the Evidence produced by the accused, however I hope that will not be the case. General Gates arrived in Albany last Monday, our affairs there appear to be in a prosperous state. General Starks and the Militia under his command have distinguished themselves by uncommon Bravery.

That Action equals any that has been done since the commencement of the War. Much Generalship was displayed in placing the men and through the whole affair. The Militia likewise behaved well in Tyron County under General Hercuman[1] I was informed by Col. Bartlett that the New Hampshire Militia refused to go to act under the continental officers then commanding and had Liberty from the government to act as an Independent corps.

Our Assembly has ordered about 200 light horse & 1400 Militia to joyn the Northern Army to serve two months from the time they joyn, and Your State have ordered a large reinforcement, I hope they will send a force between Burgoyne's Army and the Lakes & cut off their retreat. I make no doubt they will soon give a good account of them.

I see by the resolution of Congress that General Gates was appointed to that command by the vote of eleven States & but one dissent which that was may be easily guessed.

Source: Samuel Adams Papers, reel 2, Manuscripts and Archives Division, New York Public Library. Astor, Lenox, and Tilden Foundations.

1. Probably a reference to General Nicholas Herkimer (c. 1728–77), a New York militia general who died as a result of wounds sustained in the Battle of Oriskany. —Ed.

Our affairs appear to me to be in a pretty good situation except that of the currency. we can scarce purchase the common necessaries with the paper currencies, and what are sold are enormous prices. I know of no remedy but that recommended by the committee met at Springfield viz. sinking the bills emitted by the particular States (of which there is £ 1,060,000 passing in the five eastern States) and taxing for paying the public expenses as far as may be, and this should be adopted by all the states to render it effectual. Frequent taxes will keep the money circulating, and people will be obliged to sell their commodities to procure money to pay their rates, but now it is despised because there is but little use for it

I think it will be much better to carry on the war by taxes as much as can be borne, and the rest by loans in this country, than by foreign loans. It may be best to hire some money abroad to pay our debts due for the supplies that have been imported, and to pay for any further supplies that may be wanted, but not to sell bills to merchants to import on their own account. We have very plentiful crops; people can now pay larger taxes, and seem generally willing to do it. I know no better way to preserve credit than to pay debts and not to run in debt more than is absolutely necessary. Confederation is likewise necessary to support the public credit of the United States, and if it is not done while the war lasts, I fear it will not be done at all.

Our Assembly has in comparison [?] with the agreement of the Springfield Convention laid tax payable the first of next Nov. sufficient to raise £ 90,000, also made provision to supply the families of the soldiers at the prices that were regulated by the late laws.

Those laws are now repealed, they could not well be executed because the Middle and Southern State did not adopt similar measures. Further taxes I expect will be laid at the October session. I hope Congress will early attend to the state of the currency. I hear that Mr. Phillips will not accept the office of Commissary of Hides and that no other is appointed. I fear there will be great loss sustained for want of such an officer. Robert Ogden Esq. of New Jersey, I think, would be a proper person. He is skilful in that Business. I shall be glad to hear from you as often as is convenient. I hope you will attend to your health & not neglect to ride frequently. I am glad that our good Friend R.H. Lee is reappointed a Delegate, please to present my complements to him if he is returned to Congress.

These from your sincere friend & humble servant,
Roger Sherman

Letter to Richard Henry Lee, November 3, 1777

HARTFORD

Richard Henry Lee (1732–94), an important civic leader from Virginia, was also a signer of the Declaration of Independence and the Articles of Confederation.

Sir,

I sincerely congratulate you on the signal success of our Arms in the Northern department, in the surrender of Gen. Burgoyne & his Army to General Gates. This is the Lords doing, and marvellous in our eyes: and if suitably acknowledged and improved by us to his glory, I hope will prove a happy prelude to the establishment of Peace and Liberty to these States.

Gen. Howe, I think, will be in as bad a situation as Burgoyne if he cant get his ships up to Philadelphia. I dont doubt but that our Brave General, will carefully guard every avenue to prevent his retreat.

Kind Providence has blessed us in this part of the country with plentiful crops of provisions, the people chearfully bear their burthens and fatigues in carrying on the war and are willing to be taxed high for that purpose.

The low credit of our paper currency, occasioned partly by inimical persons and partly by ambitious ones, is our greatest Embarrassment, and I think that might be soon remedied if Congress would recommend to all the states to sink their own bills & tax themselves to a certain & sufficient amount for carrying on the war, and draw in as much as may be by the loan offices, and collect the Taxes frequently appropriate about 3 million dollars annually to be burnt to lessen the Quantity in circulation until the whole be sunk Which would be in less than twelve years. Such provision being made & published would have an immediate effect to give credit & stability to the currency. Care should be taken that the two first emissions should be stopt in the loan offices and not re-issued, for it will be difficult to get Silver or Gold to redeem them when the fixed periods arrive.

The mode adopted by Congress for proportioning the Quotas of the Several States according to the value of their Lands I think impracticable. The number

Source: Lee-Ludwell Papers, Virginia Historical Society.

of Inhabitants, I think, will be the best that can be devised. The wealth of a people I believe will generally be found to be nearly in proportion to the numbers that can be supported in a state—& Wealth principally arises from the labour of men.

As to the Negros, I should be willing to do what appears equitable. If for the present it should be agreed to exclude all under ten years old or any other age that may be agreed on & include the rest until a more equitable rule can be devised, & not make a perpetual rule at present would it not answer better than to have the Confederation delayed, for I am persuaded that the States can neither agree to nor practice the mode voted by Congress, & nothing effectual can be done to fix the credit or the currency or to raise necessary supplies until some Rule of proportion is adopted. I doubt not of your readiness to do whatever you shall judge may conduce to the general good and I am sure your Influence will have great weight in this affair.

I am with great truth & Regard,
Your friend and humble servant,
Roger Sherman

Report of the New Haven Convention, January 30, 1778

During the War for Independence, Sherman actively participated in state and national debates about how to finance the war effort. He argued for the virtues of hard money and against inflation. Like many civic leaders, he believed the latter could be contained by price controls. In 1777, Congress urged all of the northern states to send delegates to a January 1778 meeting in New Haven. New Hampshire, Massachusetts, Rhode Island, New York, New Jersey, Pennsylvania, and Connecticut complied with the request, and the latter appointed Sherman, William Hillhouse, and Benjamin Huntington to represent the state. The convention elected Sherman chairman and, after a week of meetings, instructed him, Robert Treat Paine, Nathaniel Peabody, and Benjamin Huntington to "draw up a report of the doings of this Convention." The New Haven Convention proposed strict limitations on wages and prices and approved a letter urging Congress to redeem Continental bills. Congress acknowledged the report but refused to act on it. Sherman's account book contains the only known draft of this document. It is in his handwriting and is dated January 29, one day before the final report was approved by the convention. There is little doubt that he played a major role in drafting the text.[1]

Met according to adjournment.

The Convention resumed the consideration of the report of the committee &c., which being read, paragraph by paragraph, was approved and is as follows, *viz:*

When we see self-love, that first principle planted in the humane breast by the all wise Creator for our benefit and preservation, through misapplication

Source: Charles J. Hoadly, ed., *The Public Records of the State of Connecticut* (Hartford, Conn.: Press of the Case, Lockwood & Brainard Co., 1894), 1: 613–19.

1. Charles J. Hoadly, ed., *The Public Records of the State of Connecticut* (Hartford, Conn.: Press of the Case, Lockwood & Brainard Co., 1894), 1: 521–28, 612, 613–19; Sherman Account Book, Sherman Papers, box 1, folder 4, Yale University, 60–61. Hillhouse (1728–1816) and Huntington were both influential political leaders in Connecticut. Peabody (1741–1823) was a medical doctor who held a variety of offices in New Hampshire. Paine (1731–1814) was a lawyer and politician from Massachusetts.

and corruption, perverted to our destruction, we feel the necessity of correcting so pernicious an error and directing the operation of it in such a manner as that our self and social love may be the same.

The application of this remark to the present state of our public affairs is obvious.

The free born inhabitants of America, opprest by the tyranny of Great Britain, found it necessary for the support of their liberties to declare themselves independent. To support that independency, it was necessary to raise and maintain an expensive army, and to issue large emissions of paper bills to defray the expences. Upon the support and success of this army, under God, depends the whole we are contending for, and on the credit of our currency depends immediately the support of our army; when therefore the principle of self-love impells the individuals of a community to exact and receive for their services or commodities such prices as exceed that proportion of prices, at which the army was raised and established, and to set no other bounds to their demands than what the necessity of the times will suffer them to receive, and to withold and conceal their necessary commodities, unless their demands are complied with, is it not evident that this self love and attention to their supposed self interest have exceeded their true bounds; and tend not only to the destruction of the welfare of the community, but also of the individuals?

Can a man in any reasonable view be considered as a friend to the American cause, who continually practices and with all his efforts supports such conduct, which if adopted by the community in general must work the destruction of that cause?

Can the officers and soldiers support themselves by their pay at the present high prices of the necessaries of life?

Can the community possibly afford to increase that pay, seeing bills with which they are paid must hereafter be redeemed in silver and gold, at the expressed value? Can all the other expences of the war be supported at so high a rate?

Must not therefore the rate of all expences be reduced to their original standard? and do not therefore those persons who, by their clamours, oppositions and engrossings labour to obstruct the reducing of prices, give evident proof that they are in fact enemies to the very cause they otherwise pretend to support? do such persons well consider what is always said of the man who, zealously professing Christianity, lives in continued practice of the breach of its precepts?

Induced by such like reflections, and feeling their obligation to superintend the welfare of the American States, the Hono[ble] American Congress by their resolves of November 22[d] last, premising the necessity of reducing the quantity of circulating medium, in order to support its value, have recommended to the several States, in the strongest terms, to raise the sum of five million dollars by taxes, and to refrain from the further emission of bills of credit, to cancel the bills emitted by particular States, to support the war by taxes and loans; and for an immediate remedy of the exorbitant evils complained of, have recommended to the States of America in three divisions, to appoint Commissioners to regulate and ascertain, the price of labour, manufactures, internal produce, and commodities imported from foreign parts, military stores excepted, and also regulate the charges of inn-holders. The Commissioners therefore of New Hampshire, Massachusetts Bay, Rhode Island and Providence Plantations, Connecticut, New York, New Jersey, and Pennsylvania, have met in Convention at New Haven, on the 15th day of Jany in pursuance of said requisition of Congress, and while attending to the injunctions of their commission, have not been insensible of the principles upon which an opposition to the regulation of prices by law is founded; and though this measure is executed by them in compliance with the requisitions of the Honble Congress, yet as the government of America is not only founded on the good will of the people but by the wisdom and sincerity of its administration recommends itself to their understanding and approbation, they thought it not amiss to address this measure to the feelings and apprehensions of the inhabitants. It is evident that those principles on which such an opposition is founded were fully considered by the Grand Council of America, that they viewed the reducing the quantity of circulating medium by stopping the currency of the bills of the particular States, and supporting the future expences by taxation and loaning as the essential remedy, and as what in time must work the desired effect, especially among a virtuous people, but that our present exigences require an immediate reduction of prices, which, though by those who are actuated by no better principle than contracted self-love may be considered as infringing the principles of trade and liberty, is nevertheless a salutary measure in connection with the others and practiced by all the States.

To the several Legislatures of the American States, therefore, is now sounded the loudest call, which the voice of true self love and self defence can utter, immediately to exert themselves to relieve the inhabitants of that plea for high prices, the undue quantity of money, by stopping the circulation of their States money, by levying large taxes, and assessing them with such equality as to admit of the highest taxes practicable. To the inhabitants of these States, this voice clearly announces the necessity of the above measure and of a regulation of prices by law. Why do we complain of a partial infringement of liberty manifestly tending to the preservation of the whole? Must the lunatick run uncontrouled to the destruction of himself and neighbours merely because he is under the operation of medicines which may in time work his cure? and indeed without the use of those medicines will the confinement cure him? Must we be suffered to continue the exaction of such high prices to the destruction of the common cause, and of ourselves with it, merely because the reduction of the quantity of our currency may in time redress the evil; and because any other method may be complained of as an infringement of liberty? Is there any alternative but the existence and increase of those evils before recited, on the one hand, or the regulation of prices by law on the other, till they become regulated by the reduction of quantity of the currency? Will the present inhabitants of this earth, or generation yet unborn, by any representations be persuaded to believe that a person or people are duly penetrated with the importance of their liberties, who will not comply with and exert themselves to support such a system of expedience as required by Congress? The same Commissioners therefore, being deeply imprest with the importance and wisdom of said resolves of Congress and, taken collectively and coöperating together, of their efficacy to produce the desired end, and having the firmest confidence in the several legislatures represented in this Convention, that they will forthwith without pretentions or delays whatsoever stop the currency of all the bills of credit, by them emitted, small change under a dollar only excepted, and call them in by loans or taxes, and emitting no more bills on their own credit, small change excepted, exert themselves to support the war by taxes and loans, and that the good people, the inhabitants of these States, will remember their first love for liberty, and their solemn fervent voluntary engagements to support the same with life and fortune, and that they will exert themselves, that this whole system of regulation shall be carried into execution to the support of the cause, have agreed to the following rates of prices to the articles hereafter mentioned.

The Commissioners, very desirous of accommodating this regulation as much as may be to the conveniencies of immediate practice, have stated these prices much higher than any one will suppose they ought to be; they have endeavoured to avoid too great a revulsion, expecting when the juditious and spirited exertions of the several legislatures shall have reduced the quantity of the circulating medium, that there will not only be no occation for this regulation, but that the prices will naturally fall from the high rates at which we have stated them, to their original standard.

From this regulation certain articles of foreign production are excepted, being in the opinion of the Commissioners equally necessary for the army and inhabitants of these States as military stores, and the charge and risk of importing them being so great, various and uncertain—hoping their prices will be so far governed by the estimate of other articles as to preserve a due proportion.

Therefore, resolved, FIRSTLY, That the various kinds of labour of farmers, mechanicks and others be set and affixed at rates not exceeding seventy five *per cent.* advance from what their respective labour was in the same places in the several States aforesaid through the various seasons of the year 1774.

SECOND, That the price of teaming and all kinds of land transportation shall not exceed the rate of five twelveths of a continental dollar for the carriage of twenty hundred neat weight per mile, including all expences attending the same.

THIRD, That all kinds of American manufactures and internal produce, not particularly mentioned and regulated by this Convention, be estimated at rates not exceeding 75 *per cent.* advance from the prices they were usually sold at in the several parts of these respective States aforesaid in the year 1774, excepting only salt, cordwood, charcoal, mutton, lamb, veal, small meats, and poultry of all kinds, roots and vegetables; the price of which may better be regulated by the respective Legislatures, if they shall judge it expedient, than by this Convention.

FOURTHLY, That the price of hemp, flax, sheeps wool, all kinds of woollen and linen clothes, hosiery of all kinds, felt hats, wire and wool cards, manufactured in America, shall not exceed the rate of *cent per cent.* advance from the price they bore in the several parts of the States aforesaid in the year 1774.

FIFTHLY, That the price of all kinds of European goods, wares and merchandize imported from foreign parts, or brought into the States by capture, or otherwise, shall not exceed the rates of one continental dollar for each shilling sterling prime cost of such goods in Europe, exclusive of all other charges, when sold from the importer or captor, excepting only the following articles, *viz:* all kinds of woollen and linen goods and checks suitable for the army, drugs and medicine, duck of all kinds, cordage, tin plates, copperas, files, alum, brimstone, felt hats, nails, window glass, salt, steel, wire, wool and cotton cards, and naval and military stores.

SIXTHLY, That all woollen cloth, blankets, linning, shoes, stockings, hats and other articles of cloathing suitable for the army, heretofore imported, which are or shall be seized and taken by order of authority for the use of the army, shall be estimated at the above rate with the addition of the stated allowance for land carriage (if any there be) to the place where taken.

SEVENTHLY, That the price of the following articles at the first port of delivery, or place of manufacture within these States, shall not exceed the rates to them affixed respectively. Good West India rum three dollars p^r gallon by wholesale. Good merchantable N. E. rum two dollars p^r gallon by d^o. Best muscovado sugars thirty three dollars and one third of a dollar p^r hundred gross w^t, and all other sugars in usual proportion according to quality. Best molasses one dollar and half p^r gallon by wholesale. Coffee not to exceed three fourths of a dollar *per lb.* by the hundred. Good merchantable Geneva not to exceed two dollars per gallon. Good merchantable brandy two dollars per gallon. Good merchantable whiskey one dollar and one sixth per gallon. All other distill'd spirits not herein enumerated not exceeding two dollars p^r gallon.

EIGHTHLY, That no trader, retailer or vender of foreign goods, wares or merchandize, shall be allowed more than at the rate of 25 *per cent.* advance upon the price such goods, wares, or merchandize are or shall be first sold for by the importer or captor, agreeable to this regulation, with the addition only of the cost and charge of transportation by land at the rate of five twelveths of a dollar p^r mile for transporting twenty hundred neat w^t, from the first port of delivery to the place where the same shall be sold and delivered by retail.

NINTHLY, That innholders be not allowed more than 50 *per cent.* advance on the wholesale price of all liquors, or other foreign articles herein stated, and by them sold in small quantities, allowing as aforesaid for charges of transportation; and for all other articles of entertainment, refreshment, and forage, not to exceed 75 *per cent.* advance on the prices the same were at in the same place in the year 1774.

TENTHLY, That the articles enumerated in the following table shall not be sold or disposed of at higher prices in the respective States and places therein named, than at the rate set down and affixed to such articles, respectively, with the addition only for the stated allowance for land carriage, if any there shall be. The said sums being estimated in lawful money at six shillings p^r dollar.

Resolved, That it be recommended to the several Legislatures of the States, that they cause the laws they may enact to carry these resolves into execution to be in force from and after the 20th of March next, with such penalties annexed as they may judge effectual.

The committee appointed to prepare a letter to the Hono^{ble} Continental Congress reported a draught which, being read and amended, was approved and ordered to be signed by the President, and is as follows, (*viz:*)

NEW HAVEN, Jany 30th, 1778.

Sir—The Commissioners appointed by the several States of New Hampshire, Massachusetts Bay, Rhode Island and Providence Plantations, Connecticut, New York, New Jersey, and Pennsylvania, in pursuance of a resolution of the Honble Congress of the 22^d November last, have convened at New Haven in Connecticut, and proceeded upon the business assigned them of regulating the price of labour &c. We now enclose a copy of our proceedings.

The Congress must be sensible that it is almost impossible, to fix the price of labour, produce and foreign commodities, in such a manner as to give sat-

Viz.	State of New Hampshire.	State of Massachusetts Bay.	State of Rhode Island and Providence p^{ln}	States of Connecticut, New York, New Jersey, Pennsylvania.
Good merchantable wheat, peas and white beans p^r bushel.	13s.	12s.		9s. 9d.
Merchantable wheat flour p^r hundred, gross w^t.	36s.	33s. 4d.		27s.
Merchantable rye or rie meal p^r bushel.	7s. 6d.	7s.		6s. 6d.
Merchantable indian corn or indian meal p^r bushel.	5s. 6d.	5s. 3d.		4s. 6d.
Merchantable oats p^r bushel	3s. 9d.	3s. 6d.		3s.
Pork well fatted and weighing from 110lb to 150lb p^r hog.	8d.	7¼d.		5½d.
D^o weighing from 150lb to 200lb	8¼d.	7½d.		6d.
D^o weighing more than 200lb p^r hog, p^r lb.	9d.	8d.		6½d.
American made cheese of the best quality.	10d.	10d. | 9d.		9d.

Through all the States above named.

Best grass fed beef with hide and tallow.	35s.	P^r hundred w^t, and in proportion for that of an inferior quality.
Good butter p^r the firkin or cask	1s. 3d.	} per lb.
D^o by the single lb or small quantity.	1s. 4d.	
Raw Hides p^r lb.	4½d.	and other skins in usual proportion.
Good well tanned sole leather.	2s. p^r lb	Skins and all kinds of curried leather in due proportion.
Mens neat's leather shoes of the common sort.	12s. p^r p^r	
Mens calf skin shoes of the best quality.	15s.	P^r pair. Women and children's shoes in due proportion.
Bloomery iron at the place of manufacture.	£48.0.0	p^r tun, and in proportion for a less quantity.
Refined iron at the place of manufacture.	£56.0.0	p^r tun, and in proportion for a less quantity.
Pig iron at the place of manufacture.	£18.0.0	p^r tun.
Best American manufactured steel fit for edge tools.	2s.	p^r lb
Common steel manufactured in America.	1s. 4d.	p^r lb
Best stall beef with the hide and tallow.	48s.	p^r hundred w^t, and in proportion for that of an inferior quality untill the 1st day of July next.

isfaction to the many persons interested; hence must arise great jealousies, disputes, and contentions, and there will be great danger that the end and design of such a measure will be frustrated, unless the other measures recommended by Congress are adopted.

We are, therefore, sincerely glad that Congress have accompanied the resolution above referred to, with sundry others which, if complied with, must produce the happiest effects; particularly that Congress have thought it necessary that the quantity of money in circulation should be reduced, and for this purpose have recommended to the United States to effect this salutary and necessary measure by taxation, by refraining from any further emissions of bills of credit, and calling in by loan or taxes and cancelling the paper money they have already emitted. Permit us to express our sentiments on this occation, that unless their three last measures are complied with, and vigorously carried into execution, the regulation of the prices of labour, produce and merchandize will be fruitless; it will be to no purpose; in short, it will be impossible to carry it into execution, no truth being more evident, as the Congress justly observes, than that where the quantity of money of any denomination exceeds what is useful for a medium of commerce, its comparative value must be proportionably reduced, consequently the price of goods must proportionably rise; and in case government, under such circumstances, and when the medium of trade is in such a fluctuating situation, should without taking any other measures, to give stability to the medium, fix the prices of goods, the people would justly complain; as in effect it would be obliging them to sell their produce and merchandize for less than the real value. Our proceeding, therefore, in regulating prices are founded on a *full dependence* that the other measures aforesaid will be *immediately* complied with by the several States; and we beg leave to submit it to the consideration of Congress, whether it will not be necessary for this purpose to renew and enforce their recommendations to the United States, to exert themselves immediately to stop the currency of all the paper bills emitted by them respectively, and which are not upon interest, and to redeem them by giving treasurers notes upon interest, and by taxes, to refrain from making any further emissions, and by taxation to reduce the quantity of continental bills as fast as possible. We beg leave to observe that in the course of our deliberation we have found ourselves under the necessity of deviating from the letter of the fifth resolve of Congress of the 22^d November last, by excepting out of the regulation certain articles of foreign produce. Our reasons are as follows: The charge and risk of importing them is so great, various and uncertain, as to render it very difficult; and tho' it appeared to Congress that military stores only should be excepted, yet many of these articles we have excepted, being absolutely necessary for the army, such indeed as the army cannot possibly do without, and as some few others of them are so necessary for the good people of these States that, in order the better to reconcile them to the regulation we have recommended, we thought it indispensably necessary that every encouragement should be given, and every impediment to the importation of them removed, and we hope it will meet with your approbation.

Permit us to mention that the Convention have been informed of some abuses in the departments of commissary, quarter-master and forage-master: many deputies being dispersed throughout the country, it has been suggested that they are idly interfering with each other in purchases and bidding on the other, and by no means so industrious and careful in securing and saving from waste the articles purchased as they ought to be.

Before we conclude, we beg leave to mention that the public have never yet been notified when the continental bills are to be redeemed, except the two first emissions, their being at an uncertainty about this matter has been complained of as having a tendency to lessen the credit of the bills, whereas if they were to be ascertained when they were to be redeemed, especially if it was at a short period, it would give them a confidence in the money and greatly tend to establish the currency.

In the name and by order of the Convention,

I am your most Obed^t. Hum^l Servt,

THO^s. CUSHING, Pres^d.

The Hon^l Henry Laurens, Esq.

Congressional Resolution Recommending the
Promotion of Morals, October 12, 1778

The Continental Congress did not have the power to directly promote religion and morality in the nation at large. However, it did have the power to recommend that the states do so, and it utilized this power from time to time, as evidenced here.

On motion, That Congress come to the following resolutions:

"Whereas true religion and good morals are the only solid foundations of public liberty and happiness:

"*Resolved,* That it be, and it is hereby earnestly recommended to the several states, to take the most effectual measures for the encouragement thereof, and for the suppressing of theatrical entertainments, horse racing, gaming, and such other diversions as are productive of idleness, dissipation, and a general depravity of principles and manners.

"*Resolved,* That all officers in the army of the United States, be, and hereby are strictly enjoined to see that the good and wholesome rules provided for the discountenancing of prophaneness and vice, and the preservation of morals among the soldiers, are duly and punctually observed."

The previous question, being moved on the preamble and the first resolution, passed in the negative.

The question being then put on the first resolution with the preamble, and the yeas and nays being required by Mr. [Daniel] Roberdeau,

New Hampshire,			*Connecticut,*		
Mr. Bartlett,	ay } ay		Mr. Sherman,	ay	ay
Massachusetts Bay,			Ellsworth,	ay	
Mr. S. Adams,	ay		*New Jersey,*		
Gerry,	ay } ay		Mr. Witherspoon,	ay	ay
Holten,	ay		Scudder,	ay	
Rhode Island,					
Mr. Marchant,	ay } ay				

Source: *JCC,* 12: 1001–3.

Pennsylvania,
Mr. R. Morris,	ay	
Roberdeau,	ay	ay
J. Smith,	no	
Clingan,	ay	

Maryland,
Mr. Henry,	no	*

Virginia,
Mr. Harvie,	no	
R. H. Lee,	ay	div.
M. Smith,	ay	
Griffin,	no	

North Carolina,
Mr. Harnett,	no	no
Williams,	no	

South Carolina,
Mr. Laurens,	ay	ay
Mathews,	ay	

Georgia,
Mr. Walton,	ay	
Telfair,	no	ay
Langworthy,	ay	

So it was resolved in the affirmative.

On the question put to agree to the second resolution,

The yeas and nays being required by Mr. G[ouverneur] Morris,

New Hampshire,
Mr. Bartlett,	ay	ay

Massachusetts Bay,
Mr. S. Adams,	ay	
Gerry,	ay	ay
Holten,	ay	

Rhode Island,
Mr. Marchant,	ay	ay

Connecticut,
Mr. Sherman,	ay	ay
Ellsworth,	ay	

New York,
Mr. Lewis,	ay	div.
G. Morris,	no	

New Jersey,
Mr. Witherspoon,	ay	
Elmer,	ay	ay
Scudder,	ay	

Pennsylvania,
Mr. R. Morris,	ay	
Reed,	ay	
Roberdeau,	ay	ay
James Smith,	no	
Clingan,	ay	

Delaware,
Mr. M'Kean,	ay	ay

Maryland,
Mr. Henry,	ay	*

Virginia,
Mr. Harvie,	no	
R. H. Lee,	ay	div.
M. Smith,	ay	
Griffin,	no	

North Carolina,
Mr. Penn,	ay	
Harnett,	no	no
Williams,	no	

South Carolina,
Mr. Laurens,	ay	ay
Mathews,	ay	

Georgia,
Mr. Walton,	ay	
Telfair,	no	ay
Langworthy,	ay	

So it was resolved in the affirmative.

On motion to re-consider the first resolution, the question being put, and the yeas and nays being required by Mr. G[ouverneur] Morris,

New Hampshire,
Mr. Bartlett,   no } no

Massachusetts Bay,
Mr. S. Adams,   no ⎫
Gerry,   no ⎬ no
Holten,   no ⎭

Rhode Island,
Mr. Marchant,   no } no

Connecticut,
Mr. Sherman,   no ⎫ no
Ellsworth,   no ⎭

New York,
Mr. Lewis,   ay ⎫ ay
G. Morris,   ay ⎭

New Jersey,
Mr. Witherspoon,   no ⎫
Elmer,   no ⎬ no
Scudder,   no ⎭

Pennsylvania,
Mr. R. Morris,   no ⎫
Reed,   no ⎪
Roberdeau,   no ⎬ no
James Smith,   ay ⎪
Clingan,   no ⎭

Delaware,
Mr. M'Kean,   no } no

Maryland,
Mr. Henry,   ay } *

Virginia,
Mr. Harvie,   ay ⎫
R. H. Lee,   no ⎪ div.
M. Smith,   no ⎬
Griffin,   ay ⎭

North Carolina,
Mr. Penn,   ay ⎫
Harnett,   ay ⎬ ay
Williams,   ay ⎭

South Carolina,
Mr. Laurens,   no ⎫ no
Mathews,   no ⎭

Georgia,
Mr. Walton,   no ⎫
Telfair,   ay ⎬ no
Langworthy,   no ⎭

So it passed in the negative.

Letter to Benjamin Trumbull, October 20, 1778

PHILADELPHIA

Benjamin Trumbull (1735–1820) was a Congregational minister from New Haven.

Dear Sir

I received Yours of the 5th Instant by the Post. It would have been very Agreeable to me to have had an interview with you when at New Haven but my Stay there was So Short that I could not wait on you at your House. The affair of our Finances is in a difficult Situation, one Committee has made report on the Subject to which Several amendments were proposed, and the whole is recommitted, the last Committee have not reported, and what will be Ultimately concluded on is uncertain—it is generally Agreed that a time not exceeding twenty years Should be fixed for the redemption of the whole by annual taxes, tis thought by Some that the taxes Should be highest at first and decrease as the money appreciates. Others think they Should be equal as the ability of the Country to pay will increase by means of the increase of Numbers and wealth as fast as the Bills will appreciate. How to lessen the quantity in circulation while the war continues is the greatest difficulty, it has been proposed to Stop the currency of so many emissions as we wish to sink and give notes on Interest for them as our State did their Bills. Others think this would be a dangerous experiment. Some think Sufficient loans might be voluntarily obtained if the lenders were Assured that they Should be paid an equivalent in value, & that the Bills brought in Should be burnt. Some think that it would be difficult to ascertain the comparative value at the time of lending and time of payment. If we had a foreign loan of 4 or 5 million pounds Sterling in Europe on which to draw Bills we might Sell them at the current Exchange & in that way draw in & sink the currency at the rate it has been issued out: but in our present Situation it is uncertain whether Such a loan can be procured as the Security to the lenders would depend on our Supporting our Independency. It would be easy to obtain any Sums we might want if Peace

Source: Paul H. Smith et al., eds., *Letters of Delegates to Congress* (Washington, D.C.: Government Printing Office, 1985), 11: 92–93.

was settled with Great Britain and the independency of the States acknowledged by the British Government. Till then I think we must relye on our own resources. And if we can provide Such Sinking funds by taxes as will prevent further depreciation, & procure a Gradual appreciation it is as much as we can expect at present—that proper measures ought to be adopted without further delay I fully agree with you, As to the mode of doing justice to Creditors I hope the States will be able [to] devise some way consistent with the general good; there are many persons who are good Friends to our cause who have Suffered & do Still Suffer greatly & Some Orphans; some who have rented houses & other real Estates for Years are reduced to great Straits by the depreciation, and ought to be relieved in Some way or other. Certainly debtors can pay an equivalent in value as easy as tho' the money had not depreciated. I have now nothing to lose in that way but wish that none may have cause to complain of the want of public justice. We have no news here.

I am with due regards to Your Self & family, Your humble Servant,

Roger Sherman

Letter from Roger Sherman and Benjamin Huntington to Jonathan Trumbull Sr., July 22, 1780

PHILADELPHIA

This letter from Connecticut's delegates to the Continental Congress was written in Sherman's hand but signed by both representatives.

Sir,

The Journals of Congress for June last are Printed and will be forwarded to your Excellency in the usual Channel together with such Copies as are ordered Immediately.

It is with Concern we observe the Exigences of the Public have been such as obliged our State to Issue large Emissions of Paper Bills which with what will Issue in Pursuance of the Resolutions of the 18th of March last may Endanger the Public Credit. The only Way to avoid this Evil is speedily to Draw in those Bills by Taxes and not Suffer them on any Account to Re-Issue.

Paper Money does it's Office when it goes out in Payment and ought to be among the People as a Medium of Trade no longer than to find it's Way into their Pockets, and like private Security should be destroyed when Returned into the Office it Issued from, This is doing Business in Sight of the People and Every Man who Pays his Tax knows he does it Discharge of much of his Public Debt. But to Re-Issue Bills taken in by Loans & Taxes Accumulates the Public Debt in a Way not open to the Inspection of the People. They see the Bills are not Redeemed and are told they never will be. The Credit of the State is Scrupled and Depreciation Ensues. The People loose their Confidence in Government, The Laws are Enervated, Military Opperations Prevented, Justice Impeeded, Trade Embarrased, the Morals of the People Corrupted, Men of Integrity in Office Abused and Resigning whilst Peculators Ride in Coaches. These Evils and the Sources from whence they arise, so lately Experienced all serve to Point out the Way to avoid them in future. The Design of Congress in Limiting the Amount of Circulating Bills within the United States will be Wholly Defeated by Emissions from Particular States unless

Source: Paul H. Smith et al., eds., *Letters of Delegates to Congress* (Washington, D.C.: Government Printing Office, 1988), 15: 484.

their Amount is Limited within the Bounds and Issued in Lieu of the Quotas Assigned by Congress, and be in Fact drawn in before the General Currency Issues.

Congress have Established a new Regulation of the Quarter Master's Department, it's now in the Press and will be Transmitted to your Excellency as Early as Possible, it is Expected this new arrangement of that Department will save great Expence to the Public.

We are with the greatest Respect, your Excellency's Most Huml Sevt,

Roger Sherman

Benj Huntington

Letter to Oliver Ellsworth, September 5, 1780

PHILADELPHIA

A major political and legal figure in Connecticut, Oliver Ellsworth (1745–1807) was a longtime ally of Roger Sherman. He and Sherman are credited with crafting the Connecticut Compromise in the Federal Convention of 1787. John Adams reported "that the late Chief Justice Ellsworth told me that he had made Mr. Sherman his model in his youth."[1]

I received your letter of the 20th ultimo yesterday. I wrote you by Brown the 2d Instant & have nothing new to add. We are in hopes our loss at the southward is not so great as was apprehended by accounts from N. York. Tis said, that they did not view it as a total defeat of our army, but that the militia gave way & they pursued the continental Troops some miles, and made some prisoners. I hope next news to hear that most of the continental Troops have escaped.

The affair of Howel's is fully represented to the Governor. He was recommended by Dr. Smith who has been acquainted with him from his Infancy. Howel lodged at Mrs. Cheeseman's during his stay here. He appears to be a modest agreeable young gentleman. He obtained his goods by drawing a prize in a British State Lottery. We understood that they amounted to some thousands of pounds N. York currency but not so much as three thousand Sterling. He told me that he should sell them for continental currency, the New Bills, or any money current in these States. I understood that he intended to dispose of his goods and settle in this city to practice Physic.

No person is more against carrying on a trade with the Enemy or any person within their lines than I am. Yet I think every citizen of these States who is within their power has a right to claim protection from the States if he can

Source: Historical Society of Pennsylvania autograph collection, collection no. 0022A, Historical Society of Pennsylvania.

1. John Adams to John Sanderson, November 19, 1822, in *Biography of the Signers to the Declaration of Independence*, ed. Robert Waln and John Sanderson (Philadelphia: R. W. Pomeroy, 1822), 3: 298.

escape with his effects, and ought to meet with every encouragement if he has not by any crime forfeited the protection of his country. I make no doubt that Doctor Howel had an honest intention to risk his Interest with these States, and to contribute his proportion toward carrying on the war—in case he met with kind treatment—but he may be prosecuted to desperation. I hope justice will be done to him & the public.

The Assembly of this State are now met, and I hope they will take measures to introduce the new money into circulation in good credit. The form for printing the Bill is so worn that it became necessary to make a new one, which is now preparing. While the [press?] is employed in finishing the quotas of Massachusetts & Connecticut, the next will be for this State, Virginia & Rhode Island. If the States dont immediately issue the Bills, all our operations must stop, for there is no money in the Treasury nor any other resource.

A new arrangement of the hospitals on an Economical plan will take place in a few days.

I hear that Mr. Peabody is near his end, being in the last stage of a consumption, at Morristown.

There are complaints of the want of meat in the army which I did not expect at this season.

I am with great respect,
Your humble servant,
Roger Sherman

P.S. It is of great importance that the people of the States should have the fullest confidence in Congress, I never knew better harmony among the Several Members, than at present, nor more universal attention to the public good, & no appearance of party spirits. R.S.

Letter from John Sullivan to George Washington, July 2, 1781

PHILADELPHIA

A native of New Hampshire, John Sullivan (1740–95) served as a member of the first and second Continental Congresses and as a general under George Washington, then was returned to Congress in 1780. In this correspondence, he notes that Sherman opposed increasing the number of lashes that could be given to soldiers because of the "principles Laid Down in the Levitical Law" (a reference to Deuteronomy 25:3, "Forty stripes he may give him, and not exceed.")

Dear General

Though I have nothing Important to write your Excellency at This moment I take the Liberty by his Excellency the Chevalier de La Luzerne to assure you of my Earnest wishes for your Success against New York & That Every Effort of mine Shall be Employed while I remain in Congress to Second your attempt & to fulfil (or Even if possible to Anticipate) your wishes: my time in Congress will Soon Expire and my Domestic Concerns forbid my Suffering myself to be rechosen. Of Course the Service I may render to your operations must be within a few weeks in which time I Shall be happy to Employ myself in that useful manner. I Suppose that the Resolutions respecting the augmentations of the powers of a Court Martial have reached you. The Report of the Committee impowered the Court to Inflict five hundred Lashes But this was Rejected upon the principles Laid Down in the Levitical Law Strongly urged by Roger Shearman Esqr &ca & though a great majority of Congress were for it the Question was Lost for want of the assent of Seven States. This relation will Convince you of the Incompetence of Some Members in the American Senate as well as of the Absurdity of Some parts of the Confederation.

I have had the Honor of Seeing Mrs. Washington yesterday & to Day; She

Source: Paul H. Smith et al., eds., *Letters of Delegates to Congress* (Washington, D.C.: Government Printing Office, 1990), 17: 368–69.

was fatigued with her Journey & was Indisposed when She Arrived, but Seems perfectly recovered. Our news from the Southward Continue to be agreable & Seem to be as well Authenticated as possible without official Information.

I have the honor to be with the most perfect Esteem Dear Genl Your Excellencys Most obedient Servant,

Jno. Sullivan

Letter from Roger Sherman and Richard Law to Jonathan Trumbull Sr., October 25, 1781

PHILADELPHIA

This letter, written by Sherman and signed by both Sherman and Law, includes news of Congress's reaction to General Charles Cornwallis's surrender at Yorktown.

Sir

We have the honor now to transmit to Your Excellency An official Account of the Surrender of Lord Cornwallis and the Army under his Command. The dispatches from General Washington were received yesterday morning, and at two O'Clock in the afternoon Congress went in a body to the Lutheran Church, where Divine Service (Suitable to the Occasion) was performed, by the Reverend Mr. Duffield one of the Chaplains of Congress. The Supreme Executive Council & Assembly of this State, The Minister of France & his Secretary and a great number of the Citizens Attended. In the Evening the City was Illuminated. This great Event we hope will prove a happy presage of a Compleat Reduction of the British forces in these States, and prepare the way for the Establishment of an honorable Peace. We mentioned in our last that Mr. McKean had resigned the Chair. He was by a Unanimous Vote yesterday morning requested to resume it, and Act as President until the first Monday in Novr. next, which he has accepted.

We have the honor to be, with the highest Respect, Your Excellency's Most Obedient & very humble Servants,

Roger Sherman
Richard Law

Source: Paul H. Smith et al., eds., *Letters of Delegates to Congress* (Washington, D.C.: Government Printing Office, 1991), 18: 165.

Call for Prayer and Fasting, October 26, 1781

The following call for prayer was written by John Witherspoon (1723–94), a Scottish clergyman and president of the College of New Jersey (now Princeton University); Joseph Montgomery (1733–94), a Presbyterian minister from Pennsylvania; James Varnum (1748–89), a political and military leader from Massachusetts; and Sherman. The Continental and Confederation Congresses regularly issued calls for prayer and fasting, but this is the only one Sherman helped craft. The final draft was penned by Witherspoon. Strikethroughs indicate material removed from the draft by Congress.

The committee, consisting of Mr. Witherspoon, Mr. Montgomery, Mr. Varnum, Mr. Sherman, appointed to prepare a recommendation for setting apart a day of public thanksgiving and prayer, reported the draught of a proclamation, which was agreed to as follows:

PROCLAMATION

Whereas, it hath pleased Almighty God, the ~~supreme Disposer of all Events,~~ father of mercies, remarkably to assist and support the United States of America in their important struggle for liberty, against the long continued efforts of a powerful nation: it is the duty of all ranks to observe and thankfully acknowledge the interpositions of his Providence in their behalf. Through the whole of the contest, from its first rise to this time, the influence of divine Providence may be clearly perceived in many signal instances, of which we mention but a few.

In revealing the councils of our enemies, when the discoveries were seasonable and important, and the means seemingly inadequate or fortuitous; in preserving and even improving the union of the several states, on the breach of which our enemies placed their greatest dependence; in increasing the number, and adding to the zeal and attachment of the friends of Liberty; in granting remarkable deliverances, and blessing us with the most signal success, when affairs seemed to have the most discouraging appearance; in raising up for us a powerful and generous ally, in one of the first of the European powers; in confounding the councils of our enemies, and suffering them to pursue such measures as have most directly

Source: *JCC*, 21: 1074–76.

contributed to frustrate their own desires and expectations; above all, in making their extreme cruelty ~~of their officers and soldiers~~ to the inhabitants of those states, when in their power, and their savage devastation of property, the very means of cementing our union, and adding vigor to every effort in opposition to them.

And as we cannot help leading the good people of these states to a retrospect on the events which have taken place since the beginning of the war, so we ~~beg~~ recommend in a particular manner ~~that they may observe and acknowledge~~ to their observation, the goodness of God in the year now drawing to a conclusion: in which

~~A mutiny in the American Army was not only happily appeased but became in its issue a pleasing and undeniable proof of the unalterable attachment of the people in general to the cause of liberty since great and real grievances only made them tumultuously seek redress while they abhorred the thoughts of going over to the enemy, in which~~ the Confederation of the United States has been completed ~~by the accession of all without exception~~ in which there have been so many instances of prowess and success in our armies; particularly in the southern states, where, notwithstanding the difficulties with which they had to struggle, they have recovered the whole country which the enemy had overrun, leaving them only a post or two ~~upon~~ on or near the sea: in which we have been so powerfully and effectually assisted by our allies, while in all the conjunct operations the most perfect ~~union and~~ harmony has subsisted in the allied army: in which there has been so plentiful a harvest, and so great abundance of the fruits of the earth of every kind, as not only enables us easily to supply the wants of the army, but gives comfort and happiness to the whole people: and in which, after the success of our allies by sea, a General of the first Rank, with his whole army, has been captured by the allied forces under the direction of our ~~illustrious~~ Commander in Chief.

It is therefore recommended to the several states to set apart the 13th day of December next, to be religiously observed as a Day of Thanksgiving and Prayer; that all the people may assemble on that day, with grateful hearts, to celebrate the praises of our gracious Benefactor; to confess our manifold sins; to offer up our most fervent supplications to the God of all grace, that it may please Him to pardon our offences, and incline our hearts for the future to keep all his laws; to comfort and relieve all our brethren who are in distress or captivity; to prosper our husbandmen, and give success to all engaged in lawful commerce; to impart wisdom and integrity to our counsellors, judgment and fortitude to our officers and soldiers; to protect and prosper our illustrious ally, and favor our united exertions for the speedy establishment of a safe, honorable and lasting peace; to bless all seminaries of learning; and cause the knowledge of God to cover the earth, as the waters cover the seas.[1]

---

1. This report, in the writing of John Witherspoon, is in the *Papers of the Continental Congress,* No. 24, folio 463.

Letter to Lyman Hall, January 20, 1784
ANNAPOLIS

In his last year in the Confederation Congress, Sherman voted to ratify the Treaty of Paris before leaving the body for good on June 4, 1784. Lyman Hall (1724–90), originally from Connecticut, became an important political leader in Georgia.

Sir

I Sincerely congratulate you upon the return of Peace, whereby the rights we have long contended for are fully established on very honorable and beneficial terms.

The definitive Treaty of peace between Great Britain and the United States was ratified in Congress last week, and the ratification forwarded to New York to go by a French Packet which was to sail this day. It was unanimously ratified by Nine States, no more being represented, a Proclamation & recommendations pursuant thereto have been agreed to, and ordered to be forwarded to the Several States by the Secretary. There are but 8 States now represented, one of the Members from Delaware went home last Saturday, on account of Sickness in his family. There are Several important matters to be transacted, interesting to all the States. I hope that members will come on from Georgia as soon as possible. The impost on foreign goods recommended by Congress for raising a revenue for payment of the interest of the monies borrowed on the Credit of the United States, is fully complied with by the States of Massachusets, New Jersey, Pennsylvania, Delaware, Maryland and Virginia. New Hampshire has likewise Agreed to it in a Committee of the whole but the act was not compleated when the Delegate from that State came away. The Assemblys of Connecticut, and New York are now sitting. Congress are in hopes to adjourn by the first of May, and have a recess 'till next fall, in case all the States transmit their acts for enabling Congress to levy and collect the Duties seasonably for them to make an ordinance for carrying it into effect, that being a matter of the utmost importance for Supporting the National Credit of the

Source: Paul H. Smith et al., eds., *Letters of Delegates to Congress* (Washington, D.C.: Government Printing Office, 1994), 21: 296–97.

united States, and doing justice to the public Creditors both at home and in Europe; and I apprehend it will be impracticable to raise a Sufficient revenue in the ordinary way of taxing. Raising money by imposts, takes it at the fountain head, and the consumer pays it insensibly and without murmering. I wish the result of your State on that requis[it]ion may be transmitted as soon as possible. The disposition and Settlement of the western territory is another object that will come under the consideration of Congress. The State of Virginia has Ceded to the United States all the Lands claimed by that State North-West of the Ohio on terms acceptable to Congress.

Enclosed is a Copy of the act of Massachusetts for enabling Congress to levy an impost which I think is well Guarded. I have also enclosed a Letter from Governor Trumbull on public Service. I am with Great Esteem & respect, Your humble Servant,

Roger Sherman

[*P.S.*] One of the members of Congress had the Massachusetts act above referred to but has Mislaid it so that I cant obtain a Copy, but I will transmit it when it comes to hand.   R.S.

The Continental
and Confederation
Congresses and the
Articles of Confederation

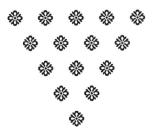

Sherman served 1,543 days in the Continental and Confederation Congresses, more than all but four other men.[1] He was intimately involved with virtually every significant policy and document approved by these bodies. The previous chapter focused on Sherman's contributions relevant to the War for American Independence. This one highlights his ongoing involvement in the Wyoming Valley and Vermont controversies and his role in drafting and defending the Articles of Confederation.

Students of the American founding rarely treat the Articles of Confederation as anything other than a failed constitution.[2] Yet its drafters did not expect it to fail, and they approached their work quite seriously. Although the Articles were eventually replaced, under them Congress won a war with Great Britain

1. John G. Rommel, *Connecticut's Yankee Patriot: Roger Sherman* (Hartford: American Revolution Bicentennial Commission of Connecticut, 1979), 28.

2. A major exception to this generalization is the historian Merrill Jensen's *The Articles of Confederation: An Interpretation of the Social-Constitutional History of the American Revolution, 1774–1781* (Madison: University of Wisconsin Press, 1940), which provides an excellent overview of the creation and ratification of the document.

and passed one of the most important pieces of legislation in American history—the Northwest Ordinance (1787).

On June 11, 1776, Congress appointed Sherman, Benjamin Franklin, John Adams, Thomas Jefferson, and Robert Livingston to a committee to write the Declaration of Independence. The next day, it selected one delegate from each state to be on a committee charged with preparing the "form of a confederation to be entered into between these colonies."[3] Sherman was assigned to this committee, along with Josiah Bartlett, Samuel Adams, Stephen Hopkins, Robert Livingston, John Dickinson, Thomas McKean, Thomas Stone, Thomas Nelson, Joseph Hewes, Edward Rutledge, and Button Gwinnett.[4] The following day, Sherman, John Adams, Benjamin Harrison, James Wilson, and Edward Rutledge were elected to the Board of War and Ordinance—one of the busiest of all congressional committees. Note that only Sherman served on all three of these committees.[5]

John Dickinson wrote the first major draft of the Articles of Confederation. He did not do so in a vacuum, but unfortunately, few records of the committee's deliberations exist. We do know that the debates were serious, as indicated by a letter written by Josiah Bartlett noting that "[a]s it is a very important business, and some difficulties have arisen, I fear it will take some time before it will be finally settled."[6] The committee eventually came to a consensus, and on July 12 a draft of the Articles of Confederation in Dickinson's handwriting was submitted to Congress. This was printed and debated, amended significantly, and then reprinted on August 20. Because of the war, Congress did not address the Articles again until April 8, 1777. They were debated sporadically throughout the spring and summer, but it was not until that fall that Congress returned to the document in earnest. In November, one last committee consisting of Richard Henry Lee, James Duane, and James Lovell was appointed to put the text into its final form.

Both Dickinson's draft of the Articles and the final version provided for "one state, one vote." This issue was hotly contested, with some delegates arguing for representation based on population. Not surprisingly, this view was generally held by delegates from large states. Delegates from smaller states insisted on equality of representation, contending that the confederation was one of equal, sovereign states. Sherman suggested a compromise. According to John Adams, he

3. *JCC,* 5: 431.
4. Ibid., 433.
5. Ibid., 438.
6. Josiah Bartlett to John Langdon, June 17, 1776, in *The Papers of Josiah Bartlett,* ed. Frank C. Mevers (Hanover, N.H.: University Press of New England, 1979), 76.

thinks we ought not to vote according to numbers. We are representatives of States, not individuals. States of Holland. The consent of every one is necessary. Three Colonies would govern the whole, but would not have a majority of strength to carry those votes into execution. The vote should be taken two ways; call the Colonies, and call the individuals, and have a majority of both.[7]

Sherman's proposal exhibited a sound recognition that the new national government would need the support of both small and large states if it was to be successful. But the small states won the debate, and the Articles retained "one state, one vote," a victory that eventually contributed to the collapse of the confederation. However, Sherman's idea resurfaced at the Constitutional Convention and was eventually adopted as the Connecticut Compromise.

On November 17, 1777, after extensive debates about sovereignty, western lands, and taxes, Congress approved the final version of the Articles of Confederation and sent them to the states for ratification. Maryland refused to accept them until all of the states with western claims agreed to cede them to Congress. Once Virginia, the last holdout, surrendered its claims, Maryland agreed to ratify the Articles. They went into effect on March 1, 1781.[8]

One of the most important attacks on the Articles of Confederation was made by Pelatiah Webster in his pamphlet *A Dissertation on the Political Union and Constitution of the Thirteen United States, of North-America*, published under the pseudonym "A Citizen of Philadelphia" in 1783. Sherman, under the pseudonym "A Connecticut Farmer," responded with *Remarks on a Pamphlet Entitled "A Dissertation on the Political Union and Constitution of the Thirteen United States of North America by a Citizen of Philadelphia"* . . .[9] Surprisingly, prior to the publication of *Roger Sherman and the Creation of the American Republic* (2013), no scholar had ever attributed this pamphlet to him, even though Joseph Sabin and Charles Evans agree that he wrote it.[10]

In his pamphlet, Sherman made a brief digression where he criticized the

7. Jensen, *Articles*, 141; Adams, *Works of John Adams*, 2: 499.

8. Jensen, *Articles*, 161–238.

9. The full title is *Remarks on a Pamphlet Entitled "A Dissertation on the Political Union and Constitution of the Thirteen United States of North America by a Citizen of Philadelphia" With some brief OBSERVATIONS, Whether all the Western Lands, not actually purchased or conquered by the Crown of GREAT BRITAIN, antecedent to the late Cession, made to the Thirteen United States of NORTH-AMERICA, ought not to be considered as ceded to the Thirteen States* jointly—*And whether all the confiscated Estates of those People, by some termed* Loyalists, *are to be considered as forfeited to the States in which they were resident, or to all the States included in the Confederation.*

10. On Sherman's authorship see Joseph Sabin, *Bibliotecha Americana: A Dictionary of Books Relating to America* (New York: Sabin, 1891), 19: 461; Charles Evans, *American Bibliography* (New York: Columbia Press, 1890), 6: 326; and Hall, *Roger Sherman and the Creation of the American Republic*, 73–77.

recent decision by a commission created under the Articles of Confederation that sided with Pennsylvania over Connecticut in the Wyoming Valley dispute. He offered a stirring argument about the right of the "original natives" to sell their land to whomever they wished, in this case the Susquehannah Company. The argument seems out of place because Webster did not mention the controversy in his pamphlet, but he had written about the issue elsewhere, and he and Sherman had corresponded about it. The digression is significant as it prompted Webster to write a friend noting that "Mr. Sherman of Connecticut has replied to my pamphlet, being displeased with my views concerning the western lands. I enclose you a copy of his pamphlet."[11] This letter is a critical piece of evidence identifying Sherman as "A Connecticut Farmer."

11. Sabin, *Bibliotecha Americana*, 461. See also Roger Sherman to John Franklin, February 21, 1784, in *Susquehannah Company Papers*, 7: 364–65; Pelatiah Webster to Roger Sherman, April 20, 1784, in Ibid., 7: 392–93.

Letter to Volkert P. Douw, November 24, 1775

PHILADELPHIA

Volkert P. Douw (1720–1801) of Albany, New York, was appointed Indian commissioner for the Northern Department in July 1775.

Sir

I Suppose the President has transmitted to you the resolutions of the Congress on the Several matters mentioned in Your letter. I would only inform You That in Settling Mr. Deans account of past Services and expences, nothing was allowed him on account of what he paid of Mr. Spencer's expences who travelled with him among the Indians, but as you mentioned nothing of it in your letter, that matter was left to be settled between him and Mr. Spencer, or by the Commissioners.

Mr. Dean Informed that said Spencer had Sometime past been employed as a blacksmith among the Indians and that Some of them were desirous that he Should come and reside among them again, that he understands their language which is a material circumstance in favour of employing him if he is otherwise qualified & willing to undertake, but that is left with the Commissioners. It is important that who ever are employed among them Should be persons of a good Moral Character, friendly to American libertys and to the Missionaries that reside among them. I have no doubt but that the Commissioners will pay due attention to every thing in their department which may conduce to the public good. Mr. Timothy Edwards of Stockbridge is appointed a Commissioner instead of Major Hawley who declined the Service. I am Sir with due regards Your humble Servant

Roger Sherman

Source: Paul H. Smith et al., eds., *Letters of Delegates to Congress* (Washington, D.C.: Government Printing Office, 1977), 2: 384.

Letters to Zebulon Butler, 1776

PHILADELPHIA

Zebulon Butler (1731–95) was an important leader of the Connecticut settlers in the disputed Wyoming Valley. He served in the Connecticut General Assembly from 1774 to 1776 and as a lieutenant colonel and colonel in the War for Independence. Tensions between settlers from Pennsylvania and Connecticut had become so high by 1775 that violence erupted and two people were killed.

January 19, 1776

Sir,

The enclosed Paper contains several resolutions of the Congress and an Act of the Assembly of Connecticut, Colo. Dyer informs me that he Sent Copies of the Resolves of Congress immediately after they were passed to you and to the Magistrates in the County of Northumberland. We have had an Account of an attack on our people by Some of the Pennsylvanians who were repulsed with the loss of two men killed, but have heard nothing from the Connecticut people relative to that Action or whether they Sustained any loss. There is a report here that your people have given Some disturbance to the Settlers under Pennsylvania, I Should be Glad of a particular account from you of the Situation of affairs relative to that unhappy controversy which tends to weaken the Union of the Colonies at the present alarming Crisis. I hope you will do all in your power to prevent any disturbance being given to the Settlers under Pennsylvania by our people and that the resolutions of the Congress be duly observed. You will observe that the Assembly of Connecticut have Shortened the western limit of Westmoreland. I would advise that no Jurisdiction be exercised over the Settlers under Pennsylvania with in the limits of P. Town if any be contrary to their mind. Colo. Dyer and Mr. Dean have left Congress,

Source: Paul H. Smith et al., eds., *Letters of Delegates to Congress* (Washington, D.C.: Government Printing Office, 1978), 3: 115–16, 283–84; 5: 38.

the time they were appointed for being expired, and Oliver Wolcot and Saml. Huntington Esqrs. are now attending in their Stead. You will observe that the Congress have recommended that all the effects taken and detained from any persons on the Controverted lands be restored, it will be proper to apply to the Magistrates who took Cognizance of that matter for restitution or to the Sheriff who had the Goods in Custody, and if they are not restored that the Case be represented to the Congress and if any thing hath been taken from the people of Pennsylvania by the Connecticut people that the same be restored. I am sir with due regards, Your humble Servant,

Roger Sherman

February 19, 1776

Sir

I wrote to You the 19th of January last & enclosed a Newspaper containing Several resolutions of the Congress and an Act of the General Assembly of Connecticut, I now enclose an attested Copy of Said Act. Mr. Gore has been here some time expecting some direction from Governor Trumbull, in consequence of a message You Sent by Mr. Avery. I mentioned the matter to the Governor in a letter soon after Mr. Gore came here and have this Day receiv'd a letter from him, wherein is the following paragraph viz, "I was not made Acquainted with Mr. Gore's going to Congress, and expectations of any thing from me, relative to his Petition from the Committee of Westmoreland. Is there any thing more can be done by this Colony to quiet that contest than is already? It appears to me the Honorable Congress will lay their hand upon it, and do every thing needful that Justice may be done, and any future attacks on our peaceable people at that place prevented."

Mr. Gore has Concluded to leave the Petition and depositions with the President of the Congress, and return home to morrow. I dont know what further can be done by Congress, unless to recommend to the Assembly or Committee of Safety of this Colony to enquire into the matter and See that the resolutions of Congress already passed be duly observed. When the late attack happened the people in Northumberland County had not been made acquainted with the last resolutions of Congress past about the 20th of December. I hope they will desist from further Hostilities, and remain quiet, until the Controversy is decided. I wrote to You before, advising that application be made to the Magistrates or the Sheriff at Sunsbury or both for restitution of the Goods or effects taken at Warriours Run, and if not restored to complain to Congress. I dont hear of any preparations or intentions to give You further trouble but it is best to keep a good look out. I Shall take the first opportunity to inform what is done in Congress relative to the representation You have Sent by Mr. Gore—or of any future plots of the Land jobbers to disturb you, that may come to my knowledge. I Suppose the Militia with you are furnished with Arms and Ammunition according to Law, for your own & your Country's defence. We have no late news from England but all the accounts that we have had agree that the Ministry design to continue the war against us. We have large reinforcements marching to Canada, & we have accounts of some arriving there. General Lee with about 3000 Troops are in New York for the Defence of that City. I am Sir Your humble Servant

Roger Sherman

August 20, 1776

Sir

I received by Mr Swift Your Letter of the 6th Instant with the representation made by the Authority, Selectmen & Committee of Inspection concerning their apprehentions of trouble from the Indians, upon which we applied to Congress to raise Some Companies upon the Continental Establishment. The application was referred to the Delegates of Connecticut and Pennsylvania who reported for raising three Companies in the Town of Westmoland to be under the Command of a Major, which now lies before Congress not acted upon, as also a report for raising a Battallion in Pennsylvania for Defence of the Frontiers of that State. Since these applications were made we have had favourable accounts from the Indians that they refused to comply with the Solicitations of Butler & others to take up arms against the colonies and are determined to remain Neuter. I dont know what will be finally done about raising Troops to defend the Frontiers, but if any are raised in Pennsylvania 'tis probable You will be allowed to raise three Companies. We shall pay proper attention to the affair and if anything is done about it Shall give You the earliest Notice. I hope your people will have restitution of their effects taken at the Warriours run, after the State of Pennsylvania hath Settled a regular Government.

I remain Your humble Servant,

Roger

Articles of Confederation, 1778

Sherman was on the committee originally tasked with drafting the Articles of Confederation. He signed the Articles on July 9, 1778, along with delegates from the states that had agreed to ratify it. With Maryland's ratification, the new national constitution went into effect on March 1, 1781.

To all to whom these Presents shall come, we the undersigned Delegates of the States affixed to our names send greeting. Whereas the Delegates of the United States of America in Congress assembled did on the fifteenth day of November in the Year of our Lord One Thousand Seven Hundred and Seventy seven, and in the Second Year of the Independence of America agree to certain articles of Confederation and perpetual Union between the States of New Hampshire, Massachusetts-bay, Rhode Island and Providence Plantations, Connecticut, New York, New Jersey, Pennsylvania, Delaware, Maryland, Virginia, North-Carolina, South-Carolina, and Georgia in the Words following, viz. "Articles of Confederation and perpetual Union between the States of New Hampshire, Massachusetts-bay, Rhode Island and Providence Plantations, Connecticut, New-York, New-Jersey, Pennsylvania, Delaware, Maryland, Virginia, North-Carolina, South-Carolina and Georgia.

Art. I. The Stile of this confederacy shall be "The United States of America."

Art. II. Each State retains its sovereignty, freedom and independence, and every Power, Jurisdiction and right, which is not by this confederation expressly delegated to the United States, in Congress assembled.

Art. III. The said States hereby severally enter into a firm league of friendship with each other, for their common defence, the security of their Liberties, and their mutual and general welfare, binding themselves to assist each other, against all force offered to, or attacks made upon them, or any of them, on account of religion, sovereignty, trade, or any other pretence whatever.

Art. IV. The better to secure and perpetuate mutual friendship and inter-

Source: Bruce Frohnen, ed., *The American Republic: Primary Sources* (Indianapolis, Ind.: Liberty Fund, 2002), 200–204.

course among the people of the different States in this union, the free inhabitants of each of these States, paupers, vagabonds and fugitives from Justice excepted, shall be entitled to all privileges and immunities of free citizens in the several States; and the people of each State shall have free ingress and regress to and from any other State, and shall enjoy therein all the privileges of trade and commerce, subject to the same duties, impositions and restrictions as the inhabitants thereof respectively, provided that such restriction shall not extend so far as to prevent the removal of property imported into any State, to any other State of which the owner is an inhabitant; provided also that no imposition, duties or restriction shall be laid by any State, on the property of the United States, or either of them.

If any Person guilty of, or charged with treason, felony, or other high misdemeanor in any State, shall flee from Justice, and be found in any of the United States, he shall upon demand of the Governor or executive power, of the State from which he fled, be delivered up and removed to the State having jurisdiction of his offence.

Full faith and credit shall be given in each of these States to the records, acts and judicial proceedings of the courts and magistrates to every other State.

Art. V. For the more convenient management of the general interests of the United States, delegates shall be annually appointed in such manner as the legislature of each State shall direct, to meet in Congress on the first Monday in November, in every year, with a power reserved to each State, to recall its delegates, or any of them, at any time within the year, and to send others in their stead, for the remainder of the Year.

No State shall be represented in Congress by less than two, nor by more than seven Members; and no person shall be capable of being a delegate for more than three years in any term of six years; nor shall any person, being a delegate, be capable of holding any office under the United States, for which he, or another for his benefit receives any salary, fees or emolument of any kind.

Each State shall maintain its own delegates in a meeting of the States, and while they act as members of the committee of the States.

In determining questions in the United States, in Congress assembled, each State shall have one vote.

Freedom of speech and debate in Congress shall not be impeached or questioned in any Court, or place out of Congress, and the members of Congress shall be protected in their persons from arrests and imprisonments, during the time of their going to and from, and attendance of Congress, except for treason, felony, or breach of the peace.

Art. VI. No State without the consent of the United States in Congress assembled, shall send any embassy to, or receive any embassy from, or enter into any conference, agreement, or alliance or treaty with any King, Prince or State; nor shall any person holding any office of profit or trust under the United States, or any of them, accept of any present, emolument, office or title of any kind whatever from any King, Prince or foreign State; nor shall the United States in Congress assembled, or any of them, grant any title of nobility.

No two or more States shall enter into any treaty, confederation or alliance whatever between them, without the consent of the United States in Congress assembled, specifying accurately the purposes for which the same is to be entered into, and how long it shall continue.

No State shall lay any imposts or duties, which may interfere with any stipulations in treaties, entered into by the United States in Congress assembled, with any King, Prince or State, in pursuance of any treaties already proposed by Congress, to the courts of France and Spain.

No vessels of war shall be kept up in time of peace by any State, except such number only, as shall be deemed necessary by the United States in Congress assembled, for the defence of such State, or its trade; nor shall any body of forces be kept up by any State in time of peace, except such number only, as in the judgment of the United States, in Congress assembled, shall be deemed requisite to garrison the forts necessary for the defence of such State; but every State shall always keep up a well regulated and disciplined militia, sufficiently armed and accoutered, and shall provide and constantly have ready for use, in public stores, a due number of field pieces and tents, and a proper quantity of arms, ammunition and camp equipage.

No State shall engage in any war without the consent of the United States in Congress assembled, unless such State be actually invaded by enemies, or shall have received certain advice of a resolution being formed by some nation of Indians to invade such State, and the danger is so imminent as not to admit of a delay, till the United States in Congress assembled can be consulted: nor shall any State grant commissions to any ships or vessels of war, nor letters of marque or reprisal, except it be after a declaration of war by the United States in Congress assembled, and then only against the kingdom or State and the subjects thereof, against which war has been so declared, and under such regulations as shall be established by the United States in Congress assembled, unless such State be infested by pirates, in which case vessels of war may be fitted out for that occasion, and kept so long as the danger shall continue, or until the United States in Congress assembled shall determine otherwise.

Art. VII. When land-forces are raised by any State for the common defence, all officers of or under the rank of colonel, shall be appointed by the legislature of each State respectively by whom such forces shall be raised, or in such manner as such State shall direct, and all vacancies shall be filled up by the State which first made the appointment.

Art. VIII. All charges of war, and all other expenses that shall be incurred for the common defence or general welfare, and allowed by the United States in Congress assembled, shall be defrayed out of a common treasury, which shall be supplied by the several States, in proportion to the value of all land within each State, granted to or surveyed for any person, as such land and the buildings and improvements thereon shall be estimated according to such mode as the United States in Congress assembled, shall from time to time direct and appoint. The taxes for paying that proportion shall be laid and levied by the authority and direction of the legislatures of the several States within the time agreed upon by the United States in Congress assembled.

Art. IX. The United States in Congress assembled shall have the sole and exclusive right and power of determining on peace and war, except in the cases mentioned in the sixth article—of sending and receiving ambassadors—entering into treaties and alliances, provided that no treaty of commerce shall be made whereby the legislative power of the respective States shall be restrained from imposing such imposts and duties on foreigners, as their own people are subjected to, or from prohibiting the exportation or importation of any species of goods or commodities whatsoever—of establishing rules for deciding in all cases, what captures on land or water shall be legal, and in what manner prizes taken by land or naval forces in the service of the United States shall be divided or appropriated—of granting letters of marque and reprisal in times of peace— appointing courts for the trial of piracies and felonies committed on the high seas and establishing courts for receiving and determining finally appeals in all cases of captures, provided that no member of Congress shall be appointed a judge of any of the said courts.

The United States in congress assembled shall also be the last resort on appeal in all disputes and differences now subsisting or that hereafter may arise between two or more States concerning boundary, jurisdiction or any other cause whatever; which authority shall always be exercised in the manner following: Whenever the legislative or executive authority or lawful agent of any State in controversy with another shall present a petition to Congress, stating the matter in question and praying for a hearing, notice thereof shall be given by order of Congress to the legislative or executive authority of the other State in controversy, and a day assigned for the appearance of the parties by their lawful agents, who shall then be directed to appoint, by joint consent, commissioners or judges to constitute a court for hearing and determining the matter in question; but if they cannot agree, Congress shall name three persons out of each of the United States, and from the list of such persons each party shall alternately strike out one, the petitioners beginning, until the number shall be reduced to thirteen; and from that number not less than seven, nor more than nine names as Congress shall direct, shall in the presence of Congress be drawn out by lot, and the persons whose names shall be so drawn or any five of them, shall be commissioners or judges, to hear and finally determine the controversy, so always as a major part of the judges who shall hear the cause shall agree in the determination; and if either party shall neglect to attend at the day appointed, without showing reasons which Congress shall judge sufficient, or being present shall refuse to strike, the Congress shall proceed to nominate three persons out of each State, and the secretary of Congress shall strike in behalf of such party absent or refusing; and the judgment and sentence of the court to be appointed, in the manner before prescribed, shall be final and conclusive; and if any of the parties shall refuse to submit to the authority of such court, or to appear to defend their claim or cause, the court shall nevertheless proceed to pronounce sentence, or judgment, which shall in like manner be final and decisive, the judgment or sentence and other proceedings being in either case transmitted to Congress, and lodged among the Acts of Congress for the security of the parties concerned: provided that every commissioner, before he sits in judgment, shall take an oath to be administered by one of the judges of the supreme or superior court of the State, where the cause shall be tried, "well and truly to hear and determine the matter in question, according to the best of his judgment, without favor, affection or hope of reward": provided also that no State shall be deprived of territory for the benefit of the United States.

All controversies concerning the private right of soil claimed under different grants of two or more States, whose jurisdictions as they may respect such lands, and the States which passed such grants are adjusted, the said grants or either of them being at the same time claimed to have originated antecedent to such settlement of jurisdiction, shall on the petition of either party to the Congress of the United States, be finally determined as near as may be in the same manner as is before prescribed for deciding disputes respecting territorial jurisdiction between different States.

The United States in Congress assembled shall also have the sole and exclusive right and power of regulating the alloy and value of coin struck by their own authority, or by that of the respective States—fixing the standard of weights and measures throughout the United States.—regulating the trade and managing all affairs with the Indians, not members of any of the States, provided that the legislative right of any State within its own limits be not infringed or violated—establishing and regulating post-offices from one State to another, throughout all the United States, and exacting such postage on the papers passing thro' the same as may be requisite to defray the expenses of the said office—appointing all officers of the land forces, in the service of the United States, excepting regimental officers—appointing all the officers of the naval forces, and commissioning all officers whatever in the service of the United States—making rules for the government and regulation of the said land and naval forces, and directing their operations.

The United States in Congress assembled shall have authority to appoint a committee, to sit in the recess of Congress, to be denominated "A Committee of the States," and to consist of one delegate from each State; and to appoint such other committees and civil officers as may be necessary for managing the general affairs of the United States under their direction—to appoint one of their number to preside, provided that no person be allowed to serve in the office of president more than one year in any term of three years; to ascertain the necessary sums of money to be raised for the service of the United States, and to appropriate and apply the same for defraying the public expenses—to borrow money, or emit bills on the credit of the United States, transmitting every half year to the respective States an account of the sums of money so borrowed or emitted—to build and equip a navy—to agree upon the number of land forces, and to make requisitions from each State for its quota, in proportion to the number of white inhabitants in such State; which requisition shall be binding, and thereupon the legislature of each State shall appoint the regimental officers, raise the men and cloath, arm and equip them in a soldier like manner, at the expense of the United States, and the officers and men so cloathed, armed and equipped shall march to the place appointed, and within the time agreed on by the United States in Congress assembled. But if the United States in Congress assembled shall, on consideration of circumstances, judge proper that any State should not raise men, or should raise a smaller number than its quota, and that any other State should raise a greater number of men than the quota thereof, such extra number shall be raised, officered, cloathed, armed and equipped in the same manner as the quota of such State, unless the legislature of such State shall judge that such extra number cannot be safely spared out of the same, in which case they shall raise officers, cloath, arm and equip as many of such extra number as they judge can be safely spared. And the officers and men so cloathed, armed and equipped, shall march to the place appointed, and within the time agreed on by the United States in Congress assembled.

The United States in Congress assembled shall never engage in a war, nor grant letters of marque and reprisal in time of peace, nor enter into any treaties or alliances, nor coin money, nor regulate the value thereof, nor ascertain the sums and expenses necessary for the defence and welfare of the United States, or any of them, nor emit bills, nor borrow money on the credit of the United States, nor appropriate money, nor agree upon the number of vessels of war, to be built or purchased, or the number of land or sea forces to be raised, nor appoint a commander in chief of the army or navy, unless nine States assent to the same; nor shall a question on any other point, except for adjourning from day to day be determined, unless by the votes of a majority of the United States in Congress assembled.

The Congress of the United States shall have power to adjourn to any time within the year, and to any place within the United States, so that no period of adjournment be for a longer duration than the space of six months, and shall publish the Journal of their proceedings monthly, except such parts thereof relating to treaties, alliances or military operations as in their judgment require secrecy; and the yeas and nays of the delegates of each State on any question shall be entered on the Journal, when it is desired by any delegate; and the delegates of a State, or any of them, at his or their request shall be furnished with a transcript of the said Journal, except such parts as are above excepted, to lay before the legislatures of the several States.

Art. X. The Committee of the States, or any nine of them, shall be authorized to execute, in the recess of Congress, such of the powers of Congress as the United States in Congress assembled, by the consent of nine States, shall from time to time think expedient to vest them with; provided that no power be delegated to the said committee, for the exercises of which, by the articles of confederation, the voice of nine States in the Congress of the United States assembled is requisite.

Art. XI. Canada acceding to this confederation, and joining in the measures of the United States, shall be admitted into, and entitled to all the advantages of this union; but no other colony shall be admitted into the same, unless such admission be agreed to by nine States.

Art. XII. All bills of credit emitted, monies borrowed and debts contracted by, or under the authority of Congress, before the assembling of the United States, in pursuance of the present confederation, shall be deemed and considered as a charge against the United States, for payment and satisfaction whereof the said United States, and the public faith are hereby solemnly pledged.

Art. XIII. Every State shall abide by the determinations of the United States in Congress assembled, on all questions which by this confederation are submitted to them. And the Articles of this confederation shall be inviolably observed by every State, and the union shall be perpetual; nor shall any alteration at any time hereafter be made in any of them; unless such alteration be agreed to in a Congress of the United States, and be afterwards confirmed by the legislatures of every State.

And whereas it hath pleased the Great Governor of the World to incline the hearts of the legislatures we respectively represent in Congress, to approve of, and to authorize us to ratify the said articles of confederation and perpetual union. KNOW YE that we the undersigned delegates, by virtue of the power and authority to us given for that purpose, do by these presents, in the name and in behalf of our respective constituents, fully and entirely ratify and confirm each and every of the said articles of confederation and perpetual union, and all and singular the matters and things therein contained. And we do further solemnly plight and engage the faith of our respective constituents, that they shall abide by the determinations of the United States in Congress assembled, on all questions, which by the said confederation are submitted to them. And that the articles thereof shall be inviolably observed by the States we respectively represent, and that the union shall be perpetual. In Witness whereof we have hereunto set our hands in Congress. Done at Philadelphia in the State of Pennsylvania the ninth Day of July in the Year of our Lord one Thousand seven Hundred and Seventy-eight, and in the third year of the independence of America.

Letter to Benjamin Trumbull, August 18, 1778

PHILADELPHIA

The following letter reflects Sherman's aversion to inflation and his support for hard money.

The affair of our currency is to be considered in Congress to-day. What will be done to restore and support its credit is uncertain. We can't lessen the quantity much while the army is kept up. I trust the fullest assurance ought and will be given for redeeming it in due time and for exchanging gold and silver for what shall be outstanding at the period fixed for its redemption at the expressed value. The whole that has been emitted is a little more than 60,000,000 dollars. I think a period of about 14 or 15 years should be fixed for sinking the whole. That taxes for about 6 million dollars per annum for 4 years, 5 million dollars for five years and four million dollars per annum for the residue of the period should be immediately laid to be collected as a sinking fund with liberty for each State to raise more than their annual quota and be allowed 6 per cent interest for the time they may anticipate the payment. That each of the States that have not called in their Bills do it immediately and refrain from further emissions and tax themselves for current expenses. Besides liberty may be given for the people to bring in as many of the Bills as they please into loan offices, with assurance that the whole that is brought in shall be burnt. That all unnecessary expenses be retrenched and the best economy introduced. That the future expense of the war be defrayed as far as may be by taxes and the residue by emissions—and if the war ceases this year, which I think not improbable, our finances may soon be put on a good footing. Provision ought to be made in the meantime by each State to prevent injustice to creditors and salary men.

Source: Lewis H. Boutell, *The Life of Roger Sherman* (Chicago: A. C. McClurg, 1896), 106–7.

Letter from Roger Sherman and Oliver Ellsworth to Jonathan Trumbull Sr., October 15, 1778

PHILADELPHIA

This letter, written in Sherman's hand, contains political intelligence about a number of issues.

Sir

We were honored with your Excellency's Letter of the 5th Inst. Your Letter to Congress, and the memorial accompanying it are referred to Messrs. R. H. Lee, Samuel Adams, Josiah Bartlet and Oliver Elsworth who have not yet made report. Hope Such determination will be made thereon as will be reasonable & Satisfactory—of which we will give Your Excellency the earliest Notice by the Post. The affair of Finance is yet unfinished, The arrangement of a Board of Treasury is determined on but the officers are Not Yet appointed. Tomorrow is assigned for their Nomination. The members of Congress are United in the great Object of Securing the Liberties and Independence of the States, but are Sometimes divided in opinion about particular measures. The Assembly of New Jersey in their late session did not Ratify the Confederation, nor has it been done by Maryland & Delaware States. These and some other of the States are dissatisfied, that the Western ungranted Lands Should be claimed by particular States, which they think ought to be the common Interest of the United States, they being defended at the common expence. They further Say, that if Some provision is not now made for Securing Lands for the Troops who Serve during the war, they Shall have to pay large Sums to the States who claim the vacant Lands to Supply their Quotas of the Troops. Perhaps if the Assembly of Connecticut Should Resolve to make grants to their own Troops, and those raised by the States of Rhode Island, New Jersey, Delaware and Maryland in the Lands South of Lake Erie and west of the Lands in Controversy with Pennsylvania, Free of any purchase money or Quit rents to the Government of Connecticut, it might be Satisfactory to those States, and be no damage to the State of Connecticut. A Tract of Thirty Miles

Source: Paul H. Smith et al., eds., *Letters of Delegates to Congress* (Washington, D.C.: Government Printing Office, 1985), 11: 58–59.

East and West across the State would be Sufficient for the purpose, and that being Settled under good regulations would enhance the value of the rest; These could not be claimed as Crown Lands, both the Fee and Jurisdiction having been Granted to the Governor & Company of Connecticut.

We are Sir with great respect, Your Excellency's most obedt & most hble Servts.

Roger Sherman
Oliver Ellsworth

Letter to Elisha Payne, October 31, 1778

PHILADELPHIA

Born and raised in Connecticut, Elisha Payne (1731–1807) moved to what was then Cardigan, New Hampshire, in 1774. He became an advocate for Vermont independence and later served as chief justice of the Vermont Supreme Court.

Sir

I take the liberty to address you on a Subject which to me appears to be of a very dangerous and alarming nature. I am informed that the Inhabitants of a number of Towns in the State of New Hamshire on the East side of Connecticut River, have withdrawn from the Jurisdiction of that State, and joined with the people of the Grants, on the west Side of the River in forming a distinct State. The Strength of the united States lies in their union; they by their joint efforts under the Smiles of Divine Providence have made a Succesful resistance to the power of Great Britain Aided by foreign Mercenaries: but if Intestine divisions and contentions take place among them, will they not become an easy prey to a formidable enemy?

Whether the State of New Hamshire or New York have a right of Jurisdiction over the New Hamshire Grants on the west Side of Connecticut River, or whether by the neglect of the former to Claim and Support its Jurisdiction against the latter, the people have a right to form themselves into a distinct State, I shall not give any opinion, those questions will I Suppose at a proper time be judicially decided.

But for people Inhabiting within the known & acknowleged boundaries of any of the united States to Seperate without the consent of the State to which they belong, appears to me a very unjustifiable violation of the Social compact, and pregnant with the most ruinous consequences. Sir I dont know whether you live in one of the revolted Towns, but as you are in that vicinity, I trust from my acquaintance with your love of Order, and regard for the welfare of Your Country, You will use Your influence to discourage every thing that in

Source: Paul H. Smith et al., eds., *Letters of Delegates to Congress* (Washington, D.C.: Government Printing Office, 1985), 11: 152.

your opinion may be injurious to the true Interest of these States. If the present Constitutions of any of the States is not So perfect as could be wished, they may & probably will by common consent be amended; but in the mean time & under present circumstances, it appears to me indispensibly necessary that civil Government Should be vigorously Supported. I hope you will excuse the freedom I have taken on this occasion, as my Sole motive is the public good. I am with Esteem & regard, Your humble Servant.

Letter to Jonathan Trumbull Sr., July 22, 1780

PHILADELPHIA

Many of Sherman's letters to Governor Trumbull focus on financial matters and finding proper supplies for the army. The following is a good example of such a letter.

Sir

Your Excellency's Several Letters to the President of Congress of the 10th Instant were received and publickly read. No measures have Yet been taken by the Board of Treasury, for Sending Commissioners to Settle accounts in the Several States, which they are fully authorized to do by a late resolution of Congress. As I am at present a Member of that Board I Shall do every thing in my power to forward that Business, which has been too long delayed. Your Excellency's Letter of the 8th of June last was referred to a Committee who reported thereon the 6th of July. "That all the Crediters of these united States who have not been paid their just demands, Shall be intitled to recieve in the present money, to the full value of the Sums due to them respectively, at the time they ought to have been paid." When the report was taken up in Congress there was no objection to making just Allowance for the depreciation, but that it was Necessary to point out Some mode for the adjustment of the Sums due, and therefore it was recommitted—and will I suppose be again reported on very Soon. Congress Seem disposed to do justice in every Case as far as is practicable.

Our affairs have been considerably retarded and Embarrassed for want of money, and for want of proper Arrangements of the Staff departments.

A New Arrangement of the Quarter Masters Department has lately been Established, which provides for the receiving, Safe keeping and transportation of the provisions and other Supplies to be purchased by the Several States, pursuant to the resolution of the 25th of February last, and for procuring other Supplies. All the officers Employed will be on Salary & not Commissions,

Source: Paul H. Smith et al., eds., *Letters of Delegates to Congress* (Washington, D.C.: Government Printing Office, 1988), 15: 489–91.

issuing posts in the Country are to be discontinued, I believe it will be a means of Saving considerable expence if duly executed, tho' not So much as could be wished. New arrangements are also ordered for the commissary's and Medical departments, to be made by the Committee at Head Quarters, & reported to Congress.

We are Informed that Admiral Graves has lately arrived at New York with Six Ships of the Line from 60 to 80 Guns. General Washington writes that his arrival will make no alteration in his Plan of operations. We have had Accounts of the Arrival of the French Fleet at New port, on the 10th Instant, but no particulars, in what force or in what condition. We hear from New York, that one 74 Gun Ship of Graves's fleet was Sunk by the French fleet, and that the French fleet is much Shattered. The people in the Several States Seem to be animated to Vigorous exertions; A few months or weeks may be productive of very important events to this Country. May the Omnipotent disposer of all events overrule them for the best good of these States.

I understand that of late the Army have been well Supplied with provisions. I am Sorry that the State of Connecticut have had occasion to emit So large a Sum in Bills of Credit previous to their being furnished with the Bills prepared by order of Congress, but am Glad to hear that they have laid So large a Tax to be paid in the New Bills, I esteem that to be a very wise measure, to introduce the Bills into circulation with full credit, and ought to be imitated by all the other States. I am fully perswaded that no way can be devised, in our circumstances to Support the value of a paper currency but by taxing to the full amount of our expenditures, after having emitted a Sufficient Sum for a Medium of trade which is limited by the resolution of Congress to ten millions of dollars for the thirteen States, and if the particular States extend their emissions beyond their quotas of that Sum, it will in my opinion give a fatal blow to the Credit of the whole paper currency, and involve us in worse evils than we have heretofore experienced. Therefore I think that No Supposed necessity, or other consideration Whatsoever Should induce any State in the least degree to exceed the limit fixed by the united States by the resolution of the 18th of March last.

I am sensible that it was Necessary to make Some State emissions before those Bills were prepared, but then I think they Should be considered as part of their quotas of the ten Million dollars. The resources of this Country are great and may be drawn out in So equable a Manner by the Wisdom of the Legislatures of the Several States as fully to answer the exigencies of our affairs, without being very burthensome to the people. It may be necessary to run in debt for Some foreign articles, but I think not for any that are to be procured in this Country. I Shall return home by the middle of August So as to attend the circuit if relieved by the arrival of another Delegate. Mr. Root writes me that he dont expect to come 'till the beginning of October. I have wrote to General Wolcot but have not yet received an Answer.

The bank Set up here for the Supply of the Army I hope will be attended with Some good effect—they purchase flour delivered in this City at £80 Pennsylvania currency, in continental Bills, per Ct, which at 60 for 1 is equal to 21/4 lawful money of Connecticut. Of the New Bills have been Sent to Connecticut about half their quota, to New Hamshire their whole quota, to Massachusetts including what is now Sent by Brown 540,000 dollars. The quota for N. York is done, but not Sent forward, the quota for New Jersy will be printed next. Eight States have Adopted the Measure, and we hear that Virginia has, which will make nine. Delaware has not yet, and we have No Account from N. Carolina. South Carolina is Not in a condition to do it at present.

Gates will be able to Collect such a force as to re-establish Civil Government there.

I am with great respect and Esteem, Your Excellency's Obedient humble Servant,

Roger Sherman

Letter from Roger Sherman and Benjamin Huntington to Jonathan Trumbull Sr., August 22, 1780

PHILADELPHIA

This letter, written in Sherman's hand and signed by Sherman and Huntington, contains information about a variety of political issues—including Congress's negotiations with other nations.

Sir

The Inclosed Papers Contain the most Recent Intelligence we have of a Publick Nature from abroad. The Armed Neutrality of so many Powerful Nations in Europe together with the Commotions in England are by no means Discouraging to these States.

A Letter from Mr Jay at the Spanish Court Dated at Madrid the 27th of May last mentions that in Conference with a Spanish Minister he Recd. Encouragement that the Bills of Congress Drawn on him to the Amount of one Hundred Thousand Pounds Sterling would (with some Difficulty) be honored That they had also Conferred on the Subject of a Treaty but Came to no Conclusion.

Congress have Recalled their Committee from Head Quarters which will Prevent any further Correspondence with those Gentlemen in that Capacity.

Majr Genll Green has Resigned his Office of Quarter Master General and Col Pickeron is appointed & in the Execution of that Trust.

All the States (Excepting Delaware) as far Southward as Virginia Inclusively have Adopted the Resolutions of Congress of the 18th of March and will be furnished as fast as Possible with their Several Quotas of the New Bills which are Exceedingly wanted in Every Department.

If every State would Tax themselves to the Extent of their Abilities Relieving the Poor as far as Possible we should find it the Best Resource in our Power to obtain Supplies and Save the Continent from that Enthralment of Debt which may be Expected from Loans. This Doctrine (tho Trite) is no less Important than True and Deserves the most Serious Attention.

Source: Paul H. Smith et al., eds., *Letters of Delegates to Congress* (Washington, D.C.: Government Printing Office, 1988), 15: 614–15.

The Current Expences of the War are Chiefly of our own Services, Provisions & Manufactures which do not much Exceed our Annual Exports in Time of Peace. This alone is Demonstration that our Internal Resources are nearly Equal to our Necessities and might with Proper Management be so applied as to Prevent an Innormous National Debt to Foreigners who may hereafter Claim the Honor & Merit of our whole Salvation as Due to them and Surprize us with unexpected Demands.

At Present we have but a Small Prospect of Loans from Spain and as Mr Lawrens has lately Sailed for Holland the Suceess of his Negotiations will not soon be Known.

We are with Sentiments of the highest Esteem & Respect your Excellency's Most Humble Servants.

Roger Sherman
Benj Huntington

Letter to Josiah Bartlett, July 31, 1781
PHILADELPHIA

Josiah Bartlett (1729–95) was a physician and political leader in New Hampshire. He signed the Declaration of Independence and later served as both chief justice of the New Hampshire Supreme Court and governor of the state.

Sir

Enclosed is a copy of an act of the General Court of the Massachusetts, respecting the State of Vermont, the matter has been debated for Several days past in Congress, on a report of a Committee, to whom was referred a Letter from the President of Your State. The Committee reported as their opinion, "that copies of the Act of Massachusetts be Sent to the States of New Hamshire and New York and that the expediency of passing Similar acts be referred to them. And in case they relinquish their Claims of Jurisdiction over the Grants on the west Side of Connecticut River, Bounded, East by Said River, North by Latitude forty five degrees, West by lake Champlain and the west lines of Several Townships Granted by the Governor of New Hampshire, to the North west corner of Massachusetts; and South by the North line of Massachusetts; Congress will Guaranty the Land & Jurisdiction belonging to the Said States respectively lying without the Said limits, against all claims & Encroachments of the people within those limits." What will be Ultimately done in Congress is uncertain. Some Gentlemen are for declaring Vermont an Independent State, others, for explicitly recommending to the States aforesaid to relinquish their claims of Jurisdiction, others, only for referring it to their consideration as reported by the Committee, and Some few are against doing any thing that will tend to make a new State. I am of opinion that a Speedy, & Amicable Settlement of the controversy would conduce very much to the peace & welfare of the united States, And that it will be difficult if not impracticable to reduce the people on the east side of the River to Obedience to the Government of New Hamshire until the other dispute is Settled, that the

Source: Paul H. Smith et al., eds., *Letters of Delegates to Congress* (Washington, D.C.: Government Printing Office, 1990), 17: 461–62.

longer it remains unsettled, the more difficult it will be to remedy the evils, but if the States of New Hamshire & New York would follow the example of Massachusetts, respecting the Grants on the west of Connecticut River, waiting for a recommendation of Congress, the whole controversy would be quieted, very much to the advantage and Satisfaction of the united States, and that the Inhabitants of New Hamshire and New York living without the limits of the disputed territory would return to their Allegiance. The British Ministry esteem it as object of Great importance to them, to engage the people of Vermont in their Interest, and have accordingly Instructed Gen. Clinton & Gen. Haldiman to use their best endeavours for that end. And tho' I dont think the people have any inclination to come under the British Yoke, or to do anything injurious to this Country, yet if left in their present Situation, they may be led to take Steps very prejudicial to the United States . . . I think it very unlikely, that Congress can attend to the Settlement of the dispute by a Judicial decision, during the War, for though the parties were heard last fall respecting their claims, yet it cannot now be determined upon the right, without a new hearing, because there are many New Members that were not then present.

I am credibly Informed that a great Majority of the members of the Legislature of the State of New York at their last winter session were willing to relinquish their claim of Jurisdiction over that district, and that they Should be admitted to be a Seperate State, but the Governor for Some reasons prevented an act passing at that time. We have No News remarkable here. Paper currency is very much at an end, Some of the New Bills are bought & Sold, but Silver and Gold are the only currency—the prices of Commodities are much fallen, many articles are as low, as before the war. I Send you two of the last News papers. And am with Great Esteem & Regard, Your humble Servant,

Roger Sherman

P.S. Since writing the foregoing Congress have recommitted the report. New York delegates arrived to day—They are instructed to move for a decision of the affair of Vermont.

Sherman's Notes on Information Desired by François Barbé-Marbois, 1781

In 1781, François de Marbois, the secretary of the French legation in Philadelphia, sent a set of queries to a variety of American civic leaders. Only Thomas Jefferson responded with a book-length manuscript (known today as Notes on Virginia*). Sherman, like the rest of his colleagues who wrote to Marbois, offered shorter answers.*

We do not have Marbois's original letter to Sherman, but one of Sherman's personal notebooks in the Library of Congress contains the following notes on his questions.

Articles on which Mr. De Marbois desires some details

1. An exact description of the limits and boundaries of Connecticut.

2. The memoirs published in its name, in the time of its being colony, and the pamphlets to its interior or exterior affairs.

3. A notice of its counties, townships, villages, rivers, rivulets, and how far they are navigable. Also of the cascades, caverns, mountains, productions, trees, plants, fruits and other natural riches.

4. The number of its Inhabitants to and the proportion between the whites and blacks.

5. The different religions received in the state.

6. The Colleges and public establishments, the roads, buildings, etc.

7. The particular customs and manners that may happen to have been received in that state.

8. The present state of manufacturing, commerce, & exterior trade.

9. A notice of the best imports of the state, how big are the vessels they can receive.

10. A notice of the commercial productions, peculiar to that State, and of those objects the inhabitants are obligated to draw from Europe and from other parts of the world.

11. The weights measures & the currency of hard money some details relating to the exchange with Europe.

12. The public income & expenses.

Source: Roger Sherman Papers, Manuscript Division, Library of Congress.

13. The measures taken with regard to the Estates of the rebels, commonly called Tories.

14. The Marine & Navigation.

15. A notice of the mines and other subterranean riches.

16. Some samples of the mines and of the extraordinary stones, in short a notice of all that can increase the progress of human knowledge?

17. A description of the Indians in the state, before the European settlements, and of those who are still remaining, an indication of the Indian monuments discovered in that state.

Draft Letter to François Barbé-Marbois, November 18, 1782

NEW HAVEN

We do not have the final version of Sherman's letter to Marbois, but the Massa-chusetts Historical Society owns the following draft. Sherman apparently sent Mar-bois a polished version of the letter along with a copy of Connecticut's charter and several other texts.

Sir

I have not been unmindful of your request concerning some details respect-ing the state of Connecticut, but have not been able to obtain an account of all the articles about which you desire to be informed, but having now an opportunity by Mr. Webster I transmit an account of such as I have obtained.

1   As to the Boundaries of the State, as contained in a Charter from King Charles II, dated April 23, 1762. No. 1.

2   There has been no History of this state published, Mr. Benjamin Trum-bull a Clergyman of this Town has Collected materials and began to write one—there are Several Histories of New-England that mention some circum-stances relating to Connecticut. Mr. Prince of Boston began a Chronological history of New England but did not live to finish it . . . I send you all that he published.

3 & 4 I have enclosed the names of the Counties with the number of Towns and Inhabitants in each County, in the years 1756, 1774, & 1782.   No. 1 & 2.

The principal River are Connecticut, Navigable to Hartford about 45 miles from the sea. 2 Thames Navigable from New London to Norwich about 14 miles. 3 Housatonnick, which falls into the Sound between Milford & Strat-ford. Navigable 10 miles to Darby.

There is a sea coast of about 100 miles and many Harbours for Trading Vessels, but none convenient for Ships of War, except New London which I suppose will admit of Ships of Burthen & would contain a large Fleet.

5   The Religion professed by the people in General is in matters of Faith the same as the Presbyterians, in Scotland as to Church Govt. & Discipline

Source: Miscellaneous Bound Collection, Massachusetts Historical Society.

they are congregational, of these Some are consociated & some are Independent. There are also a number of Episcopal Chhs the same as in England, & some ananbaptists and a very few Quakers.

6   There is but one College, a particular account you have in President Clap's History. Public schools are kept in every Town & Parish.

7   The customs and manners are nearly the same as in other parts of the United States

8   The principal manufactures are Coarse linens & Wollens. Potash. Salt Petre, of which more than 100 Tons has been made in Connecticut Since the present war, & a Sufficient quantity of G. Powder. Most kinds of Iron ware is also manufactured here, such as Cannon, & Cast Iron of all kinds & Edge Tools Such as Axes Sythes &c.

10   The Productions are Beef, Pork, Wheat, Rye, Indian Corn, Oats, Flax, Hemp, and every other kind which are produced in the middle and Northern States.

Imported from Europe. Woolen Cloths, fine Linens, Silks, Fire Arms, Nails, Cutlery, and many articles of the same kind as are made here—as they can be imported cheaper than they can be made, in time of peace

The weights & measures are the Same as in England, and the Currency is chiefly French, Spanish, Porteguez & English coins. the currency is hard money only at present. Spanish Dollars pass at 6s. French Crowns at 6/8 and French Guinea at 27/—.

12   The public expences in time of Peace for the Support are about £7000 currency. The money is raised by Taxes on the Polls & Estates of the Inhabitants.

besides these expences each Town & Parish raise Taxes for Support of the Poor & of the Clergy.

13   The Estates of the Rebels who have joined the Enemy or voluntarily taken protection under them are forfeited to the State, & disposed of for the expence of the war

14   The Marine & Navigation at present is very inconsiderable but increasing, I have not obtained an amount of what it was before the war—

15   There are plenty of good Iron mines but no other of any value have yet been discovered.

There were Some Thousands of Indians in the Several parts of this State at the Time of its first Settlement by the white people, but they Gradually decreased. there were 1363 in the year 1774. I have not heard of any remarkable monuments found among them

[By Roger Sherman]

Pelatiah Webster, *A Dissertation on the Political Union and Constitution of the Thirteen United States, of North-America*, Published under the Pseudonym "A Citizen of Philadelphia," 1783

Pelatiah Webster (1725–95) was born in Connecticut, graduated from Yale, and served as a minister for several years before moving to Philadelphia in 1755 to engage in business.

A Dissertation, &c.

I. *The supreme authority of any state must have power enough to effect the ends of its appointment,* otherwise these ends cannot be answered, and *effectually secured*, at best they are precarious—but at the same time,

II. The supreme authority ought to be *so limited and checked*, if possible as to prevent the *abuse of power, or the exercise of powers that are not necessary to the ends of its appointment,* but hurtful and oppressive to the subject—but to limit a supreme authority so far as to diminish its dignity, or lessen its power of doing good, would be to destroy or at least to corrupt it, and render it *ineffectual* to its ends.

III. A number of sovereign states uniting into one commonwealth, and appointing a supreme power to manage the affairs of the union, *do necessarily and unavoidably part with and transfer over to such supreme power, so much of their own sovereignty, as is necessary to render the ends of the union effectual,* otherwise their confederation will be a union without bands of union, like a cask without hoops, that may and probably will fall to pieces, as soon as 'tis put to any exercise which requires strength—Just so every member of civil society parts with many of his natural rights, that he may enjoy the rest in greater security under the protection of society. The union of the Thirteen United States of America is of mighty consequence to the security, sovereignty and even liberty of each of them, and of all the individuals who compose them; united under a natural well adjusted and effectual constitution, they are a

Source: Pelatiah Webster, *A Dissertation on the Political Union and Constitution of the Thirteen United States, of North-America* (Philadelphia: T. Bradford, 1783).

strong, rich, growing power, with great resources and means of defence, which no foreign power will easily attempt to invade or insult; they may easily command respect, and as their exports are mostly either raw materials or provisions, and their imports mostly finished goods, their trade becomes a capital object with every manufacturing nation of Europe, and all the southern colonies of America, their friendship and trade will of course be courted, and each power in amity with them will contribute to their security; their union is of great moment in another respect, they thereby form a superintending power among themselves, that can moderate and terminate disputes that may arise between different states, without having recourse to the dreadful decision of the sword.— I don't mean here to go into a detail of all the advantages of our union, they offer themselves on every view and are important enough to engage every honest prudent mind, to secure and establish that union by every possible method, that we may enjoy the full benefit of it, and be rendered happy and safe under the protection it affords.

This union, however important, cannot be supported without a constitution founded on principles of natural truth, fitness and utility. If there is one article wrong in such constitution, it will discover itself in practice, by its baleful operation, and destroy or at least injure the union. Many nations have been ruined by the errors of their political constitutions. Such errors first introduce wrongs and injuries which soon breed discontents, which gradually work up into mortal hatred and resentments, inveterate parties are formed, which of course make the whole community a house divided against itself, which soon falls either a prey to some enemies without, who watch to devour them, or else crumble into their original constituent parts, and loose all respectability, strength and security. 'Tis as physically impossible to secure to civil society, good cement of union, duration and security, without a constitution founded on principles of natural fitness and right, as to raise timbers into a strong compact building, which have not been framed upon true geometrick principles, for if you cut one beam a foot too long or too short, not all the authority and all the force of all the carpenters can ever get it into its place, and make it fit in with proper simmetry there. As the fate then of all governments depends much on their political constitutions, they become an object of mighty moment to the happiness and well-being of society; and as the framing of such a constitution requires great knowledge of the rights of men and societies, as well as of the interests, circumstances and even prejudices of the several parts of the community or commonwealth, for which it is intended; it becomes a very complex subject, and of course requires great steadiness and comprehension of thought, as well as great knowledge of men and things to do it properly. I shall however attempt it with my best abilities, and hope from the candor of the public to ascape censure, if I cannot merit praise.

I BEGIN with my first and great principle, viz. *That the constitution must vest powers in every department sufficient to secure and make effectual the ends of it.* The supreme authority must have the power of making war and peace—of appointing armies and navies—of appointing officers both civil and military—of making contracts—of emitting, coining and borrowing money—of regulating trade and making treaties with foreign powers—of establishing post-offices—and in short of doing every thing which the well-being of the commonwealth may require, and which is not compatible to any particular state, all of which require money, and can't possibly be made effectual without it, they must therefore of necessity be vested with *a power of taxation.* I know this is a most important and weighty trust, a dreadful engine of oppression, tyranny and injury, when ill used; yet from the necessity of the case, it must be admitted, for to give a supreme authority a power of making contracts without any power of payment—of appointing officers civil and military, without money to pay them—a power to build ships, without any money to do it with—a power of emitting money, without any power to redeem it—or of borrowing money, without any power to make payment, &c. &c. Such a solecism in government, is so naturally absurd, that I really think to offer further arguments on the subject, would be to insult the understanding of my readers—to make all these payments dependent on the votes of thirteen popular assemblies, who will undertake to judge of the propriety of every contract, and every occasion of money, and grant or withhold supplies according to their opinion, and at the same time, the operations of the whole Thirteen, stopped by the vote of a single one of them; I say this renders all supplies so precarious, and the public credit so extremely uncertain, as must in its nature render all efforts in war, and all regular administration in peace, utterly impracticable, as well as most pointedly ridiculous, Is there a man to be found, who would lend money or render personal services, or make contracts on such precarious security; indeed we have a proof of fact, the strongest of all proofs, a fatal experience—the surest though severest of all schoolmasters, which renders all other proof or arguments on this subject quite unnecessary—the present broken state of our finances—public debts and bankruptcies—enormous and ridiculous depreciation of public securities, with the total annihilation of our public credit,—prove beyond all contradiction the vanity of all recourse to the several assemblies of the states. The recent instance of the duty of five per cent on imported goods struck dead, and the bankruptcies which ensued on the single vote of Rhode-Island, affords another proof, of what 'tis certain may be done again in like circumstances.

I have another reason why a power of taxation or of raising money, ought to be vested in the supreme authority of our commonwealth, viz. the monies necessary for the public ought to be raised by a duty imposed on imported goods, not a bare five per cent or any other per cent on all imported good indiscriminately, but a duty much heavier on all articles of luxury or mere ornament, and which are consumed principally by the rich or prodigal part of the community, such as silks of all sorts, muslins, cambricks, lawns, superfine cloths, spirits, wines, &c. &c. Such an impost would ease the husbandman, the mechanic and the poor, would have all the practical effects of a sumptuary law, would mend the oeconomy and increase the industry of the community, would be collected without the shocking circumstances of collectors and their warrants, and make the quantity of tax paid always, depend on the choice of the person who pays it.

This tax can be laid by the supreme authority much more conveniently than by the particular assemblies, and would in no case be subject to their repeals or modifications, and of course the public credit would never be dependent on or liable to bankruptcy by the humours of any particular assembly,—in an essay on finance, which I design soon to offer to the public, this subject will be treated more fully.

The delegates which are to form that august body, which are to hold and exercise the supreme authority, ought to be appointed by the states in any manner they please in which they should not be limited by any restrictions; their own dignity and the weight they will hold in the great public councils, will always depend on the abilities of the persons, they appoint to represent them there; and if they are wise enough to choose men of sufficient abilities, and respectable characters, men of sound sense, extensive knowledge, gravity and integrity, they will reap the honor and advantage of such wisdom; but if they are fools enough to appoint men of trifling or vile characters, of mean abilities, faulty morals or despicable ignorance, they must reap the fruits of such folly, and content themselves to have no weight, dignity or esteem in the public councils; and what is more to be lamented by the commonwealth, to do no good there. I have no objection to the states electing and recalling their delegates as often as they please, but think it hard and very injurious both to them and the commonwealth, that they should be obliged to discontinue them after three years service, if they find them on that trial to be men of sufficient integrity and abilities; a man of that experience is certainly much more qualified to serve in the place, than a new member of equal good character can be; experience makes perfect in every kind of business—old experienced statesmen, of tried and approved integrity and abilities, are a great blessing to a state—they acquire great authority and esteem as well as wisdom, and very much contribute to keep the system of government in good and salutary order; and this furnishes the strongest reason why they should be continued in the service, on Plato's great maxim, that the man best qualified to serve ought to be appointed—I am sorry to see a contrary maxim adopted in our American councils, to make the highest reason that can be given for continuing a man in the public administration, assigned as a constitutional and absolute reason for turning him out, seems to me to be a solecism of a piece with many other reforms, by which we set out to surprize the world with our wisdom. If we should adopt this maxim in the common affairs of life, it would be found inconvenient, e. g. if we should make it a part of our constitution, that a man who has served a three years apprenticeship to the trade of a taylor or shoemaker, should be obliged to discontinue that business for the three successive years, I am of opinion the country would soon be cleared of good shoemakers and taylors.—Men are no more born statesmen than shoemakers or taylors— experience is equally necessary to perfection in both. It seems to me that a man's inducements to qualify himself for a public employment, and make himself master of it, must be much discouraged by this consideration, that let him take whatever pains to qualify himself in the best manner, he must be shortly turned out, and of course it would be of more consequence to him, to turn his attention to some other business which he might adopt when his present appointment should expire; and by this mean the commonwealth is in danger of losing the zeal, industry and shining abilities, as well as services of their most accomplished and valuable men. I hear that the state of Georgia has improved on this blessed principle, and limited the continuance of their governors to one year; the consequence is, they have already the ghosts of departed governors stalking about in every part of their state, and growing more plenty every year, and as the price of every thing is reduced by its plenty, I can suppose governors will soon be very low there.—This doctrine of rotation was first proposed by some sprightly geniuses of brilliant politics, with this cogent reason, that by introducing a rotation in the public offices, we should have a great number of men trained up to public service; but it appears to me that it will be more likely to produce many jacks at all trades, but good at none. I think that frequent elections are a sufficient security against the continuance of men in public office whose conduct is not approved, and there can be no reason for excluding those whose conduct is approved, and are allowed to be better qualified than any men who can be found to supply their places.

Another great object of government, is the apportionment of burdens and benefits, for if a greater quota of burden or a less quota of benefit than is just and right be allotted to any state, this ill apportionment will be an everlasting source of uneasiness and discontent. In the first case, the over burdened state will complain, in the last case all the states, whose quota of benefits is underated will be uneasy; and this is a case of such delicacy, that it cannot be safely trusted to the arbitrary opinion or judgment of any body of men however august. Some natural principle of confessed equity, and which can be reduced to a certainty, ought if possible to be found and adopted, for it is of the highest moment to the commonwealth, to obviate, and if possible, wholly to take away such a fruitful and common source of infinite disputes, as that of apportionment of quotas has ever proved in all states of the earth.—The value of lands may be a good rule, but the ascertainment of that value is impracticable; no assessment can be made which will not be liable to exception and debate—to adopt a good rule in any thing which is impracticable, is absurd, for 'tis physically impossible that any thing should be good for practice, which can't be practiced at all;— but if the value of lands were capable of certain assessment; yet to adopt that value as a rule of apportionment of quotas, and at the same time to except from valuation large tracts of sundry states of immense value, which have all been defended by the joint arms of the whole empire, and for the defence of which no additional quota of supply is to be demanded of those states to whom such lands are secured by such joint efforts of the states, is in its nature un- reasonable, and will open a door for great complaint; 'tis plain without argu- ment, that such states ought either to make grants to the commonwealth of such tracts of defended territory, or sell as much of it as will pay its proper quota of defence, and pay such sums into the public treasury; and this ought to be done, let what rule of quota soever, be adopted with respect to the cultivated part of the united states, for no proposition of natural right and justice can be plainer than this, that every part of valuable property which is defended, ought to contribute its quota of supply for that defence. If then the value of cultivated lands is found to be an impracticable rule of apportionment of quotas, we have to seek for some other, equally just and less exceptionable. It appears to me, that the number of living souls or human persons of whatever age, sex or condition, will afford us a rule or measure of apportionment which will forever increase or decrease with the real wealth of the states, and will of course be a perpetual rule not capable of corruption, by any circumstances of future time, which is a vast consideration in forming a constitution which is designed for perpetual duration, and which will in its nature be as just as to the inhabited parts of each state, as that of the value of lands or any other that has or can be mentioned.—Land takes its value not merely from the goodness of its soil, but from innumerable other relative advantages, among which the population of the country may be considered as principal, as lands in a full settled country will always (*caeteris paribus*) bring more than lands in thin settlements—on this principle, when the inhabitants of Russia, Poland, &c.

sell real estates, they do not value them as we do, by the number of acres, but by the number of people who live on them,—where any piece of land has many advantages, many people will croud there to obtain them, which will create many competitors for the purchase of it, which will of course raise the price. Where there are fewer advantages, there will be fewer competitors, and of course a less price; and these two things will forever be proportionate to each other, and of course the one will always be a sure index of the other. The only considerable objection I have ever heard to this, is, that the quality of inhabitants, differ in the different states, and 'tis not reasonable that the black slaves in the southern states should be estimated on a par with the white freemen in the northern states. To discuss this question fairly, I think it will be just to estimate the neat value of the labour of both, and if it shall appear that the labour of the black person produces as much neat wealth to the southern state, as the labour of the white person does to the northward state, I think it will follow plainly, that they are equally useful inhabitants in point of wealth; and therefore in the case before us, should be estimated alike,—and if the amazing profits which the southern planters boast of receiving from the labour of their slaves on their plantations are true, the southern people have greatly the advantage in this kind of estimation, and as this objection comes principally from the southward, I should suppose that the gentlemen from that part will blush to urge it any further.

That the supreme authority should be vested with powers to terminate and finally decide controversies arising between different states, I take it, will be universally admitted, but I humbly apprehend that an appeal from the first instance of tryal ought to be admitted in causes of great moment, on the same reasons that such appeals are admitted in all the states of Europe. It is well known to all men versed in courts, that the first hearing of a cause, rather gives an opening to that evidence, and reason which ought to decide it, than such a full examination and thorough discussion, as should always precede a final judgment, in causes of national consequence. A detail of reasons might be added, which I deem it unnecessary to enlarge on here.

The supreme authority ought to have a power of peace and war, and forming treaties and alliances with all foreign powers, which implies a necessity of their also having sufficient powers to inforce the obedience of all subjects of the United States to such treaties and alliances, with full powers to unite the force of the states and direct its operations in war, and to punish all transgressors in all these respects; otherwise by the imprudence of a few, the whole commonwealth may be embroiled with foreign powers, and the operations of war may be rendered useless, or fail much of their due effect: All these I conceive will be easily granted, especially the latter, as the power of

Congress to appoint and direct the army and navy in war, with all departments thereto belonging, and punishing delinquents in them all, is already
admitted into practice in the course of the present unhappy war, in which we
have been long engaged.

But now the great and most difficult part of this weighty subject remains to
be considered, viz. how this supreme authority is to be constituted in such
manner that they may be able to exercise with full force, and effect the vast
powers committed to them, for the good and well-being of the United States,
and yet be so checked and restrained from exercising these powers to the injury
and ruin of the states, that we may with safety trust them with a commission
of such vast magnitude;—and may almighty wisdom direct my pen in this
arduous discussion.

1st. The men who compose this important council, must be delegated from
all the states, and it is to be wished that none might be appointed that were
not adequate to this weighty business; but a little knowledge of human nature,
and a little acquaintance with the political history of mankind, will soon teach
us that this is not to be expected. The representatives appointed by popular
elections are commonly not only the legal, but real substantial representatives
of their electors, i. e. there will commonly be about the same proportion of
grave, sound, well qualified men,—trifling desultory men,—wild or knavish
schemers,—and dull ignorant fools in the delegated assembly, as in the body
of electors. I know of no way to help this, and such delegates must be admitted,
as the states are pleased to send; and all that can be done, is when they get
together, to make the best of them. We will suppose then they are all met in
Congress, clothed with that vast authority which it is necessary to the well-
being, and even existence of the union that they should be vested with, how
shall we impower them to do all necessary and effectual good, and restrain
them from doing hurt? To do this properly, I think we must recur to those
natural motives of action, those feelings and apprehensions which usually occur
to the mind at the very time of action; for distant consequences, however
weighty, are often too much disregarded. *Truth loves light, and is vindicated by
it. Wrong shrouds itself in darkness, and is supported by delusion.* An honest well
qualified man loves light, can bear close examination and critical enquiry, and
is best pleased when he is most thoroughly understood: A man of corrupt
design, or a fool of no design hates close examination and critical enquiry; the
knavery of the one and the ignorance of the other is discovered by it, and they
both usually grow uneasy, before the investigation is half done. I don't believe
there is a more natural truth in the world, than that divine one of our saviour,
he that doeth truth, cometh to the light. I would therefore recommend that mode
of deliberation, which should naturally bring on the most thorough and critical

discussion of the subject, previous to passing the act; and for that purpose humbly propose,

2dly, That the Congress shall consist of two chambers, an upper and lower house, or senate and commons, with the concurrence of both necessary to every act, and that every state send one or more delegates to each house; this will subject every act to two discussions before two distinct chambers of men equally qualified for the debate—equally masters of the subject, and of equal authority in the decision.—These two houses will be governed by the same natural motives and interests, viz. the good of the commonwealth and the approbation of the people. Whilst at the same time the emulation naturally arising between them, will induce a very critical and sharp-sighted inspection into the motions of each other. Their different opinions will bring on conferences between the two houses, in which the whole subject will be exhausted in arguments pro and con, and shame will be the portion of obstinate convicted error. Under these circumstances, a man of ignorance or evil design will be afraid to impose on the credulity, inattention or confidence of his house, by introducing any corrupt or indigested proposition which he knows he must be called on to defend, against the severe scrutiny, and poignant objections of the other house. I do not believe the many hurtful and foolish legislative acts which first or last have injured all the states on earth, have originated so much in corruption as indolence, ignorance, and a want of a full comprehension of the subject, which a full prying and emulous discussion would tend in a great measure to remove: This naturally rouses the lazy and idle, who hate the pain of close thinking, animates the ambitious to excel in policy and argument, and excites the whole to support the dignity of their house, and vindicate their own propositions. I am not of opinion that bodies of elective men, which usually compose parliaments, diets, assembles, congresses, &c. are commonly dishonest; but I believe it rarely happens that there are not designing men among them, and I think it would be much more difficult for them to unite their partizans in two houses and corrupt or deceive them both, than to carry on their designs where there is but one unalarmed, unapprehensive house to be managed; and as there is no hope of making these bad men good, the best policy is to embarrass them, and make their work as difficult as possible—In these assemblies are frequently to be found sanguine men, upright enough indeed, but of strong wild projection, whose brains are always teeming with utopian, chimerical plans and political whims, very destructive to society, I hardly know a greater evil than to have the supreme councils of a nation played off on such mens wires; such baseless visions at best end in darkness, and the dance, though easy and merry enough at first, rarely fails to plunge the credulous simple followers into sloughs and bogs at last. Nothing can tend more effectually to obviate these evils, and to mortify and cure such magotty brains, than to see the absurdity of their projects exposed, by the several arguments and keen satire which a full, emulous and spirited discussion of the subject will naturally produce: We have had enough of these geniuses in the short course of our politics, both in our national and provincial councils, and have felt enough of their evil effects to induce us to wish for any good method to keep ourselves clear of them in future.

The consultations and decisions of national councils are so very important, that the fate of millions depends on them; therefore no man ought to speak in such assemblies, without considering that the fate of millions hangs on his tongue,—and of course a man can have no right in such august councils to utter indigested sentiments, or indulge himself in sudden unexamined flights of thought; his most tried and improved abilities are due to the state, who have trusted him with their most important interests. A man must therefore be most inexcuseable, who is either absent during such debates, or sleeps, or whispers, or catches flies during the argument, and just rouses when the vote is called to give his yea or nay, to the weal or woe of a nation.—Therefore 'tis manifestly proper, that every natural motive that can operate on his under-standing, or his passions, to engage his attention and utmost efforts, should be put in practice, and that his present feelings should be raised by every motive of honor and shame, to stimulate him to every practicable degree of diligence and exertion, to be as far as possible useful in the great discussion.—I appeal to the feelings of every reader, if he would not (were he in either house) be much more strongly and naturally induced to exert his utmost abilities and attention to any question which was to pass through the ordeal of a spirited discussion of another house, than he would do, if the absolute decision depended on his own house, without any further enquiry or challenge on the subject.

As Congress will ever be composed of men delegated by the several states, it may well be supposed that they have the confidence of their several states, and understand well the policy and present condition of them; it may also be supposed that they come with strong local attachments, and habits of thinking limitted to the interests of their particular states: It may therefore be supposed they will need much information, in order to their gaining that enlargement of ideas, and great comprehension of thought which will be necessary to enable them to think properly on that large scale, which takes into view the interests of all the states:—The greatest care and wisdom is therefore requisite to give them the best and surest information, and of that kind that may be most safely relied on, to prevent their being deluded or prejudiced by partial representations, made by interested men who have particular views. This information may perhaps be best made by the great ministers of state, who ought to be men of the greatest abilities and integrity, their business is confined to their several departments, and their attention engaged strongly and constantly to all the several parts of the same; the whole arrangement, method and order of which, are formed, superintended, and managed in their offices, and all informations relative to their departments center there; these ministers will of course have the best information, and most perfect knowledge of the state of the nation, as far as it relates to their several departments, and will of course be able to give the best information to Congress, in what manner any bill proposed, will effect the public interest in their several departments, which will nearly comprehend the whole. The Financier manages the whole subject of revenues and expenditures—the secretary of state takes knowledge of the general policy and internal government—the minister of war presides in the whole business of war and defence—and the minister of foreign affairs regards the whole state of the nation, as it stands related to or connected with all foreign powers. I mention a secretary of state, because all other nations have one, and I suppose we shall need one as much as they, and the multiplicity of affairs which naturally fall into his office will grow so fast, that I imagine we shall soon be under necessity of appointing one—to these I would add judges of law, and chancery; but I fear they will not be very soon appointed—the one supposes the existence of law, and the other of equity—and when we shall be altogether convinced of the absolute necessity of the real and effectual existence of both these, we shall probably appoint proper heads to preside in those departments—I would therefore propose,

3dly, That when any bill shall pass the second reading in the house in which it originates, and before it shall be finally enacted, copies of it shall be sent to each of the said ministers of state, in being at the time, who shall give said house in writing, the fullest information in their power, and their most explicit sentiments of the operation of the said bill on the public interest, as far as relates to their respective departments, which shall be received and read in said house and entered on their minutes, before they finally pass the bill; and when they send the bill for concurrence to the other house, they shall send therewith the said informations of the said ministers of state, which shall likewise be read in that house before their concurrence is finally passed.—I do not mean to give these great ministers of state a negative on Congress, but I mean to oblige Congress to receive their advices before they pass their bills, and that every act shall be void that is not passed with these forms; and I further propose, that either house of Congress may, if they please, admit the said ministers to be present and assist in the debates of the house, but without any right of vote, in the decision.

It appears to me, that if every act shall pass so many different corps of discussion before 'tis compleated, where each of them stake their characters on the advice or vote they give, there will be all the light thrown on the case, which the nature and circumstances of it can admit, and any corrupt man will find it extremely difficult to foist in any erroneous clause whatever; and every ignorant or lazy man will find the strongest inducements to make himself master of the subject, that he may appear with some tolerable degree of character in it, and the whole will find themselves in a manner compelled, diligently and sincerely to seek for the real state of the facts, and the natural fitness and truth arising from them, i. e. the whole natural principles on which the subject depends, and which alone can endure every test, to the end that they may have not only the inward satisfaction of acting properly and usefully for the states, but also the credit and character which is or ought ever to be annexed to such a conduct. This will give the great laws of Congress the highest probability, presumption and means of right, fitness and truth, that any laws whatever can have at their first enaction, and will of course afford the highest reason for the confidence and acquiesence of the states, and all their subjects in them; and being grounded in truth and natural fitness, their operation will be easy, salutary and satisfactory—and if experience shall discover errors in any law (for practice will certainly discover such error if there be any) the legislature will always be able to correct them, by such repeals, amendments or new laws as shall be found necessary; but as 'tis much easier to prevent mischiefs than to remedy them, all possible caution, prudence and attention should be used, to make the laws right at first.

4thly. There is another body of men among us whose business of life, and whose full and extensive intelligence, foreign and domestic, naturally makes them more perfectly acquainted with the sources of our wealth, and whose particular interest are more intimately and necessarily connected with the general prosperity of the country, than any other order of men in the states—I mean the *Merchants*; and I could wish that Congress might have the benefit of that extensive and important information which this body of men are very capable of laying before them.—Trade is of such essential importance to our interests, and so intimately connected with all our staples great and small, that no sources of our wealth can flourish, and operate to the general benefit of the community without it. Our husbandry, that grand staple of our country, can never exceed our home consumption without this—'tis plain at first sight, that the farmer will not toil and sweat through the year to raise great plenty of the produce of the soil, if there is no market for his produce, when he has it ready for sale, i. e. if there are no merchants to buy it. In like manner the manufacturer will not lay out his business on any large scale, if there is no merchant to buy his fabricks when he has finished them; a vent is of the most essential importance to every manufacturing country—the merchants therefore become the natural negociators of the wealth of the country, who take off the abundance and supply the wants of the inhabitants;—and as this negociation is the business of their lives, and the source of their own wealth, they of course become better acquainted with both our abundance and wants, and are more interested in finding and improving the best vent for the one, and supply of the other, than any other men among us, and they have a natural interest in making both the purchase and supply as convenient to their customers as possible, that they may secure their custom, and thereby increase their own business. It follows then, that the merchants are not only qualified to give the fullest and most important information to our supreme legislature, concerning the state of our trade—the abundance and wants—the wealth and poverty of our people, i. e. their most important interests, but are the most likely to do it fairly and truely, and to forward with their influence, every measure which will operate to the convenience and benefit of our commerce, and oppose with their whole weight and superior knowledge of the subject, any wild schemes which an ignorant or arbitrary legislature may attempt to introduce, to the hurt and embarrassment of our intercourse both with one another, and with foreigners.

The states of *Venice* and *Holland* have ever been governed by merchants, or at least their policy has ever been under the great influence of that sort of men. No states have been better served as appears by their great success, the ease and happiness of their citizens, as well as the strength and riches of their commonwealth: The one is the oldest, and the other the richest state in the world of equal number of people—the one has maintained sundry wars with the grand Turk—and the other withstood the whole power of France, and the capitols of both have long been the principal marts of the several parts of Europe in which they are situated, and the banks of both are the best supported, and in the best credit of any banks in Europe, though their countries or territories are very small, and their inhabitants but a handful when compared with the great states in their neighbourhood.—Merchants must from the nature of their business, certainly understand the interests and resources of their country, the best of any men in it; and I know not of any one reason why they should be deemed less upright or patriotic, than any other rank of citizens whatever. I therefore humbly propose, that if the merchants in the several states are disposed to send delegates from their body, to meet and attend the sitting of Congress: That they shall be permitted to form a *chamber* of *commerce* and their advice to Congress be demanded and admitted, concerning all bills before Congress, as far as the same may affect the trade of the states.—I have no idea that the continent is made for Congress: I take them to be no more than the upper servants of the great political body, who are to find out things by study and enquiry as other people do; and therefore I think it necessary to place them under the best possible advantages for information, and to require them to improve all those advantages, to qualify themselves in the best manner possible, for the wise and useful discharge of the vast trust and mighty authority reposed in them; and as I conceive the advice of the merchants to be one of the greatest sources of necessary information, which is any where placed within their reach, it ought by no means to be neglected, but so husbanded and improved, that the greatest possible advantages may be derived from it:— Besides this, I have another reason why the merchants ought to be consulted, I take it to be very plain that the husbandry and manufactures of the country must be ruined, if the present weight of taxes is continued on them much longer, and of course a very great part of our revenue must arise from imposts on merchandize, which will fall directly within the merchants sphere of business, and of course their concurrence and advice will be of the utmost consequence, not only to direct the properest mode of levying those duties, but also to get them carried into quiet and peaceable execution. No men are more conversant with the citizens, or more intimately connected with their interests, than the merchants, and therefore their weight and influence will have a mighty effect on the minds of the people. I do not recollect an instance, in which the court of London ever rejected the remonstrances and advices of the merchants, and did not suffer severely for their pride. We have some striking instances of this in the disregarded advices and remonstrances of very many English merchants against the American war, and their fears and apprehensions we see verified, almost like prophecies, by the event.—I know not why I should continue this argument any longer, or indeed why I have urged it so long, inasmuch as I cannot conceive that Congress or any body else will deem it below the dignity of the supreme power to consult so important an order of men, in matters of the first consequence, which fall immediately under their notice, and in which their experience, and of course their knowledge and advice is preferable to that of any other order of men.—Besides the benefits which Congress may receive from this institution, a chamber of commerce, composed of members from all trading towns in the states, if properly instituted and conducted, will produce very many, I might almost say, innumerable advantages of singular utility to all the states—it will give dignity, uniformity, and safety to our trade, establish the credit of the bank—secure the confidence of foreign merchants—prove in very many instances a fruitful source of improvement of our staples and mutual intercourse—correct many abuses—pacify discontents—unite us in our interests, and thereby cement the general union of the whole commonwealth—will relieve Congress from the pain and trouble of deciding many intricate questions of trade which they don't understand, by refering them over to this chamber, where they will be discussed by an order of men, the most competent to the business of any that can be found, and most likely to give a decision that shall be just, useful and satisfactory. It may be objected to all this, that the less complex and the more simple every constitution is, the nearer it comes to perfection: This argument would be very good, and afford a very forcible conclusion, if the government of men was like that of the Almighty, always founded on wisdom, knowledge and truth; but in the present imperfect state of human nature, where the best of men know but in part, and must recur to advice and information for the rest, it certainly becomes necessary to form a constitution on such principles, as will secure that information and advice in the best and surest manner possible. It may be further objected that the forms herein proposed, will embarrass the business of Congress, and make it at best slow and dilatory. As far as this form will prevent the hurrying a bill through the house without due examination, the objection itself becomes an advantage—at most these checks on the supreme authority, can have no further effect than to delay or destroy a good bill, but cannot pass a bad one; and I think it much better in the main, to loose a good bill than to suffer a bad one to pass into a law.—Besides it is not to be supposed, that clear plain cases will meet with embarrassment, and 'tis most safe that untried, doubtful, difficult matters should pass through the gravest and fullest discussions, before the sanction of law is given to them;—but what is to be done if the two houses grow jealous and ill-natured, and after all their information and advice, grow out of humour and insincere, and no concurrence can be obtained—I answer, sit still and do nothing till they get into better humour: I think this much better than to pass laws in such a temper and spirit, as the objection supposes.—It is however an ill compliment to so many grave personages, to suppose them capable of throwing aside their reason, and giving themselves up like children to the controul of their passions; or if this should happen for a moment, that it should continue any length of time, is hardly to be presumed of a body of men placed in such high stations of dignity and importance, with the eyes of all the world upon them—but if they should after all, be capable of this, I think it madness to set them to making laws, during such fits—its best when they are in no condition to do good, to keep them from doing hurt,—and if they don't grow wiser in reasonable time, I know of nothing better than to be ashamed of our old appointment and make a new one. But what if the country is invaded, or some other exigency happens so pressing, that the safety of the state requires an immediate resolution?—I answer what would you do if such a case should happen, where there was but one house unchecked but equally divided, so that a legal vote could not be obtained. The matter is certainly equally difficult and embarrassed in both cases: But in the case proposed, I know of no better way than that which the Romans adopted on the like occasion, viz. that both houses meet in one chamber and choose a dictator, who should have and exercise the whole power of both houses, till such time as they should be able to concur in displacing him, and that the whole power of the two houses should be suspended in the mean time.

I further propose, that no grant of money whatever shall be made, without an appropriation and that rigid penalties (no matter how great, in my opinion the halter would be mild enough) shall be inflicted on any person however august his station, who should give order, or vote for the payment, or actually pay one shilling of such money to any other purpose, than that of its appropriation, and that no order whatever, of any superior in office shall justify such payment, but every order shall express what funds 'tis drawn upon, and what appropriation 'tis to be charged to, or the order shall not be paid:—This kind of embezzlement is of so fatal a nature, that no measures or bounds are to be observed in curing it, when ministers will set forth the most specious and necessary occasions for money, and induce the people to pay it in full tale; and when they have gotten possession of it, to neglect the great objects for which it was given, and pay it, sometimes squander it away for different purposes, oftentimes for useless, yea hurtful ones, yea often even to bribe and corrupt the very officers of government, to betray their trust, and contaminate the state, even in its public offices—to force people to buy their own destruction, and pay for it with their hard labour—the very sweat of their brow, is a crime of so high a nature, that I know not any gibbet too cruel for such offenders.

I would further propose, that the aforesaid great ministers of state, shall compose a council of state, to whose number Congress may add three others, viz. one from New-England, one from the middle states, and one for the southern states, one of which to be appointed president by Congress;—to all of whom shall be committed the supreme executive authority of the states, (all and singular of them ever accountable to Congress) who shall superintend all the executive departments, and appoint all executive officers, who shall ever be accountable to and removeable for just cause, by them or Congress, i. e. either of them.

I propose further, that the powers of Congress, and all the other departments acting under them, shall all be restricted to such matters of general necessity and utility to all the states only, as cannot come within the jurisdiction of any particular state, or to which the authority of any particular state is not competent; so that each particular state shall enjoy its sovereignty and supreme authority to all intents and purposes, excepting only those high authorities and powers by them delegated to Congress, for the purposes of the general union. There remains one very important article still to be discussed, viz. what methods the constitution shall point out, to enforce the acts and requisitions of Congress, through the several states; and how the states which refuse or delay obedience to such acts or requisitions shall be treated: This I know is a particular of the greatest delicacy, as well as of the utmost importance, and therefore, I think, ought to be decidedly settled by the constitution, in our coolest hours, whilst no passions or prejudices exist, which may be excited by the great interests, or strong circumstances of any particular case which may happen. I know that supreme authorities are liable to err, as well as subordinate ones. I know that courts may be in the wrong as well as the people; such is the imperfect state of human nature, in all ranks and degrees of men; but we must take human nature as it is, it cannot be mended, and we are compelled, both by wisdom and necessity, to adopt such methods as promise the greatest attainable good, though perhaps not the greatest possible, and such as are liable to the fewest inconveniencies, though not altogether free of them. This is a question of such magnitude, that I think it necessary to premise the great natural principles on which its decision ought to depend.—In the present state of human nature, all human life is a life of chances; 'tis impossible to make any interest so certain, but there will be a chance against it, and we are in all cases obliged to adopt a chance against us, in order to bring ourselves within the benefit of a greater chance in our favour, and that calculation of chances which is grounded on the great natural principles of truth and fitness, is of all others the most likely to come out right.

1. *No laws of any state whatever, which do not carry in them a force which extends to their effectual and final execution, can afford a certain or sufficient security to the subject:* This is too plain to need any proof.

2. *Laws or ordinances of any kind, (especially of august bodies of high dignity and consequence) which fail of execution, are much worse than none;* they weaken the government; expose it to contempt; destroy the confidence of all men, natives and foreigners in it, and expose both aggregate bodies and individuals, who have placed confidence in it, to many ruinous disappointments, which they would have escaped, had no law or ordinance been made: Therefore,

3. To appoint a Congress with powers to do all acts necessary for the support and uses of the union; and at the same time to leave all the states at liberty to obey them or not with impunity, is in every view, the grossest absurdity, worse than a state of nature, without any supreme authority at all, and at best a ridiculous effort of childish nonsense: And of course,

4. Every state in the union is under the highest obligations to obey the

supreme authority of the whole, and in the highest degree amenable to it, and subject to the highest censure for disobedience.—Yet all this notwithstanding, I think the soul that sins should die, i. e. the censure of the great supreme power, ought to be so directed, if possible, as to light on those persons, who have betrayed their country, and exposed it to dissolution, by opposing and rejecting that supreme authority, which is the band of our union, and from whence proceeds the principle strength and energy of our government. I therefore propose, that every person whatever, whether in public or private character, who shall by public vote or other overt act, disobey the supreme authority, shall be amenable to Congress, shall be summoned and compelled to appear before Congress, and on due conviction, suffer such fine, imprisonment or other punishment, as the supreme authority shall judge requisite. It may be objected here, that this will make a member of assembly accountable to Congress for his vote in assembly; I answer, it does so, *in this only case,* viz. when that vote is to disobey the supreme authority: No member of assembly can have right to give such a vote, and therefore ought to be punished for so doing—When the supreme authority is disobeyed, the government must loose its energy and effect, and of course the empire must be shaken to its very foundation. A government which is but half executed, or whose operations may all be stopped by a single vote, is the most dangerous of all institutions.—See the present *Poland* and ancient *Greece,* buried in ruins, in consequence of this fatal error in their policy. A government which has not energy and effect, can never afford a protection or security to its subjects, i. e. must ever be ineffectual to its own ends.

I cannot therefore admit, that the great ends of our union should lie at the mercy of a single state, or that the energy of our government should be checked by a single disobedience, or that such disobedience should ever be sheltered from censure and punishment; the consequence is too capital, too fatal to be admitted. Even though I know very well that a supreme authority with all its dignity and importance, is subject to passions like other lesser powers, they may be and often are heated, violent, oppressive, and very tyrannical; yet I know also, that perfection is not to be hoped for in this life, and we must take all institutions with their natural defects, or reject them altogether: I will guard against these abuses of power as far as possible, but I cannot give up all government or destroy its necessary energy for fear of these abuses. But to fence them out as far as possible, and to give states as great a check, on the supreme authority as can consist with its necessary energy and effect, I propose that any state may petition Congress to repeal any law or decision which they have made, and if more than half the states do this, the law or decision shall be repealed, let its nature or importance be however great, excepting only such acts as create funds for the public credit, which shall never be repealed till their end is effected, or other funds equally effectual are substituted in their places; but Congress shall not be obliged to repeal any of these acts, so petitioned against, till they have time to lay the reasons of such acts before such petitioning states, and to receive their answer; because such petitions may arise from sudden heats, popular prejudices, or the publication of matters false in fact, and may require time and means of cool reflection and the fullest information, before the final decision is made: But if after all, more than half the states persist in their demand of a repeal, it shall take place.—The reason is, the uneasiness of a majority of states affords a strong presumption that the act is wrong, for uneasiness arises much more frequently from wrong than right; but if the act was good and right, it would still be better to repeal and loose it, than to force the execution of it against the opinion of a major part of the states; and lastly, if every act of Congress is subject to this repeal, Congress itself will have stronger inducement not only to examine well the several acts under their consideration, but also to communicate the reasons of them to the states, than they would have, if their simple vote gave the final stamp of irrevocable authority to their acts.

Further I propose, that if the execution of any act or order of the supreme authority shall be opposed by force in any of the states, which God forbid! It shall be lawful for Congress to send into such state a sufficient force to suppress it.—On the whole, I take it that the very existence and use of our union, essentially depends on the full energy and final effect of the laws made to support it; and therefore I sacrifice all other considerations to this energy and effect, and if our union is not worth this purchase, we must give it up—the nature of the thing does not admit any other alternative. I do contend that our union is worth this purchase—*with it*, every individual rests secure under its protection, against foreign or domestic insult and oppression—*without it*, we can have no security against the oppression, insult and invasion of foreign powers, not any single state is of importance enough to be an object of treaty with them; or if it was, could it bear the expence of such treaties, or support any character or respect in a dissevered state: We shall loose all respectability among the nations abroad. We have a very extensive trade which can't be carried on with security and advantage, without treaties of commerce and alliance with foreign nations. We have an extensive western territory which can't be defended against the invasion of foreign nations, bordering on our frontiers, who will cover it with their own inhabitants, and we shall loose it forever, and our extent of Empire be thereby restrained; and what is worse, their numerous posterity will in future time drive ours into the sea, as the *Goths* and *Vandals* formerly conquered the Romans in like circumstances, unless we have force of the union to repel such invasions. We have without the union, no security against the inroads and wars of one state upon another, by which our wealth and strength, as well as ease and comfort, will be devoured by enemies growing out of our own bowels. I conclude then, that the union is not only of the most essential consequence to the well-being of the states in general, but to that of every individual citizen of them, and of course ought to be supported, and made as useful and safe as possible, by a constitution which admits that full energy and final effect of government which alone can secure its great ends and uses.

In a dissertation of this sort, I would not wish to descend to minutiae, yet there are some small matters which have important consequences, and therefore ought to be noticed. 'Tis necessary that Congress should have all usual and necessary powers of self preservation and order, e. g. to imprison for contempt, insult, or interruption, &c. and to expel their own members for due causes, among which I would rank that of non-attendance on the house, or partial attendance without such excuse as shall satisfy the house. Where there is such a vast authority and trust devolved on Congress, and the grand and most important interests of the Empire rest on their decisions, it appears to me highly unreasonable that we should suffer their august consultations to be suspended, or their dignity, authority and influence lessened by the idleness, neglect and non-attendance of its members, for we know that the acts of a thin house do not usually carry with them the same degree of weight and respect as those of a full house; besides I think, when a man is deputed a delegate in Congress, and has undertaken the business, the whole Empire becomes of course possessed of a right to his best and constant services, which if any member refuses or neglects, the Empire is injured and ought to resent the injury, at least so far as to impel and send him home, that so his place may be better supplied.

I have one argument in favour of my whole plan, viz. 'tis so formed that no men of dull intellects, or small knowledge, or of habits too idle for constant attendance, or close and steady attention, can do the business with any tolerable degree of respectability, nor can they find either honor, profit or satisfaction in being there, and of course, I could wish that the choice of the electors might never fall on such a man, and if it should, that he might have sense enough (of pain at least, if not of shame) to decline his acceptance; for after all that can be done, I don't think that a good administration depends wholly on a good constitution and good laws, for insufficient or bad men will always make bad work, and a bad administration, let the constitution and laws be ever so good; the management of able, faithful and upright men alone, can cause an administration to brighten, and the dignity and wisdom of an Empire to rise into respect; make truth the line and measure of public decisions; give weight and authority to the government, and security and peace to the subject.

We now hope that we are on the close of a war of mighty effort and great distress, against the greatest power on earth, whet into the most keen resentment, and savage fierceness, which can be excited by wounded pride, and which usually rises higher between brother and brother offended, than between strangers in contest. Twelve of the thirteen United States have felt the actual and cruel invasions of the enemy, and eleven of our capitols have been under their power first, or last, during the dreadful conflict; but a good Providence, our own virtue and firmness, and the help of our friends, have enabled us to rise superior to all the power of our adversaries, and made them seek to be at peace with us.

During the extreme pressures of the war, indeed many errors in our administration have been committed, when we could not have experience and time for reflection, to make us wise; but these will easily be excused, forgiven and forgotten, if we can now while at leisure, find virtue, wisdom and foresight enough to correct them, and form such establishments, as shall secure the great ends of our union, and give dignity, force, utility and permanency to our Empire. 'Tis a pity we should lose the honor and blessings which have cost us so dear, for want of that wisdom and firmness in measures, which are essential to our preservation. 'Tis now at our option, either to fall back into our original atoms, or form such an union, as shall command the respect of the world, and give honor and security to all our people.

This vast subject lies with mighty weight on my mind, and I have bestowed on it my utmost attention, and here offer the public the best thoughts and sentiments I am master of. I have confined myself in this dissertation, intirely to the nature, reason and truth of my subject, without once adverting to the reception it might meet with from men of different prejudices or interests. To find the truth, not to carry a point has been my object. I have not the vanity to imagine that my sentiments may be adopted; I shall have all the reward I wish or expect—if my dissertation shall throw any light on the great subject, shall excite an emulation of enquiry, and animate some abler genius to form a plan of greater perfection, less objectionable and more useful.

Philadelphia, February 16, 1783.

Roger Sherman, *Remarks on a Pamphlet Entitled "A Dissertation on the Political Union and Constitution of the Thirteen United States of North America by a Citizen of Philadelphia,"* 1784

Much of this pamphlet is obviously a response to Webster's essay, but Sherman also digresses and criticizes the recent decision by a commission created under the Articles of Confederation that sided with Pennsylvania over Connecticut in the Wyoming Valley dispute.

To the Freemen and Citizens of the State of Connecticut.

GENTLEMEN,

There has lately appeared *A Dissertation on the political Union, and Constitution of the Thirteen United States of North-America,* written by a Citizen of Philadelphia, which (for political reasons I conclude,) has been reprinted in this state; which pamphlet contains maxims and sentiments inconsistent with, and subversive of the *sovereignty, freedom* and *independence* of these states, calculated to subvert our happy constitution, and to introduce a system or form of government more *sovereign, arbitrary* and *despotic.* I have waited with impatience for some abler pen to detect and expose the secret designs of this author. None appearing, I now present you with the remarks I made, when I first read that Dissertation.

But before I enter upon that subject I would just observe to you, that in founding this new and rising empire, we ought carefully to avoid those errors which have brought ruin on our Parent State.

The national debt of Great-Britain is become so immensely large, that it is not in her power any longer to enslave us, or to tyrannize over the nations of Europe; which has been accumulated by granting exorbitant salaries to the officers of the crown, and supporting a host of *placemen* and *pensioners,* that since the last war, the interest of the national debt will not admit of any abate-

Source: [Roger Sherman], *Remarks on a Pamphlet Entitled "A Dissertation on the Political Union and Constitution of the Thirteen United States of North America by a Citizen of Philadelphia"* (New Haven, Conn.: Timothy Green, 1784).

ment of taxes; but on the other hand, new ones must be devised, or additions made to former taxes for the support of government in peace, which must distress the poor—drive out many of their manufacturers and useful members of society—sink the value of their lands, if not bring on national bankruptcy; and such as cannot seek an asylum elsewhere, must sink down into the most abject state of vassalage and slavery—And the same causes will produce the same effects in every region under the sun.

In the *first place* therefore, if we would avoid their *fate*, let us carefully avoid those measures which have brought on her *ruin.*—*Rome* no sooner became *luxurious*, but she lost her *liberty*, which was every thing worth preserving.—High salaries and emoluments of office do not always convey *wisdom, prudence, and skill in the arts of government.*—Luxury in those who *govern*, will contaminate the body of the people, and fraud, injustice and oppression will be introduced among the common people, to supply the want of the revenues of office among the *great.*—In order therefore to prevent any further the accumulation of our debt, contracted during the war, it would be more to the honour of the states, to copy after the prudent oeconomy of the States of *Holland* while they were loaded with a heavy debt, than to *mimic* the pomp, or assume the parade and pegeantry of the courts of *Europe.*

In the *next place*, if we would support our national credit *abroad*, and regain that confidence which ought forever to be put in public credit at *home*, let us be *just*—do strict justice both to the officers and soldiers of our *brave army*, who have *fought, bled* and *suffered*, in the cause of their country; make speedy and ample provision for the payment of the *interest*, and sinking the principle both of our *national* and *internal* debt, as soon as they can be adjusted, and ascertained to *satisfaction*—which will secure us the favour and protection of heaven, and make us respectable both at home and abroad.

Our public debt although large, with proper oeconomy may be discharged in the compass of a few years, without distressing the states, provided the several legislatures adopt measures to draw out their wealth, without disgusting them to such a degree, as to refuse submission—which will be the greatest calamity that can befal us, which a careful examination of the expenditure of public monies, and strictly calling to account all public defaulters, will have the greatest tendency to prevent.—The consternation into which these states were thrown, by this *bloody, cruel* and *unnatural* war, will and ought to be a sufficient excuse for the expenditure of large sums to little or no profit.—But all *criminal* defaulters, who have appropriated public monies to their own private advantages, or to the aggrandizement of their families, ought publicly to be stigmatized with *indelible reproach.*

A late writer has justly observed, *"That the art of supporting government, and maintaining authority is a delicate art, and requires more circumspection than is generally thought necessary: They who* GOVERN *are perhaps too much accustomed to hold men in* CONTEMPT, *and regard them too much as slaves, subdued and bent down by* NATURE, *while they are only so by* HABIT; *if you lay on a* NEW LOAD, *take care they do not shake it off with* FURY *and with* INTEREST, *forget not that the* LEVER OF POWER, *has no other support than* OPINION; *that the power of those who* GOVERN *is in reality but the power of those who* SUFFER GOVERNMENT. *Remind not people sleeping in their chains, to lift up their eyes to truths too terrible for you; and while they are* OBEYING, *bring not to their remembrance their right to* COMMAND, *when the moment of their rousing shall arrive; when they shall have thought in earnest, that they are not made for their magistrates, but their magistrates for them; when they shall once be able to bring themselves together, to feel the communication of kindred minds; and to pronounce with a voice unanimous, we will not have this law; this practice is offensive, medium is no more; you must be constrained, by an unavoidable alternative, either to punish or to yield; either to be tyrannical, or weak, and your authority thence forward detested or despised.*"—To which I would only add—Human nature, vile as it is, (mankind are so far convinced of the necessity of civil government,) will submit to be governed by just and equitable laws, but will be stubborn and fractious when they are unjust, unreasonable and oppressive—and in this consists the art of governing, more especially a *commonwealth*; and from this quarter republican rulers may look out to prevent trouble in due season, before it is too late. It is an old saying, but a true one, all men cannot *judge*, but they can all *feel*. Nothing will produce a quicker sensation among a free people, who have been accustomed to *eating, drinking,* and being *cloathed,* than to be abridged of those necessary articles, for the private emolument of a few individuals.

It must be acknowledged the highest wisdom in these states, to encourage and promote *frugality, industry, agriculture,* and our own *manufactures*; and to suppress by every judicious measure, *luxury* and *dissipation* of every kind. To accomplish these important views, I must for my own part highly approve of an *impost* recommended by our honourable Continental Congress, in which each state ought to be uniform as to the impost imposed. But whether such an impost laid by Congress, and collected by officers by them appointed; or to be collected by officers appointed by the authority of the state, accountable to our own legislature, to be appropriated to the discharging our quota of the national debt, as soon as the same shall be ascertained, or to be paid into the Continental treasury, to be applied to such uses as they think proper, I must submit to the good sense and integrity of the legislature of the state, on which I think I can safely rely.

The *necessaries* of life are few and simple—The conveniencies of life many—

The luxuries of life still more, and they are such as corrupt the morals of the people.—Encourage industry, and by a sort of necessary consequence, you make mankind frugal and virtuous.—To discharge our quota of the national debt by an impost on all goods or produce of foreign growth imported, every man may choose how much of the national debt he will pay, which will be in exact proportion, to the foreign articles of commerce which he purchases for his own consumption: If my circumstances will permit, and my pride and vanity prompts me to wear a cloth of 40s. per yard, I pay in that article four times as much as my neighbour, who contents himself with a cloth of 10s. which will answer all the purposes of life as well, and in some cases much better, than what cost four times that sum.—But at the same time, if the citizens of these states are unwilling to pay our quota of debt, or to support government, by taxing the luxuries of life, which will gradually and insensibly induce us to be frugal and industrious, it will be to little purpose to enact laws for that end.—To enact laws one session of the assembly, to be repealed the next, only enervates government, and renders the legislature contemptible.— I should therefore think it best, before in *democratical* governments, before any new mode of taxation is adopted by the legislature—to print the bill designed to be passed into a law, with the reasons on which it is founded, and to let the people at large have an opportunity to weigh the reasons of it, before any undue prejudices arise in their minds, or are excited by designing men, and they generally will make a good judgment. But to frame a law, which will give a general uneasiness and disgust, it will be impracticable to execute it.—Perhaps this may be thought too much beneath the dignity of the legislature of the state; but if my memory doth not betray me, it has been, on some occasions, practised by the British parliament, and if it had always been practised both by them, and the several assemblies of these states, it would often have saved them the trouble of frequent repeals. Paying of money, with the greater part of the citizens of this state, is a very serious matter, and those who are best able, are easier led than drove.—It is firmly rivited on my mind, the body of the freemen and citizens of this state are *honest,* and truly willing to pay their quota of the public debt, *justly* due, and shall continue of that opinion, until I see just grounds to alter my sentiments; and for my own part, I am desirous that they should choose the mode in which it shall be done.—If the landed interest of this state, choose their landed interest, stock, &c. should be subjected to pay the public debt;—from which we can scarcely obtain a support for the real necessities of our families, I am content; *provided* we are not subjected to an *assessment,* which would soon involve us in new troubles. Should they rather prefer that mode pointed out by Congress, which certainly will place the greatest burden on the rich and luxurious, I shall for my own part perfectly acquiesce in their choice, *provided* the laws are so calculated, as not to subject the private houses of citizens to *search warrants,* which never ought to be permited in a *free state,* for any thing short of *felony,* as it wears the highest badge of *tyranny* that can possibly be exhibited.

The citizens of this state have long been anxious for a new mode of taxation, and I am for my own part willing that mode should be fairly left to their option and choice. But am fully of opinion, a little calm reflection will incline them to adopt an *impost,* which lays the greatest part of the burden on the rich and luxurious, and has a natural tendency, to promote *industry, oeconomy,* and our own *manufactures.* The appropriation of which is the *prerogative* of the authority that *grants*; the collecting the same authority doubtless will retain in their own hands—and the sooner we comply with it, the sooner we shall be able to discharge our quota of the debt with honour to the state.—But creating many Continental *offices* and *officers,* with large emoluments of office is diametrically opposite to the true spirit and genius of a *republican* government, and tends to enlarge our debt.—The more wheels or springs in any machine, to perform the necessary movements, and the more complicated the structure, the more easily put out of order, and the more difficult to discover and repair the defect.—It is the same with regard to government.—The fewer the laws—the more simple the form of government the better.—The whole code of laws which related to the civil polity of the *Jews* might be comprised in less compass than any one of the five books of *Moses,* although *they were as the stars of heaven for multitude, and as the sand on the sea shore innumerable.*—Their Judges were the elders of their cities, who held their sessions in their gates, and their causes determined without long, tedious and expensive processes.

In the *second place,* if these states expect to maintain their *sovereignty, freedom* and *independence,* they ought carefully and explicitly to instruct their representatives to pay the strictest regard to the articles of our foederal union, and to regulate all their public acts agreeable thereto, as they are the *palladium* of all our civil rights and privileges, and the only band of our *union,* which they should strictly keep *inviolate,* as we regard our PUBLIC FAITH. And I submit it to the wisdom of the legislature of the state whether it may not answer very salutary purposes that a constant correspondence be supported between the several assemblies of the states, and a uniformity maintained in their instructions to the Delegates of Congress upon any general, grand and important concerns which relate to all the states in the *union.*

Tyranny, oppression and *arbitrary power,* make their advances by slow progressive measures, and often under the most specious pretences. They never recede, but keep gradually advancing.—Every deviation therefore, or extention of power, beyond the limits of our most happy constitution, will be attended with the most dangerous consequences.

I will now advert to the remarks on the pamphlet lately published, which I conceive to be of dangerous tendency; which I have attempted with a view to prevent its taking effect, which I should have rejoiced to have seen done by some abler pen.—All I request is your acceptance of the sincere intentions of

THE AUTHOR.

Remarks on a Pamphlet, entituled, &c.

The articles of our foedaral union were drawn up by Congress, and adopted by the states, amidst the *confusions* of a most *bloody, cruel,* and *unnatural* war, when the attention of Congress who drew, and the states who adopted them, was frequently drawn off by continual *alarms, burning of towns, slaughter* and *bloodshed:* No marvel then that every inconveniency attending them when reduced into practice, could not be foreseen, either by those who drew, or those who adopted them; at which period, it would not have been well accepted, had any one discovered, and had ventured to call into question, the propriety of any one of the thirteen articles of our confederation.

It may therefore be adviseable, now we are released from the distressing scenes of war, deliberately to examine, revise, correct and amend them, in every instance, in which when reduced into practice, they may be found—inconsistent with each other—not capable of being carried into execution—or inconsistent with the general sense and understanding of those who adopted them. And every man not an enemy to his country, who in any measure tenders its peace and future happiness, will readily give his consent, if the present articles of our foedaral union are found on a *fair trial,* deficient, in either of the foregoing particulars that they should with *care* and *due deliberation,* be revised, corrected, and amended. For, as a late writer observes, "No government has the prerogative to be *immutable*—No power how respectable soever, *created yesterday,* or a *thousand years* ago, which may not be abrogated *to-morrow*—No government is authorized to regard the state as its *property*—whoever thinks otherwise devotes himself, his family, and his childrens children to misery, allowing to his ancestors a right to stipulate for him, when he did not exist, and arrogating to himself a right to stipulate for his posterity before they existed—All authority in this world began either by the *consent* of the *subjects,* or the *power* of their *master,* in both the one or the other they may justly end— there being no prescription in favor of *tyranny* against *liberty.*"

The author of the dissertation on which I remark, has not proposed any one alteration of the articles of our foederal union thro'out his whole dissertation, but what he proposes for the enlargement of the powers of Congress, by which it is very evident he has high notions of *prerogative* in those who *govern*, how much soever he may be concerned to maintain the natural and constitutional rights of his *fellow subjects*; and rather seems to *banter* than to *support* even their right to choose their own representatives, either in the assemblies of the states, or delegates in Congress.

The Honorable Continental Congress having stiled the Confederacy in the *first* article, THE UNITED STATES OF AMERICA; by the *second* they have taken due care to secure the rights of the separate states in the following words: "*Each state retains its* SOVEREIGNTY, FREEDOM, *and* INDEPENDENCE, and every *power, jurisdiction* and *right,* not *expressly* delegated to the *United States in Congress assembled.*" Every power therefore not *expressly* delegated to Congress by the articles of confederation, still remains to be exercised by the states separately: and in this consists their *sovereignty, freedom* and *independence.*

It cannot be difficult to determine what powers the states have *expressly* delegated to Congress, a careful review of the *ninth* article will solve the difficulty, and if any thing is *doubtfully* expressed, they ought as soon as possible to be explained to the sense and understanding which Congress had when they *draughted,* and which the states had when they *adopted* them. Or if on a *fair trial* it appears that Congress are not vested with all those powers necessary to execute the grand and important ends and designs for which the states entered into confederation, the powers of Congress most certainly must be enlarged, with that care and caution necessary on so important occasion.—But for Congress to *assume,* or for the states to *submit,* to any extension of power, beyond the powers delegated to Congress, will have an effectual tendency to *subvert* the constitution, and destroy what the states highly value, viz. their own *sovereignty, freedom,* and *independence.*

The author of that dissertation on which I am about to remark, says, fol. 5, "*The supreme authority*" (by which he means Congress) "*must have the power of making war and peace—of appointing armies and navies.*" These powers by the 9th article are expressly delegated—"*of appointing officers civil and military.*" Congress in draughting the articles of our foederal union, reserved in their own hands the right of appointing the *general* officers of our armies—The officers of our navies, when we have any in existence, and the states have *expressly* delegated that power to them, to whom in fact it with great propriety belongs, and could not be exercised in any other way but by the supreme authority of the commonwealth—But it never entered into their minds I presume, as it is not even suggested in the articles, their having any power of appointing the *civil officers* of the states, which is a *prerogative,* I presume, the states never will resign, so long as they have any desire to retain their sovereignty, freedom, and independence.—Indeed was the bestowment of places of *honor* and *profit* the gift of the supreme authority of the states, let it be *King, Congress, Stateholder, Regent,* or *Dictator,* or by what name soever called, they would (so long as mankind have any fondness for *honor,* and the *emoluments of office*) have it in their power to *bribe* the assembly of the states, and every one who oppose any usurped authority or undue extension of power beyond the limits of the constitution by which they are governed; but in a *republican* government it saps it to the very foundation. So long as all public measures are open to the examination of the body of the electors, and the bestowment of places of trust left to their representatives, and the emoluments of office kept within reasonable bounds, so long a commonwealth may be governed with safety, in peace and good order; but grant to the supreme authority in any form of government whatever, the sole prerogative of the bestowment of all places civil and military, the prerogative of annexing the emoluments of office, and the bestowment of *pensions,* and their subjects are slaves to all intents and purposes whatever.— True it is a people may be happy under any form of government, so long as *good men* govern, but whenever they become corrupt—if vested with the power of bestowing all offices civil and military, and at the same time they hold the purse-strings, or which is the same thing, have such grants of money settled for life as will enable the chief magistrate, or supreme authority, to grant *pensions* to such as will be the tools and creatures of his court—no matter what the form of government is, or whether governed by a *King* or *Congress,* whenever the supreme authority becomes corrupt, and are desirous of extending their power beyond the bounds prescribed by the constitution, they always have it in their power to effect it. This author proceeds and says, *"They must have the power of making contracts—emitting, coining, and borrowing money— of regulating trade, and making treaties with foreign powers—of establishing post- offices.*—These powers Congress are already *expressly* vested with by the articles of confederation; but these do not seem fully to satisfy the desire of this author. He then proceeds and says, *"In short of doing every thing, which the well being of the commonwealth may require, and which is not compatible, to any particular state, all which require money, and cannot be effected without it, they must therefore of* NECESSITY *be vested with the power of* TAXATION."

This author may remember the Honorable Continental Congress drew up the articles of our foederal union, they doubtless well understood what powers were necessary to be vested in their hands, *"which the well being of the com- monwealth required, and which was not compatible to any particular state,"* at least they understood that matter as well as this author can be supposed to under- stand it; at the same time they fully understood the foundation of our opposition to the unconstitutional measures of the British parliament, and they well knew the confidence placed in them by the states, as the *guardians* of all our civil and natural rights, and they then retained in their own hands, by the articles of our foederal union, all those powers they thought necessary to be lodged in their hands, which we could with safety commit to them, and still the states retain their *sovereignty, freedom,* and *independence,* and they are all *judiciously* and very *expressly* pointed out in the 9th article, viz. "The sole and exclusive right and power of determining on peace and war—of sending and receiving embassadors—entering into treaties and alliances—of establishing rules for deciding in all cases, what captures on land and water shall be legal, and in what manner prizes taken by land or naval forces in the service of the United States shall be divided or appropriated—of granting letters of marque and reprisals in times of peace—appointing courts for the trial of piracies and felonies committed on the high seas, and establishing courts for receiving and determining finally appeals in all cases of captures"—and have made Congress itself "the last resort on appeal in all disputes and differences now subsisting, or that may hereafter arise between two or more states concerning boundary, jurisdiction, or any other cause whatever;" and in consequence of that authority reserved in their own hands, by public accounts, they have already finally determined, that the state of Connecticut have no just and legal claim, by virtue of their grant or charter by letters patent from king Charles the second, (extending its limits from Narraganset-bay on the east, to the South-Sea on the west) to hold any lands by virtue of said grant, west of the state of New-York—although I conclude, it must be conceded, the Susquehannah company made the first purchase of the right of soil from the natives, who were *heretofore* reputed the *lords of the see,* which is, in my opinion, virtually denying, that the original natives have any right to the lands of North-America.—In which judgment of our Honorable Continental Congress I could however fully acquiesce, provided they proceed to judge, and finally to determine, that all grants of lands, made by any of their *most gracious majesties the* KINGS *of* GREAT-BRITAIN *to any of their loving subjects,* shall not extend beyond what their *majesties* had actually *purchased* or *conquered* from the natives, antecedent to their several *grants,* or has since been purchased by any of the subjects of these states, by virtue of a proper licence granted them for that end, and that all the lands, not as yet purchased, or conquered by the joint efforts of the United States, and now ceded by *Great-Britain* to the Thirteen United States of *North-America,* be considered as the property of the aboriginal natives, who were the first discoverers and have the right of *prime occupancey,* and that the right of pre-emption of the soil from the natives, which was all that Great-Britain could cede to us, and that *only* to the exclusion of British subjects, might be and remain the joint interest of the Thirteen United States of *North-America*, by virtue of the late treaty and cession, for I never yet could discover either from *reason* or *revelation*, or from the laws of *nature* and *nations*, that the kings of Great-Britain had any more right to grant to any of his *loving subjects*, all the lands lying between certain latitudes of *North-America*, from the Atlantic on the east, to the South-Seas on the west, which gave his subjects a right to drive out the natives, the original proprietors of the soil, because they did not practice *agriculture* and occupied an extent of territory more than they judged necessary in order to support them by *hunting*, than his SUBLIME HIGHNESS the GRAND SEIGNIOR at this present day has to *re-grant* the same lands to any of his *loving subjects* not inhabited by the subjects of any MAHOMETAN PRINCE, which would give them a right to drive us back into the interior parts of this continent, because we have not the knowledge of the culture of *poppies*, and the manufacture of *opium*, but instead thereof make use of *wine* to the dishonor of their prophet *Mahomet.*—This right, power, or prerogative, call it what they please, claimed by the *Christian princes* of *Europe*, I can by no means acknowledge, unless they are able to shew that North-America was distributed to them, "*when the Most High divided unto the* NATIONS *their* INHERITANCE *when he separated the sons of* ADAM."—But to return from this digression—

The states have likewise *expressly* delegated to Congress "the sole and exclusive right of regulating the alloy, and value of coin struck by their own authority—fixing the standard of weights and measures—regulating the trade and managing all affairs with the Indians—establishing and regulating post-offices—appointing all officers of the land forces in the service of the United States, *excepting regimental officers*—appointing all officers of the naval forces, and commissioning all officers whatever in the service of the United States—making rules for the government and regulation of the said land and naval forces, and directing their operations—to appoint a committee of the states—and such other committees, and civil officers as may be necessary, for the managing the general affairs of the United States, under their direction—to appoint one of their number to preside—to *ascertain* the necessary sums of money to be raised for the service of the United States, and to *appropriate* and *apply* the same for defraying the public expences—to borrow money, or emit bills on the credit of the United States, *transmitting every half year to the respective states an account of the sums of money so borrowed or emitted*—to build and equip a navy—to agree upon the number of land forces."—These are all the *prerogatives* which the honorable Continental Congress asked, or saw necessary to be vested in their hands, as they had the general superintendency of all the United States; and indeed it was all they judged the states could delegate with safety, and leave any business for the several assemblies of the states to transact, except *the regulating of fences, restraining of swine, and preventing old women keeping too many geese, to the nusance of the public.* The foregoing enumerated powers the states have by the 9th article expressly delegated to Congress, and they are as extensive as the *prerogatives* of the crown of *Great-Britain,* about which they make so much noise and bustle; excepting the appointing all officers *civil* and *military,* which in a commonwealth would be altogether *inconsistent,* and for that reason I judge, they did not think would have been prudent for them to ask, or safe for these states to grant: in none of which enumerated articles of delegated powers is the power of *taxation* once mentioned or even hinted at. This power however, this author says, "*They must of* NECESSITY *be vested with.*" However he honestly confesses, and says, fol. 5, "*This is a most important and weighty trust, a dreadful engine of* OPPRESSION, TYRANNY *and* INJURY *when ill used; yet from the* NECESSITY *of the case it must be admitted, for to give a supreme authority, a power of making contracts, without any power of payment—of appointing officers civil and military, without any money to pay them—a power to build ships, without any money to do it with—a power of emitting money, without any power to redeem it—or a power to borrow money, without any power to pay it, &c. &c. such a solecism in government,* (he thinks) *is so naturally absurd, to offer further arguments on the subject, would be to insult the understanding of his readers.*" This author ought to have known *king George the third,* our late gracious sovereign, has all these prerogatives, and no other I can now recollect, excepting the prerogative of appointing, *all officers civil* and *military,* by which, together with a certain sum of money, granted him by his first parliament for life, at the beginning of his reign, which for many years has been usual, in order to gain the favour of their *young prince,* and to enable him to grant it back into the pockets of his favourites by *pensions*; by which two *powerful arguments,* the *kings* of *England,* for a succession of reigns, have gained a majority in the house of commons; or which is the same thing, their *ministers* have gained it,

"For ministers by *kings appointed,*
  are under them the *Lord's anointed*;
Therefore it is the self same thing,
  to *resist* the *minister* or *king.*

By which they have wrecked the civil constitution of that kingdom, the work of ages; and all their boasted liberties are sunk and absorbed by ministerial tools and hirelings, corrupted by their own money, which has been purchased at the expence of the best blood of that nation. Notwithstanding this prince has not in his power, to tax his subjects a single copper without the concurrence of his parliament. Nor have I ever seen, or read any speech, made to his parliament, that he has ever moved to have the *power of taxation,* added to his other royal prerogatives, which this *patriotic author,* says must of *necessity* be vested in Congress,—a power which Congress themselves never once mentioned in the articles of our foederal union; which power, was it once vested in Congress, they might have it in their power, to establish as many *pensioners* as they please; and if the time should ever arrive when they should aspire at greater powers than those with which they are already vested, it would be in their power, as effectually to destroy our present happy constitution, as the nation from whom we derive our original have destroyed their own—and enslave a nation that a few individuals may riot in luxury and excess.

I would just recite a few passages from a late writer on the civil constitution of England, who says, "The king of England has the prerogative of commanding armies, and equipping fleets—but without the concurrence of his parliament he cannot maintain them—he can bestow places and employments—but without his parliament he cannot pay the salleries annexed to them—he can declare war—but without his parliament it is impossible for him to carry it on—in a word, the royal prerogative, destitute as it is, of *imposing taxes,* is like a ship completely equipt, but from which the parliament at pleasure can draw off all the water, and leave it aground, or set it afloat, by granting subsidies." Now let any one run the parallel between the prerogatives of the *King of Great-Britain,* and our *Honorable Continental Congress,* their prerogatives are the same, with this exception, the King of Great-Britain has the prerogative of appointing all officers both *civil* and *military,* our Honorable Continental Congress thought proper only to retain the prerogative of appointing a part, leaving the rest to the states, and 1 thing the division judiciously made—Congress have the prerogative to declare war—but the states, who most certainly have both a *natural* and *constitutional* right to judge of the righteousness of it, may either grant or refuse to grant money to carry it on.—The several assemblies of the states by our constitution, in many respects, stand in the same situation, and have the same restraint on *Congress* that the parliament or rather the commons of England once had on the crown;—that authority which *grants money,* most certainly have a right to *refuse granting,* when they can neither see the *necessity or righteousnss* of the measure for which it is to be granted—This right originates from the reason and nature of things, and is a *self-evident* truth.—Again, Congress are vested with power to build and equip a navy—but we shall have little need of a navy, if what this author says in fol. 4 is just, and I conceive in this instance at least he judges right, viz. That these states *"will command respect, that our exports are either raw materials, or provisions, and their imports mostly finished goods, our trade becomes a capital object, with every manufacturing nation of* EUROPE, *and all the southern colonies of*

America, our friendship and trade will of course be courted, and each power in amity with us will contribute to our security." And if we take proper care not to intermeddle in the *politics* and *broils* of European courts, this doubtless will be our happy situation for *ages.*—This being our case and situation, may not the assemblies of these states, with great propriety, consistent with the articles of our foederal union, refuse to grant money for the building a navy in time of profound peace, should Congress adopt such a measure, merely for the sake of transporting our *American Embassadors* to and from the courts of Europe, or with a view to render ourselves respectable, as a *maritime power*, while we lie under a heavy debt, both to our *generous allies*, as well as to *domestic creditors?* They most certainly may, and ought to do it, under such circumstances—and if the assemblies of the states are warranted and justified in this case, they certainly are in every case, where *granting* of monies is their right and prerogative.

Although the king of England has not the power of *taxation*, he has made out, not only to support the dignity of his crown, but to ravage the ocean with his fleets, and to carry fire and sword on to the continent, in support of his German dominions, at the expence of the blood and treasure of the nation, in which they are in reality, no more interested than *America* is in the quarrels of the *Nabobs* of *Asia*; all which he has effected by his having the *prerogative* of appointing all officers *civil* and *military*, and by means of a custom which has long prevailed, that at the beginning of every reign, the parliament (to court the favor of the young prince) grant him a *fixed permanent revenue for life*, by which he is enabled to grant *Pensions* to so many of his parliament to make them the creatures and tools of his power, as to obtain a majority, and by that means to rule and govern the nation in as despotic a manner as the most absolute monarch of *Europe*. This evil our patriotic Congress, who drew the articles of our confederation, foresaw, in some future period might happen to these states, and for that reason, no doubt, did not think the power of *taxation* could safely be lodged in the hands of Congress, where the representation is so *small*, the *interests, tempers*, and *dispositions* of the states so *diverse.*—Can this author, or any one else imagine the power of *taxation* of this state could be safely lodged in the hands of two delegates, was every member of Congress as upright as we can conceive it possible for the human heart to be, in the present state of this world.—For my own part I respect and revere Congress, and am willing they should be vested with as many *hereditary duties* as the crown of England, and if that will satisfy this author, I am willing they should have the very same, viz. "A few hereditary duties on the exportation of wool, a branch of which in the reign of George I. was fixed at seven thousand pounds—a duty of two shillings on every ton of wine imported—the wrecks of ships, the owners unknown—whales and sturgeons thrown on the coast—

swans swimming on public rivers—and a few feudal relicks, compose the whole *appropriated* revenue of the crown of England—and if these will satisfy this author, without the power of *taxation*, for my own part should be content they should be granted to Congress; that in no one instance, either in point of *prerogative*, or *appropriated revenues*, they should be less respectable than the monarch of Britain.

The king of England by having the right of nominating and appointing all officers *civil* and *military*, and by a *moderate* grant of parliament of about a million sterling annually settled upon him during life, is enabled to grant so many *pensions* as to purchase his parliament, and thereby to destroy the best civil constitution, in many respects, that ever was composed and established on this side *Mount-Sinai*—an establishment from our peculiar circumstances, we in these states cannot copy after or adopt, and therefore it is the duty of every individual to guard against all innovations, or any infringements that may be attempted to be made on our civil constitution, which the wisdom of Congress have devised and judiciously draughted, and the states solemnly adopted, which we ought carefully to guard and maintain, otherwise our ruin will be of ourselves.

This author doth not even pretend we have already vested Congress with the power of *taxation*, but says they must be vested with it from *necessity*, and urges reasons to support that *necessity*; but there are others *weak* and *silly* enough to assert, they are already vested with that power, and found their opinion on these words in the 9th article, "to ascertain the necessary sums of money to be raised for the *service* of the United States, and to appropriate and apply the same for defraying the public expences."—But whoever founds his opinion on those words, must be ignorant of the true end and design of our confederation, and the spirit and meaning of those words in the 9th article.

The true end and design of our confederation I take to be this, viz. To unite the strength of the separate states under Congress as their *general Head*, and to delegate to them the direction of the operations of our military and naval forces against the power of Great-Britain.—And this I take it was the general sense and understanding of the states who adopted the articles of our foederal union, and the whole tenor of the articles themselves support this opinion.— Congress are to determine the number of *troops* necessary for the *service* of the states—What *service?* The *service* of the war and general defence—and for that end they were to make requisition to each state for their *quota*, "and to ascertain the necessary sums of money to be raised for the *service*" of the war, and to appropriate and apply the same; that matter not being *compatible to any particular state*, by constitution is vested in congress, whose right it properly is, and is *expressly* delegated to them.—But this our author cannot put up with, without their being vested with the power of *taxation*: who says, fol. 6, *"This would make all payments dependant on* THIRTEEN POPULAR ASSEMBLIES." And adds, "*The present broken state of our finances—public debt, and bankrupt- cies—enormous and ridiculous depreciation of public securities, with a total anni- hilation of our public credit—prove beyond all contradiction the* VANITY *of all recourse to the several assemblies of the states—the recent instance of the duty of 5 per cent. on imported goods* STRUCK DEAD, *and the Bankruptcies which ensued, on the single vote of* RHODE-ISLAND." What bankruptcies ensued on Rhode-Island's negativing the impost act, which was to have been collected by officers appointed by Congress, and applied at their discretion, in which the states could have no power to appropriate to the payment of their quota of debt contracted during the war, agreeable to the 8th article, the author can better say than I can pretend—but that the depreciation of bills—failure of public credit, and many bankruptcies ensued before the impost was asked for by Congress, or denied by Rhode-Island, are facts that are notorious, which many attribute to the want of seasonable and adequate taxation, which, creating a demand, would at least have retarded the depreciation of our bills. Our author however appears much out of humour with the state of Rhode-Island for preventing the operation of the *impost act*, and is desirous to enlarge the powers of Congress to prevent the like mischief in future; but at the same time seems desirous "*to restrain them from doing any mischief in the exercise of those* VAST *powers*, with which he seems very sollicitous Congress should be vested—This he thinks the *most difficult part of the weighty subject he had undertaken*," and puts up a short ejaculatory prayer, "*That Almighty Wisdom would direct his pen in the arduous discussion*," *fol.* 12. And in truth and reality, the framing a perfect and complete system of government for a rising empire, is a most arduous and very important subject; and as he seems desirous of Divine Aid, I would rec- ommend it to him *once more* to consult his bible, and duly weigh and consider the civil polity of the *Hebrews*, which was planned by Divine Wisdom, for the government of that people although their territory was small; by preventing an undue monopoly of lands by their reversion to the original proprietors in the lineal descent of the families at the *jubilee*, (which was every half century) it supported vast numbers of inhabitants within very narrow limits—their laws were few and simple—their judges the elders of their cities, well acquainted with the credibility of the parties and their evidences—they held their courts in the places of greater concourse, the gates of the city, and their processes were neither lengthy nor expensive.

Our author having informed us with what powers the supreme authority ought to be vested, in the next place has undertaken to let us know how this supreme authority is to be *constituted* so as to do no mischief with that vast authority with which he has cloathed them: he carefully avoids using the word *elected*, as he seems to have a mortal hatred of *popular elections*, in which process he is very methodical and says, 1st. *"The men who compose this important council must be* DELEGATED, *not elected, from all the states, and it is to be wished, that none might be* APPOINTED, *that were not adequate to this weighty business; but a little knowledge of human nature, and a little acquaintance with the political history of mankind, will soon teach us, that this is not to be expected. The representatives appointed by* POPULAR ELECTIONS, *are commonly, not only the* LEGAL, *but the* REAL, SUBSTANTIAL *representatives of their electors, i. e. there will commonly be about the same proportion of* GRAVE, SOUND, WELL QUALIFIED *men—*TRIFLING DESULTORY *men—*WILD *or* KNAVISH *schemers—and* DULL IGNORANT *fools* in the delegated assembly, as in the *body* of *electors."* What a motly mixture this of which our *supreme authority* and the assemblies of the states are composed!—A most severe *burlesque* obliquely cast on our Honorable Continental *Congress,* and the *assemblies* of the states, if the account given of them by this author is just! What a pity it is we have made choice of a *democratical* form of government, and that all our civil rulers were not made so by *birth,* or *hereditary right,* and that *kings, lords, dukes, barons, earls,* and *knights,* were not the *natural* and *spontaneous* growth of *North-America;* and all their *virtues* such as *knowledge, integrity, skill* in the *arts of government,* but above all, their exemplary *piety,* and firm attachment to the doctrines of *revelation,* and the *civil constitution* of the *Christian religion* as established by our *ancestors;* and that they were not all made *hereditary* to descend with their lands to all *generations.* But what adds to our misfortune he says *"he knows no way to help this;"* if that is truly the case, we are in a very *pitiable situation* truly! But for once I will just hint at a few things, which if our legislatures should think worthy of a trial, I presume many advantages will arise from them, and without some attention, to some or all of them, a commonwealth never was, nor ever will be continued long, without *intrigues, cabals,* and *factions.* In the *first* place, no office or place of trust should be made *lucrative,* any further than to support the dignity of the station with *decency* and *honor,* but not to enrich themselves or families, by the emoluments of office. *Secondly,* Let all transactions of a public nature, both in Congress and the assemblies of the states, be open to the free examination of all the electors—a printed journal both of Congress and the assemblies of the states, with the *yeas* and *nays* to every interesting question that comes before them—No man is worthy of public trust that has not an opinion of his own, or is afraid to let that opinion be known to his electors—this will make him careful, that he judges and acts according to TRUTH, of which the body of the electors in this state besure, taken collectively, are better judges, both of men and measures, than our author seems to imagine; only let them have the means of knowledge, instead of being abused by *bowing, cringing, fawning courtiers,* who are always of the opinion of the majority present, unless they happen to mistake their numbers.—There is not a single proposition in our author's whole dissertation more just than this, "TRUTH *loves* LIGHT, *and is vindicated by it,* WRONG *shrouds itself in* DARKNESS, *and is supported by* DELUSION." *Lastly,* Let there be a regular account of the expenditure of all public monies, *annually* laid before Congress and the Assemblies of the states, as those who pay money most certainly have a right to know how, and *to what use it is applied.*

These means of knowledge, of men and measures, being afforded to the electors of these states, I presume there are sufficient numbers in each state, who are men of *ability, integrity* and *discernment,* who can distinguish by those helps, (which are in the power of the legislatures to afford) *"the grave, sound, well-qualified men,* from *trifling, desultory men,* and *wild knavish schemers,* from *dull ignorant fools:"* who would be faithful to enlighten their less discerning, but honest neighbours, and in that manner regulate their choice better than the *sly, insinuating, intriguing patriots* of the present day do, by the means of knowledge we enjoy in this state: and this I judge would be more to the satisfaction of the *freemen of this state,** and would have a greater tendency to serve the interest of the states, than what he proposes under his *second* general head, viz. *"That the Congress shall consist of* TWO CHAMBERS, *an* UPPER *and* LOWER HOUSE, *or a* SENATE *and* COMMONS, *with the concurrence of both necessary to every act, and that every state send one or more delegates to each house."* This he says, *"will subject every act to two discussions, before two distinct chambers of men,* EQUALLY *qualified for the debate,* EQUALLY *masters of the subject, and of* EQUAL *authority in the decision,"* and if *equal* in all respects, I cannot at present see the necessity of building two chambers to hold them.—But another difficulty arises in my mind, as our author has not as *yet* pointed out any new mode to *constitute* these delegates, if *elected* in our present mode, they will still remain not only the *legal,* but the *real substantial representatives of their electors,* so that I do not see any real advantages obtained by the *division,* as both chambers it seems, must be filled with men of *equal* abilities, and of *equal* authority, unless as they are equal in all respects, it must be supposed the houses will be *complaisant* to each other, and frequently change chambers, which will afford some little amusement in time of peace, when but little business that is

---

* I may, perhaps, be told, Congress do publish such a journal—I would just ask for information, Has that journal ever been *once* laid before the General Assembly *officially,* as we had reason to expect by the 9th article? If it has not, at whose door doth the neglect lie?

urgent, will by our constitution, lie before them, and may prove salutary by changing the air.

Our author under his *second general head,* it must be owned, manages the division of Congress with some *art;* however he now and then a little drops his *mask.* In page 15 he has found out Congress *"will stand in need of much information,"* and has devised a plan to furnish them with the *"best and surest information, and of that kind that may be most safely relied upon,"* which information he thinks may be best made through the medium of certain *ministers of state* which he has planned out; and *first* mentions a *financier* as being uppermost on his mind, who manages the whole business of *revenues* and *expenditures,* which high and important office, our author no doubt intends to fill, as he tells us, fol. 7, he is about soon to publish an essay on *finance,* on which subject doubtless he will *shine,* and it being attended with a decent sallery, it must be supposed it would be agreeable to him to fit at the head of the *American treasury;* but more especially, should the states be so happy as to see with him, the *necessity* to vest Congress with the power of *taxation,* which would save the states the trouble of collecting their own *quota* of the continental debt, and fall directly into the continental treasury, under his own immediate inspection.

He in the next place supposes a *secretary of state* would likewise be very necessary to give *information;* who would have the knowledge of the *general policy,* and *internal government*—To these he adds a *minister of war,* who must preside in the business of *war* and *defence*—of this minister however, by his own account, we shall stand but in little need, as *"all the manufacturing nations of Europe, will court our friendship, and contribute to our security,"* for which reason it will hardly answer to maintain the dignity of that minister, purely to conduct a war with the *sachems* of the interior parts of *America,* who I fancy will stand in as much fear of the United States, as the manufacturing nations of Europe (for their *own advantage*) will *court our friendship and contribute to our security."*—To these *great ministers of state,* this author would have added JUDGES of LAW and CHANCERY—All these GREAT MINISTERS of STATE he would have to serve as ATTENDANTS on the two chambers of Congress, to give them the *best information* in their several departments of office, whose opinion he would oblige Congress always to take, before they finally pass any bill, without which formality being duly attended to, the act of Congress to be *void.* But at the same time he is so careful to guard the dignity of the *two chambers* of Congress, as not to enable these *great ministers* of *state* to negative any act of Congress, how contrary soever the same may be to their *opinion* and *advice*—so that these great ministers of state are more for *ornament,* and to add to the *dignity* of Congress, than any real utility, like the *mantling to a coat of arms.* Vid. fol. 16, 17. And to fill up the *rear* of these great ministers of state, he adds a *chamber of commerce,* composed of *merchants,* to give *information* likewise to Congress, respecting *trade* and *commerce.* So that in reality all these *great ministers of state* are only to serve Congress in quality of INFORMING OFFICERS. And to this fabric of his own structure, in fol. 24, he adds a COUNCIL of STATE, composed of all the aforesaid GREAT MINISTERS of STATE; to which number it shall be the *prerogative* of Congress to add three others, viz. one from the *New-England states,* one from the *middle states,* and one from the *southern states;* one of which three it shall be the *prerogative* of the *president* of Congress to appoint: "*to all of whom shall be committed the* SUPREME EX-ECUTIVE AUTHORITY *of the states, (all and singular of them ever accountable to Congress) who shall superintend all the executive officers, who shall ever be accountable to, or removeable for just cause by them, or Congress,* i. e. *either of them.*" This will keep this *supreme executive authority* in due *decorum,* and oblige them always to do the thing that is *just* and *right,* at least what shall be so judged by the *council* of *state* and *congress,* both of whom will have the power to remove them for any *malfeasances,* which will be a greater restraint than if they were chosen by *popular elections.*

Our author having displayed much skill in the arts of government, by the addition of all these *ministers* and *officers* of *state,* to encrease the *dignity* and add *importance* to Congress; in the next place proposes measures to be adopted to enforce the *strictest obedience* to the requisitions of Congress. In fol. 24 he says, "*There remains one very important article to be discussed, viz.* "*What methods the constitution shall point out to* ENFORCE *the acts and requisitions of Congress thro' the several states; and how the states which* REFUSE *or* DELAY OBEDIENCE *to such acts or requisitions, shall be treated.*" This he says, "*is a particular of the* GREATEST DELICACY, *as well as the* UTMOST IMPORTANCE, *and ought to be decidedly settled in our* COOLEST HOURS." In this I perfectly agree with our author; but *great, delicate* and *important,* as it appears to him to be, he has undertaken the *job;* and in fol. 25 he says, "*To appoint a Congress with powers to do all acts necessary for the support and uses of the union; and at the same time to leave all the states at liberty to obey them or not with impunity, is in every view the grossest absurdity, worse than a state of nature, without any supreme authority at all, and at best a ridiculous effort of childish nonsense; and of course, every state in the union is under the highest obligations to obey the supreme authority, and in the highest degree amenable to it, and subject to the highest censure for disobedience; yet all this notwithstanding I think,* the soul that sins should die. *The censure of the* GREAT SUPREME POWER *ought to be so directed, if possible, as to light on those persons, who have* BETRAYED *their country, and exposed it to* DISSOLU-TION, *by opposing that supreme authority, which is the band of our union, and from whence proceeds the principal strength and energy of our government;* I there-

fore propose that EVERY PERSON, *whether in* PUBLIC *or* PRIVATE CHARAC-
TER, *who by* PUBLIC VOTE, *or other* OVERT ACT DISOBEYS *the* SUPREME
AUTHORITY *shall be amenable to Congress, shall be summoned and* COMPELLED
to appear before Congress, and on due CONVICTION *suffer such* FINE, IMPRIS-
ONMENT, *or other* PUNISHMENT *as the* SUPREME AUTHORITY *shall judge
requisite. It may be objected here,* (and I think very justly) *that this will make a
member of assembly accountable in Congress for his vote in assembly; I answer, it
doth so in this case only, viz. When that vote is to* DISOBEY *the* SUPREME AU-
THORITY.—*No member of assembly can have a right to give such a vote, and
therefore ought to be* PUNISHED *for so doing.—A government which is but half
executed, or whose operations may be stopped by a* SINGLE STATE, *is the most
dangerous of all institutions—I cannot therefore admit, that the great ends of our
union should lie at the mercy of a single state.*"—What is got into the head of
this good citizen of *Philadelphia?* What doth he make of our Honorable Continental Congress who draughted the articles of our *confederation,* that they
should make such egregious blunders, as to form such a lax form of government? Has he the vanity to think Congress who framed the articles of our
foederal union, could not have foreseen these intolerable blunders and defects
in our constitution, and provided a proper remedy? they certainly would. But
this *supposed defect,* is in reality our greatest *safeguard;* and if there is any defect,
it is in his own *opticks.* He expressly owns, fol. 26, *The supreme authority are
subject to passions like other lesser powers; they may, and often are,* HEATED,
VIOLENT, OPPRESSIVE, *and very* TYRANNICAL; *and seems disposed to* FENCE
them out as far as possible, and to give the states as great a CHECK *on the supreme
authority, as can consist with its necessary energy.*—This is the very *fence* and
check which Congress, in their wisdom, saw *necessary* to provide, for the safety
and security of the states, when framing our civil constitution; and we greatly
rejoice in their *wisdom, prudence,* and *precaution.*—It is the very same *fence* and
check provided for the *seven united provinces* of *Holland.*—No state in the confederation, I presume, will oppose, or neglect to carry into execution, any
resolution of Congress which they judge to be for the general good of the states
included in the union; and until they can see it, he cannot blame them if they
oppose it; but especially if they judge such requisition inconsistent with the
articles of our foederal union, when he himself owns *the supreme authority may
be, and often are, heated, violent, oppressive, and very tyrannical.*—I cannot conceive why our author should be so very *fretful* and out of *humour* with our
present happy constitution; I fear his expectations were too much raised as a
financier; that the disappointment occasioned by *Rhode-Island's* negativing the
Impost Act in the very form pointed out by Congress, has ruffled him too
much; and that he did not write this part of his Dissertation "*in his coolest*

hours." I never yet have learned that the state of Rhode-Island have ever refused to fund their *quota* of the national debt, and to make speedy and ample provision for the payment of the interest, and gradual sinking of the principal, as soon as their quota is made out, agreeable to the 8th article of the Confederation.—For my own part, it would greatly affect me to see any member of our honorable Assembly *dragged* down to Congress, with all the whole retinue of evidences *pro* and *con,* merely for denying the authority of Congress, and voting accordingly, (when at the same time he thought, and perhaps very justly, that Congress had no constitutional right to make such a requisition) and be subjected to fine, imprisonment, and corporeal punishment. This would make our worthy members *awfully* afraid to support our own constitutional rights, our *sovereignty, freedom,* and *independence,* secured to us by the second article of our foederal union, which we have not *expressly* delegated to Congress by the ninth. Our author would have discovered more *lenity,* and more of a *christian frame and temper of mind,* if he had been willing to pass over such an error, (if, on strict scrutiny, it should prove to be an error) to have the offender only publicly reproved by the speaker, from his *chair,* for an error of that kind, committed through *ignorance* or *inadvertence*; as he can be considered only as the *legal, real* and *substantial* representative of the *common herd* of his *electors:*— For which reason, in behalf of such *state offenders,* I would humbly supplicate the several legislatures of the states not to admit of such an alteration in the articles of our foederal union, until our honorable Continental Congress shall discover the necessity of such a measure, and recommend the same to be adopted by the states.

Some have suggested, that this author may possibly be employed, by our honorable Congress, to try how far the citizens of these states would submit to such arbitrary and despotic measures: But such suggestions I reject with contempt and disdain. It must be impossible that Congress, who drafted the articles of our foederal union, and so carefully guarded the states against all arbitrary and despotic measures, should so soon attempt to subvert our happy constitution; much less would they improve so whimsical a writer as our author appears to be, to effect the design; and that without ever once moving to the assemblies of the states for any enlargement of their powers; which, no doubt, they would most readily comply with, if necessary. This state, in order to enable Congress to proportion the quota of debt to each state, I am told, on requisition, have already acceded to the alteration of the 8th article,* that speedy

---

* The 8th article of Confederation, originally adopted by the states, is, That in all charges of war, and all other expences incurred for the common defence, the quota of each state was to be in proportion to the value of lands, &c. This estimate would have been attended with great

provision may be made for the payment of the interest, and gradual sinking the principal, of our whole debt, contracted during the war.—I rather think him some gentleman of a *sovereign, arbitrary, tyrannical* turn of mind, and unhappily *vindictive*; of which he has given a convincing evidence, in fol. 27, in these words—"*Further, I propose, that if the execution of any act or order of the supreme authority shall be opposed by force, in any of the states (which God forbid) it shall be lawful for Congress to send into such state a sufficient force to suppress it.*"—Here, again, our author *interlardes* this *sanguinary proposal* with a short ejaculatory prayer to Almighty God; but then I do not understand him to mean to prevent the operation of his proposal, but that God would *forbid* or *prevent* any state from opposing, by force, the execution of any act of Congress: Which, from the present views I have of the temper and disposition of any of our states, there is not the least danger of; besure so long as they regulate their requisitions by the articles of our foederal union; which Congress themselves *drafted*, and which the states have solemnly adopted. But should Congress ever make any resolutions contrary to the articles of our foederal union, through inadvertence; as this author says, fol. 24, "*I know that supreme authorities are* LIABLE *to err as well as lesser ones*;" or should they, from lust of power, and spirit of domination, become "*over-heated, violent, oppressive, and very tyrannical,*" (as in fol. 26 he owns they may) I should think it their indispensible duty to *resist all unconstitutional extension of power*; although not unto *blood.* But should the states adopt this *sanguinary proposal* of our author, Congress would *constitutionally* be vested with power to enter with an armed force, and shed the blood of any of our sister states, merely for supporting the *constitutional rights* of the states. As Congress have wisely avoided all *sanguinary* measures, in drafting the articles of our union, I should not think it below the dignity of their high station, to manifest their disapprobation of so *sanguinary* a proposal.

This proposal gave me a more violent shock, as I happened to read it just as the news arrived, that 1500 of our continental troops, with a proper train of artillery, were on full march for *Philadelphia* to suppress the turbulent behavour of a part of the *Philadelphia* line of the army, and to protect the honorable Continental Congress from their insults. If the form of civil government in that state is so *lax,* and their citizens not disposed to support it against insults; as the officers of that state are on *half pay* during life, and they can support a

---

expence, and liable to exceptions;—Congress, therefore, moved to the states, That the quota of expence should be in proportion to the number of white and other free inhabitants, and three fifths of the slaves: Which alteration, in proportioning the quota of the states, I am told, has been adopted by the legislature of this state.

body of troops with a small additional expence, it may be well for them to take that method to do it; but I do not think it adviseable or necessary for the states to support an army for that purpose: A mild administration rarely wants an armed force to support it: The rectitude of the measures of Congress, and the Assemblies of the states, will always afford them the surest protection; and wherever the civil power of a state cannot support itself from insult, without a military force to awe their subjects into submission, there is much reason to fear either their civil constitution is deficient, or something is wrong in the administration.—Standing armies may be necessary to support tyranny, oppression, and arbitrary government; but to have recourse to arms in a civil government, is shocking to humanity!—They may be necessary with a *felon*, an *individual*; but with a sister state, a whole community of the same family, the bare mentioning of arms presents to my view the bloody scenes in which we have been involved by our *parent state!*—The unhappy effects of which, time itself will not repair, or obliterate from our minds.

I think none who duly attends to the whole scope and drift of this author, but will easily discover his design is to subvert our present constitution, and to introduce in its room, a government more arbitrary, sovereign, and despotic. His dividing Congress into two Chambers, he seems to think, will make them *wonderful wise*; and is much better disposed towards them than when in one house, and subjects of *popular elections.* However, he finds some difficulty even then: He has found out these two Chambers, *equal*, in all respects, may "*grow jealous and ill-natured, and after all their information and advice, grow out of humour and insincere, and no concurrence can be obtained.*" But he has luckily found out a remedy even in that case, viz. "*Sit still, and do nothing, till they get into better humour.*" This I think as bad a situation, as to have the proceedings of Congress suspended a small period by the vote of a *single state.* But before he arrives to the bottom of page 22, he has discovered a remedy for to cure the two Houses of their *sulky humour:* They must first agree to come into one house, and *lovingly* choose "A Dictator, *who shall have and exercise the whole power of both Houses, till such time as they shall be able to concur in displacing him; and that the whole power of the two Houses be suspended in the mean time.*" (Fol. 22.) Here our author has wholly dropt his *mask:* The two Chambers being furnished with A Dictator by the joint election of both Houses, he is to remain *Dictator* until the Houses can agree to displace him; which period, I presume, will never arrive; for he is to be vested with the *power of both Houses*, so long as they remain out of humour; of course the power of *taxation* will be his *exclusive prerogative*; by means whereof, he will have it in his power to keep the two Houses out of humour, until he makes himself a PERPETUAL DICTATOR. There is no chimera in all this—our author is consistent in his own plan—and his views are *apparent*—to reduce us to an ABSOLUTE MONARCHY; and his plan, carried into execution, will effect the thing.

I trust an *absolute monarch* is not what would be the choice of my fellow citizens: It most certainly would not be my choice, unless I could be assured always of a *wise* and *good Prince*. In a commonwealth, if small, and the electors personally acquainted with public characters, the people may enjoy great happiness; but when a commonwealth becomes *numerous*—their concerns *great and important*—the desire of *riches, honors* and *power* increasing with their numbers,—if the electors have not the means to obtain the knowledge of the public characters of rulers, by their votes given when acting in their public character, the choice of the electors (which, in general, in these northern states, is the main body of the citizens) will be very precarious and uncertain: Discontent and uneasiness will ensue—factions form and increase—frequent alterations and change in civil rulers will ensue;—the greatest calamity that can befal an elective state, or commonwealth, as no man, fit to *rule* or *govern*, will suffer himself to be *mob'd* in, and *mob'd* out, according as the several parties and factions succeed by their intrigues in courting the populace, and imposing on the credulity of their electors: And what will next ensue, courts of justice may, in the same manner, be contaminated,—which must compleat their ruin. An open line of conduct in a commonwealth, subject to the examination of the electors, is the only *barrier* against *tyranny*,—which, in a commonwealth, is the most cruel and oppressive of any species of tyranny whatever.

The form of government planned by Congress, and adopted by the states, is the only form we could adopt under our circumstances: And the honor and dignity of Congress, as a private citizen, I am determined to support, as much as the *sovereignty, freedom,* and *independence* of the states, and every *power, jurisdiction* and *right,* which they have not *expressly* delegated to Congress. But as every deviation from the articles of our foederal union makes a dangerous precedent in future, the defects in the articles of confederation can be known only by *practice:* And it is time enough to make alterations in our system of government, when the defects are made evident.

I must now revert to some things said by this author, which I have passed over, before I conclude these remarks. He says, (fol. 9,) *"Another great object of government, is the apportionment of burdens and benefits,—and that an ill apportionment will be an everlasting source of uneasiness and discontent."*—Again, *"The value of lands may be a good rule, but the ascertainment of that value is impracticable; no assessment can be made which will not be liable to exceptions and debates."*

This observation of our author is doubtless right; the same objections arose in my mind when I first read the 8th article of our foederal union. And our author says, in fol. 10, viz. *"That the number of living souls, or human persons, of whatever age, sex, or condition, will afford us a rule which will forever encrease or decrease with the real wealth of the states; and, of course, will be a perpetual rule, not capable of corruption by any circumstances of future time."*

This mode of proportioning the quota of debt *first* suggested to the public by this author, is *since* recommended by Congress, with this alteration, viz. Two fifth parts of the slaves to be exempted from the *capitation*; the reasons of which exemption do not at present occur to my mind. If I mistake not, Congress have laid a prohibition on the importation of *African slaves*; but this exemption seems rather an encouragement to the owners to progapate them in preference to *horses* or other *stock*; and they are improved for the same purposes in tilling ground in the southern, as oxen are in the northern states, and supported at less expence through our long and tedious winters: And at present I cannot see the reasons of the exemption of two fifth parts from the capitation; but otherwise, this proposal of our author, I acknowledge, would be perfectly reasonable, was all the lands ceded by the late treaty, which were not actually purchased or conquered by the Crown antecedent to the cession, to be considered as the joint interest of all the states in the confederation: But if the western lands ceded by the late treaty, not purchased or conquered by the Crown antecedent to the cession, are to be considered as belonging to those states, by virtue of their ancient grants from the Crown; I cannot as yet discover either the justice or equity, that those states which are circumscribed on every side by the adjoining states, whose lands are all located and fully settled, should pay, by that mode of computing the quota, for so large an extent of territory, gained and defended at the joint expence of all those states, who have not gained one foot of land by the cession;—much less can I see what right the King of Great-Britain had to grant to the *Virginia* and *Plymouth* companies, all the lands lying between certain latitudes in North-America, from the Atlantic Ocean on the east, to the South Sea on the west, not inhabited by the subjects of any *christian prince*; when the aboriginal natives were the first *discoverers*, and had the right of *prime occupancy*; who they do not seem to consider as having any more right to the soil than the *moose, deer, bears* and *foxes* which range the forests.

I well know the Princes of Europe have come into some compacts, that when the subjects of any Prince make a discovery of lands heretofore unknown to the nations of Europe, whether inhabited by any of the human race or not, they take possession of it, in some formal manner, for their Prince; either by giving it some *christian* or *saint's* name, setting up a crucifix, &c. Such sort of compacts, made by the Princes of Europe, may be binding on them on the eastern side of the Atlantic, but do not appear in the same light to the Americans, who, heretofore, have been wont to believe, "*That God hath made of one blood, all nations of the earth, and hath determined the bounds of their habitation.*" And many of us, to this day, think the natives who were the *first discoverers*, and had the right of *prime occupancy*, unless they have sold the same, or that it has been justly conquered, are still vested with the right of soil; and that a patent from the Crown will not justly give us a right to drive them from their habitations. I well know it is said, here was vacant territory of which they stood in no need; but as they lived by fishing, fowling, and hunting, and not furnished with the best conveniencies of taking game, they only are the proper judges of the extent of territory necessary for grazing. By the same rule of reasoning, the Americans may say, that *Britons* are chiefly *manufacturers*, and ought to be cooped up within narrower limits; and may as justly seize on their *parks* and open fields, and divest them thereof, as to dispossess the *Sachems* of America of their hunting ground, and knock their brains out if they refuse to quit the soil—which people, at least many of them, have as just notions of *right* and *wrong*, as the subjects of European Princes. If this reasoning is just, (and at least it appears so to me) no state has a right to one foot of lands, beyond what was purchased or conquered by the Crown antecedent to the cession,—and that cession means no more than ceding to the states the right of pre-emption from the natives (as it is termed) to the exclusion of British subjects. Whether that cession is made to the Thirteen States as joint tenants, or to Congress to hold the same in trust for the confederate states, as I have not seen the Definitive Treaty, I cannot say,—or whether Congress are already vested with power, by the articles of our foederal union, to make a disposition of the same, I shall leave to *civilians* to judge. But when this author says (fol. 10,) such states as by treaty have gained large extent of territory, "*ought either to make grants to the commonwealth of such tracts of defended territory, or sell as much of it as will pay its proper quota of defence, and pay such sums into the public treasury,*" (if what I have urged on that head has any weight, it is the joint interest of all the states already) to use his own expression is "*the grossest absurdity, and at best a ridiculous effort of childish nonsense.*"

The same may with great justice be said with regard to the forfeited estates of *loyalists*; the crime of which they were guilty, was not a crime committed against any state separately, but against all the states included in the confederation; otherwise how we in this state have seized the estates of *loyalists* belonging to the states of *New-York* and *Boston,* and confiscated the same, or by what rule of *right* it could be done, unless the crime is considered as a crime committed against the confederation, and not against this state individually, I know not; which forfeitures I could wish might be appropriated to repair the losses that individuals have sustained by the burning of towns on our sea coasts by *Britons,* and the desolations on our frontiers by their *Indian* allies. Which thought I humbly submit to the wisdom of Congress, and to the justice and compassion of the several assemblies of the states.

As for those unhappy people termed *Loyalists,* who have shed the blood of their country, and robbed, plundered and distressed their friends, their estates are but an inconsiderable compensation for their repeated outrages, they never ought to be permitted to reside among us, and I leave them to be punished by their own reflections. But all such as went over to our enemies from principles of the *Christian religion,* believing it unlawful to resist the civil magistrate, and all such as through fear of the power of *Britain,* and from a consciousness of the inability and unpreparedness of the states to resist, went within their lines, but have neither shed blood, nor aided and assisted the enemy, (of which I make no doubt there are many) I could wish (I write it *openly* and *freely*) that their property may be *restored,* and their persons *protected*; and I think I may be countenanced in this sentiment from a sentence in that form of prayer prescribed by the *Saviour of the world,* which from the phraseology, it appears to have been the design of the *Divine Author,* that daily use should be made of it by all his *followers.*

Letter to Ezra Stiles, May 11, 1784

ANNAPOLIS

Ezra Stiles (1727–95) was a Congregational minister and author and was president of Yale College from 1778 to 1795.

Sir

I take the liberty to introduce to you the Honorable Thomas Jefferson Esqr. late Governor of Virginia. Now a Minister Plenepotentiary of the united States for negociating Treaties of Commerce with Great Britain and Several other European Powers in conjunction with Mr. Adams and Doctr. Franklin. He is the bearer of this Letter, and is now on his way to Boston, there to embark for Europe. He wishes to gain what acquaintance he can with the country as he passes through. He is a Gentleman, of much Philosophical as well as poli[ti]cal knowlege . . . and I doubt not you will be very agreably entertained with his conversation. You will be pleased to intro[d]uce him to such other Gentlemen in the City of New Haven as you may think proper.

I am Sir with great esteem & respect, Your humble Servant,

Roger Sherman

Source: Paul H. Smith et al., eds., *Letters of Delegates to Congress* (Washington, D.C.: Government Printing Office, 1994), 21: 608–9.

The Constitutional
Convention

In 1784, Roger Sherman defended the Articles of Confederation against Pelatiah Webster's wide-ranging attacks. By 1787, the failure of states to provide funds requested by Congress, problems with trade and currency, and events like Shays' Rebellion had convinced him that the Articles needed to be strengthened. As an advocate of local government, Sherman arrived in Philadelphia presuming that the Articles simply needed to be amended. Shocked by Madison's nationalist Virginia Plan, he joined wholeheartedly in the spirited debate. By the end of the Constitutional Convention, he had spoken more times than all but three delegates. Had he not missed the deliberations of July 20–26 because of a quick trip to Connecticut, he probably would have been the most loquacious of all the delegates.[1]

On May 12, 1787, Connecticut's General Assembly appointed William Samuel Johnson, Oliver Ellsworth, and Erastus Wolcott to represent the state. However, Wolcott refused to attend the convention, citing "the Small Pox" to which "he would be greatly exposed in the City."[2] At the council's insistence, Sherman was chosen to replace him, and the full slate of delegates was formally approved on May 16, 1787. Unlike every state except Maryland, Connecticut's General Assembly permitted any of the delegates to act on behalf of the state

---

1. Unidentified author, "Constitutional Convention, 1787," *Historical Magazine* 5 (January 1861): 19.

2. James H. Hutson, ed., *Supplement to Max Farrand's The Records of the Federal Convention of 1787* (New Haven, Conn.: Yale University Press, 1987), 3, 4.

(most states required a minimum of two or three delegates, with Pennsylvania requiring four). Like several other states, the legislature specified that the trio had been appointed "for the sole and express purpose of revising the Articles of Confederation."[3]

Although the delegates were supposed to arrive in Philadelphia on May 14, a quorum was not present until May 27, and Sherman did not arrive until May 30. He was appalled by Madison's Virginia Plan, which had been introduced the previous day. Madison and a few other leading lights—notably James Wilson and Alexander Hamilton—had become convinced that the United States needed a powerful national government that could act independently of the states. Throughout his career, Sherman had consistently urged Connecticut's General Assembly to meet its obligations to the national government, yet nationalists recognized that he would oppose concentrating too much power there. Jeremiah Wadsworth, for instance, wrote to Massachusetts delegate Rufus King:

> I am satisfied with the appointment [of Connecticut's delegates]—except Sherman who, I am told, is disposed to patch up the old scheme of Government. This was not my opinion of him, when we chose him: he is as cunning as the Devil, and if you attack him, you ought to know him well; he is not easily managed, but if he suspects you are trying to take him in, you may as well catch an Eel by the tail.[4]

Wadsworth was correct in his assessment of Sherman, with respect to both his view of national power and his ability as a legislator.

Throughout the summer Sherman argued for limited national government, and he weighed in on virtually every controversial issue. David Brian Robertson has demonstrated that when Madison and Sherman clashed, Sherman won more battles than he lost. And even when he lost, he often forced compromises that made the Constitution palatable to most Americans. Indeed, Robertson concludes that the "political synergy between Madison and Sherman . . . may have been necessary for the Constitution's adoption."[5] Similarly, the historian Jack Rakove has observed that "America has had more Shermans in its politics than Madisons, and arguably too few of either, but it was the rivalry between their competing goals and political styles that jointly gave the Great Convention much of its drama and fascination—and also permitted its achievement."[6]

3. Collier, *Roger Sherman's Connecticut*, 228, 233.

4. Farrand, *Records*, 3: 33–34.

5. Robertson, "Madison's Opponents and Constitutional Design," 242; Robertson, *The Constitution and America's Destiny*.

6. Rakove, *Original Meanings*, 92.

The excerpts that follow are Madison's records of Sherman's most significant contributions at the Constitutional Convention.[7] Remarks by other founders are included to provide the context necessary for understanding Sherman's arguments. Of course, there is no substitute for reading Madison's account of the Constitutional Convention in its entirety, and several excellent books have been written that tell this fascinating story in a narrative fashion.[8] Following the excerpts from the debates is a document containing notes taken by Sherman for use in the convention.

7. It is important to keep in mind that these selections are from Madison's unofficial notes of the proceedings of the Constitutional Convention. He was not an unbiased observer, and he has even been accused of altering his notes later in life for political purposes. Hutson, *Supplement*, xx–xxxi. The footnotes contain notes by convention delegate William Pierce of Georgia.

8. See, for instance, Richard Beeman, *Plain, Honest Men: The Making of the Constitution* (New York: Random House, 2009); Clinton Rossiter, *1787: The Grand Convention* (1966; reprint, New York: W. W. Norton, 1987); and Rakove, *Original Meanings*.

Excerpts from Debates at the Constitutional Convention of 1787

The following excerpts include some of Sherman's most important contributions in the debates over the new federal constitution.

All excerpts are from Gaillard Hunt, ed., The Writings of James Madison *(New York: J. P. Putnam's Sons, 1900), hereafter cited as* Writings.

Wednesday, May 30

Roger Sherman (from Connecticut) took his seat.

The House went into Committee of the Whole on the State of the Union. Mʳ Gorham was elected to the Chair by Ballot.

The propositions of Mʳ Randolph which had been referred to the Com̃ittee being taken up. He moved on the suggestion of Mʳ G. Morris, that the first of his propositions to wit "Resolved that the articles of Confederation ought to be so corrected & enlarged, as to accomplish the objects proposed by their institution; namely, common defence, security of liberty, and general welfare,— should be postponed, in order to consider the 3 following:

 1. that a union of the States merely federal will not accomplish the objects proposed by the articles of Confederation, namely common defence, security of liberty, & genˡ welfare.

 2. that no treaty or treaties among the whole or part of the States, as individual Sovereignties, would be sufficient.

 3. that a *national* Government ought to be established consisting of a *supreme* Legislative, Executive & Judiciary.

The motion for postponing was seconded by Mʳ Govʳ Morris and unanimously agreed to.

Some verbal criticisms were raised agˢᵗ the first proposition, and it was agreed on motion of Mʳ Butler seconded by Mʳ Randolph, to pass on to the third, which underwent a discussion, less however on its general merits than on the force and extent of the particular terms *national & supreme.*

Mʳ Charles Pinkney wished to know of Mʳ Randolph, whether he meant to abolish the State Governᵗˢ altogether. Mʳ R. replied that he meant by these general propositions merely to introduce the particular ones which explained the outlines of the system he had in view.

Mʳ Butler said he had not made up his mind on the subject, and was open to the light which discussion might throw on it. After some general observations he concluded with saying that he had opposed the grant of powers to

Source: *Writings,* 3: 37–40.

Cong: heretofore, because the whole power was vested in one body. The proposed distribution of the powers into different bodies changed the case, and would induce him to go great lengths.

Gen: Pinkney expressed a doubt whether the act of Cong: recoṁending the Convention, or the Commissions of the Deputies to it, could authorize a discussion of a system founded on different principles from the federal Constitution.

M: Gerry seemed to entertain the same doubt.

M: Gov: Morris explained the distinction between a *federal* and *national, supreme,* Gov:; the former being a mere compact resting on the good faith of the parties; the latter having a compleat and *compulsive* operation. He contended that in all Communities there must be one supreme power, and one only.

M: Mason observed that the present confederation was not only deficient in not providing for coercion & punishment ag.st delinquent States; but argued very cogently that punishment could not in the nature of things be executed on the States collectively, and therefore that such a Gov: was necessary as could directly operate on individuals, and would punish those only whose guilt required it.

M.r Sherman[1] who took his seat today, admitted that the Confederation had not given sufficient power to Cong: and that additional powers were necessary; particularly that of raising money which he said would involve many other powers. He admitted also that the General & particular jurisdictions ought in no case to be concurrent. He seemed however not to be disposed to make too great inroads on the existing system; intimating as one reason, that it would be wrong to lose every amendment, by inserting such as would not be agreed to by the States.

---

1. "M: Sherman exhibits the oddest shaped character I ever remember to have met with. He is awkward, un-meaning, and unaccountably strange in his manner. But in his train of thinking there is something regular, deep, and comprehensive; yet the oddity of his address, the vulgarisms that accompany his public speaking, and that strange new England cant which runs through his public as well as his private speaking make everything that is connected with him grotesque and laughable;—and yet he deserves infinite praise,—no Man has a better Heart or a clearer Head. If he cannot embellish he can furnish thoughts that are wise and useful. He is an able politician and extremely artful in accomplishing any particular object;—it is remarked that he seldom fails. I am told he sits on the Bench in Connecticut, and is very correct in the discharge of his Judicial functions. In the early part of his life he was a Shoe-maker;—but despising the lowness of his condition, he turned Almanack maker, and so progressed upwards to a Judge. He has been several years a Member of Congress, and discharged the duties of his Office with honor and credit to himself, and advantage to the State he represented. He is about 60." —Pierce's Notes, *Am. Hist. Rev.,* iii., 326.

Thursday, May 31

William Pierce, from Georgia took his seat.

In Committee of the whole on Mr. Randolph's propositions.

The 3ᵈ Resolution "that the national Legislature ought to consist of two branches" was agreed to without debate or dissent, except that of Pennsylvania, given probably from complaisance to Docᵗ Franklin who was understood to be partial to a single House of Legislation.

Resol: 4. first clause, "that the members of the first branch of the National Legislature ought to be elected by the people of the several States," being taken up,

Mʳ Sherman opposed the election by the people, insisting that it ought to be by the State Legislatures. The people he said, immediately should have as little to do as may be about the Government. They want information and are constantly liable to be misled.

Mʳ Gerry. The evils we experience flow from the excess of democracy. The people do not want virtue, but are the dupes of pretended patriots. In Massᵗˢ it had been fully confirmed by experience that they are daily misled into the most baneful measures and opinions by the false reports circulated by designing men, and which no one on the spot can refute. One principal evil arises from the want of due provision for those employed in the administration of Governmᵗ It would seem to be a maxim of democracy to starve the public servants. He mentioned the popular clamour in Massᵗˢ for the reduction of salaries and the attack made on that of the Govʳ though secured by the spirit of the Constitution itself. He had he said been too republican heretofore: he was still however republican, but had been taught by experience the danger of the levelling spirit.

Mʳ Mason argued strongly for an election of the larger branch by the people. It was to be the grand depository of the democratic principle of the Govᵗ It was, so to speak, to be our House of Commons—It ought to know & sympathize with every part of the community; and ought therefore to be taken not

Source: *Writings*, 3: 45–49, 54–55.

only from different parts of the whole republic, but also from different districts of the larger members of it, which had in several instances particularly in Virg:, different interests and views arising from difference of produce, of habits &c &c. He admitted that we had been too democratic but was afraid we s^d. incautiously run into the opposite extreme. We ought to attend to the rights of every class of the people. He had often wondered at the indifference of the superior classes of society to this dictate of humanity & policy, considering that however affluent their circumstances, or elevated their situations, might be, the course of a few years, not only might but certainly would, distribute their posterity throughout the lowest classes of Society. Every selfish motive therefore, every family attachment, ought to recommend such a system of policy as would provide no less carefully for the rights and happiness of the lowest than of the highest orders of Citizens.

M: Wilson contended strenuously for drawing the most numerous branch of the Legislature immediately from the people. He was for raising the federal pyramid to a considerable altitude, and for that reason wished to give it as broad a basis as possible. No government could long subsist without the confidence of the people. In a republican Government this confidence was peculiarly essential. He also thought it wrong to increase the weight of the State Legislatures by making them the electors of the national Legislature. All interference between the general and local Governm^ts should be obviated as much as possible. On examination it would be found that the opposition of States to federal measures had proceeded much more from the officers of the States, than from the people at large.

M: Madison considered the popular election of one branch of the national Legislature as essential to every plan of free Government. He observed that in some of the States one branch of the Legislature was composed of men already removed from the people by an intervening body of electors. That if the first branch of the general legislature should be elected by the State Legislatures, the second branch elected by the first—the Executive by the second together with the first; and other appointments again made for subordinate purposes by the Executive, the people would be lost sight of altogether; and the necessary sympathy between them and their rulers and officers, too little felt. He was an advocate for the policy of refining the popular appointments by successive filtrations, but thought it might be pushed too far. He wished the expedient to be resorted to only in the appointment of the second branch of the Legislature, and in the Executive & judiciary branches of the Government. He thought too that the great fabric to be raised would be more stable and durable, if it should rest on the solid foundation of the people themselves, than if it should stand merely on the pillars of the Legislatures.

M! Gerry did not like the election by the people. The maxims taken from the British Constitution were often fallacious when applied to our situation which was extremely different. Experience he said had shewn that the State legislatures drawn immediately from the people did not always possess their confidence. He had no objection however to an election by the people if it were so qualified that men of honor & character might not be unwilling to be joined in the appointments. He seemed to think the people might nominate a certain number out of which the State legislatures should be bound to choose.

M! Butler thought an election by the people an impracticable mode.

On the question for an election of the first branch of the national Legislature, by the people,

Mass!ˢ ay. Connec! div! N. York ay. N. Jersey no. Pen! ay. Delaw! div! V! ay. N. C. ay. S. C. no. Georg! ay. . . .

M! Randolph disclaimed any intention to give indefinite powers to the national Legislature, declaring that he was entirely opposed to such an inroad on the State jurisdictions, and that he did not think any considerations whatever could ever change his determination. His opinion was fixed on this point.

M! Madison said that he had brought with him into the Convention a strong bias in favor of an enumeration and definition of the powers necessary to be exercised by the national Legislature; but had also brought doubts concerning its practicability. His wishes remained unaltered; but his doubts had become stronger. What his opinion might ultimately be he could not yet tell. But he should shrink from nothing which should be found essential to such a form of Gov! as would provide for the safety, liberty and happiness of the community. This being the end of all our deliberations, all the necessary means for attaining it must, however reluctantly, be submitted to.

On the question for giving powers, in cases to which the States are not competent—Mass!ˢ ay. Con! div! (Sherman no Elseworth ay) N. Y. ay. N. J. ay. P! ay. Del. ay. V! ay. N. C. ay. S. Carolina ay. Georg! ay.

Friday, June 1

William Houston from Georgia took his seat.

The Committee of the whole proceeded to Resolution 7. "that a national Executive be instituted, to be chosen by the national Legislature for the term of —————— years &c to be ineligible thereafter, to possess the Executive powers of Congress &c."

M͘ Pinkney was for a vigorous Executive but was afraid the Executive powers of the existing Congress might extend to peace & war &c which would render the Executive a monarchy, of the worst kind, to wit an elective one.

M͘ Wilson moved that the Executive consist of a single person. M͘ C. Pinkney seconded the motion, so as to read "that a National Ex. to consist of a single person, be instituted.

A considerable pause ensuing and the Chairman asking if he should put the question, Doc͘ Franklin observed that it was a point of great importance and wished that the gentlemen would deliver their sentiments on it before the question was put.

M͘ Rutlidge animadverted on the shyness of gentlemen on this and other subjects. He said it looked as if they supposed themselves precluded by having frankly disclosed their opinions from afterwards changing them, which he did not take to be at all the case. He said he was for vesting the Executive power in a single person, tho' he was not for giving him the power of war and peace. A single man would feel the greatest responsibility and administer the public affairs best.

M͘ Sherman said he considered the Executive magistracy as nothing more than an institution for carrying the will of the Legislature into effect, that the person or persons ought to be appointed by and accountable to the Legislature only, which was the depository of the supreme will of the Society. As they were the best judges of the business which ought to be done by the Executive department, and consequently of the number necessary from time to time for

Source: *Writings*, 3: 56–59, 62–64.

doing it, he wished the number might not be fixed, but that the legislature should be at liberty to appoint one or more as experience might dictate.

M.ʳ Wilson preferred a single magistrate, as giving most energy dispatch and responsibility to the office. He did not consider the Prerogatives of the British Monarch as a proper guide in defining the Executive powers. Some of these prerogatives were of a Legislative nature. Among others that of war & peace &c. The only powers he considered strictly Executive were those of executing the laws, and appointing officers, not appertaining to and appointed by the Legislature. . . .

The next clause in Resolution 7, relating to the mode of appointing, & the duration of, the Executive being under consideration,

M.ʳ Wilson said he was almost unwilling to declare the mode which he wished to take place, being apprehensive that it might appear chimerical. He would say however at least that in theory he was for an election by the people. Experience, particularly in N. York & Mass.ᵗˢ, shewed that an election of the first magistrate by the people at large, was both a convenient & successful mode. The objects of choice in such cases must be persons whose merits have general notoriety.

M.ʳ Sherman was for the appointment by the Legislature, and for making him absolutely dependent on that body, as it was the will of that which was to be executed. An independence of the Executive on the supreme Legislature, was in his opinion the very essence of tyranny if there was any such thing.

M.ʳ Wilson moves that the blank for the term of duration should be filled with three years, observing at the same time that he preferred this short period, on the supposition that a re-eligibility would be provided for.

M.ʳ Pinkney moves for seven years.

M.ʳ Sherman was for three years, and ag.ˢᵗ the doctrine of rotation as throwing out of office the men best qualified to execute its duties.

M.ʳ Mason was for seven years at least, and for prohibiting a re-eligibility as the best expedient both for preventing the effect of a false complaisance on the side of the Legislature towards unfit characters; and a temptation on the side of the Executive to intrigue with the Legislature for a re-appointment.

M.ʳ Bedford was strongly opposed to so long a term as seven years. He begged the Committee to consider what the situation of the Country would be, in case the first magistrate should be saddled on it for such a period and it should be found on trial that he did not possess the qualifications ascribed to him, or should lose them after his appointment. An impeachment he said would be no cure for this evil, as an impeachment would reach misfeasance only, not incapacity. He was for a triennial election, and for an ineligibility after a period of nine years.

Saturday, June 2

M: Sherman contended that the national Legislature should have power to remove the Executive at pleasure.

Source: *Writings,* 3: 74.

Monday, June 4 in Committee of the Whole

The Question was resumed on motion of Mʳ Pinkney, 2ᵈᵉᵈ by Mʳ Wilson, "shall the blank for the number of the Executive be filled with a single person?"

Mʳ Wilson was in favor of the motion. It had been opposed by the gentleman from Virgᵃ (Mr. Randolph) but the arguments used had not convinced him. He observed that the objections of Mʳ R. were levelled not so much agˢᵗ the measure itself, as agˢᵗ its unpopularity. If he could suppose that it would occasion a rejection of the plan of which it should form a part, though the part were an important one, yet he would give it up rather than lose the whole. On examination he could see no evidence of the alledged antipathy of the people. On the contrary he was persuaded that it does not exist. All know that a single magistrate is not a King. One fact has great weight with him. All the 13 States tho agreeing in scarce any other instance, agree in placing a single magistrate at the head of the Governᵗ The idea of three heads has taken place in none. The degree of power is indeed different; but there are no co-ordinate heads. In addition to his former reasons for preferring a Unity, he would mention another. The *tranquility* not less than the vigor of the Govᵗ he thought would be favored by it. Among three equal members, he foresaw nothing but uncontrouled, continued, & violent animosities; which would not only interrupt the public administration; but diffuse their poison thro' the other branches of Govᵗ, thro' the States, and at length thro' the people at large. If the members were to be unequal in power the principle of opposition to the Unity was given up. If equal, the making them an odd number would not be a remedy. In Courts of Justice there are two sides only to a question. In the Legislative & Executive departmᵗˢ questions have commonly many sides. Each member therefore might espouse a separate one & no two agree.

Mʳ Sherman. This matter is of great importance and ought to be well considered before it is determined. Mʳ Wilson he said had observed that in each State a single magistrate was placed at the head of the Govᵗ It was so he admitted, and properly so, and he wished the same policy to prevail in the

Source: *Writings*, 3: 79–84.

federal Gov! But then it should be also remarked that in all the States there was a Council of advice, without which the first magistrate could not act. A council he thought necessary to make the establishment acceptable to the people. Even in G. B. the King has a Council; and though he appoints it himself, its advice has its weight with him, and attracts the Confidence of the people.

M! Williamson asks M! Wilson whether he means to annex a Council.

M! Wilson means to have no Council, which oftener serves to cover, than prevent malpractices.

M! Gerry was at a loss to discover the policy of three members for the Executive. It w^d be extremely inconvenient in many instances, particularly in military matters, whether relating to the militia, an army, or a navy. It would be a general with three heads.

On the question for a single Executive it was agreed to Mass^{ts} ay. Con! ay. N. Y. no. Pen^a ay. Del. no. Mary^d no. Virg^a ay. (M! R. & M! Blair no—Doc^r M^{c}C^g Mr M. & Gen. W. ay. Col. Mason being no, but not in the house, Mr Wythe ay but gone home). N. C. ay. S. C. ay. Georg^a ay.

First Clause of Proposition 8th relating *to a Council of Revision* taken into consideration.

M! Gerry doubts whether the Judiciary ought to form a part of it, as they will have a sufficient check agst encroachments on their own department by their exposition of the laws, which involved a power of deciding on their Constitutionality. In some States the Judges had actually set aside laws as being agst the Constitution. This was done too with general approbation. It was quite foreign from the nature of ye office to make them judges of the policy of public measures. He moves to postpone the clause in order to propose "that the National Executive shall have a right to negative any Legislative act which shall not be afterwards passed by —— parts of each branch of the national Legislature."

M! King seconds the motion, observing that the Judges ought to be able to expound the law as it should come before them, free from the bias of having participated in its formation.

Mr Wilson thinks neither the original proposition nor the amendment goes far enough. If the Legislative Exetv & Judiciary ought to be distinct & independent, The Executive ought to have an absolute negative. Without such a self-defence the Legislature can at any moment sink it into non-existence. He was for varying the proposition in such a manner as to give the Executive & Judiciary jointly an absolute negative.

On the question to postpone in order to take M! Gerry's proposition into consideration it was agreed to, Mass^s ay. Con! no. N. Y. ay. P^a ay. Del. no. Mary^d no. Virg^a no. N. C. ay. S. C. ay. G^a ay.

Mr. Gerry's proposition being now before Committee, M: Wilson & M: Hamilton move that the last part of it (viz. "wch s! not be afterw^ds passed "unless by —— parts of each branch of the National legislature") be struck out, so as to give the Executive an absolute negative on the laws. There was no danger they thought of such a power being too much exercised. It was mentioned by Col: Hamilton that the King of G. B. had not exerted his negative since the Revolution.

M: Gerry sees no necessity for so great a controul over the legislature as the best men in the Community would be comprised in the two branches of it.

Doc: Franklin, said he was sorry to differ from his colleague for whom he had a very great respect, on any occasion, but he could not help it on this. He had had some experience of this check in the Executive on the Legislature, under the proprietary Government of Pen: The negative of the Governor was constantly made use of to extort money. No good law whatever could be passed without a private bargain with him. An increase of his salary, or some donation, was always made a condition; till at last it became the regular practice, to have orders in his favor on the Treasury, presented along with the bills to be signed, so that he might actually receive the former before he should sign the latter. When the Indians were scalping the western people, and notice of it arrived, the concurrence of the Governor in the means of self-defence could not be got, till it was agreed that his Estate should be exempted from taxation: so that the people were to fight for the security of his property, whilst he was to bear no share of the burden. This was a mischevous sort of check. If the Executive was to have a Council, such a power would be less objectionable. It was true, the King of G. B. had not, as was said, exerted his negative since the Revolution; but that matter was easily explained. The bribes and emoluments now given to the members of parliament rendered it unnecessary, every thing being done according to the will of the Ministers. He was afraid, if a negative should be given as proposed, that more power and money would be demanded, till at last eno' would be gotten to influence & bribe the Legislature into a compleat subjection to the will of the Executive.

M: Sherman was ag^st enabling any one man to stop the will of the whole. No one man could be found so far above all the rest in wisdom. He thought we ought to avail ourselves of his wisdom in revising the laws, but not permit him to overrule the decided and cool opinions of the Legislature.

Tuesday, June 5

Propos. 15. for *"recommending Conventions under appointment of the people to ratify the new Constitution"* &c. being taken up,

M⸢ Sherman thought such a popular ratification unnecessary: the articles of Confederation providing for changes and alterations with the assent of Cong⸢ and ratification of State Legislatures.

M⸢ Madison thought this provision essential. The articles of Confed⸢ themselves were defective in this respect, resting in many of the States on the Legislative sanction only. Hence in conflicts between acts of the States, and of Cong⸢ especially where the former are of posterior date, and the decision is to to be made by State tribunals, an uncertainty must necessarily prevail, or rather perhaps a certain decision in favor of the State authority. He suggested also that as far as the articles of Union were to be considered as a Treaty only of a particular sort, among the Governments of Independent States, the doctrine might be set up that a breach of any one article, by any of the parties, absolved the other parties from the whole obligation. For these reasons as well as others he thought it indispensable that the new Constitution should be ratified in the most unexceptionable form, and by the supreme authority of the people themselves. . . .

Mr. Rutlidge hav⸢ obtained a rule for reconsideration of the clause for establishing *inferior* tribunals under the national authority, now moved that that part of the clause in the propos. 9. should be expunged: arguing that the State tribunals might and ought to be left in all cases to decide in the first instance the right of appeal to the supreme national tribunal being sufficient to secure the national rights & uniformity of Judgm⸢ᵗˢ: that it was making an unnecessary encroachment on the jurisdiction of the States and creating unnecessary obstacles to their adoption of the new system. Mr. Sherman 2ᵈᵉᵈ the motion.

M⸢ Madison observed that unless inferior tribunals were dispersed throughout the Republic with *final* jurisdiction in *many* cases, appeals would be multiplied to a most oppressive degree; that besides, an appeal would not in many

Source: *Writings,* 3: 94–98.

cases be a remedy. What was to be done after improper Verdicts in State tribunals obtained under the biassed directions of a dependent Judge, or the local prejudices of an undirected jury? To remand the cause for a new trial would answer no purpose. To order a new trial at the Supreme bar would oblige the parties to bring up their witnesses, tho' ever so distant from the seat of the Court. An effective Judiciary establishment commensurate to the legislative authority, was essential. A Government without a proper Executive & Judiciary would be the mere trunk of a body, without arms or legs to act or move.

Mr. Wilson opposed the motion on like grounds. He said the admiralty jurisdiction ought to be given wholly to the national Government, as it related to cases not within the jurisdiction of particular states, & to a scene in which controversies with foreigners would be most likely to happen.

Mr. Sherman was in favor of the motion. He dwelt chiefly on the supposed expensiveness of having a new set of Courts, when the existing State Courts would answer the same purpose.

Mr. Dickinson contended strongly that if there was to be a National Legislature, there ought to be a national Judiciary, and that the former ought to have authority to institute the latter.

On the question for Mr. Rutlidge's motion to strike out "inferior tribunals"

Massts. divided. Cont. ay. N. Y. divd. N. J. ay. Pa. no. Del. no. Md. no. Va. no. N. C. ay. S. C. ay. Geo. ay.

Wednesday, June 6 in Committee of the Whole

M.ʳ Pinkney according to previous notice & rule obtained, moved "that the first branch of the national Legislature be elected by the State Legislatures, and not by the people;" contending that the people were less fit Judges in such a case, and that the Legislatures would be less likely to promote the adoption of the new Government, if they were to be excluded from all share in it.

M.ʳ Rutlidge 2.ᵈᵉᵈ the motion.

M.ʳ Gerry. Much depends on the mode of election. In England the people will probably lose their liberty from the smallness of the proportion having a right of suffrage. Our danger arises from the opposite extreme: hence in Mass.ᵗˢ the worst men get into the Legislature. Several members of that Body had lately been convicted of infamous crimes. Men of indigence, ignorance & baseness, spare no pains, however dirty to carry their point ag.ˢᵗ men who are superior to the artifices practised. He was not disposed to run into extremes. He was as much principled as ever ag.ˢᵗ aristocracy and monarchy. It was necessary on the one hand that the people should appoint one branch of the Gov.ᵗ in order to inspire them with the necessary confidence. But he wished the election on the other to be so modified as to secure more effectually a just preference of merit. His idea was that the people should nominate certain persons in certain districts, out of whom the State Legislatures sh.ᵈ make the appointment.

M.ʳ Wilson. He wished for vigor in the Gov.ᵗ, but he wished that vigorous authority to flow immediately from the legitimate source of all authority. The Gov.ᵗ ought to possess not only 1.ˢᵗ the *force,* but 2.ᵈˡʸ the *mind or sense* of the people at large. The Legislature ought to be the most exact transcript of the whole Society. Representation is made necessary only because it is impossible for the people to act collectively. The opposition was to be expected he said from the *Governments,* not from the Citizens of the States. The latter had parted as was observed (by M.ʳ King) with all the necessary powers; and it was immaterial to them, by whom they were exercised, if well exercised. The State

Source: *Writings,* 3: 99–105.

officers were to be the losers of power. The people he supposed would be rather more attached to the national Gov! than to the State Gov!ˢ as being more important in itself, and more flattering to their pride. There is no danger of improper elections if made by *large* districts. Bad elections proceed from the smallness of the districts which give an opportunity to bad men to intrigue themselves into office.

M! Sherman. If it were in view to abolish the State Gov!ˢ the elections ought to be by the people. If the State Gov!ˢ are to be continued, it is necessary in order to preserve harmony between the National & State Gov!ˢ that the elections to the former sh! be made by the latter. The right of participating in the National Gov! would be sufficiently secured to the people by their election of the State Legislatures. The objects of the Union, he thought were few, 1. defence ag!ᵗ foreign danger, 2 ag!ᵗ internal disputes & a resort to force, 3. Treaties with foreign nations 4 regulating foreign commerce, & drawing revenue from it. These & perhaps a few lesser objects alone rendered a Confederation of the States necessary. All other matters civil & criminal would be much better in the hands of the States. The people are more happy in small than in large States. States may indeed be too small as Rhode Island, & thereby be too subject to faction. Some others were perhaps too large, the powers of Gov! not being able to pervade them. He was for giving the General Gov! power to legislate and execute within a defined province.

Col. Mason. Under the existing Confederacy, Cong! represent the *States* and not the *people* of the States: their acts operate on the *States*, not on the individuals. The case will be changed in the new plan of Gov! The people will be represented; they ought therefore to choose the Representatives. The requisites in actual representation are that the Rep! should sympathize with their constituents; sh! think as they think, & feel as they feel; and that for these purposes sh! even be residents among them. Much he s! had been alledged ag!ᵗ democratic elections. He admitted that much might be said; but it was to be considered that no Gov! was free from imperfections & evils; and that improper elections in many instances were inseparable from Republican Gov!ˢ. But compare these with the advantage of this Form in favor of the rights of the people, in favor of human nature. He was persuaded there was a better chance for proper elections by the people, if divided into large districts, than by the State Legislatures. Paper money had been issued by the latter when the former were against it. Was it to be supposed that the State Legislatures then w! not send to the Nat! legislature patrons of such projects, if the choice depended on them.

M! Madison considered an election of one branch at least of the Legislature by the people immediately, as a clear principle of free Gov! and that this mode

under proper regulations had the additional advantage of securing better representatives, as well as of avoiding too great an agency of the State Governments in the General one. He differed from the member from Connecticut
(Mr. Sherman) in thinking the objects mentioned to be all the principal ones
that required a National Gov! Those were certainly important and necessary
objects; but he combined with them the necessity of providing more effectually
for the security of private rights, and the steady dispensation of Justice. Interferences with these were evils which had more perhaps than anything else,
produced this convention. Was it to be supposed that republican liberty could
long exist under the abuses of it practised in some of the States. The gentleman
(M! Sherman) had admitted that in a very small State, faction & oppression
w? prevail. It was to be inferred then that wherever these prevailed the State
was too small. Had they not prevailed in the largest as well as the smallest tho'
less than in the smallest; and were we not thence admonished to enlarge the
sphere as far as the nature of the Gov! would Admit. This was the only defence
agst the inconveniences of democracy consistent with the democratic form of
Gov! All civilized Societies would be divided into different Sects, Factions, &
interests, as they happened to consist of rich & poor, debtors & creditors, the
landed the manufacturing, the commercial interests, the inhabitants of this
district or that district, the followers of this political leader or that political
leader—the disciples of this religious Sect or that religious Sect. In all cases
where a majority are united by a common interest or passion, the rights of the
minority are in danger. What motives are to restrain them? A prudent regard
to the maxim that honesty is the best policy is found by experience to be as
little regarded by bodies of men as by individuals. Respect for character is
always diminished in proportion to the number among whom the blame or
praise is to be divided. Conscience, the only remaining tie is known to be
inadequate in individuals: In large numbers, little is to be expected from it.
Besides, Religion itself may become a motive to persecution & oppression.
These observations are verified by the Histories of every country antient &
modern. In Greece & Rome the rich & poor, the Creditors & debtors, as well
as the patricians & plebeians alternately oppressed each other with equal un-
mercifulness. What a source of oppression was the relation between the parent
cities of Rome, Athens & Carthage, & their respective provinces; the former
possessing the power, & the latter being sufficiently distinguished to be separate objects of it? Why was America so justly apprehensive of Parliamentary
injustice? Because G. Britain had a separate interest real or supposed, & if her
authority had been admitted, could have pursued that interest at our expence.
We have seen the mere distinction of colour made in the most enlightened
period of time, a ground of the most oppressive dominion ever exercised by

man over man. What has been the source of those unjust laws complained of among ourselves? Has it not been the real or supposed interest of the major number? Debtors have defrauded their creditors. The landed interest has borne hard on the mercantile interest. The Holders of one species of property have thrown a disproportion of taxes on the holders of another species. The lesson we are to draw from the whole is that where a majority are united by a common sentiment, and have an opportunity, the rights of the minor party become insecure. In a Republican Gov.ᵗ the majority if united have always an opportunity. The only remedy is to enlarge the sphere, & thereby divide the community into so great a number of interests & parties, that in the 1ˢᵗ place a majority will not be likely at the same moment to have a common interest separate from that of the whole or of the minority; and in the 2ᵈ place that in case they shᵈ have such an interest, they may not be apt to unite in the pursuit of it. It was incumbent on us then to try this remedy, and with that view to frame a republican system on such a scale & in such a form as will controul all the evils wᶜʰ have been experienced.

Thursday, June 7 in Committee of the Whole

M͇ Pinkney according to notice moved to reconsider the clause respecting the negative on State laws, which was agreed to, and tomorrow for fixed the purpose.

The Clause providing for y͇ appointment of the 2͟d͟ branch of the national Legislature, having lain blank since the last vote on the mode of electing it, to wit, by the 1͟s͟t͟ branch, M͇ Dickinson now moved "that the members of the 2͟d͟ branch ought to be chosen by the individual Legislatures."

M͇ Sherman seconded the motion; observing that the particular States would thus become interested in supporting the National Governm͇ and that a due harmony between the two Governments would be maintained. He admitted that the two ought to have separate and distinct jurisdictions, but that they ought to have a mutual interest in supporting each other.

M͇ Sharman opposed elections by the people in districts, as not likely to produce such fit men as elections by the State Legislatures.

Source: *Writings,* 3: 111–12, 118.

Friday, June 8

M! Sherman thought the cases in which the [executive] negative ought to be exercised, might be defined. He wished the point might not be decided till a trial at least sh! be made for that purpose

M! Wilson would not say what modifications of the proposed power might be practicable or expedient. But however novel it might appear the principle of it when viewed with a close & steady eye, is right. There is no instance in which the laws say that the individual sh! be bound in one case, & at liberty to judge whether he will obey or disobey in another. The cases are parallel. Abuses of the power over the individual person may happen as well as over the individual States. Federal liberty is to the States, what civil liberty, is to private individuals, and States are not more unwilling to purchase it, by the necessary concession of their political sovereignty, that the savage is to purchase Civil liberty by the surrender of the personal sovereignty, which he enjoys in a State of nature. A definition of the cases in which the Negative should be exercised, is impracticable. A discretion must be left on one side or the other? will it not be most safely lodged on the side of the Nat! Gov!? Among the first sentiments expressed in the first Cong! one was that Virg! is no more, that Mass!! is no [more], that P! is no more &c. We are now one nation of brethren. We must bury all local interests & distinctions. This language continued for some time. The tables at length began to turn. No sooner were the State Gov!! formed than their jealousy & ambition began to display themselves. Each endeavoured to cut a slice from the common loaf, to add to its own morsel, till at length the confederation became frittered down to the impotent condition in which it now stands. Review the progress of the articles of Confederation thro' Congress & compare the first & last draught of it. To correct its vices is the business of this convention. One of its vices is the want of an effectual controul in the whole over its parts. What danger is there that the whole will unnecessarily sacrifice a part? But reverse the case, and leave the whole at the mercy of each part, and will not the general interest be continually sacrificed to local interests?

Source: *Writings*, 3: 123–25.

Monday, June 11

M. Abraham Baldwin from Georgia took his seat. In Committee of the Whole.

The clause concerning the rule of suffrage in the Nat! Legislature postponed on saturday was resumed.

M. Sharman proposed that the proportion of suffrage in the 1st branch should be according to the respective numbers of free inhabitants; and that in the second branch or Senate, each State should have one vote and no more. He said as the States would remain possessed of certain individual rights, each State ought to be able to protect itself: otherwise a few large States will rule the rest. The House of Lords in England he observed had certain particular rights under the Constitution, and hence they have an equal vote with the House of Commons that they may be able to defend their rights. . . .

M. Sharman moved that a question be taken whether each State shall have one vote in the 2d branch. Every thing he said depended on this. The smaller States would never agree to the plan on any other principle than an equality of suffrage in this branch. M. Elsworth seconded the motion. On the question for allowing each State one vote in the 2d branch,

Mass.ts no. Con! ay. N. Y. ay. N. J. ay. P.a no. Del. ay. M.d ay. V.a no. N. C. no. S. C. no. Geo. no.

M. Wilson & M. Hamilton moved that the right of suffrage in the 2d branch ought to be according to the same rule as in the 1st branch. On this question for making the ratio of representation the same in the 2d as in the 1st branch it passed in the affirmative;

Mass.ts ay. Con! no. N. Y. no. N. J. no. P.a ay. Del. no. M.d no. V.a ay. N. C. ay. S. C. ay. Geo. ay. . . .

Resolution 14. requiring oaths from the members of the State Gov.ts to observe the Nat! Constitution & laws, being considered,

M. Sharman opposed it as unnecessarily intruding into the State jurisdictions.

Source: *Writings*, 3: 136, 144, 146.

Tuesday, June 12 in Committee of Whole

M⸳ Sharman & M⸳ Elseworth moved to fill the blank left in the 4ᵗʰ Resolution for the periods of electing the members of the first branch with the words, "every year;" Mr. Sharman observing that he did it in order to bring on some question.

M⸳ Rutlidge proposed "every two years."

M⸳ Jennifer propᵈ, "every three years," observing that the too great frequency of elections rendered the people indifferent to them, and made the best men unwilling to engage in so precarious a service.

M⸳ Madison seconded the motion for three years. Instability is one of the great vices of our republics, to be remedied. Three years will be necessary, in a Government so extensive, for members to form any knowledge of the various interests of the States to which they do not belong, and of which they can know but little from the situation and affairs of their own. One year will be almost consumed in preparing for and travelling to & from the seat of national business.

M⸳ Gerry. The people of New England will never give up the point of annual elections, they know of the transition made in England from triennial to septennial elections, and will consider such an innovation here as the prelude to a like usurpation. He considered annual elections as the only defence of the people agˢᵗ tyranny. He was as much agˢᵗ a triennial House as agˢᵗ a hereditary Executive.

M⸳ Madison, observed that if the opinions of the people were to be our guide, it wᵈ be difficult to say what course we ought to take. No member of the Convention could say what the opinions of his Constituents were at this time; much less could he say what they would think if possessed of the information & lights possessed by the members here; & still less what would be their way of thinking 6 or 12 months hence. We ought to consider what was right & necessary in itself for the attainment of a proper Governmᵗ A plan adjusted to this idea will recommend itself—The respectability of this con-

Source: *Writings,* 3: 147–50, 152–53.

vention will give weight to their recommendation of it. Experience will be constantly urging the adoption of it, and all the most enlightened & respectable citizens will be its advocates. Should we fall short of the necessary & proper point, this influential class of Citizens, will be turned against the plan, and little support in opposition to them can be gained to it from the unreflecting multitude.

M: Gerry repeated his opinion that it was necessary to consider what the people would approve. This had been the policy of all Legislators. If the reasoning of Mr. Madison were just, and we supposed a limited Monarchy the best form in itself, we ought to recommend it, tho' the genius of the people was decidedly adverse to it, and having no hereditary distinctions among us, we were destitute of the essential materials for such an innovation.

On the question for the triennial election of the 1st branch

Mass. no. (Mr King ay.) M: Ghorum wavering. Con: no. N. Y. ay. N. J. ay. P^a ay. Del. ay. M^d ay. V^a ay. N. C. no. S. C. no. Geo. ay. . . .

M: Spaight moved to fill the blank for the duration of the appointm^{ts} to the 2^d branch of the National Legislature with the words "7 years.

M: Sherman, thought 7 years too long. He grounded his opposition he said on the principle that if they did their duty well, they would be reelected. And if they acted amiss, an earlier opportunity should be allowed for getting rid of them. He preferred 5 years which w^d be between the terms of the 1st branch & of the executive

Wednesday, June 13 in Committee of the Whole

Resol: 9 being resumed

The latter parts of the clause relating to the jurisdiction of the Nat̲ᴵ tribunals, was struck out nem. con in order to leave full room for their organization.

M̲ʳ Randolph & M̲ʳ Madison, then moved the following resolution respecting a National Judiciary, viz "that the jurisdiction of the National Judiciary shall extend to cases, which respect the collection of the national revenue, impeachments of any national officers, and questions which involve the national peace and harmony" which was agreed to.

M̲ʳ Pinkney & M̲ʳ Sherman moved to insert after the words "one supreme tribunal" the words "the Judges of which to be appointed by the National Legislature."

M̲ʳ Madison, objected to an app̲ᵗ by the whole Legislature. Many of them were incompetent Judges of the requisite qualifications. They were too much influenced by their partialities. The candidate who was present, who had displayed a talent for business in the legislative field, who had perhaps assisted ignorant members in business of their own, or of their Constituents, or used other winning means, would without any of the essential qualifications for an expositor of the laws prevail over a competitor not having these recommendations, but possessed of every necessary accomplishment. He proposed that the appointment should be made by the Senate, which as a less numerous & more select body, would be more competent judges, and which was sufficiently numerous to justify such a confidence in them.

M̲ʳ Sharman & M̲ʳ Pinkney withdrew their motion, and the app̲ᵗ by the Senate was ag̲ᵈ to nem. con.

M̲ʳ Gerry moved to restrain the Senatorial branch from originating money bills. The other branch was more immediately the representatives of the people, and it was a maxim that the people ought to hold the Purse-strings. If the Senate should be allowed to originate such bills, they w̲ᵈ repeat the experiment, till chance should furnish a sett of representatives in the other branch who will fall into their snares.

Source: *Writings*, 3: 156–60.

M⁚ Butler saw no reason for such a discrimination. We were always following the British Constitution when the reason of it did not apply. There was no analogy between the H. of Lords and the body proposed to be established. If the Senate should be degraded by any such discriminations, the best men would be apt to decline serving in it in favor of the other branch. And it will lead the latter into the practice of tacking other clauses to money bills.

M⁚ Madison observed that the Comentators on the Brit: Const: had not yet agreed on the reason of the restriction on the H. of L. in money bills. Certain it was there could be no similar reason in the case before us. The Senate would be the representatives of the people as well as the 1ˢᵗ branch. If they sᵈ have any dangerous influence over it, they would easily prevail on some member of the latter to originate the bill they wished to be passed. As the Senate would be generally a more capable sett of men, it wᵈ be wrong to disable them from any preparation of the business, especially of that which was most important, and in our republics, worse prepared than any other. The Gentleman in pursuance of his principle ought to carry the restraint to the *amendment*, as well as the originating of money bills, since, an addition of a given sum wᵈ be equivalent to a distinct proposition of it.

M⁚ King differed from M⁚ Gerry, and concurred in the objections to the proposition.

M⁚ Read favored the proposition, but would not extend the restraint to the case of amendments.

M⁚ Pinkney thinks the question premature. If the Senate shᵈ be formed on the *same* proportional representation as it stands at present, they sᵈ have equal power, otherwise if a different principle sᵈ be introduced.

M⁚ Sherman. As both branches must concur, there can be no danger whichever way the Senate be formed. We establish two branches in order to get more wisdom, which is particularly needed in the finance business—The Senate bear their share of the taxes, and are also the representatives of the people. What a man does by another, he does by himself is a maxim. In Conⁱ both branches can originate in all cases, and it has been found safe & convenient. Whatever might have been the reason of the rule as to The H. of Lords, it is clear that no good arises from it now even there.

Genⁱ Pinkney. This distinction prevails in S. C. and has been a source of pernicious disputes between yᵉ 2 branches. The Constitution is now evaded, by informal schedules of amendments handed from yᵉ Senate to the other House.

M⁚ Williamson wishes for a question chiefly to prevent re-discussion. The restriction will have one advantage, it will oblige some member in the lower branch to move, & people can then mark him.

On the question for excepting money bills, as prop^d by Mr Gerry, Mass. no. Con^t no. N. Y. ay. N. J. no. Del. ay. M^d no. V^a ay. N. C. no. S. C. no. Geo. no.

Thursday, June 14 in Convention

M⸢ Patterson, observed to the Convention that it was the wish of several deputations, particularly that of N. Jersey, that further time might be allowed them to contemplate the plan reported from the Committee of the Whole, and to digest one purely federal, and contradistinguished from the reported plan. He said they hoped to have such an one ready by tomorrow to be laid before the Convention: And the Convention adjourned that leisure might be given for the purpose.

Source: *Writings,* 3: 164–65.

Friday, June 15

Mr. Patterson, laid before the Convention the plan which he said several of the deputations wished to be substituted in place of that proposed by Mr. Randolph. After some little discussion of the most proper mode of giving it a fair deliberation it was agreed that it should be referred to a Committee of the Whole, and that in order to place the two plans in due comparison, the other should be recommitted. At the earnest request of Mr. Lansing & some other gentlemen, it was also agreed that the Convention should not go into Com̃ittee of the whole on the subject till tomorrow, by which delay the friends of the plan proposed by Mr. Patterson wd. be better prepared to explain & support it, and all would have an opportuy. of taking copies.

The propositions from N. Jersey moved by Mr. Patterson were in the words following.

1. Resd. that the articles of Confederation ought to be so revised, corrected, & enlarged, as to render the federal Constitution adequate to the exigencies of Government, & the preservation of the Union.

2. Resd. that in addition to the powers vested in the U. States in Congress, by the present existing articles of Confederation, they be authorized to pass acts for raising a revenue, by levying a duty or duties on all goods or merchandizes of foreign growth or manufacture, imported into any part of the U. States, by Stamps on paper, vellum or parchment, and by a postage on all letters or packages passing through the general post-office, to be applied to such federal purposes as they shall deem proper & expedient; to make rules & regulations for the collection thereof; and the same from time to time, to alter & amend in such manner as they shall think proper, to pass Acts for the regulation of trade & commerce as well with foreign Nations as with each other: provided that all punishments, fines, forfeitures & penalties to be incurred for contravening such acts rules and regulations shall be adjudged by the Common law Judiciaries of the State in which any Offence contrary to the true intent & meaning of such Acts rules & regulations shall have been

Source: *Writings*, 3: 165–70.

committed or perpetrated, with liberty of commencing in the first instance all suits & prosecutions for that purpose in the Superior Common law Judiciary in such State, subject nevertheless, for the correction of all errors, both in law & fact in rendering Judgment, to an appeal to the Judiciary of the U. States.

3. Res.ᵈ that whenever requisitions shall be necessary, instead of the rule for making requisitions mentioned in the articles of Confederation, the United States in Congˢ be authorized to make such requisitions in proportion to the whole number of white & other free citizens & inhabitants of every age Sex and condition including those bound to servitude for a term of years & three fifths of all other persons not comprehended in the foregoing description, except Indians not paying taxes; that if such requisitions be not complied with, in the time specified therein, to direct the collection thereof in the non complying States & for that purpose to devise and pass acts directing & authorizing the same; provided that none of the powers hereby vested in the U. States in Congˢ shall be exercised without the consent of at least ———— States, and in that proportion if the number of Confederated States should hereafter be increased or diminished.

4. Res.ᵈ that the U. States in Congˢ be authorized to elect a federal Executive to consist of ———— persons, to continue in office for the term of ———— years, to receive punctually at stated times a fixed compensation for their services, in which no increase nor diminution shall be made so as to affect the persons composing the Executive at the time of such increase or diminution, to be paid out of the federal treasury; to be incapable of holding any other office or appointment during their time of service and for ———— years thereafter: to be ineligible a second time, & removeable by Congˢ on application by a majority of the Executives of the several States; that the Executives besides their general authority to execute the federal acts ought to appoint all federal officers not otherwise provided for, & to direct all military operations; provided that none of the persons composing the federal Executive shall on any occasion take command of any troops, so as personally to conduct any enterprise as General or in any other capacity.

5. Res.ᵈ that a federal Judiciary be established to consist of a supreme Tribunal the Judges of which to be appointed by the Executive, & to hold their offices during good behaviour, to receive punctually at stated times a fixed compensation for their services in which no increase nor diminution shall be made, so as to affect the persons actually in office at the time of such increase or diminution: that the Judiciary so established shall have authority to hear & determine in the first instance on all impeachments of federal Officers, & by way of appeal in the dernier resort in all cases touching the rights of Ambassadors, in all cases of captures from an enemy, in all cases of piracies & felonies on

the high Seas, in all cases in which foreigners may be interested, in the construction of any treaty or treaties, or which may arise on any of the Acts for the regulation of trade, or the collection of the federal Revenue: that none of the Judiciary shall during the time they remain in office be capable of receiving or holding any other office or appointment during their term of service, or for ———— thereafter.

6. Res^d that all Acts of the U. States in Cong^s made by virtue & in pursuance of the powers hereby & by the Articles of Confederation vested in them, and all Treaties made & ratified under the authority of the U. States shall be the supreme law of the respective States so far forth as those Acts or Treaties shall relate to the said States or their Citizens, and that the Judiciary of the several States shall be bound thereby in their decisions any thing in the respective laws of the Individual States to the Contrary notwithstanding: and that if any State, or any body of men in any State shall oppose or prevent ye carrying into execution such acts or treaties, the federal Executive shall be authorized to call forth ye power of the Confederated States, or so much thereof as may be necessary to enforce and compel an Obedience to such Acts, or an observance of such Treaties.

7. Res^d that provision be made for the admission of new States into the Union.

8. Res^d that the rule for naturalization ought to be same in every State.

9. Res^d that a Citizen of one State committing an offence in another State of the Union, shall be deemed guilty of the same offence as if it had been committed by a Citizen of the State in which the offence was committed.

Adjourned.

Monday, June 18

Mᷞ Hamilton, had been hitherto silent on the business before the Convention, partly from respect to others whose superior abilities age & experience rendered him unwilling to bring forward ideas dissimilar to theirs, and partly from his delicate situation with respect to his own State, to whose sentiments as expressed by his Colleages, he could by no means accede. This crisis however which now marked our affairs, was too serious to permit any scruples whatever to prevail over the duty imposed on every man to contribute his efforts for the public safety & happiness. He was obliged therefore to declare himself unfriendly to both plans. He was particularly opposed to that from N. Jersey, being fully convinced, that no amendment of the Confederation, leaving the States in possession of their Sovereignty could possibly answer the purpose.

Source: *Writings*, 3: 182.

Wednesday, June 20

M: Sherman 2^ded & supported M: Lansings motion. He admitted two branches to be necessary in the State Legislatures, but saw no necessity for them in a Confederacy of States. The examples were all, of a single Council. Cong: carried us thro' the war, and perhaps as well as any Gov: could have done. The complaints at present are not that the views of Cong: are unwise or unfaithful; but that their powers are insufficient for the execution of their views. The national debt & the want of power somewhere to draw forth the National resources, are the great matters that press. All the States were sensible of the defect of power in Cong: He thought much might be said in apology for the failure of the State Legislatures to comply with the Confederation. They were afraid of leaning too hard on the people, by accumulating taxes; no *constitutional* rule had been or could be observed in the quotas—the Accounts also were unsettled & every State supposed itself in advance, rather than in arrears. For want of a general system, taxes to a due amount had not been drawn from trade which was the most convenient resource. As almost all the States had agreed to the recommendation of Cong: on the subject of an impost, it appeared clearly that they were willing to trust Cong: with power to draw a revenue from Trade. There is no weight therefore in the argument drawn from a distrust of Cong: for money matters being the most important of all, if the people will trust them with power as to them, they will trust them with any other necessary powers. Cong: indeed by the confederation have in fact the right of saying how much the people shall pay, and to what purpose it shall be applied: and this right was granted to them in the expectation that it would in all cases have its effect. If another branch were to be added to Cong: to be chosen by the people, it would serve to embarrass. The people would not much interest themselves in the elections, a few designing men in the large districts would carry their points, and the people would have no more confidence in their new representatives than in Cong: He saw no reason why the State Legislatures should be unfriendly as had been suggested, to Cong: If they

Source: *Writings,* 3: 234–36.

appoint Cong^s and approve of their measures, they would be rather favourable and partial to them. The disparity of the States in point of size he perceived was the main difficulty. But the large States had not yet suffered from the equality of votes enjoyed by the small ones. In all great and general points, the interests of all the States were the same. The State of Virg^a notwithstanding the equality of votes, ratified the Confederation without, or even proposing, any alteration. Mass^{ts} also ratified without any material difficulty &c. In none of the ratifications is the want of two branches noticed or complained of. To consolidate the States as some had proposed would dissolve our Treaties with foreign Nations, which had been formed with us, as *Confederated* States. He did not however suppose that the creation of two branches in the Legislature would have such an effect. If the difficulty on the subject of representation can not be otherwise got over, he would agree to have two branches, and a proportional representation in one of them, provided each State had an equal voice in the other. This was necessary to secure the rights of the lesser States; otherwise three or four of the large States would rule the others as they please. Each State like each individual had its peculiar habits usages and manners, which constituted its happiness. It would not therefore give to others a power over this happiness, any more than an individual would do, when he could avoid it.

Thursday, June 21

M: Wilson being for making the 1ˢᵗ branch an effectual representation of the people at large, preferred an annual election of it. This frequency was most familiar & pleasing to the people. It would not be more inconvenient to them, than triennial elections, as the people in all the States have annual meetings with which the election of the National representatives might be made to coincide. He did not conceive that it would be necessary for the Nat! Leigsl: to sit constantly; perhaps not half—perhaps not one fourth of the year.

M: Madison was persuaded that annual elections would be extremely inconvenient and apprehensive that biennial would be too much so: he did not mean inconvenient to the electors; but to the representatives. They would have to travel seven or eight hundred miles from the distant parts of the Union; and would probably not be allowed even a reimbursement of their expences. Besides, none of those who wished to be re-elected would remain at the seat of Governm:; confiding that their absence would not affect them. The members of Cong: had done this with few instances of disappointment. But as the choice was here to be made by the people themselves who would be much less complaisant to individuals, and much more susceptible of impressions from the presence of a Rival candidate, it must be supposed that the members from the most distant States would travel backwards & forwards at least as often as the elections should be repeated. Much was to be said also on the time requisite for new Members who would always form a large proportion, to acquire that knowledge of the affairs of the States in general without which their trust could not be usefully discharged.

M: Sherman preferred annual elections, but would be content with biennial. He thought the Representatives ought to return home and mix with the people. By remaining at the seat of Gov: they would acquire the habits of the place which might differ from those of their Constituents.

Col. Mason observed that the States being differently situated such a rule ought to be formed as would put them as nearly as possible on a level. If elections

Source: *Writings*, 3: 248–50.

were annual the middle States would have a great advantage over the extreme ones. He wished them to be biennial; and the rather as in that case they would coincide with the periodical elections of S. Carolina as well of the other States.

Col. Hamilton urged the necessity of 3 years. there ought to be neither too much nor too little dependence, on the popular sentiments. The checks in the other branches of the Govern! would be but feeble, and would need every auxiliary principle that could be interwoven. The British House of Commons were elected septennially, yet the democratic spirit of y.ᵉ Constitution had not ceased. Frequency of elections tended to make the people listless to them; and to facilitate the success of little cabals. This evil was complained of in all the States. In Virgᵃ it had been lately found necessary to force the attendance & voting of the people by severe regulations.

On the question for striking out "three years"

Massᵗˢ ay. Conᵗ ay. N. Y. no. N. J. divᵈ Pᵃ ay. Del. no. Mᵈ no. Vᵃ ay. N. C. ay. S. C. ay. Geo. ay.

The motion for "two years" was then inserted nem. con.

Adjᵈ

Friday, June 22 in Convention

The clause in Resol. 3 "to receive fixed stipends to be paid out of the Nation! Treasury" considered.

M: Elseworth, moved to substitute payment by the States out of their own Treasurys: observing that the manners of different States were very different in the stile of living and in the profits accruing from the exercise of like talents. What would be deemed therefore a reasonable compensation in some States, in others would be very unpopular, and might impede the system of which it made a part.

M: Williamson favored the idea. He reminded the House of the prospect of new States to the Westward. They would be too poor—would pay little into the common Treasury—and would have a different interest from the old States. He did not think therefore that the latter ought to pay the expences of men who would be employed in thwarting their measures & interests.

M: Ghorum wished not to refer the matter to the State Legislatures who were always paring down salaries in such a manner as to keep out of offices men most capable of executing the functions of them. He thought also it would be wrong to fix the compensations by the constitution, because we could not venture to make it as liberal as it ought to be without exciting an enmity ag:st the whole plan. Let the Nat! Legisl: provide for their own wages from time to time; as the State Legislatures do. He had not seen this part of their power abused, nor did he apprehend an abuse of it.

M: Randolph said he feared we were going too far, in consulting popular prejudices. Whatever respect might be due to them, in lesser matters, or in cases where they formed the permanent character of the people, he thought it neither incumbent on nor honorable for the Convention, to sacrifice right & justice to that consideration. If the States were to pay the members of the Nat! Legislature, a dependence would be created that would vitiate the whole System. The whole nation has an interest in the attendance & services of the members. The Nation! Treasury therefore is the proper fund for supporting them.

Source: *Writings*, 3: 250–52.

M! King, urged the danger of creating a dependence on the States by leav^g to them the payment of the members of the Nat! Legislature. He supposed it w^d be best to be explicit as to the compensation to be allowed. A reserve on that point, or a reference to the Nat! Legislature of the quantum, would excite greater opposition than any sum that would be actually necessary or proper.

M! Sherman contended for referring both the quantum and the payment of it to the State Legislatures.

Saturday, June 23 in Convention

Gen! Pinkney moves to strike out the ineligibility of members of the 1ˢᵗ branch to offices established "by a particular State." He argued from the inconveniency to which such a restriction would expose both the members of the 1ˢᵗ branch, and the States wishing for their services; & from the smallness of the object to be attained by the restriction.

It w⁴ seem from the ideas of some that we are erecting a Kingdom to be divided agˢᵗ itself, he disapproved such a fetter on the Legislature.

M! Sherman seconds the motion. It w⁴ seem that we are erecting a Kingdom at war with itself. The Legislature ought not to [be] fettered in such a case. On the question

Masstˢ no. Con! ay. N. Y. ay. N. J. ay. Pᵃ no. M⁴ div⁴ Del. no. M⁴ ay. Vᵃ ay. N. C. ay. S. C. ay. Geo. ay.

M! Madison renewed his motion yesterday made & waved to render the members of the 1ˢᵗ branch "ineligible during their term of service, & for one year after—to such offices only as should be established, or the emoluments thereof augmented, by the Legislature of the U. States during the time of their being members." He supposed that the unnecessary creation of offices, and increase of salaries, were the evils most experienced, & that if the door was shut agˢᵗ them: it might properly be left open for the appoint! of members to other offices as an encouragem! to the Legislative service.

M! Alex: Martin seconded the Motion.

M! Butler. The amend! does not go far eno. & w⁴ be easily evaded

M! Rutlidge, was for preserving the Legislature as pure as possible, by shutting the door against appointments of its own members to offices, which was one source of its corruption.

M! Mason. The motion of my colleague is but a partial remedy for the evil. He appealed to him as a witness of the shameful partiality of the Legislature of Virginia to its own members. He enlarged on the abuses & corruption in the British Parliament, connected with the appointment of its members. He

Source: *Writings*, 3: 259–63.

c͟d͟ not suppose that a sufficient number of Citizens could not be found who would be ready, without the inducement of eligibility to offices, to undertake the Legislative service. Genius & virtue it may be said, ought to be encouraged. Genius, for aught he knew, might, but that virtue should be encouraged by such a species of venality, was an idea, that at least had the merit of being new.

M͟r͟ King remarked that we were refining too much in this business; and that the idea of preventing intrigue and solicitation of offices was chimerical. You say that no member shall himself be eligible to any office. Will this restrain him from availing himself of the same means which would gain appointments for himself, to gain them for his son, his brother, or any other object of his partiality. We were losing therefore the advantages on one side, without avoiding the evils on the other.

M͟r͟ Wilson supported the motion. The proper cure he said for corruption in the Legislature was to take from it the power of appointing to offices. One branch of corruption would indeed remain, that of creating unnecessary offices, or granting unnecessary salaries, and for that the amendment would be a proper remedy. He animadverted on the impropriety of stigmatizing with the name of venality the laudable ambition of rising into the honorable offices of the Government; an ambition most likely to be felt in the early & most incorrupt period of life, & which all wise & free Gov͟ts͟ had deemed it sound policy, to cherish, not to check. The members of the Legislature have perhaps the hardest & least profitable task of any who engage in the service of the state. Ought this merit to be made a disqualification?

M͟r͟ Sherman, observed that the motion did not go far enough. It might be evaded by the creation of a new office, the translation to it of a person from another office, and the appointment of a member of the Legislature to the latter. A new Embassy might be established to a new Court, & an ambassador taken from another, in order to *create* a vacancy for a favorite member. He admitted that inconveniences lay on both sides. He hoped there w͟d͟ be sufficient inducements to the public service without resorting to the prospect of desirable offices, and on the whole was rather ag͟st͟ the motion of M͟r͟ Madison.

Tuesday, June 26 in Convention

The duration of the 2ᵈ branch under consideration.

Mʳ Ghorum moved to fill the blank with "six years," one third of the members to go out every second year.

Mʳ Wilson 2ᵈᵉᵈ the motion.

Genˡ Pinkney opposed six years in favor of four years. The States he said had different interests. Those of the Southern, and of S. Carolina in particular were different from the Northern. If the Senators should be appointed for a long term, they wᵈ settle in the State where they exercised their functions; and would in a little time be rather the representatives of that than of the State appointᵍ them.

Mʳ Reed movᵈ that the term be nine years. This wᵈ admit of a very convenient rotation, one third going out triennially. He wᵈ still prefer "during good behaviour," but being little supported in that idea, he was willing to take the longest term that could be obtained.

Mʳ Broome 2ᵈᵉᵈ the motion.

Mʳ Madison. In order to judge of the form to be given to this institution, it will be proper to take a view of the ends to be served by it. These were first to protect the people agˢᵗ their rulers; secondly to protect the people agˢᵗ the transient impressions into which they themselves might be led. A people deliberating in a temperate moment, and with the experience of other nations before them, on the plan of Govᵗ most likely to secure their happiness, would first be aware, that those chargᵈ with the public happiness might betray their trust. An obvious precaution agˢᵗ this danger wᵈ be to divide the trust between different bodies of men, who might watch & check each other. In this they wᵈ be governed by the same prudence which has prevailed in organizing the subordinate departments of Govᵗ, where all business liable to abuses is made to pass thro' separate hands, the one being a check on the other. It wᵈ next occur to such people, that they themselves were liable to temporary errors, thro' want of information as to their true interest, and that men chosen for a

Source: *Writings*, 3: 284–88.

short term, & employed but a small portion of that in public affairs, might err from the same cause. This reflection w.^d naturally suggest that the Gov.^t be so constituted as that one of its branches might have an opp.^y of acquiring a competent knowledge of the public interests. Another reflection equally becoming a people on such an occasion, w.^d be that they themselves, as well as a numerous body of Representatives, were liable to err also, from fickleness and passion. A necessary fence ag.st this danger would be to select a portion of enlightened citizens, whose limited number, and firmness might seasonably interpose ag.st impetuous councils. It ought finally to occur to a people deliberating on a Gov.^t for themselves, that as different interests necessarily result from the liberty meant to be secured, the major interest might under sudden impulses be tempted to commit injustice on the minority. In all civilized Countries the people fall into different classes hav.^g a real or supposed difference of interests. There will be creditors & debtors; farmers, merch.^{ts} & manufacturers. There will be particularly the distinction of rich & poor. It was true as had been observ.^d (by Mr Pinkney) we had not among us those hereditary distinctions, of rank which were a great source of the contests in the ancient Gov.^{ts} as well as the modern States of Europe, nor those extremes of wealth or poverty which characterize the latter. We cannot however be regarded even at this time, as one homogeneous mass, in which every thing that affects a part will affect in the same manner the whole. In framing a system which we wish to last for ages, we sh.^d not lose sight of the changes which ages will produce. An increase of population will of necessity increase the proportion of those who will labour under all the hardships of life, & secretly sigh for a more equal distribution of its blessings. These may in time outnumber those who are placed above the feelings of indigence. According to the equal laws of suffrage, the power will slide into the hands of the former. No agrarian attempts have yet been made in this Country, but symptoms, of a levelling spirit, as we have understood, have sufficiently appeared in certain quarters, to give notice of the future danger. How is this danger to be guarded ag.st on the republican principles? How is the danger in all cases of interested coalitions to oppress the minority to be guarded ag.st? Among other means by the establishment of a body in the Gov.^t sufficiently respectable for its wisdom & virtue, to aid on such emergencies, the preponderance of justice by throwing its weight into that scale. Such being the objects of the second branch in the proposed Gov.^t he thought a considerable duration ought to be given to it. He did not conceive that the term of nine years could threaten any real danger; but in pursuing his particular ideas on the subject, he should require that the long term allowed to the 2.^d branch should not commence till such a period of life, as would render a perpetual disqualification to be re-elected little inconvenient either in a public or private view. He observed that as it was more than probable we were now digesting a plan which in its operation w.^d decide for ever the fate of Republican Gov.^t we ought not only to provide every guard to liberty that its preservation c.^d require, but be equally careful to supply the defects which our own experience had particularly pointed out.

Mr Sherman. Gov.^t is instituted for those who live under it. It ought therefore to be so constituted as not to be dangerous to their liberties. The more permanency it has the worse if it be a bad Gov.^t Frequent elections are necessary to preserve the good behavior of rulers. They also tend to give permanency to the Government, by preserving that good behavior, because it ensures their re-election. In Connecticut elections have been very frequent, yet great stability & uniformity both as to persons & measures have been experienced from its original establishm.^t to the present time; a period of more than a 130 years. He wished to have provision made for steadiness & wisdom in the system to be adopted; but he thought six or four years would be sufficient. He sh.^d be content with either.

Thursday, June 28

M⁚ Wilson. The leading argument of those who contend for equality of votes among the States is that the States as such being equal, and being represented not as districts of individuals, but in their political & corporate capacities, are entitled to an equality of suffrage. According to this mode of reasoning the representation of the boroughs in Engld which has been allowed on all hands to be the rotten part of the Constitution, is perfectly right & proper. They are like the States represented in their corporate capacity like the States therefore they are entitled to equal voices, old Sarum to as many as London. And instead of the injury supposed hitherto to be done to London, the true ground of Complaint lies with old Sarum: for London instead of two which is her proper share, sends four representatives to Parliament.

M⁚ Sherman. The question is not what rights naturally belong to man; but how they may be most equally & effectually guarded in Society. And if some give up more than others in order to obtain this end, there can be no room for complaint. To do otherwise, to require an equal concession from all, if it would create danger to the rights of some, would be sacrificing the end to the means. The rich man who enters into Society along with the poor man, gives up more than the poor man, yet with an equal vote he is equally safe. Were he to have more votes than the poor man in proportion to his superior stake the rights of the poor man would immediately cease to be secure. This consideration prevailed when the articles of Confederation were formed.

The determination of the question from striking out the word "not" was put off till tomorrow at the request of the Deputies of N. York.

Doc⁚ Franklin. M⁚ President

The small progress we have made after 4 or five weeks close attendance & continual reasonings with each other—our different sentiments on almost every question, several of the last producing as many noes as ays, is methinks a melancholy proof of the imperfection of the Human Understanding. We indeed seem to feel our own want of political wisdom, since we have been

Source: *Writings*, 3: 308–12.

running about in search of it. We have gone back to ancient history for models of Government, and examined the different forms of those Republics which having been formed with the seeds of their own dissolution now no longer exist. And we have viewed Modern States all round Europe, but find none of their Constitutions suitable to our circumstances.

In this situation of this Assembly, groping as it were in the dark to find political truth, and scarce able to distinguish it when presented to us, how has it happened, Sir, that we have not hitherto once thought of humbly applying to the Father of lights to illuminate our understandings? In the beginning of the Contest with G. Britain, when we were sensible of danger we had daily prayer in this room for the divine protection.—Our prayers, Sir, were heard, & they were graciously answered. All of us who were engaged in the struggle must have observed frequent instances of a superintending providence in our favor. To that kind providence we owe this happy opportunity of consulting in peace on the means of establishing our future national felicity. And have we now forgotten that powerful friend? or do we imagine that we no longer need his assistance? I have lived, Sir, a long time, and the longer I live, the more convincing proofs I see of this truth—*that God Governs in the affairs of men.* And if a sparrow cannot fall to the ground without his notice, is it probable that an empire can rise without his aid? We have been assured, Sir, in the sacred writings that "except the Lord build the House they labour in vain that build it." I firmly believe this; and I also believe that without his concurring aid we shall succeed in this political building no better than the Builders of Babel: We shall be divided by our little partial local interests; our projects will be confounded, and we ourselves shall become a reproach and bye word down to future ages. And what is worse, mankind may hereafter from this unfortunate instance, despair of establishing Governments by Human wisdom and leave it to chance, war and conquest.

I therefore beg leave to move—that henceforth prayers imploring the assistance of Heaven, and its blessings on our deliberations, be held in this Assembly every morning before we proceed to business, and that one or more of the Clergy of this City be requested to officiate in that Service—

M: Sharman seconded the motion.

M: Hamilton & several others expressed their apprehensions that however proper such a resolution might have been at the beginning of the convention, it might at this late day, 1. bring on it some disagreeable animadversions, & 2. lead the public to believe that the embarrassments and dissensions within the Convention, had suggested this measure. It was answered by Doc: F. M: Sherman & others, that the past omission of a duty could not justify a further omission—that the rejection of such a proposition would expose the Convention to more unpleasant animadversions than the adoption of it: and that the alarm out of doors that might be excited for the state of things within, would at least be as likely to do good as ill.

M: Williamson, observed that the true cause of the omission could not be mistaken. The Convention had no funds.

M: Randolph proposed in order to give a favorable aspect to y: measure, that a sermon be preached at the request of the convention on 4.ᵗʰ of July, the anniversary of Independence; & thenceforward prayers be used in y: Convention every morning. D: Frankⁿ 2ᵈᵉᵈ this motion. After several unsuccessful attempts for silently postponing this matter by adjournᵍ the adjournment was at length carried, without any vote on the motion.

Saturday, June 30

M⁏ Sherman. M⁏ Madison had animadverted on the delinquency of the States, when his object required him to prove that the Constitution of Cong⁏ was faulty. Cong⁏ is not to blame for the faults of the States. Their measures have been right, and the only thing wanting has been, a further power in Cong⁏ to render them effectual.

Source: *Writings,* 3: 334.

Saturday, July 7 in Convention

"Shall the clause allowing each State one vote in the 2ᵈ branch, stand as part of the Report,"? being taken up—

Mʳ Gerry. This is the critical question. He had rather agree to it than have no accommodation. A Governᵗ short of a proper national plan, if generally acceptable, would be preferable to a proper one which if it could be carried at all, would operate on discontented States. He thought it would be best to suspend the question till the Commᵉ yesterday appointed, should make report.

Mʳ Sherman Supposed that it was the wish of every one that some Genˡ Govᵗ should be established. An equal vote in the 2ᵈ branch would, he thought, be most likely to give it the necessary vigor. The small States have more vigor in their Govᵗˢ than the large ones, the more influence therefore the large ones have, the weaker will be the Govᵗ In the large States it will be most difficult to collect the real & fair sense of the people. Fallacy & undue influence will be practised with most success; and improper men will most easily get into office. If they vote by States in the 2ᵈ branch, and each State has an equal vote, there must be always a majority of States as well as a majority of the people on the side of public measures, & the Govᵗ will have decision and efficacy. If this be not the case in the 2ᵈ branch there may be a majority of States agˢᵗ public measures, and the difficulty of compelling them to abide by the public determination, will render the Government feebler than it has ever yet been.

Mʳ Wilson was not deficient in a conciliating temper, but firmness was sometimes a duty of higher obligation. Conciliation was also misapplied in this instance. It was pursued here rather among the Representatives, than among the Constituents; and it wᵈ be of little consequence if not established among the latter; and there could be little hope of its being established among them if the foundation should not be laid in justice and right.

On Question shall the words stand as part of the Report?

Massᵗˢ divᵈ Conᵗ ay. N. Y. ay. N. J. ay. Pᵃ no. Del. ay. Mᵈ ay. Vᵃ no. N. C. ay. S. C. no. Geo. divᵈ

Source: *Writings*, 3: 375–76.

Wednesday, July 11 in Convention

M᷾ Randolph's motion requiring the Legisl᷾ to take a periodical census for the purpose of redressing inequalities in the Representation was resumed.

M᷾ Sherman was ag᷾ Shackling the Legislature too much. We ought to choose wise & good men, and then confide in them.

M᷾ Rutlidge contended for the admission of wealth in the estimate by which Representation should be regulated. The Western States will not be able to contribute in proportion to their numbers; they sh᷾ not therefore be represented in that proportion. The Atlantic States will not concur in such a plan. He moved that "at the end of —— years after the 1ˢᵗ meeting of the Legislature, and of every —— years thereafter, the Legislature shall proportion the Representation according to the principles of wealth & population."

M᷾ Sherman thought the number of people alone the best rule for measuring wealth as well as representation; and that if the Legislature were to be governed by wealth, they would be obliged to estimate it by numbers. He was at first for leaving the matter wholly to the discretion of the Legislature; but he had been convinced by the observation of (M᷾ Randolph & M᷾ Mason), that the *periods & the rule,* of revising the Representation ought to be fixt by the Constitution. . . .

the next clause as to ⅗ of the negroes considered

M᷾ King being much opposed to fixing numbers as the rule of representation, was particularly so on account of the blacks. He thought the admission of them along with Whites at all, would excite great discontents among the States having no slaves. He had never said as to any particular point that he would in no event acquiesce in & support it; but he w᷾ say that if any in case such a declaration was to be made by him, it would be in this. He remarked that in the temporary allotment of Representatives made by the Committee, the Southern States had received more than the number of their white & Three fifths of their black inhabitants entitled them to.

Source: *Writings,* 3: 394, 400, 406–8.

Mʳ Sherman. S. Carolᵃ had not more beyond her proportion than N. York & N. Hampshire, nor either of them more than was necessary in order to avoid fractions or reducing them below their proportions. Georgia had more; but the rapid growth of that State seemed to justify it. In general the allotment might not be just, but considering all circumstances, he was satisfied with it.

Mʳ Ghorum. supported the propriety of establishing numbers as the rule. He said that in Massᵗˢ estimates had been taken in the different towns, and that persons had been curious enough to compare these estimates with the respective numbers of people; and it had been found even including Boston, that the most exact proportion prevailed between numbers & property. He was aware that there might be some weight in what had fallen from his colleague, as to the umbrage which might be taken by the people of the Eastern States. But he recollected that when the proposition of Congˢ for changing the 8ᵗʰ art: of the Confedⁿ was before the Legislature of Massᵗˢ the only difficulty then was to satisfy them that the negroes ought not to have been counted equally with whites instead of being counted in ratio of three-fifths only.

Mʳ Wilson did not well see on what principle the admission of blacks in the proportion of three fifths could be explained. Are they admitted as Citizens? then why are they not admitted on an equality with White Citizens? are they admitted as property? then why is not other property admitted into the computation? These were difficulties however which he thought must be overruled by the necessity of compromise. He had some apprehensions also from the tendency of the blending of the blacks with the whites, to give disgust to the people of Penᵃ, as had been intimated by his Colleague (Mʳ Govʳ Morris). But he differed from him in thinking numbers of inhabᵗˢ so incorrect a measure of wealth. He had seen the Western settlemᵗˢ of Pᵃ and on a comparison of them with the City of Philadᵃ could discover little other difference, than that property was more unequally divided among individuals here than there. Taking the same number in the aggregate in the two situations he believed there would be little difference in their wealth and ability to contribute to the public wants.

Mʳ Govʳ Morris was compelled to declare himself reduced to the dilemma of doing injustice to the Southern States or to human nature, and he must therefore do it to the former. For he could never agree to give such encouragement to the Slave Trade as would be given by allowing them a representation for their negroes, and he did not believe those States would ever confederate on terms that would deprive them of that trade.

On Question for agreeing to include ⅗ of the blacks Massᵗˢ no. Conᵗ ay. N. J. no. Pᵃ no. Del. no. Marᵈ no. Vᵃ ay. N. C. ay. S. C. no. Geo. ay.

Saturday, July 14 in Convention

M. L. Martin called for the question on the whole report, including the parts relating to the origination of money bills, and the equality of votes in the 2.ᵈ branch.

M. Gerry, wished before the question should be put, that the attention of the House might be turned to the dangers apprehended from Western States. He was for admitting them on liberal terms, but not for putting ourselves in their hands. They will if they acquire power like all men, abuse it. They will oppress commerce, and drain our wealth into the Western Country. To guard ag.ˢᵗ these consequences, he thought it necessary to limit the number of new States to be admitted into the Union, in such a manner, that they should never be able to outnumber the Atlantic States. He accordingly moved "that in order to secure the liberties of the States already confederated, the number of Representatives in the 1ˢᵗ branch, of the States which shall hereafter be established, shall never exceed in number, the Representatives from such of the States as shall accede to this Confederation.

M. King, seconded the motion.

M. Sherman, thought there was no probability that the number of future States would exceed that of the Existing States. If the event should ever happen, it was too remote to be taken into consideration at this time. Besides We are providing for our posterity, for our children & our grand Children; who would be as likely to be citizens of new Western States, as of the old States. On this consideration alone, we ought to make no such discrimination as was proposed by the motion. . . .

M. Pinkney moved that instead of an equality of votes, the States should be represented in the 2.ᵈ branch as follows: N. H. by 2 members. Mass. 4. R. I. 1. Con.ᵗ 3. N. Y. 3. N. J. 2. P.ᵃ 4. Del. 1; M.ᵈ 3. Virg.ᵃ 5. N. C. 3. S. C. 3. Geo. 2. making in the whole 36.

M. Wilson seconds the motion

Source: *Writings*, 3: 424–25, 428, 434–37.

M: Dayton. The smaller States can never give up their equality. For himself he would in no event yield that security for their rights.

M: Sherman, urged the equality of votes not so much as a Security for the small States; as for the State Gov:ts which could not be preserved unless they were represented & had a negative in the Gen:l Government. He had no objection to the members in the 2:d b. voting per capita, as had been suggested by (M: Gerry). . . .

M: Wilson would add a few words only. If equality in the 2:d branch was an error that time would correct, he should be less anxious to exclude it being sensible that perfection was unattainable in any plan; but being a fundamental and a perpetual error, it ought by all means to be avoided. A vice in the Representation, like an error in the first concoction, must be followed by disease, convulsions, and finally death itself. The justice of the general principle of proportional representation has not in argument at least been yet contradicted. But it is said that a departure from it so far as to give the States an equal vote in one branch of the Legislature is essential to their preservation. He had considered this position maturely, but could not see its application. That the States ought to be preserved he admitted. But does it follow that an equality of votes is necessary for the purpose? Is there any reason to suppose that if their preservation should depend more on the large than on the small States the security of the States ag:st the Gen:l Government would be diminished? Are the large States less attached to their existence more likely to commit suicide, than the small? An equal vote then is not necessary as far as he can conceive: and is liable among other objections to this insuperable one: The great fault of the existing confederacy is its inactivity. It has never been a complaint ag:st Cong:s that they governed over much. The complaint has been that they have governed too little. To remedy this defect we were sent here. Shall we effect the cure by establishing an equality of votes as is proposed? no: this very equality carries us directly to Congress; to the system which it is our duty to rectify. The small States cannot indeed act, by virtue of this equality, but they may controul the Gov: as they have done in Cong:s This very measure is here prosecuted by a minority of the people of America. Is then the object of the Convention likely to be accomplished in this way? Will not our Constituents say? we sent you to form an efficient Gov: and you have given us one more complex indeed, but having all the weakness of the former govern: He was anxious for uniting all the States under one Govern: He knew there were some respectable men who preferred three confederacies, united by offensive & defensive alliances. Many things may be plausibly said, some things may be justly said, in favor of such a project. He could not however concur in it himself; but he thought nothing so pernicious as bad first principles.

M: Elseworth asked two questions, one of M: Wilson, whether he had ever seen a good measure fail in Cong: for want of a majority of States in its favor? He had himself never known such an instance: the other of M: Madison whether a negative lodged with the majority of the States even the smallest, could be more dangerous than the qualified negative proposed to be lodged in a single Executive Magistrate, who must be taken from some one State?

M: Sherman, signified that his expectation was that the Gen! Legislature would in some cases act on the *federal principle*, of requiring quotas. But he thought it ought to be empowered to carry their own plans into execution, if the States should fail to supply their respective quotas.

On the question for agreeing to M: Pinkney's motion for allowing N. H. 2. Mas. 4. &c—it passed in the negative,

Mass. no. M: King ay. M: Ghorum absent. Con: no. N. J. no. P: ay. Del. no. M: ay. V: ay. N. C. no. S. C. ay. Geo. no.

Adjourned.

Tuesday, July 17 in Convention

M.ʳ Govern.ʳ Morris. moved to reconsider the whole Resolution agreed to yesterday concerning the constitution of the 2 branches of the Legislature. His object was to bring the House to a consideration in the abstract of the powers necessary to be vested in the general Government. It had been said, Let us know how the Gov.ᵗ is to be modelled, and then we can determine what powers can be properly given to it. He thought the most eligible course was, first to determine on the necessary powers, and then so to modify the Govern.ᵗ as that it might be justly & properly enabled to administer them. He feared if we proceeded to a consideration of the powers, whilst the vote of yesterday including an equality of the States in the 2.ᵈ branch, remained in force, a reference to it, either mental or expressed, would mix itself with the merits of every question concerning the powers.—This motion was not seconded. (It was probably approved by several members who either despaired of success, or were apprehensive that the attempt would inflame the jealousies of the smaller States.)

The 6.ᵗʰ Resol.ⁿ in the Report of the Com.ᵉ of the Whole relating to the powers, which had been postponed in order to consider the 7 & 8.ᵗʰ relating to the constitution of the Nat.ˡ Legislature, was now resumed.

M.ʳ Sherman observed that it would be difficult to draw the line between the powers of the Gen.ˡ Legislature, and those to be left with the States; that he did not like the definition contained in the Resolution, and proposed in place of the words "individual legislation" line 4. inclusive, to insert "to make laws binding on the people of the United States in all cases which may concern the common interests of the Union; but not to interfere with the Government of the individual States in any matters of internal police which respect the Gov.ᵗ of such States only, and wherein the general welfare of the U. States is not concerned."

M.ʳ Wilson 2.ᵈᵉᵈ the amendment as better expressing the general principle.

Source: *Writings*, 3: 444–51, 455–56.

M.ʳ Gov.ʳ Morris opposed it. The internal police, as it would be called & understood by the States ought to be infringed in many cases, as in the case of paper money & other tricks by which Citizens of other States may be affected.

M.ʳ Sherman, in explanation of his idea read an enumeration of powers, including the power of levying taxes on trade, but not the power of *direct taxation*.

M.ʳ Gov.ʳ Morris remarked the omission, and inferred that for the deficiencies of taxes on consumption, it must have been the meaning of Mr. Sherman, that the Gen.ˡ Gov.ʳ should recur to quotas & requisitions, which are subversive of the idea of Gov.ʳ

M.ʳ Sherman acknowledged that his enumeration did not include direct taxation. Some provision he supposed must be made for supplying the deficiency of other taxation, but he had not formed any.

On Question on M.ʳ Sherman's motion it passed in the negative

Mas. no. Con.ᵗ ay. N. J. no. P.ᵃ no. Del. no. M.ᵈ ay. V.ᵃ no. N. C. no. S. C. no. Geo. no.

M.ʳ Bedford moved that the 2.ᵈ member of Resolution 6. be so altered as to read, "and moreover to legislate in all cases for the general interests of the Union, and also in those to which the States are severally incompetent, "or in which the harmony of the U. States may be interrupted by the exercise of individual Legislation."

M.ʳ Gov.ʳ Morris 2.ᵈˢ the motion

M.ʳ Randolph. This is a formidable idea indeed. It involves the power of violating all the laws and constitutions of the States, and of intermeddling with their police. The last member of the sentence is also superfluous, being included in the first.

M.ʳ Bedford. It is not more extensive or formidable than the clause as it stands: *no State* being *separately* competent to legislate for the *general interest* of the Union.

On question for agreeing to M.ʳ Bedford's motion it passed in the affirmative.

Mas. ay. Con.ᵗ no. N. J. ay. P.ᵃ ay. Del. ay. M.ᵈ ay. V.ᵃ no. N. C. ay. S. C. no. Geo. no.

On the sentence as amended, it passed in the affirmative.

Mas. ay. Con.ᵗ ay. N. J. ay. P.ᵃ ay. Del. ay. M.ᵈ ay. V.ᵃ ay. N. C. ay. S. C. no. Geo. no.

The next. "To negative all laws passed by the several States contravening in the opinion of the Nat: Legislature the articles of Union, or any treaties subsisting under the authority of y.ᵉ Union."

M.ʳ Gov.ʳ Morris opposed this power as likely to be terrible to the States, and not necessary, if sufficient Legislative authority should be given to the Gen! Government.

M! Sherman thought it unnecessary; as the Courts of the States would not consider as valid any law contravening the Authority of the Union, and which the legislature would wish to be negatived.

M! L. Martin considered the power as improper & inadmissible. Shall all the laws of the States be sent up to the Gen! Legislature before they shall be permitted to operate?

M! Madison, considered the negative on the laws of the States as essential to the efficacy & security of the Gen! Gov! The necessity of a general Gov! proceeds from the propensity of the States to pursue their particular interests in opposition to the general interest. This propensity will continue to disturb the system, unless effectually controuled. Nothing short of a negative on their laws will controul it. They will pass laws which will accomplish their injurious objects before they can be repealed by the Gen! Legisl͎ or be set aside by the National Tribunals. Confidence can not be put in the State Tribunals as guardians of the National authority and interests. In all the States these are more or less depend! on the Legislatures. In Georgia they are appointed annually by the Legislature. In R. Island the Judges who refused to execute an unconstitutional law were displaced, and others substituted, by the Legislature who would be the willing instruments of the wicked & arbitrary plans of their masters. A power of negativing the improper laws of the States is at once the most mild & certain means of preserving the harmony of the system. Its utility is sufficiently displayed in the British system. Nothing could maintain the harmony & subordination of the various parts of the empire, but the prerogative by which the Crown, stifles in the birth every Act of every part tending to discord or encroachment. It is true the prerogative is sometimes misapplied thro' ignorance or a partiality to one particular part of y͎ empire; but we have not the same reason to fear such misapplications in our System. As to the sending all laws up to the Nat! Legisl: that might be rendered unnecessary by some emanation of the power into the States, so far at least as to give a temporary effect to laws of immediate necessity.

M! Gov! Morris was more & more opposed to the negative. The proposal of it would disgust all the States. A law that ought to be negatived will be set aside in the Judiciary departm! and if that security should fail; may be repealed by a Nation! law.

M! Sherman. Such a power involves a wrong principle, to wit, that a law of a State contrary to the articles of the Union would if not negatived, be valid & operative.

M! Pinkney urged the necessity of the Negative.

On the question for agreeing to the power of negativing laws of States &c. it passed in the negative.

Mas. ay. C! no. N. J. no. P? no. Del. no. M⁴ no. V? ay. N. C. ay. S. C. no. Geo. no.

M! Luther Martin moved the following resolution "that the Legislative acts of the U. S. made by virtue & in pursuance of the articles of Union, and all Treaties made & ratified under the authority of the U. S. shall be the supreme law of the respective States, as far as those acts or treaties shall relate to the said States, or their Citizens and inhabitants—& that the Judiciaries of the several States shall be bound thereby in their decisions, any thing in the respective laws of the individual States to the contrary notwithstanding" which was agreed to nem: con:

9ᵗʰ Resol: "that Nat! Executive consist of a single person," Ag⁴ to nem. con. "To be chosen by the National Legisl:"

M! Govern! Morris was pointedly agˢᵗ his being so chosen. He will be the mere creature of the Legisl: if appointed & impeachable by that body. He ought to be elected by the people at large, by the freeholders of the Country. That difficulties attend this mode, he admits. But they have been found superable in N. Y. & in Con! and would he believed be found so, in the case of an Executive for the U. States. If the people should elect, they will never fail to prefer some man of distinguished character, or services; some man, if he might so speak, of continental reputation. If the Legislature elect, it will be the work of intrigue, of cabal, and of faction; it will be like the election of a pope by a conclave of cardinals; real merit will rarely be the title to the appointment. He moved to strike out "National Legislature," & insert "citizens of the U. S."

M! Sherman thought that the sense of the Nation would be better expressed by the Legislature, than by the people at large. The latter will never be sufficiently informed of characters, and besides will never give a majority of votes to any one man. They will generally vote for some man in their own State, and the largest State will have the best chance for the appointment. If the choice be made by the Legisl⁻ᵉ a majority of voices may be made necessary to constitute an election. . . .

"For the term of 7 years," resumed.

M! Broom was for a shorter term since the Executive Magistrate was now to be re-eligible. Had he remained ineligible a 2⁴ time, he should have preferred a longer term.

Doc! McClurg moved to strike out 7 years, and insert "during good behavior." By striking out the words declaring him not re-eligible, he was put into a situation that would keep him dependent forever on the Legislature;

and he conceived the independence of the Executive to be equally essential with that of the Judiciary department.

M: Gov: Morris 2 ded the motion. He expressed great pleasure in hearing it. This was the way to get a good Government. His fear that so valuable an ingredient would not be attained had led him to take the part he had done. He was indifferent how the Executive should be chosen, provided he held his place by this tenure.

M: Broome highly approved the motion. It obviated all his difficulties

M: Sherman considered such a tenure as by no means safe or admissible. As the Executive Magistrate is now re-eligible, he will be on good behavior as far as will be necessary. If he behaves well he will be continued; if otherwise, displaced, on a succeeding election.

Wednesday, July 18

Resol. II. "that a Nat! Judiciary shall be estab? to consist of one supreme tribunal," ag? to nem. con.

"The judges of which to be appoint? by the 2? branch of the Nat! Legislature,"

M? Ghorum, w? prefer an appointment by the 2? branch to an appointm? by the whole Legislature; but he thought even that branch too numerous, and too little personally responsible, to ensure a good choice. He suggested that the Judges be appointed by the Execu^{ve} with the advice & consent of the 2? branch, in the mode prescribed by the constitution of Mas?^s This mode had been long practised in that country, & was found to answer perfectly well.

M? Wilson, still w? prefer an appointm? by the Executive; but if that could not be attained, w? prefer in the next place, the mode suggested by M? Ghorum. He thought it his duty however to move in the first instance "that the Judges be appointed by the Executive." M? Gov? Morris 2^{ded} the motion.

M? L. Martin was strenuous for an app? by the 2? branch. Being taken from all the States it w? be best informed of characters & most capable of making a fit choice.

M? Sherman concurred in the observations of M? Martin, adding that the Judges ought to be diffused, which would be more likely to be attended to by the 2? branch, than by the Executive.

M? Mason. The mode of appointing the Judges may depend in some degree on the mode of trying impeachments of the Executive. If the Judges were to form a tribunal for that purpose, they surely ought not to be appointed by the Executive. There were insuperable objections besides ag?^t referring the appointment to the Executive. He mentioned as one, that as the Seat of Gov? must be in some one State, and as the Executive would remain in office for a considerable time, for 4. 5. or 6 years at least, he would insensibly form local & personal attachments within the particular State that would deprive equal merit elsewhere, of an equal chance of promotion.

M? Ghorum. As the Executive will be responsible in point of character at

Source: *Writings*, 3: 461–63.

least, for a judicious and faithful discharge of his trust, he will be careful to look through all the States for proper characters. The Senators will be as likely to form their attachments at the seat of Gov.ᵗ where they reside, as the Executive. If they cannot get the man of the particular State to which they may respectively belong, they will be indifferent to the rest. Public bodies feel no personal responsibility, and give full play to intrigue & cabal. Rh. Island is a full illustration of the insensibility to character produced by a participation of numbers in dishonorable measures, and of the length to which a Public body may carry wickedness & cabal.

M.ʳ Gov.ʳ Morris supposed it would be improper for an impeachm.ᵗ of the Executive to be tried before the Judges. The latter would in such case be drawn into intrigues with the Legislature and an impartial trial would be frustrated. As they w.ᵈ be much about the Seat of Gov.ᵗ they might even be previously consulted & arrangements might be made for a prosecution of the Executive. He thought therefore that no argument could be drawn from the probability of such a plan of impeachments ag.ˢᵗ the motion before the House.

M.ʳ Madison suggested that the Judges might be appointed by the Executive, with the concurrence of ⅓ at least, of the 2.ᵈ branch. This would unite the advantage of responsibility in the Executive with the security afforded in the 2.ᵈ branch ag.ˢᵗ any incautious or corrupt nomination by the Executive.

M.ʳ Sherman, was clearly for an election by the Senate. It would be composed of men nearly equal to the Executive, and would of course have on the whole more wisdom. They would bring into their deliberations a more diffusive knowledge of characters. It would be less easy for candidates to intrigue with them, than with the Executive Magistrate. For these reasons he thought there would be a better security for a proper choice in the Senate than in the Executive.

Tuesday, August 7

M! Sherman was decided for fixing the time, as well as for frequent meetings of the Legislative body. Disputes and difficulties will arise between the two Houses, & between both & the States, if the time be changeable—frequent meetings of Parliament were required at the Revolution in England as an essential safeguard of liberty. So also are annual meetings in most of the American charters & constitutions. There will be business eno' to require it. The Western Country, and the great extent and varying state of our affairs in general will supply objects.

Source: *Writings*, 4: 114.

Wednesday, August 8

Mr King wished to know what influence the vote just passed was meant to have on the succeeding part of the Report, concerning the admission of Slaves into the rule of Representation. He could not reconcile his mind to the article if it was to prevent objections to the latter part. The admission of slaves was a most grating circumstance to his mind, & he believed would be so to a great part of the people of America. He had not made a strenuous opposition to it heretofore because he had hoped that this concession would have produced a readiness which had not been manifested, to strengthen the Gen! Gov! and to mark a full confidence in it. The Report under consideration had by the tenor of it, put an end to all those hopes. In two great points the hands of the Legislature were absolutely tied. The importation of slaves could not be prohibited—exports could not be taxed. Is this reasonable? What are the great objects of the Gen! System? 1. defence agst foreign invasion. 2. agst internal sedition. Shall all the States then be bound to defend each; & shall each be at liberty to introduce a weakness which will render defence more difficult? Shall one part of the U. S. be bound to defend another part, and that other part be at liberty not only to increase its own danger, but to withhold the compensation for the burden? If slaves are to be imported shall not the exports produced by their labor, supply a revenue the better to enable the Gen! Gov! to defend their Masters? There was so much inequality & unreasonableness in all this, that the people of the Northern States could never be reconciled to it. No candid man could undertake to justify it to them. He had hoped that some accommodation w^d have taken place on this subject; that at least a time w^d have been limited for the importation of slaves. He never could agree to let them be imported without limitation & then be represented in the Nat! Legislature. Indeed he could so little persuade himself of the rectitude of such a practice, that he was not sure he could assent to it under any circumstances. At all events, either slaves should not be represented, or exports should be taxable.

Source: *Writings*, 4: 133–38.

M.̱ Sherman regarded the slave trade as iniquitous; but the point of representation having been settled after much difficulty & deliberation, he did not think himself bound to make opposition; especially as the present article as amended did not preclude any arrangement whatever on that point in another place of the Report.

M.̱ Madison objected to 1 for every 40.000 inhabitants as a perpetual rule. The future increase of population if the Union sh^d be permanent, will render the number of Representatives excessive.

M.̱ Ghorum. It is not to be supposed that the Gov.̱ will last so long as to produce this effect. Can it be supposed that this vast Country including the Western territory will 150 years hence remain one nation?

Mr Elseworth. If the Gov.̱ should continue so long, alterations may be made in the Constitution in the manner proposed in a subsequent article.

M.̱ Sherman & M.̱ Madison moved to insert the words "not exceeding," before the words "1 for every 40.000. which was agreed to nem. con.

Mr Govr Morris moved to insert "free" before the word inhabitants. Much he said would depend on this point. He never would concur in upholding domestic slavery. It was a nefarious institution. It was the curse of heaven on the States where it prevailed. Compare the free regions of the Middle States, where a rich & noble cultivation marks the prosperity & happiness of the people, with the misery & poverty which overspread the barren wastes of V^a Mayr.̱ & the other States having slaves. Travel thro' y.̱ whole Continent & you behold the prospect continually varying with the appearance & disappearance of slavery. The moment you leave ye E. States & enter N. York, the effects of the institution become visible, passing thro' the Jerseys & entering P.̱ every criterion of superior improvement witnesses the change. Proceed southw^dly & every step you take thro' y.̱ great regions of slaves presents a desert increasing, with y.̱ increasing [word is illegible] proportion of these wretched beings. Upon what principle is it that the slaves shall be computed in the representation? Are they men? Then make them Citizens and let them vote. Are they property? Why then is no other property included? The Houses in this city (Philad.̱) are worth more than all the wretched Slaves which cover the rice swamps of South Carolina. The admission of slaves into the Representation when fairly explained comes to this: that the inhabitant of Georgia and S. C. who goes to the Coast of Africa, and in defiance of the most sacred laws of humanity tears away his fellow creatures from their dearest connections & damns them to the most cruel bondages, shall have more votes in a Gov.̱ instituted for protection of the rights of mankind, than the Citizen of P.̱ or N. Jersey who views with a laudable horror, so nefarious a practice. He would add that Domestic slavery is the most prominent feature in the aristocratic countenance of the proposed Constitution. The vassalage of the poor has ever been the favorite offspring of Aristocracy. And What is the proposed compensation to the Northern States for a sacrifice of every principle of right, of every impulse of humanity. They are to bind themselves to march their militia for the defence of the S. States; for their defence agst those very slaves of whom they complain. They must supply vessels & seamen in case of foreign Attack. The Legislature will have indefinite power to tax them by excises, and duties on imports: both of which will fall heavier on them than on the Southern inhabitants; for the bohae tea used by a Northern freeman, will pay more tax than the whole consumption of the miserable slave, which consists of nothing more than his physical subsistence and the rag that covers his nakedness. On the other side the Southern States are not to be restrained from importing fresh supplies of wretched Africans, at once to increase the danger of attack, and the difficulty of defence; nay they are to be encouraged to it by an assurance of having their votes in the Nat! Gov! increased in proportion, and are at the same time to have their exports & their slaves exempt from all contributions for the public service. Let it not be said that direct taxation is to be proportioned to representation. It is idle to suppose that the Gen! Gov! can stretch its hand directly into the pockets of the people scattered over so vast a Country. They can only do it through the medium of exports imports & excises. For What then are all the sacrifices to be made? He would sooner submit himself to a tax for paying for all the negroes in the U. States, than saddle posterity with such a Constitution.

Mr Dayton 2^{ded} the motion. He did it he said that his sentiments on the subject might appear whatever might be the fate of the amendment.

Mr Sherman, did not regard the admission of the Negroes into the ratio of representation, as liable to such insuperable objections. It was the freemen of the South^{n} States who were in fact to be represented according to the taxes paid by them, and the Negroes are only included in the Estimate of the taxes. This was his idea of the matter.

Mr Pinkney, considered the fisheries & the Western frontier as more burthensome to the U. S. than the slaves. He thought this could be demonstrated if the occasion were a proper one.

Mr Wilson, thought the motion premature. An agreement to the clause would be no bar to the object of it.

Question On motion to insert "free" before "inhabitants,

N. H. no. Mass. no. C^{t} no. N. J. ay. P^{a} no. Del. no. M^{d} no. V^{a} no. N. C. no. S. C. no. Geo. no.

Thursday, August 9

M: Gov: Morris observed that the States might make false returns and then make no provisions for new elections.

M: Sherman did not know but it might be best to retain the clause, though he had himself sufficient confidence in the State Legislatures. The motion of M: P. & M' R. did not prevail

Source: *Writings*, 4: 154.

Friday, August 10

Art: VI. Sect. 7. taken up.

M! Gov! Morris urged that if the yeas & nays were proper at all any individual ought to be authorized to call for them; and moved an amendment to that effect.—The small States may otherwise be under a disadvantage, and find it difficult to get a concurrence of ⅕.

M! Randolph 2^{ded} ye motion.

M! Sherman had rather strike out the yeas & nays altogether. They never have done any good, and have done much mischief. They are not proper as the reasons governing the voter never appear along with them.

M! Elseworth was of the same opinion.

Col. Mason liked the Section as it stood. it was a middle way between two extremes.

Mr Ghorum was opposed to the motion for allowing a single member to call the yeas & nays, and recited the abuses of it in Mass^{ts} 1 in stuffing the journals with them on frivolous occasions. 2 in misleading the people who never know the reasons determing the votes.

The motion for allowing a single member to call the yeas & nays was disag^d to nem. con.

Source: *Writings,* 4: 164–65.

Saturday, August 11 in Convention

M: Madison & Mr Rutlidge moved "that each House shall keep a journal of its proceedings, & shall publish the same from time to time; except such part of the proceedings of the Senate, when acting not in its Legislative capacity as may be judged by that House to require secrecy."

M: Mercer. This implies that other powers than legislative will be given to the Senate which he hoped would not be given.

M: Madison & M: R's motion was disag^d to by all the States except Virg^a

Mr Gerry & M: Sharman moved to insert after the words "publish them" the following "except such as relate to treaties & military operations." Their object was to give each House a discretion in such cases.—On this question

N. H. no. Mass. ay. C^t ay. N. J. no. P^a no. Del. no. V^a no. N. C. no. S. C. no. Geo. no.

Mr Elseworth. As the clause is objectionable in so many shapes, it may as well be struck out altogether. The Legislature will not fail to publish their proceedings from time to time. The people will call for it if it should be improperly omitted.

Mr Wilson thought the expunging of the clause would be very improper. The people have a right to know what their Agents are doing or have done, and it should not be in the option of the Legislature to conceal their proceedings. Besides as this is a clause in the existing confederation, the not retaining it would furnish the adversaries of the reform with a pretext by which weak & suspicious minds may be easily misled.

Mr Mason thought it would give a just alarm to the people, to make a conclave of their Legislature.

Mr Sherman thought the Legislature might be trusted in this case if in any.

Source: *Writings*, 4: 166–67.

Question on 1st part of the section down to "*publish them*" inclusive: Agreed to nem. con.

Question on the words to follow, to wit "except such parts thereof as may in their Judgment require secrecy." N. H. div^d Mass. ay. C^t ay. N. J. ay. P^a no. Del. no. M^d no. V^a ay. N. C. ay. S. C. no. Geo. ay.

The remaining part as to yeas & nays,—agreed to nem. con.

Monday, August 13

M: Gov: Morris moved to add to the end of the section (Art IV. S. 2) a proviso that the limitation of seven years should not affect the rights of any person now a Citizen.

Mr Mercer 2^{ded} the motion. It was necessary he said to prevent a disfranchisement of persons who had become Citizens under and on the faith & according to the laws & Constitution from being on a level in all respects with natives.

Mr Rutlidge. It might as well be said that all qualifications are disfranchisem^{ts} and that to require the age of 25 years was a disfranchisement. The policy of the precaution was as great with regard to foreigners now Citizens; as to those who are to be naturalized in future.

M: Sherman. The U. States have not invited foreigners nor pledged their faith that they should enjoy equal privileges with native Citizens. The Individual States alone have done this. The former therefore are at liberty to make any discriminations they may judge requisite.

M: Ghorum. When foreigners are naturalized it w^d seem as if they stand on an equal footing with natives. He doubted then the propriety of giving a retrospective force to the restriction.

M: Madison animadverted on the peculiarity of the doctrine of M: Sharman. It was a subtilty by which every national engagement might be evaded. By parity of reason, Whenever our public debts, or foreign treaties become inconvenient nothing more would be necessary to relieve us from them, than to new model the Constitution. It was said that the *U. S.* as such have not pledged their faith to the naturalized foreigners, & therefore are not bound. Be it so, & that the States alone are bound. Who are to form the New Constitution by which the condition of that class of citizens is to be made worse than the other class? Are not the States ye Agents? will they not be the members of it? Did they not appoint this Convention? Are not they to ratify its proceedings? Will not the new Constitution be their Act? If the new Consti-

Source: *Writings*, 4: 175–79.

tution then violates the faith pledged to any description of people will not the makers of it, will not the States, be the violaters. To justify the doctrine it must be said that the States can get rid of their obligation by revising the Constitution, though they could not do it by repealing the law under which foreigners held their privileges. He considered this a matter of real importance. It would expose us to the reproaches of all those who should be affected by it, reproaches which w.d soon be echoed from the other side of the Atlantic; and would unnecessarily enlist among the Adversaries of the reform a very considerable body of Citizens: We should moreover reduce every State to the dilemma of rejecting it or of violating the faith pledged to a part of its Citizens.

M.r Gov.r Morris considered the case of persons under 25 years, as very different from that of foreigners. No faith could be pleaded by the former in bar of the regulation. No assurance had ever been given that persons under that age should be in all cases on a level with those above it. But with regard to foreigners among us, the faith had been pledged that they should enjoy the privileges of Citizens. If the restriction as to age had been confined to natives, & had left foreigners under 25 years, eligible in this case, the discrimination w.d have been an equal injustice on the other side.

M.r Pinkney remarked that the laws of the States had varied much the terms of naturalization in different parts of America; and contended that the U. S. could not be bound to respect them on such an occasion as the present. It was a sort of recurrence to first principles.

Col. Mason was struck not like (Mr. Madison) with the *peculiarity*, but the *propriety* of the doctrine of M.r Sharman. The States have formed different qualifications themselves, for enjoying different rights of citizenship. Greater caution w.d be necessary in the outset of the Gov.t than afterwards. All the great objects w.d then be provided for. Every thing would be then set in motion. If persons among us attached to G. B. should work themselves into our Councils, a turn might be given to our affairs & particularly to our Commercial regulations which might have pernicious consequences. The Great Houses of British Merchants will spare no pains to insinuate the instruments of their views into the Gov.t.

M.r Wilson read the clause in the Constitution of Pen.a giving to foreigners after two years residence all the rights whatsoever of Citizens, Combined it with the article of Confederation making the Citizens of one State Citizens of all, inferred the obligation Pen.a was under to maintain the faith thus pledged to her citizens of foreign birth, and the just complaints which her failure would authorize: He observed likewise that the Princes & States of Europe would avail themselves of such breach of faith to deter their subjects from emigration to the U. S.

M! Mercer enforced the same idea of a breach of faith.

M! Baldwin could not enter into the force of the arguments ag^st extending the disqualification to foreigners now Citizens. The discrimination of the place of birth, was not more objectionable than that of age which all had concurred in the propriety of.

Question on the proviso of M! Gov! Morris in favor of foreigners now Citizens

N. H. no. Mass. no. C^t ay. N. J. ay. P^a ay. Del. no. Mary^d ay. V^a ay. N. C. no. S. C. no. Geo. no.

Tuesday, August 14

Mr Sherman. The Constitution sh^d lay as few temptations as possible in the way of those in power. Men of abilities will increase as the Country grows more populous and as the means of education are more diffused. . . .

Mr Sherman was not afraid that the Legislature would make their own wages too high; but too low, so that men ever so fit could not serve unless they were at the same time rich. He thought the best plan would be to fix a moderate allowance to be paid out of the Nat^l Treas^y and let the States make such additions as they might judge fit. He moved that 5 dollars per day be the sum, any further emoluments to be added by the States.

Source: *Writings*, 4: 197, 203.

Wednesday, August 15

M⁞ Gov⁞ Morris, suggested the expedient of an absolute negative in the Executive. He could not agree that the Judiciary which was part of the Executive, should be bound to say that a direct violation of the Constitution was law. A controul over the legislature might have its inconveniences. But view the danger on the other side. The most virtuous Citizens will often as members of a legislative body concur in measures which afterwards in their private capacity they will be ashamed of. Encroachments of the popular branch of the Government ought to be guarded ag⁞ˢᵗ The Ephori at Sparta became in the end absolute. The Report of the Council of Censors in Pennsylvᵃ points out the many invasions of the legislative department on the Executive numerous as the latter is, within the short term of seven years, and in a State where a strong party is opposed to the Constitution, and watching every occasion of turning the public resentments ag⁞ˢᵗ it. If the Executive be overturned by the popular branch, as happened in England, the tyranny of one man will ensue. In Rome where the Aristocracy overturned the throne, the consequence was different. He enlarged on the tendency of the legislative Authority to usurp on the Executive and wished the section to be postponed, in order to consider of some more effectual check than requiring ⅔ only to overrule the negative of the Executive.

M⁞ Sharman. Can one man be trusted better than all the others if they all agree? This was neither wise nor safe. He disapproved of Judges meddling in politics and parties. We have gone far enough in forming the negative as it now stands.

Source: *Writings,* 4: 210–11.

Thursday, August 16

M⸢ Mercer was strenuous against giving Congress power to tax exports. Such taxes are impolitic, as encouraging the raising of articles not meant for exportation. The States had now a right where their situation permitted, to tax both the imports and the exports of their uncommercial neighbours. It was enough for them to sacrifice one half of it. It had been said the Southern States had most need of naval protection. The reverse was the case. Were it not for promoting the carrying trade of the North⸢ States, the South⸢ States could let the trade go into foreign bottoms, where it would not need our protection. Virginia by taxing her tobacco had given an advantage to that of Maryland.

M⸢ Sherman. To examine and compare the States in relation to imports and exports will be opening a boundless field. He thought the matter had been adjusted, and that imports were to be subject, and exports not, to be taxed. He thought it wrong to tax exports except it might be such articles as ought not to be exported. The complexity of the business in America would render an equal tax on exports impracticable. The oppression of the uncommercial States was guarded ag⸢ by the power to regulate trade between the States. As to compelling foreigners, that might be done by regulating trade in general. The Government would not be trusted with such a power. Objections are most likely to be excited by considerations relating to taxes & money. A power to tax exports would shipwreck the whole.

M⸢ Carrol was surprised that any objection should be made to an exception of exports from the power of taxation.

It was finally agreed that the question concerning exports sh⸢ lie over for the place in which the exception stood in the report: Mary⸢ alone voting ag⸢ it[.]

Source: *Writings*, 4: 217–18.

Friday, August 17

"To make war"

M: Pinkney opposed the vesting this power in the Legislature. Its proceedings were too slow. It w⁴ meet but once a year. the H: of Rep: would be too numerous for such deliberations. The Senate would be the best depository, being more acquainted with foreign affairs, and most capable of proper resolutions. If the States are equally represented in the Senate, so as to give no advantage to the large States, the power will notwithstanding be safe, as the small have their all at stake in such cases as well as the large States. It would be singular for one authority to make war, and another peace.

Mʳ Butler. The Objections agˢᵗ the Legislature lie in a great degree agˢᵗ the Senate. He was for vesting the power in the President, who will have all the requisite qualities, and will not make war but when the Nation will support it.

M: Madison and M: Gerry moved to insert "*declare*," striking out "*make*" war; leaving to the Executive the power to repel sudden attacks.

Mʳ Sharman thought it stood very well. The Executive shᵈ be able to repel and not to commence war. "Make" is better than "declare" the latter narrowing the power too much.

M: Gerry never expected to hear in a republic a motion to empower the Executive alone to declare war.

M: Elsworth. There is a material difference between the cases of making *war* and making *peace*. It shᵈ be more easy to get out of war, than into it War also is a simple and overt declaration, peace attended with intricate & secret negociations.

M: Mason was agˢᵗ giving the power of war to the Executive because not safely to be trusted with it; or to the Senate, because not so constructed as to be entitled to it. He was for clogging rather than facilitating war; but for facilitating peace He preferred "*declare*" to "*make.*"

On the motion to insert "*declare*"—in place of "*make*," it was agreed to.

N. H. no. Mass. absᵗ Conᵗ no. Pᵃ ay. Del. ay. Mᵈ ay. Vᵃ ay. N. C. ay. S. C. ay. Geo. ay.

Source: *Writings*, 4: 227–28.

M.ʳ Pinkney's motion to strike out whole clause, disag.ᵈ to without call of States.

M.ʳ Butler moved to give the Legislature the power of peace, as they were to have that of war.

M.ʳ Gerry 2.ᵈˢ him. 8 Senators may possibly exercise the power if vested in that body, and 14 if all should be present; and may consequently give up part of the U. States. The Senate are more liable to be corrupted by an Enemy than the whole Legislature.

On the motion for adding "and peace" after "war,"

N. H. no. Mas. no. C.ᵗ no. P.ª no. Del. no. M.ᵈ no. V.ª no. N. C. no. S. C. no. Geo. no.

Adjourned

Saturday, August 18

M? Sherman thought it would be better to authorize the Legislature to assume the State debts, than to say positively it should be done. He considered the measure as just and that it would have a good effect to say something about the matter.

M? Elseworth differed from Mr Sherman. As far as the State debts ought in equity to be assumed, he conceived that they might and would be so.

Mr Sherman, took notice that the States might want their militia for defence agst invasions and insurrections, and for enforcing obedience to their laws. They will not give up this point. In giving up that of taxation, they retain a concurrent power of raising money for their own use.

M? Gerry thought this the last point remaining to be surrendered. If it be agreed to by the Convention, the plan will have as black a mark as was set on Cain. He had no such confidence in the Gen! Gov! as some gentlemen possessed, and believed it would be found that the States have not.

Col. Mason, thought there was great weight in the remarks of Mr Sherman, and moved an exception to his motion "of such part of the militia as might be required by the States for their own use."

M? Read doubted the propriety of leaving the appointment of the Militia officers in the States. In some States they are elected by the Legislatures; in others by the people themselves. He thought at least an appointment by the State Executives ought to be insisted on.

On committing to the grand Committee last appointed, the latter motion of Col. Mason, & the original one revived by Ge! Pinkney

N. H. ay. Mas. ay. C! no. N. J. no. P^a ay. Del. ay. M? div? V? ay. N. C. ay. S. C. ay. Geo. ay.

Source: *Writings*, 4: 232, 239–40.

Tuesday, August 21

M⸱ Sherman moved to add to Sect 3. the following clause "And all accounts of supplies furnished, services performed, and monies advanced by the several States to the U. States, or by the U. S. to the several States shall be adjusted by the same rule"

M⸱ Govern⸱ Morris 2ᵈˢ the motion.

M⸱ Ghorum, thought it wrong to insert this in the Constitution. The Legislature will no doubt do what is right. The present Congress have such a power and are now exercising it.

M⸱ Sherman unless some rule be expressly given none will exist under the new system.

Mʳ Elseworth. Though The contracts of Congress will be binding, there will be no rule for executing them on the States; and one ought to be provided.

Mʳ Sherman withdrew his motion to make way for one of Mʳ Williamson to add to Sect. 3. "By this rule the several quotas of the States shall be determined in settling the expences of the late war."

M⸱ Carrol brought into view the difficulty that might arise on this subject from the establishment of the Constitution as intended without the *unanimous* consent of the States

M⸱ Williamson's motion was postponed nem. con. . . .

M⸱ Dickenson. The power of taxing exports may be inconvenient at present; but it must be of dangerous consequence to prohibit it with respect to all articles and for ever. He thought it would be better to except particular articles from the power.

Mʳ Sherman. It is best to prohibit the National legislature in all cases. The States will never give up all power over trade. An enumeration of particular articles would be difficult invidious and improper

M⸱ Madison As we ought to be governed by national and permanent views, it is a sufficient argument for giving y⸱ power over exports that a tax, tho' it

Source: *Writings*, 4: 255, 260–61, 264–65.

may not be expedient at present, may be so hereafter. A porper regulation of exports may & probably will be necessary hereafter, and for the same purposes as the regulation of imports; viz, for revenue—domestic manufactures—and procuring equitable regulations from other nations. An Embargo may be of absolute necessity, and can alone be effectuated by the Gen! authority. The regulation of trade between State and State cannot effect more than indirectly to hinder a State from taxing its own exports; by authorizing its Citizens to carry their commodities freely into a neighbouring State which might decline taxing exports in order to draw into its channel the trade of its neighbours. As to the fear of disproportionate burthens on the more exporting States, it might be remarked that it was agreed on all hands that the revenue w^d principally be drawn from trade, and as only a given revenue would be needed, it was not material whether all should be drawn wholly from imports—or half from those, and half from exports. The imports and exports must be pretty nearly equal in every State—and relatively the same among the different States. . . .

Mr L. Martin, proposed to vary the Sect: 4. art VII so as to allow a prohibition or tax on the importation of slaves. 1. as five slaves are to be counted as 3 free men in the apportionment of Representatives; such a clause would leave an encouragement to this trafic. 2 slaves weakened one part of the Union which the other parts were bound to protect; the privilege of importing them was therefore unreasonable. 3. it was inconsistent with the principles of the revolution and dishonorable to the American character to have such a feature in the Constitution.

Mr Rutlidge did not see how the importation of slaves could be encouraged by this section. He was not apprehensive of insurrections and would readily exempt the other States from the obligation to protect the Southern against them. Religion & humanity had nothing to do with this question. Interest alone is the governing principle with nations. The true question at present is whether the South^n States shall or shall not be parties to the Union. If the Northern States consult their interest, they will not oppose the increase of slaves which will increase the commodities of which they will become the carriers.

Mr Elseworth was for leaving the clause as it stands, let every State import what it pleases. The morality or wisdom of slavery are considerations belonging to the States themselves. What enriches a part enriches the whole, and the States are the best judges of their particular interest. The old confederation had not meddled with this point, and he did not see any greater necessity for bringing it within the policy of the new one:

Mr Pinkney. South Carolina can never receive the plan if it prohibits the slave trade. In every proposed extension of the powers of Congress, that State has expressly & watchfully excepted that of meddling with the importation of negroes. If the States be all left at liberty on this subject, S. Carolina may perhaps by degrees do of herself what is wished, as Virginia & Maryland already have done.

Adjourned.

Wednesday, August 22 in Convention

Art VII sect 4. resumed. Mr Sherman was for leaving the clause as it stands. He disapproved of the slave trade; yet as the States were now possessed of the right to import slaves, as the public good did not require it to be taken from them, & as it was expedient to have as few objections as possible to the proposed scheme of Government, he thought it best to leave the matter as we find it. He observed that the abolition of Slavery seemed to be going on in the U. S. & that the good sense of the several States would probably by degrees compleat it. He urged on the Convention the necessity of despatching its business.

Col. Mason. This infernal traffic originated in the avarice of British Merchants. The British Gov^t constantly checked the attempts of Virginia to put a stop to it. The present question concerns not the importing States alone but the whole Union. The evil of having slaves was experienced during the late war. Had slaves been treated as they might have been by the Enemy, they would have proved dangerous instruments in their hands. But their folly dealt by the slaves, as it did by the Tories. He mentioned the dangerous insurrections of the slaves in Greece and Sicily; and the instructions given by Cromwell to the Commissioners sent to Virginia, to arm the servants & slaves, in case other means of obtaining its submission should fail. Maryland & Virginia he said had already prohibited the importation of slaves expressly. N. Carolina had done the same in substance. All this would be in vain, if S. Carolina & Georgia be at liberty to import. The Western people are already calling out for slaves for their new lands, and will fill that Country with slaves if they can be got thro' S. Carolina & Georgia. Slavery discourages arts & manufactures. The poor despise labor when performed by slaves. They prevent the immigration of Whites, who really enrich & strengthen a Country. They produce the most pernicious effect on manners. Every master of slaves is born a petty tyrant. They bring the judgment of heaven on a Country. As nations can not be rewarded or punished in the next world they must be in this. By an inevitable

Source: *Writings*, 4: 265–73.

chain of causes & effects providence punishes national sins, by national calamities. He lamented that some of our Eastern brethren had from a lust of gain embarked in this nefarious traffic. As to the States being in possession of the Right to import, this was the case with many other rights, now to be properly given up. He held it essential in every point of view that the Gen! Gov^t should have power to prevent the increase of slavery.

Mr Elseworth. As he had never owned a slave could not judge of the effects of slavery on character. He said however that if it was to be considered in a moral light we ought to go farther and free those already in the Country.—As slaves also multiply so fast in Virginia & Maryland that it is cheaper to raise than import them, whilst in the sickly rice swamps foreign supplies are necessary, if we go no farther than is urged, we shall be unjust towards S. Carolina & Georgia. Let us not intermeddle. As population increases, poor laborers will be so plenty as to render slaves useless. Slavery in time will not be a speck in our Country. Provision is already made in Connecticut for abolishing it. And the abolition has already taken place in Massachusetts. As to the danger of insurrections from foreign influence, that will become a motive to kind treatment of the slaves.

Mr Pinkney. If slavery be wrong, it is justified by the example of all the world. He cited the case of Greece Rome & other antient States; the sanction given by France England, Holland & other modern States. In all ages one half of mankind have been slaves. If the S. States were let alone they will probably of themselves stop importations. He w^d himself as a citizen of S. Carolina vote for it. An attempt to take away the right as proposed will produce serious objections to the Constitution which he wished to see adopted.

General Pinkney declared it to be his firm opinion that if himself & all his colleagues were to sign the Constitution & use their personal influence, it would be of no avail towards obtaining the assent of their Constituents. S. Carolina & Georgia cannot do without slaves. As to Virginia she will gain by stopping the importations. Her slaves will rise in value, & she has more than she wants. It would be unequal to require S. C. & Georgia to confederate on such unequal terms. He said the Royal assent before the Revolution had never been refused to S. Carolina as to Virginia. He contended that the importation of slaves would be for the interest of the whole Union. The more slaves, the more produce to employ the carrying trade; The more consumption also, and the more of this, the more revenue for the common treasury. He admitted it to be reasonable that slaves should be dutied like other imports, but should consider a rejection of the clause as an exclusion of S. Carol^a from the Union.

Mr Baldwin had conceived national objects alone to be before the Convention, not such as like the present were of a local nature. Georgia was decided on this point. That State has always hitherto supposed a Gen! Governm! to be the pursuit of the central States who wished to have a vortex for every thing—that her distance would preclude her from equal advantage—& that she could not prudently purchase it by yielding national powers. From this it might be understood in what light she would view an attempt to abridge one of her favorite prerogatives. If left to herself, she may probably put a stop to the evil. As one ground for this conjecture, he took notice of the sect of ——— which he said was a respectable class of people, who carried their ethics beyond the mere *equality of men,* extending their humanity to the claims of the whole animal creation.

M! Wilson observed that if S. C. & Georgia were themselves disposed to get rid of the importation of slaves in a short time as had been suggested, they would never refuse to Unite because the importation might be prohibited. As the section now stands all articles imported are to be taxed. Slaves alone are exempt. This is in fact a bounty on that article.

M! Gerry thought we had nothing to do with the conduct of the States as to Slaves, but ought to be careful not to give any sanction to it.

M! Dickenson considered it as inadmissible on every principle of honor & safety that the importation of slaves should be authorized to the States by the Constitution. The true question was whether the national happiness would be promoted or impeded by the importation, and this question ought to be left to the National Gov^t not to the States particularly interested. If Eng^d & France permit slavery, slaves are at the same time excluded from both those kingdoms. Greece and Rome were made unhappy by their slaves. He could not believe that the South^n States would refuse to confederate on the account apprehended; especially as the power was not likely to be immediately exercised by the Gen! Government.

M! Williamson stated the law of N. Carolina on the subject, to-wit that it did not directly prohibit the importation of slaves. It imposed a duty of £5 on each slave imported from Africa, £10 on each from elsewhere, & £50 on each from a State licensing manumission. He thought the S. States could not be members of the Union if the clause sh^d be rejected, and that it was wrong to force any thing down not absolutely necessary, and which any State must disagree to.

M! King thought the subject should be considered in a political light only. If two States will not agree to the Constitution as stated on one side, he could affirm with equal belief on the other, that great & equal opposition would be experienced from the other States. He remarked on the exemption of slaves from duty whilst every other import was subjected to it, as an inequality that could not fail to strike the commercial sagacity of the North^n & Middle States.

M! Langdon was strenuous for giving the power to the Gen¹ Gov^t He c^d not with a good conscience leave it with the States who could then go on with the traffic, without being restrained by the opinions here given that they will themselves cease to import slaves.

Gen¹ Pinkney thought himself bound to declare candidly that he did not think S. Carolina would stop her importations of slaves in any short time, but only stop them occasionally as she now does. He moved to commit the clause that slaves might be made liable to an equal tax with other imports which he thought right & wch w^d remove one difficulty that had been started.

M! Rutlidge. If the Convention thinks that N. C. S. C. & Georgia will ever agree to the plan, unless their right to import slaves be untouched, the expectation is vain. The people of those States will never be such fools as to give up so important an interest. He was strenuous agst striking out the section, and seconded the motion of Gen¹ Pinkney for a commitment.

M! Govr Morris wished the whole subject to be committed including the clauses relating to taxes on exports & to a navigation act. These things may form a bargain among the Northern & Southern States.

M! Butler declared that he never would agree to the power of taxing exports.

M! Sherman said it was better to let the S. States import slaves than to part with them, if they made that a sine qua non. He was opposed to a tax on slaves imported as making the matter worse, because it implied they were *property*. He acknowledged that if the power of prohibiting the importation should be given to the Gen! Government that it would be exercised. He thought it would be its duty to exercise the power.

M! Read was for the commitment provided the clause concerning taxes on exports should also be committed.

Mr Sherman observed that that clause had been agreed to & therefore could not be committed.

M! Randolph was for committing in order that some middle ground might, if possible, be found. He could never agree to the clause as it stands. He w^d sooner risk the constitution. He dwelt on the dilemma to which the Convention was exposed. By agreeing to the clause, it would revolt the Quakers, the Methodists, and many others in the States having no slaves. On the other hand, two States might be lost to the Union. Let us then, he said, try the chance of a commitment.

On the question for committing the remaining part of Sect. 4 & 5. of Art: 7. N. H. no. Mass. abs! Con^t ay N. J. ay P^a no. Del. no Mary^d ay. V^a ay. N. C. ay S. C. ay. Geo. ay.

M! Pinkney & Mr Langdon moved to commit Sect. 6. as to navigation act by two thirds of each House

M.ʳ Gorham did not see the propriety of it. Is it meant to require a greater proportion of votes? He desired it to be remembered that the Eastern States had no motive to Union but a commercial one. They were able to protect themselves. They were not afraid of external danger, and did not need the aid of the Southⁿ States.

M.ʳ Wilson wished for a commitment in order to reduce the proportion of votes required.

Mʳ Elseworth was for taking the plan as it is. This widening of opinions has a threatening aspect. If we do not agree on this middle & moderate ground he was afraid we should lose two States, with such others as may be disposed to stand aloof, should fly into a variety of shapes & directions, and most probably into several confederations and not without bloodshed.

On Question for committing 6 Sect. as to navigation act to a member from each State—N. H. ay. Mas. ay. Cᵗ no. N. J. no. Pᵃ ay. Del. ay. Mᵈ ay. Vᵃ ay. N. C. ay. S. C. ay. Geo. ay.

The Committee appointed were Mʳ Langdon, King, Johnson, Livingston, Clymer, Dickenson, L. Martin, Madison, Williamson, C. C. Pinkney, & Baldwin.

To this committee were referred also the two clauses above mentioned, of the 4 & 5. Sect: of Art. 7.

Thursday, August 23 in Convention

The Report of the Committee of Eleven made Aug: 21. being taken up, and the following clause being under consideration to wit "To make laws for organizing, arming & disciplining the Militia, and for governing such parts of them as may be employed in the service of the U. S. reserving to the States respectively, the appointment of the officers, and authority of training the militia according to the discipline prescribed"

Mʳ Sherman moved to strike out the last member "and authority of training &c. He thought it unnecessary. The States will have this authority of course if not given up.

Mʳ Elseworth doubted the propriety of striking out the sentence. The reason assigned applies as well to the other reservation of the appointment to offices. He remarked at the same time that the term discipline was of vast extent and might be so expounded as to include all power on the subject.

Mʳ King, by way of explanation, said that by *organizing*, the Committee meant, proportioning the officers & men—by *arming*, specifying the kind size & caliber of arms—& by *disciplining*, prescribing the manual exercise evolutions &c.

Mʳ Sherman withdrew his motion.

Mʳ Gerry. This power in the U. S. as explained is making the States drill-sergeants. He had as lief let the Citizens of Massachusetts be disarmed, as to take the command from the States, and subject them to the Genˡ Legislature. It would be regarded as a system of Despotism.

Mʳ Madison observed that "*arming*" as explained did not extend to furnishing arms; nor the term "*disciplining*" to penalties & Courts Martial for enforcing them.

Mʳ King added to his former explanation that *arming* meant not only to provide for uniformity of arms, but included the authority to regulate the modes of furnishing, either by the militia themselves, the State Governments, or the National Treasury; that *laws* for disciplining, must involve penalties and every thing necessary for enforcing penalties.

Source: *Writings*, 4: 278–80, 283–84, 286–88.

Mᵣ Dayton moved to postpone the paragraph, in order to take up the following proposition

"To establish an uniform & general system of discipline for the Militia of these States, and to make laws for organizing, arming, disciplining & governing *such part of them as may be employed in the service of the U. S.*, reserving to the States respectively the appointment of the officers, and all authority over the militia not herein given to the General Government"

On the question to postpone in favor of this proposition; it passed in the Negative

N. H. no. Mas. no. Cᵗ no. N. J. ay. P. no. Del. no. Maryᵈ ay. Vᵃ no. N. C. no. S. C. no. Geo. ay.

Mᵣ Elseworth & Mᵣ Sherman moved to postpone the 2ᵈ clause in favor of the following

"To establish an uniformity of arms, exercise & organization for the militia, and to provide for the Government of them when called into the service of the U. States"

The object of this proposition was to refer the plan for the Militia to the General Govᵗ but to leave the execution of it to the State Govᵗˢ . . .

Mᵣ Madison moved to amend the next part of the clause so as to read "reserving to the States respectively, the appointment of the officers, *under the rank of General officers*"

Mᵣ Sherman considered this as absolutely inadmissible. He said that if the people should be so far asleep as to allow the most influential officers of the militia to be appointed by the Genˡ Government, every man of discernment would rouse them by sounding the alarm to them.

Mᵣ Gerry. Let us at once destroy the State Govᵗˢ have an Executive for life or hereditary, and a proper Senate, and then there would be some consistency in giving full powers to the Genˡ Govᵗ but as the States are not to be abolished, he wondered at the attempts that were made to give powers inconsistent with their existence. He warned the Convention agˢᵗ pushing the experiment too far. Some people will support a plan of vigorous Government at every risk. others of a more democratic cast will oppose it with equal determination, and a Civil war may be produced by the conflict.

Mʳ Madison. As the greatest danger is that of disunion of the States, it is necessary to guard agˢᵗ it by sufficient powers to the Common govᵗ and as the greatest danger to liberty is from large standing armies, it is best to prevent them by an effectual provision for a good Militia.

On the Question to agree to Mᵣ Madison's motion

N. H. ay. Mas. no. Cᵗ no. N. J. no. Pᵃ no. Del. no. Mᵈ no. Vᵃ no. N. C. no. S. C. ay. Geo. ay.

On the question to agree to the "reserving to the States the appointment of the officers." It was agreed to nem: contrad:

On the question on the clause "and the authority of training the Militia according to the discipline prescribed by the U. S."—

N. H. ay. Mas. ay. C^t ay. N. J. ay. P^a ay. Del. no. M^d ay. V^a no. N. C. ay. S. C. no. Geo. no.

On the question to agree to Art. VII. Sect. 7. as reported it passed nem: contrad: . . .

Mr C. Pinkney moved to add as an additional power to be vested in the Legislature of the U. S. "To negative all laws passed by the several States interfering in the opinion of the legislature with the general interests and harmony of the Union; "provided that two thirds of the members of each House assent to the same" This principle he observed had formerly been agreed to. He considered the precaution as essentially necessary. The objection drawn from the predominance of the large States had been removed by the equality established in the Senate.

Mr Broome 2^{ded} the proposition.

Mr Sherman thought it unnecessary; the laws of the General Government being supreme & paramount to the State laws according to the plan, as it now stands.

Mr Madison proposed that it should be committed. He had been from the beginning a friend to the principle; but thought the modification might be made better.

Mr Mason wished to know how the power was to be exercised. Are all laws whatever to be brought up? Is no road nor bridge to be established without the Sanction of the General Legislature? Is this to sit constantly in order to receive & revise the State Laws?—He did not mean by these remarks to condemn the expedient, but he was apprehensive that great objections would lie agst it.

Mr Williamson thought it unnecessary, having been already decided, a revival of the question was a waste of time.

Mr Wilson considered this as the key-stone wanted to compleat the wide arch of Government we are raising. The power of self-defence had been urged as necessary for the State Governments. It was equally necessary for the General Government. The firmness of Judges is not of itself sufficient. Something further is requisite. It will be better to prevent the passage of an improper law, than to declare it void when passed.

Mr Rutlidge. If nothing else, this alone would damn and ought to damn the Constitution. Will any State ever agree to be bound hand & foot in this manner. It is worse than making mere corporations of them whose bye laws would not be subject to this shackle.

M.ʳ Elseworth observed that the power contended for wᵈ require either that all laws of the State Legislatures should previously to their taking effect be transmitted to the Gen.ˡ Legislature, or be repealable by the Latter; or that the State Executives should be appointed by the Genˡ Government, and have a controul over the State laws. If the last was meditated let it be declared.

Mʳ Pinkney declared that he thought the State Executives ought to be so appointed with such a controul, & that it would be so provided if another Convention should take place.

M.ʳ Governʳ Morris did not see the utility or practicability of the proposition of M.ʳ Pinkney, but wished it to be referred to the consideration of a Committee.

M.ʳ Langdon was in favor of the proposition. He considered it as resolvable into the question whether the extent of the National Constitution was to be judged of by the Gen.ˡ or the State Governments.

On the question for commitment, it passed in the negative.

N. H. ay. Mass.ᵗˢ no. Con.ᵗ no. N. J. no. P.ᵃ ay. Del. ay. M.ᵈ ay. Vᵃ ay. N. C. no. S. C. no. Geo. no.

M.ʳ Pinkney then withdrew his proposition.

Friday, August 24

M� Rutlidge moved to insert "joint" before the word "ballot," as the most convenient mode of electing.

M⁫ Sherman objected to it as depriving the *States* represented in the *Senate* of the negative intended them in that house.

Mʳ Ghorum said it was wrong to be considering at every turn whom the Senate would represent. The public good was the true object to be kept in view. Great delay and confusion would ensue if the two Houses shᵈ vote separately, each having a negative on the choice of the other.

M⁫ Dayton. It might be well for those not to consider how the Senate was constituted, whose interest it was to keep it out of sight.—If the amendment should be agreed to, a *joint* ballot would in fact give the appointment to one House. He could never agree to the clause with such an amendment. There could be no doubt of the two Houses separately concurring in the same person for President. The importance & necessity of the case would ensure a concurrence.

M⁫ Carrol moved to strike out "by the Legislature" and insert "by the people." M⁫ Wilson 2ᵈᵉᵈ him & on the question

N. H. no. Massᵗˢ no. Conᵗ no. N. J. no. Pᵃ ay. Del. ay. Mᵈ no. Vᵃ no. N. C. no. S. C. no. Geo. no.

Mʳ Brearly was opposed to the motion for inserting the word "joint." The argument that the small States should not put their hands into the pockets of the large ones did not apply in this case.

Mʳ Wilson urged the reasonableness of giving the larger States a larger share of the appointment, and the danger of delay from a disagreement of the two Houses. He remarked also that the Senate had peculiar powers balancing the advantage given by a joint ballot in this case to the other branch of the Legislature.

Mʳ Langdon. This general officer ought to be elected by the joint & general voice. In N. Hampshire the mode of separate votes by the two Houses was

Source: *Writings*, 4: 294–96, 298–99.

productive of great difficulties. The negative of the Senate would hurt the feelings of the man elected by the votes of the other branch. He was for inserting "joint" tho' unfavorable to N. Hampshire as a small State.

Mᵣ Wilson remarked that as the President of the Senate was to be the President of the U. S. that Body in cases of vacancy might have an interest in throwing dilatory obstacles in the way, if its separate concurrence should be required.

Mʳ Madison. If the amendment be agreed to the rule of voting will give to the largest State, compared with the smallest, an influence as 4 to 1 only, altho the population is as 10 to 1. This surely cannot be unreasonable as the President is to act for the *people* not for the *States*. The President of the *Senate* also is to be occasionally President of the U. S. and by his negative alone can make ¾ of the other branch necessary to the passage of a law. This is another advantage enjoyed by the Senate.

On the question for inserting "joint," it passed in the affirmative

N. H. ay. Massᵗˢ ay. Cᵗ no. N. J. no. Pᵃ ay. Del. ay. Mᵈ no. Vᵃ ay. N. C. ay. S. C. ay. Geo. no. . . .

Sect. 2. Art: X being taken up, the word information was transposed & inserted after "Legislature"

On motion of Mʳ Govʳ Morris, "he may" was struck out, & "and" inserted before "recommend" in the clause 2ᵈ sect 2ᵈ art: X. in order to make it the *duty* of the President to recommend, & thence prevent umbrage or cavil at his doing it.

Mʳ Sherman objected to the sentence "and shall appoint officers in all cases not otherwise provided for by this Constitution." He admitted it to be proper that many officers in the Executive Department should be so appointed—but contended that many ought not, as general officers in the army in time of peace &c. Herein lay the corruption in G. Britain. If the Executive can model the army, he may set up an absolute Government; taking advantage of the close of a war and an army commanded by his creatures. James 2ᵈ was not obeyed by his officers because they had been appointed by his predecessors not by himself. He moved to insert "or by law" after the word "Constitution."

On motion of Mʳ Madison "officers" was struck out and "to offices" inserted, in order to obviate doubts that he might appoint officers without a previous creation of the offices by the Legislature.

On the question for inserting "or by law as moved by Mʳ Sherman N. H. no. Mas. no. Cᵗ ay. N. J. no. Penᵃ no. Del. no. Mᵈ no. Vᵃ no. N. C. absent. S. C. no. Geo. no.

Mʳ Dickinson moved to strike out the words "and shall appoint to offices in all cases not otherwise provided for by this Constitution" and insert—"and shall appoint to all offices established by this Constitution, except in cases herein otherwise provided for, and to all offices which may hereafter be created by law."

Mᣳ Randolph observed that the power of appointments was a formidable one both in the Executive & Legislative hands—and suggested whether the Legislature should not be left at liberty to refer appointments in some cases, to some State authority.

Mᣳ Dickenson's motion, it passed in the affirmative N. H. no. Mas. no. Cᵗ ay. N. J. ay. Pᵃ ay. Del. no. Mᵈ ay. Vᵃ ay. N. C. absᵗ S. C. no. Geo. ay.

Mᣳ Dickinson then moved to annex to his last amendment "except where by law the appointment shall be vested in the Legislatures or Executives of the several States." Mʳ Randolph 2ᵈᵉᵈ the motion.

Mᣳ Wilson. If this be agreed to it will soon be a standing instruction from the State Legislatures to pass no law creating offices, unless the appᵗˢ be referred to them.

Mᣳ Sherman objected to "Legislatures" in the motion, which was struck out by consent of the movers.

Mᣳ Govᣳ Morris. This would be putting it in the power of the States to say, "You shall be viceroys but we will be viceroys over you"—

The motion was negatived without a Count of the States—

Ordered unanimously that the order respecting the adjournment at 4 OClock be repealed, & that in future the House assemble at 10 OC. & adjourn at 3 OC.

Adjourned

Saturday, August 25

M^{r}: Sherman thought it necessary to connect with the clause for laying taxes duties &c an express provision for the object of the old debts &c—and moved to add to the 1st clause of 1st sect. art VII "for the payment of said debts and for the defraying the expences that shall be incurred for the common defence and general welfare."

The proposition, as being unnecessary was disagreed to, Connecticut alone, being in the affirmative.

The Report of the Committee of eleven (see friday the 24th: instant) being taken up,

Genl: Pinkney moved to strike out the words, "the year eighteen hundred" as the year limiting the importation of slaves, and to insert the words "the year eighteen hundred and eight"

M^{r}: Ghorum 2^{ded} the motion

Mr Madison. Twenty years will produce all the mischief that can be apprehended from the liberty to import slaves. So long a term will be more dishonourable to the National character than to say nothing about it in the Constitution.

On the motion; which passed in the affirmative, N. H. ay. Mas. ay. C^{t} ay. N. J. no. P^{a}: no. Del. no. M^{d}: ay. V^{a}: no. N. C. ay. S. C. ay. Geo. ay.

M^{r}: Govr: Morris was for making the clause read at once, "the importation of slaves into N. Carolina, S. Carolina & Georgia shall not be prohibited &c." This he said would be most fair and would avoid the ambiguity by which, under the power with regard to naturalization, the liberty reserved to the States might be defeated. He wished it to be known also that this part of the Constitution was a compliance with those States. If the change of language however should be objected to by the members from those States, he should not urge it.

Col: Mason was not against using the term "slaves" but agst: naming N. C. S. C. & Georgia, lest it should give offence to the people of those States.

Source: *Writings*, 4: 303–6, 308–9.

M.ʳ Sherman liked a description better than the terms proposed, which had been declined by the old Cong.ˢ & were not pleasing to some people. M.ʳ Clymer concurred with M.ʳ Sherman

M.ʳ Williamson said that both in opinion & practice he was against slavery; but thought it more in favor of humanity, from a view of all circumstances, to let in S. C & Georgia on those terms, than to exclude them from the Union.

M.ʳ Gov.ʳ Morris withdrew his motion.

M.ʳ Dickenson wished the clause to be confined to the States which had not themselves prohibited the importation of slaves, and for that purpose moved to amend the clause so as to read "The importation of slaves into such of the States as shall permit the same shall not be prohibited by the Legislature of the U. S. until the year 1808"—which was disagreed to nem: con:

The first part of the report was then agreed to, amended as follows. "The migration or importation of such persons as the several States now existing shall think proper to admit, shall not be prohibited by the Legislature prior to the year 1808." N. H. Mas. Con. M.ᵈ N. C. S. C. Geo: ay N. J. P.ᵃ Del. Virgᵃ no

M.ʳ Baldwin in order to restrain & more explicitly define "the average duty" moved to strike out of the 2ᵈ part the words "average of the duties laid on imports" and insert "common impost on articles not enumerated" which was agreed to nem: cont:

M.ʳ Sherman was ag.ˢᵗ this 2ᵈ part, as acknowledging men to be property, by taxing them as such under the character of slaves.

M.ʳ King & M.ʳ Langdon considered this as the price of the 1.ˢᵗ part.

Gen.ˡ Pinkney admitted that it was so.

Col: Mason. Not to tax, will be equivalent to a bounty on the importation of slaves.

M.ʳ Ghorum thought that M.ʳ Sherman should consider the duty, not as implying that slaves are property, but as a discouragement to the importation of them.

M.ʳ Gov.ʳ Morris remarked that as the clause now stands it implies that the Legislature may tax freemen imported.

M.ʳ Sherman in answer to M.ʳ Ghorum observed that the smallness of the duty shewed revenue to be the object, not the discouragement of the importation.

M.ʳ Madison thought it wrong to admit in the Constitution the idea that there could be property in men. The reason of duties did not hold, as slaves are not like merchandize, consumed, &c

Col. Mason (in answ.ʳ to Gov.ʳ Morris) the provision as it stands was necessary for the case of convicts in order to prevent the introduction of them.

It was finally agreed nem. contrad: to make the clause read "but a tax or duty may be imposed on such importation not exceeding ten dollars for each person," and then the 2^d part as amended was agreed to.

Sect 5. art. VII was agreed to nem: con: as reported. . . .

"Shall receive ambassadors & other public Ministers," agreed to, nem. con.

Mr Sherman moved to amend the "power to grant reprieves & pardon" so as to read "to grant reprieves until the ensuing session of the Senate, and pardons with consent of the Senate."

On the question

N. H. no. Mas. no. C^t ay. P^a no. M^d no. V^a no. N. C. no. S. C. no. Geo. no.

"except in cases of impeachment" inserted nem. con: after "pardon"

On the question to agree to—"but his pardon shall not be pleadable in bar"

N. H. ay. Mas. no. C^t no. P^a no. Del. no. M^d ay. V^a no. N. C. ay. S. C. ay. Geo. no.

Adjourned

Monday, August 27 in Convention

Art X. Sect 2. being resumed,

Mr L. Martin moved to insert the words "after conviction" after the words "reprieves and pardons."

Mr Wilson objected that pardon before conviction might be necessary in order to obtain the testimony of accomplices. He stated the case of forgeries in which this might particularly happen.—Mr L. Martin withdrew his motion.

Mr Sherman moved to amend the clause giving the Executive the command of the Militia, so as to read "and of the Militia of the several States, *when called into the actual service of the U. S.*" and on the Question N. H. ay. Mas. abs^t C^t ay. N. J. abs^t P^a ay. Del. no. M^d ay. V^a ay. N. C. abs^t S. C. no. Geo. ay. . . .

Mr Dickinson moved as an amendment to sect. 2. art XI after the words "good behavior" the words "provided that they may be removed by the Executive on the application by the Senate and House of Representatives."

Mr Gerry 2^{ded} the motion

Mr Govr Morris thought it a contradiction in terms to say that the Judges should hold their offices during good behavior, and yet be removeable without a trial. Besides it was fundamentally wrong to subject Judges to so arbitrary an authority.

Mr Sherman saw no contradiction or impropriety if this were made a part of the Constitutional regulation of the Judiciary establishment. He observed that a like provision was contained in the British Statutes.

Mr Rutlidge. If the Supreme Court is to judge between the U. S. and particular States, this alone is an insuperable objection to the motion.

Mr Wilson considered such a provision in the British Government as less dangerous than here, the House of Lords & House of Commons being less likely to concur on the same occasions. Chief Justice Holt, he remarked, had *successively* offended by his independent conduct, both houses of Parliament. Had this happened at the same time, he would have been ousted. The Judges would be in a bad situation if made to depend on any gust of faction which might prevail in the two branches of our Gov^t

Source: *Writings*, 4: 309–13, 316.

M: Randolph opposed the motion as weakening too much the independence of the Judges.

M: Dickinson was not apprehensive that the Legislature composed of different branches constructed on such different principles, would improperly unite for the purpose of displacing a Judge.

On the question for agreeing to M: Dickinson's Motion

N. H. no. Mas. abs^t C: ay. N. J. abs: P^a no. Del. no. M^d no. V^a no. N. C. abs^t S. C. no. Geo. no. . . .

M: Sherman moved to insert after the words "between Citizens of different States" the words, "between Citizens of the same State claiming lands under grants of different States"—according to the provision in the 9th Art: of the Confederation—which was agreed to nem: con:

Adjourned

Tuesday, August 28 in Convention

Mʳ Sherman from the Committee to whom were referred several propositions on the 25ᵗʰ instant, made the following report:—

That there be inserted after the 4 clause of 7ᵗʰ section

"Nor shall any regulation of commerce or revenue give preference to the ports of one State over those of another, or oblige vessels bound to or from any State to enter clear or pay duties in another and all tonnage, duties, imposts & excises laid by the Legislature shall be uniform throughout the U. S."

Art XI Sect. 3, It was moved to strike out the words "it shall be appellate" to insert the words "the supreme Court shall have appellate jurisdiction,"—in order to prevent uncertainty whether "it" referred to the *supreme Court*, or to the *Judicial power.*

On the question

N. H ay. Mas. ay. Cᵗ ay. N. J. absᵗ Pᵃ ay. Del. ay. Mᵈ no. Vᵃ ay. N C ay. S. C ay. Geo. ay. . . .

Art: XII being taken up.

Mʳ Wilson & Mʳ Sherman moved to insert after the words "coin money" the words "nor emit bills of credit, nor make any thing but gold & silver coin a tender in payment of debts" making these prohibitions absolute, instead of making the measures allowable (as in the XIII art:) *with the consent of the Legislature of the U. S.*

Mʳ Ghorum thought the purpose would be as well secured by the provisions of art: XIII which makes the consent of the Genˡ Legislature necessary, and that in that mode no opposition would be excited; whereas an absolute prohibition of paper money would rouse the most desperate opposition from its partizans.

Mʳ Sherman thought this a favorable crisis for crushing paper money. If the consent of the Legislature could authorize emissions of it, the friends of paper money would make every exertion to get into the Legislature in order to license it.

Source: *Writings*, 4: 316–24.

The question being divided; on the 1ˢᵗ part—"nor emit bills of credit" N. H. ay. Mas. ay. Cᵗ ay. Pᵃ ay. Del. ay. Mᵈ divᵈ Vᵃ no. N. C. ay. S. C. ay. Geo. ay. The remaining part of Mʳ Wilson's & Sherman's motion was agreed to nem: con:

Mͬ King moved to add, in the words used in the Ordinance of Congͬ establishing new States, a prohibition on the States to interfere in private contracts.

Mʳ Govͬ Morris. This would be going too far. There are a thousand laws, relating to bringing actions—limitations, of actions & which affect contracts. The Judicial power of the U. S. will be a protection in cases within their jurisdiction; and within the State itself a majority must rule, whatever may be the mischief done among themselves.

Mͬ Sherman. Why then prohibit bills of credit?

Mͬ Wilson was in favor of Mͬ King's motion.

Mͬ Madison admitted that inconveniences might arise from such a prohibition but thought on the whole it would be overbalanced by the utility of it. He conceived however that a negative on the State laws could alone secure the effect. Evasions might and would be devised by the ingenuity of the Legislatures.

Col: Mason. This is carrying the restraint too far. Cases will happen that cannot be foreseen, where some kind of interference will be proper & essential. He mentioned the case of limiting the period for bringing actions on open account—that of bonds after a certain lapse of time—asking whether it was proper to tie the hands of the States from making provision in such cases?

Mͬ Wilson. The answer to these objections is that retrospective interferences only are to be prohibited.

Mͬ Madison. Is not that already done by the prohibition of ex post facto laws, which will oblige the Judges to declare such interferences null & void.

Mͬ Rutlidge moved instead of Mͬ King's Motion to insert—"nor pass bills of attainder nor retrospective laws" on which motion N. H. ay. Cͭ no. N. J. ay. Pᵃ ay. Del. ay. Mᵈ no. Virgᵃ no. N. C. ay. S. C. ay. Geo. ay.

Mʳ Madison moved to insert after the word "reprisal" (art. XII) the words "nor lay embargoes." He urged that such acts by the States would be unnecessary—impolitic—and unjust.

Mͬ Sherman thought the States ought to retain this power in order to prevent suffering & injury to their poor.

Col: Mason thought the amendment would be not only improper but dangerous, as the Genͬ Legislature would not sit constantly and therefore could not interpose at the necessary moments. He enforced his objection by appealing to the necessity of sudden embargoes during the war, to prevent exports, particularly in the case of a blockade.

M: Gov: Morris considered the provision as unnecessary; the power of regulating trade between State & State already vested in the Gen¹ Legislature, being sufficient.

On the question

N. H. no. Mas. ay. C: no. N. J. no. Pᵃ no. Del. ay. Mᵈ no. Vᵃ no. N. C. no. S. C. ay. Geo. no.

M: Madison moved that the words "nor lay imposts or duties on imports" be transferred from art: XIII where the consent of the Gen¹ Legislature may license the act—into art: XII which will make the prohibition of the States absolute. He observed that as the States interested in this power by which they could tax the imports of their neighbors passing thro' their markets, were a majority, they could give the consent of the Legislature, to the injury of N. Jersey, N. Carolina &c.

Mʳ Williamson 2ᵈᵉᵈ the motion.

M: Sherman thought the power might safely be left to the Legislature of the U. States.

Col: Mason observed that particular States might wish to encourage by impost duties certain manufactures for which they enjoyed natural advantages, as Virginia, the manufacture of Hemp &c.

M: Madison. The encouragement of Manufactures in that mode requires duties not only on imports directly from foreign Countries, but from the other States in the Union, which would revive all the mischiefs experienced from the want of a Gen¹ Government over commerce.

On the question

N. H. ay. Mas. no. Cᵗ no. N. J. ay. Pᵃ no. Delᵃ ay. Mᵈ no. Vᵃ no. N. C. ay. S. C. no. Geo. no.

Art: XII as amended agreed to nem: con:

Art: XIII being taken up. M: King moved to insert after the word "imports" the words "or exports," so as to prohibit the States from taxing either, & on this question it passed in the affirmative.

N. H. ay. Mas. ay. C: no. N. J. ay. P. ay. Del. ay. Mᵈ no. Vᵃ no. N. C. ay. S. C. no. Geo. no.

M: Sherman moved to add after the word "exports"—the words "nor with such consent but for the use of the U. S."—so as to carry the proceeds of all State duties on imports & exports, into the common Treasury.

Mʳ Madison liked the motion as preventing all State imposts—but lamented the complexity we were giving to the commercial system.

Mʳ Gov: Morris thought the regulation necessary to prevent the Atlantic

States from endeavoring to tax the Western States—& promote their interest by opposing the navigation of the Mississippi which would drive the Western people into the arms of G. Britain.

M.ʳ Clymer thought the encouragement of the Western Country was suicide on the old States. If the States have such different interests that they cannot be left to regulate their own manufactures without encountering the interests of other States, it is a proof that they are not fit to compose one nation.

M.ʳ King was afraid that the regulation moved by M.ʳ Sherman would too much interfere with the policy of States respecting their manufactures, which may be necessary. Revenue he reminded the House was the object of the general Legislature.

On M.ʳ Sherman's motion

N. H. ay. Mas. no. C.ᵗ ay. N. J. ay. P.ᵃ ay. Del. ay. M.ᵈ no. V.ᵃ ay. N. C. ay. S. C. ay. Geo. ay

Art XIII was then agreed to as amended.

Art. XIV was taken up.

Gen.ˡ Pinkney was not satisfied with it. He seemed to wish some provision should be included in favor of property in slaves.

On the question on Art: XIV.

N. H. ay. Mas. ay. C.ᵗ ay. N. J. ay. P.ᵃ ay. Del. ay. M.ᵈ ay. V.ᵃ ay. N. C. ay. S. C. no. Geo. divided.

Art: XV. being taken up, the words "high misdemesnor," were struck out, and "other crime" inserted, in order to comprehend all proper cases; it being doubtful whether "high misdemeanor" had not a technical meaning too limited.

M.ʳ Butler and M.ʳ Pinkney moved "to require fugitive slaves and servants to be delivered up like criminals."

M.ʳ Wilson. This would oblige the Executive of the State to do it at the public expence.

M.ʳ Sherman saw no more propriety in the public seizing and surrendering a slave or servant, than a horse.

M.ʳ Butler withdrew his proposition in order that some particular provision might be made apart from this article.

Art XV as amended was then agreed to nem: con:

Adjourned

Wednesday, August 29

Art: VII Sect. 6 by y.ᵉ Comittee of eleven reported to be struck out (see the 24 instant) being now taken up.

Mꞏ Pinkney moved to postpone the Report in favor of the following proposition—"That no act of the Legislature for the purpose of regulating the commerce of the U. S. with foreign powers among the several States, shall be passed without the assent of two thirds of the members of each House." He remarked that there were five distinct commercial interests. 1. the fisheries & W. India trade, which belonged to the N. England States. 2. the interest of N. York lay in a free trade. 3. Wheat & flour the Staples of the two middle States (N. J. & Pennᵃ). 4. Tob.ᵒ the staple of Marylᵈ & Virginia & partly of N. Carolina. 5. Rice & Indigo, the staples of S. Carolina & Georgia. These different interests would be a source of oppressive regulations if no check to a bare majority should be provided. States pursue their interests with less scruple than individuals. The power of regulating commerce was a pure concession on the part of the S. States. They did not need the protection of the N. States at present.

Mꞏ Martin 2ᵈᵉᵈ the motion

Genꞏ Pinkney said it was the true interest of the S. States to have no regulation of commerce; but considering the loss brought on the commerce of the Eastern States by the revolution, their liberal conduct towards the views of South Carolina, and the interest the weak Southⁿ States had in being united with the strong Eastern States, he thought it proper that no fetters should be imposed on the power of making commercial regulations, and that his constituents though prejudiced against the Eastern States, would be reconciled to this liberality. He had himself, he said, prejudices agˢᵗ the Eastern States before he came here, but would acknowledge that he had found them as liberal and candid as any men whatever.

Mꞏ Clymer. The diversity of commercial interests of necessity creates difficulties, which ought not to be increased by unnecessary restrictions. The

Source: *Writings*, 4: 326–28, 332–35.

Northern & middle States will be ruined, if not enabled to defend themselves against foreign regulations.

Mr Sherman, alluding to Mr Pinkney's enumeration of particular interests, as requiring a security agst abuse of the power; observed that the diversity was of itself a security, adding that to require more than a majority to decide a question was always embarrassing as had been experienced in cases requiring the votes of nine States in Congress.

Mr Pinkney replied that his enumeration meant the five minute interests. It still left the two great divisions of Northern & Southern interests. . . .

The Report of the Committee for striking out Sect. 6. requiring two thirds of each House to pass a navigation act was then agreed to, nem: con:

Mr Butler moved to insert after Art: XV. "If any person bound to service or labor in any of the U. States shall escape into another State, he or she shall not be discharged from such service or labor, in consequence of any regulations subsisting in the State to which they escape, but shall be delivered up to the person justly claiming their service or labor," which was agreed to nem: con:

Art: XVII being taken up, Mr Govr Morris moved to strike out the two last sentences, to wit "If the admission be consented to, the new States shall be admitted on the same terms with the original States. But the Legislature may make conditions with the new States, concerning the public debt which shall be then subsisting."—He did not wish to bind down the Legislature to admit Western States on the terms here stated.

Mr Madison opposed the motion, insisting that the Western States neither would nor ought to submit to a union which degraded them from an equal rank with the other States.

Col: Mason. If it were possible by just means to prevent emigrations to the Western Country, it might be good policy. But go the people will as they find it for their interest, and the best policy is to treat them with that equality which will make them friends not enemies.

Mr Govr Morris did not mean to discourage the growth of the Western Country. He knew that to be impossible. He did not wish however to throw the power into their hands.

Mr Sherman, was agst the motion & for fixing an equality of privileges by the Constitution.

Mr Langdon was in favor of the motion, he did not know but circumstances might arise which would render it inconvenient to admit new States on terms of equality.

Mr Williamson was for leaving the Legislature free. The existing *small* States enjoy an equality now, and for *that* reason are admitted to it in the Senate. This reason is not applicable to new Western States.

On M.̲ Gov.̲ Morris's motion for striking out.

N. H. ay. Mas. ay. C.̲ ay. N. J. ay. P.ª ay. Del. ay. M.ᵈ no. V.ª no. N. C. ay. S. C. ay. Geo. ay.

M.̲ L. Martin & M.ʳ Gov.̲ Morris moved to strike out of art XVII, "but to such admission the consent of two thirds of the members present shall be necessary." Before any question was taken on this motion,

M.̲ Gov.̲ Morris moved the following proposition as a substitute for the XVII Art:

"New States may be admitted by the Legislature into this Union; but no new State shall be erected within the limits of any of the present States, without the consent of the Legislature of such State, as well as of the Gen.ˡ Legislature."

The first part to Union inclusive was agreed to nem: con:

M.̲ L. Martin opposed the latter part. Nothing he said would so alarm the limited States as to make the consent of the large States claiming the Western lands, necessary to the establishment of new States within their limits. It is proposed to guarantee the States. Shall Vermont be reduced by force in favor of the States claiming it? Frankland & the Western county of Virginia were in a like situation.

On M.̲ Gov.̲ Morris's motion to substitute &c it was agreed to. N. H. no. Mass. ay. C.̲ no. N. J. no. P.ª ay. Del. no. M.ᵈ no. V.ª ay. N. C. ay. S. C. ay. Geo. ay.

Art: XVII—before the House, as amended.

M.̲ Sherman was against it. He thought it unnecessary. The Union cannot dismember a State without its consent.

Thursday, August 30

Mʳ Sherman moved to postpone the substitute for Art: XVII agreed to yesterday in order to take up the following amendment

"The Legislature shall have power to admit other States into the Union, and new States to be formed by the division or junction of States now in the Union, with the consent of the Legislature of such States." (The first part was meant for the case of Vermont to secure its admission.)

On the question, it passed in the negative

N. H. ay. Mas. ay. Cᵗ ay. N. J. no. Pᵃ ay. Del. no. Mᵈ no. Vᵃ no. N. C. no. S. C. ay. Geo. no. . . .

Art: XIX taken up.

Mʳ Govʳ Morris suggested that the Legislature should be left at liberty to call a Convention, whenever they please.

The Art: was agreed to nem: con:

Art: XX. taken up.—"or affirmation" was added after "oath."

Mʳ Pinkney moved to add to the Art:—"but no religious test shall ever be required as a qualification to any office or public trust under the authority of the U. States"

Mʳ Sherman thought it unnecessary, the prevailing liberality being a sufficient security agᵗ such tests.

Mʳ Govʳ Morris & Genˡ Pinkney approved the motion.

The motion was agreed to nem: con: and then the whole Article; N. C. only no—and Mᵈ divided

Art: XXI. taken up, viz: "The ratifications of the Conventions of —— States shall be sufficient for organizing this Constitution."

Mʳ Wilson proposed to fill the blank with "seven" that being a majority of the whole number & sufficient for the commencement of the plan.

Mʳ Carrol moved to postpone the article in order to take up the Report of the Committee of Eleven (see Tuesday Augˢᵗ 28)—and on the question

N. H. no. Mas. no. Cᵗ no. N. J. ay. Pᵃ no. Del. ay. Mᵈ ay. Vᵃ no. N. C. no. S. C. no. Geo. no.

Source: *Writings,* 4: 337–38, 344–45.

M! Gov! Morris thought the blank ought to be filled in a twofold way, so as to provide for the event of the ratifying States being contiguous which would render a smaller number sufficient, and the event of their being dispersed, which w^d require a greater number for the introduction of the Government.

M! Sherman observed that the States being now confederated by articles which require unanimity in changes, he thought the ratification in this case of ten States at least ought to be made necessary.

Friday, August 31 in Convention

Mͬ King moved to add to the end of Art: XXI the words "between the said States" so as to confine the operation of the Govͭ to the States ratifying it.

On the question

N. H. ay. Mas. ay. Cͭ ay. N. J. ay. Pᵃ ay. Mᵈ no. Virgᵃ ay. N. C. ay. S. C. ay. Geo. ay.

Mͬ Madison proposed to fill the blank in the article with "any seven or more States entitled to thirty three members at least in the House of Representatives according to the allotment made in the 3 Sect: of Art: 4." This he said would require the concurrence of a majority of both the States and the people.

Mͬ Sherman doubted the propriety of authorizing less than all the States to execute the Constitution, considering the nature of the existing Confederation. Perhaps all the States may concur, and on that supposition it is needless to hold out a breach of faith. . . .

On motion of Mͬ Sherman it was agreed to refer such parts of the Constitution as have been postponed, and such parts of Reports as have not been acted on, to a Committee of a member from each State; the Committee appointed by ballot, being, Mͬ Gilman, Mͬ King, Mͬ Sherman, Mͬ Brearly, Mͬ Govͭ Morris, Mͬ Dickinson, Mͬ Carrol, Mͬ Madison, Mͬ Williamson, Mͬ Butler, & Mͬ Baldwin.

The House adjourned

Source: *Writings*, 4: 346, 354.

Monday, September 3

The clause in the Report "To establish uniform laws on the subject of Bankruptcies" being taken up.

M⁚ Sherman observed that Bankruptcies were in some cases punishable with death by the laws of England, & He did not chuse to grant a power by which that might be done here.

M⁚ Gov⁚ Morris said this was an extensive & delicate subject. He would agree to it because he saw no danger of abuse of the power by the Legislature of the U. S.

On the question to agree to the clause

N. H. ay. Mas. ay. Cᵗ no. N. J. ay. Pᵃ ay. Mᵈ ay. Vᵃ ay. N. C. ay. S. C. ay. Geo. ay.

M⁚ Pinkney moved to postpone the Report of the Committee of Eleven (see Sepʳ 1.) in order to take up the following,

"The members of each House shall be incapable of holding any office under the U. S. for which they or any other for their benefit, receive any salary, fees or emoluments of any kind, and the acceptance of such office shall vacate their seats respectively." He was strenuously opposed to an ineligibility of members to office, and therefore wished to restrain the proposition to a mere incompatibility. He considered the eligibility of members of the Legislature to the honourable offices of Government, as resembling the policy of the Romans, in making the temple of virtue the road to the temple of fame.

On this question

N. H. no. Mas. no. Cᵗ no. N. J. no. Pᵃ ay. Mᵈ no. Vᵃ no. N. C. ay. S. C. no. Geo. no.

M⁚ King moved to insert the word "created" before the word "during" in the Report of the Committee. This he said would exclude the members of the first Legislature under the Constitution, as most of the offices wᵈ then be created.

Source: *Writings*, 4: 356–58.

Mr Williamson 2^{ded} the motion. He did not see why members of the Legislature should be ineligible to *vacancies* happening during the term of their election.

Mr Sherman was for entirely incapacitating members of the Legislature. He thought their eligibility to offices would give too much influence to the Executive. He said the incapacity ought at least to be extended to cases where salaries should be *increased,* as well as *created,* during the term of the member. He mentioned also the expedient by which the restriction could be evaded to wit: an existing officer might be translated to an office created, and a member of the Legislature be then put into the office vacated.

Mr Govr Morris contended that the eligibility of members to office w^d lessen the influence of the Executive. If they cannot be appointed themselves, the Executive will appoint their relations & friends, retaining the service & votes of the members for his purposes in the Legislature. Whereas the appointment of the members deprives him of such an advantage.

Tuesday, September 4

M. Gorham disapproved of making the next highest after the President, the vice-President, without referring the decision to the Senate in case the next highest should have less than a majority of votes. As the regulation stands a very obscure man with very few votes may arrive at that appointment

M. Sherman said the object of this clause of the report of the Committee was to get rid of the ineligibility, which was attached to the mode of election by the Legislature, & to render the Executive independent of the Legislature. As the choice of the President was to be made out of the five highest, obscure characters were sufficiently guarded against in that case; and he had no objection to requiring the vice-President to be chosen in like manner, where the choice was not decided by a majority in the first instance

M. Madison was apprehensive that by requiring both the President & vice President to be chosen out of the five highest candidates, the attention of the electors would be turned too much to making candidates instead of giving their votes in order to a definitive choice. Should this turn be given to the business, The election would, in fact be consigned to the Senate altogether. It would have the effect at the same time, he observed, of giving the nomination of the candidates to the largest States.

Source: *Writings*, 4: 364–65.

Wednesday, September 5

To the (2) clause Mr Gerry objected that it admitted of appropriations to an army, for two years instead of one, for which he could not conceive a reason, that it implied that there was to be a standing army which he inveighed against as dangerous to liberty, as unnecessary even for so great an extent of Country as this, and if necessary, some restriction on the number & duration ought to be provided: Nor was this a proper time for such an innovation. The people would not bear it.

Mr Sherman remarked that the appropriations were permitted only, not required to be for two years. As the Legislature is to be biennally elected, it would be inconvenient to require appropriations to be for one year, as there might be no Session within the time necessary to renew them. He should himself he said like a reasonable restriction on the number and continuance of an army in time of peace.

Source: *Writings*, 4: 370–71.

Thursday, September 6 in Convention

Mr King and Mr Gerry moved to insert in the (5) clause of the Report (see Sepr 4) after the words "may be entitled in the Legislature" the words following—"But no person shall be appointed an elector who is a member of the Legislature of the U. S. or who holds any office of profit or trust under the U. S." which passed nem: con:

Mr Gerry proposed as the President was to be elected by the Senate out of the five highest candidates, that if he should not at the end of his term be reelected by a majority of the Electors, and no other candidate should have a majority, the eventual election should be made by the Legislature. This he said would relieve the President from his particular dependence on the Senate for his continuance in office.

Mr King liked the idea, as calculated to satisfy particular members and promote unanimity & as likely to operate but seldom.

Mr Read opposed it, remarking that if individual members were to be indulged, alterations would be necessary to satisfy most of them.

Mr Williamson espoused it as a reasonable precaution against the undue influence of the Senate.

Mr Sherman liked the arrangement as it stood, though he should not be averse to some amendments. He thought he said that if the Legislature were to have the eventual appointment instead of the Senate, it ought to vote in the case by States, in favor of the small States, as the large States would have so great an advantage in nominating the candidates.

Mr Govr Morris thought favorably of Mr Gerry's proposition. It would free the President from being tempted in naming to offices, to Conform to the will of the Senate, & thereby virtually give the appointments to office, to the Senate.

Mr Wilson said that he had weighed carefully the report of the Committee for remodelling the constitution of the Executive; and on combining it with other parts of the plan, he was obliged to consider the whole as having a

Source: *Writings*, 4: 379–81.

dangerous tendency to aristocracy; as throwing a dangerous power into the hands of the Senate. They will have in fact, the appointment of the President, and through his dependence on them, the virtual appointment to offices; among others the Officers of the Judiciary Department. They are to make Treaties; and they are to try all impeachments. In allowing them thus to make the Executive & Judiciary appointments, to be the Court of impeachments, and to make Treaties which are to be laws of the land, the Legislative, Executive & Judiciary powers are all blended in one branch of the Government. The power of making Treaties involves the case of subsidies, and here as an additional evil, foreign influence is to be dreaded. According to the plan as it now stands, the President will not be the man of the people as he ought to be, but the minion of the Senate. He cannot even appoint a tide-waiter without the Senate. He had always thought the Senate too numerous a body for making appointments to office. The Senate, will moreover in all probability be in constant Session. They will have high salaries. And with all those powers, and the President in their interest, they will depress the other branch of the Legislature, and aggrandize themselves in proportion. Add to all this, that the Senate sitting in conclave, can by holding up to their respective States various and improbable candidates, contrive so to scatter their votes, as to bring the appointment of the President ultimately before themselves. Upon the whole, he thought the new mode of appointing the President, with some amendments, a valuable improvement; but he could never agree to purchase it at the price of the ensuing parts of the Report, nor befriend a system of which they make a part.

Friday, September 7

Section 3 (see Sepr 4). "The vice President shall be ex-officio President of the Senate"

Mr Gerry opposed this regulation. We might as well put the President himself at the head of the Legislature. The close intimacy that must subsist between the President & vice-president makes it absolutely improper. He was agst having any vice President.

Mr Govr Morris. The vice President then will be the first heir apparent that ever loved his father. If there should be no vice president, the President of the Senate would be temporary successor, which would amount to the same thing.

Mr Sherman saw no danger in the case. If the vice-President were not to be President of the Senate, he would be without employment, and some member by being made President must be deprived of his vote, unless when an equal division of votes might happen in the Senate, which would be but seldom.

Mr Randolph concurred in the opposition to the clause.

Mr Williamson, observed that such an officer as vice-President was not wanted. He was introduced only for the sake of a valuable mode of election which required two to be chosen at the same time.

Col: Mason, thought the office of vice-President an encroachment on the rights of the Senate; and that it mixed too much the Legislative & Executive, which as well as the Judiciary departments, ought to be kept as separate as possible. He took occasion to express his dislike of any reference whatever of the power to make appointments, to either branch of the Legislature. On the other hand he was averse to vest so dangerous a power in the President alone. As a method for avoiding both, he suggested that a privy Council of six members to the president should be established; to be chosen for six years by the Senate, two out of the Eastern two out of the middle, and two out of the Southern quarters of the Union, & to go out in rotation two every second year; the concurrence of the Senate to be required only in the appointment of Am-

Source: *Writings*, 4: 395–98.

bassadors, and in making treaties, which are more of a legislative nature. This would prevent the constant sitting of the Senate which he thought dangerous, as well as keep the departments separate & distinct. It would also save the expence of constant sessions of the Senate. He had he said always considered the Senate as too unwieldy & expensive for appointing officers, especially the smallest, such as tide waiters &c. He had not reduced his idea to writing, but it could be easily done if it should be found acceptable.

On the question shall the vice President be ex officio President of the Senate? N. H. ay. Mas. ay. C^t ay. N. J. no. P^a ay. Del. ay. Mar. no. V^a ay. N. C. abs^t S. C. ay. Geo. ay.

The other parts of the same Section (3) were then agreed to.

The Section 4.—to wit. "The President by & with the advice and consent of the Senate shall have power to make Treaties &c"

Mr Wilson moved to add after the word "Senate" the words, "and House of Representatives." As treaties he said are to have the operation of laws, they ought to have the sanction of laws also. The circumstance of secrecy in the business of treaties formed the only objection; but this he thought, so far as it was inconsistent with obtaining the Legislative sanction, was outweighed by the necessity of the latter.

Mr Sherman thought the only question that could be made was whether the power could be safely trusted to the Senate. He thought it could; and that the necessity of secrecy in the case of treaties forbade a reference of them to the whole Legislature.

Mr Fitzimmons 2^{ded} the motion of Mr Wilson, & on the question N. H. no. Mas. no. C^t no. N. J. no. P^a ay. Del. no. M^d no. V^a ay. N. C. no. S. C. no. Geo. no.

The first sentence as to making treaties was then Agreed to; nem: con:

Saturday, September 8 in Convention

The last Report of the Committee of Eleven (see Sep.ʳ 4) was resumed.

M.ʳ King moved to strike out the "exception of Treaties of peace" from the general clause requiring two thirds of the Senate for making Treaties

M.ʳ Wilson wished the requisition of two thirds to be struck out altogether If the majority cannot be trusted, it was a proof, as observed by M.ʳ Ghorum, that we were not fit for one Society.

A reconsideration of the whole clause was agreed to.

M.ʳ Gov.ʳ Morris was ag.ˢᵗ striking out the "exception of Treaties of peace" If two thirds of the Senate should be required for peace, the Legislature will be unwilling to make war for that reason, on account of the Fisheries or the Mississippi, the two great objects of the Union. Besides, if a majority of the Senate be for peace, and are not allowed to make it, they will be apt to effect their purpose in the more disagreeable mode, of negativing the supplies for the war.

M.ʳ Williamson remarked that Treaties are to be made in the branch of the Gov.ᵗ where there may be a majority of the States without a majority of the people. Eight men may be a majority of a quorum, & should not have the power to decide the conditions of peace. There would be no danger, that the exposed States, as S. Carolina or Georgia, would urge an improper war for the Western Territory.

M.ʳ Wilson If two thirds are necessary to make peace, the minority may perpetuate war, against the sense of the majority.

M.ʳ Gerry enlarged on the danger of putting the essential rights of the Union in the hands of so small a number as a majority of the Senate, representing perhaps, not one fifth of the people. The Senate will be corrupted by foreign influence.

M.ʳ Sherman was ag.ˢᵗ leaving the rights established by the Treaty of peace, to the Senate, & moved to annex a proviso that no such rights sh.ᵈ be ceded without the sanction of the Legislature.

Source: *Writings*, 4: 403–6, 408.

M! Gov! Morris seconded the ideas of Mr Sherman.

Mr Madison observed that it had been too easy in the present Congress, to make Treaties altho' nine States were required for the purpose.

On the question for striking "except Treaties of peace"

N. H. ay. Mass. ay. C! ay. N. J. no. P? ay. Del. no. M^d no. V? ay. N. C. ay. S. C. ay. Geo. ay

M! Wilson & Mr Dayton move to strike out the clause requiring two thirds of the Senate for making Treaties; on which,

N. H. no. Mas. no. C^t div^d N. J. no. P? no. Del. ay. M^d no. V^a no. N. C. no. S. C. no. Geo. no.

M! Rutlidge & M! Gerry moved that "no Treaty be made without the consent of ⅔ of all the members of the Senate"—according to the example in the present Cong^s

M! Ghorum. There is a difference in the case, as the President's consent will also be necessary in the new Gov!

On the question

N. H. no. Mass. no. (M! Gerry ay) C^t no. N. J. no. P? no. Del. no. M^d no. V? no. N. C. ay. S. C. ay. Geo. ay.

M! Sherman mov^d that no Treaty be made without a Majority of the whole number of the Senate. M! Gerry seconded him.

M! Williamson. This will be less security than ⅔ as now required.

M! Sherman. It will be less embarrassing.

On the question, it passed in the negative.

N. H. no. Mass. ay. C! ay. N. J. no. P? no. Del. ay. M^d no. V? no. N. C. no. S. C. ay. Geo. ay. . . .

M! Gov! Morris thought no other tribunal than the Senate could be trusted. The supreme Court were too few in number and might be warped or corrupted. He was agst a dependence of the Executive on the Legislature, considering the Legislative tyranny the great danger to be apprehended; but there could be no danger that the Senate would say untruly on their oaths that the President was guilty of crimes or facts, especially as in four years he can be turned out.

M! Pinkney disapproved of making the Senate the Court of impeachments, as rendering the President too dependent on the Legislature. If he opposes a favorite law, the two Houses will combine agst him, and under the influence of heat and faction throw him out of office.

Mr Williamson thought there was more danger of too much lenity than of too much rigour towards the President, considering the number of cases in which the Senate was associated with the President.

Mr Sherman regarded the Supreme Court as improper to try the President, because the Judges would be appointed by him.

Monday, September 10

Mʳ Sherman moved to add to the article "or the Legislature may propose amendments to the several States for their approbation, but no amendments shall be binding until consented to by the several States."

Mʳ Gerry 2ᵈᵉᵈ the motion

Mʳ Wilson moved to insert, "two thirds of" before the words "several States"—on which amendment to the motion of Mʳ Sherman

N. H. ay. Mas. no. Cᵗ no. N. J. no. Pᵃ ay. Del. ay. Mᵈ ay. Vᵃ ay. N. C. no. S. C. no. Geo. no.

Mʳ Wilson then moved to insert "three fourths of" before "the several Sts" which was agreed to nem: con: . . .

Mʳ King thought it would be more respectful to Congress to submit the plan generally to them; than in such a form as expressly and necessarily to require their approbation or disapprobation. The assent of nine States he considered as sufficient; and that it was more proper to make this a part of the Constitution itself, than to provide for it by a supplemental or distinct recommendation.

Mʳ Gerry urged the indecency and pernicious tendency of dissolving in so slight a manner, the solemn obligations of the articles of confederation. If nine out of thirteen can dissolve the compact. Six out of nine will be just as able to dissolve the new one hereafter.

Mʳ Sherman was in favor of Mʳ King's idea of submitting the plan generally to Congress. He thought nine States ought to be made sufficient: but that it would be best to make it a separate act and in some such form as that intimated by Col: Hamilton, than to make it a particular article of the Constitution.

Source: *Writings*, 4: 413–14, 417.

Wednesday, September 12

M: Williamson moved to reconsider the clause requiring three fourths of each House to overrule the negative of the President, in order to strike out ¾ and insert ⅔. He had he remarked himself proposed ¾ instead of ⅔, but he had since been convinced that the latter proportion was the best. The former puts too much in the power of the President.

Mr Sherman was of the same opinion; adding that the States would not like to see so small a minority and the President, prevailing over the general voice. In making laws regard should be had to the sense of the people, who are to be bound by them, and it was more probable that a single man should mistake or betray this sense than the Legislature. . . .

Col: Mason perceived the difficulty mentioned by Mr Gorham. The jury cases cannot be specified. A general principle laid down on this and some other points would be sufficient. He wished the plan had been prefaced with a Bill of Rights, & would second a Motion if made for the purpose. It would give great quiet to the people; and with the aid of the State declarations, a bill might be prepared in a few hours.

Mr Gerry concurred in the idea & moved for a Committee to prepare a Bill of Rights. Col: Mason 2^ded the motion.

M: Sherman, was for securing the rights of the people where requisite. The State Declarations of Rights are not repealed by this Constitution; and being in force are sufficient. There are many cases where juries are proper which cannot be discriminated. The Legislature may be safely trusted.

Col: Mason. The laws of the U. S. are to be paramount to State Bills of Rights. On the question for a Com^e to prepare a Bill of Rights

N. H. no. Mas. abs: C: no. N. J. no. P^a no. Del. no. M^d no. V^a no. N. C. no. S. C. no. Geo. no.

Source: *Writings,* 4: 438, 441–42.

Friday, September 14

Art. 1. Sect. 8. The Congress "may by joint ballot appoint a Treasurer"

M.ʳ Rutlidge moved to strike out this power, and let the Treasurer be appointed in the same manner with other officers.

M.ʳ Gorham & M.ʳ King said that the motion, if agreed to, would have a mischievous tendency. The people are accustomed & attached to that mode of appointing Treasurers, and the innovation will multiply objections to the system.

M.ʳ Govʳ Morris remarked that if the Treasurer be not appointed by the Legislature, he will be more narrowly watched, and more readily impeached.

M.ʳ Sherman. As the two Houses appropriate money, it is best for them to appoint the officer who is to keep it; and to appoint him as they make the appropriation, not by joint but several votes.

Gen.ˡ Pinkney. The Treasurer is appointed by joint ballot in South Carolina. The consequence is that bad appointments are made, and the Legislature will not listen to the faults of their own officer.

On the motion to strike out

N. H. ay. Mas. no. C.ᵗ ay. N. J. ay. P.ᵃ no. Del. ay. M.ᵈ ay. V.ᵃ no. N. C. ay. S. C. ay. Geo. ay.

Art 1 sect. 8. "but all such duties imposts & excises, shall be uniform throughout the U. S." were unanimously annexed to the power of taxation.

To define & punish piracies and felonies on the high seas, and "punish" offences against the law of nations.

M.ʳ Govʳ Morris moved to strike out "punish" before the words "offences ag.ˢᵗ the law of nations," so as to let these be *definable* as well as punishable, by virtue of the preceding member of the sentence.

M.ʳ Wilson hoped the alteration would by no means be made. To pretend to *define* the law of nations which depended on the authority of all the civilized nations of the world, would have a look of arrogance, that would make us ridiculous.

M.ʳ Gov.ʳ Morris. The word *define* is proper when applied to *offences* in this case; the law of nations being often too vague and deficient to be a rule.

Source: *Writings*, 4: 450–52, 455.

On the question to strike out the word "punish" it passed in the affirmative
N. H. ay. Mas. no. C! ay. N. J. ay. Pᵃ no. Del. ay. Mᵈ no. Vᵃ no. N. C. ay.
S. C. ay. Geo. no.

Docᵗ Franklin moved to add after the words "post roads" Art ɪ. Sect. 8.
"a power to provide for cutting canals where deemed necessary"

Mʳ Wilson 2ᵈᵉᵈ the motion

Mʳ Sherman objected. The expence in such cases will fall on the U. States,
and the benefit accrue to the places where the canals may be cut.

Mʳ Wilson. Instead of being an expence to the U. S. they may be made a
source of revenue.

Mʳ Pinkney & Mʳ Gerry, moved to insert a declaration "that the liberty of the
Press should be inviolably observed."

Mʳ Sherman. It is unnecessary. The power of Congress does not extend to
the Press. On the question, it passed in the negative

N. H. no. Mas. ay. Cᵗ no. N. J. no. Pᵃ no. Del. no. Mᵈ ay. Vᵃ ay. N. C. no.
S. C. ay: Geo. no.

Saturday, September 15 in Convention

Mr Carrol reminded the House that no address to the people had yet been prepared. He considered it of great importance that such an one should accompany the Constitution. The people had been accustomed to such on great occasions, and would expect it on this. He moved that a Committee be appointed for the special purpose of preparing an address.

Mr Rutlidge objected on account of the delay it would produce and the impropriety of addressing the people before it was known whether Congress would approve and support the plan. Congress if an address be thought proper can prepare as good a one. The members of the Convention can also explain the reasons of what has been done to their respective Constituents.

Mr Sherman concurred in the opinion that an address was both unnecessary and improper.

On the motion of Mr Carrol

N. H. no. Mas. no. C^t no. N. J. no. P^a ay. Del. ay. M^d ay. V^a ay. N. C. abs^t S. C. no. Geo. no.

Mr Langdon. Some gentlemen have been very uneasy that no increase of the number of Representatives has been admitted. It has in particular been thought that one more ought to be allowed to N. Carolina. He was of opinion that an additional one was due both to that State and to Rho: Island, & moved to reconsider for that purpose.

Mr Sherman. When the Committee of eleven reported the apportionment— five Representatives were thought the proper share of N. Carolina. Subsequent information however seemed to entitle that State to another.

On the motion to reconsider

N. H. ay. Mas. no. C^t ay. N. J. no. Pen. div^d Del. ay. M^d ay. V^a ay. N. C. ay. S. C. ay. Geo. ay. . . .

M^r McHenry & Mr Carrol moved that "no State shall be restrained from laying duties of tonnage for the purpose of clearing harbours and erecting lighthouses."

Source: *Writings*, 4: 458–59, 461–62, 467–71.

Col. Mason in support of this explained and urged the situation of the Chesapeak which peculiarly required expences of this sort.

Mʳ Govʳ Morris. The States are not restrained from laying tonnage as the Constitution now stands. The exception proposed will imply the contrary, and will put the States in a worse condition than the gentleman (Col. Mason) wishes.

Mʳ Madison. Whether the States are now restrained from laying tonnage duties, depends on the extent of the power "to regulate commerce." These terms are vague, but seem to exclude this power of the States. They may certainly be restrained by Treaty. He observed that there were other objects for tonnage Duties as the support of seamen &c. He was more & more convinced that the regulation of Commerce was in its nature indivisible and ought to be wholly under one authority.

Mʳ Sherman. The power of the U. States to regulate trade being supreme can controul interferences of the State regulations when such interferences happen; so that there is no danger to be apprehended from a concurrent jurisdiction.

Mˢ Langdon insisted that the regulation of tonnage was an essential part of the regulation of trade, and that the States ought to have nothing to do with it. On motion "that no State shall lay any duty on tonnage without the consent of Congress"

N. H. ay. Mas. ay. Cᵗ divᵈ N. J. ay. Pᵃ no. Del. ay. Mᵈ ay. Vᵃ no. N. C. no. S. C. ay. Geo. no. . . .

Art. V. "The Congress, whenever two thirds of both Houses shall deem necessary, or on the application of two thirds of the Legislatures of the several States shall propose amendments to this Constitution, which shall be valid to all intents and purposes as part thereof, when the same shall have been ratified by three fourths at least of the Legislatures of the several States, or by Conventions in three fourths thereof, as the one or the other mode of ratification may be proposed by the Congress: Provided that no amendment which may be made prior to the year 1808 shall in any manner affect the 1 & 4 clauses in the 9. Section of article 1"

Mʳ Sherman expressed his fears that three fourths of the States might be brought to do things fatal to particular States, as abolishing them altogether or depriving them of their equality in the Senate. He thought it reasonable that the proviso in favor of the States importing slaves should be extended so as to provide that no State should be affected in its internal police, or deprived of its equality in the Senate.

Col: Mason thought the plan of amending the Constitution exceptionable & dangerous. As the proposing of amendments is in both the modes to depend, in the first immediately, and in the second ultimately, on Congress, no amendments of the proper kind would ever be obtained by the people, if the Government should become oppressive, as he verily believed would be the case.

Mr Govr Morris & Mr Gerry moved to amend the article so as to require a Convention on application of ⅔ of the Sts

Mr Madison did not see why Congress would not be as much bound to propose amendments applied for by two thirds of the States as to call a Convention on the like application. He saw no objection however against providing for a Convention for the purpose of amendments, except only that difficulties might arise as to the form, the quorum &c. which in constitutional regulations ought to be as much as possible avoided.

The motion of Mr Govr Morris & Mr Gerry was agreed to nem: con: (see the first part of the article as finally past)

Mr Sherman moved to strike out of art. V. after "legislatures" the words "of three fourths" and so after the word "Conventions" leaving future Conventions to act in this matter, like the present Conventions according to circumstances. On this motion

N. H. div^d Mas. ay. C^t ay. N. J. ay. P^a no. Del. no. M^d no. V^a no. N. C. no. S. C. no. Geo—no.

Mr Gerry moved to strike out the words "or by Conventions in three fourths thereof" On this motion

N. H. no. Mas. no. C^t ay. N. J. no. P^a no. Del. no. M^d no. V^a no. N. C. no. S. C. no. Geo. no.

Mr Sherman moved according to his idea above expressed to annex to the end of the article a further proviso "that no State shall without its consent be affected in its internal police, or deprived of its equal suffrage in the Senate."

Mr Madison. Begin with these special provisos, and every State will insist on them, for their boundaries, exports &c.

On the motion of Mr Sherman

N. H. no. Mas. no. C^t ay. N. J. ay. P^a no. Del. ay. M^d no. V^a no. N. C. no. S. C. no. Geo. no.

Mr Sherman then moved to strike out art V altogether

Mr Brearley 2^{ded} the motion, on which

N. H. no. Mas. no. C^t ay. N. J. ay. P^a no. Del div^d M^d no. V^a no. N. C. no. S. C. no. Geo. no

Mr Govr Morris moved to annex a further proviso—"that no State, without its consent shall be deprived of its equal suffrage in the Senate"

This motion being dictated by the circulating murmurs of the small States was agreed to without debate, no one opposing it, or on the question, saying no

Col: Mason expressing his discontent at the power given to Congress by a bare majority to pass navigation acts, which he said would not only enhance the freight, a consequence he did not so much regard—but would enable a few rich merchants in Philadᵃ N. York & Boston, to monopolize the Staples of the Southern States & reduce their value perhaps 50 Per Cᵗ moved a further proviso that no law in the nature of a navigation act be passed before the year 1808, without the consent of ⅔ of each branch of the Legislature

On this motion

N. H. no. Mas. no. Cᵗ no. N. J. no. Pᵃ no. Del. no. Mᵈ ay. Vᵃ ay. N. C. absᵗ S. C. no. Geo. ay.

Mᵣ Randolph animadverting on the indefinite and dangerous power given by the Constitution to Congress, expressing the pain he felt at differing from the body of the Convention, on the close of the great & awful subject of their labours, and anxiously wishing for some accommodating expedient which would relieve him from his embarrassments, made a motion importing "that amendments to the plan might be offered by the State Conventions, which should be submitted to and finally decided on by another general Convention" Should this proposition be disregarded, it would he said be impossible for him to put his name to the instrument. Whether he should oppose it afterwards he would not then decide but he would not deprive himself of the freedom to do so in his own State, if that course should be prescribed by his final judgment.

Col: Mason 2ᵈᵉᵈ & followed Mᵣ Randolph in animadversions on the dangerous power and structure of the Government, concluding that it would end either in monarchy, or a tyrannical aristocracy; which, he was in doubt, but one or other, he was sure. This Constitution had been formed without the knowledge or idea of the people. A second Convention will know more of the sense of the people, and be able to provide a system more consonant to it. It was improper to say to the people, take this or nothing. As the Constitution now stands, he could neither give it his support or vote in Virginia; and he could not sign here what he could not support there. With the expedient of another Convention as proposed, he could sign.

Mᵣ Pinkney. These declarations from members so respectable at the close of this important scene, give a peculiar solemnity to the present moment. He descanted on the consequences of calling forth the deliberations & amendments of the different States on the subject of Government at large. Nothing but confusion & contrariety could spring from the experiment. The States will never agree in their plans, and the Deputies to a second Convention coming together under the discordant impressions of their Constituents, will never agree. Conventions are serious things, and ought not to be repeated. He was not without objections as well as others to the plan. He objected to the contemptible weakness & dependence of the Executive. He objected to the power of a majority only of Cong⁵ over Commerce. But apprehending the danger of a general confusion, and an ultimate decision by the sword, he should give the plan his support.

Mʳ Gerry stated the objections which determined him to withhold his name from the Constitution. 1. the duration and re-eligibility of the Senate. 2. the power of the House of Representatives to conceal their journals. 3. the power of Congress over the places of election. 4. the unlimited power of Congress over their own compensation. 5. Massachusetts has not a due share of Representatives allotted to her. 6. ³⁄₅ of the Blacks are to be represented as if they were freemen. 7. Under the power over commerce, monopolies may be established. 8. The vice president being made head of the Senate. He could however he said get over all these, if the rights of the Citizens were not rendered insecure 1. by the general power of the Legislature to make what laws they may please to call necessary and proper. 2. raise armies and money without limit. 3. to establish a tribunal without juries, which will be a Star-chamber as to Civil cases. Under such a view of the Constitution, the best that could be done he conceived was to provide for a second general Convention.

On the question of the proposition of Mʳ Randolph. All the States answered no

On the question to agree to the Constitution as amended. All the States ay.

The Constitution was then ordered to be engrossed. and the House adjourned.

Monday, September 17

The President having asked what the Convention meant should be done with the Journals &c. whether copies were to be allowed to the members if applied for. It was Resolved nem. con: "that he retain the Journal and other papers, subject to the order of Congress, if ever formed under the Constitution." The members then proceeded to sign the instrument.

Whilst the last members were signing it Doct⟨r⟩ Franklin looking towards the President's Chair, at the back of which a rising sun happened to be painted, observed to a few members near him, that Painters had found it difficult to distinguish in their art a rising from a setting sun. I have said he, often and often in the course of the Session, and the vicissitudes of my hopes and fears as to its issue, looked at that behind the President without being able to tell whether it was rising or setting: But now at length I have the happiness to know that it is a rising and not a setting Sun.

The Constitution being signed by all the members except M⟨r⟩ Randolph, M⟨:⟩ Mason and M⟨r⟩ Gerry, who declined giving it the sanction of their names, the Convention dissolved itself by an Adjournment sine die—

[Following is a literal copy of the engrossed Constitution as signed. It is in four sheets, with an additional sheet containing the resolutions of transmissal. The note indented at the end is in the original precisely as reproduced here.]

WE THE PEOPLE of the United States, in Order to form a more perfect Union, establish Justice, insure domestic Tranquility, provide for the common defence, promote the general Welfare, and secure the Blessings of Liberty to ourselves and our Posterity, do ordain and establish this Constitution for the United States of America.

Source: *Writings,* 4: 482–502.

Article. I.

Section. 1. All legislative Powers herein granted shall be vested in a Congress of the United States, which shall consist of a Senate and House of Representatives.

Section. 2. The House of Representatives shall be composed of Members chosen every second Year by the People of the several States, and the Electors in each State shall have the Qualifications requisite for Electors of the most numerous Branch of the State Legislature.

No Person shall be a Representative who shall not have attained to the Age of twenty five Years, and been seven Years a Citizen of the United States, and who shall not, when elected, be an Inhabitant of that State in which he shall be chosen.

Representatives and direct Taxes shall be apportioned among the several States which may be included within this Union, according to their respective Numbers, which shall be determined by adding to the whole Number of free Persons, including those bound to Service for a Term of Years, and excluding Indians not taxed, three fifths of all other Persons. The actual Enumeration shall be made within three Years after the first Meeting of the Congress of the United States, and within every subsequent Term of ten Years, in such Manner as they shall by Law direct. The Number of Representatives shall not exceed one for every thirty Thousand, but each State shall have at Least one Representative; and until such enumeration shall be made, the State of New Hampshire shall be entitled to chuse three, Massachusetts eight, Rhode-Island and Providence Plantations one, Connecticut five, New-York six, New Jersey four, Pennsylvania eight, Delaware one, Maryland six, Virginia ten, North Carolina five, South Carolina five, and Georgia three.

When vacancies happen in the Representation from any State, the Executive Authority thereof shall issue Writs of Election to fill such Vacancies.

The House of Representatives shall chuse their Speaker and other Officers; and shall have the sole Power of Impeachment.

Section. 3. The Senate of the United States shall be composed of two Senators from each State, chosen by the Legislature thereof, for six Years; and each Senator shall have one Vote.

Immediately after they shall be assembled in Consequence of the first Election, they shall be divided as equally as may be into three Classes. The Seats of the Senators of the first Class shall be vacated at the Expiration of the second Year, of the second Class at the Expiration of the fourth Year, and of the third Class at the Expiration of the sixth Year, so that one third may be chosen every second Year; and if Vacancies happen by Resignation, or otherwise, during the Recess of the Legislature of any State, the Executive thereof may make temporary Appointments until the next Meeting of the Legislature, which shall then fill such Vacancies.

No Person shall be a Senator who shall not have attained to the Age of thirty Years, and been nine Years a Citizen of the United States, and who shall not, when elected, be an Inhabitant of that State for which he shall be chosen.

The Vice President of the United States shall be President of the Senate, but shall have no Vote, unless they be equally divided.

The Senate shall chuse their other Officers, and also a President pro tempore, in the Absence of the Vice President, or when he shall exercise the Office of President of the United States.

The Senate shall have the sole Power to try all Impeachments. When sitting for that Purpose, they shall be on Oath or Affirmation. When the President of the United States is tried, the Chief Justice shall preside: And no Person shall be convicted without the Concurrence of two thirds of the Members present.

Judgment in Cases of Impeachment shall not extend further than to removal from Office, and disqualification to hold and enjoy any Office of honor, Trust or Profit under the United States: but the Party convicted shall nevertheless be liable and subject to Indictment, Trial, Judgment and Punishment, according to Law.

Section. 4. The Times, Places and Manner of holding Elections for Senators and Representatives, shall be prescribed in each State by the Legislature thereof; but the Congress may at any time by Law make or alter such Regulations, except as to the Places of chusing Senators.

The Congress shall assemble at least once in every Year, and such Meetings shall be on the first Monday in December, unless they shall by Law appoint a different Day.

Section. 5. Each House shall be the Judge of the Elections, Returns and Qualifications of its own Members, and a Majority of each shall constitute a Quorum to do Business; but a smaller Number may adjourn from day to day, and may be authorized to compel the Attendance of absent Members, in such Manner, and under such Penalties as each House may provide.

Each House may determine the Rules of its Proceedings, punish its Members for disorderly Behaviour, and, with the Concurrence of two thirds, expel a Member.

Each House shall keep a Journal of its Proceedings, and from time to time publish the same, excepting such Parts as may in their Judgment require Secrecy; and the Yeas and Nays of the Members of either House on any question shall, at the Desire of one fifth of those Present, be entered on the Journal.

Neither House, during the Session of Congress, shall, without the Consent of the other, adjourn for more than three days, nor to any other Place than that in which the two Houses shall be sitting.

Section. 6. The Senators and Representatives shall receive a Compensation for their Services, to be ascertained by Law, and paid out of the Treasury of the United States. They shall in all Cases, except Treason, Felony and Breach of the Peace, be privileged from Arrest during their Attendance at the Session of their respective Houses, and in going to and returning from the same: and for any Speech or Debate in either House, they shall not be questioned in any other Place.

No Senator or Representative shall, during the Time for which he was elected, be appointed to any civil Office under the Authority of the United States, which shall have been created, or the Emoluments whereof shall have been encreased during such time; and no Person holding any Office under the United States, shall be a Member of either House during his Continuance in Office.

Section. 7. All Bills for raising Revenue shall originate in the House of Representatives; but the Senate may propose or concur with Amendments as on other Bills.

Every Bill which shall have passed the House of Representatives and the Senate, shall, before it become a Law, be presented to the President of the United States; If he approve he shall sign it, but if not he shall return it, with his Objections to that House in which it shall have originated, who shall enter the Objections at large on their Journal, and proceed to reconsider it. If after such Reconsideration two thirds of that House shall agree to pass the Bill, it shall be sent, together with the Objections, to the other House, by which it shall likewise be reconsidered, and if approved by two thirds of that House, it shall become a Law. But in all such Cases the Votes of both Houses shall be determined by yeas and Nays, and the Names of the Persons voting for and against the Bill shall be entered on the Journal of each House respectively. If any Bill shall not be returned by the President within ten Days (Sundays excepted) after it shall have been presented to him, the Same shall be a Law, in like Manner as if he had signed it, unless the Congress by their Adjournment prevent its Return, in which Case it shall not be a Law.

Every Order, Resolution, or Vote to which the Concurrence of the Senate and House of Representatives may be necessary (except on a question of Adjournment) shall be presented to the President of the United States: and before the Same shall take Effect, shall be approved by him, or being disapproved by him, shall be repassed by two thirds of the Senate and House of Representatives, according to the Rules and Limitations prescribed in the Case of a Bill.

Section. 8. The Congress shall have Power To lay and collect Taxes, Duties, Imposts and Excises, to pay the Debts and provide for the common Defence and general Welfare of the United States; but all Duties, Imposts and Excises shall be uniform throughout the United States;

To borrow Money on the credit of the United States;

To regulate Commerce with foreign Nations, and among the several States, and with the Indian Tribes;

To establish an uniform Rule of Naturalization, and uniform Laws on the subject of Bankruptcies throughout the United States;

To coin Money, regulate the Value thereof, and of foreign Coin, and fix the Standard of Weights and Measures;

To provide for the Punishment of counterfeiting the Securities and current Coin of the United States;

To establish Post Offices and post Roads;

To promote the Progress of Science and useful Arts, by securing for Limited Times to Authors and Inventors the exclusive Right to their respective Writings and Discoveries;

To constitute Tribunals inferior to the supreme Court;

To define and punish Piracies and Felonies committed on the high Seas, and Offences against the Law of Nations;

To declare War, grant Letters of Marque and Reprisal, and make Rules concerning Captures on Land and Water;

To raise and support Armies, but no Appropriation of Money to that Use shall be for a longer Term than two Years;

To provide and maintain a Navy;

To make Rules for the Government and Regulation of the land and naval Forces;

To provide for calling forth the Militia to execute the Laws of the Union, suppress Insurrections and repel Invasions;

To provide for organizing, arming, and disciplining, the Militia, and for governing such Part of them as may be employed in the Service of the United States, reserving to the States respectively, the Appointment of the Officers, and the Authority of training the Militia according to the discipline prescribed by Congress;

To exercise exclusive Legislation in all Cases whatsoever, over such District (not exceeding ten Miles square) as may, by Cession of particular States, and the Acceptance of Congress, become the Seat of the Government of the United States, and to exercise like Authority over all Places purchased by the Consent of the Legislature of the State in which the Same shall be, for the Erection of Forts, Magazines, Arsenals, dock-Yards, and other needful Buildings:—And

To make all Laws which shall be necessary and proper for carrying into Execution the foregoing Powers, and all other Powers vested by this Constitution in the Government of the United States, or in any Department or Officer thereof.

Section. 9. The Migration or Importation of such Persons as any of the States now existing shall think proper to admit, shall not be prohibited by the Congress prior to the Year one thousand eight hundred and eight, but a Tax or duty may be imposed on such Importation, not exceeding ten dollars for each Person.

The Privilege of the Writ of Habeas Corpus shall not be suspended, unless when in Cases of Rebellion or Invasion the public Safety may require it.

No bill of Attainder or ex post facto Law shall be passed.

No Capitation, or other direct, Tax shall be laid, unless in Proportion to the Census or Enumeration herein before directed to be taken.

No Tax or Duty shall be laid on Articles exported from any State.

No Preference shall be given by any Regulation of Commerce or Revenue to the Ports of one State over those of another: nor shall Vessels bound to, or from, one State, be obliged to enter, clear, or pay Duties in another.

No Money shall be drawn from the Treasury, but in Consequence of Appropriations made by Law; and a regular Statement and Account of the Receipts and Expenditures of all public Money shall be published from time to time.

No Title of Nobility shall be granted by the United States: And no Person holding any Office of Profit or Trust under them, shall, without the Consent of the Congress, accept of any present, Emolument, Office, or Title, of any kind whatever, from any King, Prince, or foreign State.

Section. 10. No State shall enter into any Treaty, Alliance, or Confederation; grant Letters of Marque and Reprisal; coin Money; emit Bills of Credit; make any Thing but gold and silver Coin a Tender in Payment of Debts; pass any Bill of Attainder, ex post facto Law, or Law impairing the Obligation of Contracts, or grant any Title of Nobility.

No State shall, without the Consent of the Congress, lay any Imposts or Duties on Imports or Exports, except what may be absolutely necessary for executing it's inspection Laws: and the net Produce of all Duties and Imposts, laid by any State on Imports or Exports, shall be for the Use of the Treasury of the United States; and all such Laws shall be subject to the Revision and Controul of the Congress.

No State shall, without the Consent of Congress, lay any Duty of Tonnage, keep Troops, or Ships of War in time of Peace, enter into any Agreement or Compact with another State, or with a foreign Power, or engage in War, unless actually invaded, or in such imminent Danger as will not admit of delay.

Article. II.

Section. 1. The executive Power shall be vested in a President of the United States of America. He shall hold his Office during the Term of four Years, and, together with the Vice President, chosen for the same Term, be elected, as follows

Each State shall appoint, in such Manner as the Legislature thereof may direct, a Number of Electors, equal to the whole Number of Senators and Representatives to which the State may be entitled in the Congress: but no Senator or Representative, or Person holding an Office of Trust or Profit under the United States, shall be appointed an Elector.

The Electors shall meet in their respective States, and vote by Ballot for two Persons, of whom one at least shall not be an Inhabitant of the same State with themselves. And they shall make a List of all the Persons voted for, and of the Number of Votes for each; which List they shall sign and certify, and transmit sealed to the Seat of the Government of the United States, directed to the President of the Senate. The President of the Senate shall, in the Presence of the Senate and House of Representatives, open all the Certificates, and the Votes shall then be counted. The Person having the greatest Number of Votes shall be the President, if such Number be a Majority of the whole Number of Electors appointed; and if there be more than one who have such Majority, and have an equal Number of Votes, then the House of Representatives shall immediately chuse by Ballot one of them for President; and if no Person have a Majority, then from the five highest on the List the said House shall in like Manner chuse the President. But in chusing the President, the Votes shall be taken by States, the Representation from each State having one Vote; A quorum for this Purpose shall consist of a Member or Members from two thirds of the States, and a Majority of all the States shall be necessary to a Choice. In every Case, after the Choice of the President, the Person having the greatest Number of Votes of the Electors shall be the Vice President. But if there should remain two or more who have equal votes, the Senate shall chuse from them by Ballot the Vice President.

The Congress may determine the Time of chusing the Electors, and the

Day on which they shall give their Votes; which Day shall be the same throughout the United States.

No Person except a natural born Citizen, or a Citizen of the United States, at the time of the Adoption of this Constitution, shall be eligible to the Office of President; neither shall any Person be eligible to that Office who shall not have attained to the Age of thirty five Years, and been fourteen Years a Resident within the United States.

In Case of the Removal of the President from Office, or of his Death, Resignation, or Inability to discharge the Powers and Duties of the said Office, the Same shall devolve on the Vice President, and the Congress may by Law provide for the Case of Removal, Death, Resignation or Inability, both of the President and Vice President, declaring what Officer shall then act as President, and such Officer shall act accordingly, until the Disability be removed, or a President shall be elected.

The President shall, at stated Times, receive for his Services, a Compensation, which shall neither be encreased nor diminished during the Period for which he shall have been elected, and he shall not receive within that Period any other Emolument from the United States, or any of them.

Before he enter on the Execution of his Office, he shall take the following Oath or Affirmation:—"I do solemnly swear (or affirm) that I will faithfully execute the Office of President of the United States, and will to the best of my Ability, preserve, protect and defend the Constitution of the United States."

Section. 2. The President shall be Commander in Chief of the Army and Navy of the United States, and of the Militia of the several States, when called into the actual Service of the United States; he may require the Opinion, in writing, of the principal Officer in each of the executive Departments, upon any Subject relating to the Duties of their respective Offices, and he shall have Power to grant Reprieves and Pardons for Offences against the United States, except in Cases of Impeachment.

He shall have Power, by and with the Advice and Consent of the Senate, to make Treaties, provided two thirds of the Senators present concur; and he shall nominate, and by and with the Advice and Consent of the Senate, shall appoint Ambassadors, other public Ministers and Consuls, Judges of the supreme Court, and all other Officers of the United States, whose Appointments are not herein otherwise provided for, and which shall be established by Law: but the Congress may by Law vest the Appointment of such inferior Officers, as they think proper, in the President alone, in the Courts of Law, or in the Heads of Departments.

The President shall have Power to fill up all Vacancies that may happen during the Recess of the Senate, by granting Commissions which shall expire at the End of their next Session.

Section. 3. He shall from time to time give to the Congress Information of the State of the Union, and recommend to their Consideration such Measures as he shall judge necessary and expedient; he may, on extraordinary Occasions, convene both Houses, or either of them, and in Case of Disagreement between them, with Respect to the Time of Adjournment, he may adjourn them to such Time as he shall think proper; he shall receive Ambassadors and other public Ministers; he shall take Care that the Laws be faithfully executed, and shall Commission all the Officers of the United States.

Section. 4. The President, Vice President and all civil Officers of the United States, shall be removed from Office on Impeachment for, and Conviction of, Treason, Bribery, or other high Crimes and Misdemeanors.

Article. III.

Section. 1. The judicial Power of the United States, shall be vested in one supreme Court, and in such inferior Courts as the Congress may from time to time ordain and establish. The Judges, both of the supreme and inferior Courts, shall hold their Offices during good Behaviour, and shall, at stated Times, receive for their Services, a Compensation, which shall not be diminished during their Continuance in Office.

Section. 2. The judicial Power shall extend to all Cases, in Law and Equity, arising under this Constitution, the Laws of the United States, and Treaties made, or which shall be made, under their Authority;—to all Cases affecting Ambassadors, other public Ministers and Consuls;—to all Cases of admiralty and maritime Jurisdiction;—to Controversies to which the United States shall be a Party;—to Controversies between two or more States;—between a State and Citizens of another State;—between Citizens of different States,—between Citizens of the same State claiming Lands under Grants of different States, and between a State, or the Citizens thereof, and foreign States, Citizens or Subjects.

In all Cases affecting Ambassadors, other public Ministers and Consuls, and those in which a State shall be Party, the supreme Court shall have original Jurisdiction. In all the other Cases before mentioned, the Supreme Court shall have appellate Jurisdiction, both as to Law and Fact, with such Exceptions, and under such regulations as the Congress shall make.

The Trial of all Crimes, except in Cases of Impeachment, shall be by Jury; and such Trial shall be held in the State where the said Crimes shall have been committed; but when not committed within any State, the Trial shall be at such Place or Places as the Congress may by Law have directed.

Section. 3. Treason against the United States, shall consist only in levying War against them, or in adhering to their Enemies, giving them Aid and Comfort. No Person shall be convicted of Treason unless on the Testimony of two Witnesses to the same overt Act, or on Confession in open Court.

The Congress shall have Power to declare the Punishment of Treason, but no Attainder of Treason shall work Corruption of Blood, or Forfeiture except during the Life of the Person attainted.

Article. IV.

Section. 1. Full Faith and Credit shall be given in each State to the public Acts, Records, and judicial Proceedings of every other State. And the Congress may by general Laws prescribe the Manner in which such Acts, Records and Proceedings shall be proved, and the Effect thereof.

Section. 2. The Citizens of each State shall be entitled to all Privileges and Immunities of Citizens in the several States.

A Person charged in any State with Treason, Felony, or other Crime, who shall flee from Justice, and be found in another State, shall on Demand of the executive Authority of the State from which he fled, be delivered up, to be removed to the State having Jurisdiction of the Crime.

No Person held to Service or Labour in one State, under the Laws thereof, escaping into another, shall, in Consequence of any Law or Regulation therein, be discharged from such Service or Labour, but shall be delivered up on Claim of the Party to whom such Service or Labour may be due.

Section. 3. New States may be admitted by the Congress into this Union; but no new State shall be formed or erected within the Jurisdiction of any other State; nor any State be formed by the Junction of two or more States, or Parts of States, without the Consent of the Legislatures of the States concerned as well as of the Congress.

The Congress shall have Power to dispose of and make all needful Rules and Regulations respecting the Territory or other Property belonging to the United States; and nothing in this Constitution shall be so construed as to prejudice any Claims of the United States, or of any particular State.

Section. 4. The United States shall guarantee to every State in this Union a Republican Form of Government, and shall protect each of them against Invasion; and on Application of the Legislature, or of the Executive (when the Legislature cannot be convened) against domestic Violence.

Article. V.

The Congress, whenever two thirds of both Houses shall deem it necessary, shall propose Amendments to this Constitution, or, on the Application of the Legislatures of two thirds of the several States, shall call a Convention for proposing Amendments, which, in either Case, shall be valid to all Intents and Purposes, as Part of this Constitution, when ratified by the Legislatures of three fourths of the several States, or by Conventions in three fourths thereof, as the one or the other Mode of Ratification may be proposed by the Congress; Provided that no Amendment which may be made prior to the Year One thousand eight hundred and eight shall in any Manner affect the first and fourth Clauses in the Ninth Section of the first Article; and that no State, without its Consent, shall be deprived of it's equal Suffrage in the Senate.

Article. VI.

All Debts contracted and Engagements entered into, before the Adoption of this Constitution, shall be as valid against the United States under this Constitution, as under the Confederation.

This Constitution, and the Laws of the United States which shall be made in Pursuance thereof; and all Treaties made, or which shall be made, under the Authority of the United States, shall be the supreme Law of the Land; and the Judges in every State shall be bound thereby, any Thing in the Constitution or Laws of any State to the Contrary notwithstanding.

The Senators and Representatives before mentioned, and the Members of the several State Legislatures, and all executive and judicial Officers, both of the United States and of the several States, shall be bound by Oath or Affirmation, to support this Constitution; but no religious Test shall ever be required as a Qualification to any Office or public Trust under the United States.

Article. VII.

The Ratification of the Conventions of nine States, shall be sufficient for the Establishment of this Constitution between the States so ratifying the Same.

The Word, "the," being interlined between the seventh and eighth Lines of the first Page, The Word "Thirty" being partly written on an Erazure in the fifteenth Line of the first Page, The Words "is tried" being interlined between the thirty second and thirty third Lines of the first Page and the Word "the" being interlined between the forty third and forty fourth Lines of the second Page.

done in Convention by the Unanimous Consent of the States present the Seventeenth Day of September in the Year of our Lord one thousand seven hundred and Eighty seven and of the Independence of the United States of America the Twelfth In witness whereof We have hereunto subscribed our Names,

Attest WILLIAM JACKSON Secretary

G° WASHINGTON—Presid^t and deputy from Virginia

New Hampshire	JOHN LANGDON NICHOLAS GILMAN
Massachusetts	NATHANIEL GORHAM RUFUS KING
Connecticut	W^M SAM^L JOHNSON ROGER SHERMAN
New York . . .	ALEXANDER HAMILTON
New Jersey	WIL: LIVINGSTON DAVID BREARLEY. W^M PATERSON. JONA: DAYTON
Pennsylvania	B FRANKLIN THOMAS MIFFLIN ROB^T MORRIS GEO. CLYMER THO^S FITZSIMONS JARED INGERSOLL JAMES WILSON GOUV MORRIS
Delaware	GEO. READ GUNNING BEDFORD JUN JOHN DICKINSON RICHARD BASSETT JACO. BROOM
Maryland	JAMES MCHENRY DAN OF ST THO JENIFER DANL CARROLL
Virginia	JOHN BLAIR JAMES MADISON JR.
North Carolina	W^M BLOUNT RICH^D DOBBS SPAIGHT HU WILLIAMSON

South Carolina
- J. RUTLEDGE
- CHARLES COTESWORTH PINCKNEY
- CHARLES PINCKNEY
- PIERCE BUTLER

Georgia
- WILLIAM FEW
- ABR BALDWIN

Sherman's Proposals

Max Farrand reports that the following document was found among Sherman's papers, presumably in his handwriting. He suggests that it reflects "the ideas of the Connecticut delegation in forming the New Jersey Plan."[1] Jack Rakove, on the other hand, believes it is associated with Sherman's proposals of July 17.[2]

That, in addition to the legislative powers vested in congress by the articles of confederation, the legislature of the United States be authorised to make laws to regulate the commerce of the United States with foreign nations, and among the several states in the union; to impose duties on foreign goods and commodities imported into the United States, and on papers passing through the post office, for raising a revenue, and to regulate the collection thereof, and apply the same to the payment of the debts due from the United States, and for supporting the government, and other necessary charges of the Union.

To make laws binding on the people of the United States, and on the courts of law, and other magistrates and officers, civil and military, within the several states, in all cases which concern the common interests of the United States: but not to interfere with the government of the individual states, in matters of internal police which respect the government of such states only, and wherein the general welfare of the United States is not affected.

That the laws of the United States ought, as far as may be consistent with the common interests of the Union, to be carried into execution by the judiciary and executive officers of the respective states, wherein the execution thereof is required.

That the legislature of the United States be authorised to institute one supreme tribunal, and such other tribunals as they may judge necessary for the purpose aforesaid, and ascertain their respective powers and jurisdictions.

Source: Max Farrand, ed., *The Records of the Federal Convention of 1787* (New Haven, Conn.: Yale University Press, 1966), 3: 615–16.

1. Farrand, *Records*, 3: 615–16.
2. Rakove, *Original Meanings*, 380.

That the legislatures of the individual states ought not to possess a right to emit bills of credit for a currency, or to make any tender laws for the payment or discharge of debts or contracts, in any manner different from the agreement of the parties, unless for payment of the value of the thing contracted for, in current money, agreeable to the standard that shall be allowed by the legislature of the United States, or in any manner to obstruct or impede the recovery of debts, whereby the interests of foreigners, or the citizens of any other state, may be affected.

That the eighth article of the confederation ought to be amended agreeably to the recommendation of congress of the   day of   .

That, if any state shall refuse or neglect to furnish its quota of supplies, upon requisition made by the legislature of the United States, agreeably to the articles of the Union, that the said legislature be authorised to order the same to be levied and collected of the inhabitants of such state, and to make such rules and orders as may be necessary for that purpose.

That the legislature of the United States have power to make laws calling forth such aid from the people, from time to time, as may be necessary to assist the civil officers in the execution of the laws of the United States; and annex suitable penalties to be inflicted in case of disobedience.

That no person shall be liable to be tried for any criminal offence, committed within any of the United States, in any other state than that wherein the offence shall be committed, nor be deprived of the privilege of trial by a jury, by virtue of any law of the United States.

Ratification Debates

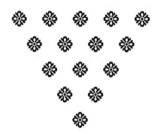

Sherman initially opposed popular ratification of the Constitution, noting that "the articles of Confederation provid[e] for changes and alterations with the assent of Congs. and ratification of State Legislatures."[1] After ratification by state conventions was approved, he contended that because the states were "now confederated by articles which require unanimity in changes, he thought the ratification in this case of ten States at least ought to be made necessary."[2] Sherman lost both battles, although the delegates did eventually agree that the Constitution should be ratified by a supermajority of nine out of thirteen states. After the Constitution was signed on September 17, 1787, Sherman returned to Connecticut to argue for its approval.

On September 26, Sherman and Oliver Ellsworth sent a printed copy of the proposed Constitution to Connecticut governor Samuel Huntington, "to be laid before the legislature of the state."[3] After discussing the proposed Constitution and related documents, the General Assembly adopted a resolution requiring towns to hold meetings on November 12 to elect delegates to a state ratification convention. Each town could elect the same number of delegates as it had members in the lower house of the legislature. Sherman, Ellsworth, and William Samuel Johnson (who had just begun to serve as president of Columbia College) were all elected—thus making Connecticut one of only two states to send all of their Federal Convention delegates to the state rati-

1. Farrand, *Records,* 1: 122.

2. Ibid., 2: 468–69.

3. Merrill Jensen, ed., *The Documentary History of the Ratification of the Constitution,* vol. 3, *Ratification of the Constitution by the States: Delaware, New Jersey, Georgia, Connecticut* (Madison: State Historical Society of Wisconsin, 1978), 363.

fying convention (New York was the other). The delegates were to convene in Hartford on January 3, 1788.

As in many states, newspapers in Connecticut were filled with essays on the proposed Constitution. Unlike most states, Connecticut had virtually no anti-Federalist essayists, and the newspapers were so dominated by Federalists that few out-of-state anti-Federalist pieces were printed. The presses did reprint Federalist essays from other states, notably those by Tench Coxe, James Wilson, and John Hancock. Ellsworth led the Federalist defense of the Constitution in Connecticut with his thirteen "Letters of a Landholder" essays. In a few rare instances, out-of-state anti-Federalist essays were published so they could be refuted. For instance, Ellsworth requested that Elbridge Gerry's letter to the Massachusetts General Court be published so he could respond to it.[4]

Sherman's contribution to the flood of Federalist literature included five essays published from November 14 to December 20 under the pseudonym "Countryman." He also wrote "Observations on the New Federal Constitution" as "A Citizen of New Haven" during Connecticut's ratification convention. These essays are reprinted here.

Delegates to Connecticut's ratification convention gathered at the State House in Hartford on January 3, 1788. After approving election certificates they moved to the North Meeting House, where they unanimously agreed to examine the Constitution passage by passage but to vote only on the entire document. Unfortunately for scholars, no official record of the debates was kept, and newspapers reported only a few speeches in support of the Constitution (and none by Sherman). Sherman did participate in the debates, however, as indicated by a *Connecticut Courant* article noting that "all the objects to the Constitution vanished before the learning and eloquence of a Johnson, the genuine good sense and discernment of a Sherman, and the Demosthenian energy of an Ellsworth."[5] The reporter was obviously biased, but the sense of Federalist domination conveyed in this account was accurate, as evidenced by the January 9 vote of 128–40 to ratify the Constitution. Connecticut thus became the fifth state to approve the document.[6]

4. Ibid., 372–73, 456–57.

5. Ibid., 554.

6. For details about the ratification of the Constitution in Connecticut, see ibid., 315–614, and Christopher Collier, *All Politics Is Local: Family, Friends, and Provincial Interests in the Creation of the Constitution* (Hanover, N.H.: University Press of New England, 2003).

Roger Sherman and Oliver Ellsworth to Samuel Huntington, September 26, 1787

NEW LONDON

This letter to Governor Huntington was forwarded by him to Connecticut's General Assembly, along with a copy of the Constitution. It was also published in the New Haven Gazette *on October 25, 1787, and was reprinted in seven other Connecticut papers.*

We have the honor to transmit to Your Excellency a printed copy of the Constitution formed by the Federal Convention, to be laid before the legislature of the state.

The general principles which governed the Convention in their deliberations on the subject are stated in their letter addressed to Congress.

We think it may be of use to make some further observations on particular parts of the Constitution.

The *Congress* is differently organized; yet the whole number of members, and this state's proportion of suffrage, remain the same as before.

The equal representation of the states in the Senate and the voice of that branch in the appointment to offices will secure the rights of the lesser as well as the greater states.

Some additional powers are vested in Congress, which was a principal object that the states had in view in appointing the Convention those powers extend only to matters respecting the common interests of the Union and are specially defined, so that the particular states retain their *Sovereignty* in all other matters.

The objects for which Congress may apply monies are the same mentioned in the eighth Article of the Confederation, viz., for the common defense and general welfare, and for payment of the debts incurred for those purposes. It is probable that the principal branch of revenue will be duties on imports; what may be necessary to be raised by direct taxation is to be apportioned on the

Source: Merrill Jensen, ed., *The Documentary History of the Ratification of the Constitution*, vol. 3, *Ratification of the Constitution by the States: Delaware, New Jersey, Georgia, Connecticut* (Madison: State Historical Society of Wisconsin, 1978), 352. Reprinted with permission of the Wisconsin Historical Society.

several states according to the numbers of their inhabitants, and altho Congress may raise the money by their own authority, if necessary, yet that authority need not be exercised if each state will furnish its quota.

The restraint on the legislatures of the several states respecting emitting bills of credit, making anything but money a tender in payment of debts, or impairing the obligation of contracts by *ex post facto* laws was thought necessary as a security to commerce, in which the interest of foreigners as well as the citizens of different states may be affected.

The Convention endeavored to provide for the energy of government on the one hand and suitable checks on the other hand to secure the rights of the particular states, and the liberties and properties of the citizens. We wish it may meet the approbation of the several states and be a mean of securing their rights and lengthening out their tranquility.

Letter to William Floyd, n.d.

William Floyd (1734–1821) was a member of the New York State Senate. He later served with Sherman in the U.S. House of Representatives.

Perhaps a better [constitution] could not be made upon mere speculation. It was consented to by all the states present in Convention, which is a circumstance in its favor so far as any respect is due to this. If upon experience, it should be found deficient, it provides an easy and peaceable mode of making amendments. If it should not be adopted, I think we shall be in deplorable circumstances. Our credit as a nation is sinking. The resources of the country could not be drawn out to defend against a foreign invasion nor the forces of the Union to prevent a civil war; but if the Constitution should be adopted and the several states choose some of their wisest and best men from time to time to administer the government, I believe it will not want any amendment. I hope that Kind Providence, that guarded these states thro a dangerous and distressing war to peace and liberty, will still watch over them and guide them in the way of safety.

Source: Merrill Jensen, ed., *The Documentary History of the Ratification of the Constitution*, vol. 3, *Ratification of the Constitution by the States: Delaware, New Jersey, Georgia, Connecticut* (Madison: State Historical Society of Wisconsin, 1978), 353. Reprinted with permission of the Wisconsin Historical Society.

Letter to Unknown Recipient, December 8, 1787

NEW HAVEN

The recipient of the following letter is unknown. It is particularly interesting as Sherman offers his first sustained response to those who objected to the ratification of the Constitution.

Dear Sir,

I am informed that you wish to know my opinion with respect to the new constitution lately formed by the federal convention, and the objections made against it.

I suppose it is the general opinion that the present government of the united States is not sufficient to give them credit and respectability abroad or security at home. But little faith or confidence can be placed in a government that has only power to enter into engagements, but no power to fulfil them.

To form a just opinion of the new constitution it should be considered, whether the powers to be thereby vested in the federal government are sufficient, and only such as are necessary to secure the common interests of the States; and whether the exercise of those powers is placed in safe hands. In every government there is a trust, which may be abused; but the greatest security against abuse is, that the interest of those in whom the powers of government are vested is the same as that of the people they govern, and that they are dependent on the suffrage of the people for their appointment to, and continuance in office. This is a much greater security than a declaration of rights, or restraining clauses upon paper.

The rights of the people under the new constitution will be secured by a representation in proportion to their numbers in one branch of the legislature, and the rights of the particular State governments by their equal representation in the other branch.

The President, Vice President, and Senators, tho chosen for fixed periods, are re-eligible as often as the electors shall think proper, which will be a very

Source: Roger Sherman (1721–93) Collection (MS 447), box 1, folder 9, Manuscripts and Archives, Yale University Library.

great security for their fidelity in office, and will likewise give much greater stability and energy to government than an exclusion by rotation. The greatest possible security that a people can have for their civil rights and liberties, is, that no laws can be made to bind them, nor any taxes be imposed upon them without their consent by representatives chosen by themselves. This was the great point contended for in our contest with Great Britain; and will not this be fully secured to us under the new constitution?

Declarations of rights in England were charters granted by Princes, or acts of Parliament made to limit the prerogatives of the crown, but not to abridge the powers of the legislature. These observations duly considered will obviate most of the objections that have been made against the constitution. The powers vested in the federal government are only such as respect the common interests of the Union, and are particularly defined, so that each State retains its sovereignty in what respects its own internal government, and a right to exercise every power of a sovereign State not delegated to the united States. And tho' the general government in matters within its jurisdiction is paramount to the constitutions & laws of the particular States, yet all acts of the Congress not warranted by the constitution would be void. Nor could they be enforced contrary to the sense of a majority of the States. One excellency of the constitution is that when the government of the united States acts within its proper bounds it will be the interest of the legislatures of the particular States to support it, but when it over leaps those bounds and interferes with the rights of the State governments, they will be powerful enough to check it; but distinction between their jurisdictions will be so obvious, that there will be no great danger of interference.

The unanimity of the convention is a remarkable circumstance in favour of the constitution, that all the States present concurred in it, and all the members but three out of forty two signed it, and Governor Randolph, declared, that tho' he did not think fit to sign it, he had no fixed determination to oppose it, nor have I heard that he has since made any opposition to it.

The other two Honorable Gentlemen whom I esteem for their patriotism and good sense have published their objections, which deserve some notice; and I think the foregoing observations on the principles of the constitution must evince that their fears are groundless. The peoples right of election is doubly secured, the legislatures of the particular States have right to regulate it, and if they should fail to do it properly, it may be done by Congress. And what possible motive can either have to injure the people in the exercise of that right. The qualifications of the electors are to remain as fixed by the State constitutions. It is objected that the number of representatives will be too small—but it is my opinion that it will be quite large enough if extended as far as the constitution will admit, the present number in both branches will consist of ninety one members which is the same number that the States have a right to elect under the confederation, and I have heard no complaint that the number is not sufficient to give information, of the circumstances of the States and to transact the general affairs of the union; nor have any of the States thought fit to keep up the full representation that they are entitled to nor will the additional powers of congress make it necessary to increase the number of members they will have the additional powers of regulating commerce, establishing a uniform rule of naturalization, and laws on the subject of bankruptcies, and to provide for the punishment of counterfeiting coins and securities of the united States, and to prescribe a uniform mode of organizing, arming and training the Militia under the authority of the several States, and to promote the progress of science by securing, to persons for a limited time the benefit of their writings & inventions. The other powers are the same as Congress have under the articles of confederation with this difference, that they will have authority to carry into effect, what they have now a right to require to be done by the States.

It was thought necessary in order to carry into effect the laws of the union, and to preserve justice and harmony among the States, to extend the judicial powers of the confederacy, they cannot be extended beyond the enumerated cases, but may be limited by Congress, and doubtless will be restricted to such cases of importance & magnitude as cannot safely be trusted to the final decision of the courts of the particular States, the Supreme Court may have a circuit through the States to make the trials as convenient, and as little expensive to the parties as may be; and the trial by jury will doubtless be allowed in cases proper for that mode of trial, nor will the people in general be at all affected by the judiciary of the united States, perhaps not one to an hundred of the citizens will ever have a cause that can come within its jurisdiction, for all causes between citizens of the Same States, except where they claim lands under grants of different States, must be finally decided by the courts of the State to which they belong.

The power of making war and raising and supporting armies is now vested in Congress, who are not restrained from keeping up armies in time of peace, but by the new constitution no appropriation of money for that purpose can be in force longer than two years, but the security is that the power is in the legislature who are the representatives of the people and can have no motive to keep up armies unnecessarily.

In order to [have] a well regulated government, the legislature, should be dependant on the people, and be vested with a plenetude of power, for all the purposes, for which it is instituted, to be exercised for the public good, as occasion may require, powers are dangerous only when trusted in officers not under the controul of the laws; but by the new constitution, Congress are vested with power to make all laws which shall be necessary and proper for carrying into execution, all the powers vested in the government of the united States, or in any department or officer thereof.[1]

---

1. The letter simply ends at this point. —Ed.

Draft of "Observations on the New Federal Constitution," 1787[?]

The following observations are taken from a draft written in Sherman's hand. It is not clear when he penned them or for what purpose, but he clearly drew from this draft for his January 7, 1788, essay written under the pseudonym "A Citizen of New Haven" (pages 491–95 of this book).

Observations on the New Federal Constitution

A conviction that the present confederation is deficient to give respectability and security to the united States was the motive with the several States to appoint a convention to make amendments.

It was deficient in the organization of the government, and with respect to the powers necessary for the common defence and general welfare of the union.

One principal defect in the government was the want of a supreme Executive power. Congress exercises that power when sitting, and a committee of the States in the recess of Congress, which has been found to be very inadequate for the purposes of government. The frequent changing the members of that body & their being vested with legislative as well as executive authority, renders their administration slow, unstable, and precarious.

But the want of sufficient power was still a greater evil. They had power to enter into engagements but no power to fulfil them, and there is no security in trusting to the legislatures of the several States to provide for the exigencies of the union upon requisition. The want of a power to regulate commerce with foreign nations, and among the several States, and to enforce a due observation of treaties has been very detrimental to the interests of the States & the cause of lessening their national credit. These defects will be supplied by the new Constitution if adopted. There are some other powers vested in the general government which relate to the common interests of the union, and are par-

Source: Roger Sherman (1721–93) Collection (MS 447), box 1, folder 9, Manuscripts and Archives, Yale University Library.

ticularly defined, so that each state retains its sovereignty in what concerns its own internal government, and a right to exercise every power of a sovereign state, not delegated to the government of the united States. And although the government of the united States in matters within its jurisdiction is paramount to the constitutions and laws of the particular States, yet all acts of the Congress not warranted by the Constitution would be void, nor could they be enforced contrary to the sense of a majority of the States. When the general government acts within its proper jurisdiction it will be the interest of the legislatures of the several States to support it, and they will be a check sufficiently powerful to prevent unconstitutional incroachments on the rights & privileges of the particular States. But the jurisdiction of each will be so easily distinguished that there will be no great danger of Interference.

In order to a well regulated government the legislature should be properly constituted, and vested with plenary powers for all the purposes for which it is instituted, to be exercised for the public good as occasion may require. The greatest possible security that a people can have for the enjoyment of their civil rights and liberties, is that no laws can be made to bind them or taxes be imposed on them without their consent by representatives of their own chusing. This was the great point contended for in our controversy with Great Britain, and this will be fully secured to us under the new constitution. The rights of the people will be secured by a representation in proportion to their numbers in one branch of the Congress, and the rights of the several States by their equal representation in the other branch. This will be a much greater security than a declaration of rights or restraining clauses on paper.

A farther security will be that the representatives, & the people they represent, will have one common interest, and will participate in the benefits and burthens of the public measures.

The President and Vice President as well as the members of Congress tho' chosen for fixed periods will be re-eligible as often as the Electors shall think proper, which will be a great security for their fidelity in office, and will give much greater stability and energy to government than an exclusion by rotation, and will always be an operative and effectual security against arbitrary government, either Monarchical or Aristocratic. There is as much security in the new Constitution as in the present against keeping up standing armies in time of peace, it can't be done without the consent of Congress, with this additional security that it will require the concurrence of two branches, and that no law appropriating money for that purpose can be in force for more [than] two years.

The liberty of the Press not being under the regulation of Congress will be in no danger. There are but few powers vested in the new government but what the present Congress have power to do or require to be done. The new powers are to regulate Commerce, provide for a uniform practice with respect to naturalization, Bankruptcies, and forming and training the Militia, and for the punishment of certain crimes against the united States, and for promoting the progress of science in the mode therein pointed out. These appear to be necessary for the common benefit of the union and can't be effectively provided for by the particular States; therefore the objection that the convention exceeded the authority given by the States is groundless, for though they have formed a new Instrument including the former and additional powers, yet it is no more than an amendment of the present constitution in those matters wherein it was really deficient.

The objects of expenditure are the same as under the present constitution, and why should this system be more expensive than the present? The number of the members of Congress is the same—that number may be increased with the increase of the people, but then it is probable that the wealth of the State will be proportionally increased.

The executive is vested in a single person; whose support will not probably exceed the present allowance to the President of Congress and the pay of a committee of the States. The subordinate officers need not be more numerous, nor have larger salaries than at present. The expense of collecting the impost will be transferred from the particular States to the united States but need not be greater than at present. The principal sources of revenue will be imposts on goods imported, and sale of the Western lands, which probably will be sufficient to pay the debts & expenses of the united States if properly managed. So long as peace continues; but should there be occasion to resort to direct taxation, each State's quota will be ascertained according to a rule which has been approved by eleven of the States, and should any state neglect to furnish its quota, Congress may raise it by a tax in the same manner as the state ought to have done. And what remedy more easy and equitable could be devised to obtain the supplies from a delinquent state?

Some have objected that the representation will be inadequate, but the States have never thought fit to keep up the full representation they are intitled to in Congress; and of what possible advantage can it be to have a very large assembly to transact the few general matters that will come under the direction of Congress, sufficient information may be had from the legislatures of the several States in all matters that the members of Congress are not personally acquainted with. The regulating the time, place, & mode of elections seems to be as well secured as possible. The legislature of each state may do it, & if they neglect to do it properly, it may be done by Congress, and what possible motive can either have to injure the people in the exercise of that right? The qualifications of the electors will remain as fixed by the constitutions or laws of the several States.

The power of the President to grant pardons extends only to offences against the united States, with exception of Impeachments, which is a sufficient security for seclusion of offenders from office; therefore no great mischief can be apprehended from that quarter. The partial negative of the President on the acts of Congress and the recession in consequence thereof may be very useful to prevent laws being passed without mature deliberation. The Vice President while he acts as President of the Senate will have nothing to do in the executive department, his being elected by the suffrage of all the States will incline him to regard equally the Interests of all—and when the members of the Senate are equally divided on a question, who so proper to give a casting voice, as one who represents all the States.

"Letters of a Countryman,"
November 14–December 20, 1787

The following five essays were published in the New Haven Gazette *in the weeks leading up to Connecticut's ratification convention, which began on January 3, 1788. In them, Sherman responds to anti-Federalist objections to the Constitution.*

A Countryman, I.

THURSDAY, NOVEMBER 14, 1787.

TO THE PEOPLE OF CONNECTICUT.

You are now called on to make important alterations in your government, by ratifying the new federal constitution.

There are, undoubtedly, such advantages to be expected from this measure, as will be sufficient inducement to adopt the proposal, provided it can be done without sacrificing more important advantages, which we now do or may possess. By a wise provision in the constitution of man, whenever a proposal is made to change any present habit or practice, he much more minutely considers what he is to *lose* by the alterations, what effect it is to have on what he at present possesses, than what is to be *hoped* for in the proposed expedient.

Thus people are justly cautious how they exchange present advantages for the hope of others in a system not yet experienced.

Hence all large states have dreaded a division into smaller parts, as being nearly the same thing as ruin; and all smaller states have predicted endless embarrassment from every attempt to unite them into larger. It is no more than probable that if any corner of this State of ten miles square, was now, and long had been independent of the residue of the State, that they would consider

Source: Paul Leicester Ford, ed., *Essays on the Constitution of the United States Published During Its Discussion by the People, 1787–1788* (New York: Burt Franklin, 1892), 215–28.

a proposal to unite them to the other parts of the State, as a violent attempt to wrest from them the only security for their persons or property. They would lament how little security they should derive from sending one or two members to the legislature at Hartford & New Haven, and all the evils that the Scots predicted from the proposed union with England, in the beginning of the present century, would be thundered with all the vehemence of American politics, from the little ten miles district. But surely no man believes that the inhabitants of this district would be less secure when united to the residue of the State, than when independent. Does any person suppose that the people would be more safe, more happy, or more respectable, if every town in this State was independent, and had no State government?

Is it not certain that government would be weak and irregular, and that the people would be poor and contemptible? And still it must be allowed, that each town would entirely surrender its boasted independence if they should unite in State government, and would retain only about one-eightieth part of the administration of their own affairs.

Has it ever been found, that people's property or persons were less regarded and less protected in large states than in small?

Have not the Legislature in large states been as careful not to over-burden the people with taxes as in small? But still it must be admitted, that a single town in a small state holds a greater proportion of the authority than in a large.

If the United States were one single government, provided the constitution of this extensive government was as good as the constitution of this State now is, would this part of it be really in greater danger of oppression or tyranny, than at present? It is true that many people who are *great men* because they go to Hartford to make laws for us once or twice in a year, would then be no greater than their neighbours, as much fewer representatives would be chosen. But would not the people be as safe, governed by their representatives assembled in New York or Philadelphia, as by their representatives assembled in Hartford or New Haven? Many instances can be quoted, where people have been unsafe, poor and contemptible, because they were governed only in small bodies; but can any instance be found where they were less safe for uniting? Has not every instance proved somewhat similar to the so much dreaded union between England and Scotland, where the Scots, instead of becoming a poor, despicable, dependent people, have become much more secure, happy, and respectable? If then, the constitution is a good one, why should we be afraid of uniting, even if the Union was to be much more complete and entire than is proposed?

A Countryman, II.

THURSDAY, NOVEMBER 22, 1787.

To the People of Connecticut.

It is fortunate that you have been but little distressed with that torrent of impertinence and folly, with which the newspaper politicians have over whelmed many parts of our country.

It is enough that you should have heard, that one party has seriously urged, that we should adopt the *New Constitution* because it has been approved by *Washington* and *Franklin:* and the other, with all the solemnity of apostolic address to *Men, Brethren, Fathers, Friends and Countryman,* have urged that we should reject, as dangerous, every clause thereof, because that *Washington* is more used to command as a soldier, than to reason as a politician—*Franklin is old,* others are *young*—and *Wilson* is *haughty.* You are too well informed to decide by the opinion of others, and too independent to need a caution against undue influence.

Of a very different nature, tho' only one degree better than the other reasoning, is all that sublimity of *nonsense* and *alarm,* that has been thundered against it in every shape of *metaphoric terror,* on the subject of a *bill of rights,* the *liberty of the press, rights of conscience, rights of taxation and election, trials in the vicinity, freedom of speech, trial by jury,* and a *standing army.* These last are undoubtedly important points, much too important to depend on mere paper protection. For, guard such privileges by the strongest expressions, still if you leave the legislative and executive power in the hands of those who are or may be disposed to deprive you of them—you are but slaves. Make an absolute monarch—give him the supreme authority, and guard as much as you will by bills of rights, your liberty of the press, and trial by jury;—he will find means either to take them from you, or to render them useless.

The only real security that you can have for all your important rights must be in the nature of your government. If you suffer any man to govern you who is not strongly interested in supporting your privileges, you will certainly lose them. If you are about to trust your liberties with people whom it is necessary to bind by stipulation, that they shall not keep a standing army, your stipulation is not worth even the trouble of writing. No bill of rights ever yet bound the supreme power longer than the *honeymoon* of a new married couple, unless the *rulers were interested* in preserving the rights; and in that case they have always been ready enough to declare the rights, and to preserve them when they were declared.—The famous English *Magna Charta* is but an act of parliament, which every subsequent parliament has had just as much constitutional power to repeal and annul, as the parliament which made it had to pass it at first. But the security of the nation has always been, that their government was so formed, that at least *one branch* of their legislature must be strongly interested to preserve the rights of the nation.

You have a bill of rights in Connecticut (i. e.) your legislature many years since enacted that the subjects of this state should enjoy certain privileges. Every assembly since that time, could, by the same authority, enact that the subjects should enjoy none of those privileges; and the only reason that it has not long since been so enacted, is that your legislature were as strongly interested in preserving those rights as any of the subjects; and this is your only security that it shall not be so enacted at the next session of assembly: and it is security enough.

Your General Assembly under your present constitution are supreme. They may keep troops on foot in the most profound peace, if they think proper. They have heretofore abridged the trial by jury in some cases, and they can again in all. They can restrain the press, and may lay the most burdensome taxes if they please, and who can forbid? But still the people are perfectly safe that not one of these events shall take place so long as the members of the General Assembly are as much interested, and interested in the same manner, as the other subjects.

On examining the new proposed constitution, there can be no question but that there is authority enough lodged in the proposed Federal Congress, if abused, to do the greatest injury. And it is perfectly idle to object to it, that there is no bill of rights, or to propose to add to it a provision that a trial by jury shall in no case be omitted, or to patch it up by adding a stipulation in favor of the press, or to guard it by removing the paltry objection to the right of Congress to regulate the time and manner of elections.

If you cannot prove by the best of all evidence, viz., by the *interest of the rulers*, that this authority will not be abused, or at least that those powers are not more likely to be abused by the Congress, than by those who now have the same powers, you must by no means adopt the constitution:—No, not with all the bills of rights and with all the stipulations in favor of the people that can be made.

But if the members of Congress are to be interested just as you and I are, and just as the members of our present legislatures are interested, we shall be just as safe, with even supreme power (if that were granted) in Congress, as in the General Assembly. If the members of Congress can take no improper step which will not affect them as much as it does us, we need not apprehend that they will usurp authorities not given them to injure that society of which they are a part.

The sole question, (so far as any apprehension of tyranny and oppression is concerned) ought to be, how are Congress formed? how far have you a control over them? Decide this, and then all the questions about their power may be dismissed for the amusement of those politicians whose business it is to catch flies, or may occasionally furnish subjects for *George Bryan's* Pomposity, or the declamations of *Cato—An Old Whig—Son of Liberty—Brutus—Brutus junior— An Officer of the Continental Army,*—the more contemptible *Timoleon,* and the residue of that rabble of writers.

A Countryman, III.

THURSDAY, NOVEMBER 29, 1787.

TO THE PEOPLE OF CONNECTICUT.

The same thing once more—I am a plain man, of few words; for this reason perhaps it is, that when I have said a thing I love to repeat it. Last week I endeavored to evince, that the only surety you could have for your liberties must be in the nature of your government; that you could derive no security from bills of rights, or stipulations, on the subject of a standing army, the liberty of the press, trial by jury, or on any other subject. Did you ever hear of an absolute monarchy, where those rights which are proposed by the pigmy politicians of this day, to be secured by stipulation, were ever preserved? Would it not be mere trifling to make any such stipulations, in any absolute monarchy?

On the other hand, if your interest and that of your rulers are the same, your liberties are abundantly secure. Perhaps the most secure when their power is most complete. Perhaps a provision that they should never raise troops in time of peace, might at some period embarrass the public concerns and en- danger the liberties of the people. It is possible that in the infinite variety of events, it might become improper strictly to adhere to any one provision that has ever been proposed to be stipulated. At all events, the people have always been perfectly safe without any stipulation of the kind, when the rulers were interested to make them safe; and never otherwise.

No people can be more secure against any oppression in their rulers than you are at present; and no rulers can have more supreme and unlimited au- thority than your general assembly have.

When you consult on the subject of adopting the new constitution, you do not enquire whether the powers therein contained can be safely lodged in any hands whatever. For not only those very powers, but all other powers, are already in the general assembly. - - - - The enquiry is, whether Congress is by this new constitution so formed that a part of the power now in the general assembly would be as well lodged in Congress. Or, as was before said, it depends on how far the members are under your control; and how far their interest and yours are the same; to which careful attention must be given.

A Countryman, IV.

THURSDAY, DECEMBER 6, 1787.

TO THE PEOPLE OF CONNECTICUT.

If the propriety of trusting your government in the hands of your representatives was now a perfectly new question, the expediency of the measure might be doubted. A very great portion of the objections which we daily find made against adopting the new constitution (and which are just as weighty objections against our present government, or against any government in existence) would doubtless have their influence; and perhaps would determine you against trusting the powers of sovereignty out of your own hands.

The best theory, the best philosophy on the subject, would be too uncertain for you to hazard your freedom upon.

But your freedom, in that sense of the expression (if it could be called sense), is already totally gone. Your Legislature is not only supreme in the usual sense of the word, but they have *literally, all the powers of society.* Can you—can you *possibly* grant anything new? Have you any power which is not already granted to your General Assembly? You are indeed called on to say whether a part of the powers now exercised by the General Assembly, shall not, in future, be exercised by Congress. And it is clearly much better for your interest, that Congress should experience those powers than that they should continue in the General Assembly, provided you can trust Congress as safely as the General Assembly.

What forms your security under the General Assembly? Nothing save that the interest of the members is the same as yours. Will it be the same with Congress? There are essentially only two differences between the formation of Congress and of your General Assembly. One is, - - - that Congress are to govern a much larger tract of country, and a much greater number of people, consequently your proportion of the government will be much smaller than at present. The other difference is - - - that the members of Congress when elected, hold their places for two, four and six years, and the members of Assembly only six and twelve months.

The first of these differences was discussed pretty fully in the first number, (when there was no idea of proceeding thus far on the subject), and has all the force as an objection against the powers of Congress, that it would have if applied to a proposal to give up the sovereignty of the several towns of the state, (if such sovereignty had existed,) and unite in state government.

It would be only a repetition to enter into a consideration of this difference between Congress and your Assembly.

It has been suggested that the six or eight members which we shall send to Congress will be men of property, who can little feel any burthens they may lay on society. How far is this idea supported by experience? As the members are to pay their proportion, will they not be as careful of laying too great burthens as poorer people? Are they less careful of their money than the poor? This objection would be much stronger against trusting the power out of your hands at all. If the several towns were now independent, this objection would be much more forcible against uniting in state government, and sending one or two of your most wealthy men to Hartford or New Haven, to vote away your money. But this you have tried, and found that assemblies of representatives are less willing to vote away money than even their constituents. An individual of any tolerable economy, pays all his debts, and perhaps has money beforehand. A small school district, or a small parish, will see what sum they want, and usually provide sufficiently for their wants, and often have a little money at interest.

Town voters are partly representatives, i. e. many people pay town taxes who have no right to vote, but the money they vote away is principally their own. The towns in this state tax themselves less willingly than smaller bodies. They generally however tax themselves sufficiently to nearly pay the demands against them within the year, very seldom raise money beforehand by taxes. The Generally Assembly of this state could never be induced to *attempt* to do more than pay the annual interest of what they owe, and occasionally sink very small parts of the principal, and they never in fact did thus much, and we are all witnesses that they are full as careful of the public money as we can wishs It never was a complaint that they were too ready to allow individuals large sums. A man who has a claim against a town, and applies to a town-meeting, is very likely to obtain justice: but he who has a claim against the state, and applies to the General Assembly, stands but a poor chance to obtain justice. Some rule will be found to exclude his claim,—or to lessen it,—or he will be paid in a security - - - not worth half the money.

You have uniformly experienced that your representatives are as careful, if not more so, of your money, than you yourselves are in your town-meetings; but still your representatives are generally men of property, and those of them who are most independent, and those whom you have sent to Congress, have not been by any means the least careful.

A Countryman, V.

TUESDAY, DECEMBER 20, 1787.

TO THE PEOPLE OF CONNECTICUT.

You do not hate to read Newspaper Essays on the new constitution, more than I hate to write them. Then *we will be short* - - - which I have often found the *best* expression in a dull sermon, except the *last*.

Whether the mode of election pointed out in the proposed constitution is well calculated to support the principles which were designed to be established in the different branches of the legislature, may perhaps be justly doubted:— and may perhaps in some future day be discussed.

The design undoubtedly was, that the house of representatives should be a *popular* assembly,—that the senate should, in its nature, be somewhat more permanent, and that the two houses should be completely independent of each other. These *principles* are right.—for the present we will suppose they will be supported—there then remains to be considered no considerable difference between the constitutional government which is proposed, and your present government, except that the time for which you choose your present rulers is only for six and twelve months, and the time for which you are to choose your continental rulers is for two, four and six years.

The convention were mistaken if they supposed they should lessen the evils of tumultuous elections by making elections less frequent. But are your liberties endangered by this measure? Philosophy may mislead you. Ask experience. Are not the liberties of the people of England as safe as yours?—They are not as free as yours, because much of their government is in the hands of *hereditary majesty* and *nobility*. But is not that part of the government which is under the control of the commons exceedingly well guarded? But still the house of commons is only a third branch—the *only* branch who are appointed by the people—and they are chosen but once in *seven years*. Is there then any danger to be apprehended from the length of time that your rulers are to serve? when none are to serve more than six years - - - one whole house but two years, and your President but four.

The great power and influence of an hereditary monarch of Britain has spread many alarms, from an apprehension that the commons would sacrifice the liberties of the people to the money or influence of the crown: but the influence of a powerful *hereditary* monarch, with the national Treasury—Army—and fleet at his command—and the whole executive government - - - and one-third of the legislative in his hands constantly operating on a house of commons, whose duration is never less than *seven years*, unless this same monarch should *end* it, (which he can do in an hour,) has never yet been sufficient to obtain one vote of the house of commons which has taken from the people the *liberty of the press*, - - - *trial by jury*, - - - *the rights of conscience, or of private property.*

Can you then apprehend danger of oppression and tyranny from the too great duration of the power of *your* rulers?

"Observations on the New Federal Constitution,"
January 7, 1788

The Connecticut ratification convention met in Hartford from January 3 to January 9, 1788. In the midst of the debates, the Connecticut Courant, *a Hartford paper, published the following essay by Roger Sherman under the pseudonym "A Citizen of New Haven." It was republished on December 25, 1788, in the* New Haven Gazette *under the pseudonym "A Citizen of New Haven, II."*

A Citizen of New Haven

CONNECTICUT COURANT, 7 JANUARY

Observations on the new Federal CONSTITUTION.

In order to form a good constitution of government, the legislature should be properly organized and be vested with plenary powers for all the purposes for which the government is instituted to be exercised for the public good as occasion may require.

The greatest security that a people can have for the enjoyment of their rights and liberties is that no laws can be made to bind them nor any taxes be imposed upon them without their consent by representatives of their own choosing, who will participate with them in the public burthens and benefits; this was the great point contended for in our controversy with Great Britain, and this will be fully secured to us by the new Constitution. The rights of the people will be secured by a representation in proportion to their numbers in one branch of the legislature, and the rights of the particular states by their equal representation in the other branch.

The President and Vice President as well as the members of Congress will be eligible for fixed periods and may be reelected as often as the electors shall

Source: Merrill Jensen, ed., *The Documentary History of the Ratification of the Constitution,* vol. 3, *Ratification of the Constitution by the States: Delaware, New Jersey, Georgia, Connecticut* (Madison: State Historical Society of Wisconsin, 1978), 524–27. Reprinted with permission of the Wisconsin Historical Society.

think fit, which will be a great security for their fidelity in office, and will give greater stability and energy to government than an exclusion by rotation, and will be an operative and effectual security against arbitrary government, either monarchial or aristocratic.

The immediate security of the civil and domestic rights of the people will be in the governments of the particular states. And as the different states have different local interests and customs which can be best regulated by their own laws, it would not be expedient to admit the federal government to interfere with them any further than may be necessary for the good of the whole. The great end of the federal government is to protect the several states in the enjoyment of those rights against foreign invasion, and to preserve peace and a beneficial intercourse among themselves, and to regulate and protect their commerce with foreign nations.

These were not sufficiently provided for by the former Articles of Confederation, which was the occasion of calling the late Convention to make amendments. This they have done by forming a new Constitution containing the powers vested in the federal government under the former, with such additional powers as they deemed necessary to attain the ends the states had in view in their appointment. And to carry those powers into effect, they thought it necessary to make some alterations in the organization of the government; this they supposed to be warranted by their commission.

The powers vested in the federal government are particularly defined, so that each state still retains its sovereignty in what concerns its own internal government and a right to exercise every power of a sovereign state not particularly delegated to the government of the United States. The new powers vested in the United States are to regulate commerce; provide for a uniform practice respecting naturalization, bankruptcies, and organizing, arming, and training the militia, and for the punishment of certain crimes against the United States; and for promoting the progress of science in the mode therein pointed out. There are some other matters which Congress has power under the present Confederation to require to be done by the particular states, which they will be authorized to carry into effect themselves under the new Constitution. These powers appear to be necessary for the common benefit of the states and could not be effectually provided for by the particular states.

The objects of expenditure will be the same under the new Constitution as under the old; nor need the administration of government be more expensive. The number of members of the Congress will be the same, nor will it be necessary to increase the number of officers in the executive department or their salaries. The supreme executive will be in a single person who must have an honorable support, which perhaps will not exceed the present allowance to the President of Congress and the expense of supporting a committee of the states in the recess of Congress.

It is not probable that Congress will have occasion to sit longer than two or three months in a year, after the first session which may perhaps be something longer. Nor will it be necessary for the Senate to sit longer than the other branch. The appointment of officers may be made during the session of Congress, and trials on impeachment and making treaties will not often occur and will require but little time of the Senate to attend to them. The security against keeping up armies in time of peace will be greater under the new Constitution than under the present, because it can't be done without the concurrence of two branches of legislature, nor can any appropriation of money for that purpose be in force for more than two years, whereas there is no restriction under the present Confederation.

The liberty of the press can be in no danger, because that is not put under the direction of the new government.

If the federal government keeps within its proper jurisdiction, it will be the interest of the state legislatures to support it, and they will be a powerful and effectual check to its interfering with their jurisdictions. But the objects of the federal government will be so obvious that there will be no great danger of any interference.

The principal sources of revenue will be imposts on goods imported and sale of the western lands, which probably will be sufficient to pay the debts and expenses of the United States while peace continues. But if there should be occasion to resort to direct taxation, each state's quota will be ascertained according to a rule which has been approved by the legislatures of eleven of the states, and should any state neglect to furnish its quota, Congress may raise it by a tax in the same manner as the state ought to have done; and what remedy more easy and equitable could be devised to obtain the supplies from a delinquent state?

Some object that the representation will be too small, but the states have never thought fit to keep half the number of representatives in Congress that they are entitled to under the present Confederation; and of what advantage can it be to have a large assembly to transact the few general matters that will come under the direction of Congress? The regulating the time, place, and manner of elections seems to be as well secured as possible. The legislature of each state may do it, and if they neglect to do it in the best manner, it may be done by Congress; and what motive can either have to injure the people in the exercise of that right? The qualifications of the electors are to remain as fixed by the constitutions and laws of the several states.

It is by some objected that the executive is blended with the legislature, and that these powers ought to be entirely distinct and unconnected, but is not this a gross *error* in politics? The united wisdom and various interests of a nation should be combined in framing the laws. But the execution of them should not be in the whole legislature; that would be too troublesome and expensive, but it will not thence follow that the executive should have no voice or influence in legislation. The supreme executive in Great Britain is one branch of the legislature and has a negative on all the laws. Perhaps that is an extreme that ought not to be imitated by a republic, but the partial negative vested in the President by the new Constitution on the acts of Congress, and the consequent revision, may be very useful to prevent laws being passed without mature deliberation.

The Vice President, while he acts as President of the Senate, will have nothing to do in the executive department. His being elected by all the states will incline him to regard the interests of the whole, and when the members of the Senate are equally divided on any question, who so proper to give a casting vote as one who represents all the states?

The power of the President to grant pardons extends only to offenses against the United States, which can't be productive of much mischief, especially as those on impeachment are excepted, which will exclude offenders from office.

It was thought necessary in order to carry into effect the laws of the Union, to promote justice, and preserve harmony among the states, to extend the judicial powers of the United States to the enumerated cases, under such regulations and with such exceptions as shall be provided by law, which will doubtless reduce them to cases of such magnitude and importance as cannot be safely trusted to the final decision of the courts of the particular states. The Constitution does not make it necessary that any inferior tribunals should be instituted, but it may be done if found necessary. Tis probable that the courts of the particular states will be authorized by Congress to try causes under the laws of the Union, as has been heretofore done in cases of piracy, etc., and the Supreme Court may have a circuit to make trials as convenient and as little expensive as possible to the parties; nor is there anything in the Constitution to deprive them of trial by jury in cases where that mode of trial has been heretofore used. All cases in the courts of common law between citizens of the same state, except those claiming lands under grants of different states, must be finally decided by the courts of the state to which they belong, so that it is not probable that more than one citizen to a thousand will ever have a cause that can come before a federal court.

Every department and officer of the federal government will be subject to the regulation and control of the laws, and therefore the people will have all possible security against oppression. Upon the whole, the Constitution appears to be well framed to secure the rights and liberties of the people and for preserving the governments of the individual states, and, if well administered, to restore and secure public and private credit, and to give respectability to the states both abroad and at home. Perhaps a more perfect one could not be formed on mere speculation; and if upon experience it shall be found deficient, it provides an easy and peaceable mode to make amendments. Is it not much better to adopt it than to continue in present circumstances? Its being agreed to by all the states that were present in Convention is a circumstance in its favor, so far as any respect is due to their opinions.

"Observations on the Alterations Proposed as Amendments to the New Federal Constitution," December 4, 1788

With North Carolina's vote to ratify the Constitution on November 26, 1788, twelve of the thirteen states had ratified the document. Some states simply ratified it, but others also proposed amendments to be considered by the first federal Congress. In this essay published in the New Haven Gazette, *Sherman, once again writing under the pseudonym "A Citizen of New Haven," offers his views on these proposals.*

A Citizen of New Haven, I.

THURSDAY, DECEMBER 4, 1788.

Observations on the Alterations Proposed as Amendments to the new Federal Constitution.

Six of the states have adopted the new constitution without proposing any alteration, and the most of those proposed by the conventions of other states may be provided for by congress in a code of laws without altering the constitution. If congress may be safely trusted with the affairs of the Union, and have sufficient powers for that purpose, and possess no powers but such as respect the common interest of the states (as I have endeavored to show in a former piece), then all the matters that can be regulated by law may safely be left to their discretion, and those will include all that I have noticed except the following, which I think on due consideration will appear to be improper or unnecessary.

1. It is proposed that the consent of two-thirds or three-fourths of the members present in this branch of the congress shall be required for passing certain acts.

On which I would observe, that this would give a minority in congress power to controul the majority, joined with the concurrent voice of the president, for

Source: Paul Leicester Ford, ed., *Essays on the Constitution of the United States Published During Its Discussion by the People, 1787–1788* (New York: Burt Franklin, 1892), 233–36.

if the president dissents, no act can pass without the consent of two-thirds of the members in each branch of congress; and would not that be contrary to the general principles of republican government?

2. That impeachments ought not to be tried by the senate, or not by the senate alone.

But what good reason can be assigned why the senate is not the most proper tribunal for that purpose? The members are to be chosen by the legislatures of the several states, who will doubtless appoint persons of wisdom and probity, and from their office can have no interested motives to partiality. The house of peers in Great Britian try impeachments and are also a branch of the legislature.

3. It is said that the president ought not to have power to grant pardons in cases of high treason, but the congress.

It does not appear that any great mischief can arise from the exercise of this power by the president (though perhaps it might as well have been lodged in congress). The president cannot pardon in case of impeachment, so that such offenders may be excluded from office notwithstanding his pardon.

4. It is proposed that members of congress be rendered ineligible to any other office during the time for which they are elected members of that body.

This is an objection that will admit of something plausible to be said on both sides, and it was settled in convention on full discussion and deliberation. There are some offices which a member of congress may be best qualified to fill, from his knowledge of public affairs acquired by being a member, such as minister to foreign courts, &c., and on accepting any other office his seat in congress will be vacated, and no member is eligible to any office that shall have been instituted or the emoluments increased while he was a member.

5. It is proposed to make the president and senators ineligible after certain periods.

But this would abridge the privilege of the people, and remove one great motive to fidelity in office, and render persons incapable of serving in offices, on account of their experience, which would best qualify them for usefulness in office—but if their services are not acceptable they may be left out at any new election.

6. It is proposed that no commercial treaty should be made without the consent of two-thirds of the senators, nor any cession of territory, right of navigation or fishery, without the consent of three-fourths of the members present in each branch of congress.

It is provided by the constitution that no commercial treaty shall be made by the president without the consent of two-thirds of the senators present, and as each state has an equal representation and suffrage in the senate, the rights of the state will be as well secured under the new constitution as under the old; and it is not probable that they would ever make a cession of territory or any important national right without the consent of congress. The king of Great Britian has by the constitution a power to make treaties, yet in matters of great importance he consults the parliament.

7. There is one amendment proposed by the convention of South Carolina respecting religious tests, by inserting the word *other*, between the words *no* and *religious* in that article, which is an ingenious thought, and had that word been inserted, it would probably have prevented any objection on that head. But it may be considered as a clerical omission and be inserted without calling a convention; as it now stands the effect will be the same.

On the whole it is hoped that all the states will consent to make a fair trial of the constitution before they attempt to alter it; experience will best show whether it is deficient or not, on trial it may appear that the alterations that have been proposed are not necessary, or that others not yet thought of may be necessary; everything that tends to disunion ought to be avoided. Instability in government and laws tends to weaken a state and render the rights of the people precarious.

If another convention should be called to revise the constitution, 'tis not likely they would be more unanimous than the former; they might judge differently in some things, but is it certain that they would judge better? When experience has convinced the states and people in general that alterations are necessary, they may be easily made, but attempting it at present may be detrimental if not fatal to the union of the states.

The judiciary department is perhaps the most difficult to be precisely limited by the constitution, but congress have full power to regulate it by law, and it may be found necessary to vary the regulations at different times as circumstances may differ.

Congress may make requisitions for supplies previous to direct taxation, if it should be thought to be expedient, but if requisitions be made and some states comply and others not, the noncomplying states must be considered and treated as delinquents, which will tend to excite disaffection and disunion among the states, besides occasioning delay; but if congress lay the taxes in the first instance these evils will be prevented, and they will doubtless accommodate the taxes to the customs and convenience of the several states.

Some suppose that the representation will be too small, but I think it is in the power of congress to make it too large, but I believe that it may be safely trusted with them. Great Britian contains about three times the number of the inhabitants in the United States, and according to Burgh's account in his political disquisitions, the members of parliament in that kingdom do not exceed

131, and if 69 more be added from the principal cities and towns the number would be 200; and strike off those who are elected by the small boroughs, which are called the rotten part of the constitution by their best patriots and politicians, that nation would be more equally and better represented than at present; and if that would be a sufficient number for their national legislature, one-third of that number will be more than sufficient for our federal legislature who will have few general matters to transact. But these and other objections have been considered in a former paper, before referred to. I shall therefore conclude this with my best wishes for the continuance of the peace, liberty and union of these states.

A Citizen of New Haven.

Roger Sherman as a Member of Congress

Connecticut was the only state to send each of its Federal Convention delegates to serve in the legislature created by the new Constitution. William Samuel Johnson and Oliver Ellsworth, Sherman's legal mentor and his protégé, respectively, were selected by the General Assembly to be Connecticut's first U.S. senators. The state elected members of the House of Representatives as it had elected delegates to the Confederation Congress: Freemen nominated candidates in November, and in December they cast ballots for five of the top twelve nominees. Sherman was fourth on the list of nominees and second in the general, at-large election. His election was bittersweet because it forced him to choose between serving in the House of Representatives and continuing to serve as a judge on Connecticut's Superior Court. He petitioned the General Assembly for an exception to the 1784 statute prohibiting holding both offices, but his plea was rejected. Thus, in February 1789, after twenty-three years on the bench, he resigned from the Superior Court.

Sherman arrived in the nation's temporary capital of New York City on March 5, 1789. At sixty-nine years of age, he was the oldest member of Congress. No representative or senator had more experience in the Continental and Confederation Congresses than "father Sherman." In spite of his age, he jumped into the business of putting flesh on the skeleton of the new national government. Indeed, in the first Congress, he spoke more often than any other member of the House of Representatives except for James Madison. He made particularly important contributions to debates over representation, executive

501

power, revenue, debt, the proper scope of the national government, and the Bill of Rights.[1]

Sherman was reelected to the House of Representatives in 1790. When Congress moved from New York to Philadelphia, William Samuel Johnson resigned from the Senate in order to remain president of Columbia College. Sherman was appointed to his seat, and he served in the Senate from June 13, 1791, until his death on July 23, 1793. Because Senate debates were secret at that time, it is difficult to say much about his Senate service. He apparently continued his campaign to keep the House of Representatives small and helped investigate General Arthur St. Clair's disastrous defeat by Native Americans. He regularly corresponded with his son-in-law Simeon Baldwin about the creation of the federal judiciary, but most of their letters center on the possibility of Baldwin being appointed to the bench. Sherman resided in Philadelphia until illness finally necessitated his return to New Haven in April 1793.[2]

During the era in which Sherman served in Congress, the House and Senate kept journals, but these contain only sparse records of motions and contested votes. Accordingly, most of the following excerpts are from letters written by Sherman or newspaper accounts of congressional speeches in the House. Several newspapers covered congressional proceedings, including the *Congressional Register*, the *Gazette of the United States*, the *Daily Advertiser*, and the *New York Gazette*. None of them recorded speeches verbatim, and their accounts sometimes vary. Unless there is an obvious contradiction or problem, I draw from whichever source seems to be the most accurate. It is noteworthy that Sherman thought these newspapers were "[l]iable to make some mistakes," but he did "not think them guilty of unfairness."[3]

Because many of Sherman's letters address multiple subjects, I include most of them in the first section of this chapter, placing them in chronological order. The remainder of the chapter is organized by subject matter.

---

1. Linda Grant de Pauw et al., eds., *The Documentary History of the First Federal Congress* (Baltimore: Johns Hopkins University Press, 1972–2012), 14: 508–12; 16: 781 (hereafter cited as *DHFFC*).

2. Collier, *Roger Sherman's Connecticut*, 314–15.

3. *DHFFC*, 13: 1015.

Letters

The letters in this section were written when Roger Sherman was a member of Congress. The first federal Congresses were particularly important as members had to flesh out the new republic's political institutions, put the nation on firm financial footing, and consider amendments to the recently ratified Constitution. The last letter in this section was sent to Sherman by George Washington less than two months before Sherman's death.

Letter to Samuel Huntington, January 7, 1789

NEW HAVEN

Sir,—I have a grateful sense of the honor done me by the freemen of this State in electing me one of their representatives in the Congress of the United States. This fresh instance of their confidence lays me under an additional obligation to devote my time to their service. The trust I esteem very weighty and important in the present situation of public affairs. I could therefore have wished that their choice had been fixed on some other person in my stead, better able to sustain the weight and perform the services of that office, especially as I hold another in the State which as the law now stands is incompatible with holding this at the same time. I wish to employ my time in such service as may be most beneficial and acceptable to my country. Much of my time since the commencement of the late war has been employed at a distance from home, and as I have a numerous family to provide for, it would be most agreeable to me to be in a situation wherein I might pay some attention to their affairs. But if the honorable the Legislature shall think fit to provide that my acceptance of this office shall not vacate my office in the Superior Court until their further pleasure shall be made known, I will accept the trust to which I have been elected by the freemen, (I do not wish to hold any office otherwise than subject to their pleasure) but if in their wisdom they shall not think fit to make such provision, I shall desire a little further time to consider and advise on the matter. I have the honor to be with great respect your excellency's most obedient and humble servant,

ROGER SHERMAN.

Source: Lewis H. Boutell, *The Life of Roger Sherman* (Chicago: A. C. McClurg, 1896), 191–92.

Letter to Oliver Wolcott, May 14, 1789

NEW YORK

SIR,—As the proceedings of Congress are daily published in the papers in this city, and from them in the papers of the other States, I cannot give your honor any new information respecting them. Much time was lost by the non-attendance of members at the beginning of the session, so that seasonable provision could not be made by an impost law to embrace the spring importations.

The House of Representatives entered upon that subject immediately after they formed, and have agreed upon the rates of the impost on the various articles, in doing which they had respect to revenue, and the encouraging the manufactures of these States. Much time was necessarily taken up in adjusting those rates to suit the circumstances of the different parts of the Union. A spirit of harmony and accommodation has been manifested, and the business has been done to general satisfaction, except as to the duty on molasses which at first was fixed at 6 cents per gallon, which gave great dissatisfaction to the members from Massachusetts and occasioned much debate, till at length it was altered to 5 cents. It was the general sense of the House that were it not for the distillation of that article into rum it ought to be lower, but as a considerable branch of the revenue was to be derived from distilled spirits it was urged, that if molasses was not rated in a greater proportion to imported rum than some other articles, it would tend to diminish the revenue on that branch by increasing the manufacture of it in the country, and so lessening the importation; and that it would operate unequally on the different parts of the Union, as in those parts where the distillery is not carried on the people would pay a higher tax on the spirits which they consume than the citizens of the other States.

All classes of citizens here appear to be well pleased with the new Government, and especially with the President's address.

There has been a joint committee to consider what style shall be annexed to the offices of President and Vice President, who reported that it is not proper to annex any style or title other than the style of office in the Consti-

Source: Lewis H. Boutell, *The Life of Roger Sherman* (Chicago: A. C. McClurg, 1896), 202–4.

tution, which was unanimously approved by the House and dissented to by a majority of the Senate—on which a committee of conference was appointed, and the committee from the Senate agreed to report that the address of the Senate should be made to the President, only by the style of office.

The House have this day agreed to engross the bill for laying duties on goods imported, which is to be read a third time to-morrow—having previously agreed to a deduction of 10 per cent of the duties on goods imported in vessels built in the United States and belonging to citizens thereof.

Letter to Simeon Baldwin, August 22, 1789

NEW YORK

Simeon Baldwin (1761–1851) married Sherman's daughter Rebecca in 1787. They were the parents of Roger Sherman Baldwin (1793–1863).

Dear Sir,

I received Yours of the 18ᵗʰ. The house have gone through the consideration of amendments, and a committee of 3 is appointed to prepare a resolve for introducing them to the States, and so to arrange the several articles as that each may be passed upon distinctly by the States, and any one that is adopted by three fourths of the legislatures may become a part of the Constitution. They have concluded that they shall be supplement to the constitution if not be incorporated.

I was at home when the salaries of the members & officers of the house were considered—the allowance to the door-keepers is not as was at first reported, but is a daily allowance during the session.

The Secretary of the Senate and Clerk of the House I think should likewise have been paid by the day—the bill is in the Senate & will probably undergo some amendments.

I wish you would take administration on William's Estate. It must be represented insolvent & a time limited for exhibiting the claims.

I suppose the former creditors would be entitled to their proportion if there was any thing worthy their attention. What was formerly assigned to the trustees will belong wholly to those who were creditors at the time of passing the Insolvent act—and there is no duty incumbent on the trustees to do anything in behalf of creditors respecting the other part of the Estate.

The expence for sickness & funeral charges & the charges of administering must be paid in full if there is assets sufficient, and remainder if any be divided to the creditors who shall exhibit their claims by the time limited.

Source: Roger Sherman (1721–93) Collection (MS 447), box 1, folder 12, Manuscripts and Archives, Yale University Library.

I have had no opportunity to enquire to the points of law you mention, but shall attend to it and write again.

Yours respectfully,

Roger Sherman

Letter to Samuel Huntington, September 17, 1789
NEW YORK

Your Excellency has doubtless Seen the amendments proposed to be made to the Constitution as passed by the House of Representatives, enclosed is a copy of them as amended by the Senate, wherein they are considerably abridged & I think altered for the better.

The present session draws near to a close, the 22d Inst. being the time fixed by both Houses for adjournment Some Bills for laws and other business begun will be continued to next session; but the arrangements that will be compleated will enable the Executive to administer the Government in the recess of Congress.

It was impossible to make any Special appropriation for paying the Interest of the public debt without further information than can be obtained at present, the Secretary of the Treasury will be directed to make proper Statements and report to the Next session.

The Salaries of Some of the Officers are higher than I thought was necessary or proper considering the State of the finances and the just and meritorious demands of the creditors who have long been kept out of their dues, especially Such of them as originally loaned their money, or rendered Services or Specific Supplies. & Still hold their Securities. I dont know whether any discrimination will or ought to be made between them & others, but if there Should I think it ought not to be made for the benefit of the public, but of the original creditors who were necessitated to Sell their Securities at a discount.

I was absent when the Bill for fixing the compensation of the members & officers of Congress was brought in and passed the House, the Senate concurred with an alteration that in the year 1795 the pay of a Senator Should be augmented one dollar a day. on this principle that a Senator ought to have higher pay than a Representative, though they were willing to dispense with it during their continuance in office, a great majority of the House of Representatives thought the principle not admissible, but on conference rather than

Source: *DHFFC*, 17: 1564, 1567. © 2004 Johns Hopkins University Press. Reprinted by permission of Johns Hopkins University Press.

lose the Bill it was agreed by way of accommodation to limit the continuance of the law to Seven years, so that the extra pay of a Senator will continue but one year.

The pay is fixed at one dollar a day more than was last Stated by the Legislature of the State of Connecticut which is perhaps as Oeconomical a State as any in the union, and I suppose the members from that State would have been content with that allowance, if they had to provide only for themselves, but the members from those States who had formerly *been* allowed Eight dollars a day thought it hard to be reduced to Six. but mutual concession was necessary. It's is important that a full representation be kept up, and it is well known that in Connecticut as well as in other States, it was difficult out of Seven Members to keep up a representation by two. and Some could not be induced to attend at all.

The judiciary Bill which had passed the Senate was this day concurred with by the House of Representatives with Some Small alterations—The Salaries of the Judges have been this day reported but not considered by the House. The Enclosed papers contain the news of the day.

Letter to Richard Law, October 3, 1789
NEW HAVEN

DEAR SIR;—Congress closed the session last Tuesday, having made such arrangements as will enable the Executive to administer the Government. They could not obtain sufficient information to make any appropriations for the interest of the public debts, but have directed the Secretary of the Treasury to report the necessary statements for that purpose, to the next session.

The Judiciary Act passed with but *little alteration from the original draft*. I suppose you will be furnished with a copy of it. You are appointed District Judge for Connecticut. The salary is something more than you now receive from the State and can't be diminished.

Your honor will have the appointment of a Clerk who must reside at Hartford or New Haven. Simeon Baldwin, Esq., of this city, with whom you are well acquainted, would execute the office well, and I believe, to good acceptance, if he should be appointed. If your honor shall think fit to confer that office on him the favor will be gratefully acknowledged by him, and

Your sincere friend and humble servant,

ROGER SHERMAN.

Source: Lewis H. Boutell, *The Life of Roger Sherman* (Chicago: A. C. McClurg, 1896), 225–26.

Letter to Samuel Huntington, March 6, 1790

The proceedings of Congress being daily published in the news papers, your Excellency has I conceive been fully informed of the progress they have made in the public business, Several new laws have passed both Houses, & have been approved by the President, there are a number of Bills that have been formed & passed one or other of the Houses that are yet unfinished. A Bill passed the Senate yesterday accepting a large Cession of western territory made by the State of North-Carolina, 'tis said it contains about 18 millions of Acres exclusive of the Grants that have been made in it by that State—The report of the Secretary has been under consideration for some time respecting a provision for the national debt. There has been a long debate respecting a discrimination between the Securities in the hands of the original creditors and those which have been tranfered—but it was finally decided by a large majority against a discrimination, the motives were that the Securities were by government made transferable, & payable to the bearer, and therefore the tranfer vested the whole property in the purchaser, if there was no fraud or compulsion. That they were in the early Stages of the loans many of them purchased at par. in a way of commerce or in payment of debts, and others at So Small a discount. as to be equal to the full value considering all circumstances. that the very low rate at which they Sold commenced about the time of issuing the final Settlement certificates to the Army, and were chiefly confined to the Army Securities, so that no common market price could be fixed without great inequality & injustice in many Instances, and a particular inquiry into the circumstances of every case would be impracticable; besides the public faith had been pledged after the transfers in most of the cases of Speculation. by issuing new Securities to the purchasers in their own names, to the amount of about 5 million dollars; upward of 3 millions of which were registered to foreigners in their own names. It was therefore concluded that government could do nothing to impair or alter the contracts consistent with good faith. The assumption of the debts of the

Source: *DHFFC*, 18: 753–54. © 2012 Johns Hopkins University Press. Reprinted by permission of Johns Hopkins University Press.

Several States incurred for the common defence during the late war, is now under consideration. The Secretary of the Treasury has been directed to report what funds can be provided for them in case they Should be assumed, his report is contained in one of the enclosed papers. He Supposes that Sufficient provision may be made for the whole debt without resorting to direct taxation; if So—I think it must be an advantage to all the States, as well as to the creditors. Some have Suggested that it will tend to increase the power of the federal government & lessen the importance of the State governments, but I dont See how it can operate in that manner, the constitutions are so framed that the government of the united States & those of the particular States are friendly, & not hostile, to each other, their jurisdictions being distinct, & respecting different objects, & both Standing upon the broad basis of the people, will act for *their* benefit in their respective Spheres without any interference. and the more Strength each have to attain their ends of their Institutions the better for both, and for the people at large.

I have ever been of opinion that the Governments of the particular States ought to be Supported in their full vigour, as the Security of the civil & domestic rights of the people more immediately depend on them, that their local interests & customs can be best regulated and Supported by their own laws; and the principal advantages of the federal government, is, to protect the Several States in the enjoyment of those rights, against foreign invasion, and to preserve peace & and a beneficial intercourse between each other, and to protect & regulate their commerce with foreign nations. I shall be always happy to receive your Excellency's Instructions respecting any public affairs in the transaction of which I may be concerned.

Letter to William Ellery, June 29, 1790

William Ellery (1727–1820) was an attorney and judge from Rhode Island. He served as customs collector for the port of Newport, Rhode Island, from 1790 until his death.

I received your favr. of the the 21st. instant I am glad that we Succeeded in obtaining Your Appointment to the Office of Collector. It is an important trust, which I doubt not will be executed with fidelity, I have had the pleasure of an interview with the Senators from your State, and am pleased with the Sentiments that they expressed on public affairs.

I hope there will be an agrement to provide for the State debts before Congress closes the present session. The matter of weights & measures, & Coinage, was ea[r]ly taken up in Congress, and referred to the Secretary of State. He has not Yet reported upon it, but he lately Shewed me a report which he had prepared, but I believe no law will be passed upon it this session A Committee of both Houses have reported, the business necessary to be finished before Congress adjourn, ~~wh~~ they Suppose it may be accomplished by the 15th of July. I dont think a war will take place between Spain & Britain, neither of them are prepared for it.

Provision is made by Congress for intercourse with foreign nations [*Foreign Intercourse Act HR-52*]. & I Suppose Some kind of Minister will be Sent to London—I hope France will not be involved in a war. before they have Settled a free & effective Government. I think it will be an important event to the European Nations in general, as well as to us. These States, I hope will enjoy peace, until the time when the Nations Shall learn war no more.

Source: *DHFFC*, 19: 1961–62. © 2012 Johns Hopkins University Press. Reprinted by permission of Johns Hopkins University Press.

Letter to Samuel Huntington, November 2, 1790

NEW HAVEN

Sir

I was honored with your Excellency's Letter of the 29th of last month giving notice that I am duly Elected a Representative of this State in the Congress of the United States, for two years to commence on the fourth day of March next.

I have a high sense of the honor done me by the Free Men of this State, in this repeated mark of their confidence, and do accept the trust, wishing that my services in that important office may merit their approbation.

I am Sir with very great Respect
Your Excellency's Obedient,
humble servant
Roger Sherman

Source: Simon Gratz autograph collection, collection no. 0250A, Historical Society of Pennsylvania.

Letter to William Williams, February 11, 1791

PHILADELPHIA

Dear Sir

I received your much esteemed favour of 1 instant yesterday. I should have commenced a correspondence with you before this time, had it not been that the proceedings and debates in Congress were more fully communicated in the Newspapers than they could be by letter, as well as all other occurrences of importance.

But I seldom see the papers from Connecticut or hear much of the politics of that State; in the time of the war I always received by your letters the most full account of public measures and also of the motives and springs of action from which they originated, and the principal agents by which they were effected, to my great satisfaction. I shall ever retain a grateful remembrance of our former friendship while we were fellow labourers in the common cause of our country in several departments.

I am also very sensible of the Indefatigable exertions of your brother the late sheriff, in the service of the United States, and his sharing in the common calamity by a delay and depreciation of his pay.

Your nephew at Hartford executed the office of Deputy Sheriff to good satisfaction when he attended the Superior Court, and I believe to general satisfaction in other respects, and I wish that the United States may avail themselves of his services, in the collection of the revenue. I am not in the line of appointment to offices, I mentioned him to Mr. Trumbull who concurs with me as to his qualifications. The new revenue Bill has not yet passed the Senate it is like to undergo considerable alterations in that House and what offices will be ultimately established is not yet known to me. I shall bear in mind your request.

You and I have borne the burden & heat of the Day but the most faithful and painful services are soon forgotten when they are past, and young persons are rising up who would be willing to crowd us off of the stage to make room for themselves, but they can't deprive us of the consolation arising from a consciousness of having done our duty.

Source: Williams Family Papers, 1700–1903, Connecticut Historical Society, Hartford, Connecticut.

A Bill for establishing a National Bank has passed both Houses, and a bill to admit Kentucky into the union. Vermont has adopted the Constitution and applied for admission, their application is referred to a committee by each House. This session will end the third day of March. The House of Representatives have passed a Bill fixing the time for the next meeting of Congress to the first Monday in November next.

I am Sir with great respect & esteem

Your Friend & humble servant

Roger Sherman

Letter to Samuel Huntington, November 21, 1791
PHILADELPHIA

Sir,

The President's Speech at the opening of the present session of Congress gives a favourable View of public affairs, and particularly that the revenues are likely to be adequate to their objects, so that no additional burdens need be imposed on the People.

Both branches of Congress are nearly full, and have so arranged the principal business of the session that each have taken a proportion of it, and are forwarding it with the usual dispatch.

The house of Representatives after some days debate, have passed a vote for fixing the number of Representatives, for the next, and succeeding elections, under the present census, at one for every 30,000 Inhabitants, which will make the whole to be about 112. The members were divided on the question 35 being for it & 23 against it, two members that were for a less number, who were present at the debate, were absent when the vote is taken. I understand that some members intend to move to lessen the number when the bill is considered in the House; I am not able to make any conjecture what will be the opinion of the Senate on the subject.

It appears to one that no advantage can be derived from so great an increase of the number, sufficient to countervail the expence, as the jurisdiction of Congress is limited to a few objects that concern the States in general, a less number might give the necessary information, and more conveniently transact the public business. Increasing the number will not increase the *Powers* of that branch of the legislature; but it will lessen the weight and responsibility of each individual member. I wish that the number was so fixed by the constitution as not to be varied by Congress. When the Constitution was formed the number of the Representatives, was in proportion to the number of Senators as five to two. At that rate the Representatives should be increased at the next election to 75, which being apportioned to the several States, would not lessen the number first assigned to Connecticut, nor vary their proportion or suffrage in

Source: Simon Gratz autograph collection, collection no. 0250A, Historical Society of Pennsylvania.

either house, from thus or allowing one Vote to each State. If the Constitution should be altered so as always to preserve the like proportion between the numbers in each house as at first, I think it would be a real amendment; and the expence would be about 40,000 dollars per. *annum* less, than if the amendment heretofore recommended, should be ratified; which sum might be applied toward sinking the national debt.

We have no late accounts from the hostile Indians in the territory Northwest of the Ohio; a treaty with the Cherokee Nation has been lately concluded which will probably secure peace to the southwestern Frontier. Mr. Hammond a Minister, plenipotentiary from his British Majesty has had an audience, and has been announced by the President of the United States.

By the latest accounts from France, the new Constitution of Government has been ratified by the King, and will probably secure to the people of that nation the peaceable enjoyment of Civil and religious liberty; which may probably have a good effect on the other nations of Europe, and strengthen the Alliance between France and these States.

The public papers here contain but little news.—I have enclosed a morning and an evening Paper of this day.

I am Sir with much respect and Esteem
Your Excellency's Obedient
Humble Servant
Roger Sherman

Letter to Samuel Huntington, January 2, 1792
PHILADELPHIA

Sir,

I have received your Letter of the 22^d of last month. I lately conversed with the Secretary of the Treasury on the state of the revenues and expenditures of the United States, and he says, the present revenues will be sufficient to pay all the expenses, and the interest of the foreign and Domestic debts, including the state debts assumed; and that the whole amount of the loans will be applied for sinking the principal, that the foreign debts can be discharged by new loans, so as to lessen the capital sum, and the annual interest. The credit of the funded is very high at present, and our credit abroad is said to be equal to any state in Europe.

The defeat of our Army under General St. Clair is a very sad disaster. I suppose their march into the wilderness to establish a Port at or near the Miame Town was in consequence of a plan concocted at the seat of government, how much was left to the General's discretion, I am not informed. The ultimate object was to secure the frontier settlements and to induce the Indians to make a treaty of peace.

I fear it will be more difficult to attain that end now than before the expedition. I believe the future measures to be taken are not yet determined on.

The Legislature of Virginia have ratified the Amendments of the Constitution so that they are now become a part of the Constitution, having been ratified by eleven States. The Bill for fixing the number of Representatives and apportioning them among the States was lost between the two houses.

The legislature of Pennsylvania can't yet agree upon the mode of chusing a Senator to Congress, the Representatives contend for a joint vote of the members of the two branches, and the Senate for a concurrent vote. It appears clearly to me that the Senate are right in their opinion.

Enclosed is a Pamphlet containing an account of the number Inhabitants in the counties & other lesser districts in the several States.

Source: Miscellaneous Bound Collection, Massachusetts Historical Society.

The depredations and distresses in the French Islands are very great, and evince the impolicy of the slave-trade, and I hope it will be a warning to them & others concerned in it to discontinue it, and totally to abolish slavery in due time.[1]

The President has nominated Thomas Pinkney of South Carolina to be a Minister plenepotentiary to the Court of Great Britain, and Governeur Morris a Minister of the same grade to the Court of France, and Mr. Short now Charge de Affairs of France, to be a resident Minister at the Hague. The Senate have several days had the matter under consideration but have not yet given their opinion.

There may be some probability of obtaining a treaty of former with Great Britain if a Minister should be sent there, and possibly the obstacles which prevent carrying the Treaty of peace into full effect may be removed.

But I do not think it will be for the interest of the United States to support Ministers at Foreign Courts where they have no special business to transact.

---

1. This sentence was written and then crossed out by Sherman. —Ed.

Letter to Samuel Huntington, March 7, 1792

PHILADELPHIA

Sir,

I received your letter of the 24th of last Month. A Bill has passed into a law, making further provision for the protection of the frontier settlements, authorizing the President to raise three additional regiments if he shall judge it necessary. The whole is left very much to his discretion, the additional forces are to be discharged as soon as peace can be made with the hostile Indians . . . I suppose that every reasonable endeavor will be made to attain that desirable end.

Congress [intends?] to close this session by the first tuesday of April next, and ordered an arrangement of the business to be reported by a committee of both Houses. Their report is contained in the enclosed paper—one half of the matters contained in the report as necessary to be finished this session, have been already acted upon in one or both Houses.

We have no foreign news remarkable, except a letter from the King in France informing, that he has accepted the new constitution, & expressing his friendship to the United States.

I received a Letter yesterday from Capt. Seth Harding dated at Cape Francis 6th of February last. He writes that the people there are in a very distressed situation, and he can see no reason why it will not continue so, for a long time, the Negros kill, burn & destroy all before them, and have the sole command of the country—there has been upwards of two thousand white people killed, the number of blacks that have been killed is uncertain. He says 500 troops have arrived from France, but in his opinion 12000 would not be sufficient to subdue the Negros.

This shews the bad effects of slavery and I hope it will tend to its abolition.

The enclosed Federal Gazette contains a law regulating the Election of President and Vice President of the United States. The Bill for fixing the

Source: William Buell Sprague autograph collection, collection no. 0623, Historical Society of Pennsylvania.

number of Representatives is not yet finished—one passed the House and was negatived by the Senate—another on the same principles has passed the House of Representatives and is now before the Senate.

I am with great Respect

Your Excellency's obedient, humble servant,

Roger Sherman

Letter to Samuel Huntington, May 8, 1792

PHILADELPHIA

SIR,—The Congress will close their session this day. It has been about six weeks longer than I at first expected. Many bills have been passed of a public nature, and considerable time has been spent on private applications. Measures have been taken to lessen that branch of business in future, by enabling the executive departments to give relief. The first bill that passed the two Houses for fixing the number of Representatives at one hundred and twenty was disapproved by the President; that is the only instance in which he has exercised his power of negative. The last act fixes the number at one hundred and five, allowing the State of Connecticut to choose seven. The Indian war has made it necessary to increase the imposts on some articles, part of which is limited to two years. Measures will be taken by the Executive to obtain a conference with the hostile tribes of Indians in order to settle a permanent peace.

The enclosed paper contains a copy of the law for regulating the Militia of the several States. Another act is passed for calling them into service on necessary occasions, which I have not a copy of, but all the laws will soon be transmitted to your Excellency officially by the Secretary of State. Mr Thomas Pinckney who is appointed Minister to the Court of Great Britain is now in this city. He says he expects to embark for London within about six weeks. I don't learn that much progress has been made in any negotiations with the British Minister here. If we could get possession of the Western Posts, I believe it would be a favorable circumstance for obtaining and preserving peace with the Indians. I am Sir with the most perfect respect,

Your Excellency's obedient humble servant,

ROGER SHERMAN.

Source: Simon Gratz autograph collection, collection no. 0250A, Historical Society of Pennsylvania.

Letter to Samuel Huntington, December 10, 1792

PHILADELPHIA

Sir,

Enclosed is a Plan reported by the Secretary of Treasury for paying a part of the principal of the national debt, the report has not yet been considered by Congress. I think it would be a desirable object to pay the public debt as fast as circumstances will admit, without resorting to taxes that will be inconvenient to the people.

If peace could be made with the hostile Indians, perhaps the present revenues might pay the principal of the six percent funded debt as fast as the Law will admit. By accounts lately received from the chiefs of the six nations who were at the late council of the Indian Tribes Northwest of the Ohio, the hostile Indians have agreed to hold a conference next spring with the United States— in order to settle a peace, and that hostilities shall cease in the mean time.

The commissioners for settling accounts between the United States & the Individual States have reported that they can complete the settlement with in the time limited by the law made for that purpose. Your Excellency has a view of the present state of public affairs; in the President's speech, and the proceedings of Congress are published at large in the news papers.

The Electors in N. Jersey, Pennsylvania, Delaware & Maryland have been unanimous in voting for George Washington & John Adams for President and Vice President (except one in this state who did not vote for Mr. Adams).

It is probable that Congress may rise in February, soon after the Election of President and Vice President. The latest accounts from France are dated the last of September. Important news is daily expected from that country.

I am with great respect
Your Excellency's obedient,
humble servant,
Roger Sherman

Source: Simon Gratz autograph collection, collection no. 0250A, Historical Society of Pennsylvania.

Letter from George Washington to Roger Sherman, March 1, 1793

The President of the United States to Roger Sherman, Senator for the State of Connecticut

Certain matters touching the public good, requiring that the Senate shall be convened on Monday the 4th instant, you are desired to attend at the Senate Chamber in Philadelphia on that day, then and there to receive and deliberate on such communications as shall be made to you on my part.

Source: Miscellaneous Bound Collection, Massachusetts Historical Society.

Debates in Congress

Miscellaneous

When the House of Representatives began meeting in March 1789, it faced several major tasks and numerous minor ones. This section includes accounts of speeches Sherman gave on a variety of topics. In many cases I include comments from his colleagues to provide context. The speech on Gouverneur Morris's appointment as minister to France was recorded by New York senator Rufus King (1755–1857).

Congressional Chaplains

29 April 1789

Mr. SHERMAN moved, that the House now proceed to the nomination and choice of a Chaplain—upon which it was voted, that Friday next, be the time assigned for the choice, and in the mean time that nominations be made.

Mr. LAURANCE nominated, Reverend Doctor JOHN ROGERS.

Mr. GOODHUE nominated, Reverend Mr. LINN.

Source: *DHFFC,* 10: 332. © 1992 Johns Hopkins University Press. Reprinted by permission of Johns Hopkins University Press.

2 May 1789

On motion of Mr. Sherman, the house proceeded to the order of the day, viz. The appointment of a Chaplain to the house of Representatives and on calling up the ballots it appeared that the

Rev. Mr. Wm. Lynn, had 27 votes.

Rev. Mr. Rogers, 19.

Wherefore the Rev. Mr. Lynn was declared to be duly appointed, and the Clerk was directed to notify the Senate thereof, and then the house adjourned till Monday next, in order to give the committee time to bring forward business.

Source: *DHFFC*, 10: 391. © 1992 Johns Hopkins University Press. Reprinted by permission of Johns Hopkins University Press.

Oaths

6 May 1789

On motion of Mr. Sherman, the house took into consideration the amendments of the Senate, to the bill for regulating the time and manner of administering certain oaths.

On the following amendment, viz. Be it enacted, That the members of the several state legislatures, and all executive and judicial officers of the several states, who have been heretofore chosen or appointed, or who shall be chosen or appointed before the first day of August next, and who shall then be in office, shall within one month thereafter, take the same oath or affirmation, except where they shall have taken it before; which may be administered by any person authorised by the law of the state in which such office shall be holden, to administer oaths. And the members of the several state legislatures, and all executive and judicial officers of the several states, who shall be chosen or appointed after the said first day of August, shall, before they proceed to execute the duties of their respective offices, take the foregoing oath or affirmation, which shall be administered by the person or persons, who by the law of the state shall be authorised to administer the oath of office, and the person or persons so administering the oath hereby required to be taken, shall cause a record or certificate thereof to be made, in the same manner as by the law of the state, he or they shall be directed to record or certify the oath of office.
. . .

MR. SHERMAN

Was not afraid of being charged with inconsistency, he had voted against a similar clause when the bill was before the house, but he was convinced now of its propriety, he thought it more eligible to have a general provision for taking the oath, than particular ones. It also appeared necessary to point out the oath itself, as well as the time and manner of taking it—no other legislature is competent to all these purposes; but if they were, there is a propriety in the

Source: *DHFFC,* 10: 481, 486. © 1992 Johns Hopkins University Press. Reprinted by permission of Johns Hopkins University Press.

supreme legislature's doing it. At the same time, if the state legislatures take it up, it cannot operate disagreeably upon them, to find all their neighbouring states obliged to join them in supporting a measure they approve. What a state legislature may do, will be good as far as it goes; on the same principle, the constitution will apply to each individual of the state officers, they may go without the direction of the state legislature to a Justice and take the oath voluntarily; this I suppose would be binding upon them—but this is not satisfactory, the government ought to know that the oath has been properly taken, and this can only be done by a general regulation. If it is in the discretion of the state legislatures to make laws to carry the declaration of the constitution into execution, they have the power of refusing, and may avoid the positive injunctions of the constitution. As our power in this particular extends over the whole union, it is most proper for us to take the subject up and make the proper provision for carrying it into execution, to the intention of the constitution.

John Adams

17 September 1789

Mr. SHERMAN, in the conversation on this motion, observed that he had a high esteem for the person of the present Vice President, as a man of abilities, integrity and patriotism. His eminent services during the whole course of the late contest, were a sufficient eulogium, and rendered any other unnecessary. He had, he said, in an uncommon degree, one virtue which was rarely found; a faculty of uniting dignity with oeconomy. He thought therefore that it was unnecessary, at present, to allow the Vice President so large a salary as six thousand dollars, especially, considering the present low state of our finances.

Source: *DHFFC*, II: 1479. © 1992 Johns Hopkins University Press. Reprinted by permission of Johns Hopkins University Press.

NATIONAL CAPITAL

28 September 1789

The house then proceeded to consider the amendments proposed by the senate, to the bill for establishing the seat of government of the United States.

Mr. Sherman.

In our deliberations on this occasion, we should have an eye to the general accommodation of the union, and the best way of defraying the expence. The place fixed upon by the senate, he presumed, was known to the members generally; hence they were able to judge of its eligibility at the first view: It certainly possessed some advantages over the other situation; and, he believed, it was as central, if not more so, than the Susquehanna, as it respected the present inhabitants; the air, and soil, in that neighborhood, were quite as agreeable as the other. But there was an access, by water, from every part of the United States, which furnished a very great convenience; but beside this, those who came from the southern states, had generally an inland navigation, with a short distance to come by land from the Head of Elk; so the citizens of the eastern states, in the like manner, would be accommodated by coming thro' the Sound, and crossing to Amboy, on which route they would have but about 70 miles land carriage; a distance nearly equal with the other. He admitted that Germantown was not quite so near to the Western Territory as the Susquehanna was; but he contemplated a very distant day before it would be settled, and much longer before the inhabitants would have frequent occasion of travelling to the seat of government. Added to the advantages he had mentioned, there were good buildings, and convenience for arsenals and ship-yards, with abundance of artificers on the spot; these considerations, taken together, induced him to think it best to concur with the senate.

With respect to the change which the senate had proposed, in the mode of obtaining the money requisite to defray the expence of raising the public buildings, he thought it a prudent alteration, considering the present situation of

Source: *DHFFC*, ɪɪ: 1510–12. © 1992 Johns Hopkins University Press. Reprinted by permission of Johns Hopkins University Press.

the treasury: The senate, no doubt, considering this circumstance, as well as that the state of Pennsylvania would be benefited by this selection, beyond her equal proportion; and that she ought, therefore, to contribute something for the advantage it procured her.

Mr. Smith [*Md.?*]

Thought the honorable gentleman rather inconsistent in his argument to-day. If he recollected right, the gentleman had formerly urged in favor of the Susquehanna, that it was not accessible by vessels from sea; and now he recommends this quality as an advantage in favor of the Delaware. The gentleman admits, that this position is not quite so near the Western Territory, as the one chosen by the house; but then, he thinks no inconvenience will arise, inasmuch that it will be some years before it is peopled: But how does this comport with the principle laid down by an almost unanimous vote of the house? At the beginning of this business, we declared that a due regard should be had to the Western Territory; he now tells us, as an argument in favor of the senate's amendment, that we should have no regard to it at all. He thinks the change made in the manner of obtaining the money favorable; but what advantage will accrue to the United States from Pennsylvania's granting 100,000 dollars, when congress will have to purchase the land on which they are to sit down? Land, in the neighborhood of Philadelphia, he had been told, was worth 40 or 50l. an acre. The 100,000 dollars, given by Pennsylvania, would not go far in a purchase at this rate. He thought the government would have a better bargain in buying cheap lands on the Susquehanna; or, perhaps, they might have been got there for nothing. He thought this alteration unfavorable to the public treasury, which could illy supply such a demand upon it.

But he had an objection which would go against fixing in the neighborhood of any large city. The federal town would, in such case, be no more than a suburb. Could any one expect Germantown to rival Philadelphia? No, it would be swallowed up in it. The public ministers, and all the officers of government, that could afford it, would reside in Philadelphia; for they are generally found to prefer a large, handsome, well-built city to a small village. Now, he would submit whether it was consistent with the dignity of the nation to place themselves in such a situation? Beside, the state of Pennsylvania had fixed boundaries, into which they would not admit congress; should the house, then, to shew their deference and respect to her, go precisely to those boundaries, and say they are content? Why, if Germantown is central, do we not say we will go to Philadelphia; that city would undoubtedly afford more accommodation, and could be but five miles short of the centre? No, we are not to go there, because the state of Pennsylvania has proscribed us; we must go to the very line she has marked out for us, and accept her cession upon her own terms. It would be more consistent with the dignity of congress to select the place, and wait where we are well accommodated, till the state should consent to give it.

He hoped the large majority which had agreed to the Susquehanna, would continue firm, and not suffer a dereliction of the object they had so ably supported.

Mr. Sherman

Begged to answer a few words to the gentleman; he was charged with inconsistency, because he had said the Susquehanna was safe from vessels of war; but this was not an objection, in his mind, to any place; he only mentioned it to obviate the objection in the minds of those who entertained it: For his part, he did not fear the effects of an invasion; because, he believed, and trusted, that many years would pass away before the United States were involved again in war. The gentleman might also remember, that the eastern members always thought the Susquehanna south and westward of the true centre, but were content to go that far for the sake of accommodation; but now the senate had agreed with them in that opinion, he thought it but reasonable to meet them, and adopt their proposition.

NEWSPAPERS

8 July 1790

On motion of Mr. Sherman, the House went into committee on the engrossed bill from the Senate, concerning the residence of government.

The first section of the bill being read,

Mr. *Sherman* said he wished to have it explained. It ought to be made appear that the Potowmack would be the most proper and convenient place for the seat of government. To him it appeared too far to the southward to be considered either as the centre of population or of territory. He supposed the centre of population would be not far from Philadelphia. He was willing, however, for the sake of accommodation to go to a place southward of the centre, that is, to Baltimore. He then moved that the words "On the River Potowmack at some place between the Eastern branch [*Anacostia*] and Connogocheague" should be obliterated, in order to insert "the town of Baltimore."

Mr. *Burke* seconded the motion.

Mr. *Lee* wished to know, in case the gentleman's motion should succeed, what place was intended as a temporary residence.

Mr. *Sherman* replied, that he was willing to go to Philadelphia, as soon as it should appear proper to do so. He thought, however, that the government ought to remain some time longer at New-York, and he urged several reasons tending to prove that the present time was not a proper one for removing the seat of government.

Source: *DHFFC*, 13: 1634–35. © 1995 Johns Hopkins University Press. Reprinted by permission of Johns Hopkins University Press.

17 April 1790

The report of the committee on the accounts presented by the printers for newspapers supplied the house was taken up.

Mr. SHERMAN moved that the report be accepted.

Mr. GERRY observed that a free press is of the greatest importance to the people, and all proper encouragement ought to be given it; that the practice of Congress in taking the newspapers upon a liberal plan conduced to this object; that the most beneficial consequences had resulted to the government from that information which their constituents had received thro this medium. Gentlemen have observed that persons at the seat of government derive an advantage from the early intelligence which that circumstance enables them to obtain—but it will not be denied that all parts of the union have as good a right to political intelligence, as the spot where Congress happens to be; no mode of conveying this intelligence can be devised which is attended with so much facility as this: and no citizen can grudge the expence; it does not amount perhaps to more than the fraction of a farthing, on an average. The information conveyed through this channel has afforded the greatest satisfaction to our constituents—it is expected from us, and is what they have a right to—and so great has been the anxiety on some occasions for news from Congress, in some of the towns in the Eastern States, that I have been informed (said he) that half a dollar has been given for a newspaper. The last session of Congress, complaints were made of the partiality and misrepresentations of the printers, and justly; in their accounts of the debates some of the members were held up in a ridiculous point of light and great injustice was done thro the inaccuracy of those partial publications. This session matters have been better conducted; the debates have been more impartially handed to the public—the printers publish on both sides, and are willing to correct their mistakes. If no other advantage was to be derived from a general encouragement—this freedom and impartiality being obtained, is a sufficient indemnification for the trifling ex-

Source: *DHFFC*, 13: 1019–21. © 1995 Johns Hopkins University Press. Reprinted by permission of Johns Hopkins University Press.

pence. If one or two printers only, were to have public encouragement; or the exclusive printing of newspapers for Congress—it would preclude the public in all probability from that full and impartial information to which they are entitled; it would tend to giving the house an undue controul over the press, or perhaps make it the tool of a party. Mr. Gerry made many other remarks, and concluded by observing, with respect to any saving to the public—the expence was so trifling compared to the advantage, that he thought it a very contemptible object of economy, in a national point of view; and moved to reject the clause which proposed that Congress should not be supplied with any more papers at the public expence.

Mr. BENSON said he hoped the resolution would be agreed to with an amendment, which he moved, by striking out what relates to supplying the Senate; he was for leaving that part of the business to themselves; he gave a short account of the origin of Congress being supplied with papers. Under the old confederation he said, Congress was considered as a diplomatic body—the members were amenable to the States who sent them; Congress could not compel their punctual attendance—hence the expedient of taking the papers to keep the members together, from the time of meeting, till they formed a house; but he observed this did not apply to the present Congress, who are a differently organized body, and the introduction of newspapers interrupted public business. He adverted to the odd appearance the charge must make in the account of public expences.

Mr. SMITH (S.C.) offered a variety of observations to shew the ill policy of adopting the report—enlarged on the advantages derived to the people from the diffusion of the information contained in the newspapers which were transmitted by the members.

Mr. SHERMAN observed that he did not particularly recollect the origin of Congress taking the newspapers, but the punctuality of the members at present rendered any such expedient unnecessary. He objected to the papers being read in Congress; but if it is thought necessary that Congress should be supplied with the papers as heretofore, the members may receive them at their lodgings, and there they may read them before they come to Congress; as to the observation that the printers are more impartial this session than they were the last—he did not think there was much in that—he thought that they had always aimed to be impartial—he conceived it was for their interest to be so; it is true they are liable to commit errors, and some have been printed in the debates, but when they have been pointed out, they were willing to publish corrections, and in many cases have done it. He did not think that the members sending the papers to their constituents conduced so much to diffuse information, as the republications which took place in consequence of the printers sending their papers to each other; this answered the purpose to much greater extent.

The motion for striking out what relates to the Senate, was negatived.

The question being divided—the first part of the report respecting payment for the papers was agreed to—the latter part was negatived.

In committee of the whole on the bill to regulate the post-office of the United States.

The committee made considerable progress in the discussion of the bill but did not finish it.

Appointment of Gouverneur Morris

January 1792

Speech of Mr. Sherman.

Some observations respecting Mr. Morris' appointment having been already made, I shall explain the reasons why I shall not vote for his appointment, and that I may not be misunderstood I shall class my remarks under two heads, one having respect to Mr. Morris' natural capacity, & the other his moral character.

I ought in the first place to observe, that I bear Mr. Morris no ill will—I have personally known him for several years; I have served with him in Congress, & was with him in the Convention of 1787. I have never been borne down by his superior Talents, nor have I experienced any mortifications from the manner in which he has treated me in debate. I wish him and all mankind holy and happy. I allow that he possesses a sprightly mind, a ready apprehension, and that he is capable of writing a good letter and forming a good Draft. I never have heard that he has betrayed a Trust, or that he lacks integrity—indeed I have not known him in any individually responsible station—In the State Legislature, in Congress, & in the Convention of 1787, he was one of many, and in the office of Finance his principal was responsible, and nothing for or against him can be inferred from these stations.

With regard to his moral character, I consider him an irreligious and profane man—he is no hypocrite and never pretended to have any religion. He makes religion the subject of ridicule and is profane in his conversation. I do not think the public have as much security from such men as from godly and honest men—It is a bad example to promote such characters; and although they may never have betrayed a trust, or exhibited proofs of a want of integrity, and although they may be called men of honor—yet I would not put my trust in them—I am unwilling that the country should put their Trust in them, and because they have not already done wrong, I feel no security that they will not do wrong in future. General Arnold was an irreligious and profane character—

Source: *The Life and Correspondence of Rufus King* (New York: G. P. Putnam's Sons, 1894), I: 419–21.

he was called a man of honor, but I never had any confidence in him, nor did I ever join in promoting him. I remember he sued a man at New Haven for saying he had the foul disease—and it was urged that the Jury should give heavy damages, because Arnold was a man of honor and high-minded—but this same Arnold betrayed his Trust when he had an opportunity and would have delivered up the Commander in chief & betrayed his country. And the like has happened from other such characters; and I am against their being employed and shall therefore vote against Mr. Morris.

Monroe. His manners not conciliatory—his character well known & considered as indiscreet—upon the grounds of character he was twice refused as a Member of the Treasury board, once at Trenton & afterwards at New York—Besides he is a monarchy man & not suitable to be employed by this country, nor in France. He went to Europe to sell lands and Certificates.

Burr. I merely state a fact. It has been asserted and without any injunction of secresy, that Mr. Morris conducted himself so offensively in his intercourse with the Eng. Ministers, that they were offended & refused, after an abrupt breaking up of an interview, to renew it.

Vote on Gov. Morris's Appointment to Paris.

Ayes.	*No.*
N. H. Langdon	Wingate N. H.
R. I. Foster	Strong Mass.
Con. Ellsworth	Cabot same
N. Y. King	Stanton R. I.
N. J. Rutherford	Sherman Con.
N. I. Dickinson	Burr N. Y.
Penn. Morris	Robinson Vermt.
Del. Read	Monroe Virg.
Del. Basset	Lee
Mard. Henry	Few Georg.
Mard. Carroll	Gunn same—11.
N. C. Johnson	
N. C. Hawkins	☞ Govr. Morris Appt.
S. C. Izard	Min to France
S. C. Butler—16	Jany. 1792

Excerpts from Congressional Debates over the Scope of National Power

One of the most contentious issues at the Federal Convention, during the ratification debates, and in the first federal Congress was the extent of the national government's power. The following passages offer some insight into Sherman's position on this question.

20 April 1789

HUNTINGTON: Made a long time ago, a discovery from observation that—from Cook's observations of variation of compass and by spheric trigonometry, 14 degrees from the poles of the earth. It was not a discovery of Cook, taken up by others. He is the person who first made the calculation. The degree of longitude. It is so easy to use. This intersection being calculated and reduced to tables will bring the longitude—The only difficulty is, need observation of variations. Unless the needle interrupted, in general the principle true. This being done, that by a table calculated showing the degrees of magnitude will point to the degree of longitude. Not strange not discovered before. The variations long known. The motion of the magnet is late discovery. He merits no further than presuming on rules of trigonometry. He has discovered the theory of the revolution of ———. So much is certainly the fact. His desire of going to Baffin's Bay is this: The magnetic point is within the compass of that bay. I have no imagination discover the visible thing. But no doubt if had the opportunity of going there with proper instruments he might make discovery that useful. Had no imagination that any great immediate advantage would arise from it.

SHERMAN: I had opportunity to view the map and globe, the principle of scheme. There is something ingenious. If the needle will point directly at this magnetic point, considerable use made in ascertaining the longitude. It as yet uncertain, and I don't think a voyage to the north would make a discovery that would help the matter. It would be ascertained by taking observations in different parts of globe, comparing these observations to matters could be ascertained. It appears gone as far as proper to go at this time, as far as warranted by the Constitution. This report of committee will show that they supposed his discovery worthy attention and giving the exclusive right to benefit by the discovery. If have a right to go further and lay out money it must be upon—

Source: *DHFFC*, 10: 212–13. © 1992 Johns Hopkins University Press. Reprinted by permission of Johns Hopkins University Press.

Gentleman has fruitful invention. Large sums might be expended which finally might be to no advantage. The committee thought fit to go as far as this to promote the progress; they did not think proper to give any further power to encourage this useful discovery.

SHERMAN: It is—

TUCKER: Divide the question.

3 February 1790

MR. SHERMAN

Thought that the interests of the state, where the emigrant intended to reside, ought to be consulted, as well as the interests of the general government. He presumed it was intended by the convention, who framed the constitution, that the congress should have the power of naturalization, in order to prevent particular states receiving citizens, and forcing them upon others, who would not have received them in any other manner; it was therefore meant to guard against an improper mode of naturalization, rather than receive them upon easier terms than those pursued by the several states. Now, the regulation provided for in this bill, entitles all free white persons, which includes emigrants, and even those who are likely to become chargeable; it certainly never would be undertaken by congress, to compel the states to receive, and support this class of persons; it would therefore be necessary, that some clause should be added to the bill to counteract such a general proposition.

Source: *DHFFC*, 12: 147. © 1995 Johns Hopkins University Press. Reprinted by permission of Johns Hopkins University Press.

5 May 1790

Mr. Gerry suggested the propriety of reading those reports on petitions, from the heads of departments, which negative the prayers of such petitions, as well as those in favor of granting them—as, he observed, the contrary practice is in fact delegating a very extraordinary power to executive officers. After some debate Mr. Gerry submitted the following proposition in substance—"That the reports on memorials and petitions not determined upon in one session may be called up in a subsequent session."

On motion of Mr. Smith, (S.C.) that part of the President's speech which respects the encouragement of science and literature was read. He then moved that it should be referred to a select committee.

Mr. Stone enquired what part of the Constitution authorised Congress to take any steps in a business of this kind—for his part he knew of none. We have already done as much as we can with propriety—We have encouraged learning, by giving to authors an exclusive privilege of vending their works—this is going as far as we have power to, by the Constitution.

Mr. Sherman said that a proposition to vest Congress with power to establish a National University was made in the General Convention—but it was negatived—It was thought sufficient that this power should be exercised by the States in their separate capacity.

Mr. Page observed, that he was in favor of the motion. He wished to have the matter determined whether Congress has or has not a right to do anything for the promotion of science and literature—He rather supposed they had such a right—but if on investigation of the subject, it shall appear they have not, I should consider the circumstance said he, as a very essential defect in the Constitution—and should be for proposing an amendment—for on the diffusion of knowledge and literature depend the liberties of this country, and the preservation of the Constitution.

The House adjourned without a decision on this motion.

Source: *DHFFC*, 13: 1220–21. © 1995 Johns Hopkins University Press. Reprinted by permission of Johns Hopkins University Press.

3 June 1790

[*Committee report on the petition of John F. Amelung*]

CARROLL: In favor of Amelung.

SMITH: Oppose it because it goes too far. They too hasty and precipitate. Congress can borrow money but can't lend any. It a matter of doubt whether right to lend money. Soon exhaust the twelve million that ordered to borrow. The gentlemen moved a considerable impost to imported glass to encourage this manufacture. Said they would derive benefit from that manufacture. This reason the matter improper.

SHERMAN: Don't think authorized by the Constitution to advance money for this purpose. Particularly can't advance money for encouragement of useful arts. But if had authority it not proper to use it on this occasion. We involved in debt and agreed to a loan yesterday of twelve million. We want to hire money, to (deliver) creditors of their debts. If to undertake to advance money to encourage projects of any kind, set example, don't know where to stop. The Congress was very doubtful of advancing money. It was moved to have power to open canals beneficial to inland navigation but Congress would not agree to it. Two glass works in C[onnecticut]. G[overnment] raised 1300 for each toward assisting them. If anything done the particular state should offer the assistance. Give great uneasiness to advance money in one state to encourage— That matter inexpedient and we not in condition to advance money.

CARROLL: A member of the committee and if I was to go into the history of proceedings of that committee and make an inference of what the committee—from what actually passed there, the house would be as little inclined to (bow to) assumption of state debts as to act on this subject now. However, waive saying anything on this subject because the letter and spirit our sole guide. The gentleman contends that the power of this house to assume the state debts is under that clause of Constitution which (goes generally to duty). Duties for the general welfare (new/now).

Source: *DHFFC*, 13: 1539–41. © 1995 Johns Hopkins University Press. Reprinted by permission of Johns Hopkins University Press.

SHERMAN: The sentiment I held was that state debts were debts of United States.

CARROLL: The sentiment laid down would bear out in this case. Did not understand there was difficulty on the subject. Gentlemen will be cautious before they determine upon it. Anxious as I am that this manufacture should succeed, if doubt of the Constitutionality, I should relinquish readily, but as we are proceeding on this business and not that sentiment, hope duly considered and made proposition of the house. The gentlemen from South Carolina and Connecticut have observed that these objects are principally attended to by the several states. Something done in Connecticut. Maryland has given encouragement to this very manufacture. They granted loan of money and exempted its property from taxation. But when entered into this confederation, it was not expected that the manufactures were to be protected and brought to perfection by the particular states, but looked up to this government for assistance. Temporary aid of states but of little value compared with the action of the legislature.

VINING: States what Mr. Carroll stated, that policy to encourage these by bounties. Suppose this man to suspend his operation for the want of three thousand pounds. I ask if impolitic to give it? It of public benefit and advantage. It happens to be in one state. The success of manufacture—It must bring manufactures of all kinds, to settle far country, to establish manufactures and prevent enormous importation. This encouragement proper. Does it say will not lend money? Suppose money to ———. When debts paid we may have more money than applies to exigencies. Suppose a country (that settled, if in war) and suppose that government wants money. Has not every country that power? Necessary to existence. Are afraid to encourage manufactures lest discourage British commerce. I wish to provide everything that can. The true wealth of country lies in manufactures and agriculture. Wish to meet people as they meet us, to encourage immigration and get here all kinds of trades. What sum is it? Is it too much? Are you afraid of future applications? Can't claim the advantage of principle because very few cases like this can occur. If have a right and ability we will lend this man. Can't be done as well by the states. They not (advance) in their powers. It the general utility of the object which congress ought to consider. If deserve encouragement will receive it. That the first instance and will receive that consideration from the house which it deserves. Can't conceive unconstitutional. They must be left to the wisdom of judges.

BOUDINOT: Duty to examine every circumstance. If matter rightly understood to be viewed in different point of light. It requires attention of the house. This man came from Germany. Consider the effect of failure on immigration. He expended his capital—large quantity of capital. Not establish a correspondent throughout the states. He now doing that. ——— ——— fears the high price of grain. What the consequence of stopping him? We have 500 persons turned loose without employ. Have discouragement held up to every kind—If Constitution in the way, refuse him. But if this true, we guilty of unconstitutional advantages. What is bounty to—Have we not had it in favor of particular manufactures? Collect taxes for general welfare. Is not this providing for it in particular manner? View it another point of light. We raise by impost a certain sum to pay the interest of our debt. This money we told must come into treasury. Any injury to suffer part of this money to go to use? We depend on foreigners for this manufacture, must be useful. So to be wished could establish a manufacture of this kind (in every state) by loan of 8000 dollars. From examination into circumstances formed a (conception) of importance of it and effect on your revenue, the increase of population, etc. Should encourage him. It set up on waste land near mountains. It settling that part of country which not fit for purpose of agriculture. Five hundred people a great object.

VINING: It was unanimously thought a proper principle that congress should give something to the Baron. Can congress give and can't lend? It would be absurd. Another thing the C[onstitution] says, (United States will pay your debts; we will not be paid our debts). I appeal to the candor of that gentleman. Though as a gratuity he would give him something, not as bargain or contract. Will he give in one case and not lend in another? We could borrow for 4 and lend for 6.

SHERMAN: The general welfare extended to everything. I look on it restrictive clause because they have the powers only herein granted. Though the power given to congress to raise armies yet they will not do unless for the general welfare.

8 February 1791

The bill for incorporating the subscribers of the bank, which was sent from the Senate, under consideration. On the question—shall the bill pass.

Mr. WILLIAMSON moved to commit the first section for the purpose of altering the time or manner of subscribing, so that the holders of State securities, assumed to be paid by the United States, may be on a footing with the holders of other securities, formerly called National Securities.

If April was the time fixed for opening the subscription, he conceived that the holders of State securities would not have it in their power to partake of the advantage of making their first payment in evidences of the assumed debt; because it cannot be ascertained before the beginning of October, whether the sum limited by law for the subscription of each State, would include the whole of their state paper. If they became subscribers, they would labour under the disadvantage, he conceived, of laying down the first payment all in hard cash.

Mr. FITZSIMONS said that each subscriber to the bank, to the amount of 2000 dollars, by paying 500 dollars, had two years given him for the payment of the remaining 1500.

Mr. WILLIAMSON agreed that this was the case, yet the holder of continental paper would still have it in his power to lay down one fourth of the first payment in cash, and the remainder in paper.

Mr. LAURANCE remarked that if this inconvenience really existed it was small compared to that of putting off the time of subscribing to the bank. But he thought it could be obviated by regulations at the Treasury.

Mr. SHERMAN conceived that this plan of a National Bank had not been thought of for the benefit of individuals. It was intended to be of public benefit, and he conceived its execution should not be deferred because a few individuals might suffer some trifling inconvenience by its being carried into immediate execution. But he said the sum to be subscribed was so considerable that many months would elapse before the subscription would be full, and this would

Source: *DHFFC*, 14: 382–83. © 1996 Johns Hopkins University Press. Reprinted by permission of Johns Hopkins University Press.

allow sufficient time to the holders of state paper to become subscribers with every advantage.

Mr. LEE said he thought it the duty of the House to take every possible step to facilitate the admission of subscribers from every part of the Union, in order to render the advantage to be derived from a concern in the bank more generally diffused. He therefore conceived that a provision to entitle each state, for a certain time, to subscribe to the bank for a certain amount, proportioned to their representation or population, would be expedient. By this means he conceived that if this bank was to have any influence in government, it would not be confined to the spot in which it was established, but be collected from every part of the union. Great advantage, at any rate, would undoubtedly be derived to holders of continental paper, who might become subscribers to the bank, from receiving the interest of their paper as creditors of the United States, and also their dividend for the same paper as stock-holders in the bank. They would receive 10 per cent. upon the whole on that property. If this was the case every citizen, he thought, should have an equal chance for a share in this advantage; and the subscription book should not be opened to receive, without limitation, the vast quantity of funded stock, collected in the cities of New-York and Philadelphia, to the exclusion of holders of securities in the more remote cities and states. If no limiting provision of the kind he proposed was adopted, the bill he was convinced would breed discontent. He did not wish to sound an alarm; but thought it his duty to express his opinion that gentlemen might be on their guard before they pursued a measure so evidently partial, and which he feared would occasion discontent and confusion.

Note to James Madison, 1791

During the debate over the constitutionality of a national bank, Sherman passed the following note to James Madison. Madison apparently inserted "a necessary &" (in brackets below) in front of "a proper measure" and returned the note to Sherman.

You will admit that Congress have power to provide by law, for raising, de-positing & applying money for the purposes enumerated in the constitution, & generally of regulating the Finances.

That they have power so far as no particular rules are pointed out, in the constitution to make such rules & regulations as they may Judge necessary & proper to effect these purposes. The only question that remains is—Is a Bank a [a necessary &] proper measure for effecting these purposes? And is not this a question of expediency rather than of right?

[Note in a different hand:]

Feb. 4, 1791. This handed to J. M. by Mr. Sherman during the debate on the constitutionality of the Bill for a National Bank. The line marked X given up by him on the objection of J. M.[1] The interlineation of "*a necessary &*" by J. M. to which he gave no answer other than a smile.

Source: Roger Sherman (1721–93) Collection (MS 447), box 1, folder 21, Manuscripts and Archives, Yale University Library.

1. The line referred to reads, "& generally of regulating the Finances." —Ed.

Finances

The new federal government had to resolve the issue of state debts from the War for Independence and find revenue for the national government. Many in Congress saw the western lands as an important source of revenue for the United States, but the government also had to adopt a policy for making this land available to settlers. Sherman was intimately involved in these debates, as suggested by the following excerpts.

Public Credit/State Debt

28 January 1790

MR. SHERMAN

Hoped the business would be conducted in such a way, as to be concluded before the end of the present session. As to obtaining the sense of the state legislatures, he did not think that a necessary thing. The people appointed the members of this house, and their situation enabled them to consult and judge better what was for the public good, than a number of distinct parts, void of relative information, and under the influence of local views. He supposed that congress contained all the information necessary to determine this, or any other national question. As to the first observation of the gentleman from Georgia, that speculations had been carried on to a great extent, he had only to observe, that this had been the case from the time when the public securities were first issued, and he supposed it would continue to be done, until the holders were satisfied with what was done to secure the payment.

As to the state debts, it was a subject which he apprehended would not be ultimately decided, till the sense of the people was generally known, and on this occasion, it might be well to be acquainted with the sense of the state legislatures; he hoped therefore that it would be the case. But with regard to the foreign, and domestic continental debts, he did not hesitate to say, it was proper for congress to take them into consideration as speedily as possible; for the sooner they are discussed, the sooner will the house make up their judgment thereon. He believed they were possessed of all the facts they could be possessed of, and therefore any great delay was improper. He was in favor of making the business the order of the day for Monday week.

Source: *DHFFC*, 12: 109–10. © 1995 Johns Hopkins University Press. Reprinted by permission of Johns Hopkins University Press.

9 February 1790

MR. SHERMAN.

The motion, before the committee, relates to the second resolution: The objects brought into view, by the gentleman last up, are many of them unconnected with it, though they are severally objects of great importance. I think, whatever doubts there may be with respect to the advantage or disadvantage of a public debt, we can none of us hesitate to decide, that provision of some kind ought to be made, for what we have already incurred: It is true, if we were now about to borrow money, it would be highly prudent to consider, whether the anticipation should not be repaid by a speedy collection of taxes, or duties to the amount; but when a debt is acquired, beyond our present ability to discharge, we ought to make some provision for its gradual extinction, but, in the interim, we ought to pay punctually the interest; now, this resolution goes no further.

Some of the propositions which follow, go further than this; they propose perpetual annuities, and talk of irredeemable stock; now, this is more than I am willing to agree to, because I think it prudent for us to get out of debt as soon as we can: But then I do not suppose we can raise money enough to pay off the whole principal and interest in two, three, or ten years. If I am right in this, we ought to agree to some mode of paying the interest in the interim. . . .

MR. SCOTT.

I find myself obliged to consider the government of the United States in a very different situation, with respect to our foreign and domestic creditors; with repect to the foreign debt, we, the representatives of the United States, are vested with full power, and we are bound in duty to provide for the punctual payment according to the nature of the contract: But, when I turn my eyes to the domestic debt, I find myself in a very different situation. I conceive myself

Source: *DHFFC,* 12: 208–9, 214–15, 223–24. © 1995 Johns Hopkins University Press. Reprinted by permission of Johns Hopkins University Press.

a mere arbiter, among the individuals of which the union is composed. A part of the people have claim upon somebody; I think that claim is against the people at large, and we are not only to provide for the payment of that claim, if just, but to determine, if that claim is just or not; one part of the community applies to us to recover of the other what is due to it; the other says, the debt is too large, it is more than is justly due; you must try and determine between us, and say, what part is just, and what is not; this brings clearly into my view the whole subject, as a thing within the power of congress to new model or modify it, if we find that justice demands it; but we have no such authority with respect to the foreign debt; it is very clear to me, that we have the power to administer justice and impartiality among the members of the union; and this will lead me freely to assert, that we have not only authority, but it is our duty, if, on examination, we find that not more than half the sum that is claimed, is justly claimed, to strike off the other half. If we find, on full investigation, that the whole is just, we must, no doubt, provide for the payment of it; in such sort as to do complete justice, which of these may be found to be the case in reality, when well examined, I will not pretend to say; but, at any rate, we are in the dark at present, inasmuch as we do not know the real amount. We cannot say, whether it is possible for us to pay it; we cannot know whether it is just or not, until we know what the claim is, as to quantity and quality. I do believe we are now walking on the brink of a precipice, that will be dangerous for us to step too fast upon.

I wish the subject to be duly considered, I wish every man in this house was of the same opinion with me, in one respect, that we are judges to determine matters of right and equity, we are, in fact, as a court of law; can we propose to decide with wisdom, whether the claims are just or not until the claims are exhibited? I presume we cannot. I am clear for going into the consideration of a resolve of the kind now before us when these doubts are removed from my mind. Rationally, I cannot consider in what manner the debt can be paid, until these points are settled; I do not perceive how we can say any thing about it; perhaps the resolutions might be worded in such a way as to give all the credit to the public securities, which they could derive from a more precise funding system, while, at the same time, sufficient room should be left for settling the great points, which I have in contemplation. I have no idea, mr. chairman, that these securities can be raised to their nominal value by the most explicit vote of this house; I do not believe they can acquire that stability which some gentlemen imagine. I am led to view the subject in this light from experience: I have seen within a few days, a warrant from the treasury, not to mention too particularly the sum, that would lead to the discovery of the circumstance I am about to mention; I shall say, the warrant was for one hundred dollars, payable in the month of March, it was sold for eighty dollars cash, here was a loss of twenty dollars, of one-fifth of the whole, upon a note, which neither the seller nor buyer could suppose would be refused punctual payment; now, if this is the case with public debts of such a certain nature, we cannot reasonably expect, that funding our debts will raise the public securities to any thing near their nominal value; indeed, I believe, it would have very little effect upon them. Men in business would give little more for a certificate drawing four dollars per cent. per annum, than they would now: supposing then, the public credit will be unaffected in a great degree, by the present measure; I would propose, to take time for the purpose of ascertaining the justice of their claims. I will, therefore, move to amend the resolution now before you, sir, by adding these words to it "as soon as the same is ascertained and duly liquidated." . . .

Mr. Sherman.

I do not differ much in principle, from the gentleman who spake last, from Pennsylvania (mr. Scott) but, I do not extend my views so far as he extends his, in the exercise of the power, which he contends is vested in this body. I look upon it, that every legislature acts in a threefold capacity: They have a power to make laws for the good government of the people, and a right to repeal, and alter those laws as public good requires; in another capacity, they have a right to make contracts; but here I must contend, that they have no right to violate, alter or abolish; but they have a right to fulfil them. The legislature stands in another capacity, or what is called judicial, between the union at large, and those creditors with whom she has entered into situations; there can be no other solemn judge on such occasions, because no court of law is capable of giving redress; they cannot issue an execution against the sovereign power, and enforce their decrees; therefore, any creditor who has money due to him from the state, has a right, by petition, to apply to the legislature, who has the sole power of ordering the money out, and of doing him justice. When applied to in that manner, the legislature has a right to examine, or appoint another to examine, how far the claim is just or unjust. This power has been exercised, with respect to the greatest part of the claims against the United States; there has been a liquidation of these accounts, and the specie value has been ascertained of the depreciated security. When bills of credit were first emitted, it was declared that they should be redeemed with specie, indeed they passed as such at first; but the opinion of their real value was changed by common consent, those that were put into the continental loan-offices, were always payable in the same species of money. If they had been paid in paper currency, the owners of them would have suffered a loss and injury: In justice, therefore, to the holders, the government agreed to fix the value of the loans according to the current rate of paper bills, at the time they were left in the office: All certificates were ordered to be liquidated in this manner, the same could not be done in favor of those who had left their other property with the public, and took the continental bills as a security; because they passed as a circulating medium, and went from one hand to another, by which means every one who received them, and kept them, though a small space of time, suffered loss; in that way it operated as a tax, and perhaps as equitable and as just a one as could have been any way apportioned; therefore it could not have been supposed equitable, that the last possessor should receive for these bills, the nominal sum in specie. The government, therefore, interfered in order to do justice; but when they had entered into a contract, founded on specie value, liquidated and ascertained, I don't see but what the public are bound by that contract, as much as an individual, and that they cannot reduce it down in either principal or interest, unless by an arbitrary power, and in that case there never will be any security in the public promises. If we should now agree to reduce the domestic debt to 4 per cent. the world may justly fear that we may, on some future occasion, reduce it to two; if this government once establishes such a principle, our credit is inevitably gone for ever. I presume the gentleman does not found his motion upon the idea, that there has been fraud and injustice committed on the one side, or imbecility or oversight on the other; if there was, it would be a good reason why an enquiry should take place in such cases; but though the legislature may judge of accounts exhibited against the government, and determine on them, their power ought not to be extended to judge of those already acknowledged; unless it be for the special reasons which I have just mentioned. From these considerations, I should be inclined to vary the motion for amendment, and insert the word liquidated before domestic debt, so as to provide permanent funds for the payment of interest on the liquidated part of the debt only.

23 February 1790

MR. SHERMAN.

If we can make provision for these debts, it will be a desirable object to assume them; it will, at the same time, ease the states of a very great burthen, and put all ranks of creditors on the same footing; and this last will have an effect to prevent speculation, inasmuch as there will be but one uniform object for men to trade in; there will be no difficult variety in the nature of the stock. But, at the same time, I think the debts to be assumed, ought to consist of those only which were incurred for common or particular defence during the last war; and not those debts which a state may have incurred for the support of its government, the protection and encouragement of its manufactures, or for amending and opening highways—clearing the obstructions in the navigation of rivers—or any other local purpose, undertaken merely for the benefit of one or two states.

I have no objection to agreeing to the general proposition at this time; but I am not quite so well satisfied with respect to the time when the provision ought to be made for paying the interest thereon; but as that matter is not immediately before the committee, I shall not touch upon it at present.

It appears to me, that the objections of the gentleman from Maryland, are not sufficient to prevent our adoption of this proposition. His first objection is, that it will give a greater degree of importance to the general government, while it will lessen the consequence of the state governments: Now, I don't believe it will have that effect; I consider both governments as standing on the broad basis of the people, they were both instituted by them, for their general and particular good. The representatives in congress draw their authority from the same source as the state legislatures, they are both of them elected by the people at large; the one to manage their national concerns, and the other their domestic, which they find can be better done, by being divided into lesser

Source: *DHFFC*, 12: 507–8, 513–15. © 1995 Johns Hopkins University Press. Reprinted by permission of Johns Hopkins University Press.

communities, than the whole union; but to effect the greater concerns, they have confederated; therefore, every thing which strengthens the federal government, and enables it to answer the end for which it was instituted, will be a desirable object with the people; it is well known, we can extend our authority no further than to the bounds the people have assigned: If we abuse this power, doubtless, the people will send others to correct our faults, or, if necessary, alter the system; but we have every reason to believe the people will be pleased with it; and none suppose that the state governments will object. They are the supreme power, within their own jurisdiction, and they will have authority over the states, in all cases, not given to the general government, notwithstanding the assumption of the state debts. If it was a question, between two different countries, and we were going to give the British parliament power, by assuming our debts, of levying what taxes they thought proper, and the people of America were to have no voice in the appointment of the officers, who were to administer the affairs of the government, the experiment would be dangerous to this country; but as the business is to be conducted by ourselves, there can be no ground for apprehension. The people of the United States are like masters, prescribing to their servants the several branches of business they would have each perform: It would not comport with their interest if the federal government was to interfere with the government of particular states; while, on the other hand, it would injure their interests to restrict the general government from performing what the federal constitution allows them. It is the interest of each and of the whole, that they both should be supported within their proper limits.

Another objection is, that we are to pay the whole by imposts, and that this mode will be unequal: I apprehend this is not well founded; because the consumers of imported goods, comprises all the inhabitants of the United States, and the consumption is, in a great degree, proportioned to the abilities of the citizen. The rich man, with his dependents, consumes more; there is more waste too in such a family, than in the oeconomy and frugality of the poor: If this is the fact, the rich contribute revenue in a proportion, and of consequence, the burthen of the tax is born generally and equally, by those who derive benefit from the late revolution.

Another objection is, that we are not authorised by the constitution to assume the state debts. By the confederation, congress were authorised to raise money; but not being able to effect this, in an immediate and direct manner, they did it mediately, through the intervention of the state governments; so that, in fact, these debts are to be looked upon as the absolute debts of the union; however, I should have no objection to qualify the mode of expressing our opinion, in such way as to confine the assumption to those debts alone which were contracted by the states for the common defence. Those debts, as was observed by the gentleman from Pennsylvania, will ultimately be assumed, and it is as well to be charged with them, in the first instance, especially if doing so, in the first instance, will promote the general good.

Another objection is, that the debts of the states are of different value. I take it, sir, that no debt will be assumed, but what is liquidated and reduced to specie value, and, although we differ in nominal accounts, yet a dollar is every where equal: As to the inequality of the market rate, it may have been occasioned by some states not having made equal provision for their debts, when compared to the provision of other states; but as the debts are all equally meritorious, an equality of provision ought to be made. That some creditors have hitherto suffered, is no reason why they should continue to suffer; so I can see no weight in this objection. But he supposes that some creditors will prefer holding the state for their money, rather than the United States; if it should be the case, it will make no difference on the final settlement, because the states will only be debited for that part of the debt which their creditors had subscribed into the general fund. But I see no good reason for supposing that the creditors of the states will refuse to subscribe. They have an election, it is true, but the terms must appear to them so advantageous, considering all things, as to induce them to accept the plan.

I have no difficulty, in my mind, respecting the assumption; but as to the time of doing it, I am not so well satisfied. I have not a doubt of our ability, because if the whole debt must be paid by the joint efforts of the state and general governments, the same money may be raised, with greater ease, by the general government alone; this point being conceded, I shall add nothing further at this time.

26 February 1790

Mr. Sherman

Supposed, from the arguments of the gentlemen in opposition, that they thought it was in contemplation to assume the debts of the states, contracted for private purposes; he believed this was not the intention of the resolution— at least it was not his intention; he meant to assume nothing more than the debts of the respective states, which were properly charged against the United States.

Source: *DHFFC*, 12: 595. © 1995 Johns Hopkins University Press. Reprinted by permission of Johns Hopkins University Press.

1 March 1790

Mr. Sherman

Judged it was best to pass over the propositions as they stood; because they were in a simple form, for he feared if they were too minutely detailed, or modified with opposite qualities, the business would acquire such a degree of complexity as to render it difficult to proceed. He was dissatisfied with the amendment, because it contemplated what would be very inconvenient, not to say oppressive and unjust. He said the circulation of the revenue would be very agreeable to the greater proportion of the inhabitants; because the evidences of the state debts were generally in the hands of the original holders: He had made particular enquiry into this circumstance, and so far as it respected Connecticut, he was led to believe it was true of nineteen-twentieths: There was one hundred thousand dollars, specie, in the hands of the original holders in the very town in which he lived: He believed very little beside the army debt had been transferred in that state; and even of the army debt, it was only that portion which fell into the hands of the soldiers.

Source: *DHFFC*, 12: 612. © 1995 Johns Hopkins University Press. Reprinted by permission of Johns Hopkins University Press.

27 March 1790

The proposition for assuming the State debts being under consideration.

Mr. SHERMAN. As the Secretary has given us the necessary information respecting the provision for payment of interest on the State debts—the assumption it is to be presumed will be agreeable to the States in general; having them all placed on one footing, and one system of revenue pervading the union—the resources will be brought forward with more justice and equality, with more certainty and effect, than on any other plan—and the belief that this measure will be agreeable to the people is strengthened by the idea that the States are averse to excises—without which no provision can be made (except dry taxes) to pay the State creditors their interest; the subject has been fully discussed and I think that we are now prepared for a decision, and I cannot but hope that we shall adopt the proposition before the committee.

In committee of the whole on the report of the Secretary of the Treasury for making provision for the support of the public credit.

The first alternative in the 5th [*6th*] proposition, was read with the amendment proposed by Mr. Boudinot, viz.

To receive a certificate drawing an interest of 6 per cent. per annum, payable in 10 years for the other ⅓ of the debt, which certificate shall be received as specie, in payment for the lands in the western territory.

Mr. Sherman observed, that if the alternative proposed by the Secretary, is adopted, one third part of the debt, principal and interest, will be extinguished; but the amendment contemplates an encrease of the debt, for one third at an interest will in the course of 10 years amount to an enormous sum. He adverted to the several alternatives, and supposed that among the number every description of creditors will be satisfied. If the alternative should be adopted, he should

Source: *DHFFC*, 12: 662, 672, 679–81. © 1995 Johns Hopkins University Press. Reprinted by permission of Johns Hopkins University Press.

move to strike out the 20 cents per acre—to leave the price a blank in order to wait for the report of the Secretary on the subject of the western territory.

In committee of the whole on the report of the Secretary of the Treasury, for making provision for the support of the public credit—the following proposition was read, viz.

To have the whole sum funded at an annuity, or yearly interest of four per cent, irredeemable by any payment exceeding five dollars per annum on account both of principal and interest; and to receive as a compensation for the reduction of interest, fifteen dollars and eighty cents. payable in lands, as in the preceding case.

The motion to reject the proposition was discussed.

Mr. Sherman. This proposition is to fund the debt at 4 per cent and if the evidences of the debt are to go out of the country, I should be in favor of having as much of it funded at that rate as possible. He thought the proposition a favorable one in this view and he was against striking out.

Mr. Sedgwick. The irredeemable quality of this proposition appears to be the chief objection in the minds of gentlemen—since it appears conceded on all hands, that a strict literal compliance with the precise terms of the original contract at the present moment cannot be made, and a modification of it is the necessary result—it becomes a subject of enquiry how we shall best meet the ideas and acquiescence of the creditors, and conciliate the approbation of our constituents. In this view, holding out different alternatives appears to be a proper measure, and among those alternatives the principle of irredeemability seems to offer itself, as a mean of acquiring the concurrence of a particular class of creditors—others will prefer other modes of funding their demands—hence the advantage, propriety and justice of holding out various propositions; and as he was fully persuaded that the public opinion would concur in every decision which appears to be the result of calm deliberation and a thorough investigation of the State of our country and the circumstances of our constituents, he doubted not that 99 out of 100, of the public creditors would subscribe to the loans; the principal is not strictly irredeemable—it provides for a gradual extinction of the debt, and within a period which will be as short as any person can contemplate, as within the probable capacity of the country to do it.

Mr. Fitzsimons after premising that the several propositions appeared to depend on each other; said, with respect to irredeemability, he had his doubts.

He did not think that this idea would meet the approbation of the people; on the other hand, they generally conceived that a public debt was a great public disadvantage, and would be for getting rid of the burthen as soon as possible, the habitual mode of reflecting on this subject is opposed to a perpetual debt; I confess I have my difficulties respecting this principle; I could wish that the period could be shortened, so that the eventual extinction should take place as soon as the abilities of the people would admit of it.

Mr. Madison was in favor of reducing the number of the alternatives, a simple, unembarrassed system is to be prefered.

Mr. Seney also objected to the adoption of the several propositions as in the report; it would render the funding system complex, and introduce such a series of calculations, as to convert the whole into an intricate science, which would be above the comprehension of persons in general; and being made an object by particular persons would give them great advantage in speculating in the funds; for these reasons he hoped the proposition would be struck out.

Mr. Sherman observed that if the whole debt was in the hands of the citizens of the United States he should think it unnecessary to introduce the irredeemable principal into the system; but as between 4 and 5 millions are in the hands of foreigners, and it is as necessary that that part should be funded as well as the rest, to induce them to reloan at 4 per cent. and to accommodate some part of the plan to their ideas, he thought as this part of the system would not operate to the injury of the United States he was in favor of its adoption. He thought it best that the debt should be kept in the United States as much as possible: he considered it an unfavorable circumstance to have it in the hands of foreigners; but as they were in possession of such a proportion he was for making the best terms that we could.

Mr. Page reprobated different propositions; he was in favor of a simple plain system, commensurate to the apprehension of men of plain, common understanding. He contrasted the different species of paper with different sorts of coin, and shewed there was no similarity.

12 April 1790

On the assumption of the state debts.

SHERMAN: Good deal said upon—good deal of concern to see the house so equally divided on a matter of this importance. It appears to me have a bad aspect in the government.

The support of public credit by providing for the payment of debt of United States was one object that had considerable influence in leading to the establishment of this government. If the government fail in making proper provision for it and rendering justice to the creditors it would disappoint the expectations of many of the best friends to the government and people in general.

The debt contracted by states for carrying on war ought to be provided, ought not to be postponed till the settlement of accounts. The claims as good against the United States as any other creditors'. If they left to be provided for by the states I believe great reason to expect equal justice will not be done. Some states able to provide for creditors and would do as well as United States. The case would be different in other states. Some from peculiar circumstances during the war have been obliged to take greater burden than other states in proportion. They likewise suffered from depredation of enemy and weakness, so that none is able now to provide for payment of debts they been obliged to contract. It appears to be hardship for those states that been struggling under unequal burdens to leave them still to bear them singly, as can't be known until the accounts liquidated which debtors and which creditors. It very pertinent that many of the debts contracted by United States, security given by individual states. The states that been so unequally burdened must bear it, else the creditors, as meritorious as any, their debts unprovided for. Their case would give great uneasiness; it have tendency to weaken the government and embarrass public measures. On the other hand, if all the debts assumed due to individuals and the liquidation of public accounts should be carried on and brought to a close, I believe the states be satisfied with it. Don't think any state have reason

Source: *DHFFC*, 13: 982–84, 988. © 1995 Johns Hopkins University Press. Reprinted by permission of Johns Hopkins University Press.

to complain. But to oblige some to take greater proportion of the debts now due and bear them longer when at the same time not known that ought to do, they have reason to complain, and no good reason can be given.

Some gentlemen supposed that the debts of particular states never will or can be liquidated. If that the case, that never are to be settled, it wields a conclusive argument why we ought to assume the debts contracted for the purpose of union. Because if never can ascertain how much each ought to bear, we ought to take the burden up equally. At present we can know what the unpaid debts are, but can't tell who paid most. Pay out of common stock the most equitable—Do see any reason why should be done any other way? The states made great exertions and since the war made great exertions to extinguish principal and pay interest. It presumed made exertions in proportion to ability. It appears no good reason to suppose that accounts not liquidated. There is Board appointed that going on. If any further provision necessary to such liquidation, that proposed by this proposition—that those measures be taken and accompany its other measures. Certainly Congress can make provision for liquidating and settling accounts.

Gentleman said no rule to fix the quotas of states. Now I take it that fixed by the past resolutions of Congress. That the quota that each state was to pay of public expense was to be according to the rule that fixed by Articles of Confederation, that ultimately fixed upon by the states—the same rule that taxes in future expense—was the ratio by which their past advances were to be settled. A resolution passed in November '77 which all the requisitions referred to, which settled the rule beyond a doubt. (Quote.) The 8th article of confederation declared a rule—that the value of real estates—but it was declared by Congress impracticable. They recommended to several states to alter that article and fix on number of inhabitants, modified. There was eleven states agreed to that alteration, two did not. At the —— of this C[ongress], one rule which recommended is agreed to, and by that rule what not paid out of common stock, where no means of ascertaining quota, is to be done by number of inhabitants. There was another resolution giving direction how the quotas should be settled passed by late Congress in '84, June 3. From this it appears that Congress did not expect the states charged with requisitions. They sometimes fully complied with, sometimes partially. Only credited with the sum advanced or supplies rendered, not charged with requisitions. Their accounts should be debited for sums received from the United States. Therefore, according to this every state be a creditor state more or less. All states made considerable advances. Now in the payment of these sums, they're paid out of common stock and then no need of ascertaining the quotas. Only the gross sum due will be to be paid and as far as can't be paid out of common stock—

that is, impost—must be out of tax. There rule for it; so full provision made for the settlement of these accounts.

Upon the whole, more just and politic to assume the states' debts that been (held) by the states where gave notice that were incurred for support of war. Give more general satisfaction and more justice to the several states and people at large than anything we could do, then go on with liquidation of accounts and thus final justice be done to all the states.

SHERMAN: Would move in that manner. *"And that any further provision that may be necessary for the speedy, just, and final settlement of the accounts of the several states with the United States ought at the same time to be made."* This provision only to fix certain principles. When the principles agreed to, then the provision necessary to be made will carry them into effect. Therefore the more simple they are the better. The proposition goes so far that with "further provision necessary for speedy, just, and final settlement—ought to be provided at the time we assume the state debts."

28 April 1790

The following observations were made by Mr. SHERMAN, *the 12th inst.*

When I see the house so equally divided on so important a subject, it gives me great concern on account of the threatening aspect it has on the peace and welfare of the government.

The support of public credit by a provision for doing justice to the creditors of the United States, was one great object that led to the establishment of the present government, and should it fail of doing justice to so great a proportion of them as are involved in this provision, it would lose the confidence of many of its best friends, and disappoint the expectations of the people in general.

I consider the debts incurred by the several states in support of the war, and for the common defence and general welfare, as the debts of the United States, and that those creditors have as just and meritorious a claim on the union for payment as any creditors whatever. A great part of them were assumed by the states in behalf of the United States, in consequence of requisitions of Congress.

I shall not now go into a particular discussion of the proposition before the committee, (every thing having been already said that may reflect light on the subject) but shall only state the reasons on which I shall give my vote in the affirmative.

The measure appears to me both just and politick. Just, with respect to the *creditors,* whose debts are due for services and supplies rendered in support of the common cause of the union, which therefore ought to be paid out of the same common funds, as the other creditors of the United States, and although some of the states would be able to provide for their creditors as well as the United States, yet that is not the case as to those whose exertions, sufferings and burthens have been much greater, than the others, and it would not give satisfaction to assume the debts of some states, and not of others.

The measure will be *just* with respect to the several *States,* because each will bear *only* its just proportion of the present burthen, and their past exertions

Source: *DHFFC,* 13: 1008–10. © 1995 Johns Hopkins University Press. Reprinted by permission of Johns Hopkins University Press.

and expenditures, will be equitably adjusted in the final settlement of their accounts, for which effectual provision is to be made by the same act that provides for the assumption of the debts.

The policy of the measure consists in its tendency to promote justice and harmony, and confidence in the government, in alleviating the burthens of a number of the States, who from their situation and circumstances during the war, were necessitated to make greater exertions, and were subjected to greater sufferings and expenditures than the other States, and by putting all the funds necessary for paying the debts under one direction, to facilitate the collection and render them more productive and less embarrassing to commerce. The principal resource for pay (the impost) is in possession of the general government.

But if the state debts are not assumed, the states which have heretofore borne the greatest burthens, will be left still to sustain those unequal and grievous burthens, or their creditors will be left without any provision for satisfying their claims either of which would be unreasonable, and occasion great uneasiness, which will tend to embarrass and obstruct the measures of government.

It has been said, let those States wait until their accounts with the United States shall be settled, and then receive security for the balances that may be due to them; But why should those States be subjected to greater burthens at present, than the other States? As it is not known which are Debtor or Creditor States, why not bear the burthen equally until that can be ascertained? If there is to be no settlement, I think it is a conclusive argument that the whole public debt should be assumed by the United States. It ought to be presumed that the States have made exertions according to their abilities, and in due proportion until the contrary appears, and that can no otherwise appear, but by a settlement of the accounts; and until that is done I can see no good reason why any State should bear more than its just proportion of the existing debts, whether contracted by the United States, or by the individual States, if incurred for the common defence, or general welfare of the Union. It is said there is no rule established to ascertain the quotas of the several States; but I think the rule is fixed by the resolutions of the late Congress, of the 22d of November 1777, and the third of June 1784, and the provision in the new Constitution for apportioning direct taxes.

14 April 1790

SHERMAN: This the most advantageous, provided the creditors accept of it. Creditors not another option to accept? Three alternatives. This one. Don't suppose suit all but many will be well suited. So far as accepted, the debt extinguished. What the consequence if two-thirds funded and issued certificates for the remainder? That a year's interest accumulated. That that part must be paid or breach of public faith. Can't get that sum together to pay the interest. It also a subject of speculation. The creditor gets nothing for it. It be a burden and be injurious to both. As to the disadvantage of bringing land to market, no disadvantage if can get the price at all. If can't, still hold it. If gentlemen think the land not high enough, raise it. Said encourage emigration to the western territory. Don't think it have that effect any more than if land office opened and they could get land from the Secretary. Those who had land, who purchased—but don't think we ought to hold up this invidious distinction. Number of settlers there. They within the union. They not lost. They will be advantageous in another point of view. If but few people there, keep up army. But they able to defend themselves. Save great expense in that way. Think make it very well. The creditors have option. If (owe debt and have house and land), he have the same security as before. But if choose to take my (horse) or land when offer, think it best to accept it.

Source: *DHFFC*, 13: 1046. © 1995 Johns Hopkins University Press. Reprinted by permission of Johns Hopkins University Press.

16 April 1790

SHERMAN: Appears to me that different parts of argument of the same gentlemen contradictory to the other. One, it will be wrong to the creditor to offer land for one-third. Another is, be a great loss because it is to allow much more of them. Now don't think United States so far is (among cruel masters). I believe private people valued much more. If the United States could make any advantage, it would be advantage to the creditor to receive them. One gentleman observes it would not fulfil contract. We been all this time promising new modification and do not know that would not be fulfilment of the old one. New modification, gentlemen say, no alternative. Yet the last resolution—it goes on this principle, not to promise more to pay now than 4 per cent on whole or 6 on two-thirds. Would be dangerous to fund or pay higher interest immediately. It will not be (candor). Not proposed to depart from contract but fulfil as fast as can. I believe many creditors think this forms an advantageous bargain and willing to accept it. Gentlemen object that would be disadvantage to revenue—to discourage emigration. Think make little difference as to emigration whether this to be had or not, because those who disposed to, go, and not go. But if account for what saved, we never make as much as ten years' interest. Never have this government make a promise but what sees the way clear in performing it. I believe as far as Secretary proposes to make engagements the government able to comply with it. More money than (be laid). Four per cent better than a promise for 6 per cent as paid hereafter. Think it right that a composition—Don't think they could question our candor. No doubt but in the power of government to pay the debt in full.

Source: *DHFFC*, 13: 1053. © 1995 Johns Hopkins University Press. Reprinted by permission of Johns Hopkins University Press.

21 April 1790

SHERMAN: We should pay it with less sum to pay the whole. The longer it lays in interest the more it will take. If probable we could pay it sooner than 19 years, would have no objection to pay it sooner. I believe interest of money will fall. In Europe they hire money at 4 per cent. The United States hired money at 4 per cent. Think at 5 per cent public security is better than private security at 6 per cent. If states establish credit, certain of interest, they prefer 5 per cent to 6 on private security. If lay out in land not more than 4 per cent unless in new country. It might been hired before the war for 5 per cent in this city when the security was good. The want of security during the war, the (tender) money.

FITZSIMONS: Two circumstances insisted upon, without sufficient reason. One is that rate of interest will not fall. The other is that irredeemable quality of debt don't make more valuable. Not a single (iota) argued for the truth of these opinions. Reason and experience against both. At this moment general interest 6 per cent. I would ask any gentleman whether he does not conceive that 5 per cent received quarterly is not really more beneficial than 6 from private debtor. There not a gentleman but admit it. Be the security however good, the money seldom paid punctually, the interest for the time in arrear. If has occasion to make use of (complete), can't command at short notice all these advantages he has. It within the knowledge of many gentlemen that in many states could borrow 5 per cent, if the person could rely on interest. Is there any reason why not in as good circumstances in future? The probability is that be in better. England borrowed at 8 per cent, found it difficult to get at that; in few years they borrowed at 4, the common rate of interest.

With respect to irredeemable quality, experience against his argument. The loans made in Europe was one of the conditions. Is it not reasonable? If wishes to place his money at interest, would it be convenient that the person should have it in power to return it at the end of year? At a loss to know what use to

Source: *DHFFC*, 13: 1129–34, 1148–49. © 1995 Johns Hopkins University Press. Reprinted by permission of Johns Hopkins University Press.

make of it. Expense of (freight, commission, and induction) would be 1 per cent. We do know that was condition made by the lenders that should not be obliged to receive it back. The experience full at that point.

PAGE: Think 8 better than any other. If disposed to lend should wish to have in my power to receive rather 8 than 6 per annum. Immense amount collected at 8 during his life. They collect little but the interest of securities. Such person lend sooner to have 8 than 6. That a temptation and in favor of the republic. With respect to interest, no man can calculate the rate of interest for some years to come. The state of rate of interest may be totally different. New (science) in Europe, new fad in America. Point out one circumstance— the fad of speculation which swallows up all the money that can be brought into any state. Immense sum in Virginia. The men who want money, unless public security, can seldom find it. Speculators make I know not what, but more than any other person.

6 per cent—carried in the affirmative.

MADISON: Important question. It unfortunate that should delay part of debt. As part received in proportion —— —— if fill with 10. One third bear no interest for ten years and principal not discharged for 30, 40, or 50 years. In this shape, it probable in my judgment that the citizens who receive this paper will set very little value upon it indeed, much less value than intrinsically worth. Those who can make accurate calculation and can afford to lay out of money would alone be the purchasers. Foreigners chiefly come under that description. They ought to fear little in the first instance. Ten years has raised up enormous debt, for which receive very little at the first, for we must pay the principal and interest. Think safely shorten the term; if now able to pay 6 per cent on two thirds, the situation of this country might enable us to pay 6 per cent on the remaining one third—than 10 years. I should not myself from any idea I have of capacity of the country—think the shorter term proper.

7 years—unanimously.

Fitzsimons' *33⅓ dollars* agreed to.

SHERMAN: Move an amendment to the last resolution. That next after the word "resolved"—*"That the debts contracted by the several states for the common defense and benefit of union ought to be considered as part of the domestic debt of the union."* Then follows the resolution as it stands there. *Correct also, "that present provision ought to be made for the immediate debt of the United States."*

LEE objects to the order.

PAGE: Should wait till go into the house. In this place it is improper. Hope not insist on doing it here. If disappointed now, their members may renew it. If fair majority, consider how like to be carried. Embarrassing every attempt to go forward. It might be disadvantageous to themselves—dreadful expense.

LIVERMORE, the chairman, says it is in order.

SHERMAN: This matter been fully debated as to the general question of assumption. It be unnecessary to go very particularly into it again. The objections that were against it under the general proposition that was made before will be obviated. One, respecting the extent of them: some received accounts from, others not. The whole supposed 25 million, but that was uncertain. But thought imprudent to assume so large a sum without knowing how it would be. Thus, propose to assume only certain sums of state debts in order to render it convenient for the several states to provide for the remainder. Some states were obliged to assume for the United States much larger sum and greater expense than other states. They did it cheerfully. They knew every state should exert itself, had confidence, knew justice be done fully. If had not this confidence, never should obtain the object of all. Now exceedingly hard to leave these states to groan under these burdens, especially as those funds taken by the United States. Impost exclusively in the hands of union. If the United States should assume such part of the debts of particular states as would leave the burden pretty nearly equal, and so much as to be willing to forward settlement of accounts, in order to have complete liquidation, it appears to me give the greatest satisfaction and possible justice that can be done under present circumstances. If the states should be left—they would be unable—They ought to be provided for. Ought not to postpone till settlement of accounts, should pay as much out of common funds as we can. It is true that particular states have a right by the Constitution to lay excise. But if go into any considerable extent upon imported articles, it must interfere with the impost and embarrass the commerce of the union. Some states lay higher excise than others; if laid high in some states and low in others, it would embarrass the commerce of those states and would be detrimental to the union. These states have part of burden taken from them, might be satisfied. If unable to do justice, the creditors be unequal. Justice and good policy require it. Therefore hope adopted.

As to the sums, I have made an estimate on the other side of what sums the state debts consist of as far as he received accounts, and the sum to be assumed to apportion the burden more equally. But as it stands blank, the committee fill it up with lower sums than the whole. What I propose was about 19 million. If less assumed, or apportionment different, the committee has matter before them, they may assume 16, 17, 18 million—as find most expedient.

MADISON: Wish to know whether means to fix any general principle by which the proportion of the whole debt is to be determined, or fix a ratio by which the apportionment to be made to the several states, or means that so much to be given or taken just as majority can agree. Don't find any principle laid down to guide us. A very material question indeed whether the apportionment to the several states is to depend on the arbitrary determination of majority or fixed principle contained in the resolution itself.

SHERMAN: Here is account that Secretary has reported of what the debts are. States what his intention to give.

JACKSON: Was in hopes that united to defeat the (chore) of assumption and (chore) of payment; find intend to bring in answer. A letter from Governor to Secretary of Treasury—Georgia stands in no need of them. Any modification that would prepare as bad as the original proposition for assumption. The state debt does not amount to 300,000. She sank the greatest part latterly. What the consequence of modification, which that government have to—$\frac{5}{65}$ths of? She have a debt four times as large as to pay. Would this do for one state? If the injustice in one part there is injustice in the whole. If some, it ought all to be assumed. I dislike the modification more than the original proposition. I trust those who oppose the assumption from principle must see it must be opposed in light of injustice. Notwithstanding gentleman calls it necessary, yet other part right to say will not pay your debts.

WILLIAMSON: Not the same thing, but much worse. We now going to see whether —— accounts. Treating them with partial justice whether can prevail on gentlemen to alter. What the effect of assuming part? It answers this purpose: persons, before the Secretary's report known in this house—persons having heard it—set off to North Carolina with money, been buying up at two shillings. It will (cover) as many of them as have come to the northward. But the unfortunate citizens who knew nothing of this, who hold securities, it will not (cover) them. Let them get it when accounts settled. That one of the pretty distinctions. What the other? Some states whose representatives not fully agreed. That state to have all paid. Another state to have certain sum which answers certain purpose at least. If the object had been to relieve the states, do unequal justice, and I do not believe harm herself by partial justice and giving to particular states. I would expect to see motion on this measure, that an account according to the present ratio will be paid to the state, or will be allowed a certain sum only, which will distribute to whom owe money until the accounts should be settled. Then, if 25 million due, the proportion, so much to New Hampshire, others—so that would relieve the states and do justice to the citizens. It would done equal justice in that case. The state would get the relief equal to the interest. With that allowance each state would be able to stumble along. But if undertake to judge and say that will have so many among the rest as you can, an arbitrary measure without any rule or measure— is this not a favoritism to carry a point, not carried by the common means of deciding a question? Value the plain way of going forward. I surprised—not surprised that persevere in assumption, but should not expect in this particular manner, so exceptionable.

SHERMAN: Other blanks left. I only made a proposition which thought relieve the states in some measure. It lies open to fill blanks with the whole debt—no objection. Take off in proportion according to quotas. Should consider what we leave upon the states. If all in the hands of union we going to give it in certain proportion, should consider how much can bear and provide for. Would leave it so that could provide easily. Think the state creditors not —— because the state can make full provision. But if gentlemen think it best to assume whole, will not object to it.

The committee then took into consideration the following proposition, being one of the alternatives proposed by the Secretary of the Treasury.

"To have 66⅔ dollars funded immediately at annuities or yearly interest of 6 per cent. irredeemable by any payment exceeding four dollars and two thirds of a dollar per annum on account both of principal and interest; and to have at the expiration of ten years 26 dollars, and 88 hundredths funded at the like interest and rate of redemption." The proposition being amended to read as follows, was agreed to.

"To have sixty-six dollars and two thirds of a dollar funded immediately at an annuity or yearly interest of six per cent. irredeemable by any payment exceeding six dollars and two thirds of a dollar per annum on account both of principal and interest; and to have, at the end of seven years, thirty-three dollars and one third of a dollar funded at the like interest and rate of redemption."

Mr. *Sherman* then proposed to modify the resolution so as to admit of the following proposition—"That the debts contracted by the several states for the common defence and benefit of the union, ought to be considered as a part of the domestic debt of the United States: that proper provision ought to be made for the immediate debt of the United States; and that the faith of government ought to be pledged to make provision, at the next session, for so much of the debts of the respective states as shall have been subscribed upon any of the terms expressed in the last resolution; provided that subscriptions shall not be received for a greater amount, than the following sums, viz.

That the remainder ought to be left to the respective states to provide for, until a final settlement of their accounts with the United States, for which settlement effectual provision ought now to be made.

Provided that no debts be assumed but such as have been liquidated in specie value, and evidenced by notes or certificates issued by authority of the respective states, before the   day of   1790.

Assumption of the State Debts,
not exceeding the sums in the last column.

	Due as per Sec'ry's Report.	Sums to be assumed.
		DOLLARS
N. Hampshire	300,000	300,000
Massachusetts	5,226,801	4,000,000
Connecticut	1,951,173	1,600,000
New-York	1,167,575	1,000,000
New-Jersey	788,680	750,000
Pennsylvania	2,200,000	2,000,000
Delaware		100,000
Maryland	800,000	750,000
Virginia	3,680,743	3,000,000
N. Carolina		1,600,000
S. Carolina	5,386,232	4,000,000
Georgia		200,000
		19,300,000

And if the creditors of any state shall not subscribe to the amount of the debt of such state to be assumed as aforesaid, such state shall receive interest at the rate of 4 per cent per annum, on the remainder of said sum, until a final settlement of its accounts with the United States, to be applied to the payment of interest to its non-subscribing creditors, for which, and for the sums that may be assumed, the respective states shall be accountable to the United States."

Mr. Sherman being called upon to ascertain in what proportion he meant to fill up the blanks, read the following as a statement of the debts owing by the states, and the proportions he wanted assumed.

22 April 1790

SEDGWICK [SHERMAN?]: If it ever was contemplated in Congress or held up to the view of people as a measure that was to be attempted? Know the convention which framed the Constitution—what they made it was to give powers, not to point out how execute them; leave to those who appointed to administer the government to execute the powers as they think proper. They find that everything provided in the Constitution necessary for the purpose. It was mentioned that in the Convention (talked of) in committee consisting of member from each state, but it was objected that that matter would be left to the general government. What should be right in that respect? Two parts that point to this business. One the preamble. *"We the people."* This an essential to establish justice—to the union and to the several states. *"To lay and collect taxes."* If they are not the debts of United States they ought not to be assumed. But if they are contracted for general benefit of union with expectation of having them reimbursed—here another part which explicit—*"all debts contracted."* Great part of these debts for supply and pay of army and raising men, furnishing supplies upon the recommendation of Congress, which always understood to be the debts of United States. They were obliged to recommend, could not fix rule. Some states obliged to make exertions themselves, they could not apply to continental body. All those things necessary for carrying on the war and necessary to defend the states. Gentlemen say let justice be done in liquidation. New government to take up matter to pay debts, the accounts can[not?] be settled till an apportionment and census taken. But it seems necessary from the situation of particular states that burdened with greater proportion to other states and for the creditors that they should be considered and provided for so far as to leave the burden tolerable. Gentlemen say one objection, it does not go to the whole of the debt. Gentlemen should consider may be the whole amount. If that the sense of majority, to be completed according to their wishes. If gentlemen suppose operate better, they agree to it.

Source: *DHFFC*, 13: 1155–56. © 1995 Johns Hopkins University Press. Reprinted by permission of Johns Hopkins University Press.

23 April 1790

SHERMAN: The whole leads off from the true principle on which the question should stand. Don't think it matter of importance, whether the fact stated yesterday is true or not true can[not?] have any weight. If had exerted double to Massachusetts and paid up the whole—what paid is to be liquidated, and when final settlement then known which have balance due to them and which have not. Can't draw conclusion that apply in the present case. The former government stand on the authority of the governments of individual states, and the individual states received the funds. They could borrow money but no means of payment. But since that the people have altered. The government don't stand on the authority of different states at all. People at large, therefore, superseded the old Congress. In this new Congress they took from the state governments one principal fund for paying the debts—that is, the impost— and diverted to the government of United States. Put their resources into the hands of government, so that have the command of the whole. They are de- livered in trust, to do what? To pay the debts, provide for common defense. Now the debts that remain unpaid that properly the debts of the United States for supplies rendered to the union in the course of the war, these remain debts against the United States. They not able to pay them. If leave the great burden of debts on the states it make such a convulsion in the government as will be— be very difficult for the (reparation) to proceed, such an abandonment of the claims of creditors that never can be justified.

Gentlemen have said that as the house nearly equally divided it be safer to negative the measure. Let gentlemen obtain information, but no ground for the house to give an order. *Quote Bland's amendment—carried.*

Source: *DHFFC*, 13: 1190–91. © 1995 Johns Hopkins University Press. Reprinted by permission of Johns Hopkins University Press.

25 May 1790

SHERMAN: Answer some objections which were made when the matter under consideration before. State first the reasons in favor of adopting the measure.

One, debts contracted for benefit of United States, therefore justice requires that should be assumed. The proposition proposes that such only be assumed.

Another reason, some states took upon them greater sums than others and beyond their ability to pay. It is true of Massachusetts and South Carolina. From local circumstances they obliged to take upon themselves a great proportion of national debt. Some other states done the same.

3. That the funds are by the Constitution put under federal government, and this done by the authority of the people for paying off debts of United States, of which these part, and debts follow the funds.

4. Excise and impost best managed under one direction.

5th reason, equal justice ought to be done to all, but this can't be done by all the states being unequally deprived of revenue.

6. Grounded on good policy as well as justice. Produce harmony, attach them to government, and facilitate the operation of government.

Notice a few objections. Said the accounts ought first to be settled. I allow that no payment ought to be made till accounts settled—Nor to individual creditors. It not intended that any division made to any state but merely those who have debts contracted by the states for United States have their claims funded. These creditors have as good claims on justice as any of the other creditors, and not in their power to compel settlement. And that they should be held out till that done is inconsistent with every idea of justice.

Another objection, that when the states took the debts on themselves—This may grant under some explanation. When undertook them, not as quota, but as occasion happened—that requisitions—It was necessary that the states should interpose and take up debts in behalf of union. They took larger and smaller proportions. They expected there would be adjustment of accounts and that

Source: *DHFFC*, 13: 1392–96. © 1995 Johns Hopkins University Press. Reprinted by permission of Johns Hopkins University Press.

would be likely every state should pay own quota. But a revolution in government. Then the funds in the hands of states. But since the impost taken away, and all the other funds put into the power of general government for express purpose of paying debt of United States. These debts of United States and should be paid out of these funds.

It been objected that a new project, not mentioned in the Constitution, that when the assumption mentioned in the general convention that I opposed it. Now the novelty of the measure is argument against it. If justice requires it, if ever so new, ought to be adopted. When mentioned in the convention I did object to it. When I objected to it, this was reason, Congress have full power to do what just. That satisfied the person who moved it.

MADISON: I never said nor mean to insist—I alluded to another gentleman, from the state of Massachusetts.

SHERMAN: I had not made up my mind whether best to adopt or not to adopt. The merits not entered into very far.

Another objection is that the states most urgent for this measure are not incapacitated by adopting the new Constitution from paying their debts. The only states which expect—are Massachusetts and South Carolina. It not proposed to pay any of them more than their proportion. These two states intolerably burdened. Only in favor of these two states. These two states chiefly depend upon the impost, of which wholly deprived.

Connecticut don't wish more than her just proportion. The debt of New Hampshire will not amount to half of her proportion, but she in favor of the measure on principles of justice and policy, not in self-interest. The whole debt of Virginia assumed, which amounts to her full proportion. So that the interest of that state will be no further affected than by the transfer of our general funds. The states no less—North Carolina have her full quota assumed. This provision been founded on month's collection. I think must be satisfactory.

But an argument was advanced that must appear to have some degree of fallacy. It appears with an ill grace as it comes from the gentleman that advances it. It is in respect to the ratio in which these states contribute by way of impost. This principle fully confounded by the report of committee of which he a member. Journal, A[pril] '83 where he says the tax ultimately paid by the consumers. Read the report. Journal, April 29, 1783.

One objection—objected that difficult to discriminate state debts. Of what use is it? If some be assumed, if assumed in due proportion, no injustice can take place. The proposition proposes not to receive them in one or two cases—

Objection that if —— ——. Partial assumption will leave those who poor and unable to come forward—will be left without remedy. To that may be answered that the most of these debts which properly debts of union will be assumed. It will take in the whole of the claims of the creditors, or very nearly. But now the objection is that burdened beyond their ability. If small balance due by some states, yet they be able to make provision for those creditors, so that no difficulty, the states and creditors will be satisfied. If took up small part there would be difficulty, but if assume the whole, perhaps amounting to 20 million of dollars—so that those who come first—We appoint commissioners so that each have fair opportunity. Another objection, that the debts of Georgia being without interest—Though if any weight in it, exists in favor of assumption. If they not paid interest they ought to be put on footing with others as soon as possible. That argument ought not to be urged.

It said that Virginia paid specie requisitions and principal of part of her state debt. She ought not to be burdened with those that didn't make like application. That answered, because her whole quota to be assumed, so puts no burden on it. Paid out of common funds, that the only alteration. North Carolina and Connecticut should have each of them, as much as Virginia, that about equal to representation, at their just proportion. A number of other states which not debts to the amount of their quota. They had not occasion to take as much of the debt as other states. These states will take part of the burden of Massachusetts and South Carolina. Those who not took their proportion will come in debt of those who have too much. Other states made great exertions since the war in paying requisitions and sinking state debts.

He does not propose direct tax nor excise. I think some reliance ought to be placed on this officer. He supposes that provision can be made for the state debts, better if assumed than if made —— the debt that necessarily allowed to be the debt of the union. If concede all revenue will be [in] power of United States, and will be best managed by them, think may trust to the opinion of the officer.

They contracted for the benefit of union, provision must be made for them all. We ought to consider how can be best paid out of common stock, have no murmuring, no ground of complaint—all be satisfied. No doubt but its sources are sufficient to pay interest and sink principal if properly managed. No doubt be so managed under the government of union so that universal satisfaction.

There is western territory, principal source of sinking the debt in the course of years. I look upon public debt to be a public evil. Don't wish it continued any longer than can be paid off, the sooner paid off the better. The gentleman made an observation concerning the expense of collecting excise. In England cost 10 per cent. S[mith] says it costs but 5 per cent—10 per cent impost.

It been objected that the c[ontinental] paper in large trading towns—get into the hands of foreigners. It most likely to be the case with those who wish to live on the interest of their money. There such people throughout the United States and will center in those. There is corporate bodies for promoting literature—They purchase in. But, however, they won't get out of the hands of proper owners without their consent, and if well funded won't go out of their hands without proper compensation. Everyone right to dispose of own property without control. Some gets into the hands of foreigners. The United States can't restrain that.

It objected that the provision intended to be made was not to be made the present session, but only declare that at next session provision made for these debts. That according to the report of Secretary of Treasury—that the actual funds used not appropriated at this time, but see how much be subscribed between this and next session. But it was said that could not bind our successors. It have this advantage, the creditors see they are not neglected, that their claims be attended to. Prevent them getting out of their hands at under rate. They consider justice will be done. If abandoned, then discouraged, then speculators bring upon them—Many of them where they can't find states making provision—

Another objection, that as the house divided it would be safer to determine against than in favor with small majority. Now appears quite the reverse, because people governed by their feelings more than reasoning and calculation. If a bare majority should carry the question in favor of assumption, what ground of unease to any citizen? There no more to be paid than what justly due. They will feel no new burden. But if not assumed, there will be separate states that groaning under burdens that will be felt. Here a class of creditors no provision made for their claims. It naturally excites uneasiness, such an uneasiness as make government very uneasy and operation of government go on very heavily. Therefore appears safer and likely to produce harmony to decide in favor of assumption, though small majority.

Another objection, that several legislatures been in session and had not applied, except South Carolina. Believe that never ought to apply. We should be left to own deliberation. All interference from abroad except private measures—The members never ought to be influenced by anything but that taken up for general good of union. That will satisfy the people at large and the state legislatures.

The sum stands blank. States may consider how filled up. Think the best to assume near the whole that comes under (subscription) of the states—20 million. Be able to provide for that whole—The officer of finance gives no better—No state found fault in c[ommittee]. It better for the other creditors to have all funded under one direction than the contrary. Therefore hope will adopt the proposition.

Roger Sherman, Notes for a Speech

The debates on this Subject have given me great concern on account of the threatning Aspect it has on the Government, when I See the house so equally divided in Sentiment, on so important a Subject. and so little prospect of an accommodation.

The Support of public credit by a provision for doing justice to the public creditors was one great object that led to the establishment of the present government, and if it Should fail of doing that justice, it would lose the confidence of many of its best friends, & disappoint the raised expectations of the people in general, both at home & abroad. I consider the debts incurred by the Several States in Support of the War as a part of the national debt. & that a provision for them ought not to be postponed, until a Settlement of the accounts of the States with the United States.

I am sensible that difficulties, and delays may attend the Settlement of those accounts, on any plan that can be adopted; nor is perfect equity to be expected. but in great national affairs, smaller inconveniencies must be dispensed with. If the States had not by their mutual confidence in each other, Surmounted much greater difficulties, than than these, they never would have accomplished the revolution; but each made all possible exertions in confidence that final justice would be done.

I Shall not now go into a particular discussion of the proposition before Committee, every thing that may reflect light on the Subject having been repeatedly Said already. I Shall only State the principles. that induce me to be in favour of the assumption of the State debts. Such of them I mean as Shall have been liquidated by the respective States at their just value in Specie. This measure under present circumstances appears to me both just and politic. The assumption is *just* with respect to the creditors whose debts are due for Services & Supplies rendered in Support of the common cause of the Union, which there fore ought to be paid out of the common funds. and tho' some of the

Source: *DHFFC*, 19: 1213–15. © 2012 Johns Hopkins University Press. Reprinted by permission of Johns Hopkins University Press.

States might provide as well for their creditors, as the united States could. yet that is not the case as to others, & it would not give Satisfaction to assume the debts of Some States & not of others.

The measure will be just with respect to the Several States, because each will bear only its just proportion of the present burthen, and their past exertions will be equitably adjusted in the final Settlement of their accounts. which is already provided for, & any further provision that may be necessary for carrying it into effect; is proposed now to be made.

The policy of the measure will consist in its tendancy, by doing equal justice to the creditors to promote harmony among them, & secure their confidence in the Government; and in allieviating the burthens of a number of the States, who from their Situation & circumstances were necessitated during the war, to make greater exertions, and were Subjected to greater Sufferings & expenditures than the other States: But if those debts are not Assumed those States will be left to Sustain their unequal burthens; or their creditors be left without any provision for Satisfying their claims, either of which must produce great uneasiness & dissatisfaction which will tend greatly to embarrass & obstruct the measures of government. weaken or str. govt.

It has been Said let those States wait until their Accounts Shall be Settled, & then receive the balances that may be due to them. But why Should those States be Subjected to greater burthens at present than the other States? As it is not known which are Dr. or Cr. States, why not bear the burthen equally until that can be ascertained?

It is Said there is no rule established to determine the quotas of the States, & that it is uncertain whether there ever can or will be a Settlement. I think the rule in the constitution to proportion direct taxes, is an established rule to determine the quotas of the States as to past as well as future expenditures: but if there is to be no Settlemt. I think it a conclusive argument, that the whole public debt Should be assumed by the union. for all the States made great exertions during the war, perhaps as great as their circumstances & abilities would admit, & they have likewise contributed Since the peace toward the payment of the debts contracted during the war. by the united States as well as by themselves individually, and must it not be presumed that each has done its due proportion until the contrary appears, and that can no otherwise appear than by a Settlement of the accounts; & until that is done I can See no good reason why any State Should bear more than its just proportion of the existing debts, whether contracted by the union or the States individually. if incurred for the Common defence.

Imposts

16 April 1789

MR. SHERMAN.

The gentlemen object to these articles because they are necessary, and cannot be furnished in quantities equal to the demand; but I am of opinion if they cannot now be had in such plenty as is wished for, they may in a very short time; every state can manufacture them, although they may not make nail-rods. Connecticut has excellent iron ore of which bars are made, but she gets nail-rods from this city, others can do the like; and until every state can supply themselves, by their own industry, for which purpose they have every thing at their hands, it may not be amiss for the government to get some revenue from the consumption of foreign nails.

Source: *DHFFC*, 10: 160–61. © 1992 Johns Hopkins University Press. Reprinted by permission of Johns Hopkins University Press.

17 April 1789

SHERMAN: It appears prudent to insert glass. That article great deal used, and perhaps more than necessary, and even if tends to lessen the use of it, it would not be great oppression to the people. To encourage manufacture it would bear something of revenue to be laid upon it. I think impost better than direct taxation. Observed odious, but it is odious on account of collection. Where pay (assessment), they pay more freely than direct tax. I think we might, by encouraging the manufacture of this article—might save money in the country, and as we have (method) and manufacture set up—window glass—politic to give some encouragement to the manufacturing of it, and hope in few years will be able to do without importing any and in the meantime raise revenue on what imported. Lay equal in proportion to ability to pay. Large houses— we must have some articles and necessaries to be consumed as well as superfluities. This operates well in both respects, as to raising revenue and encouraging manufactures.

Source: *DHFFC*, 10: 171–72. © 1992 Johns Hopkins University Press. Reprinted by permission of Johns Hopkins University Press.

25 April 1789

MR. SHERMAN.

The probable amount of the duties we have agreed to, will not in my opinion exceed 2,000,000 dollars, this sum is insufficient to answer the public exigencies, therefore I should be sorry to reduce much upon any article: In this case it is not intended perhaps to make a great reduction, it is only to shew a preference to our allies, but if the discrimination on tonnage is not sufficient for that purpose, I would rather make a discrimination on any other article than ardent spirits; the importation of which does not deserve encouragement from any part of the world.

Source: *DHFFC*, 10: 314. © 1992 Johns Hopkins University Press. Reprinted by permission of Johns Hopkins University Press.

27 April 1789

MR. SHERMAN.

Had not made up his mind on the subject; but he thought it necessary that some way should be devised of coming at a proportionable duty on country rum, otherwise the preference it would obtain by the lowness of the price, must occasion a considerable diminution of the revenue by lessening the consumption of foreign rum. If an excise was an agreeable tax, perhaps it might be so managed as to answer the end; but he feared it was a disagreeable one in some states, and ought therefore to be well considered before it was laid. He would while he was up mention another idea. He had said in a former debate, that he would rather give our allies a preference over other foreign nations in any article than spirits. Molasses is an article principally imported from the colonies of nations in alliance; a discrimination therefore in favor of such molasses would be a substantial benefit, and he recommended it in lieu of that on brandy.

Source: *DHFFC*, 10: 335. © 1992 Johns Hopkins University Press. Reprinted by permission of Johns Hopkins University Press.

4 May 1789

MR. SHERMAN

Was opposed to the discrimination. In his opinion the great principle in making treaties with foreign powers, was to obtain equal and reciprocal advantages to what were granted, and in all our measures to gain this object, the principle ought to be held in view. If the business before the house was examined, it would appear to be rather founded on principles of resentment, because the nation of Great Britain has neglected or declined forming a commercial treaty with us. He did not know that she discriminates between these states and other powers who are not in treaty with her, and therefore did not call upon us for retaliation; if we are treated in the same manner as those nations we have no right to complain. He was not opposed to particular regulations to obtain the object which the friends of the measure had in view, but he did not like this mode of doing it; because he feared it would injure the interest of the United States.

Source: *DHFFC*, 10: 428. © 1992 Johns Hopkins University Press. Reprinted by permission of Johns Hopkins University Press.

9 May 1789

MR. SHERMAN.

After this subject had been debated in a committee of the whole, and then in the House upon the report, and every argument that could be thought of had been urged, both on the general and particular amount of the duties proposed, and the probable effects of a deduction, I did not expect to have heard the same debate take place again. Gentlemen have a large field to display their abilities in, but I do not think it contains any new matter that will induce a single gentleman to alter his opinion on the subject. The great object is to raise a sum of money adequate to supply our wants; and let us dispute as we will about the mode, the fact is it must be raised; the people have sent their representatives here for this purpose, it is for their benefit that we raise the money, and not for any peculiar advantage to ourselves; the objects are to pay the debts, and to provide for the general welfare of the community. The first of these objects I take to be, that we pay our debts. There are many very meritorious characters who furnished us with essentials in the hour of imminent danger, who, from the imbecility of our former government, have not been able to get even the interest of what they loaned us. I believe it is the first wish of the people throughout the United States to do justice to the public creditors, and to do it in such a manner, that each may contribute an equal part according to his abilities. We have very considerable arrearages due on this account, upon not only the domestic but foreign debt; there are several instalments not yet discharged, and considerable of the interest not yet paid. No statement can be made of the expences of government, so as to ascertain what quantity of revenue will be demanded on that head; but saying that, they will be much the same under this government as the former, we shall have occasion for a very considerable sum to defray the expences. I believe we are not able to make a very accurate calculation of what the system, proposed in the bill, will yield. The late Congress contemplated a million of dollars from this source, which,

Source: *DHFFC*, 10: 567–69, 580–81. © 1992 Johns Hopkins University Press. Reprinted by permission of Johns Hopkins University Press.

in aid of the requisition, they suppose sufficient for the purpose of paying the instalments of the national debt and interest; but that sum alone will now be found very short of what is wanted without the aid of direct taxes. It is very material that we lay the burthen as equal as possible, in whatever mode we pursue to obtain a revenue: a great deal of care has been taken in distributing the proportion with equity; I apprehend, therefore, that we shall not be able to make it much more equitable by any alteration than it is at present. I think also that the people will pay more freely a duty of this nature than they will in direct taxes; if the gentlemen prevail in getting the duties lowered to what the late Congress proposed, they will find themselves obliged to have recourse to direct taxation, for a million and an half, or two million, of dollars. It then only remains for us to consider, whether it will be more agreeable to the people to reduce the impost in this manner, and raise the deficiency by direct taxes. If these duties are to be considered as a tax on the trading part of the community alone they are improper; but this I believe is not the case, the consumer pays them eventually, and they pay no more than what they chuse, because they have it in their power to determine the quantity of taxable articles they will use. A tax left to be paid at discretion must be more agreeable than any other. The merchant considers that part of his capital applied to the payment of the duties the same as if employed in trade, and gets the same profit upon it as on the original cost of the commodity.

As to the tax on distilled spirit, it will be felt as little as any other whatever; and from this source we are to expect a very considerable proportion of the revenue. If we attend to what every body says abroad, we shall have a great deal to do, but there is a great variety of opinions. I have received information from a gentleman of knowledge and experience on this point, and he says, that it is his opinion, and the general opinion of those about him, that the duty on distilled spirits is too low by one-half: the same are the sentiments even of the importers of this article. The duty on it cannot be said to be unequal, as it has been contended on other articles, it is pretty generally consumed throughout the United States. The state I belong to is at a considerable distance from the West-Indies, yet they consume no inconsiderable quantity, but much more than I wish she did. The gentleman from South-Carolina seems to suppose, that the duty will bear harder upon his state than upon others. I cannot think it will be the case, but if they do consume more, they should agree to a high duty in order to lessen the consumption. As to the subject of collection, they refer us to what was done under the government of Britain, in my opinion the comparison does not hold good; it was thought lawful by the people of America to evade those duties because they were unconstitutionally laid; they were not represented in the parliament of Great Britain, and it is a principle that taxation is founded upon representation. As to the collection of the State duties since the peace, I think the governments have laboured under greater disadvantages than the United States will under this system; the duties that were collected by them went into the treasury of the particular state into which the goods were imported; the people who consumed those goods in other states, thought it a peculiar hardship to pay into their funds, what they thought ought to belong to the United States, the great embarrassment arose from this inequality; under the present system each state will pay alike, and will be alike benefitted.

One gentleman has observed, that there is not money enough to pay all the duties imposed in this bill; but is it not as easy to introduce money as merchandize? When there is a demand for it, the merchants will bring it in, for they can as well bring less of a commodity and more money; so that, if this should take place, the objection will be done away. It is in this way that we must be supplied with cash, because we have neither gold nor silver mines to draw it from, if we get it, it must be imported, and will be imported, if it is more advantageous than the importation of other articles.

I think we ought to rely a great deal on the virtue of our constituents; they will be convinced of the necessity of a due collection of the revenue; they will know that it must be done in this way, or it will be by direct taxation. I believe the people will prefer this mode of raising revenue, and will give all the assistance in the execution of the law that is in their power; and as the mercantile part of the people will see that it is equally laid, though it may be something higher than the states have hitherto required, they will submit themselves to our ordinance, and use their influence to aid the collection. I know there will be some characters concerned in an illicit trade, acting without principle, but I think we can restrain them. If there is a degree of infamy attached to the wretches concerned in smuggling, and the practice is detested by the community, a man will scarcely be able to carry on such trade with advantage. It appears to me, therefore, that we had best let the system remain as it is, the duties are reasonable, and will operate as equitable on the people at large, as is in our power to devise; it will at the same time, as it raises revenue, tend to enrich the country, by promoting the industry and oeconomy of our citizens. . . .

MR. AMES

Contended that it would be the particular interest of one set of men to evade the payment of the duties, as mankind was governed by interest, it required all the attention of the government to prevent a breach of the law, because, when the banks and bulwarks of defence were once broken down, the full tide of clandestine commerce would overflow the country. Gentlemen recollected the circumstances which attended the depreciation of the late Continental money; some persons, from motives of interest or necessity, first made a distinction between it and specie, and although every exertion was made by the patriotic among our citizens to prevent the alarming evil, yet every thing was insufficient, they were at length obliged to acquiesce in measures they could not prevent. This was the case on that occasion, and will be the case whenever our laws or regulations run counter to private interest.

Mr. Sherman

The gentleman from Massachusetts (Mr. Ames) has said that because we cannot raise the whole sum necessary to supply our wants, we should be content to stop half way, I know we shall not be able to obtain money enough by the impost to pay off our whole debt, but then I wish to raise as much as possible in this way. I believe the people are able to pay as much as the necessities of the government require, if they are not, we shall never restore the public credit, which is one of the chief ends of our appointment. I believe they are not only able but willing to contribute sufficient for this purpose, the resources of this country are very great if they are properly called into action, and although they may not be so great as those of Britain, yet it should be remembered that nation has occasion for twelve times as much revenue as the United States.

Gentlemen have had recourse to popular opinion in support of their arguments. Popular opinion is founded in justice, and the only way to know if the popular opinion is in favour of a measure, is to examine whether the measure is just and right in itself. I think whatever is proper and right the people will judge of and comply with. The people wish that the government may derive respect from the justice of its measures, they have given it their support on this account. I believe the popular opinion is in favour of raising a revenue to pay our debts, and if we do right they will not neglect their duty; therefore the arguments that are urged in favour of a low duty, will prove that the people are contented with what the bill proposes. The people at this time pay a higher duty on imported rum, than what is proposed in this system, even in Massachusetts; it is true, it is partly laid by way of excise, but I can see no reason against doing it in this way as well as the other.

The article of molasses is a good deal used in that country, but I do not think it so much a necessary of life but what every citizen could live without it; and I believe the people would be very well contented to contribute their proportion of the public expences by a small duty on that article; those who consume foreign luxuries are generally able to pay for them. When gentlemen have recourse to public opinion to support their arguments, they generally find means to accommodate it to their own; the reason why I think public opinion is in favour of the present measure is, because this regulation in itself is reasonable and just.

Some gentlemen think a system of moderate duties will be capable of improvement, every subsequent year they may be encreased, and so become more and more productive. If we were on the eve of a future war, in which it is presumeable our expences would encrease, such policy might be proper; but as we want it only to pay a certain debt, the demand will decrease, and we shall have less occasion for an encrease of revenue.

I think if we should not support public credit now we have the ability, the people will lose all confidence in the government. When they see public bodies shrink from their duty, what can be expected but they will neglect theirs also? It cannot be for the interest of the people of the United States that they should continue to pay a high interest, and suffer an accumulation of the principal of the national debt till some distant period. Will any gentleman assure us that the people will then be better able to pay it off than at present? have they any certain evidence that we shall grow richer as we delay the establishment of our credit, and the payment of our debts? I think they have not; therefore it is best to get out of debt as fast as possible, and while we have the command of funds amply sufficient for the purpose.

12 May 1789

SHERMAN: Offer few words in support of this offer. I voted against 6 cents. Attended carefully to the debates. I was in doubt whether 6 cents would be higher in proportion on this article than articles in general. Another motive, that part of this article consumed by poor people. I am still of opinion that 6 cents not too high as relates to distilleries. Much better to (commute) it. Lay a duty on distiller. I would vote for 3 on molasses. —— ——. Then a duty on rum distilled from molasses which makes the proportion equal to what it was at 6 cents. Is this supported by the disposition of Massachusetts? They did likewise on foreign rum, 12 pence, their money, 6 pence at half. Not so great a burden as to discourage. They are better able to judge than people of other states which most proper, to separate the two objects. The question is whether it does not lay too high on poor people. Don't think the weight of argument lies against discouraging fisheries, unless people consume less of that molasses. Can any gentleman suppose it would lessen the consumption much? I don't think it would. If reduce the consumption as much as that, would be but small proportion. If reduce 2 cents then only as 1 shilling to eight. For my part I should be willing to have duty equalized as can; if I was to look and act partially, I should have this article low. This article which state I belong to imports. Then think 3 on molasses and 4 on rum, as long as connected in one motion. The principle of accommodation two sides—the committee near divided. Won't the other part be dissatisfied as their part would be for 5 cents? I should. I thought I ought to pay that justice in the house. I wish for a motion to divide the duty—"on all rum distilled from molasses, blank cents."

Source: *DHFFC*, 10: 621. © 1992 Johns Hopkins University Press. Reprinted by permission of Johns Hopkins University Press.

13 May 1789

PARKER: Sorry the Constitution allowed importation at all. Contrary to republican principles. I move an addition, "On all slaves 10 dollars for each slave so imported."

SCOTT: Second.

CADWALADER: Second the motion.

SMITH [S.C.]: So important, hoped it would be omitted as proceeded so far. It is matter of most serious consequence for the state to which I come. No one thing done would more affect the state than the question now proposed. Hope withdraw for the present.

SHERMAN: Don't like to see the human beings among goods, wares, and merchandise. Seems improper. Make it proper subject.

Source: *DHFFC*, 10: 633. © 1992 Johns Hopkins University Press. Reprinted by permission of Johns Hopkins University Press.

14 May 1789

SHERMAN: If gentlemen of opinion—The Constitution does not consider them as property—speak as persons. They can lay so much a head in any state that brought in from any place, as ⸺ citizens as they will. Congress have power to (pass), however, for citizenship. Can't prevent migration further than 10 dollars. There are some others besides blacks that ought to be regulated. Convicts—mischievous tendency. Some regulation respecting that so far as can go. I think different subject and ought to take up in different point of view. Congress have right to lay direct tax and excise but not proper to bring all into one law.

Source: *DHFFC*, 10: 638. © 1992 Johns Hopkins University Press. Reprinted by permission of Johns Hopkins University Press.

27 June 1789

MR. SHERMAN

Was well convinced there was a large and decided majority in both houses, and that it was the universal voice of the union, that America should meet commercial restrictions with commercial restrictions; but there might be some disagreement about the best way to effect this point. He did not think it the voice of the people that congress should lay the commerce of a nation under disadvantages, merely because we had no treaty with them; it could not appear a solid reason in the minds of gentlemen, if they considered the subject carefully; therefore it was not the proper principle for the government to act upon. He would mention one that appeared to him more equitable, namely, lay a heavy duty upon all goods coming from any port or territory to which the vessels of the United States are denied access; this would strike directly at objects which the honorable gentleman had in view, without glancing upon other ports to which we were allowed access.

Source: *DHFFC*, II: 1078. © 1992 Johns Hopkins University Press. Reprinted by permission of Johns Hopkins University Press.

13 May 1790

SHERMAN: The matter of discrimination fully discussed last session. Same opinion now. Should have no objection to discrimination on their principle if foundation for it. If could be shown that our vessels paid a lower tonnage in France, would—Keep up to this one principle, treat them as they treat us. Not contend for treaty; never court for it; never use measures to compel them against their will. Consider what regulations they made and meet them as far as for our own advantage. If Spain, Portugal, though not in treaty should admit our vessels in lower tonnage than France or Holland, why should we make discrimination on that account? It said yesterday that consider—beyond duty we expect from the bill—It is to encourage the sale of ships. France not enough. She willing to purchase from us. If Britain suffers, it be their own fault. She may avail themselves by taking off restrictions. They may be our carriers in our vessels. Besides, not operate in favor of France because I don't find that many of their vessels enter our ports. Very few. So operates against Britain than any other, more than any other. Anything that opposes her directly, as not trading with our vessels. She no friend. Wish to treat her as friend, but to hold to such a discrimination.

Source: *DHFFC,* 13: 1287–88. © 1995 Johns Hopkins University Press. Reprinted by permission of Johns Hopkins University Press.

27 December 1790

Mr. PARKER objected to the third. It was laying, he said, a partial tax upon the produce of land; Congress might as well tax wheat.

Mr. SHERMAN observed, that it was necessary an additional revenue should be raised on some article; the impost on other foreign importation, he conceived, had been carried as far as expedient, and he could not think of a more proper article for a heavy duty than spirits; it could not injure the people; on the contrary, it would check the consumption, and thereby prove very beneficial: But if no duty was laid on the same article made at home, the revenue would not be benefited, as our own stills could furnish all that might be consumed, and the consumption would not be lessened, as it could be afforded by our own distillers as cheap as when imported.

Mr. MADISON thought the proposition for this additional duty founded on good principles; he was in favor of it. Yet the ease of collecting direct taxes, he said, was a circumstance much in their favor.

Source: *DHFFC*, 14: 190. © 1996 Johns Hopkins University Press. Reprinted by permission of Johns Hopkins University Press.

6 January 1791

Mr. Sherman. The objections to this article seem to be, that there is no necessity for encreasing the revenue, and that, if there was, this would not be the best mode of doing it. I believe, these opinions will be found, on examination, to be ill-grounded. But the gentleman from Georgia seems to think, we are not disposed to enter into such an examination, but that it is meant to carry the measure by a silent majority. If this had been a new subject, and had never employed the attention of the House, there might possibly be some ground for the observation. But when it is considered, that it was fully discussed, though not adopted, last session, the charge becomes totally unfounded. That it was not adopted, arose from contingencies perfectly no doubt in the recollection of every member. It was intended, at the last session, to make provision for the payment of the interest on the debt of the United States, and exclusively of the debts of the particular States. Many of those gentlemen, who were the friends of the assumption, concurred in striking out of the revenue plan the scheme of the excise, under an idea, that if the states were to continue to sustain the whole burthen of the debts they had contracted in the common cause of the confederacy during the late war, then this source of revenue ought to be left to them, in order to enable them to discharge the same. And it will be remembered, that the decision, in favor of the assumption of the state debts, was made so near the close of the last session, that the plan of additional revenue could not conveniently have been gone through. From this history of the business, it must be discovered, that the present subject had its full share of discussion. If so, can gentlemen insinuate, that there is a disposition to carry a vote by a silent majority, especially if nothing new is urged, in addition to the arguments, which have been already fully answered? Ought it not, on the contrary, to be thought unreasonable to take up so much more of the time of the House, in repeating what must be in the recollection of every gentleman?

The House, at the last session, gave special directions to the Secretary of

Source: *DHFFC*, 14: 246–47. © 1996 Johns Hopkins University Press. Reprinted by permission of Johns Hopkins University Press.

the Treasury, to report, what further provision would be necessary to complete the engagements of the United States. He has done it; and it appears from his report, that it is necessary to collect the money contemplated in this bill. It is true, there has been some surplus in the collection, beyond the calculation. But this cannot be conclusive evidence, as to the sum, which may be raised the next year: and it is incumbent on government to provide enough. There never ought to be a deficiency, as such an accident may tend to injure public credit: whereas if a surplusage accrues, it may be well applied in sinking the principal; so that the United States can suffer no injury from such an event. But I apprehend there may not be the surplus, which gentlemen please themselves with: for I very much doubt, if any man within these walls has more accurate or better information, than that officer, whose duty it is to have congnizance of these affairs.

As to the propriety of the duty itself, I think gentlemen are mistaken. They call it an excise, and then declaim against the measure. Call it by what name you will, you cannot change its nature: and this duty is not of the nature of that excise, which has become odious in Europe, and against which a popular clamor is excited. Those excises follow the articles into the hands of the consumer. All retailers and tavern-keepers are exposed to the visits of the excise-officers, who, in consequence of such multiplied business, are necessarily numerous; and this occasions no inconsiderable degree of the uneasiness so often expressed. But care is taken, in this bill, to collect the excise at the fountain-head. The distillers and importers are to pay the duty; and it affects none others of the community. In this case, the odium has no ground, whereon to rest itself; and falls, of consequence, to nothing.

As to the public voice, I believe it to be clearly in favour of a tax on ardent spirits; at least nine-tenths of the people approve this sentiment. And in order to make the tax operate equally, it is necessary, that it be laid on spirits distilled in the United States, as well as on that which is imported; otherwise the consumers of the former pay nothing, while the consumers of the latter pay all. It is necessary likewise on another account: it would lose to the government a great part of the revenue rising from imported spirits, inasmuch as it would operate as a bounty on home-made spirits, and encrease the consumption of the one, at the expense of the other. I believe it is not an object, that deserves the particular encouragement of the government, to encrease the manufacture or distillation of ardent spirits. It will be enough for us, to keep up its relative condition, as we found it, when the government commenced its operation.

Western Lands

13 July 1789

Mr. Sherman

Thought it best to delay the decision of this subject. It is certainly a matter of high importance to the union, that this land be disposed of, in the best manner, no doubt but if it is properly managed, it will pay the principal and interest of all the debts of the United States, said he, but I have great objection to the manner of settlement proposed by the honorable gentleman from Pennsylvania: I think it would tend to greater advantage, to settle the country gradually, in compact bodies, as the inhabitants can be spared from the other parts of the union. But this business ought to be managed with a degree of caution, least we open a door to that field of speculation, in the certificates of the United States, by which the holders of the securities may be treated with injustice.

It will be a better plan to settle the country by townships; so far I would be willing to go; and also make arrangements for compleating the survey of those tracts already disposed of; perhaps it might be well to give some of the township lots to settlers, without any charge, reserving others to sell at some future day, when they become more valuable, in consequence of the settlement around them; I apprehend we should get more money in this way than in that proposed. If men are to take out warrants, and lay them where they please, the pitches will brake up the ground, and we shall be forced to sell after a while, for less money, because the lands will be picked and nothing but the refuse left; beside, people not knowing where others have located, may take up the same lots, and lay a foundation for eternal law-suits, and discontent.

Source: *DHFFC*, II: 1108–9. © 1992 Johns Hopkins University Press. Reprinted by permission of Johns Hopkins University Press.

20 January 1790

MR. SHERMAN

Thought the best way to manage this business, was to refer it to the secretary of the treasury, as was proposed. He said that the unappropriated land in the western territory was a great fund of wealth, and which if properly disposed of might extinguish the national debt, and be peopled with a valuable class of citizens; but if from a mistaken policy it was thrown away upon foreign adventurers or speculators, the public would get nothing for them, as had been the case heretofore, in the sale of large districts, where the expences attending the surveys &c. left very little profit to the United States. It is true such measures may induce a number of foreigners to come among us, but then it ought to be remembered that such are generally persons of different education, manners, and customs from the citizens of the union, and not so likely to harmonize in a republican government, as might be wished; consequently any considerable accession of this class of settlers might tend to disturb the harmony and tranquillity, and embarrass the operations of the government. He thought it was worthy of enquiry, whether America stood in need of emigrants to people her territory; he supposed the notorious rapid population of the present inhabitants, was of itself sufficient for the purpose, it must have struck the observation of every gentleman, that they were daily throwing off vast numbers, and extending the settlements into that country which some gentlemen seemed to think could not be too early cultivated. But nevertheless, he was willing to let foreigners come in gradually, and in the same way he was inclined to dispose of the lands. He thought it would be most judicious to lay off a district at a time, reserving some lots which, with the increasing population of the surrounding ones, would encrease in value, and ultimately these reserved lots would bring more into the Treasury than the others. He wished the business to go to the Secretary of the Treasury, because he supposed he had the most information respecting it.

Source: *DHFFC*, 12: 51–52. © 1995 Johns Hopkins University Press. Reprinted by permission of Johns Hopkins University Press.

Bill of Rights

On June 8, 1789, James Madison encouraged his colleagues to take "into consideration the subject of amendments to the constitution."[1] Sherman responded
that he understood that some of his colleagues thought it their duty to discuss
a bill of rights, but he had "strong objections to being interrupted in completing
the more important business."[2] Madison, nevertheless, went ahead and made
his famous speech proposing a bill of rights. The House declined to move
forward at that time, and the issue was tabled. Sherman wanted to make sure
it remained tabled, so he arranged to have his essays against adding a bill of
rights republished in the *New York Packet* and several New England papers
during the summer of 1789.[3]

Undeterred by Sherman's literary efforts, on July 21 Madison "[b]egged the
house to indulge him in the further consideration of amendments to the constitution."[4] Sherman again objected, pointing out that eleven states had ratified
the Constitution and that a majority of them did not propose amendments.
Madison was again put off, although this time the House approved a motion
by Fisher Ames to form a select committee composed of one member from
each state to consider amendments.[5] Sherman was appointed to represent Connecticut. There are no records of the committee's deliberations, but the committee did produce a draft bill of rights in Sherman's handwriting. This is the
only handwritten draft of the Bill of Rights known to exist. The draft is undated but was likely penned between July 21 and July 28.[6] The printed report
from the select committee differs significantly from the draft in Sherman's
hand. It was this report that was debated by the House in August. Sherman
also served on the three-person House committee charged with arranging the
amendments proposed by the House, and on the six-person conference committee charged with reconciling the House and Senate versions of the Bill of
Rights.[7]

---

1. *DHFFC,* 11: 811.

2. Ibid., 11: 815.

3. Ibid., 11: 821–27, 836; 4: 3–4, 9–12; Collier, *Roger Sherman's Connecticut,* 297; *DHFFC,* 16: 682,
975, 1041.

4. *DHFFC,* 11: 1158.

5. Ibid., 11: 1158–63.

6. Ibid., 4: 4; 16: 1099–100. For a discussion of the extent to which the draft reflects Sherman's
views or those of the committee, see Hall, *Roger Sherman and the Creation of the American Republic,*
135–37.

7. *DHFFC,* 11: 1292; 19: 1430, 1827.

Correspondence between Henry Gibbs and Roger Sherman, 1789

Sherman sent copies of his "Citizen of New Haven" essays (found on pages 491–99 of this volume) to Henry Gibbs (1749–94), a Massachusetts merchant, and encouraged him to have them republished in Massachusetts. Gibbs's response prompted a second letter that reveals some of Sherman's thoughts on the proposed bill of rights.

Letter to Henry Gibbs, June 1, 1789

The enclosed Letter came enclosed to me I Suppose from one of my family—an extract from my last has found its way from the Salem Paper—into one of the papers in this City, I wrote it in haste without any view to its publication, but I think the publishing it may be of Some use.

I now enclose two News papers, of the 20th & 24th of March, containing Obeservations on the New Federal Constitutions, and the alterations proposed as amendments Signed *A Citizen of New Haven* for your perusal, and if you Shall think it may be useful, that they may be published in the Salem Paper, & any other Papers in your State—It will be best to put the whole into one Paper, and I wish to have one of them transmitted to me when You write again—I believe the contention about amendments of the Constitution has pretty much Subsided every where, and I trust the people will be Still more reconciled to it, as the Laws that will from time to time be made under it Shall be published.

The Impost & Tonage Laws are not yet finished but I hope will be, very Soon.

Source: *DHFFC*, 16: 682. © 2004 Johns Hopkins University Press. Reprinted by permission of Johns Hopkins University Press.

Letter from Henry Gibbs to Roger Sherman, July 16, 1789

Your favor of the 1rst. Ult. came seasonably to hand as has also that of the 7th. Inst. the former inclosed the pieces under the signature of "a Citizen of New Haven" which I immediately handed to our Printers & which were publish'd in their papers of June 30th. & July 7th. I am far from wishing that the Beauty of our new System should be marred by the many preposterous Alterations which have been propos'd. but as it was adopted by some of the States in full Confidence that the subject of Amendments would be soon constitutionally enter'd upon, I hope Congress will not delay canvassing the matter any longer than their more important Business renders necessary. All Ambiguity of Expression certainly ought to be remov'd; Liberty of Conscience in religious matters, right of trial by Jury, Liberty of the Press &c. may perhaps be more explicitly secur'd to the Subject & a general reservation made to the States respectively of all the powers not expressly delegated to the general Government. These indeed may be tho't by most to be the spirit of the Constitution, but there are some who have their fears that the loose manner of expression in some instances will not sufficiently guard the rights of the Subject from the invasion of corrupt Rulers hereafter. Some such explanatory & reserving Clauses may therefore without giving umbrage to the friends of the new plan of Government tend greatly to conciliate the minds of many of it's Opponents. As to any essential Alterations neither time nor Capacity will allow of my forming an Opinion respecting them. We sympathise with you Sir, on the melancholly occasion of your Son's [*William*] Death as also on the unfortunate Incidents of his Life & sincerely wish you that Comfort in your other Children which an all-wise Providence has in some respects deny'd you in the Deceas'd. We have lately made a little excursion into the Country, found our Friends at Concord all well. We are rejoic'd at the news of Sister [*Rebecca*] Sherman's being in better Health & wish her a Confirmation of that desirable Blessing. *** I am desir'd by a Friend to ask you whether it is probable any thing will be done respecting the Domestic Debt before the expected recess of Congress.

Source: *DHFFC*, 16: 1041. © 2004 Johns Hopkins University Press. Reprinted by permission of Johns Hopkins University Press.

Letter to Henry Gibbs, August 4, 1789

I received your letter of the 19th *Ultimo* & the papers accompanying the Same. You have doubtless before this Seen the amendments to the Constitution reported by the Committee—they will probaly be harmless & satisfactory to those who are fond of Bills of rights, I dont like the form in which they are reported to be incorporated in the Constitution, that Instrument being the act of the people, ought to be kept intire—and amendments made by the legislatures Should be in addition by way of Supplement. As to the Domestic [*de*]bt it will doubtless be provided for as soon as possible—and a Committee of ways and means is appointed. but I dont think there will be money to make any payment soon—and I hope the present Congress will never make any engagement but Such as they can punctually perform.

Source: *DHFFC,* 16: 1237–38. © 2004 Johns Hopkins University Press. Reprinted by permission of Johns Hopkins University Press.

EXCERPTS FROM CONGRESSIONAL DEBATES OVER
THE BILL OF RIGHTS, JUNE 8–JULY 21, 1789

8 June 1789

Mr. Madison

This day Mr. Speaker, is the day assigned for taking into consideration the subject of amendments to the constitution. As I considered myself bound in honor and in duty to do what I have done on this subject, I shall proceed to bring the amendments before you as soon as possible, and advocate them until they shall be finally adopted or rejected by a constitutional majority of this house. With a view of drawing your attention to this important object, I shall move, that this house do now resolve itself into a committee of the whole, on the state of the union, by which an opportunity will be given, to bring forward some propositions which I have strong hopes, will meet the unanimous approbation of this house, after the fullest discussion and most serious regard. I therefore move you, that the house now go into a committee on this business. . . .

Mr. Sherman.

I do not suppose the constitution to be perfect, nor do I imagine if congress and all the legislatures on the continent were to revise it, that their united labours would make it perfect. I do not expect any perfection on this side the grave in the works of man; but my opinion is, that we are not at present in circumstances to make it better. It is a wonder that there has been such unanimity in adopting it, considering the ordeal it had to undergo; and the unanimity which prevailed at its formation, is equally astonishing; amidst all the members from the twelve states present at the federal convention, there were only three who did not sign the instrument to attest their opinion of its goodness. Of the eleven states who have received it, the majority have ratified it without proposing a single amendment; this circumstance leads me to suppose that we shall not be able to propose any alterations that are likely to be adopted by nine states; and gentlemen know before the alterations take effect, they must be agreed to by the legislatures of three-fourths of the states in the

Source: *DHFFC*, 11: 811, 834, 818–27. © 1992 Johns Hopkins University Press. Reprinted by permission of Johns Hopkins University Press.

union. Those states that have not recommended alterations will hardly adopt them, unless it is clear that they tend to make the constitution better; now how this can be made out to their satisfaction I am yet to learn; they know of no defect from experience. It seems to be the opinion of gentlemen generally, that this is not the time for entering upon the discussion of amendments: our only question therefore is, how to get rid of the subject; now for my own part I would prefer to have it referred to a committee of the whole, rather than a special committee, and therefore shall not agree to the motion now before the house.

Mr. Gerry moved, that the business lie over until the 1st. day of July next, and that it be the order for that day. . . .

Mr. Madison.

I am sorry to be accessory to the loss of a single moment of time by the house. If I had been indulged in my motion, and we had gone into a committee of the whole, I think we might have rose, and resumed the consideration of other business before this time; that is, so far as it depended on what I proposed to bring forward. As that mode seems not to give satisfaction, I will withdraw the motion, and move you, sir, that a select committee be appointed to consider and report such amendments as are proper for Congress to propose to the legislatures of the several States, conformably to the 5th article of the constitution. I will state my reasons why I think it proper to propose amendments; and state the amendments themselves, so far as I think they ought to be proposed. If I thought I could fulfill the duty which I owe to myself and my constituents, to let the subject pass over in silence, I most certainly should not trespass upon the indulgence of this house. But I cannot do this; and am therefore compelled to beg a patient hearing to what I have to lay before you. And I do most sincerely believe that if congress will devote but one day to this subject, so far as to satisfy the public that we do not disregard their wishes, it will have a salutary influence on the public councils, and prepare the way for a favorable reception of our future measures. It appears to me that this house is bound by every motive of prudence, not to let the first session pass over without proposing to the state legislatures some things to be incorporated into the constitution, as will render it as acceptable to the whole people of the United States, as it has been found acceptable to a majority of them. I wish, among other reasons why something should be done, that those who have been friendly to the adoption of this constitution, may have the opportunity of proving to those who were opposed to it, that they were as sincerely devoted to liberty and a republican government, as those who charged them with wishing the adoption of this constitution in order to lay the foundation of an aristocracy or despotism. It will be a desirable thing to extinguish from the bosom of every member of the community any apprehensions, that there are those among his countrymen who wish to deprive them of the liberty for which they valiantly fought and honorably bled. And if there are amendments desired, of such a nature as will not injure the constitution, and they can be ingrafted so as to give satisfaction to the doubting part of our fellow citizens; the friends of the federal government will evince that spirit of deference and concession for which they have hitherto been distinguished.

It cannot be a secret to the gentlemen in this house, that, notwithstanding the ratification of this system of government by eleven of the thirteen United States, in some cases unanimously, in others by large majorities; yet still there is a great number of our constituents who are dissatisfied with it; among whom are many respectable for their talents, their patriotism, and respectable for the jealousy they have for their liberty, which, though mistaken in its object, is laudable in its motive. There is a great body of the people falling under this description, who at present feel much inclined to join their support to the cause of federalism, if they were satisfied in this one point: We ought not to disregard their inclination, but, on principles of amity and moderation, conform to their wishes, and expressly declare the great rights of mankind secured under this constitution. The acquiescence which our fellow citizens shew under the government, calls upon us for a like return of moderation. But perhaps there is a stronger motive than this for our going into a consideration of the subject; it is to provide those securities for liberty which are required by a part of the community, I allude in a particular manner to those two states who have not thought fit to throw themselves into the bosom of the confederacy: it is a desirable thing, on our part as well as theirs, that a re-union should take place as soon as possible. I have no doubt, if we proceed to take those steps which would be prudent and requisite at this juncture, that in a short time we should see that disposition prevailing in those states that are not come in, that we have seen prevailing in those states which are.

But I will candidly acknowledge, that, over and above all these considerations, I do conceive that the constitution may be amended; that is to say, if all power is subject to abuse, that then it is possible the abuse of the powers of the general government may be guarded against in a more secure manner than is now done, while no one advantage, arising from the exercise of that power, shall be damaged or endangered by it. We have in this way something to gain, and, if we proceed with caution, nothing to lose; and in this case it is necessary to proceed with caution; for while we feel all these inducements to go into a revisal of the constitution, we must feel for the constitution itself, and make that revisal a moderate one. I should be unwilling to see a door opened for a re-consideration of the whole structure of the government, for a re-consideration of the principles and the substance of the powers given; because I doubt, if such a door was opened, if we should be very likely to stop at that point which would be safe to the government itself: But I do wish to see a door opened to consider, so far as to incorporate those provisions for the security of rights, against which I believe no serious objection has been made by any class of our constituents. Such as would be likely to meet with the concurrence of two-thirds of both houses, and the approbation of three-fourths of the state legislatures. I will not propose a single alteration which I do not wish to see take place, as intrinsically proper in itself, or proper because it is wished for by a respectable number of my fellow citizens; and therefore I shall not propose a single alteration but is likely to meet the concurrence required by the constitution.

There have been objections of various kinds made against the constitution: Some were levelled against its structure, because the president was without a council; because the senate, which is a legislative body, had judicial powers in trials on impeachments; and because the powers of that body were compounded in other respects, in a manner that did not correspond with a particular theory; because it grants more power than is supposed to be necessary for every good purpose; and controuls the ordinary powers of the state governments. I know some respectable characters who opposed this government on these grounds; but I believe that the great mass of the people who opposed it, disliked it because it did not contain effectual provision against encroachments on particular rights, and those safeguards which they have been long accustomed to have interposed between them and the magistrate who exercised the sovereign power: nor ought we to consider them safe, while a great number of our fellow citizens think these securities necessary.

It has been a fortunate thing that the objection to the government has been made on the ground I stated; because it will be practicable on that ground to obviate the objection, so far as to satisfy the public mind that their liberties will be perpetual, and this without endangering any part of the constitution, which is considered as essential to the existence of the government by those who promoted its adoption.

The amendments which have occurred to me, proper to be recommended by congress to the state legislatures, are these:
***
The first of these amendments, relates to what may be called a bill of rights; I will own that I never considered this provision so essential to the federal constitution, as to make it improper to ratify it, until such an amendment was added; at the same time, I always conceived, that in a certain form and to a

certain extent, such a provision was neither improper nor altogether useless. I am aware, that a great number of the most respectable friends to the government and champions for republican liberty, have thought such a provision, not only unnecessary, but even improper, nay, I believe some have gone so far as to think it even dangerous. Some policy has been made use of perhaps by gentlemen on both sides of the question: I acknowledge the ingenuity of those arguments which were drawn against the constitution, by a comparison with the policy of Great-Britain, in establishing a declaration of rights; but there is too great a difference in the case to warrant the comparison: therefore the arguments drawn from that source, were in a great measure inapplicable. In the declaration of rights which that country has established, the truth is, they have gone no farther, than to raise a barrier against the power of the crown, the power of the legislature is left altogether indefinite. Altho' I know whenever the great rights, the trial by jury, freedom of the press, or liberty of conscience, came in question in that body, the invasion of them is resisted by able advocates, yet their Magna Charta does not contain any one provision for the security of those rights, respecting which, the people of America are most alarmed. The freedom of the press and rights of conscience, those choicest privileges of the people, are unguarded in the British constitution.

But altho' the case may be widely different, and it may not be thought necessary to provide limits for the legislative power in that country, yet a different opinion prevails in the United States. The people of many states, have thought it necessary to raise barriers against power in all forms and departments of government, and I am inclined to believe, if once bills of rights are established in all the states as well as the federal constitution, we shall find that altho' some of them are rather unimportant, yet, upon the whole, they will have a salutary tendency.

It may be said, in some instances they do no more than state the perfect equality of mankind, this to be sure is an absolute truth, yet it is not absolutely necessary to be inserted at the head of a constitution.

In some instances they assert those rights which are exercised by the people in forming and establishing a plan of government. In other instances, they specify those rights which are retained when particular powers are given up to be exercised by the legislature. In other instances, they specify positive rights, which may seem to result from the nature of the compact. Trial by jury cannot be considered as a natural right, but a right resulting from the social compact which regulates the action of the community, but is as essential to secure the liberty of the people as any one of the pre-existent rights of nature. In other instances they lay down dogmatic maxims with respect to the construction of the government; declaring, that the legislative, executive, and judicial branches shall be kept separate and distinct: Perhaps the best way of securing this in practice is to provide such checks, as will prevent the encroachment of the one upon the other.

But whatever may be the form which the several states have adopted in making declarations in favor of particular rights, the great object in view is to limit and qualify the powers of government, by excepting out of the grant of power those cases in which the government ought not to act, or to act only in a particular mode. They point these exceptions sometimes against the abuse of the executive power, sometimes against the legislative, and, in some cases, against the community itself; or, in other words, against the majority in favor of the minority.

In our government it is, perhaps, less necessary to guard against the abuse in the executive department than any other; because it is not the stronger branch of the system, but the weaker: It therefore must be levelled against the legislative, for it is the most powerful, and most likely to be abused, because it is under the least controul; hence, so far as a declaration of rights can tend to prevent the exercise of undue power, it cannot be doubted but such declaration is proper. But I confess that I do conceive, that in a government modified like this of the United States, the great danger lies rather in the abuse of the community than in the legislative body. The prescriptions in favor of liberty, ought to be levelled against that quarter where the greatest danger lies, namely, that which possesses the highest prerogative of power: But this is not found in either the executive or legislative departments of government, but in the body of the people, operating by the majority against the minority.

It may be thought all paper barriers against the power of the community, are too weak to be worthy of attention. I am sensible they are not so strong as to satisfy gentlemen of every description who have seen and examined thoroughly the texture of such a defence; yet, as they have a tendency to impress some degree of respect for them, to establish the public opinion in their favor, and rouse the attention of the whole community, it may be one mean to controul the majority from those acts to which they might be otherwise inclined.

It has been said by way of objection to a bill of rights, by many respectable gentlemen out of doors, and I find opposition on the same principles likely to be made by gentlemen on this floor, that they are unnecessary articles of a republican government, upon the presumption that the people have those rights in their own hands, and that is the proper place for them to rest. It would be a sufficient answer to say that this objection lies against such provisions under the state governments as well as under the general government; and there are, I believe, but few gentlemen who are inclined to push their theory so far as to say that a declaration of rights in those cases is either ineffectual or improper. It has been said that in the federal government they are unnecessary, because the powers are enumerated, and it follows that all that are not granted by the constitution are retained: that the constitution is a bill of powers, the great residuum being the rights of the people; and therefore a bill of rights cannot be so necessary as if the residuum was thrown into the hands of the government. I admit that these arguments are not entirely without foundation; but they are not conclusive to the extent which has been supposed. It is true the powers of the general government are circumscribed, they are directed to particular objects; but even if government keeps within those limits, it has certain discretionary powers with respect to the means, which may admit of abuse to a certain extent, in the same manner as the powers of the state governments under their constitutions may to an indefinite extent; because in the constitution of the United States there is a clause granting to Congress the power to make all laws which shall be necessary and proper for carrying into execution all the powers vested in the government of the United States, or in any department or officer thereof; this enables them to fulfil every purpose for which the government was established. Now, may not laws be considered necessary and proper by Congress, for it is them who are to judge of the necessity and propriety to accomplish those special purposes which they may have in contemplation, which laws in themselves are neither necessary or proper; as well as improper laws could be enacted by the state legislatures, for fulfilling the more extended objects of those governments. I will state an instance which I think in point, and proves that this might be the case. The general government has a right to pass all laws which shall be necessary to collect its revenue; the means for enforcing the collection are within the direction of the legislature: may not general warrants be considered necessary for this purpose, as well as for some purposes which it was supposed at the framing of their constitutions the state governments had in view. If there was reason for restraining the state governments from exercising this power, there is like reason for restraining the federal government.

It may be said, because it has been said, that a bill of rights is not necessary, because the establishment of this government has not repealed those declarations of rights which are added to the several state constitutions: that those rights of the people, which had been established by the most solemn act, could not be annihilated by a subsequent act of that people, who meant, and declared at the head of the instrument, that they ordained and established a new system, for the express purpose of securing to themselves and posterity the liberties they had gained by an arduous conflict.

I admit the force of this observation, but I do not look upon it to be conclusive. In the first place, it is too uncertain ground to leave this provision upon, if a provision is at all necessary to secure rights so important as many of those I have mentioned are conceived to be, by the public in general, as well as those in particular who opposed the adoption of this constitution. Beside some states have no bills of rights, there are others provided with very defective ones, and there are others whose bills of rights are not only defective, but absolutely improper; instead of securing some in the full extent which republican principles would require, they limit them too much to agree with the common ideas of liberty.

It has been objected also against a bill of rights, that, by enumerating particular exceptions to the grant of power, it would disparage those rights which were not placed in that enumeration, and it might follow by implication, that those rights which were not singled out, were intended to be assigned into the hands of the general government, and were consequently insecure. This is one of the most plausible arguments I have ever heard urged against the admission of a bill of rights into this system; but, I conceive, that may be guarded against. I have attempted it, as gentlemen may see by turning to the last clause of the 4th resolution.

It has been said, that it is unnecessary to load the constitution with this provision, because it was not found effectual in the constitution of the particular states. It is true, there are a few particular states in which some of the most valuable articles have not, at one time or other, been violated; but it does not follow but they may have, to a certain degree, a salutary effect against the abuse of power. If they are incorporated into the constitution, independent tribunals of justice will consider themselves in a peculiar manner the guardians of those rights; they will be an impenetrable bulwark against every assumption of power in the legislative or executive; they will be naturally led to resist every encroachment upon rights expressly stipulated for in the constitution by the declaration of rights. Beside this security, there is a great probability that such a declaration in the federal system would be inforced; because the state legislatures will jealously and closely watch the operations of this government, and be able to resist with more effect every assumption of power than any other power on earth can do; and the greatest opponents to a federal government admit the state legislatures to be sure guardians of the people's liberty. I conclude from this view of the subject, that it will be proper in itself, and highly politic, for the tranquility of the public mind, and the stability of the government, that we should offer something, in the form I have proposed, to be incorporated in the system of government, as a declaration of the rights of the people.

In the next place I wish to see that part of the constitution revised which declares, that the number of representatives shall not exceed the proportion of one for every thirty thousand persons, and allows one representative to every state which rates below that proportion. If we attend to the discussion of this subject, which has taken place in the state conventions, and even in the opinion of the friends to the constitution, an alteration here is proper. It is the sense of the people of America, that the number of representatives ought to be encreased, but particularly that it should not be left in the discretion of the government to diminish them, below that proportion which certainly is in the power of the legislature as the constitution now stands; and they may, as the population of the country encreases, increase the house of representatives to a very unwieldy degree. I confess I always thought this part of the constitution defective, though not dangerous; and that it ought to be particularly attended to whenever congress should go into the consideration of amendments.

There are several lesser cases enumerated in my proposition, in which I wish also to see some alteration take place. That article which leaves it in the power of the legislature to ascertain its own emolument is one to which I allude. I do not believe this is a power which, in the ordinary course of government, is likely to be abused, perhaps of all the powers granted, it is least likely to abuse; but there is a seeming impropriety in leaving any set of men without controul to put their hand into the public coffers, to take out money to put in their pockets; there is a seeming indecorum in such power, which leads me to propose a change. We have a guide to this alteration in several of the amendments which the different conventions have proposed. I have gone therefore so far as to fix it, that no law, varying the compensation, shall operate until there is a change in the legislature; in which case it cannot be for the particular benefit of those who are concerned in determining the value of the service.

I wish also, in revising the constitution, we may throw into that section, which interdicts the abuse of certain powers in the state legislatures, some other provisions of equal if not greater importance than those already made. The words, "No state shall pass any bill of attainder, ex post facto law, &c." were wise and proper restrictions in the constitution. I think there is more danger of those powers being abused by the state governments than by the government of the United States. The same may be said of other powers which they possess, if not controuled by the general principle, that laws are unconstitutional which infringe the rights of the community. I should therefore wish to extend this interdiction, and add, as I have stated in the 5th resolution, that no state shall violate the equal right of conscience, freedom of the press, or trial by jury in criminal cases; because it is proper that every government should be disarmed of powers which trench upon those particular rights. I know in some of the state constitutions the power of the government is controuled by such a declaration, but others are not. I cannot see any reason against obtaining even a double security on those points; and nothing can give a more sincere proof of the attachment of those who opposed this constitution to these great and important rights, than to see them join in obtaining the security I have now proposed; because it must be admitted, on all hands, that the state governments are as liable to attack these invaluable privileges as the general government is, and therefore ought to be as cautiously guarded against.

I think it will be proper, with respect to the judiciary powers, to satisfy the public mind on those points which I have mentioned. Great inconvenience has been apprehended to suitors from the distance they would be dragged to obtain justice in the supreme court of the United States, upon an appeal on an action for a small debt. To remedy this, declare, that no appeal shall be made unless the matter in controversy amounts to a particular sum: This, with the regulations respecting jury trials in criminal cases, and suits at common law, it is to be hoped will quiet and reconcile the minds of the people to that part of the constitution.

I find, from looking into the amendments proposed by the state conventions, that several are particularly anxious that it should be declared in the constitution, that the powers not therein delegated, should be reserved to the several states. Perhaps words which may define this more precisely, than the whole of the instrument now does, may be considered as superfluous. I admit they may be deemed unnecessary; but there can be no harm in making such a declaration, if gentlemen will allow that the fact is as stated, I am sure I understand it so, and do therefore propose it.

These are the points on which I wish to see a revision of the constitution take place. How far they will accord with the sense of this body, I cannot take upon me absolutely to determine; but I believe every gentleman will readily admit that nothing is in contemplation, so far as I have mentioned, that can endanger the beauty of the government in any one important feature, even in the eyes of its most sanguine admirers. I have proposed nothing that does not appear to me as proper in itself, or eligible as patronised by a respectable number of our fellow citizens; and if we can make the constitution better in the opinion of those who are opposed to it, without weakening its frame, or abridging its usefulness, in the judgment of those who are attached to it, we act the part of wise and liberal men to make such alterations as shall produce that effect.

Having done what I conceived was my duty, in bringing before this house the subject of amendments, and also stated such as I wish for and approve, and offered the reasons which occurred to me in their support; I shall content myself for the present with moving, that a committee be appointed to consider of and report such amendments as ought to be proposed by congress to the legislatures of the states, to become, if ratified by three-fourths thereof, part of the constitution of the United States. By agreeing to this motion, the subject may be going on in the committee, while other important business is proceeding to a conclusion in the house. I should advocate greater dispatch in the business of amendments, if I was not convinced of the absolute necessity there is of pursuing the organization of the government; because I think we should obtain the confidence of our fellow citizens, in proportion as we fortify the rights of the people against the encroachments of the government.

21 July 1789

MR. MADISON

Begged the house to indulge him in the further consideration of amendments to the constitution, and as there appeared, in some degree, a moment of leisure, he would move to go into a committee of the whole on the subject, conformably to the order of the 8th of last month.

MR. AMES

Hoped that the house would be induced, on mature reflection, to rescind their vote of going into committee on the business, and refer it to a select committee: It would certainly tend to facilitate the business. If they had the subject at large before a committee of the whole, he could not see where the business was likely to end. The amendments proposed were so various, that their discussion must inevitably occupy many days, and that at a time when they can be illy spared; whereas a select committee could go through and cull out those of the most material kind, without interrupting the principal business of the house. He therefore moved, that the committee of the whole be discharged, and the subject referred to a select committee.

MR. SEDGWICK

Opposed the motion, for the reasons given by his colleague, observing that the members from the several states proposing amendments, would no doubt drag the house through the consideration of every one, whatever their fate might be after they were discussed, now gentlemen had only to reflect on this, and conceive the length of time the business would take up, if managed in this way.

MR. WHITE

Thought no time would be saved by appointing a select committee. Every member would like to be satisfied with the reasons upon which the amend-

Source: *DHFFC*, II: 1158–59. © 1992 Johns Hopkins University Press. Reprinted by permission of Johns Hopkins University Press.

ments offered by the select committee are grounded, consequently the train of argument which gentlemen have in contemplation to avoid, must be brought forward.

He did not presume to say the constitution was perfect, but it was such as had met with the approbation of wise and good men in the different states. Some of the proposed amendments were also of high value, but he did not expect they would be supported by two thirds of both houses, without undergoing a thorough investigation. He did not like to refer any business to a select committee, until the sense of the house had been expressed upon it, because it rather tended to retard than dispatch it, witness the collection bill which had cost them much time, but after all had to be deserted.

Mr. Sherman.

The provision for amendments made in the fifth article of the constitution, was intended to facilitate the adoption of those which experience should point out to be necessary. This constitution has been adopted by eleven states, a majority of those eleven have received it without expressing a wish for amendments; now, is it probable that three fourths of the eleven states will agree to amendments offered on mere speculative points, when the constitution has had no kind of trial whatever? It is hardly to be expected that they will: Consequently we shall lose our labour, and had better decline having any thing farther to do with it for the present.

But if the house are to go into a consideration, it had better be done in such a way as not to interfere much with the organization of the government.

Draft House Committee Report in Sherman's Hand, July 21–28, 1789

Report it as their Opinion, that the following articles be proposed by by Congress to the legislatures of the Several States to be adopted by them as amendments of the Constitution of the United States, and when ratified by the legislatures of three fourth's (at least) of the Said States in the union, to become a part of the constitution of the United States, pursuant to the fifth Article of the Said Constitution.

1   The powers of Government being derived from the people, ought to be exercised for their benefit, and they have an inherent and unalienable right, to change or amend their political constitution, when ever they judge such change will advance their interest & happiness.

2   The people have certain natural rights which are retained by them when they enter into society, Such are the rights of conscience in matters of religion; of acquiring property, and of pursuing happiness & safety; of Speaking, writing and publishing their Sentiments with decency and freedom; of peaceably Assembling to consult their common good, and of applying to Government by petition or remonstrance for redress of grievances. Of these rights therefore they Shall not be deprived by the Government of the United States.

3   No person shall be tried for any crime whereby he may incur loss of life or any infamous punishment, without Indictment by a grand Jury, nor be convicted but by the unanimous verdict of a Petit Jury of good and lawful men freeholders of the vicinage or district where the trial shall be had.

4   After a census Shall be taken, each State Shall be allowed one representative for every thirty thousand Inhabitants of the description in the Second Section of the first Article of the Constitution, until the whole number of representatives Shall amount to   but never to exceed   .

Source: *DHFFC*, 16: 1099–100. © 2004 Johns Hopkins University Press. Reprinted by permission of Johns Hopkins University Press.

5 The Militia shall be under the government of the laws of the respective States, when not in the actual Service of the United States, but Such rules as may be prescribed by Congress for their uniform organisation & discipline shall be observed in officering and training them. but military Service Shall not be required of persons religiously Scrupulous of bearing arms.

6 No Soldier Shall be quartered in any private house, in time of Peace, nor at any time, but by authority of law.

7 ~~No~~ Excessive bail shall not be required, nor excessive fines imposed, nor cruel & unusual punishments inflicted in any case.

8 Congress shall not have power to grant any monopoly or exclusive advantages of Commerce to any person or Company; nor to restrain the liberty of the Press.

9 In Suits at common law in courts acting under the Authority of the United States, issues of fact Shall be tried by a Jury if either party request it.

10 No law that Shall be passed for fixing a compensation for the members of Congress except the first, Shall take effect until after the next election of representatives *posterior* to the passing Such law.

11 The legislative, executive and judiciary powers vested by the Constitution in the respective branches of the Government of the United States, shall be exercised according to the distribution therein made, so that neither of said branches shall assume or exercise any of the powers peculiar to either of the other branches.

And the powers not delegated to the government of the United States by the Constitution, nor prohibited by it to the particular States, are retained by the States respectively. nor Shall [*illegible*] any the exercise of power by the government of the united States ~~the~~ [*illegible*] particular instances here in enumerated by way of caution be construed to imply the contrary.

Final House Committee Report, July 28, 1789

[1] IN the introductory paragraph before the words, "*We the people*," add, "Government being intended for the benefit of the people, and the rightful establishment thereof being derived from their authority alone."

[2] ART. I, SEC. 2, PAR. 3—Strike out all between the words, "*direct*" and "*and until such*," and instead thereof insert, "After the first enumeration there shall be one representative for every thirty thousand until the number shall amount to one hundred; after which the proportion shall be so regulated by Congress that the number of Representatives shall never be less than one hundred, nor more than one hundred and seventy-five, but each State shall always have at least one Representative."

[3] ART. I, SEC. 6—Between the words "*United States*," and "*shall in all cases*," strike out "*they*," and insert, "But no law varying the compensation shall take effect until an election of Representatives shall have intervened. The members."

[4] ART. I, SEC. 9—Between PAR. 2 and 3 insert, "No religion shall be established by law, nor shall the equal rights of conscience be infringed."

[5] "The freedom of speech, and of the press, and the right of the people peaceably to assemble and consult for their common good, and to apply to the government for redress of grievances, shall not be infringed."

[6] "A well regulated militia, composed of the body of the people, being the best security of a free State, the right of the people to keep and bear arms shall not be infringed, but no person religiously scrupulous shall be compelled to bear arms."

[7] "No soldier shall in time of peace be quartered in any house without the consent of the owner, nor in time of war but in a manner to be prescribed by law."

[8] "No person shall be subject, except in case of impeachment, to more than one trial or one punishment for the same offence, nor shall be compelled

Source: *DHFFC*, 4: 27–31. © 1986 Johns Hopkins University Press. Reprinted by permission of Johns Hopkins University Press.

to be a witness against himself, nor be deprived of life, liberty, or property without due process of law; nor shall private property be taken for public use without just compensation."

[9] "Excessive bail shall not be required, nor excessive fines imposed, nor cruel and unusual punishments inflicted."

[10] "The right of the people to be secure in their person, houses, papers and effects, shall not be violated by warrants issuing, without probable cause supported by oath or affirmation, and not particularly describing the places to be searched, and the persons or things to be seized."

[11] "The enumeration in this Constitution of certain rights shall not be construed to deny or disparage others retained by the people."

[12] ART. 1, SEC. 10, between the 1st and 2d PAR. insert, "No State shall infringe the equal rights of conscience, nor the freedom of speech, or of the press, nor of the right of trial by jury in criminal cases."

[13] ART. 3, SEC. 2, add to the 2d PAR. "But no appeal to such court shall be allowed, where the value in controversy shall not amount to one thousand dollars; nor shall any fact, triable by a Jury according to the course of the common law, be otherwise re-examinable than according to the rules of common law."

[14] ART. 3, SEC. 2—Strike out the whole of the 3d paragraph, and insert— "In all criminal prosecutions the accused shall enjoy the right to a speedy and public trial, to be informed of the nature and cause of the accusation, to be confronted with the witnesses against him, to have compulsory process for obtaining witnesses in his favor, and to have the assistance of counsel for his defence."

[15] "The trial of all crimes (except in cases of impeachment, and in cases arising in the land or naval forces, or in the militia, when in actual service in time of war or public danger) shall be by an impartial jury of freeholders of the vicinage, with the requisite of unanimity for conviction, the right of challenge and other accustomed requisites; and no person shall be held to answer for a capital, or otherwise infamous crime, unless on a presentment or indictment by a Grand Jury; but if a crime be committed in a place in the possession of an enemy, or in which an insurrection may prevail, the indictment and trial may by law be authorized in some other place within the same State; and if it be committed in a place not within a State, the indictment and trial may be at such place or places as the law may have directed."

[16] "In suits at common law the right of trial by jury shall be preserved."

[17] "Immediately after ART. 6, the following to be inserted as ART. 7."

"The powers delegated by this Constitution to the government of the United States, shall be exercised as therein appropriated, so that the Legislative shall never exercise the powers vested in the Executive or the Judicial; nor the Executive the powers vested in the Legislative or Judicial; nor the Judicial the powers vested in the Legislative or Executive."

[18] "The powers not delegated by this Constitution, nor prohibited by it to the States, are reserved to the States respectively."

[19] ART. 7 to be made ART. 8.

Extract from the Journal,
JOHN BECKLEY, CLERK

EXCERPTS FROM CONGRESSIONAL DEBATES OVER
THE BILL OF RIGHTS, AUGUST 13–22, 1789

13 August 1789

MR. SHERMAN.

I believe, mr. chairman, this is not the proper mode of amending the constitution. We ought not to interweave our propositions into the work itself, because it will be destructive of the whole fabric. We might as well endeavor to mix brass, iron and clay, as to incorporate such heterogeneous articles; the one contradictory to the other. Its absurdity will be discovered by comparing it with a law: would any legislature endeavor to introduce into a former act, a subsequent amendment, and let them stand so connected. When an alteration is made in an act, it is done by way of supplement; the latter act always repealing the former in every specified case of difference.

Beside this, sir, it is questionable, whether we have the right to propose amendments in this way. The constitution is the act of the people, and ought to remain entire. But the amendments will be the act of the state governments; again all the authority we possess, is derived from that instrument; if we mean to destroy the whole and establish a new constitution, we remove the basis on which we mean to build. For these reasons I will move to strike out that paragraph and substitute another.

The paragraph proposed, was to the following effect; Resolved by the senate and house of representatives of the United States in congress assembled, That the following articles be proposed as amendments to the constitution; and when ratified by three fourths of the state legislatures shall become valid to all intents and purposes, as part of the same.

Under this title, the amendments might come in nearly as stated in the report, only varying the phraseology so as to accommodate them to a supplementary form.

MR. MADISON.

Form, sir, is always of less importance than the substance; but on this occasion, I admit that form is of some consequence, and it will be well for the

Source: *DHFFC*, ii: 1221–22, 1229–31. © 1992 Johns Hopkins University Press. Reprinted by permission of Johns Hopkins University Press.

house to pursue that, which upon reflection, shall appear to be the most eligible. Now it appears to me, that there is a neatness and propriety in incorporating the amendments into the constitution itself; in that case the system will remain uniform and entire; it will certainly be more simple, when the amendments are interwoven into those parts to which they naturally belong, than it will if they consist of separate and distinct parts; we shall then be able to determine its meaning without references or comparison; whereas, if they are supplementary, its meaning can only be ascertained by a comparison of the two instruments, which will be a very considerable embarrassment, it will be difficult to ascertain to what parts of the instrument the amendments particularly refer; they will create unfavorable comparisons, whereas if they are placed upon the footing here proposed, they will stand upon as good foundation as the original work.

Nor is it so uncommon a thing as gentlemen suppose, systematic men frequently take up the whole law, and with its amendments and alterations reduce it into one act. I am not, however, very solicitous about the form, provided the business is but well completed. . . .

MR. SHERMAN.

If I had looked upon this question as mere matter of form, I should not have brought it forward or troubled the committee with such a lengthy discussion. But, sir, I contend that amendments made in the way proposed by the committee are void: No gentleman ever knew an addition and alteration introduced into an existing law, and that any part of such law was left in force; but if it was improved or altered by a supplemental act, the original retained all its validity and importance in every case where the two were not incompatible. But if these observations alone should be thought insufficient to support my motion, I would desire gentlemen to consider the authorities upon which the two constitutions are to stand. The original was established by the people at large by conventions chosen by them for the express purpose. The preamble to the constitution declares the act: But will it be a truth in ratifying the next constitution, which is to be done perhaps by the state legislatures, and not conventions chosen for the purpose. Will gentlemen say it is "We the people" in this case, certainly they cannot, for by the present constitution, we nor all the legislatures in the union together, do not possess the power of repealing it: All that is granted us by the 5th article is, that whenever we shall think it necessary, we may propose *amendments to the constitution*; not that we may propose to repeal the old, and substitute a new one.

Gentlemen say it would be convenient to have it in one instrument that people might see the whole at once; for my part I view no difficulty on this point. The amendments reported are a declaration of rights, the people are secure in them whether we declare them or not; the last amendment but one provides that the three branches of government shall each exercise its own rights, this is well secured already; and in short, I do not see that they lessen the force of any article in the constitution, if so, there can be little more difficulty in comprehending them whether they are combined in one, or stand distinct instruments.

Mr. Smith [S.C.]

Read extracts from the amendments proposed by several of the state conventions at the time they ratified the constitution, from which he said it appeared that they were generally of opinion that the phraseology of the constitution ought to be altered; nor would this mode of proceeding repeal any part of the constitution but such as it touched, the remainder will be in force during the time of considering it and ever after.

As to the observations made by the honorable gentleman from Georgia, respecting the amendments made to the constitution of Great-Britain, they did not apply—the cases were nothing like similar, and consequently could not be drawn into precedent. The constitution of Britain is neither the magna charta of John, nor the Habeas Corpus act, nor all the charters put together; it is what the parliament wills; it is true there are rights granted to the subject that cannot be resumed, but the constitution or form of government may be altered by the authority of parliament, whose power is absolute without controul.

Mr. Seney

Was afraid the house would consume more time than was at first apprehended in discussing the subject of amendments, if he was to infer any thing from what had now taken place: He hoped the question would soon be put and decided.

Mr. Vining

Was an enemy to unnecessary debate, but he conceived the question to be an important one, and was not displeased with the discussion that had taken place; he should, however, vote in favor of the most simple mode.

Mr. Gerry.

The honorable gentleman from Connecticut, if I understand him right, says that the words, "We the people" cannot be retained if congress should propose amendments, and they be ratified by the state legislatures: Now if this is a fact, we ought most undoubtedly adopt his motion; because if we do not, we cannot obtain any amendment whatever. But upon what ground does the gentleman's position stand? The constitution of the United States was proposed by a convention met at Philadelphia, but with all its importance it did not possess as high authority as the president, senate, and house of representatives of the union: For that convention was not convened in consequence of any express will of the people, but an implied one, through their members in the state legislatures. The constitution derived no authority from the first convention; it was concurred in by conventions of the people, and that concurrence armed it with power, and invested it with dignity. Now the congress of the United States are expressly authorised by the sovereign and uncontrollable voice of the people, to propose amendments whenever two-thirds of both houses shall think fit: Now if this is the fact, the propositions of amendment will be found to originate with a higher authority than the original system. The conventions of the states respectively have agreed for the people, that the state legislatures shall be authorised to decide upon these amendments in the manner of a convention. If these acts of the state legislatures are not good because they are not specifically instructed by their constituents, neither were the acts calling the first and subsequent conventions.

Does he mean to put amendments on this ground, that after they have been ratified by the state legislatures they are not to have the same authority as the original instrument; if this is his meaning, let him avow it, and if it is well founded, we may save ourselves the trouble of proceeding in the business. But for my part I have no doubt but a ratification of the amendments, in any form, would be as valid as any part of the constitution. The legislatures are elected by the people; I know no difference between them and conventions, unless it be that the former will generally be composed of men of higher characters than may be expected in conventions; and in this case, the ratification by the legislatures would have the preference.

Now if it is clear that the effect will be the same in either mode, will gentlemen hesitate to approve the most simple and clear? It will undoubtedly be more agreeable to have it all brought into one instrument, than have to refer to five or six different acts.

MR. SHERMAN.

The gentlemen who oppose the motion say we contend for matter of form; they think it nothing more; now we say we contend for substance, and therefore cannot agree to amendments in this way. If they are so desirous of having the business compleated, they had better sacrifice what they consider but a matter of indifference to get gentlemen to go more unanimously along with them in altering the constitution.

The question on Mr. Sherman's motion was now put and lost.

14 August 1789

MR. MADISON.

If it be a truth, and so self evident that it cannot be denied; if it be recognized, as is the fact in many of the state constitutions; and if it be desired by three important states, to be added to this, I think they must collectively offer a strong inducement to the mind desirous of promoting harmony, to acquiesce with the report; at least some strong arguments should be brought forward to shew the reason why it is improper.

My worthy colleague says the original expression is neat and simple; that loading it with more words may destroy the beauty of the sentence, and others say it is unnecessary, as the paragraph is complete without it, be it so in their opinion; yet, still it appears important in the estimation of three states, that this solemn truth should be inserted in the constitution. For my part, sir, I do not think the association of ideas any ways unnatural; it reads very well in this place, so much so that I think gentlemen who admit it should come in somewhere, will be puzzled to find a better place.

MR. SHERMAN

Thought they ought not to come in in this place. The people of the United States have given their reasons for doing a certain act; here we propose to come in and give them a right to do what they did on motives which appeared to them sufficient to warrant their determination—to let them know that they had a right to exercise a natural and inherent privilege which they have asserted in a solemn ordination and establishment of the constitution. Now if this right is indefeasible, and the people have recognized it in practice, the truth is better asserted than it can be by any words whatever—the words "We the people" in the original constitution are copious and expressive as possible; any addition will only drag out the sentence without illuminating it; for these reasons it may be hoped the committee will reject the proposed amendment.

Source: *DHFFC*, II: 1242–43, 1249–51. © 1992 Johns Hopkins University Press. Reprinted by permission of Johns Hopkins University Press.

The question on the first paragraph of the report was put and carried in the affirmative, 27 to 23.

Second paragraph in the report was read as follows;

Art. 1. Sect. 2. Par. 3. Strike out all between the words "direct" and "and until such" and instead thereof insert "after the first enumeration, there shall be one representative for every 30,000, until the number shall amount to 100. After which the proportion shall be so regulated by congress that the number of representatives, shall never be less than one hundred, nor more than one hundred and seventy-five; but each state shall always have at least one representative."

Mr. Vining.

The duty, sir, which I owe to my constituents, and my desire to establish the constitution on a policy, dictated by justice and liberality, which will ever secure domestic tranquillity, and promote the general welfare, induces me to come forward with a motion, which I rest upon its own merits. Gentlemen who have a magnanimous policy in view, I trust will give it their support; and concede to what is proper in itself, and likely to procure a greater degree of harmony. I therefore move you, sir, to insert after the words "one hundred and seventy-five," these words, "That where the number of inhabitants of any particular state amounts to 45,000, they shall be entitled to two representatives." This motion was negatived without a division. . . .

Mr. Sherman

Said if they were now forming a constitution, he should be in favor of one representative for 40,000 rather than 30,000; the proportion by which the several states are now represented in this house, was founded on the former calculation; in the convention that framed the constitution, there was a majority in favor of 40,000, and though there were some in favour of 30,000 yet that proposition did not obtain until after the constitution was agreed to, when the president had expressed a wish that 30,000 should be inserted, as more favorable to the public interest; during the contest between 30 and 40,000, he believed there were not more than nine states who voted in favour of the former.

The objects of the federal government were fewer than those of the state governments; they did not require an equal degree of local knowledge; the only case, perhaps, where local knowledge would be advantageous, was in laying direct taxes; but here they were freed from an embarrassment, because the arrangements of the several states might serve as a pretty good rule on which to found their measures.

So far was he from thinking a hundred and seventy-five insufficient, that he was about to move for a reduction, because he always considered that a small body deliberated to better purpose than a greater one.

MR. MADISON

Hoped gentlemen would not be influenced by what had been related to have passed in the convention; he expected the committee would determine upon their own sense of propriety; though as several states had proposed the number of two hundred, he thought some substantial reason should be offered to induce the house to reject it.

MR. LIVERMORE

Said that he did not like the amendment as it was reported; he approved of the ratio being one for 30,000, but he wished the number of representatives might be increased in proportion as the population of the country increased, until the number of representatives amounted to two hundred.

MR. TUCKER

Said the honorable gentleman who spoke last had anticipated what he was going to remark. It appeared to him that the committee had looked but a very little way forward when they agreed to fix the representation at one hundred members, on a ratio of one to every 30,000 upon the first enumeration; he apprehended the United States would be found to comprehend near 3,000,000 of people, consequently they would give a hundred members, now, by the amendment, it will lay in the power of congress to prevent any addition to that number; if it should be a prevalent opinion among the members of this house that a small body was better calculated to perform the public business than a larger one, they will never suffer their members to increase to a hundred and seventy-five, the number to which the amendment extended.

MR. GERRY

Expressed himself in favour of extending the number to two hundred, and wished that the amendment might be so modified as to insure an increase in proportion to the increase of population.

MR. SHERMAN

Was against any increase; he thought that if a future house should be convinced of the impropriety of increasing this number to above one hundred, they ought to have it at their discretion to prevent it, and if that was likely to be the case, it was an argument why the present house should not decide. He did not consider that all that had been said with respect to the advantages of a large representation was founded upon experience; it had been intimated that a large body was more incorruptible than a smaller one; this doctrine was not authenticated by any proof, he could invalidate it by an example notorious to every gentleman in this house; he alluded to the British house of commons, which altho' it consisted of upwards of 500 members, the minister always contrived to procure votes enough to answer his purpose.

15 August 1789

The house resolved itself into a committee of the whole, and resumed the consideration of the report of the committee on the subject of amendments.

Mr. BOUDINOT in the chair.

The fourth proposition under consideration being as follows:

Article 1. Sect. 9. Between paragraph 2 and 3 insert "no religion shall be established by law, nor shall the equal rights of conscience be infringed."

MR. SILVESTER

Had some doubts of the propriety of the mode of expression used in this paragraph; he apprehended that it was liable to a construction different from what had been made by the committee, he feared it might be thought to have a tendency to abolish religion altogether.

MR. VINING

Suggested the propriety of transposing the two members of the sentence.

MR. GERRY

Said it would read better if it was, that no religious doctrine shall be established by law.

MR. SHERMAN

Thought the amendment altogether unnecessary, inasmuch as congress had no authority whatever delegated to them by the constitution, to make religious establishments, he would therefore move to have it struck out.

MR. CARROLL.

As the rights of conscience are in their nature of peculiar delicacy, and will little bear the gentlest touch of the governmental hand; and as many sects have

Source: *DHFFC*, II: 1260–61, 1267–68. © 1992 Johns Hopkins University Press. Reprinted by permission of Johns Hopkins University Press.

concurred in opinion that they are not well secured under the present constitution, he said he was much in favor of adopting the words; he thought it would tend more toward conciliating the minds of the people to the government than almost any other amendment he had heard proposed. He would not contend with gentlemen about the phraseology, his object was to secure the substance in such a manner as to satisfy the wishes of the honest part of the community.

MR. MADISON

Said he apprehended the meaning of the words to be, that congress should not establish a religion, and enforce the legal observation of it by law, nor compel men to worship God in any manner contrary to their conscience; whether the words were necessary or not he did not mean to say, but they had been required by some of the state conventions, who seemed to entertain an opinion that under the clause of the constitution, which gave power to congress to make all laws necessary and proper to carry into execution the constitution, and the laws made under it, enabled them to make laws of such a nature as might infringe the rights of conscience, or establish a national religion, to prevent these effects he presumed the amendment was intended, and he thought it as well expressed as the nature of the language would admit. . . .

MR. SHERMAN.

It appears to me, that the words are calculated to mislead the people by conveying an idea, that they have a right to control the debates of the legislature; this cannot be admitted to be just, because it would destroy the object of their meeting. I think, when the people have chosen a representative, it is his duty to meet others from the different parts of the union, and consult, and agree with them to such acts as are for the general benefit of the whole community; if they were to be guided by instructions, there would be no use in deliberation, all that a man would have to do, would be to produce his instructions and lay them on the table, and let them speak for him, from hence I think it may be fairly inferred, that the right of the people to consult for the common good can go no further than to petition the legislature or apply for a redress of grievances. It is the duty of a good representative to enquire what measures are most likely to promote the general welfare, and after he has discovered them to give them his support; should his instructions therefore coincide with his ideas on any measure, they would be unnecessary; if they were contrary to the conviction of his own mind, he must be bound by every principle of justice to disregard them.

17 August 1789

The house went into a committee of the whole, on the subject of amendments. The 3d clause of the 4th proposition in the report was taken into consideration, being as follows; "A well regulated militia, composed of the body of the people, being the best security of a free state; the right of the people to keep and bear arms shall not be infringed, but no person, religiously scrupulous, shall be compelled to bear arms."

Mr. Gerry.

This declaration of rights, I take it, is intended to secure the people against the mal-administration of the government; if we could suppose that in all cases the rights of the people would be attended to, the occasion for guards of this kind would be removed. Now I am apprehensive, sir, that this clause would give an opportunity to the people in power to destroy the constitution itself. They can declare who are those religiously scrupulous, and prevent them from bearing arms.

What, sir, is the use of a militia? It is to prevent the establishment of a standing army, the bane of liberty. Now it must be evident, that under this provision, together with their other powers, congress could take such measures with respect to a militia, as make a standing army necessary. Whenever government mean to invade the rights and liberties of the people, they always attempt to destroy the militia, in order to raise an army upon their ruins. This was actually done by Great Britain at the commencement of the late revolution. They used every means in their power to prevent the establishment of an effective militia to the eastward. The assembly of Massachusetts, seeing the rapid progress that administration were making, to divest them of their inherent privileges, endeavored to counteract them by the organization of the militia, but they were always defeated by the influence of the crown.

Source: *DHFFC*, II: 1285–90. © 1992 Johns Hopkins University Press. Reprinted by permission of Johns Hopkins University Press.

Mr. Seney

Wished to know what question there was before the committee, in order to ascertain the point upon which the gentleman was speaking?

Mr. Gerry

Replied, that he meant to make a motion, as he disapproved of the words as they stood. He then proceeded, No attempts that they made, were successful, until they engaged in the struggle which emancipated them at once from their thraldom. Now, if we give a discretionary power to exclude those from militia duty who have religious scruples, we may as well make no provision on this head; for this reason he wished the words to be altered so as to be confined to persons belonging to a religious sect, scrupulous of bearing arms.

Mr. Jackson

Did not expect that all the people of the United States would turn Quakers or Moravians, consequently one part would have to defend the other, in case of invasion; now this, in his opinion, was unjust, unless the constitution secured an equivalent, for this reason he moved to amend the clause, by inserting at the end of it "upon paying an equivalent to be established by law."

Mr. Smith, (of S.C.)

Enquired what were the words used by the conventions respecting this amendment; if the gentleman would conform to what was proposed by Virginia and Carolina, he would second him: He thought they were to be excused provided they found a substitute.

Mr. Jackson

Was willing to accommodate; he thought the expression was, "No one, religiously scrupulous of bearing arms, shall be compelled to render military service in person, upon paying an equivalent."

Mr. Sherman

Conceived it difficult to modify the clause and make it better. It is well-known that those who are religiously scrupulous of bearing arms, are equally scrupulous of getting substitutes or paying an equivalent; many of them would rather die than do either one or the other—but he did not see an absolute necessity for a clause of this kind. We do not live under an arbitrary government, said he, and the states respectively will have the government of the militia, unless when called into actual service; beside, it would not do to alter it so as to exclude the whole of any sect, because there are men amongst the quakers who will turn out, notwithstanding the religious principles of the society, and defend the cause of their country. Certainly it will be improper to prevent the exercise of such favorable dispositions, at least whilst it is the practice of nations to determine their contests by the slaughter of their citizens and subjects.

MR. VINING

Hoped the clause would be suffered to remain as it stood, because he saw no use in it if it was amended so as to compel a man to find a substitute, which, with respect to the government, was the same as if the person himself turned out to fight.

MR. STONE

Enquired what the words "Religiously scrupulous" had reference to, was it of bearing arms? If it was, it ought so to be expressed.

MR. BENSON,

Moved to have the words "But no person religiously scrupulous shall be compelled to bear arms" struck out. He would always leave it to the benevolence of the legislature—for, modify it, said he, as you please, it will be impossible to express it in such a manner as to clear it from ambiguity. No man can claim this indulgence of right. It may be a religious persuasion, but it is no natural right, and therefore ought to be left to the discretion of the government. If this stands part of the constitution, it will be a question before the judiciary, on every regulation you make with respect to the organization of the militia, whether it comports with this declaration or not? It is extremely injudicious to intermix matters of doubt with fundamentals.

I have no reason to believe but the legislature will always possess humanity enough to indulge this class of citizens in a matter they are so desirous of, but they ought to be left to their discretion.

The motion for striking out the whole clause being seconded, was put, and decided in the negative, 22 members voting for it, and 24 against it.

MR. GERRY

Objected to the first part of the clause, on account of the uncertainty with which it is expressed: A well-regulated militia being the best security of a free state, admitted an idea that a standing army was a secondary one. It ought to read "a well regulated militia, trained to arms," in which case it would become the duty of the government to provide this security, and furnish a greater certainty of its being done.

Mr. Gerry's motion not being seconded, the question was put on the clause as reported, which being adopted,

Mr. Burke

Proposed to add to the clause just agreed to, an amendment to the following effect: "A standing army of regular troops in time of peace, is dangerous to public liberty, and such shall not be raised or kept up in time of peace but from necessity, and for the security of the people, nor then without the consent of two-thirds of the members present of both houses, and in all cases the military shall be subordinate to the civil authority." This being seconded,

Mr. Vining

Asked whether this was to be considered as an addition to the last clause, or an amendment by itself? If the former, he would remind the gentleman the clause was decided; if the latter, it was improper to introduce new matter, as the house had referred the report specially to the committee of the whole.

Mr. Burke

Feared that what with being trammelled in rules, and the apparent disposition of the committee, he should not be able to get them to consider any amendment; he submitted to such proceeding because he could not help himself.

Mr. Hartley

Thought the amendment in order, and was ready to give his opinion of it. He hoped the people of America would always be satisfied with having a majority to govern. He never wished to see two-thirds or three-fourths required, because it might put it in the power of a small minority to govern the whole union.

The question on mr. Burke's motion was put, and lost by a majority of 13.

The 4th clause of the 4th proposition was taken up as follows: "No soldier shall in time of peace, be quartered in any house, without the consent of the owner, nor in time of war but in a manner to be prescribed by law."

Mr. Sumter

Hoped soldiers would never be quartered on the inhabitants, either in time of peace or war, without the consent of the owner: It was a burthen, and very oppressive, even in cases where the owner gave his consent; but where this was wanting, it would be a hardship indeed: Their property would lie at the mercy of men irritated by a refusal, and well disposed to destroy the peace of the family.

He moved to strike out all the words from the clause but "No soldier shall be quartered in any house without the consent of the owner."

Mr. Sherman

Observed that it was absolutely necessary that marching troops should have quarters, whether in time of peace or war, and that it ought not to be put in the power of an individual to obstruct the public service; if quarters were not to be obtained in public barracks, they must be procured elsewhere. In England, where they paid considerable attention to private rights, they billetted the troops upon the keepers of public houses, and upon private houses also, with the consent of the magistracy.

Mr. Sumter's motion being put was lost by a majority of 16.

Mr. Gerry

Moved to insert between "but" and "in a manner" the words "by a civil magistrate" observing that there was no part of the union but what they could have access to such authority.

Mr. Hartley

Said those things ought to be entrusted to the legislature; that cases might arise where the public safety would be endangered by putting it in the power of one person to keep a division of troops standing in the inclemency of the weather for many hours, therefore he was against inserting the words.

Mr. Gerry said either his amendment was essential, or the whole clause was unnecessary.

On putting the question 13 rose in favor of the motion, 35 against it, and then the clause was carried as reported.

The 5th clause of the 4th proposition was taken up, viz. "no person shall be subject, in case of impeachment, to more than one trial or one punishment for the same offence, nor shall be compelled to be a witness against himself, nor be deprived of life, liberty or property, without due process of law, nor shall private property be taken for public use without just compensation."

Mr. Benson

Thought the committee could not agree to the amendment in the manner it stood, because its meaning, appeared rather doubtful, it says that no person shall be tried more than once for the same offence, this is contrary to the right heretofore established, he presumed it was intended to express what was secured by our former constitution, that no man's life should be more than once put in jeopardy for the same offence, yet it was well known, that they were intitled to more than one trial; the humane intention of the clause was to prevent more than one punishment, for which reason he would move to amend it by striking out the words "one trial or."

Mr. Sherman

Approved of the motion, he said, that as the clause now stood, a person found guilty could not arrest the judgment, and obtain a second trial in his own favor, he thought that the courts of justice would never think of trying and punishing twice for the same offence, if the person was acquitted on the first trial, he ought not to be tried a second time, but if he was convicted on the first, and any thing should appear to set the judgment aside, he was intitled to a second, which was certainly favorable to him. Now the clause as it stands would deprive him of this advantage.

18 August 1789

The 8th proposition in the words following, was considered, "Immediately after art. 6, the following to be inserted as art. 7."

"The powers delegated by this constitution to the government of the United States, shall be exercised as therein appropriated, so that the legislative shall not exercise the powers vested in the executive or the judicial; nor the executive the power vested in the legislative or judicial; nor the judicial the powers vested in the legislative or executive."

Mr. SHERMAN conceived this amendment to be altogether unnecessary, inasmuch as the constitution assigned the business of each branch of the government to a separate department.

MR. MADISON

Supposed the people would be gratified with the amendment, as it was admitted, that the powers ought to be separate and distinct, it might also tend to an explanation of some doubts that might arise respecting the construction of the constitution.

Mr. LIVERMORE, thinking the clause subversive of the constitution, was opposed to it, and hoped it might be disagreed to.

On the motion being put, the proposition was carried.

The 9th proposition in the words following was considered, "The powers not delegated by the constitution, nor prohibited by it to the states, are reserved to the states respectively."

MR. TUCKER

Proposed to amend the proposition by prefixing to it, "all powers being derived from the people," thought this a better place to make this assertion than the introductory clause of the constitution, where a similar sentiment was proposed by the committee. He extended his motion also, to add the

Source: *DHFFC*, 11: 1300–1301. © 1992 Johns Hopkins University Press. Reprinted by permission of Johns Hopkins University Press.

word "expressly" so as to read "The powers not expressly delegated by this constitution."

MR. MADISON

Objected to this amendment, because it was impossible to confine a government to the exercise of express powers, there must necessarily be admitted powers by implication, unless the constitution descended to recount every minutiae. He remembered the word "expressly" had been moved in the convention of Virginia, by the opponents to the ratification, and after full and fair discussion was given up by them, and the system allowed to retain its present form.

MR. SHERMAN

Coincided with mr. Madison in opinion, observing that corporate bodies are supposed to possess all powers incident to a corporate capacity, without being absolutely expressed.

MR. TUCKER

Did not view the word "expressly" in the same light with the gentleman who opposed him; he thought every power to be expressly given that could be clearly comprehended within any accurate definition of the general power.

Mr. TUCKER's motion being negatived,
***

21 August 1789

Mr. SHERMAN renewed his motion for adding the amendments to the constitution by way of supplement.

Hereupon ensued a debate similar to what took place in the committee of the whole [*on 13 August*] but on the question, mr. Sherman's motion was carried by two-thirds of the house, of consequence it was agreed to. . . .

MR. SHERMAN

Moved to alter the last clause so as to make it read, the powers not delegated to the United States, by the constitution, nor prohibited by it to the states, are reserved to the states respectively, or to the people.

This motion was adopted without debate. . . .

MR. SEDGWICK

Moved to amend the motion by giving the power to congress to alter the times, manner and places of holding elections, provided the states made improper ones; for as much injury might result to the union from improper regulations, as from a neglect or refusal to make any; it is as much to be apprehended that the states may abuse their powers, as that the United States may make an improper use of theirs.

MR. AMES

Said, that inadequate regulations were equally injurious, as having none; and that such an amendment as was now proposed, would alter the constitution; it would vest the supreme authority in places where it was never contemplated.

MR. SHERMAN

Observed, that the convention were very unanimous in passing this clause, that it was an important provision, and if it was resigned it would tend to subvert the government.

Source: *DHFFC*, 11: 1308, 1310, 1313. © 1992 Johns Hopkins University Press. Reprinted by permission of Johns Hopkins University Press.

Mr. Madison

Was willing to make every amendment that was required by the states, which did not tend to destroy the principles, and the efficacy of the constitution; he conceived that the proposed amendment would have that tendency, he was therefore opposed to it.

22 August 1789

The house resumed the consideration of the amendments to the constitution. When

Mr. Tucker

Moved the following as a proposition to be added to the same. "The congress shall never impose direct taxes but where the monies arising from the duties, imposts and excise are insufficient for the public exigencies, nor then until congress shall have made a requisition upon the states to assess, levy, and pay their respective proportions of such requisitions. And in case any state shall neglect, or refuse to pay its proportion, pursuant to such requisition, then congress may assess, and levy such states proportioned, together with the interest thereon at the rate of 6 per cent. per annum, from the time of payment prescribed by such requisition." . . .

Mr. Sherman

Remarked that if congress should exercise this power, the taxes would be laid by the immediate representatives of the people; neither would it be necessary to adopt one uniform method of collecting direct taxes. The several states might be accommodated by a reference to their respective modes of taxation.

The question upon the paragraph being called for from every part of the house, the ayes and noes were taken.

Source: *DHFFC*, II: 1319, 1323. © 1992 Johns Hopkins University Press. Reprinted by permission of Johns Hopkins University Press.

Conference Committee Report and House Resolution

Conference Committee Report

September 24, 1789
The Committees of the two Houses appointd to confer on thier different votes on the Amendments proposed by the Senate to the Resolution proposing Amendments to the Constitution, and disagreed to by the House of Representatives, have had a conferrence, and have agreed that it will be proper for the House of Representatives to agree to the said Amendments proposed by the Senate, with an Amendment to their fifth Amendment, so that the third Article shall read as follows "Congress shall make no law *respecting an establishment of Religion,* or prohibiting the free exercise thereof; or abridging the freedom of Speech, or of the Press; or the right of the people peaceably to assemble and ~~to~~ petition the Government for a redress of grievancies;" And with an Amendment to the fourteenth Amendment proposed by the Senate, so that the eighth Article, as numbered in the Amendments proposed by the Senate, shall read as follows "In all criminal prosecutions, the accused shall enjoy the right to a speedy & publick trial *by an impartial jury of the district wherein the crime shall have been committed, as the district shall have been previously asscertained by law,* and to be informed of the nature and cause of the accusation; to be confronted with the witnesses against him; and to have compulsory process for obtaining Witnesses ~~against him~~ in his favour, & ᵗᵒ have the assistance of counsel for his defence."

The Committees were also of Opinion that it would be proper for both Houses to agree to amend the first Article, by striking out the word "*less*" in the last line but one, and inserting in its place, the word "more," and accordingly recommend that the said Article be reconsidered for that purpose.

Source: *DHFFC,* 4: 47–48. © 1986 Johns Hopkins University Press. Reprinted by permission of Johns Hopkins University Press.

House Resolution

SEPTEMBER 24, 1789

RESOLVED, That the President of the United States be requested to transmit to the executives of the several states which have ratified the Constitution, copies of the amendments proposed by Congress to be added thereto; and like copies to the executives of the states of Rhode-Island and North-Carolina.

Amendments to the Constitution, September 28, 1789

The Conventions of a number of the States, having at the time of their adopting the Constitution, expressed a desire, in order to prevent misconstruction or abuse of its powers, that further declaratory and restrictive clauses should be added: And as extending the ground of public confidence in the Government, will best ensure the benificent ends of its institution

RESOLVED by the Senate and House of Representatives of the United States of America, in Congress assembled, two thirds of both Houses concurring, that the following Articles be proposed to the Legislatures of the several States, as amendments to the Constitution of the United States, all or any of which Articles, when ratified by three fourths of the said Legislatures, to be valid to all intents and purposes, as part of the said Constitution; vizt.

ARTICLES in addition to, and amendment of the Constitution of the United States of America, proposed by Congress, and ratified by the Legislatures of the several States, pursuant to the fifth Article of the original Constitution.

ARTICLE THE FIRST. After the first enumeration required by the first Article of the Constitution, there shall be one Representative for every thirty thousand, until the number shall amount to one hundred, after which, the proportion shall be so regulated by Congress, that there shall be not less than one hundred Representatives, nor less than one Representative for every forty thousand persons, until the number of Representatives shall amount to two hundred, after which the proportion shall be so regulated by Congress, that there shall not be less than two hundred Representatives, nor more than one Representative for every fifty thousand persons.

ARTICLE THE SECOND. No law, varying the compensation for the services of the Senators and Representatives, shall take effect, until an election of Representatives shall have intervened.

Source: *DHFFC,* 4: 1–2. © 1986 Johns Hopkins University Press. Reprinted by permission of Johns Hopkins University Press.

ARTICLE THE THIRD. Congress shall make no law respecting an establishment of religion, or prohibiting the free exercise thereof; or abridging the freedom of speech, or of the press, or the right of the people peaceably to assemble, and to petition the Government for a redress of grievances.

ARTICLE THE FOURTH. A well regulated militia, being necessary to the security of a free State, the right of the people to keep and bear arms, shall not be infringed.

ARTICLE THE FIFTH. No Soldier shall, in time of peace be quartered in any House, without the consent of the owner, nor in time of war, but in a manner to be prescribed by law.

ARTICLE THE SIXTH. The right of the people to be secure in their persons, houses, papers, and effects, against unreasonable searches and seizures, shall not be violated, and no warrants shall issue, but upon probable cause, supported by oath or affirmation, and particularly describing the place to be searched and the persons or things to be seized.

ARTICLE THE SEVENTH. No person shall be held to answer for a capital, or otherwise infamous crime, unless on a presentment or indictment of [a] Grand Jury, except in cases arising in the land or naval forces, or in the militia, when in actual service in time of war or public danger; nor shall any person be subject for the same offence to be twice put in jeopardy of life or limb; nor shall be compelled in any criminal case to be a witness against himself, nor be deprived of life, liberty, or property, without due process of law; nor shall private property be taken for public use, without just compensation.

ARTICLE THE EIGHTH. In all criminal prosecutions, the accused shall enjoy the right to a speedy and public trial, by an impartial jury of the State and district wherein the crime shall have been committed; which district shall have been previously ascertained by law, and to be informed of the nature and cause of the accusation; to be confronted with the witnesses against him; to have compulsory process for obtaining witnesses in his favor, and to have the assistance of counsel for his defence.

ARTICLE THE NINTH. In suits at common law, where the value in controversy shall exceed twenty dollars, the right of trial by jury shall be preserved, and no fact tried by a jury, shall be otherwise re-examined in any Court of the United States, than according to the rules of the common law.

ARTICLE THE TENTH. Excessive bail shall not be required, nor excessive fines imposed, nor cruel and unusual punishments inflicted.

ARTICLE THE ELEVENTH. The enumeration in the Constitution, of certain rights, shall not be construed to deny or disparage others retained by the people.

ARTICLE THE TWELFTH. The powers not delegated to the United States by the Constitution, nor prohibited by it to the States, are reserved to the States respectively, or to the people.

FREDERICK AUGUSTUS MUHLENBERG
Speaker of the House of Representatives

Call for Prayer, September 25, 1789

The day after the House passed the final version of the First Amendment, Elias Boudinot proposed that the president recommend a public day of thanksgiving and prayer. After debate, the House agreed and appointed Boudinot, Sherman, and Peter Silvester to a committee to meet with senators on the matter. The Senate concurred with the House's motion, and Congress requested that President Washington issue what became his famous 1789 Thanksgiving Day Proclamation.[1]

MR. BOUDINOT

Said he could not think of letting the session pass over without offering an opportunity to all the citizens of the United States, of joining, with one voice, in returning to Almighty God their sincere thanks for the many blessings he had poured down upon them. With this view, therefore, he would move the following: Resolved, that a joint committee of both houses be directed to wait upon the president of the United States, to request that he would recommend to the people of the United States, a day of public Thanksgiving and Prayer, to be observed by acknowledging, with grateful hearts, the many signal favors of Almighty God, especially by affording them an opportunity peaceably to establish a constitution of government for their safety and happiness.

MR. BURKE

Did not like this mimicking European customs, where they made a mere mockery of thanksgivings: Two parties at war, frequently sung *te deum* for the same event; tho' to one it was a victory, and to the other a defeat.

Source: *DHFFC*, 11: 1500–1501. © 1992 Johns Hopkins University Press. Reprinted by permission of Johns Hopkins University Press.

1. *DHFFC*, 11: 1500–1501; Daniel L. Dreisbach and Mark David Hall, eds., *The Sacred Rights of Conscience: Selected Readings on Religious Liberty and Church-State Relations in the American Founding* (Indianapolis, Ind.: Liberty Fund, 2009), 453–54.

Mr. Boudinot

Was sorry to hear arguments drawn from the abuse of a good thing, against the use of it: He hoped no gentleman would make a serious opposition to a measure both prudent and just.

Mr. Tucker

Thought the house had no business to interfere in a matter which did not concern them. Why should the president direct the people to do what, perhaps, they have no mind to do? They may not be inclined to return thanks for a constitution, until they have experienced that it promotes their safety and happiness. We do not yet know but they may have reason to be dissatisfied with the effects it has already produced; but whether this be so or not, it is a business with which congress have nothing to do; it is a religious matter, and, as such, is proscribed as to us. If a day of thanksgiving must take place, let it be done by the authority of the several states; they know best what reason their constituents have to be pleased with the establishment of this constitution.

Mr. Sherman

Justified the practice of thanksgiving, on any signal event, not only as a laudable one in itself, but as warranted by a number of precedents in holy writ: For instance, the solemn thanksgivings and rejoicings which took place in the time of Solomon, after the building of the temple, was a case in point. This example he thought worthy of christian imitation on the present occasion; and he would agree with the gentleman who moved the resolution.

Mr. Boudinot quoted farther precedents from the practice of the late congress; and hoped the motion would meet a ready acquiescence.

The question was now put on the resolution, and it was carried in the affirmative;

***

Executive Power

The first significant battle concerning presidential power was sparked on May 19, 1789, when representatives began discussing the organization of the executive branch. James Madison proposed a "department of foreign affairs; at the head of which there should be an officer, to be called, the secretary to the department of foreign affairs, who shall be appointed by the president, by and with the advice and consent of the senate; and to be removable by the president."[1] *No one doubted that there would be such an officer, or that he would be appointed by the president with the advice and consent of the Senate. The critical issue, as William Smith immediately pointed out, was whether the president could unilaterally remove the secretary. The Constitution does not address the removal of executive branch officials by the president, and the issue remained hotly contested in American constitutional law well into the twentieth century.*

As is evident from the first set of texts, Sherman tenaciously argued against giving the president the power to remove members of the executive branch. However, his motion to strike the words "to be removable by the president" from the bill lost by a vote of 20–34.[2] *A similar battle was fought in the Senate, where a tie vote on the issue was broken in favor of presidential power by Vice President John Adams on July 16. The following day, Adams wrote Sherman a letter politely criticizing portions of his January 7, 1788, essay, "Observations on the New Federal Constitution," which addressed presidential power and republican government.*[3] *This instigated a fascinating correspondence, which is reprinted here.*

The third and final set of excerpts related to executive power addresses miscellaneous issues including (1) which branch should determine how many ambassadors are sent overseas, (2) how treaties should be negotiated, and (3) what would happen if the offices of the presidency and the vice presidency were vacant at the same time.

---

1. *DHFFC*, 10: 725–26.

2. Ibid., 11: 917, 977, 1024.

3. Sherman had published a revised version of this essay on December 25, 1788, but the quote with which Adams starts his essay is clearly from the earlier essay. Charles Francis Adams erroneously suggests that a letter from Sherman, not Sherman's essay, started this correspondence. *Works of John Adams*, 6: 437.

EXCERPTS FROM CONGRESSIONAL DEBATES OVER
THE EXECUTIVE'S POWER TO REMOVE
APPOINTED OFFICERS

17 June 1789

MR. SHERMAN.

I consider this as a very important subject in every point of view, and therefore worthy of full discussion. In my mind it involves three questions. First, whether the president has by the constitution the right to remove an officer appointed by and with the advice and consent of the senate? No gentleman contends but the advice and consent of the senate is necessary to make the appointment in all cases, unless in inferior offices where the contrary is established by law, but then they alledge that although the consent of the senate is necessary to the appointment, the president alone by the nature of his office has the power of removal. Now it appears to me, that this opinion is ill founded, because this provision was intended for some useful purpose, and by that construction would answer none at all. I think the concurrence of the senate as necessary to appoint an officer as the nomination of the president; they are constituted as mutual checks, each having a negative upon the other.

I consider it as an established principle, that the power which appoints can also remove, unless there are express exceptions made. Now the power which appoints the judges cannot displace them, because there is a constitutional restriction in their favor; otherwise the president, by and with the advice and consent of the senate, being the power which appointed them, would be sufficient to remove them. This is the construction in England, where the king had the power of appointing judges; it was declared to be during pleasure, and they might be removed when the monarch thought proper. It is a general principle in law as well as reason, that there should be the same authority to remove as to establish. It is so in legislation; where the several branches whose concurrence was necessary to pass a law, must concur in repealing it. Just so I take it to be in cases of appointment; and the president alone may remove when he alone appoints, as in the case of inferior offices to be established by law.

Source: *DHFFC*, II: 916–18. © 1992 Johns Hopkins University Press. Reprinted by permission of Johns Hopkins University Press.

Here another question arises, whether this officer comes within the description of inferior officers? Some gentlemen think not; because he is the head of the department of foreign affairs. Others may perhaps think that as he is employed in the executive department in aid of the president, he is not such an officer as is understood by the term heads of departments; because the president is the head of the executive department, in which the secretary of foreign affairs serves. If this is the construction which gentlemen put upon the business, they may vest the appointment in the president alone, and the removal will be in him of consequence. But if this reasoning is not admitted, we can by no means vest the appointment or removal either in the chief magistrate alone. As the officer is the mere creature of the legislature, we may form it under such regulations as we please, with such powers and duration as we think good policy require; we may say he shall hold his office during good behaviour, or that he shall be annually elected; we may say he shall be displaced for neglect of duty, and point out how he should be convicted of it—without calling upon the president or senate.

The third question is, if the legislature has the power to authorise the president alone to remove this officer, whether it is expedient to invest him with it? I do not believe it is absolutely necessary that he should have such power; because the power of suspending would answer all the purposes which gentlemen have in view by giving the power of removal. I do not think that the officer is only to be removed by impeachment, as is argued by the gentleman from South-Carolina (Mr. Smith); because he is the mere creature of the law, and we can direct him to be removed on conviction of mismanagement or inability, without calling upon the senate for their concurrence: But I believe if we make no such provision, he may constitutionally be removed by the president, by and with the advice and consent of the senate, and I believe it would be most expedient for us to say nothing in the clause on this subject.

18 June 1789

MR. SHERMAN.

The importance of this question requires mature deliberation; the more I have heard it discussed, the more convinced I am that the clause ought to be struck out. If we suppose (and gentlemen do suppose on this side of the question), that the power is vested in the president by the constitution, why should we intermeddle in the matter? Why are we officiously to intrude our opinions upon the president? Are we to suppose he is unacquainted with his duty, and is to be taught it by our superior wisdom? I apprehend that the electors who chose the president, thought him competent to understand his duty; what then can induce us to give our advice unasked? If he was in doubt, and was to apply to us for such a purpose, there might be some propriety in it. The convention, who formed this constitution, thought it would tend to secure the liberties of the people, if they prohibited the president from the sole appointment of all officers. They knew that the crown of Great Britain, by having that prerogative, has been enabled to swallow up the whole administration; the influence of the crown upon the legislature subjects both houses to its will and pleasure; perhaps it may be thought by the people of that kingdom, that it is best for the executive magistrate to have such kind of influence; if so, it is very well, and we have no right to complain that it is injurious to them, while they themselves consider it beneficial. But this government is different, and intended by the people to be different. I have not heard any gentleman produce an authority from law or history which proves, that where two branches are interested in the appointment, that one of them has the power of removal. I remember that the gentleman from Massachusetts (Mr. Sedgwick) told us, that the two houses, notwithstanding the partial negative of the president, possessed the whole legislative power; but will the gentleman infer from that, that because the concurrence of both branches is necessary to pass a law, that a less authority can repeal it? This is all we contend for.

Source: *DHFFC*, II: 977–78. © 1992 Johns Hopkins University Press. Reprinted by permission of Johns Hopkins University Press.

Some gentlemen suppose, if the president has not the power by the constitution, we ought to vest it in him by law. For my part I very much doubt if we have the power to do this. I take it we would be placing the heads of departments in a situation inferior to what the constitution contemplates; but if we have the power, it will be better to exercise it than attempt to construe the constitution: But it appears to me, that the best way will be to leave the constitution to speak for itself whenever occasion demands.

It has been said, that the senate are merely an advisory body. I am not of this opinion, because their consent is expressly required; if this is not obtained an appointment cannot be made. Upon the whole, I look upon it necessary, in order to preserve that security which the constitution affords to the liberty of the people, that we avoid making this declaration, especially in favor of the president, as I do not believe the constitution vests the authority in him alone.

19 June 1789

MR. SHERMAN.

I wish, mr. chairman, that the words may be left out of the bill, without giving up the question either way as to the propriety of the measure. Many of the honorable gentlemen who advocate this clause have labored to shew, that the president has, constitutionally, the power of removal; if it be a well-founded opinion, they ought not to let the words remain in the bill, because they are of such a nature as to imply that he had not the power before it was granted him by the law.

If gentlemen would consent to make a general law, declaring the proper mode of removal, I think we should acquire a greater degree of unanimity, which, on this occasion, must be better than carrying the question against a large minority.

The call for the question being now very general, it was put, shall the words "to be removable by the president," be struck out?

It was determined in the negative; being yeas 20—noes 34.

Source: *DHFFC,* II: 1024. © 1992 Johns Hopkins University Press. Reprinted by permission of Johns Hopkins University Press.

Correspondence between John Adams and Roger Sherman, 1789

Letter from John Adams to Roger Sherman, July 17, 1789

I have read over with Pleasure, your Observations on the new federal Constitution, and am glad of an opportunity to communicate to you my opinion of some Parts of them. it is by a free and friendly Intercourse of Sentiments that the Friends of our Country may hope for Such an Unanimity of Opinion and Such a Concert of Exertions, as may Sooner or later produce the Blessings of good Government.

You Say "it is by Some objected, that the Executive is blended with the Legislature, and that those Powers ought to be entirely distinct and unconnected, but is not that a gross Error in Politicks? The united Wisdom and various Interests of a nation Should be combined in framing the Laws, by which all are to be governed and protected, though it would not be convenient to have them executed by the whole Legislature. The Supreme Executive in Great Britain is one branch of the Legislature, and has a negative on all the Laws; perhaps that is an extreme not to be imitated by a Republic, but the Negative vested in the President by the new Constitution, on the Acts of Congress, and the consequent Revision, may be very useful to prevent Laws being passed without mature deliberation; and to preserve stability in the Administration of Government. And the Concurrence of the Senate in the Appointment to office, will Strengthen the hands of the Executive, and Secure the Confidence of the People, much better than a Select Council and will be less expensive."

Is it then "an extreme not to be imitated by a Republic, to make the Supreme Executive a Branch of the Legislature, and give it a Negative on all the Laws"? if you please We will examin this Position, and See whether it is well founded. in the first Place what is your definition of a Republic? Mine is this, *A Government, whose Sovereignty is vested in more than one Person.* Governments are divided into *Despotisms, Monarchies,* and *Republics.* A *Despotism* is a Government, in which the three Divisions of Power, the Legislative, Executive and

Source: *DHFFC,* 16: 1053–54. © 2004 Johns Hopkins University Press. Reprinted by permission of Johns Hopkins University Press.

Judicial are all vested in one Man. A *Monarchy* is a Government, where the Legislative and Executive Powers are vested in one Man; but the Judicial, in other Men, in all Governments the Sovereignty is vested in that Man or Body of Men, who have the Legislative Power. in Despotisms and Monarchies therefore, the Legislative Authority, being in one Man, the Sovereignty is in one Man. in Republicks, as the Sovereignty [*lined out*] that is the Legislative Power is always vested in more than one, it may be vested in as many more as you please. in the United States it might be vested in two Persons, or in three Millions or in any intermediate Number, and in every such supposeable Case the Government would be a Republic. in conformity to these Ideas Republics have been divided into three different Species, monarchical, Aristocratical and Democratical Republics. England is a Republic: a monarchical Republic it is true: but a Republic Still: because the Sovereignty, which is the Legislative Power, is vested in more than one Man. it is equally divided indeed between the one, the few, and the many: or in other Words between the three natural Divisions of Mankind in every Society; the monarchical, the Aristocratical and the Democratical. it is essential to a monarchical Republic, that the Supream Executive Should be a Branch of the Legislature, and have a Negative on all the Laws. I Say essential because, if Monarchy were not an essential Part of the Sovereignty the Government would not be a monarchical Republic. Your Position therefore is clearly and certainly an Error, because the Practice of G. Britain in making their Supreme Executive a Branch of the Legislative and giving it a Negative on all the Laws, must be imitated, by every Monarchical Republic.

I will pause here if you please—but if you will give me leave, I will write you another Letter or two upon this subject.

Letter from John Adams to Roger Sherman, July 18, 1789

In my Letter of yesterday, I think it was demonstrated that the English Constitution is a Republic, and that the Regal Negative upon the Laws is essential to that Republic: because that without it, that Government would not be what it is a monarchical Republic and consequently could not preserve the Ballance of Power between the Executive and Legislative Powers, nor that other Ballance, which is in the Legislature between the one, the few and the many, in which two Ballances the Excellence of that form of Government, consist.

Let us now enquire, whether the new Constitution of the United States is, or is not a monarchical Republic, like that of G. Britain. The Monarchical, and the Aristocratical Power, in our Constitution, it is true are not hereditary: but this makes no difference in the nature of the Power, in the nature of the Ballance, or in the name of the Spirit of Government. it would make no difference in the Power of a Judge, or Justice, or General, or Admiral, whether his Commission were for Life or years. his authority, during the time it lasted would be the same, whether it were for one year or twenty, or for Life, or descendible to his eldest son. The People The Nation, in whom all Power resides originally, may delegate their Power, for one year, or for ten years, for years or for Life or may delegate it in fee simple, or fee Tail, if I may so express my self or during good behaviour, or at Will, or till further orders. A nation might unanimously create a Dictator or Despot, for one year, or more, or for Life, or for Perpetuity with hereditary descent. in Such a Case, the Dictator for one year, would as really be a Dictator during the Time, his Power lasted, as the other would be whose Power was perpetual and descendible. a Nation in the Same manner might create a Simple Monarch, for years, Life or Perpetuity, and in either Case the Creature would be equally a Simple Monarch during the Continuance of his Power. So the People of England might create King, Lords and commons, for a year, or for Several years, or for Life—and

Source: *DHFFC*, 16: 1061–63. © 2004 Johns Hopkins University Press. Reprinted by permission of Johns Hopkins University Press.

in any of these Cases, their Government would be a monarchical Republic, or if you will a limited Monarchy, during its continuance, as much as it is now, when the King and Nobles are hereditary. They might make their house of commons hereditary too. what the Consequence of this would be it is easy to foresee but it would not in the first moment make any change in the legal Power nor in the name of the Government.

Let us now consider what our Constitution is: and see whether any other name can with propriety be given it: than that of a monarchical Republic, or if you will a limited Monarchy. The Duration of our President is neither perpetual nor for Life, it is only for four years: but his Power, during those four years, is much greater than that of an Avoyer, a Consul a Podesta a Doge, a Statholder, nay than a King of Poland. nay than a King of Sparta. I know of no first Magistrate in any Republican Government except in England and Neuchattel, who possesses a constitutional Dignity, Authority and Power comparable to his. The Power of Sending and receiving Ambassadors of raising and commanding Armies and Navies, of nominating appointing and commissioning all offices—of managing The Treasures, the internal and external affairs of the nation—nay the whole Executive Power, co extensive with the Legislative Power is vested in him and he has the Right and his is the Duty to take Care that the Laws be faithfully executed. These Rights and Duties, these Prerogatives and Dignities, are so transcendant, that they must naturally and necessarily excite in the Nation all the Jealousy, Envy, Fears, Apprehensions and opposition, that is so constantly observed in England against the Crown.

That these Powers are necessary I readily Admit. That the Laws cannot be executed with out them: that the Lives, Liberties, Properties and Character of the Citizens cannot be Secure, without their Protection is most clear. But it is equally certain I think that they ought to have been Still greater, or much less. The Limitations upon them, in the Cases of War, Treaties, and Appointment to Office and especially the Limitation, on the Presidents Independence as a branch of the Legislature, will be the destruction of this Constitution, and involve us in Anarchy, if not amended. I shall pass over all these particulars for the present, except the last: because that is now the Point in dispute between you and me.

Longitude and the Philosophes Stone, have not been sought with more Earnestness by Philosophes, than a *Guardian of the Laws* has been Studied by Legislators from Plato to Montesquieu. but every Project has been found to be no better, than committing the Lamb to the Custody of the Wolf, excepting that one, which is called *a ballance of Power.* a Simple Sovereignty, in one, a few, or many has no ballance, and therefore no Laws. a divided Sovereignty without a ballance, or in other Words, where the division is unequal is always at War, and consequently has no Laws. in our Constitution the Sovereignty, i.e. the Legislative Power is divided, into three Branches. The House and Senate are equal, but the third Branch, tho essential is not equal. The President must pass Judgment upon every Law—but in Some Cases his Judgment may be overruled. These Cases will be Such as attack, his constitutional Power, it is therefore certain he has not equal Power to defend himself, nor the Constitution or the Judicial Power, as the Senate and House have.

Power naturally grows. Why? because human Passions are insatiable. but that Power alone can grow which is already too great, that which is unchecked. that which has no equal Power to controul it. The Legislative Power in our Constitution, is greater than the Executive, it will therefore encroach—because both Aristocratical and democratical Passions are insatiable. The Legislative Power will increase, the Executive will diminish. in the Legislature, the Monarchical Power is not equal, either to the Aristocratical, or democratical—it will therefore decrease, while the others will increase. indeed I think the Aristocratical Power is greater than either the Monarchical or Democratical. that will therefore Swallow up the other two.

In my Letter of yesterday, I think it was proved, that a Republic might make the Supream Executive an integral Part of the Legislature. in this it is equally demonstrated as I think, that our Constitution ought to be amended by a decisive adoption of that Expedient.

If you dont forbid me, I shall write you again.

Letter from John Adams to Roger Sherman, July 20, 1789

There is a Sense, and a degree, in which the Executive, in our Constitution, is blended with the Legislature: The President, has the Power of Suspending a Law; of giving the two Houses an Oppertunity to pause, to think, to collect themselves, to reconsider a rash Step of a Majority; he has the Right to Urge all his Reasons against it, by Speech or Message; which becoming Public is an appeal to the Nation—But the rational Objection, here is not that the Executive is ~~not~~ blended with the Legislature: but that it is not *enough* blended: that it is not *incorporated* with it, and made an *essential* Part of it. If it were an *integral* Part of it it might negative a Law, without much Noise, Speculation, or Confusion among the People. But as it now Stands, I beg you, to consider— it is almost impossible that a President Should ever have the Courage to make use of his partial negative. what a Situation would a President be in, to maintain a Controversy against a Majority of both Houses, before the Tribunal of the Public. To put a Stop to a Law, that more than half the Senate and House, and consequently We may Suppose more than half the Nation, had set their hearts upon? it is moreover possible, that more than two thirds of the Nation, the Senate and House, may in times of Calamity Distress, Misfortune and ill success of the Measures of Government from the momentary Passion and Enthusiasm, demand a Law which will wholly Subvert the Constitution. The Constitution of Athens was overturned in such a moment by Aristides himself. The Constitution Should guard against a Possibility of its Subversion. But we may take Stronger ground and assert that it is probable, that Such Cases will happen, and that the Constitution will in fact be Subverted, in this way. Nay I go farther and Say, that from the constitution of human nature and the constant Course of human affairs, it is certain, that our Constitution will be Subverted, if not amended, and that in a very Short time, merely for Want of a decisive negative in the Executive.

There is another Sense, and another Degree, in which the Executive is

Source: *DHFFC*, 16: 1079–82. © 2004 Johns Hopkins University Press. Reprinted by permission of Johns Hopkins University Press.

blended with the Legislature, which is liable to great and just Objection; which excites alarms, Jealousies and Apprehensions in a very great degree. I mean 1. the Negative of the Senate, upon Appointments to office; 2. the Negative of the Senate upon Treaties, and 3. the Negative of the two Houses upon War. I Shall confine my self at present to the first. The Negative of the Senate upon Appointments, is liable to the following Objections. 1. It takes away, or a least it lessens the Responsibility of the Executive—our Constitution obliges me to Say, that it lessens the Responsibility of the President. The blame of an hasty, injudicious, weak or wicked appointment, is Shared So much between him and the Senate, that his part of it will be too Small. Who can censure him, without censuring the Senate, and the Legislatures who appoint them? all their Friends will be interested to vindicate the President, in order to Screen them from censure. & besides if an Impeachment is brought before them against any officer are they not interested to acquit him, least some part of the Odium of his Guilt Should fall upon them, who advised to his appointment.

2. It turns the Minds and Attention of the People, to the Senate, a Branch of the Legislature, in Executive matters. it interests another Branch of the Legislature in the management of the Executive. it divides the People, between the Executive and the Senate: whereas all the People ought to be united to watch the Executive, to oppose its Encroachments, and resist its ambition. Senators and Representatives, and their Constituents, in short the Aristocratical and Democratical Divisions of Society ought to be united, on all occasions to oppose the Executive, or the Monarchical Branch when it attempts to overleap its Limits. But how can this Union be effected, when the Aristocratical Branch has pledged its Reputation to the Executive by consenting to an appointment.

3. It has a natural Tendency, to excite Ambition in the Senate. An Active, ardent Spirit, in that House, who is rich, & able; has a great Reputation and influence; will be solicited by Candidates for office. not to introduce the Idea of Bribery, because, tho it certainly would force itself in, in other Countries, and will, probably, here when We grow populous and rich, yet it is not yet, I hope to be dreaded. But Ambition must come in already. A Senator of great Influence, will be naturally ambitious, and desirous of increasing his Influence. Will he not be under a Temptation to Use his Influence with the President as well as his Brother Senators, to appoint Persons to office in the several States who will exert themselves in Elections to get out his Ennemies or opposers both in Senate and House of Representatives, and to get in his Friends, perhaps his Instruments? Suppose a Senator, to aim at the Treasury office, for himself, his Brother, Father, or Son—suppose him to aim at the President's Chair, or Vice Presidents, at the next Election—or at the office of War, foreign or do-

mestic affairs, will he not naturally be tempted to make use of his whole Patronage his whole Influence, in Advising to appointments, both with President and senators to get Such Persons nominated, as will exert themselves for Elections of President Vice President, senators and H. of Representatives to increase his Interest and promote his Views. in this Point of View I am very apprehensive that this defect in our Constitution will have an un happy Tendency to introduce Corruption of the grossest Kinds both of Ambition and Avarice into all our Elections. And this will be the worst of Poisons to our Constitution—it will not only destroy the present form of Government, but render it almost impossible to substitute in its Place any free Government, even a better limited Monarchy, or any other than a Despotism or a Simple Monarchy.

4. To avoid the Evil under the last head it will be in danger of dividing the Continent, into two or three Nations, a Case that presents no Prospect but of perpetual War.

5. This Negative on Appointments, is in danger of involving the Senate in Reproach, Obloquy, Censure and Suspicion, without doing any good. Will the Senate use their Negative or not. if not; why Should they have it—many will censure them for not using it. many will ridicule them. call them Servile &c.— if they do Use it. The very first Instance of it, will expose the Senators, to the Resentment not only of the disappointed Candidate and all his Friends; but of the President and all his Friends; and these will be most of the officers of Government, through the nation.

6. We Shall very soon have Parties formed—a Court and Country Party. and these Parties will have names given them, one Party in the House of Representatives will support the President and his Measures and Ministers— the other will oppose them. a Similar Party will be in senate—these Parties will Struggle with all their Art, perhaps with Intrigue—perhaps with Corruption at Every Election to increase their own Friends and diminish their opposers. Suppose Such Parties formed in senate, and then consider what Factious divisions We shall have there, upon every Nomination.

7. The Senate have not time. The Convention & Indian Treaties.

You are of opinion "that the concurrence of the Senate in the Appointment to office, will Strengthen the hands of the Executive, and secure the Confidence of the People, much better than a Select Council, and will be less expensive" but in every one of these Ideas, I have the Misfortune to differ from you. 1. it will weaken the hands of the Executive, by lessening the Obligation, Gratitude and Attachment of the Candidate to the President by dividing his attachment between the Executive and Legislative which are natural Ennemies. officers of Government instead of having a Single Eye and undivided attachment to the Executive Branch, as they ought to have consistent with Law and the Constitution, will be constantly tempted to be factious with their factious Patrons in the Senate. The Presidents own officers in a thousand Instances will oppose his just and constitutional Exertions, and Screen themselves under the Wings of their Patrons and Party in the Legislature. Nor will it Secure the Confidence of the People. The People will have more confidence in the Executive, in Executive matters than in the Senate. The People will be constantly jealous of factious Schemes in the Senators to unduly influence the Executive, and of corrupt bargains between the senate and Executive, to serve each others private Views. The People will also be jealous that the Influence of the senate will be employed to conceal, connive and defend Guilt in Executive Offices, instead of being a guard and watch upon them and a terror to them. a Council selected by the President himself at his Pleasure, from among the Senators, Representatives and Nation at large, would be purely responsible. in that Case, the Senate as a Body would not be compromised. The senate would be a Terror to Privy Councillors. its Honour would never be pledged to support any Measure or Instrument of the Executive, beyond Justice, Law, and the Constitution. Nor would a privy Council be more expensive. The whole Senate must now deliberate on every Appointment and, if they ever find time for it, you will find that a great deal of time will be required and consumed in this service. Then the President might have a constant Executive Council now he has none.

I Said under the Seventh head that the Senate would not have time. You will find that the whole Business of this Government will be infinitely delayed, by this Negative of the Senate on Treaties and appointments. Indian Treaties and Consular Conventions have been already waiting for months and the senate have not been able to find a moment of time to attend to them. and this Evil must constantly increase, so that the Senate must be constantly Sitting, and must be paid as long as they Sit.

But I have tired your Patience. Is there any Truth or Importance in these broken hints and crude surmises? or not? To me they appear well founded and very important.

Letter to John Adams, July 20, 1789

I was honored with your letters of the 17th. & 18 Inst. and am much obliged to you for the observations they contain. The Subject of Government is an important one, and necessary to be well understood, by the citizens & especially by the legislators of these States. I Shall be happy to receive further light on the Subject, and to have any errors that I may have entertained corrected.

I find that writers on government differ in their difinition of a *Republic.* Entick's Dictionary defines it. *"A commonwealth, without a King"* I find you do not agree to the negative part of his definition. What I meant by it was a government under the authority of the people—consisting of legislative executive and judiciary powers, the legislative powers vested in an assembly consisting of one or more branches, who together with the executive are appointed by the people, and dependent on them for continuance by ~~frequent~~ periodical elections, agreably to an established Constitution, and that what especially denominates it a *Republic* is its dependence on the *public* or *people* at *large,* without any hereditary powers. But it is not of so much importance by what appellation the government is distinguished, as to have it well constuded to Secure the rights, and advance the happiness of the community. I fully agree with you Sir, that it is optional with the people of a State, to establish any form of Government they please, to vest the powers *in one, a few* or *many,* and for a limited or unlimited time, and the individuals of the State will be bound to yield obedience to such government while it continues; but I am also of opinion that they may alter their frame of government when they please, any former act of theirs, however explicit to the contrary notwithstanding.

But what I principally have in view is to submit to your consideration the reasons that have inclined me to think that the qualified negative given to the executive by our constitution is better than an absolute negative; In Great Britain where there are the rights of the nobility as well as the rights of the common people to Support, it may be necessary that the crown Should have

Source: *DHFFC,* 16: 1089–91. © 2004 Johns Hopkins University Press. Reprinted by permission of Johns Hopkins University Press.

a compleat negative to preserve the balance; but in a *Republic* like ours, wherein is no higher rank than that of common citizens, unless distinguished by appointment to office what occasion can there be for such a balance? It is true that some men in every Society, have Natural and acquired abilities Superiour to others, and greater wealth. yet these give them no legal claim to offices in preference to others, but will doubtless give them Some degree of influence, and justly, when they are men of integrity, and may procure them [*lined out*] appointments to places of trust in the government, yet they having only the Same common rights with the other citizens What competition of Interests can there be to require a balance? besides while the real estates are divideable among all the children, or other kindred in equal degrees and Entails are not admitted, it will operate as an agrarian law, and the influence arising from great estates in a few hands or families, will not exist to such a degree of extent or duration as to form a System, or have any great effect.

In order to trace moral effects to their causes & *vice versa* it is necessary to attend to principles as they operate on mens minds. Can it be expected that a chief Magistrate of a free and enlightened people on whom he depends for his election and continuance in office, would give his negative to a law passed by the other two branches of the legislature if he had power? But the qualified negative given to the Executive by our Constitution, which is only to produce a revision, will probably be exercised on proper Occasions, and the legislature have the benefit of the President's reasons in their further deliberations on the Subject, and if a Sufficient number of the members of either house should be convinced by them to put a negative upon the Bill it would add weight to the Presidents opinion & render it more Satisfactory to the people—but if two thirds of the members of each house after considering the reasons offered by the President Should adhere to their former opinion, will not that be the most Safe foundation to rest the decision upon? on the whole it appears to me that the *power* of a compleat negative if given would be a dormant and useless one and that the provision in the constitution, is calculated to operate with proper weight, and will produce beneficial effects.

The negative vested in the Crown of Great Britain has never been exercised Since the revolution [*of 1688*], and the great influence of the Crown in the legi[*s*]lature of that nation is derived from another Source, that of appointment to all offices of honor & profit, which has rendered the power of the Crown nearly absolute—So that the Nation is in fact governed by the Cabinet Council, who are the creatures of the Crown, the consent of Parliament is necessary to give Sanction to their measures, and this they easily obtain by the influence aforesaid. If they should carry their points so far as directly to affect personal Liberty or private property the people would be alarmed and oppose their progress, but this forms no part of their System, the principal object of which is *revenue,* which they have carried to an enormous height. Where ever the chief Magisgrate may appoint to offices without controul, his government, may become absolute or at least oppressive therefore the concurrence of the Senate is made requisite by our Constitution.

I have not time or room to add, or apologize.

Letter to John Adams, n.d.

I received your letter of the 20th Inst. I had in mine of the Same date communicated to you my Ideas on that part of the Constitution, limiting the Presidents power of negativing the acts of the legislature—And just hinted Some thoughts on the propriety, of the provision made for the appointment to offices, which I esteem to be a power nearly as important as legislation.

If that was vested in the President alone, he might were it not for his periodical election by the people render himself despotic. It was a Saying of one of one of the Kings of England. That while the King could appoint the Bishops and judges he might have what Religion and Law he pleased.

It appears to me the Senate is the most important branch in the government, for aiding & Supporting the Executive, Securing the rights of the individual States, the government of the united States, and the liberties of the people. The Executive Magistrate is to execute the laws, the Senate being a branch of the legislature will naturally incline to have them duly executed, and therefore will advise to Such appointments as will best attain that end. from the knowledge of the people in the Several States, they can give the best information who are qualified for Offices, and though they will as you justly observe in Some degree lessen his responsibility, yet their advice may enable him to make such judicious appointments as to render responsibility less necessary.

The Senators being eligible by the legislatures of the several States, and dependent on them for reelection will be vigilant in Supporting their rights against infringement by the legislature or executive of the united States. and the government of the Union being federal, and Instituted by the Several States for the advancement of their Interests, they may be considered as so many pillars to support it, and by the exercise of the State governments peace and good order may be preserved in places most remote from the Seat of the Federal government, as well as at the centre. And the Municipal and federal rights of the people at large will be regarded by the Senate, they being elected by the immediate representatives of the people, & their rights will be best

Source: *DHFFC*, 16: 1148–50. © 2004 Johns Hopkins University Press. Reprinted by permission of Johns Hopkins University Press.

Secured, by a due execution of the laws. What temptation can the Senate be under to be partiality in the trial of officers whom they had a voice in the appointment of, can they be disposed to favour a person who has violated his trust & their confidence? The other evils that you mention that may resulting from this power appear to me but barely possible. The Senators will doubtless be in general Some of the most respectable citizens in the States for wisdom & probity, Superiour to mean and unworthy conduct—and instead of undue influence to procure appointments for themselves or their friends, they will consider that a fair and upright conduct will have the best tendency to preserve the confidence of the people & of the States. They will be disposed to be diffident in recommending their friends & kindred, lest they Should be Suspected of partiality, and the other Members will feel the Same kind of reluctance, lest they Should be thought unduly to favour a person because related to a member of their body. So that their friends and relations would not Stand so good a chance for appointment to offices according to their merit as others.

The Senate is a convenient body to advise the President from the Smalness of its numbers. And I think the laws would be better framed & more duly administred if the Executive and judiciary officers were in general members of the legislature, in case there should be no interference as to the time of attending to their Several duties—this I have learned by experience in the government in which I live & by observation of others differently constituted.

I see no principles in our Constitution that have any tendency to Aristocracy, which if I understand the term, is, A government by Nobles independent of the people, which cant take place in either respect without a total Subversion of the Constitution, and as both branches of Congress are elegible from the Citizens at large & wealth is not a requisite qualification, both will commonly be composed of members of Similar Circumstances in Life. And I See no reason why the Several brancheses of the government Should not maintain the most perfect harmony, their powers being all directed to one end the advancement of the public good.

If the President alone was vested with the power of appointing all officers, and was left to Select a Council for himself he would be liable to be deceived by flatterers and pretenders to Patriotism, who would have no motive but their own emolument, they would wish to extend the powers of the Executive to encrease their own importance, and however upright he might be in his intentions, there would be great danger of his being misled, even to the Subversion of the Constitution, or at least to introduce such *evils* as to interrup the harmony of the government & deprive him of the confidence of the people. but I have Said enough upon these Speculative points, which nothing but experience can reduce to a certainty.

Excerpts from Congressional Debates over Miscellaneous Issues Related to Executive Power

19 January 1790

MR. SHERMAN

Was inclined to think that the legislature ought to determine how many ministers should be employed abroad, nor did he think it would be any abridgment of the executive power so to do.

Source: *DHFFC*, 12: 37. © 1995 Johns Hopkins University Press. Reprinted by permission of Johns Hopkins University Press.

26 January 1790

Mr. Sherman.

The establishment of every treaty requires the voice of the senate, as does the appointment of every officer for conducting the business; these two objects are expressly provided for in the constitution, and they lead me to believe, that the two bodies ought to act jointly in every transaction which respects the business of negociation with foreign powers. But the bill provides for the president to do it alone, which is evidently a deviation from the apparent principle of the constitution. And what do gentlemen urge as an argument to induce the committee to adopt their idea? Why, that the singleness of the officer, who appropriates and disburses the public money, will ensure a higher degree of responsibility than the mode recommended (at least by inference) by the constitution. This argument would extend to prove, that a single person ought to exercise the powers of this house, consequently it goes too far. There is something more required than responsibility in conducting treaties. The constitution contemplates the united wisdom of the president and the senate, in order to make treaties for the benefit of the United States: The more wisdom there is employed, the greater security there is that the public business will be well done. As to the circumstance of drawing money out of the treasury, it is of little consequence; but if a discretionary power is to be exercised in apportioning the salaries of the ministers, there will be more security in connecting the senate with the president.

Source: *DHFFC*, 12: 79. © 1995 Johns Hopkins University Press. Reprinted by permission of Johns Hopkins University Press.

15 January 1791

In committee of the whole—on the bill declaring what officer, in case of vacancy of the offices of President, and Vice-President, shall act as President.

Mr. Boudinot in the chair.

THE first clause of the bill being read, which contains a blank to be filled up with the officer, who shall act as President.

Mr. Smith (S.C.) observed, that by the constitution the vacancy is to be filled with an officer of the United States: This narrows the discussion, said he, very much. But he conceived there was a previous question necessary to be determined, and that was, whether the person appointed to supply the vacancy should hold the office during the time for which the President and Vice-President was elected; or whether he was to hold the office only till a new election could take place: He thought that by the Constitution, a new election was not to take place till the term for which the President and Vice-President had been elected, was expired.

He then descanted on the respective offices of the Chief Justice, Secretary of State, and Secretary of the Treasury—and by several particulars shewed, that the appointment would most naturally devolve on the Secretary of State. He accordingly moved that the blank be filled with the words "The Secretary of State."

Mr. Livermore observed, that in considering this question, he thought no reference should be had to the officers which had been mentioned—for as it was supposed that the case contemplated would not happen once in a 100 years, he conceived that the present characters, who now hold the above offices, would be entirely out of the question. He had in view a different person, and that was the President of the Senate, *pro tempore*—and moved that the blank be filled with this person.

Mr. White observed, that the Constitution says the vacancy shall be filled by an officer of the United States. The President, *pro tempore*, of the Senate,

Source: *DHFFC*, 14: 271–72. © 1995 Johns Hopkins University Press. Reprinted by permission of Johns Hopkins University Press.

is not an officer of the United States. Besides this will give one branch of the legislature the power of electing a President: This he conceived was contrary to the Constitution—as both branches have a right to an equal voice in the appointment in this case. This will introduce the very evil intended to be guarded against.

Mr. Williamson said the motion was directly repugnant to the Constitution. Why not chuse the Speaker of this House?

Mr. Livermore said, he was well aware of the objections offered by the gentlemen: He could have wished the Constitution had pointed out the person. But he conceived that the Senate was the only body that could do this business. If either of the officers mentioned, should be the person designated to supply the vacancy, it would be in the power of the Vice-President, by virtue of the power of removing officers, absolutely to appoint a successor, without consulting either branch of the legislature.

Mr. Sherman observed, that this matter is left with the legislature—the whole power of the people, in case of the vacancy, devolves on the legislature. The particular officer is not pointed out: It lays with Congress to say who it shall be. The President of the Senate is an officer of the United States. In case of the death of a Governor and Lieutenant Governor, it is common in the several States for the oldest counsellor to preside. He instanced the case of the abdication of James IId. Adverting to the constitution, he shewed that the appointment of Vice-President, in certain cases devolves on the Senate—who will of course be President. The vacancy may be filled for a longer or shorter time, and this appears to be a question previous in its nature to be determined.

13 January 1791

Mr. SHERMAN was of opinion, that putting the chief magistracy into the hands of a subordinate officer was by no means proper. As to the observations made by the gentleman last up on the arrangements in the government of the Western Territory, he did not think they could be applied to the present case: That government was a subordinate one, and a kind of legislative power was vested in the governor, of selecting from the laws, and regulations of the different states such as he thought requisite for the government of those he had under his care.

He was in favor of giving the supreme executive in case of accident, to the President of the senate: The government would certainly suffer fewer inconveniences by that arrangement than if the head of a department was put in. The Vice-President, by the constitution succeeds to the President; the President of the senate to the office of the first, it was therefore very natural that he should also exercise the duties of the second in case of vacancy.

To designate any officer, as possible successor to the President, he said, would be giving him too much dignity, and raising him in a manner even above the legislature.

Source: *DHFFC*, 14: 320. © 1995 Johns Hopkins University Press. Reprinted by permission of Johns Hopkins University Press.

Militia Bill

EXCERPTS FROM CONGRESSIONAL
DEBATES OVER MILITIA BILL

*The Constitution gives Congress the power "[t]o provide for calling forth the Militia
to execute the Laws of the Union, suppress Insurrections and repel Invasions" and
"[t]o provide for organizing, arming, and disciplining, the Militia, and for governing such Part of them as may be employed in the Service of the United States,
reserving to the States respectively, the Appointment of the Officers, and the Authority of training the Militia according to the discipline prescribed by Congress."[1]
The debate in the House of Representatives over the Militia Bill of 1790 provides
insight into Sherman's views on a number of matters, including federalism, the
right to bear arms, and religious exemptions.*

---

1. U.S. Constitution, Article I, Section 8.

16 December 1790

Mr. Sherman thought it better to leave the matter open as it now stands, than adopt an opinion that might be ill founded, and would certainly occasion a considerable expence. He believed it to have been the intention of the Convention, who put this article into the constitution, that the United States were to be put to no expence about the militia, except when they were called forth into the actual service of the union. It is true, that article is not expressed with as much certainty as might be wished; but it will be difficult to fix upon the construction which the gentleman from North Carolina has attempted. The militia are to be organized under the laws of the United States, but it is reserved to the particular states to appoint the officers, and train them on exercise days, so that congress have nothing to do with their government, except that part of them which may be employed in the service of the United States. What relates to arming and disciplining them, means nothing more than providing, by a general regulation, the nature and uniformity of the arms, which ought to be of one caliber.

Upon the whole, he thought there were so few free men in the United States incapable of procuring themselves a musquet, bayonet and cartouchbox, as to render any regulation by the general government respecting them improper. If the people were left to themselves, he was pretty certain the necessary warlike implements would be provided without inconvenience or complaint, whereas if they were furnished by Congress, the public arsenals would be speedily drained, & from the careless manner in which many persons are disposed to treat such public property, he apprehended they would be speedily lost or destroyed. The expence and inconvenience of the measure would in his opinion, far overbalance any probable good which might be expected to result from it—and he would much rather vote at once, for exempting all persons unable to procure arms for themselves, from the operation of the law. . . .

Source: *DHFFC,* 14: 60–61, 67. © 1996 Johns Hopkins University Press. Reprinted by permission of Johns Hopkins University Press.

Mr. Sherman said it was the practice of the state legislatures, to exempt their own legislatures, and professors, and teachers in colleges and academies, and some others mentioned in the clause, and he conceived a seat in the general government to be as high in rank as either of them; it was also necessary that the members of it should be exempted, he was therefore against the amendment, tho' he had no objection to strike out the whole, and leave it to the discretion of the state legislatures who to exempt.

17 December 1790

Mr. Sherman contended, that every power still remained in the people and the state governments, except what had been given up to the United States by the new constitution. The house was not about to relinquish to the state governments any part of its power; but merely to acknowledge a power, that remained in the state legislatures. He asked, if gentlemen imagined, that the state governments had given out of their hands the command of the militia, or the right of declaring who should bear arms? He conceived it to be the privilege of every citizen, and one of his most essential rights, to bear arms, and to resist every attack upon his liberty or property, by whomsoever made. The particular states, like private citizens, have a right to be armed, and to defend, by force of arms, their rights, when invaded. A militia existed in the United States, before the formation of the present constitution: and all that the people have granted to the general government, is the power of organizing such militia. The reason of this grant was evident; it was in order to collect the whole force of the union to a point, the better to repel foreign invasion, and the more successfully to defend themselves.

The United States have no command over the militia of the particular states, except when they are called out into actual service, in defence of the union; and that exception, which reserves to the states the right of appointing the officers, and training the militia, according to the rule prescribed by Congress, is not to be understood as giving up to Congress every thing respecting the militia, besides what is so reserved; because it is palpable, from the same clause, that the states must have the command over the whole, at all times, except when they are employed in the service of the United States; and even then the power of the United States is confined to such part only as are actually in such service.

From this view of the subject, he thought, it would be as well to exempt such characters severally, as were usually exempted by the respective states, and

Source: *DHFFC*, 14: 92–93. © 1996 Johns Hopkins University Press. Reprinted by permission of Johns Hopkins University Press.

leave it to the states to exempt others, if they thought it reasonable. He joined the gentleman from Virginia, in supposing that the states would not exonerate one half its citizens, as the burthen must in that case be doubled on the other half.

He admitted the authority of Congress fully to organize and arm, and discipline the militia; the two latter he conceived ought to be uniform, to enable the whole to act in concert: But he saw no real necessity for a strict uniformity with respect to the particular size and bodily strength of each individual; which was what some gentlemen's arguments went to prove.

20 December 1790

Mr. Sherman did not view four company days and two battalion days in a year, as any great sacrifice, when it was given for so valuable a consideration as the acquisition of military skill, he tho't no person could justly complain of such a burthen—neither, said he, is there any inequality in making a difference of two training days; for altho' it may appear to exempt men above the age of 25 from attending so often as those between 18 and 25, yet it must be considered, that such exempts, have borne a considerable burthen during the late war, of which the junior class did not participate, and after a few years the burthen will be perfectly equal, with regard to every citizen in the union.

As to the discrimination in favour of students at college, he would just observe, that it was an indulgence in favour of literature, which it justly merited, and what had been extended to them by all enlightened nations where such establishments as a national militia obtained, it was the practice of these states before the revolution, and one worthy, in his opinion of being continued.

Source: *DHFFC*, 14: 107–8. © 1996 Johns Hopkins University Press. Reprinted by permission of Johns Hopkins University Press.

21 December 1790

Mr. SENEY said, Maryland, he thought, should have two inspectors, instead of one, as provided by the section; that state, he observed, was divided by a wide and sometimes dangerous bay, which could not at all times be crossed. Two inspectors were given to Maryland, one to reside on the eastern, the other on the western shore.

Mr. LAURANCE saw an impropriety in providing the same allowance to all the inspectors, without regard to the quantum of duty to be performed. The duty, he observed, of an inspector in the state of Rhode-Island, could not be near so great as that of the inspector in the state of New-York. He moved that their different salaries be fixed and specified in the bill.

It was agreed; and the blanks left to be filled with such sums as shall be deemed proper, when the house chuse to take that part of the bill into consideration.

Mr. SHERMAN was of opinion that some of the duties, by this section to devolve on inspectors, ought to be left to the states to exercise. Their duty should be confined to superintending the exercise and manoeuvres.

Mr. BLOODWORTH was averse to appointing an officer to be directed by state laws. He should be appointed by the state.

Mr. WADSWORTH said, in his opinion, that he ought to be a continental officer, and conduct himself in his office in conformity to the laws passed by the states.

Mr. SMITH moved that that clause which leaves the appointment of this officer to the president be stricken out, and that it only be specified that such an officer shall be appointed.

Mr. BOUDINOT considered this officer as appointed to assist the president. It was necessary that the commander in chief should be acquainted with the state of the militia, throughout the continent; it was impossible for him to gather this information without assistance, the officer was appointed for that

Source: *DHFFC*, 14: 116–18. © 1996 Johns Hopkins University Press. Reprinted by permission of Johns Hopkins University Press.

purpose, he should be considered as a continental officer, and as such was to be paid by the general government.

Mr. SMITH said, if his motion prevailed of having this officer appointed by the states he would also move that his salary be paid by them. He was to all intents and purposes, a militia officer, and as such was in the appointment of the states.

Mr. LAURANCE wished the clause struck out, and the power of the duty of inspector left to the adjutant general: In New-York this was the case. His salary should be in proportion greater, having then double duty to perform.

Mr. BOUDINOT said, he thought the duty too great, and the salary such an officer would require more than the states would consent to give, the officer would not be appointed, and the President could not receive the necessary information. The inspector was not a militia officer; but appointed to collect the information the President should want, for the benefit of the union.

Mr. FITZSIMONS gave it as his opinion, that the officer should be under the appointment of the President.

Mr. SHERMAN said, there appeared to be a distrust of this inspector, unless appointed by the President; he thought there could be no just foundation for entertaining this opinion, if he should be appointed by the states. He was certainly appointed for the good of the union; but if the several states did [*not*] pay his salary, the expence would in the end devolve on the United States.

It was agreed to leave the appointment to the states.

Mr. STONE moved that that clause giving to inspectors the rank of lieutenant colonel be struck out. He observed, that since the appointment of those officers was left to the states, the house could certainly not with propriety fix the rank.

Mr. WADSWORTH hoped it would not be struck out. He observed, that as the house had the power of organizing the militia, and were about determining that there should be inspectors, they could with the same propriety say what rank those inspectors should hold. He was as much averse as any man to granting unnecessary titles; but where great trust was reposed, and severe duty required, there rank should also follow. These inspectors were placed in a very important station, which they could not properly fill without the weight of some military rank.

Mr. STONE withdrew his motion.

Mr. BLOODWORTH moved that the rank of brigadier should be given to them, agreed.

Mr. BENSON moved for an additional clause to the bill, for granting to the President of the United States, the power of calling out the militia into the service of the United States, &c. to repel invasions or suppress insurrection.

Mr. SHERMAN observed that the proposed clause was not explicit enough. The general government by the constitution had not the power of calling out the militia to suppress insurrections in the states, without the special request of the states.

Mr. BLOODWORTH hoped the additional section would not be adopted, it would be he said, a dangerous provision.

Mr. BENSON agreed to withdraw his motion for the present, to bring it before the house, when the principles of the bill came to be discussed by them.

The committee rose [*and*] reported the bill with sundry amendments. The speaker resumed the chair.

Mr. FITZSIMONS proposed giving the bill with the amendments to a special committee to report thereon.

Mr. MADISON said it would be improper to refer it to a committee, without first agreeing to the principles of the bill.

Mr. LIVERMORE was also against leaving it to a committee. The principles of the bill were by no means settled. Three-fourths of it he looked upon as useless. The house, he conceived, had no business to enter minutely into particulars of the business, further than warranted by the constitution.

The report of the committee was ordered to lie on the table.

22 December 1790

Mr. MADISON proposed an amendment, specially to exempt by a clause in the bill, those conscientiously scrupulous of bearing arms. It was the boast, he said, and pride of the federal constitution, that the rights of man had been attended to. It was the glory of the country, that it had secured to its inhabitants the rights of conscience. The people in whose behalf I now speak, added he, deserve that some attention should be shewn them, upon this delicate point, liberty of conscience, even if it proceeded from motives of gratitude. They have had it in their power to lay restrictions on the conscientious principles of others; they have never done it. They might have made their religion the established one, when power was in their hands. If he consulted his own feelings, he would be inclined, he said, to exempt them and require no equivalent; but he thought this would be impracticable in the house, and might give dissatisfaction to other sects out of doors.

It had been said, he observed, by an honorable member from Georgia, (Mr. Jackson) in the course of the debate, that "if such an exemption should take place, the greatest part of the inhabitants of the United States would apostatize to enjoy the privileges granted to Quakers; that he himself might be tempted to put on Quakerism;" he was sure the Gentleman did not consult his own, did not consult the human heart when he made this declaration, or he never could have supposed that an enlightened people would wittingly act against the voice of their reason and conscience to avoid a duty of that nature: Not one in a thousand, he was confident, would abuse the privilege.

It was impossible, he observed, to force this people into the field against their will—the house might as well make a virtue of necessity, and grant them the privilege. It was possible to oppress their sect, but never to make them bear arms. If this amendment was in order, the principle, he conceived, was fairly before the house, he hoped it would be adopted.

Source: *DHFFC*, 14: 127, 132–34. © 1996 Johns Hopkins University Press. Reprinted by permission of Johns Hopkins University Press.

Mr. SHERMAN approved of the amendment, thought the exemption could come in with great propriety in the first section.

Mr. Sherman observed, that most of the powers, delegated to the government of the United States by the constitution, were altogether distinct from the local powers, retained by the individual states. But in the case of the militia it was different. Both governments are combined in the authority necessary to regulate that body. The national government is to provide for organizing, arming and disciplining the militia, and for governing such part of them, as may be employed in the service of the United States. But then it is to be observed, that the states do respectively and expressly reserve out of such power, the right of appointing officers and the authority of training the militia: so that the concurrence of both governments is evidently necessary, in order to form and train them. Now in governing the militia, the states have at times, other than when they are in the actual service of the United States, an indisputable title to act as their discretion shall dictate. And here it was an allowable supposition, that the particular states would have the greatest advantage of judging of the disposition of their own citizens, and who are the most proper characters to be exempted from their government. He admitted, however, that the general government had (under that clause of the constitution, which gave the authority to exercise all powers necessary to carry the particularly enumerated powers into effect) a right to make exemptions of such officers of the government, whose duties were incompatible with those of militia men. Every thing, besides this, he believed, was vested in the particular states: and he would ask gentlemen whether it was not a desirable thing to give satisfaction on these points? and whether they ought not to avoid stretching the general power, which he had mentioned, beyond what was absolutely necessary to answer the end designed?

With respect to the objection, made by the gentleman from New Hampshire, that the effect of the amendment could not be foreseen, he would remark, that he had constructed the nation [*motion*], so as to speak in the present sense; and all that was necessary in order that an officer in any state should know who were exempted from militia duty, was to look into what was the law of the state at the moment of his enquiry, and into the law of the United States, for the exemptions of the officers of the United States. And here he would just add, that, if the gentleman from Virginia would extend his motion for amending the amendment, so as to include all the proper officers of the general government, executive, legislative, and judicial, he would have no objection to incorporate it with the original motion.

An accommodation on this point took place between the gentlemen, and the two motions were blended and made into one; whereupon Mr. Giles rose, and said, he had now greater objections to the motion than before; and was well persuaded, that if the gentleman (Mr. Sherman) attended to its consequences, he would find that it was not only extremely dissimilar in its principles, but tended to overthrow the very doctrine laid down in the first proposition, which was intended to decide, whether, under the division of the authority for forming and raising the militia, the power of making exemptions remained in the state governments, or was granted by the constitution to the government of the United States. Now in the compromised proposition, there appears to be a mixture of power. The first part seems to declare, that the states ought to make the exemptions; yet the subsequent part absolutely exercises it on the part of the United States. If then the power of exemption be either ceded to the general government, or reserved to the state governments, the amendment must fall to the ground. But this was not his only objection. He conceived, that whether the power of exemption was in the state or federal government, there was one description of men mentioned in the proposition, which could not be exempted or further privileged by the house. He alluded to the members of the legislature of the United States. The privilege of these persons was taken up, and duly considered by the convention, who then decided, what privileges they were entitled to: And this house cannot pretend to give themselves other or greater, than those granted to them by the constitution. It is under this clause, said he, that every thing, necessary or proper to be done for the members of Congress, was done. "The Senators and Representatives shall receive a compensation for their services, to be ascertained by law, and paid out of the treasury of the United States. They shall in all cases, except treason, felony, and breach of the peace, be privileged from arrest, during their attendance at the session of their respective houses, and in going to, or returning from the same; and for any speech or debate in either house, they shall not be questioned in any other place." Now, if the convention took up this subject (as it is plain from the foregoing clause that they did) it is reasonable to presume, that they made a full declaration of all our privileges; and it is improper to suppose, that we are possessed of similar powers with the convention, and able to extend our own privileges. I conceive, that every inconvenience, which would attend the want of an exemption in the bill, is completely remedied by the constitution; and therefore it is impolitic to make an useless regulation. But there is another principle, upon which it is likewise impolitic. The members of this house ought to sympathize with the people on every regulation, which is here adopted. If we exempt ourselves in one instance, I do not see where we are to stop. Establish the principle, that we may exempt ourselves from militia duty; and it follows, that we may equally exonerate ourselves from every other duty, which we ought to bear in common with our constituents. By giving such just and accumulated causes of complaint, we should in the end subvert the constitution, which we are bound to support.

For these reasons, I think the clause now more exceptionable than it was at first; and hope it may not be agreed to.

23 December 1790

The House, having resolved itself into a Committee of the whole on the militia-bill, took into consideration the amendments proposed by Mr. Madison, in order to exempt persons religiously scrupulous of bearing arms from being formed into militia, as an amendment to Mr. Sherman's amendment to the first section of the bill, for leaving the general power of exemption to the particular states, after Congress had exempted, in particular, certain officers of the general government.

Mr. Laurance rose, and declared himself against all the amendments, because he conceived this an improper place to insert them. Although he thought, that Congress had a right to make the exemptions proposed, yet, on the principle of expediency, he was of opinion they might grant such part to be performed through the agency of the states, as the states, from their local capacity, were better capable of determining, so as to accommodate more conveniently their respective inhabitants. He was as well inclined to respect the rights of conscience, as any man; and thought, that persons religiously scrupulous of bearing arms, ought to be exempted from the performance of militia duty. Yet he would not vote for the last amendment, because it was not proper to insert it in the section, and because it was one of the exemptions, which might be as well determined by the states, to whom it seemed intended to leave all the business of exemption, except what related to the officers of the Union.

Mr. Madison hoped, as the gentleman agreed in the principle, that he would not vote against the amendment, until he saw how the question was determined, with respect to granting to the several states a concurrent jurisdiction with the United States, in making exceptions. If he was to apprehend, that the loss of his motion would be the consequence of inserting it [*in*] this place, he would withdraw it: and upon reflection he did so, as he was not disposed to sacrifice substance to form.

Mr. Sherman objected to the idea which the gentlemen had expressed. He

Source: *DHFFC*, 14: 164–65. © 1996 Johns Hopkins University Press. Reprinted by permission of Johns Hopkins University Press.

did not conceive, when Congress left to the states the business of making exemptions, that they "granted" them any thing. He was of opinion, that the states already possessed the power of making such exemptions: and so did the general government, so far as related to its own officers, if they considered the duties of such officers to be incompatible with their attendance upon the militia. Congress, however, does not draw this power from that clause of the constitution, which authorises them to organize the militia. But from that, which enables them to make all laws necessary to carry the government into full effect.

Some gentlemen had said, that the militia would not be uniform, if it was left to the states to make exemptions. From whence is it that they insist upon the necessity of uniformity? Certainly not from the constitution; for that says not a word respecting such equality. Uniformity is, nevertheless, desireable; and under the amendment, it will be attained so far as to answer every useful purpose: for after the states have made their exemptions, the residue of the militia will be uniform: the several corps will consist of like numbers, throughout the union. The arms, the accoutrements, and the discipline will be alike; and what greater uniformity ought to be required, to give efficacy to the militia? He apprehended, gentlemen pressed the point of uniformity, because they found it mentioned in the title of the bill, and not because it was made absolutely necessary by any constitutional necessity.

Theological Writings
and Final Days

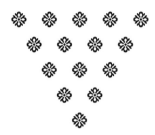

The Reformed (Calvinist) theological tradition was a significant force in eighteenth-century New England. Sydney Ahlstrom, in his magisterial history of religion in America, estimates that the Reformed tradition was "the religious heritage of three-fourths of the American people in 1776."[1] Similarly, Yale historian Harry Stout states that prior to the War for Independence, "the vast majority of colonists were Reformed or Calvinist."[2] Sherman, like most of his New England colleagues, was a member of this tradition.[3]

Sherman formally joined the Congregational church of his youth shortly before he moved to New Milford, Connecticut. He transferred his church membership to the local Congregational church there. Joining a Congregational church in the mid-eighteenth century was not simply a formality, and church members made every effort to elect only pious men as church leaders

---

1. Sydney E. Ahlstrom, *A Religious History of the American People* (Garden City, N.Y.: Doubleday, 1975), 1: 426.

2. Harry S. Stout, "Preaching the Insurrection," *Christian History* 15 (1996): 17.

3. Some scholars, notably Roger Finke and Rodney Stark, have argued that on "the eve of the Revolution only about 17 percent of Americans were churched." Roger Finke and Rodney Stark, *The Churching of America, 1776–1990: Winners and Losers in Our Religious Economy* (New Brunswick, N.J.: Rutgers University Press, 1992), 15. This estimate is widely cited even though there are good reasons to doubt its accuracy. I discuss this debate in detail in *Roger Sherman and the Creation of the American Republic*, 27–32. See also James H. Hutson, *Forgotten Features of the Founding: The Recovery of Religious Themes in the Early American Republic* (Lanham, Md.: Lexington Books, 2003), 118, and Patricia U. Bonomi and Peter R. Eisenstadt, "Church Adherence in the Eighteenth Century British Colonies," *William and Mary Quarterly*, 3rd ser., 39 (April 1982): 275.

(unlike Anglican churches in the South, where local gentry were routinely appointed as church leaders regardless of their devotion to the faith). Sherman was by all appearances an active member of the church. He was chosen "Deacon upon trial" in 1755 and "was established Deacon" in 1757. He was regularly elected clerk of the ecclesiastical society and served on the school and other committees.[4]

After moving to New Haven in 1760, Sherman transferred his church membership to White Haven, a New Light Congregational church, where he was "by the vote of the Church received to full communion in Gospel Ordinances and Privileges."[5] Jonathan Edwards Jr. was chosen as minister of this church in 1768. As was the case with his more famous father, Edwards's emphasis on theology and his concern with piety tended to drive away parishioners. Ezra Stiles estimated that White Haven had 480 members in 1772, but by 1789 the congregation had shrunk to "nineteen men and their families."[6] Edwards's biographer contends that "the major reason he was not dismissed in the late 1780's or early 1790's was the fact that he received strong support from Roger Sherman."[7] Among other things, Sherman wrote several letters defending Edwards's theological positions and his conduct.

Sherman had an abiding interest in theology. An inventory of his belongings made shortly after his death reveals that about a third (about fifty books) consisted of Bibles, concordances, catechisms, confessions of faith, volumes of sermons, and works by prominent Reformed theologians (notably, Jonathan Edwards Sr.).[8] He corresponded on religious matters throughout his life, and

4. Records of New Milford/First Congregational Church, Connecticut Church Records, reel #582, 5, Connecticut State Library. The Massachusetts Historical Society has a copy of the important Old Light "Resolves of the General Consociation Convened at Guilford, November 24th, 1741," which was copied in Sherman's hand in 1746. In 1742, Connecticut's General Assembly responded to the Resolves by passing anti-itinerancy laws that remained in place until 1750. Both documents are in Stephen Nissenbaum, ed., *The Great Awakening at Yale College* (Belmont, Calif.: Wadsworth, 1972), 128–32, 136–39. That Sherman would copy this eight-page document in 1746 suggests an interest in the proper scope of religious liberty, but it is unclear whether he supported or opposed the Resolves. General Consociation of Connecticut Churches Collection, Massachusetts Historical Society.

5. Records of the Congregational Church at White Haven, Connecticut Church Records, reel #577, 24, Connecticut State Library.

6. Ezra Stiles, *The Literary Diary of Ezra Stiles*, ed. Franklin Bowditch Dexter (New York: Charles Scribner's Sons, 1901), 3: 546.

7. Robert L. Ferm, *Jonathan Edwards the Younger: 1745–1801: A Colonial Pastor* (Grand Rapids, Mich.: Eerdmans, 1976), 139.

8. No theologian was better represented in Sherman's library than Jonathan Edwards Sr. His collection included (using the short citations from the inventories): *Life* [*of David Brainerd?*], *On*

toward the end of it he wrote and published a sermon and engaged in an extensive theological debate with the theologian Samuel Hopkins. The book closes with letters and other texts from Sherman's final years. From a political perspective, his life must have been a cause for great satisfaction. Sherman was an influential member of Congress, serving a country whose freedom he had helped earn under a constitution he had helped write. But on the home front all was not well. His first son failed at business, became an alcoholic, and was divorced by his wife. His second son ran Roger Sherman's New Haven store into bankruptcy, abandoned his post as paymaster in the War for Independence, was divorced from his wife, and was dead by 1789. The third son succeeded only in contrast to his brothers; he served with honor in the War for Independence and as a surveyor, managing to fail only at business. Fortunately, Sherman's daughters fared much better. Perhaps it is because of this turmoil that there are far more personal and intimate letters from the last years of Sherman's life than there are from his earlier years.[9]

Sherman was ill throughout the spring of 1793, but on April 15 he participated in his final public act—laying the cornerstone for South College at Yale. He died on July 23, 1793, and was buried with New Haven's equivalent of a state funeral on July 25. Jonathan Edwards Jr. gave the eulogy, reflecting with some insight that Sherman

> could with reputation to himself and improvement to others converse on the most important subjects of theology. I confess myself to have been often entertained, and in the general course of my long and intimate acquaintance with him to have been much improved by his observations on the principal subjects of doctrinal and practical divinity.
>
> But his proper line was politics. For usefulness and excellence in this line, he was qualified not only by his acute discernment and sound judgment, but especially by his knowledge of human nature. He had a happy talent of judging what was feasible and what was not feasible, or what men would bear, and what they would not bear in government. And he had a rare talent of prudence, or of timing and adopting his measures to the attainment of his end.[10]

---

the Will, History of Redemption, Religious Affections, Edwards Against Chauncey, and 15 Sermons by President Edwards. "Division of the Books belonging to the Estate of Roger Sherman Esq. Made November 14, 1794," photostatic copy in the Sherman Collection, box 1, folder 16, Yale University. There is also "Inventory of Pamphlets belonging to the Estate of the Late Roger Sherman, Esq. Including bound Book[s]," in Roger Sherman Papers, Library of Congress.

9. Collier, Roger Sherman's Connecticut, 317–23, 329–32. Of course, it is possible that there were personal letters from Sherman's early life that were lost or remain undiscovered.

10. Tyron Edwards, ed., The Works of Jonathan Edwards, D.D.: Late President of Union College (Boston: John P. Jewett, 1854), 2: 183.

Letter to Joseph Bellamy, July 23, 1772

NEW HAVEN

Joseph Bellamy (1719–90), a student of Jonathan Edwards Sr.'s, was an important New Light minister and theologian. He was the minister of a Congregational church in Bethlehem, Connecticut, from 1740 until 1790.

Rev-Sir

I received your Letter by your son yesterday, am sorry to hear that Mr. Brimsmade is in such distressed circumstances.

Mr. Lockwood I hear Died last Monday.

You mention that your letter was wrote in great haste. I beg leave to make some further remarks on the affair of Dismissing Ministers, for your consideration, & Opinion when I come to your House.

You consider the covenant between a Minister & People to be made to continue only during the people's pleasure; and if that is the tenor of the Covenant your conclusions are doubtless right.

But I take it to be the general understanding of the people in this Country, that the tenor of the Covenant is, that it shall continue during the Life of the Minister, or at least so long as he is capable to officiate. If so, the call is not, if you will settle with us we will attend your Ministry and Support you, 'till we give you notice to depart; But so long as you live, behave well & perform the work of the Ministry: and upon the Minster's agreeing to the terms he is understood to Covenant, to behave well, & perform the Ministerial work according to his ability during Life. And this Covenant I take to be of the nature of other Contracts in general, to bind each party according to the tenor of it.

And that this has been the general Sense of the Country I think appears from Judgments of Courts given on such contracts. For Instance, when Mr. Palmer left Cornwell & turned to the Chh of England, the people recovered Damages for breach of Covenant, tho' he plead that he could not in Conscience continue in the Ministry with them.

Source: Jonathan Edwards Collection, GEN MSS 151, box 28, folder 1538, Beinecke Rare Book and Manuscript Library, Yale University.

And when Mr. Sprout left the 4th Society in Guilford by advice of a mutual Council, the people would not comply with the advice, & consent to Dismiss him, but recovered Damages against him for breach of Covenant. So on the other hand. The Society of Canan in Fairfield County were desirous of Mr. Siliman's Dismission & refused to pay his salary—but they were compelled by the Genl. Assembly to pay it not only for the time then past but for the future till he resigned.

And Mr. Ives's people at Norwich desired him to depart, applied to Councils to get him Dismissed and refused to pay him his Salary—but he recovered Judgment for it at Law several times, and until by agreement he Resigned.

I mention these only to shew the General Sense of the Colony that the continuance of a peoples obligation to their Minister does not depend on their own will, but remains in force 'till discharged by mutual agreement or something is done by the minister to forfeit his Rights to the benefits of it. Nor do I know of one Instance to the contrary. If therefore this be the true understanding of the parties contracting must they not beholden to perform accordingly: Unless such a contract is in the nature of it unlawful?

As to the Instances in the Apostolic times, of Ministers Sent to preach to persons not converted to Christianity, and the directions given them, as, *If they persecute you in one city flee unto another*—*If they receive you not shake of the Dust of your feet &c* they seem not to apply to the Case in Question. And after particular Churches were gathered, and Elders were ordained in every Chh. We have their respective Duties pointed out, but I don't recollect any Instance mentioned in Scripture of Elders being deposed or dismissed, nor any Rules for doing it, except for Heresy or Scandal.

Mr. King, on the Constitution &c. of the primitive Chh. in the three first Centuries, sums up what he quotes from the Fathers on this subject in these words viz "But now excepting these three causes, of *Apostacy, Heresy,* and *Immorality,* it is Schism in a Parish to leave their Minister, or to set up another Bishop against him; for tho' they at first chose their Bishop, yet their Bishop being on their choice approved and Confirmed by the Neighbouring Bishops, they could not dethrone him, without truly assigning one of these forementioned causes." Page 166.

Now if there is any Law Divine or Humane, or practice of the Christian Church, or anything in the Nature of the Relation, to Contradict this I should be glad to see it produced. I am sensible there may be Instances wherein it may be best for a Well Qualified Minister to Resign with the Consent of the people—as on a prospect of a Minster's Usefulness being more extensive elsewhere—or when a people think that they can be better Suited & better Edified by another Minister: provided no Injustice be done to either party—but the expediency of Such a Resignation depends rather upon Probability, than certainty of advantage, & being meer matter of Judgment if the parties can't be convinced that it is best & either party refuses to consent I don't see how it can take place without manifest violation of an express obligation lawfully & voluntarily entered into—as I understand the tenor of the Covenant.

I hope to have the pleasure of Seeing you when I come to Litchfield—Miss Sherman will be well pleased with a visit from Miss Bellamy at Commencement. These with Suitable regards to your Self and Family

From your humble Servt

Roger Sherman

White Haven Church Documents

Sherman was a member of White Haven Church in New Haven. In 1788, the church approved a new confession of faith and a church covenant. One of Sherman's notebooks in the Library of Congress has what appear to be drafts of each document. Although they are very similar, there are some substantial differences. The notebook is undated, but it is likely that Sherman was involved in revising both documents. I provide Sherman's draft of each document, as well as the confession of faith adopted by the church in 1788 and the covenant adopted in 1796 (I was unable to find a copy of the 1788 covenant).

Confession of Faith in Sherman's Hand

I believe that there is one only living and true God, existing in three persons, the Father, the Son, and the Holy-Ghost, the same in substance, equal in power and glory. That the Scriptures of the old and new testaments are a revelation from God, and a compleat rule to direct us how we may glorify and enjoy him. That God has foreordained whatsoever comes to pass, so as, thereby he is not the author or approver of sin. That He created all things, and preserves and governs all creatures and all their actions, in a manner perfectly consistent with the freedom of will in moral agents, and the usefulness of means. That he made man at first perfectly holy, that the first man sinned, and as he was the public head of his posterity, they all became sinners in consequence of his first transgression, are wholly indisposed to that which is good & inclined to evil, and on account of sin are liable to all the miseries of this life, to death, and to the pains of hell forever.

I believe that God having elected some of mankind to eternal life, did send his own son to become man, die in the room and stead of sinners, and thus to lay a foundation for the offer of pardon and salvation to all mankind, so as, all may be saved who are willing to accept the Gospel offer: also by his special grace and Spirit, to regenerate, sanctify and enable to persevere in holiness, all who shall be saved; and to procure in consequence of their repentance and faith in himself, their justification by the virtue of his atonement, as the only meritorious cause.

I believe a visible church to be a congregation of those who make a credible profession of their faith in christ, and obedience to him, joined by the bond of the covenant.

That a church of christ hath power to chuse its own officers, to admit members, and to administer discipline upon offenders according to the rules of christ; either by admonition or excommunication.

I believe that the sacraments of the new testament are baptism and the

Source: Roger Sherman Papers, Manuscript Division, Library of Congress.

Lord's supper, that baptism is a sign and seal of engrafting into Christ, of a participation of his benefits, and of the obligation of the subjects to be the Lord's.

That in the Lord's supper the worthy receivers are by faith made partakers of all the benefits of Christ, to their growth in grace.

I believe that the souls of believers are at their death made perfectly holy, and immediately taken to glory: that at the end of this world there will be a resurrection of the dead, and a final judgment of all mankind, when the righteous shall be publickly acquitted by Christ the Judge and admitted to everlasting life and glory, and the wicked be sentenced to everlasting punishment.

Confession of Faith Adopted by White Haven, 1788

1. I believe there is one only living and true God, infinite, eternal, unchangeable in his being, wisdom, power, holiness, justice, goodness and truth, and that this God exists in three persons, the Father, the Son, and the Holy Ghost, the same in essence and equal in glory.

2. That the Scriptures of the Old and New Testaments are a revelation from God, and a perfect rule to direct how we may glorify and enjoy him.

3. That God hath foreordained and worketh all things according to his eternal purpose and the counsel of his own will.

4. That he created all things, and preserves and governs all creatures and all their actions in a manner consistent with man's free agency, and the use of means, so that the sinfulness of actions is imputable only to creatures and not to God, who is holy in all his works.

5. That man was at first created holy, in the image of God.

6. That the first man sinned, and he being the public head of his posterity, they all became sinners in consequence of his first transgression, and are while unregenerate wholly indisposed to that which is spiritually good, and inclined to evil; from whence proceed actual transgressions; and on account of sin are justly liable to all the miseries of this life, to death and the pains of hell forever.

7. That God, of his mere good pleasure, elected some of mankind to everlasting life, and gave his only begotten Son to assume human nature and die for sinners, that whosoever believeth in him should not perish but have everlasting life, and thereby hath laid a foundation for the offer of pardon and salvation to all mankind in the gospel; and does by his special grace and Holy Spirit regenerate, sanctify, and enable to persevere in holiness, all who shall be saved.

8. That Jesus Christ, who is God and man in one divine person, rose from the dead the third day, and ever lives to make intercession for his people, and governs all things for their good, and by the virtue of his atonement as the

Source: Samuel W. S. Dutton, *The History of the North Church in New Haven* (New Haven, Conn.: A. H. Maltby, 1842), 123–24.

only meritorious cause procures their justification, adoption and final salvation, in consequence of their repentance and faith in himself.

9. I believe that a church is a congregation of Christians professing faith in Christ and obedience to him, and joined in covenant for ordinary communion in all his ordinances; and that those who are sincere in their profession are real saints. That a church hath power to choose its own officers, to admit members, and exercise government and discipline according to the rules of the gospel.

10. I believe that the sacraments of the New Testament, baptism and the Lord's Supper, are holy ordinances instituted by Christ; that baptism is a sign and seal of the believer's faith and union with Christ, and acceptance and participation of his benefits; and of the obligation of the subjects to be the Lord's; and that the infants of members of the church are to be baptized; that in the Lord's Supper, Christ's death is shewed forth and commemorated, and the worthy receivers are by faith made partakers of all his benefits to their growth in grace.

11. I believe that the souls of believers are at their death made perfectly holy and immediately taken to glory.

12. That at the end of this world there will be a resurrection of the dead, and a final judgment of all mankind, when the righteous will be publicly acquitted by Christ the Judge, and admitted to everlasting life and glory, and the wicked will be condemned and go away into everlasting punishment.

Church Covenant in Sherman's Hand, c. 1788

I do this day publickly avouch the one only living and true God to be my God, and so far as I know my own heart I love him supremely, and am pleased with his whole character & law, and with the way of salvation by Jesus Christ as revealed in the Gospel. And by the assistance of divine grace I resolve to make his law the rule of my life, and hope I do sincerely repent of all my sins, and receive the Lord Jesus as my only saviour, trusting in the mercy of God through his atonement as the only ground of my justification and salvation.

I also think I sincerely wish the good & happiness of all mankind, and have a special love of complacency in all those who appear to be real Christians.

And furthermore through Christ strengthening me without which I can do nothing, I resolve to deny all ungodliness and worldly lusts, and give up my self to the Lord Jesus Christ to be taught and governed by him in all things.

And do further bind myself in his strength to walk with this church, in all the ordinances of Christ, and with the members thereof, as becometh a member according to the requirements of the Gospel.

I believe that baptism and the Lord's Supper are holy ordinances instituted by Christ wherein by sensible signs Christ and the benefits of the new covenant are represented, sealed, & applied to believers. That baptism is to be administered to such as make a credible profession of Christianity, and their infant seed.

Source: Roger Sherman Papers, Manuscript Division, Library of Congress.

Church Covenant Adopted by White Haven, 1796

And you do this day publicly acknowledge and choose the only living and true God to be your God; and by the assistance of Divine grace resolve to make his Law the rule of your life, hoping that you do sincerely repent of your sins, and receive the Lord Jesus Christ as your only Savior and Redeemer—trusting in the mercy of God, through his atonement as the only ground of your justification. You also hope you have a cordial love of benevolence for all mankind, sincerely desiring their best good and happiness, and a delight and complacency in those who appear to be real Christians: And through Christ strengthening you, without whom you can do nothing, you resolve to deny all ungodliness and worldly lusts, and give up yourself to the Lord Jesus Christ, to be taught and governed by him: And also bind yourself in his strength, to walk with this church in all the ordinances of Christ, and with the members thereof as becometh a member according to the requirements of the gospel. *Thus you profess and covenant.*

Then doth this church also promise you, that through the help of Christ, without whom we can do nothing, we will walk towards you in all brotherly helpfulness according to the gospel.

Thus you are admitted a member of this church, and have a right to all the privileges of it. May you have grace to improve them to the glory of God and your own edification.

Source: Samuel W. S. Dutton, *The History of the North Church in New Haven* (New Haven, Conn.: A. H. Maltby, 1842), 125–26.

Letter to John Witherspoon, July 10, 1788

NEW HAVEN

Benjamin Trumbull, a Congregational minister in New Haven, published An Appeal to the Public, Especially to the Learned, with Respect to the Unlawfulness of Divorces, in All Cases, Excepting Those of Incontinency *in 1788. Sherman may have been particularly interested in the subject because two of his sons had been divorced by their wives.*

Sir,

I here with send you Mr. Trumbull's appeal to the public respecting Divorce. Upon reading of which you will see that he supposes, divorce is not lawful in any case except for incontinency.

The law of this state admits of divorce; for fraudulent contract, Adultery, or three years wilful desertion and total neglect of duty.

Herein it agreed with the Westminster Confession of Faith article 24th. The late President Edwards was also of the same opinion, as appears by the enclosed note extracted from his writings. As the subject is important and interesting to the public as well as to individuals, I should esteem it a favour to know your opinion respecting it.

It is evident that those who admit wilful desertion as a sufficient ground for divorce, found their opinion on 1 Cor. 7.15, which they suppose contains an apostolic direction in a case not mentioned by our Lord in the Evangelists, and perfectly consistent with what he has said on the subject. They suppose that what is contained in the Evangelists, and referred to in 1 Cor. 7.10,11, as said by the Lord, imports no more, than, that no separation, or voluntary departing or putting away, except for incontinency, is lawful, or if the wife should accept a Bill of divorce from the husband, and thereupon voluntarily leave him, it would not dissolve the band of matrimony, and either party that should marry another in consequence of such a separation would be guilty of Adultery.

But in case there should be a wilful desertion of one party, either by going

Source: Miscellaneous Bound Collection, Massachusetts Historical Society.

away and leaving the other, or by cruelty and abuse compelling the other to go away, this conduct obstinately persisted in, so as totally to deprive the other of all the benefits and comforts of the marriage state; the innocent party, after using all proper means to reclaim the other, and waiting a reasonable time, and there appearing no prospect of a reconciliation, may, upon application to public authority be lawfully declared free from the band of marriage, and be at liberty to marry another.

This distinction they suppose is evident from what the apostle says in the 12th verse, *To the rest speak I, not the Lord.* This was therefore a new case on the same subject, about which our Lord had not given any direction.

As Mr. Trumbull has fully stated the arguments in support of one side of the question, I thought it might be proper to give these few hints of what has been said in support of the other side, and submit the whole to your consideration.

I am sir with great respect
and esteem your humble
servant
Roger Sherman

Letter from John Witherspoon to Roger Sherman, July 25, 1788

PRINCETON

Dear Sir,

I received a few days ago your favour of the 10th Instant with a copy of Mr. Trumbull's Discourse relating to Divorce. I have read it over with attention & am fully of opinion with Dr. Edwards that the declaration of our saviour against frivolous divorces ought not to be so interpreted that it should be impossible to liberate an innocent party any other way. As all contracts are mutual and this of marriage in a particular manner, an obstinate and perpetual refusal of performance on one side seems in the nature of things to liberate the other. Therefore the protestant churches in general and ours in particular have always admitted wilful and obstinate desertion as a cause of divorce, and have supposed the passage of the Apostle Paul to be a confirmation of this by a particular instance. This ought not to be considered as any contradiction to our saviour's declaration; on the contrary it may be considered as falling under it, for in the case of obstinate desertion Adultery may be very justly presumed in law, as the person cannot be supposed to desert in order to live the life of a monk or a nun, but from alienated affection, especially as in most cases of the kind they withdraw themselves out of the reach of observation or proof. I think Mr. Trumbull has not proved his theoretical point; but if he has given a just account of facts it would appear that either your Laws are lax upon the subject, or the courts have been lax in the execution of them, but this must depend upon the fairness and fulness of his representation which I cannot judge of with certainty in any situation.

I have the honor to be &c.

John Witherspoon

Source: Miscellaneous Bound Collection, Massachusetts Historical Society.

Letter to Rebecca Sherman, June 29, 1789

NEW YORK

Sherman wrote this letter to his wife shortly after hearing about the death of his son, and Rebecca's stepson, William.

Dear wife,

The late bereaving stroke of divine Providence in our family is very affecting to me. I should have been glad to have been with Wm. in his illness but could not. I am informed by Isaac's letter that all possible care was taken of him, and that Mr. Baldwin was very helpful in ministring to him, and he has given me a particular account of his case in his letters. I shall ever retain a grateful sense of his kindness therein.

It is my earnest Prayer that this Providence may be suitably regarded by me & all the family and especially the surviving children of our family, & his child—that they may be excited to be always in an actual readiness for death.

Our children have all been brought under the Bond of the covenant, by Baptism, but those of them who are come to years of discretion should consider that it is indispensably necessary for them to give their cordial consent to the covenant of grace and that it is their duty to make a public profession of Religion and attend all the ordinances of the Gospel, and in order to understand how this should be done in a proper manner they should search the scriptures & attend public preaching.

The sermon that I agreed with Mr. Moss to print will give much light on that subject. I would have each of the family have one, and give two to John's family one to Mr. Baldwin one to William's daughter Betsey, & to the following Persons: Dr. Stiles, Dr. Dana, Dr. Wales, Dr. Edwards, Mr. Austin, Brother Josiah, Mrs. Minon & her son. I want much to come home, but it is difficult leaving the business at present—tis supposed by some that Congress may make such arrangements by September as to adjourn to December. I can have leave of absence but should be unwilling to leave the business at present.

Source: Roger Sherman (1721–93) Collection (MS 447), box 1, folder 10, Manuscripts and Archives, Yale University Library.

I should be glad to have you write to me that I may know how you do, and what you want. I had thought of sending home a piece of India Taffity for Becca & Betsey but can't find any, the India ships are gone to New Jersey & dont expect to bring much of the goods here until the state duties expire. I received my trunk by Capt. Clark.

I am in health & affectionately yours

Roger Sherman

Letter from Elizabeth Sherman to Roger Sherman, June 29, 1789

NEW HAVEN

Sherman's daughter wrote the following letter to her father concerning William's death.

HOND. SIR; It is an hour of trying affliction with us. We all need your advice and counsel in this affecting moment. Mama has been graciously supported beyond our expectation. Thus we have reason to praise God in the midst of this most severe chastisement. It is by her desire that I write to inform you the particulars of the death and interment of my deceased brother. He appeared to have his senses and was able to speak until about six hours before his death.

Doctor Stiles, Doctor Wales and Mr. Austin all visited and conversed with him concerning the state of his mind. He expressed penitence for sins and his belief of a necessity of the atonement by Christ and seemed sincerely to desire to be enabled by the grace of God to repent of all his sins and accept of salvation upon the terms offered in the Gospel, and the last words he was heard to utter appeared to be an earnest prayer to his Creator for the salvation of his soul and at 3 o'clock on Saturday he was buried. His daughter Betsy attended as a mourner at the funeral. Mama got for her and for the rest of us hats, gloves, buckles, handkerchiefs and everything necessary for mourning except gowns. Those we borrowed. They were black silk. Now Mama wishes to know what you think proper to get for the family and whether you do not think best to get for them and for his Betsy suits of black silk and she also wishes if possible to have you come home even if you cannot stay but two days. Roger and Oliver have dark coats and other dress that is very decent. John and Isaac have no dark coats. They have black underdresses, stockings, gloves and all else that is necessary and Mama wants to know if they had not best have some dark coats. Roger has been to Mr Tomlinsons and took some patterns of the lute strings which I have enclosed. They are half yard wide. The large piece is 11/8 per ell. The other 9/6 per ell York currency, and he will make his usual deduction from

Source: Lewis H. Boutell, *The Life of Roger Sherman* (Chicago: A. C. McClurg, 1896), 221–22.

the above prices. At the same place is some English taffety for 7 pounds per piece Y. C. and marked price.

from yours affectionately,

ELIZA SHERMAN.

N. B. We cannot find any broad cloths here. If you think best to get any I suppose you can get enough in New York.

Mama is happy to inform you that Isaac has been a great comfort to her and all the family in our present distress.

Letter to Simeon Baldwin, June 29, 1789

NEW YORK

Sherman wrote the following letter to his son-in-law shortly after his son William's death.

SIR,—I received your letter of the 24th on the evening of the 25th and that of the 26th on the evening of the 28th—I am greatly obliged to you for the attention you gave to my son William in his sickness, and the early and circumstantial account given me respecting him in your letters. I had thought of returning home on receipt of your first letter but had no opportunity by land or water until it was too late to see him alive or to attend his funeral. The first account I had of his death was by a letter from my son Isaac last Saturday evening. I wish this sudden and sorrowful event may be sanctified to all the family—that we may always be prepared for so great and important a change, by choosing the good part that can never be taken away from us.

These with my love to you and Mrs. Baldwin,
    from your affectionate Parent,

ROGER SHERMAN.

Source: Lewis H. Boutell, *The Life of Roger Sherman* (Chicago: A. C. McClurg, 1896), 222–23.

Letter to Rebecca Sherman, July 23, 1789

NEW YORK

This letter by Sherman to his wife contains a mix of political news and domestic concerns.

DEAR WIFE,—I received Roger's letter of the 20th inst wherein he mentions that you had a poor turn that day but was so far recovered as to ride out. If your state of health makes it necessary, I will return home immediately, otherwise I shall stay a little longer. The bill establishing courts passed by the Senate is now before the House, and I am on a committee for considering amendments to the Constitution. The bill for fixing the pay of the members is depending and undetermined—I wish you to write me by the first post.

I received my clothes in the green box—The new jacket fits well. Coppers have taken a sudden fall here to 48 for a shilling York money, if we have any on hand I think it best to keep them for the present. I believe it would answer to take in good flax well dressed for spinning at a reasonable price—the crop won't be so good this year as last.

Yours, &c.,

ROGER SHERMAN.

Source: Lewis H. Boutell, *The Life of Roger Sherman* (Chicago: A. C. McClurg, 1896), 224–25.

"A Short Sermon on the Duty of Self Examination, Preparatory to Receiving the Lord's Supper. Wherein the Qualifications for Communion Are Briefly Considered," 1789

Sherman wrote and published, but apparently never preached, the following sermon. He also attached a few extracts from the English Puritan Richard Baxter's The Practical Works of the Late Reverend and Pious Mr. Richard Baxter *(London, 1707). There are minor variations between Baxter's original works and Sherman's extracts, but on the whole Sherman transcribed the passages accurately.*

Source: Roger Sherman, "A Short Sermon on the Duty of Self Examination, Preparatory to Receiving the Lord's Supper. Wherein the Qualifications for Communion Are Briefly Considered" (New Haven, Conn.: Able Morris, 1789).

A SHORT SERMON

On the duty of Self Examination,

preparatory to receiving the
Lord's Supper.
Wherein the qualifications for Communion
are briefly considered,
With an Appendix containing Extracts from
Mr. Richard Baxter's Work's.

Shewing the *necessity* of the personal profession of true
Christianity to entitle persons of Adult age to the privileges
of Communion with the visible Church whether
Baptized in Infancy or not.

Rom. X. 10, *For with the heart man believeth unto righteousness,*
and with the mouth Confession is made unto Salvation.

New Haven Printed and Sold

By ABEL MORSE.
M, DCC LXXXIX.

1 Cor. XI. 28

But let a man examine himself, and so let him eat of that Bread, and drink of that Cup.

Self examination previous to an approach to the holy supper of the Lord, is a necessary, tho' I fear too much a neglected duty; had not the Corinthians been remiss herein, it is not likely those disorders would have crept into their attendance on this sacred solemnity, which are mentioned and severely reproved by the Apostle in this Chapter: they sat down to the Lord's supper as tho' it had been but a common meal; and even with such greediness, as not in a decent manner to tarry for one another; and some where guilty of eating and drinking to excess.——This irreverent behaviour of theirs, which the Apostle calls eating and drinking damnation, or rather judgment to themselves, greatly provoked the Lord, who testified his displeasure against them, by visiting them with grievous temporal judgments.——"For this cause," says he, "many are weak and sickly among you, and many sleep," or are dead.

To prevent such disorders in future, as well as the consequences of them, he, among other directions, exhorts them all to examine themselves of their knowledge, temper and behaviour, that so they might no longer be guilty of profaning the body and blood of Christ.

This examination is a duty equally incumbent on us, and on all communicants:——And it ought to be done seriously, impartially, sincerely, with humility, and earnest prayer, that God by his spirit would assist our enquiries, and not suffer us to be deceived in a matter of such importance.

But what are the principal points of enquiry, about which we are to examine ourselves? The most important are the following.

1st We are to examine ourselves concerning our knowledge of the Gospel-scheme of salvation in general, and of the nature, use, and design of this ordinance in particular.

Let us examine what our knowledge of Jesus Christ, the author of our salvation is. Do we consider him as God and man, united in two distinct natures and one person forever? Do we rightly understand the mediatorial character, and the offices Jesus Christ is invested with, that he was appointed by the Father to undertake the work of redeeming lost sinners; and for this purpose was constituted a prophet to reveal the counsels of his grace;——a priest, by the sacrifice of himself to atone for our sin, and plead for pardon; and a king, to rule or reign over, and defend us; Have we right apprehensions of the covenant of redemption and grace; that the Father from all eternity, upon the foresight of the fall, determined to rescue and save a chosen number; and to this end, appointed his own Son to be mediator of the new covenant; to take upon him our nature, to be made under the law, and as the sinner's substitute, to obey the precepts, and endure the penalty thereof; thus fulfilling all the righteousness of it, for the justifying of the ungodly; and as an encouragement hereto, promised to furnish him for, assist and succeed him in the undertaking, and give him a seed to serve him?—The Son accepted the proposal, answering, "Lo I come to do thy will O God!" and in the appointed time was made man, became subject to the law, lived a holy and exemplary life, and died a cursed death on the cross; that so by compleatly answering the demand of the law, he might ransom us from hell, and purchase pardon, reconciliation with God, the adoption of children, the sanctifying, quickening and strengthening influences of the holy spirit, and eternal life in heaven for all his people.

The revelation of this transaction between the Father and the Son, with its accomplishment and happy fruits, I say the revelation and proposal hereof to us in the gospel is, for substance, what we call the covenant of grace; in which God most graciously offers, thro' Christ, to be again reconciled to us; to pardon our iniquities; to grant us the adoption of Sons, with all their present privileges and future blessedness; or, in the more comprehensive language of Scripture, that he will be to us a God, a God in covenant, to bless and make us happy forever.

But then on the other hand, in order to the enjoyment of these privileges, we are required heartily to consent to, and accept of this covenant, by sincerely repenting of all our Sins, believing in the Lord Jesus Christ, and by devoting ourselves unreservedly to his Service.—We are thus to give up our-selves to God, as his people; and in this way he will be to us a God.

Those privileges He promises on his part, and these duties are required on ours; not as a meritorious condition upon which they are to be obtained, but rather as necessary qualifications therefor, without which there is an unsuitableness in, as well as an utter impossibility of, our enjoying them.

This may lead us to enquire further, whether we have right conceptions of the deplorable state in which the Gospel of God's grace supposes, and finds mankind? Viz. a state of depravity, guilt and misery, exposed to the eternal curse of the law;--dead in trespasses and sins;--by nature prone to evil and averse to good, and entirely unable to deliver ourselves.

Again do we rightly understand the way in which we are to obtain deliverance out of this our ruined and miserable condition, Viz. by faith in Jesus Christ, which implies a firm belief of the gospel report concerning him, a hearty approbation of the whole method of salvation thro' him, a chearful consent and desire to be saved in this way, and a reliance of soul on his merits, and the mercy of God thro' him, for the whole of salvation, both from sin and hell, to be made holy as well as happy; acknowledging the whole to be of mere grace, and testifying our acceptance hereof, by a life of holy obedience to his commands.

Once more let us examine into our knowledge of the nature, use and design of this ordinance of the Supper.—I hope we none of us maintain such mistaken notions of it, as some of the Corinthians did, who looked upon it as a common feast, and designed principally for the refreshment of their bodies.—we are to consider it a religious remembrancer of Jesus Christ, of his atoning sacrifice and precious benefits.---"This do," says he, "in remembrance of me." And what those views of him are, which this ordinance was principally designed to give us, we may learn from his own explication, when he distributed the bread and wine among his disciples;—taking the bread, he says, "this is my body," that is, a memorial of my body, "which is broken for you."—And of the cup he said, "this cup is the new testament in my blood," that is, a memorial or exhibition of the new covenant ratified in my blood.---so that you see this feast was instituted in memory of a crucified Jesus, whose body was broken, and whose blood was shed for the remission of sins.

And here we have a striking representation of the amazing love of Christ, in giving his life a ransom for us;--of the infinite evil of sin, which could not be expiated at less expence;---of the strict and inflexable justice of God, which could not let sin escape without an adequate punishment; and likewise of the triumphs of the cross over sin, death and hell, which are here displayed with admirable lustre.

And various, important, and inestimable are the blessings herein exhibited to our believing view---such as pardon of sin, peace with God;---the adoption of children;-the sanctifying, guiding, comforting and quickening influences of the holy spirit,--and in a word, all needfull grace here, and full glory hereafter. ---These are all held forth to view, and offered to us in this ordinance which seems to contain the form and substance of the whole gospel in miniature.

Here we see the need we stand in of a Saviour, else why is one pro-vided?---Here we see the strictness and purity of God's law the least tittle of which cannot be abated, nor broken without satisfaction.———Here we see the fulness of Christ's atonement; the blessings purchased by it, and the freeness with which they are offered.

I have run over the particulars, as a summary of that christian knowledge, which it is peculiarly proper we should have at least, in some tolerable measure, in order to an acceptable, and understanding attendance on this ordinance. But knowledge is not all that is necessary,———we must examine farther yet; ---it is necessary that we come to the table of the Lord as true penitents for sin: Let us then in the

2d place examine ourselves respecting our repentance.

An impenitent communicant is a monster, no better than a traitor at his master's table. And there is the greatest absurdity, as well as impiety, in celebrating an ordinance in memorial of a crucified Jesus, who died a sacrifice for sin, without a relenting heart, which sincerely hates, mourns for and turns from that accursed thing which occasioned his deep humiliation and bitter agonies,---How then do we stand affected toward sin? do we see it to be infinitely base and odious in its own nature, as against God, as well as in its destructive consequences with regard to us? And does such a view cause us to mourn heartily for it, that ever we should be guilty of acting such a base unreasonable and ungrateful part against that glorious being, who has done such great things for us and to whom we are so infinitely indebted.

Does all sin appear inexpressibly hatefull in our eyes? do we loath it, and loath ourselves on account of it? so that we are ready with the leeper to cry out unclean! unclean? And does this mourning for, and hatred of sin, manifest itself to be genuine by our forsaking it? and setting ourselves with all our might to oppose and destroy it? He is not a true penitent, who does not heartily renounce all his evil ways, and bid adieu to every thing which he knows to be sinful, with a fixed determination of soul never to indulge himself therein any more; but on the other hand, that he will conscientiously and carefully endeavor to live obedient to all God's commandments.——This is that repentance we ought all to have, but especially those who approach to the table of the Lord. Moreover.

3d We should examine ourselves concerning our faith in Jesus Christ, which is requisite to a due attendance on this ordinance? Do we firmly believe the record which God has given concerning his Son? Are we earnestly desirous of, and do we sincerely and with all our hearts consent to be saved by him in that way which God has appointed thro' him? Do we chearfully place our dependance on his merits, for all those spiritual and eternal blessings which we need? Faith if there may be any comparison, is above all things necessary on such an occasion; for to what purpose is it that Jesus Christ is here set forth as a propitiation, unless we have faith to fix upon him as such and apply to our own use the benefits which are herein exhibited and offered to us, if we are destitute of this, our souls may starve and perish in the midst of all this gospel plenty.

Have we then this faith which is of such necessity and importance to us? do we receive it for an undoubted truth, that Jesus Christ was made an atoning sacrifice for sin? that he is an allsufficient Saviour? that he is an infinitely willing Saviour? that all his benefits are freely offered to us? that we are bid an hearty welcome to him? And do we with all our souls make choice of and rely upon him, as our Saviour to sanctify and govern, as well as save us from hell? this is a point which it concerns us carefully to examine into. And further.

4th. We should examine ourselves concerning our love to God and man. If we have not a supreme love to the blessed God, and our divine Redeemer, and a hearty generous charity for our fellow men, especially for those of the household of faith, we are but poorly prepared to celebrate such a feast as this.

How stands the case with us in these regards? Is the glorious author of our being, the object of our highest esteem? do we place our chief delight in him? and is our sincere and unwearied care to please him in all our ways? do we love our Lord Jesus Christ in sincerity, and give that evidence of it, which he requires, by keeping his commandments? And do we manifest ourselves to be his disciples, by our obedience to that particular command of his, that we love one another? A love of benevolence is due to all mankind, but in an especial manner are we required to love the brethren, with a pure heart fervently.

A wrathful, malicious, revengeful, uncharitable disposition, is very unbecoming a professed disciple of that meek and lowly Jesus, who laid down his life even for his enemies. Are we then possessed of, and do we seek to cultivate that charity toward our fellow men, and our fellow christians, without which we are nothing? Do we feel a benevolent disposition toward mankind in general, and our brethren in Christ Jesus in particular? Do we rejoice in each others welfare, and seek as we have opportunity to promote it?

Are we grieved at the faults of those around us, and do we try to reclaim them? Have we a mantle to cover their infirmities? Are we ready to overlook offences? and forgive those who have trespassed against us, even as God for Christ's sake hath forgiven us? to put the kindest and softest construction on the words and actions of such as we think have injured us and meant us ill? considering and weighing every alleviating circumstance in their favour.---In short have we that charity which beareth all things of an injurious nature, as far as is consistent with duty? which believeth all things and hopeth all things in favour of another, as far as there is any manner of ground for it: and endureth all things while there is any prospect of a change for the better? yea, which suffereth long and is kind, which envieth not, vaunteth not itself, is not puffed up, is not easily provoked, thinketh no evil? Let us see to it that it dwells and abounds in us.

Again.

5th. We should examine ourselves concerning our obedience to the commands of God.——In this ordinance, we as it were, swear allegiance to God, and promise that, by his assistance, we will continue faithful in his service for ever.——Has it then been our care to live answerable to these engagements? do we set the law of God before us, as the rule of our whole behaviour? And tho' we are unable now in our fallen state to keep it perfectly, yet do we strive to come as near to perfection as possible, exercising ourselves daily to maintain consciences void of offence, both toward God, and toward man? or if we have been remiss and careless in time past, do we heartily repent of and bewail before God these our miscarriages, and firmly resolve in the strength of his grace to become more circumspect and careful in time to come? and when we have done our utmost, are we sensible and ready to acknowledge, that we are unprofitable, yea guilty servants, who stand in need of a pardon, instead of meriting reward? And consequently do we look to the merits of Christ alone to render our services as well as persons acceptable.

I add in the last place; it is proper that we examine ourselves, concerning our spiritual wants when we are about to wait upon Christ in this ordinance of the supper; that so we may know what petitions to put up for relief.———This ordinance is a kind of gospel store-house, or spiritual market, in which is set forth to view, plentiful provision for the supply of all our necessities; and offered upon the condescending terms of a believing reception.———

We should then cast in our minds, what relief we stand in need of, what pardon, what comfort, what quickening, what strength, what light, support, &c. And all these wants of our souls, we should spread before the Lord, at his table, and humbly pray to have them supplied, according to the riches of grace in Christ Jesus.

Thus have we run over, tho' in a brief and imperfect manner, the most material heads of examination: And I have endeavored to do it in such a manner, as not to open too great a latitude on the one hand, nor raise unreasonable scruples of conscience on the other.

And now a little to recapitulate the whole. If upon a careful examination we find, that we have a competent understanding of the gospel way of life by Jesus Christ, and of the nature, use and design of this holy institution of the supper:———If we do heartily repent of all our sins, bewailing them before God, with a deep rooted hatred of, and turning from them to the Lord, and the practice of his commandments:-If we sincerely acknowledge Jesus Christ to be our Lord and master, believing him to be an allsufficient and infinitely suitable Saviour, as well as unspeakably willing even for us, and do earnestly desire to be interested in, and devoted to him upon the terms of the gospel: with a chearful confidence in his power and grace for salvation.———If we have reason to think we have that love to God and Christ which is a spring of chearful obedience and at the same time are of a charitable, forgiving, obliging disposition toward our fellow-men and especially our fellow christians; if we are conscious that we use our honest endeavors to live in obedience to all God's commands; and if we have any due sense of our spiritual wants, that we are in ourselves, poor and miserable, wretched and blind and naked. I say, if we can answer such enquiries as these in the affirmative; or if, so far as we know our own hearts, we have reason to conclude it is thus with us, tho' not in such measures as we desire; or, to come lower yet, If we do earnestly and above all things desire, and use our utmost endeavors that it may be so with us, we ought to come and eat of this bread and drink of this wine.

But if after the most careful examination a person shall fear that he is not a subject of God's saving grace, or in other words is not savingly converted; let such a one consider that he must judge of his spiritual state, by the exercises and affection, of his own mind, toward God and Jesus Christ, and toward the divine law and the gospel; and of these exercises he must be conscious, tho' he may not always be able to judge with certainty whether they proceed from a principal of holiness implanted in the heart in regeneration or not. The re-mainders of sinful depravity in the hearts of the regenerate greatly tend to darken the evidence of their good estate, hence the sincere and humble chris-tian is more ready to doubt of his good estate than the presumptuous hypocrite.

But any one who firmly believes, in the first place, that whatever is revealed in the gospel concerning Jesus Christ is true; if so far as he knows his own heart, he approves of the whole method of salvation by him: If he is heartily grieved for all his past sins, and is willing and determined with abhorence to forsake them: If he is earnestly desirous to have them pardoned for Christ's sake, and to be renewed in the spirit of his mind; and it is his firm resolution and desire, so far as he can judge of his own sincerity, and in a dependence on divine assistance, to walk in obedience to all God's commands for time to come; I say if he is conscious of all this, that this is his temper and these his views, desires, resolutions, and endeavors; I think he ought to come tho' he is in darkness and doubts respecting his state.

But as to such as are conscious to themselves, that they do not repent of all their sins; that there is any sin that they are not willing and determined to forsake; or that there is any known duty which they wilfully live in the neglect of, and are not resolved immediately to put it in practice, or that they do not earnestly desire an interest in Christ upon gospel terms, and are not willing and resolved, in humble dependence on divine assistance, to live entirely de-voted to his service, I say if any know this to be the case with them, they cannot come to the Lord's table without the most daring presumption and known hypocrisy.

But it is time to draw to a close; what I farther say shall be a word or two concerning the frame of mind with which we ought to approach the table of the Lord, and the business we have to transact when seated there.

As to our approach we should come with a deep sense of our exceeding great guilt and unworthiness, with a reverential awe and solemnity of soul: with composure of mind and fixedness of thought: with chearful confidence in God, as one propitious to returning sinners thro' his dear Son; we should come hungering and thirsting after righteousness, with raised expectations of having our spiritual wants supplied; with fervent charity towards one another; and a solemn consideration of the nature of the ordinance to be attended on. And when engaged in the solemnity, we are called upon to confess and bewail before God our many and great offences, which were the procuring cause of our Saviour's great sufferings; to act faith in the Lord Jesus Christ for pardon and every blessing we need; yea afresh to receive him in all his offices, as our Saviour: and deliberately, humbly, chearefully, sincerely and unreservedly to renew the surrender of ourselves to him, in that well ordered covenant which was established in his blood: admiring and thankfully acknowledging the riches of redeeming love, and earnestly imploring that divine assistance, which may enable us to live no more to ourselves, but to him that loved us, and gave himself to die for us.

Appendix:

Containing Some
Extracts from Mr. Richard Baxter's *Works* who was a very celebrated Minister of the Gospel among the *Dissenters* in *England,* in the time of the long *Parliament,* and thro' the *Reign of* Cha. IId.

Vol ist, *Question,* Whether it be necessary that they, who are baptized in Infancy, do solemnly at age, renew and own their baptismal covenant, before they have a right to the state and privilege of Adult members? and if they do not, whether they are to be numbered with christians, or apostates.

Answer ist. Church membership is the same thing in Infants as in the Adult.

2d. Infants are naturally incapable of doing all that which the adult must do, as to understand, profess, &c. themselves.

Thirdly. The Baptism of the Adults, being the most compleat, because of the maturity of the receivers, is made the standing pattern in Scripture: for God formeth his ordinances to the most perfect ordinary receivers.

Fourthly. Though an Infants be devoted acceptably to God by his Parents will, yet when he is of age it must be done by his own will.

Fifthly. Therefore a bare Infant's title ceaseth when we come to age, and the Persons title ceaseth, unless it be renewed by himself, or his own consent, the reason is because the conditions of his Infant-title then cease, For his Parents will shall go for his no longer.

Sixthly. Regularly, *ad bene esse*, the transition out of the state of Infant membership should be very solemn; and by an understanding, personal owning of the Baptismal covenant.

Seventhly. There needeth no other proof of this, than 1st. That God in Scripture never gave adult persons title to his covenant, but by their own personal covenant: and at the first institution of baptism, both went together, (personal profession and baptism) because the receivers were adult.

2d. And that Infants are capable of baptism, but not of personal profession.

3d. Therefore though they are not to repeat baptism, which was done before, yet they are bound to make that profession at age which they never made before.

Eighthly. Where this solemn owning of their covnant cannot be had (by reason of Church corruption, and magistrates prohibition) there the persons ordinarily joining with the church, in the publick profession and worship, is to be taken for an owning it.

Ninthly, He that being baptized in Infancy, doth no way at full age own his baptismal covenant, is to be taken for an Apostate: 1st Because his Infant title ceaseth: and he notoriously violateth his covenant: because he can be no adult christian that no way owneth Christ.

Tenthly. But this is to be understood of those who have opportunity, for one in a wilderness among heathens only, cannot join in publick worship, nor give testimony of his christianity to the Church.

Eleventh. Though the Sacrament of the Lord's Supper be appointed for the renewing of our covenant at age, yet is it not the first owning of the covenant by the aged: for that Sacrament belongeth neither to Infants nor Infidels: and he that claimeth it, must be an adult Church member or Christian; which those are not, who at full age no way ever owned their baptismal covenant, nor made any personal profession of Christianity.

In page 559 of the same book the same Author says, none ought to be baptized but those that either personally deliver up themselves in covenant to God the Father, Son, and Holy-Ghost, professing a true repentance, and faith and consent to the Covenant; or else are thus delivered up and dedicated and entered into covenant in their Infancy, by those that being christians themselves have so much interest in them and power of them, that their act may be esteemed as the Infant's act, and legally imputed to them as if themselves had done it. If any others are unduly baptized they have hereby no title to the pardon of sin or life eternal, nor are they taken by God to be in covenant as having no way consented to it.

Having been entered in your Infancy into the covenant of God by your Parents, you must at years of discretion, renew the covenant which by them you made, and renew it personally yourselves; and this with as great seriousness, and resolution, as if you were now first to enter and subscribe it, and as if your everlasting life or death, were to depend on the sincerity of your consent, and performance. For your infant baptismal covenant will save none of you that live to years of discretion, and do not as heartily own it in their own persons, as if they had been now to be baptized.

Page 471. Are all the members of the visible church to be admitted to this Sacrament (The Lord's Supper) or communicate?

Answ. All are not to seek it, or to take it, because many may know their unfitness, when the church or Pastors know it not: But all that come and seek it, are to be admitted by the Pastors, except such children, ideot, ignorant persons, or hereticks, as know not what they are to receive and do, and such as are notoriously wicked or scandalous, and have not manifested their repentance. But then it is presupposed, that none should be numbered with the adult members of the church, but those that have personally owned their baptismal covenant, by a credible profession of true christianity.

The acceptance and baptism of our Infants, is one of the privileges of believers: but no one hath right to this privilege (that his children be accepted into the church) upon a bare infant title, without the profession of a personal actual faith. He that cometh to God must believe that God is, and that he is a rewarder of them that diligently seek him. Therefore those that profess not this belief, consequently cannot have communion with the church. Without which it is impossible to please God. Heb. 11.5,6. therefore without a profession of faith, it is impossible to have just communion; which is purposely for the pleasing God.

There's no middle state between believers and Infidels; consenters, and refusers. How shall they escape that neglect so great salvation? Neglecting and not consenting in a capable invited subject is certain Infidelity: and therefore in the external profession we must judge accordingly.

He that will not confess Christ, even in a christian church, and a peaceable age, deserves not to be called a christian. He that is not for him is against him. It was never proved by any writer, nor ever will be, that any person at age, and natural capacity ought to be a member of the church of Christ, under the gospel, (nor under the law neither) without a shew of grace, even of faith, by his profession of consent to the holy covenant.

Question. What if I am uncertain whether my heart be sincere in this covenant which I make with God when I renounce all, and profess to prefer him before all? May I venture to covenant and profess that covenant whose sincerity I am uncertain of?

Answer. The truth of your consent is one thing, and your certainty of it is another: that it be true, is necessary to your Salvation; but not that you be sure that it is true.

One that truly consenteth and resolveth, but is afraid lest his deceitful heart is not sincere in it, this person must covenant in this uncertainty. Because all that can be expected from us is that we speak our own minds, according to the best acquaintance with them that we can get; otherwise we must forbear all thanksgiving, for special mercies, and a great part of our worship of God, till we are certain of the sincerity of our own hearts, which too many are not.

Concerning Church discipline and the Subjects of it.

I know that discipline is of excellent use, and is likely to have excellent effects: but upon whom? upon such as are fit to come under discipline, and with such I have seen its usefulness: but with the rest it makes them next to mad. They that before would patiently hear me in the plainest sharpest Sermons that I could preach, and would quietly bear any private admonition, when once they are publickly admonished and cast out, are filled with the gall of malice and indignation and never more like to profit by a Sermon.

No man is safe out of his own rank and place.

The state of catechumens or expectants is the seminary of the church, and the state of Infant Church membership, the Seminary to the state of the Adult, into which they must be seasonably and solemnly transplanted, when they are ripe and ready, and not before. In the state of expectants these may profit by preparing ordinances, and the season may come when they may be fitly transplanted: but if we put them that are infidels among actual believers, and Adult church members, that are not such, nor prepared for the station, we bring them under a discipline which will exasperate them, and turn them to be malignant enemies, and undo them forever.

A due placing of all, according to their qualifications, is the chiefest part of our Government.

Objection, Let us trust God with his own ordinances: we must do our duty, whatever come of it.

Answer. This doth but beg the *Question*: God's ordinances are not for destruction, but edification, Ministers are appointed to make disciples, and gather men to Christ and further their conversion, and not plunge them into a remedial state, and to hurry them unprepared into church Communion, that they may be thrust out again, and brought to hate the Church.——And yet I never knew the man, nor saw his face, that practiced what this objection pleads for; and exercised discipline faithfully on a whole Parish; nor do I believe that any man can do it that would. 283. When men are made to understand, that by the law of God, seconded by the common consent of the Church, and the most learned godly Pastors, that no man is to be accounted, or numbered with the adult christians, but those that make a sober, serious, understanding profession of christianity; renouncing the flesh, the world and the devil; and not contradicting and nullifying this profession by a wicked life, this will engage Parents to teach their children, and children themselves to learn what christianity is, when they cannot have the name, or the honour, and the privileges of christians, without some credible appearance of the thing.

For doubtless while christianity is in credit, the same motives that now prevail with the multitude to seem christians, and to desire the baptism of their children, will continue then, to make them desire to be numbered with christians when they are at age; and so will provoke them to do that, without which they know they cannot be esteemed christians.

284. By this means also church discipline will attain its end; it will awe and preserve the Church, and terrify offenders, and help them to repentance, and preserve the order of the church and gospel, when it is exercised upon such as are capable of it, that know the nature of it, and either are habitually disposed to profit by it, or at least understand what it was that they were engaged to, and understandingly consent to live under such a discipline; and when it is exercised upon few, and we have not such multitudes to sweep out of the church.

By this means also the ordinances will be more purely administered agreably to their nature, and the institution and so God will bless them more to his church, and own his people, with the fuller discoveries of his presence, and take pleasure in the assembles and services of his Saints.

And by this means the church & the christian religion will be more honourable in the eyes of the world, who judge by the members and professors lives, before they can judge of the thing as in it itself.

The foregoing *Extracts* are taken from the first and fourth Folio Volumns of the Author's Works, which belong to the Library of Yale-College, where the several points are more fully considered, with the arguments and Scripture proofs in support of them.

Letter from Justus Mitchell to Roger Sherman, January 26, 1790

CANAAN

Justus Mitchell (1754–1806) married the daughter of Sherman's brother, Josiah Sherman. A graduate of Yale College, Mitchell served as minister of the Church of Christ in New Canaan from 1782 until his untimely death in 1806. This letter to Roger Sherman begins with a discussion of a sermon by Josiah Sherman. Sherman responded to this missive on February 8, and Mitchell returned the favor on March 17.

Honorable & Worthy Sir,

I received your letter, which accompanied the goods, by the hand of Capt Hoit of Norwalk, and the other dated Jan. 10 with the sermon of Mr. Sherman. The goods arrived safe, except a table leg broken, which may be repaired with a trifle of expense.

I have only looked at the sermon, without much attention. It requires so much care, even to read it, that it is difficult to pay that attention to the sentiment, which is necessary, to form a just conclusion on the subject. I am not fully convinced that I ever understood my Father Sherman's sentiments in all their length. He supposes, that the law demands perfection, and the obligation is still binding on sinners; but that the Gospel doth not require the exercise of spiritual life till God hath given it in regeneration: which is to be received in the use of means. But this is a difficult sentiment for me to admit.

I suppose, that obligation, either from law or Gospel, doth not depend on the state of the heart, whether it be spiritually active or dead: when therefore I look into the Gospel, and find salvation offered to Adam's race, to be received by repentance & faith, then my obligation from the Gospel begins, whether God sends his Spirit to renew, or not. For a creature to live without this spiritual life is his own [fault?], and there is no excuse; and however impossible it is, for a sinner to exercise this spiritual life, yet here lies his blame. Now, I conceive, that because God sends his Holy Spirit to renew, without which the soul would not repent, doth not argue, that the creature is under no obligation to repent, where the Spirit is not sent.

Source: Roger Sherman Papers, Manuscript Division, Library of Congress.

If the creature is not under obligation to exercise spiritual life; till he receives it in the life of means, then the [?], and the inability, are not of the moral, but of the natural kind of moral inability [two illegible words] obligation: and I do not see why obligation from law to exercise spiritual life does not cease: and is make an obligation, lie on sinners from law to exercise this spiritual life which ceases in the Gospel, is a difficulty which I do not understand.

These are some of the turning points in the sermon, which it will be necessary to examine, and on which I should like to hear your sentiments. Mr. Sherman professes to be a Calvinist, but I have supposed he dwelt so much on the subject of means, as to crowd some other points a little out of joint. Though I had great regard for Mr. Sherman, as a good preacher, and preached thorough Calvinism when he was not laboring, some peculiarities, in his scheme. In my next, I will say something further on the sermon, which at present I must omit, for want of acquaintance with it.

The subject of moral obligation, among many divines, is denied, in some of its parts, which occasions many disputes, among common people.

By your letter, I perceive you had heard of my misfortune after I left your house,—Mr. Lambert of Milford, brought some hay to my horses; he had been butchering, & his frock was bloody, which the horse smelt, & saw; the bridle was slipped off his head, and after the first fright, seeing the carriage, he was much terrified, turned it over, and broke the box; but I had a trifle done to it, so as that we rode to my house with safety, this the care of a kind providence, we are well. Mrs. Sherman is more composed, she has been much affected with her trials, but now appears content. Her son Roger is now with us. He left your family comfortable. Your Lady, and one of your daughters, designed to have come with him & made us a visit, which would have been very agreeable to us; but for want of snow, were disappointed.

One of the letters, enclosed with this, is Mrs. Sherman's to one of her friends, containing a desire, to have the situation of her son, communicated to her friends, that if agreeable, they would consult on some measures the most likely, to be acceptable to obtain some relief without which he must leave college; containing an account of Mr. Sherman's death the state of the family etc. etc.

And a desire to have a line returned soon, to inform whither any assistance can be procured, and to have it sent to your care, and to be disposed of by you, for the benefit of Roger.

Another letter to W. Judson, which I supposed might be sent more direct from you which I shall esteem as a favor if you would see it conveyed. I could wish to have the letters which you sent to me lodged in the post office at Norwalk.

I hope your candour will excuse my freedom—I want to write with the same freedom as though I were your equal, and the state of my Father Sherman's family is such that I shall want to use the same freedom with you as if you were parent to us all, and I hope you will express your mind with perfect freedom, and advise in any matter without reserve. I esteem it a peculiar smile of divine providence, that I have such a friend with whom I may ask counsel. I should be very stupid not to acknowledge my obligations, and that of the whole family, for your great kindness in such a day of trouble, as that through which we have been passing, and the peculiar attention, and kindness of your Lady, whom I have great reason to respect, and the friendship, and respect, we have received from your children.

Mrs. Baldwin of Goshen is quite low, but the Doct. speaks encouraging in her case, thinks if she is taken good care of will recover. My Mother Sherman expected to visit her daughter, as soon, as she can go in a sleigh.

We shall esteem it a great favor to have you & your family use great freedom at our house. I esteem it, a great favor, to have you write often: I have no opportunity, to send you the money, for the freight of Mrs. Sherman's good; but expect soon to have, which I will improve. My Mother Sherman, & Mrs. Mitchell desire to be remembered to you, with their particular respects. I shall take peculiar satisfaction in writing often. It is an uncommon time of health: no news; people seem to be satisfied with the federal Government.

I remain with much respect, & esteem,

Your very humble Sevt.,

Justus Mitchell

P.S. The People in this place, have agreed, many of them to set up a library; and are collecting the money to make a small purchase of books: I want to know whether they are sold at a dear rate in New York, and whether you suppose by purchasing to considerable amount, would enable us to obtain them to any advantage; if not we should send part to New Haven; as it is probably we might obtain some late publications, which may not be found at New York.

The pulpit is supplied at Amity for 16 Sabbaths after the month of February by agreement of ministers, in different parts.

Letter to Justus Mitchell, February 8, 1790

NEW YORK

Dear Sir,

I received your letter of the 26ᵗʰ January. Am glad to hear that sister Sherman & your family are well & that her goods came so safe to hand. As to the small expense of sending them to New York she is very welcome to it, I shall not take any thing for it and I shall always be ready to render her and the rest of the family any service in my power.

I perfectly agree in sentiment with you that moral depravity or inability is no excuse for not complying with the requirements of the law or the gospel, but that blame or guilt is aggravated in proportion to the degree of it.

My brother expresses the same sentiment in page 16ᵗʰ of the copy of the sermon that I sent, in these words, "The gospel considers mankind as under this inability, or spiritual death, and considers it as their *sin,* and their *disease,* and at the same time that the gospel condemns them for it as their *sin,* as much as the law doth, yet it offers them a remedy for it as a *disease.*"

The notes of that sermon I think are very incorrect, so that his sentiments cannot be clearly understood by it. And I think you could easier make a new one from the same text than correct that [illegible word] for the press, and I believe most or all the sentiments intended to be contained in that discourse are more clearly expressed in his printed sermons. He says in his History of the War, page 49, "Regeneration is produced in the principle of the soul, by an immediate, instantaneous, irresistible operation of the spirit of God." He supposes that men are under a natural inability to comply with the requirements of the law or the gospel until they have a doctrinal knowledge of them— and this knowledge is attainable in the exercise of their natural powers in reading, hearing, & none have reason to expect to be regenerated until they have attained it in the use of means, and that they have a great encouragement to expect it in that way as he that tilleth his ground has to expect a crop—but there is no promise or absolute certainty of success in either case—but in both cases a certainty of failure of success if the means are not used. And further,

Source: Roger Sherman Papers, Manuscript Division, Library of Congress.

when men have attained a competent doctrinal knowledge of the laws & gospel their natural inability to comply is removed, and then if they do not comply they will be inexcusable.

In the latter part of his life, he seemed to have his mind deeply impressed and affected with the danger that secure sinners are in of perishing from under gospel light for want of a due attention to the means of grace of the vast importance of their being awakened to a sense of their danger & roused from a state of carnal security and attend to the gospel offers, and this zeal led him strenuously to oppose everything that he thought tended to discourage their earnest & diligent attendance on the means of grace - & perhaps he might in some instances rate the endeavours and strivings of unregenerate sinners.

I suppose that moral good or evil consists not in dormant principles, but voluntary exercises, that regeneration simply considered is not a moral virtue, but the holy exercises that flow from it are—and on the other hand no propensities in animal nature are in themselves sinful, if not indulged contrary to law. That moral good consists in right exercises of the natural powers and principles of the soul, in setting the affections on right objects & moral evil in placing the affections in wrong objects. And mankind having the power of free agency are justly accountable for the exercise of their natural powers, and they any indisposition to do what they know to be their duty can be no excuse for not doing it.

I have enquired of several book sellers what abatement they will make from their retail prices for taking a considerable number, all the answer I can get is that they will sell as low as they can possibly afford. If I had a list of the books wanted I could let you know whether they are to be had & the price.

[This letter, written in Sherman's hand, is unsigned. In the margin there is a note that indicates the letter is a copy of the original.]

Letter from Justus Mitchell to Roger Sherman, March 17, 1790

NORWALK

Honor'd & Worthy Sir,

I received your agreeable letter dated Feb. 9, and can fully agree to the sentiments which you there express respecting moral good and evil and the nature of obligation. They appear to be scriptural, and entirely remove every excuse from the sinner; and it is the only consistent ground on which we can make the various parts of scripture harmonize. Since my last I have read my Father Sherman's sermon with more attention and in the sentence preceding the first quotation in your letter on the 16th page he says, "For the sinner, before the regeneration, hath an entire moral inability, to such an exercise (that is spiritual) and he hath no natural power to remove this moral inability, nor is he required to do it, in his own strength." Though he considers spiritual death in the next sentence as being the sin and disease; yet he doth not consider him to be under any obligation to change his heart, or to exercise repentance, till the holy Spirit is sent to renew the soul. I think he considers spiritual life as a thing offered to sinners, which they are under no obligation to exercise, till it is given by God. I do not consider spiritual life to be offered in such a sense, as to lessen the sinner's obligation to exercise it: and his representation of the subject on the last page of the doctrinal part appears to me to lose sight of the sinner's obligation, in God's method of bringing home sinners to his Kingdom. He says "And if spiritual life is not offered to sinners in the Gospel upon conditions that can be performed by them, before they have spiritual life and strength, I do not see that there are any offers made to sinners in the Gospel."

I suppose the law requires sinners to exercise spiritual life, and the Gospel demands it, not as a thing offered (in such a sense as pardon, and eternal life) to the doings of sinners; but it is a qualification which the Gospel demands, to which pardon, justification, & eternal life is promised, and which qualifies the soul to receive all the Gospel offers. I think a distinction should be made between the qualification of a creature to receive, and the favor offered. If the

Source: Roger Sherman Papers, Manuscript Division, Library of Congress.

sinner exercises spiritual life; and should not be pardoned; he would not be to blame, for not being pardoned, justified, & entitled to eternal life. If a beggar is qualified to receive favors, which are not at his disposal, he is not to blame for not receiving, but if he is of such a proud spirit as to refuse offered relief he is entirely guilty, for not receiving; and it doth not alter a favor, offered whither the creature is qualified in heart to receive it or not.

Now if we consider *spiritual* life as an offered favor to certain unregenerate qualifications which doth not belong to the creature to exercise till God is pleased to bestow it; then if the sinner hath the unregenerate qualifications, but is not renewed, and so doth not receive spiritual life, he is not to blame for not repenting & believing the Gospel. If the sinner is not required to exercise *spiritual* life in his own strength, that is, without any sovereign interposition of God, then all obligation from the law ceases, and to the Gospel, till God gives spiritual life, and the creature can be blamed for nothing unless it be for not exercising such unregenerate duties, as a dead sinner may perform.

I am fully sensible that Mr. Sherman did not allow these consequences; yet I am not certain but they do follow from some things which is said in his sermon. We are not to conclude that because God said I will take away the stony heart, that the creature is therefore under no obligation to be of another temper or to exercise repentance till he renew the soul: any more than if a parent should say to his disobedient child I will compel you to obedience, that the child may therefore conclude he is not to blame for his disobedience till he is compelled, by his parent.

Though God doth bring his designs of grace to pass by the instrumentality of means, and makes use of doctrinal knowledge to convince & awaken the soul; yet this doth not alter the sinner's obligation. I think there are some inconsistencies in the sermon, as you observed in your first letter, and I fully agree with you that it would be difficult to correct it and do justice to the author.

The view which you have given of my Father Sherman's sentiments are just and very impartial, so far as I understand them, in your letter.

How far a sinner's ignorance, under the light of the Gospel, may be considered as a natural inability is difficult for me to determine. Our Savior says to the ignorant Jews, ye will not come to me, that ye might have life. They were under the influence of great errors and had but little knowledge in the Gospel; but our Savior considers their inability to be moral; and perhaps all their ignorance arose from this moral inability, and so was really of a willful kind. They were not willing to understand the Gospel. Therefore when men have the means of knowledge and yet do not know, I am inclined to consider the inability to be moral. I could wish to know your sentiments, on that subject.

I am inclined to think that it might be well to give up the thought of publishing this sermon, or of sending it to Mr. Wildman or Doc. Edwards to revise it. But I would wish your opinion as to the expediency of sending the sermon to those gentlemen, or not.

I am much obliged to you for the information concerning the books which you gave me in your letter. We have sent for them, and are to be received this week. Several gentlemen have been anxious to purchase a history of the late war, but none of us were sufficiently acquainted with the writers on that subject to be able to determine what history to get, and so deferred it, desiring your opinion, whose is the best written & which you would advise to?

I should have written before this, but have been a journey to Woodberry & have been much taken up in attending on my little daughter who hath the smallpox the natural way. She was inoculated, but did not receive the infection, and her situation is critical: and it is a trying providence: Mrs. Mitchell cannot see her, which occasions many anxious hours: I have daily to visit her at some distance; but I hope she may recover. Mrs. Sherman is at Goshen—her daughter Mrs. Baldwin is on the recovery, through divine goodness.

I remain with much respect
Your obliged friend, & humble servant
Justus Mitchell

Mrs. Mitchell desires her sincere respects to you.

Letter to Simeon Baldwin, February 4, 1790

NEW YORK

Sherman's letter to his son-in-law concerns, among other things, conflicts between his pastor, Jonathan Edwards Jr., and members of the congregation of White Haven.

Dear Sir,

I this day received a letter from my son John dated Jan. 14th enclosing one for his wife which I have forwarded to you. He writes that he has recovered his health, that Isaac is there & their prospects are good.

You wrote me some time ago that you were notified to attend a meeting of some members of our Society. I wish to be informed whether there is any new difficulty arisen, & how the members stand affected to Dr. Edwards. I esteem him one of the best of preachers that I am acquainted with, sound in the Faith, & pious, and diligent in his studies and attention to the duties of his office. I should be very sorry to have any thing done to grieve him or weaken his hands in the great and important work committed to his charge. If he should leave the Society I should expect they would be divided & broken up. I hope all the well wishers to pure religion will use their influence to preserve peace—and avoid calling Society meetings unnecessarily, as I think it would only promote dissention. Our Saviour says "Woe to the world because of offences; but woe to that man by whom the offence cometh." I am willing that any thing I have written should be made known if it will do any good, not only to the friendly but to the disaffected if there be any such. I feel well affected to all the members, and wish to have cordial harmony restored. Perhaps there is nothing more pleasing to the adversary of mankind than discord among christian brethren. I shall enclose to you next Saturday's paper, which will contain the news.

The joining with the first Society in Lectures, has been urged by some, but a majority of the church did not think it expedient. I believe it has never been moved for on the part of Dr. Dana nor do I think he would wish to have it take place. It is a matter of no great importance if there were no diversity of

Source: Roger Sherman (1721–93) Collection (MS 447), box 1, folder 13, Manuscripts and Archives, Yale University Library.

sentiment between the two Pastors, but as there really is, and as some members of our church would be dissatisfied with it, I think it would be highly criminal to insist upon it, so as to break the unity of the church. Let each preach his own lecture, & every one may attend *either*, or *both*, at pleasure.

As to Dr. Beardsley's affair, I understand he is pretty well fixed in his mind not to return to our Society, but to join the first, in which I think it is best he should be indulged. I think that Deacon Austin could do as much to reconcile matters as any member of the Society, and that it is the duty of every one to use their Influence to that end, & to strengthen the hands and encourage the heart of Dr. Edwards in his ministerial work.

I am very respectfully yours,
Roger Sherman

P.S. After writing the foregoing I received your letter of the 30th *ultimo*. I am sorry for Mr. Collen's misfortune. If he has a legal claim application must be made to Mr. O. Wolcot the Auditor, as you may see by the law for establishing the Treasury department, but if no provision is made by law, & he has an equitable claim, application must be made by Petition to Congress. Depositions & other vouchers will be admitted in evidence, & no expence attend it, except to the agent he may employ. A member will Present his petition without pay & do what may be necessary for its passing Congress.
R.S.

Letter to David Austin, March 1, 1790

NEW YORK

The following is a copy, written in Sherman's hand, of a letter he wrote to David Austin, a deacon at White Haven, concerning Jonathan Edwards Jr. and related matters.

Dear Sir,

I received your favour of the 20th Feb. & am much obliged by the free & friendly Information respecting the affairs of our Society. I am of your opinion that we do not differ much respecting the essential doctrines of religion. I am also very sensible that you have in time past exerted yourself more for the support of Dr. Edwards & his family than any other member of the Society, and therefore I expressed an ardent wish that your former friendship might be revived, and though I have no doubt that you yet bear him good will, but I want to have that cordial complacency that once existed be again restored.

You observe that I have been much absent & so have not had an opportunity to attend & be acquainted with his preaching in general of late years. I know that has been the case but I have frequently attended his ministry, & had conversation with him on religious subjects to my great satisfaction. When I have been absent I have heard many good preacher[s] which I esteem orthodox & pious, but I have found none that in all respects suits me better than Dr. Edwards. As to what you mention respecting his copying his fathers writings for the press, I think he has much served the Interest of religion in a way that must have tended to furnish his mind for serving his own people as transcribing those works must fix them in his memory much better than merely reading them. And if they yielded him some pecuniary advantage I think it a favourable circumstance, for I believe what the Society give him would not be sufficient to support his family without some other income.

I dont know what advantages his answer to Dr. Chauncey may produce to his own people or to others, that merit of it can be better Judged of when it

Source: Roger Sherman (1721–93) Collection (MS 447), box 1, folder 13, Manuscripts and Archives, Yale University Library.

is published. but I think Dr. Chauncey's sentiments on that subject very erronious, & if believed will tend to relax the restraints on vice arising from the threatenings of the divine law against impenitent sinners.

It is true I did declare it to be my opinion at first in the case of Dr. Beardsley, that such an opinion ought not to exclude a person from communion, but on further consideration of the matter, & finding a former determination of our church in point against my opinion, I have viewed it in different point of light from what I did at first. I think we are as much bound to believe the threatenings, as the promises of the gospel.

There are damnable heresies as well as practices, 2 Peter 2.1. A man that is an heretic after two admonitions is to be rejected, Titus 3.10. Knowing that he that is is subverted, and sinneth, being condemned of himself—that is as Dr. [Gayle?] observes, the evidence of his heresy appears from his own profession of his erronious principles & can't be proved any other way.

The divine punishment threatened to sinners is not greater than in the view of divine wisdom, was best to accomplish the purposes of divine goodness for advancing the glory of God & the greatest good & happiness of his intelligent creatures. And any principles that tend to diminish the influence of those sanctions must be of dangerous tendency. The apostle says knowing the terrors of the Lord we persuade men. Sin and misery was first introduced into our world—by persuading Eve to disbelieve the divine threatning—when the tempter said to her ye shall not surely die.

I have always viewed Dr. Edwards conduct in the case of Dr. Beardsley when he was nominated for a delegate—not only as proper but as an indispensible duty, & what Dr. Beardsley ought to have received in a kind & friendly light. It was well known that reports were propagated not only in New Haven but in other towns that Dr. Beardsley was a universalist. The evidence of the truth or falsehood of this report must be known only to himself and it being mentioned on that occasion when he was present, gave him opportunity to declare his sentiments, and if he had either disavowed his having ever embraced the opinion, or had then declared that he had renounced it, his character would have stood fair & his election took place—but if he at that time held to the opinion or was doubtful respecting the truth of the contrary doctrine he was unfit for that office.

The rule in the 18th Mathew is good & of undoubted authority in the cases to which it is applicable but I think it does not all respect such a case as that, but only personal injuries or such private offences that might be settled without a public confession. 1Tim 5.20 Them that sin rebuke before all, that others may fear. Gal. 2, 12-14 When Peter was come to antioch I withstood him to the face because he was to be blamed. When I saw that they walked not uprightly according to the truth of the gospel, I said unto Peter before them all, &c. As to the matter respecting joining with the first Society in the Lecture I should not esteem it a matter of much importance if there was no diversity of sentiment—whether one or two lectures were kept up I believe most of the people in the city might redeem time to attend both.

The former coalition was but a half way practice to join in lectures & not exchange on the Sabbath. I was for having a full understanding of each others sentiments & join fully or not at all.

Minutes of a letter to D. Austin, Esq.

Letter to Rebecca Sherman, March 6, 1790

Sherman's letter to his wife touches on a number of domestic concerns.

I received Your letter of the 1st. Instant Judge Cushing & his Lady are yet here, they propose going to Middletown by the next Stage—I am glad to hear that you are in better health—Carpets are 5/6 this currency for a yard Square I Shall Send you one as Soon as I draw Some money. I wish to be informed what Size will Suit. If the children make more gloves than will Sell at New Haven they may put up Some in dozens & Send them here—I will leave them to be Sold with a wholesale merchant that I deal with who may Sell them at the same price as imported ones—If Martin Skins can be procured as cheap as you mention it might be well to manufacture Muffs & Tippets for Sale— I Should be glad to have 8 or 10 pound of the Pea Coffee Sent ground, in papers to contain one or two pounds each, it is well liked here, tho' none of the family knew that it was not imported Coffee, nor Should I wish to have any thing Said about what you Send here Mrs. Polock is desirous to buy some of it. She knows what it is made of, I wish to know how much a pound it can be afforded at. I Shall Send my clothes home to wash. it has cost me but three quarters of a dollar for washing here—I believe it would be for Your health to come to New York after the ways are well Settled, you may come with our horse & Chaise & Roger or Oliver may come with you. it will be less expence than for me to come home considering the loss of time—Capt. Abraham Bradley & Capt. Bonticure are now here. Congress have under consideration the assumption of the debts of the States I believe there will be a great majority for assuming them, & then the Interest will be punctually paid in hard money. Mr. Davis has sold all the Sacramental Sermons that I left with him—I wish to have 6 more Sent & 3 or 4 Paulinus's letters to Scripturista—Send my linen drawers when you Send the green Box—I would not have you give your Self much trouble to See Judge C. & Lady, but be prepared. you would be pleased

Source: *DHFFC*, 18: 754–55. © 2012 Johns Hopkins University Press. Reprinted by permission of Johns Hopkins University Press.

with their conversation, but I Suppose they will make no Stay in town. but go out with the Stage.

I believe I Shall get a new coat made here—the Taylor will have 11/6 lawful for making it—you will See that my Society tax is paid & make Dr. Edwards Some presents, give him what Support you can within the circle of your acquaintance. his continuance with us is a matter of great importance in my mind. I am in Health.

Correspondence between Samuel Hopkins
and Roger Sherman, 1790

The publication of Jonathan Edwards Sr.'s Dissertation concerning the Nature of True Virtue *in 1765 caused significant controversy. Samuel Hopkins (1721–1803), one of Edwards's chief disciples and a leading New Divinity theologian, entered the fray in 1773 with* An Inquiry into the Nature of True Holiness. *Sherman read, or perhaps reread, the book in 1790 and initiated the following correspondence.*[1]

Source: *Correspondence between Roger Sherman and Samuel Hopkins* (Worcester, Mass.: Press of Charles Hamilton, 1889), 8–27.

1. The correspondence between Sherman and Hopkins was published for the American Antiquarian Society in 1889. Yale University Manuscripts and Archives possesses manuscripts of all three letters, and the Library of Congress (LOC) has what may be a draft of Sherman's initial letter to Hopkins. Comparison between the LOC version and the 1889 version reveals that the latter faithfully reproduces the handwritten manuscript except for minor editorial judgments and a decision not to include the following valediction before Sherman's signature: "Sir, with great respect and esteem, your friend and humble servant." These lines may simply be a formality, but they may also suggest that Sherman was personally acquainted with Hopkins.

CORRESPONDENCE

BETWEEN

ROGER SHERMAN AND SAMUEL HOPKINS.

From Proceedings of the American Antiquarian Society,
October 22, 1888.

WORCESTER, MASS., U.S.A.
PRESS OF CHARLES HAMILTON,
311 MAIN STREET.
1889.

Roger Sherman to Samuel Hopkins.

NEW YORK, JUNE 28, 1790.

DEAR SIR:—

I have lately read your book on the nature of true holiness and approve the sentiments, except in two points, which do not appear to me well founded, and which I think may have a bad tendency. One is on the nature of self love; the other, "that it is the duty of a person to be *willing* to give up his eternal interest for the Glory of God." I have also read a manuscript dialogue between a Calvinist and Semi-Calvinist on the latter subject, of which it is said you are the author. I have carefully attended to these subjects, and shall submit to your consideration the result of my inquiries.

I admit that *self love* as you have defined it, or selfishness in a depraved being that is destitute of true virtuous benevolence to others, is the source of moral evil. That this arises from the want of a good moral taste, or spiritual discernment, which occasions the person to place his happiness in wrong objects. But I consider self love as a natural principle which exists in beings perfectly holy, which by the moral law is made the measure of our love to our neighbor, and is therefore a principle distinct from general benevolence or love to others. I define *self love* to be a desire of one's own happiness, or a regard to one's own interest, which I think may be exercised in the highest possible degree consistent with the highest possible degree of disinterested love to others, by wishing perfect happiness to ourselves and others. I think these affections are distinct but not opposite. And in the great fountain of happiness there is a sufficiency to fill the capacities of all. You suppose that we ought to love ourselves and others in proportion to the importance of each in the scale of being in general. I was for sometime at a loss for a scale by which to ascertain the proportion of love due to ourselves or others; but I could find none short of the superlative degree, that is, to wish to each the highest possible degree of good and happiness which they are capable of enjoying, and to rejoice in the infinite happiness of the Deity.

I suppose a virtuous person feels the same kind of pleasure in the good and happiness of others, as in his own; not from any selfish views or motives, but from a disposition to be pleased with the happiness of being in general; this will incline him to refrain from everything injurious to others, and to do good to all as there may be opportunity and occasion; and his natural principle of *self love*, will dispose him to pay a due attention to his own interest. And as these affections are distinct and may consistently be exercised in the highest degree towards their respective objects, what necessity or room is there for degrees of comparison, or the subordination of one to the other? Both are subject to the law.—Beneficence or doing good to others, is not commensurate with benevolence towards them, for we ought to exercise the highest degree of benevolence toward that being to whom our goodness or beneficence cannot extend; and the duty of extending it to others depends upon a variety of circumstances, so that much wisdom is necessary to direct in the proper application of it. On the other point, viz. "that it is the duty of a person to be willing to give up his eternal interest for the glory of God." I do not find any such thing required of any person in the divine law or in the Gospel; but it appears to me that the contrary is enjoined. I admit that persons are required to be willing to give up their temporal interest, and to lay down their lives, when the glory of God or the advancement of his kingdom in the world require it; to these all general requirements of submission to the will of God may be applied. The Old Testament Saints and Martyrs mentioned in Heb. II. endured great sufferings in the cause of religion, but they were limited to this state of trial, and they were supported in them by their faith in a future state of happiness; they considered that they had in heaven a better, and an enduring substance, but though they had respect to this recompense of reward, yet their love to God and religion was not founded in selfish principles, but they loved them for their own amiableness and intrinsic excellence; and in the exercise of this disinterested love, consisted their happiness and reward, as well as their duty. And in Heb. 12. 2. where Jesus Christ is referred to as our example, it is said "That for the joy that was set before him he endured the cross," etc. The whole tenor of the gospel appears to me to be against a person being willing to be damned on any consideration. God commands all men everywhere to repent. He also commands them to believe on the Lord Jesus Christ, and has assured us that all who do repent and believe shall be saved. And his voice to impenitent sinners is, not, be willing to be damned, but *Turn ye, turn ye, from your evil ways; for why will ye die?* How do I know of any direction or example in the Bible for praying for Spiritual or eternal blessings, with a willingness to be denied on any consideration. But God allows his people to pray for them absolutely and has absolutely promised to bestow them on all those who are willing to accept them on the terms of the gospel, that is, in a way of free grace through the atonement. *"Ask and ye shall receive. Whosoever will, let him come and take of the waters of life freely. Him that cometh unto me I will in no wise cast out."* But there are no such absolute promises as to the bestowment of temporal favors. It is impossible that it should be for the glory of God, or consistent with the gospel dispensation to punish with endless misery any man who has a supreme love to God, and regard for his glory, which in this case is held out as the motive to be willing to be damned. It also involves in it this absurdity, that a person ought to be willing to be fixed in a state of eternal enmity to God, from a principle of supreme love to him.

The reason why any of the human race are subjected to endless punishment, is, because they have sinned and voluntarily continue finally impenitent, which is wholly their own fault. And God has declared that he has no pleasure in the death of the wicked; but that the wicked turn from his way and live. Ezek. 33. 11. Is this consistent with his requiring them to be willing to continue in sin and perish forever; for none can be damned who do not persevere in sin? I admit that it is the duty of all to acknowledge that the divine law which requires us to love God with all our heart and our neighbor as ourselves, on pain of eternal damnation is holy, just and good; and I suppose that the conscience of every sinner who shall be finally condemned by the law, will witness to the justice of the sentence, and that seems to be sufficient to answer the ends of government, without his being willing to suffer the punishment. While in a state of probation sinners are required to turn and live, which appears to me inconsistent with their being required to be willing to be damned. And I believe that it is naturally impossible for any moral agent to be willing to be separated from all good, to all evil, and if so, it can't be his duty. The revealed law of God is the rule of our duty and it may be his will to suffer events to take place with respect to us, which it would be sinful in us to be willing should take place with respect to ourselves. For instance, it is the will of God to suffer the Saints during their continuance in this life to be imperfect in holiness, yet it is their duty to be perfect, nor ought they to be willing to be unholy in any respect or degree, for that would be a willingness to transgress the divine law, and would be sinful. The like might be observed respecting all the sins which ever have been, or shall be committed in the world, and God overrules all these for good, yet neither God's suffering sin to take place, or his overruling it for good, can excuse any person in the commission of sin, much less make it his duty to be willing to commit it. This is fully illustrated in your sermons on "Sin the occasion of great good!"

Mr. Calvin's comment on the words of Saint Paul, Rom. 9. 3. is quoted in support of the lawfulness of being willing to be damned; but Calvinists do not found their faith on the authority of his opinions, that would be to entertain an opinion contrary to his, viz., That the word of God is the only rule of faith in matters of religion. Expositors differ as to the meaning of those words of Saint Paul, but if they import what Mr. Calvin supposes, may they not be considered as an hyperbole which is never understood to be literally true? And the occasion on which they were spoken was only to express in strong terms the Apostle's great affection for his nation and concern for their spiritual welfare. Besides every wish of a good man is not a good wish. Moses in a like expression, Exod. 32. 32. seems not fully to have met with the divine approbation, as appears by the answer, verse 33. "And the Lord said unto Moses whosoever hath sinned against me, him will I blot out of my book."—Holy David was displeased because the Lord had made a breach upon Uzza. And the pious prophet Jonah was angry because the Lord spared Nineveh. And patient Job had some impatient wishes that would not be justified.

But if Mr. Glasse's exposition of Rom. 9. 3. is admitted it will remove the difficulty, that is, that he himself once had wished anathema to Christ, etc.

It is further said in support of this opinion, that a number of mankind will eventually suffer endless punishment, and that all holy beings will approve the judgment of God therein, and that it ought to be approved by all. But can it be inferred from hence that it was the duty of those unhappy persons while in a state of probation to be willing to persevere in sin and suffer the just consequences of it? Are they not punished because they were willing to continue in sin? And does God punish his creatures for doing their duty? Or can it be inferred, that it is the duty of a person possessed of true holiness, to be willing to apostatize from his holiness, and abandon himself to wickedness and so plunge himself into endless misery.

It is said that it is necessary to be willing to be damned, if it should be God's will and for his glory, to evince that our love to God is supreme and disinterested; but would not the affection expressed, Psalm 73. 25. "Whom have I in heaven but thee and there is none upon earth that I desire besides thee," etc., be a much better evidence of the sincerity and disinterestedness of our love to God, than to be willing to be forever separated from his favourable presence and fixed in a state of enmity to him for our own voluntary transgression and impenitence.

These few imperfect hints will communicate to you my idea on the subjects, and if I am mistaken I wish to be enlightened. I had not the book or manuscript before me when I wrote this, so that in my reference to them, I do not recite the words, but state the sense according to my best recollection. I am, sir, with great respect and esteem, your friend and humble servant,

ROGER SHERMAN.

Samuel Hopkins to Roger Sherman.

NEWPORT, AUG. 2, 1790.

DEAR SIR:

I am gratified, and think myself honored by your address of the 28th of June last. I am pleased with your particular attention to the subject upon which you write, and the ingenuity manifested in what you have written. But your differing in judgment from me, and especially your thinking my sentiments may have a bad tendency, cannot be but disagreeable to me. However, as I apprehend my real sentiments are in some respects mistaken; and that what I have advanced on those points can be supported by Scripture and reason; and not doubting of your uprightness and candour, I am encouraged to write you on the subjects in dispute.

The self love which I have defined, in my tract on the nature of true holiness, and discarded, as wholly opposed, in every degree of it, to the divine law, and to that universal, disinterested benevolence, in which all holiness consists,—this self love you suppose to be a natural principle of human nature, and perfectly innocent, though exercised in the highest possible degree; and is really "subject to the law of God," as much as universal benevolence, and consequently must be a holy affection, I think. This, if I am not mistaken, is the difference between us on this point.

In support of my sentiment, and in opposition to the contrary, I take leave to propose the following considerations.

I. There cannot be any need of self love, supposing it to be an innocent affection; and it can answer no good end, where universal, disinterested benevolence is exercised in a proper degree. And there is, indeed, *no room* for the former, where the latter is perfect.

Universal benevolence extends to being in general as its object, and wishes the greatest possible happiness of the whole: And the greatest possible happiness of every individual being, capable of happiness, so far as is consistent with the greatest happiness of the whole. The benevolent person is himself the object of his universal benevolence, as really as any other being; and for the same reason that he wishes the greatest possible happiness to being in general, he wishes the greatest possible happiness to himself, as included in being in general. This is necessary; for to suppose otherwise is a direct contradiction. Love to being in general necessarily regards and wishes the greatest possible happiness to him who exercises this love. This is not, indeed, self love, which is a regard for one's self, *as self,* and as distinguished from all others, and to no other being; but it is the same disinterested affection which wishes the highest happiness to every individual, included in being in general; and therefore to himself, as necessarily included in the whole, and one among others.

What need then can there be of self love? It can do no more than wish and seek the greatest happiness of the person who exercises it: But this the reasonable and noble affection of universal, disinterested benevolence will do in the best and most perfect manner. Self love is excluded as wholly needless, at best; and there appears to be no use or room for it in the mind exercising love to the being in general. To suppose two distinct and different kinds of love exercised by the same person, at the same time, wishing and seeking the same greatest possible happiness to himself, is doubtless inconceivable, as it is monstrous and absurd. This view of the matter leads me to suspect that they who plead for self love as a useful principle, as consisting in a person's wishing his own highest possible happiness, and as distinct from universal benevolence, do really mean that regard to our particular interest which is necessarily included in universal benevolence; and which I mean by disinterested, benevolent affection; and that the difference is only in words, and if we could understand each other, we should be agreed. To prevent mistakes of this kind, I endeavored to explain what I meant by self love, and opposite disinterested affection, in my inquiry concerning the nature of true holiness (Sec. III., IV.) But perhaps have not distinguished with sufficient clearness, and therefore have not been understood.

I agree that this universal benevolence is exercised "in the superlative degree," wishing the greatest possible happiness to the whole, and to every individual, without any "degree of comparison," *so far as is consistent with the greatest good of the whole.*

This leads to another consideration.

II. Self love, as distinguished from universal benevolence, or disinterested, public affection, cannot be a holy and innocent affection; but must oppose the latter, because it will not subordinate a person's own private interest to the general good; or give up any degree of supposable, or possible personal happiness, however inconsistent with the greatest general good.

The greatest possible good of the whole may not be consistent with the greatest possible happiness of every individual, and certainly is not; for if it were none would suffer evil; and certainly there would be no individuals miserable forever. And whenever the interest and happiness of an individual is not consistent with the greatest happiness of the whole, or an infinitely greater good than the happiness of that particular person, it is reasonable and desirable that the interest and happiness of that individual should give way, and be given up for the sake of greater general good. And universal, disinterested benevolence will do this; for it wishes and seeks the greatest good of the whole, and of individuals, so far as is consistent with this, and no further, and therefore subordinates the interest of individuals to the greater and more important general interest and happiness. But self love which desires and seeks nothing but the greatest possible happiness of himself, and has not the least regard to the happiness of the whole, or of any other being but his own self, will not subordinate his own interest and happiness to any other interest whatever; or be willing to give up any degree of his own personal interest and happiness, for the sake of the greater happiness of the public, or of any other being. Therefore this self love always opposes universal benevolence, and the latter is, in the nature of it, contrary to the former, and directly opposes and counteracts it. And so far as the latter takes place in the heart, the other is weakened and rooted out. And perfect universal benevolence is inconsistent with every degree of self love. What can be more evident than this? The consequence is, that self love is unreasonable and sinful in every degree of it and cannot be reconciled with universal benevolence.

III. Self love cannot be a holy or right affection, or agree or consist with holy affection, because it does not desire or seek, or even discern that in which real good and happiness consists; but the contrary.

If this be true of self love, and can be made evident, all must grant that it is in its own nature an evil and vicious affection, and directly opposed to universal benevolence, which discerns and seeks the only true happiness of all, and that to the highest degree, so far as is consistent with the greatest possible happiness of the whole.

You, Sir, "Admit that self love in a depraved being, is the source of moral evil. That this arises from the want of a good moral taste, or spiritual discernment, which occasion the person to place his happiness in wrong objects."

Is it not unintelligible if not a contradiction, to say that "Self love, *in a depraved being, is the source* of moral evil?" Is not moral *depravity* moral evil? This, according to your position, must take place previous to self love becoming the source of moral evil, and in order to it. Is it not too late for self love, or anything else to be the *source* of moral evil, after moral evil exists in the mind, in its full strength? Besides, if the above were consistent, is it not perfectly unaccountable that self love, if it be a perfectly good and innocent affection, should be the positive, productive source or fountain of moral evil; and yet continue itself, innocent and good, in all the exercises of it?

But to drop all this, upon the above position the following questions may be asked.

Question 1. How can *the mere want* of a good moral taste, or spiritual discernment, *occasion* a person to place his happiness in wrong objects? It is easily seen that the want of a good moral taste will prevent a person placing his happiness in right objects, or those objects which are suited to make him truly happy. But actually to place his happiness in wrong objects, supposes not only the want of a good moral taste, but a positively wrong or bad moral taste. Whence arises this positive wrong moral taste, which leads a person to place his happiness in wrong objects? . It cannot be the production of the want of a good moral taste; for a mere negative can produce nothing that is positive. If there be nothing wrong in self love; but it is a perfectly right and good affection in every degree of it, and in its greatest possible strength; then this cannot be the source or cause of a wrong moral taste. And if the absence or want of a right moral taste cannot be the cause of a positive wrong moral taste; from what quarter or source can this come?

Question 2. In what does a right and good moral taste consist? It must consist in self love, or in disinterested benevolence, for there is no other moral disposition or affection in the mind of a moral agent but these, or that is not implied in them. And I conclude it consists in the latter. That so far as the heart is formed to disinterested benevolence, so far it has a right moral taste, or spiritual discernment. And he who is "destitute of all disposition to virtuous benevolence to others" is destitute of all right moral taste. But if self love be right and good in a moral sense, why is that destitute of all right moral taste? Or why does a wrong taste, which consists in moral blindness and delusion, and places happiness in wrong objects, take place, and lead the mind astray, where there is nothing but self love?

These questions cannot be answered to satisfaction, I believe, or the subject be cleared of insuperable difficulties in any way, but by adopting the proposition above asserted, viz.: That self love does not discern, relish and seek that good in which true happiness consists; but the contrary, which is the same as to say, that it is directly opposed to all right moral taste or spiritual discernment; and is itself wrong moral taste, in which all moral blindness consists; and which necessarily excludes all true moral discernment. Therefore it knows not, nor can know, what true happiness is; but places it in wrong objects, in that in which it does not consist, and pursues it in opposition to God, and the general good; and even the real good of the person who is under the dominion of it.

That this is the truth may be argued from the nature of self love. It excludes being in general from the mind. It has no eye to see it, no true discerning of it, or feeling towards it. Therefore it excludes all regard to God, the sum of all being. It has no true idea of disinterested universal benevolence; consequently is wholly in the dark with regard to holiness, the only happiness and beauty of the moral world; and has not the least degree of taste and relish for it; but contrary. It contracts the mind down to one infinitely little, diminutive object, which is as nothing, compared with universal being; and feels as if this *little object* was all that is worthy of regard. The constant language of this affection is, "I am, and none else besides *me*." This is to love and make the greatest lie possible; and is the sum of all moral darkness and delusion. Surely such an affection excludes all perception of true enjoyment and happiness; and all desire and taste for it; and necessarily includes as essential to it, a perfectly wrong taste, and pursuit of happiness; placing it wholly in wrong objects, where it is not to be found. And who can doubt that such an affection is the epitome and source of all moral evil?

But what the Scripture reveals on this point, is more to be relied upon; and that coincides with and confirms the reasoning above. According to that, all right taste and spiritual discerning consists in love, or disinterested benevolence. "Every one that *loveth*, knoweth God. He that loveth not knoweth not God." (1 Joh. 4. 7, 8.) The love here intended appears from the context to be disinterested benevolence. Where this is not, it is said God is not known. Consequently there is no true taste and spiritual discerning with respect to anything in the moral world. "He that hateth his brother is in darkness, and walketh in darkness, because that darkness has blinded his eyes." (Chap. 2, 11.) What is it but self love, or selfishness which hateth a brother? This is here asserted to be moral darkness itself; which darkness is not a mere negative thing. It is *sin*. It is a wrong, perverted taste, placing happiness in wrong, forbidden objects. It puts light for darkness, bitter for sweet, and sweet for bitter.

The following words of Christ, rightly considered, will be found to assert the same thing. "The light of the body is the eye; If therefore thine eye be single, thy whole body shall be full of light. But if thine eye be evil, thy whole body shall be full of darkness." (Mat. 6. 22, 23.) Here all moral darkness (for it is of this that Christ is here speaking) is said to consist in the *evil eye;* which is something positive, and not merely the want of a single eye. The evil eye is an exercise and affection of the heart, and is moral evil or sin; for "From within, out of the heart of men proceeds *an evil eye.*" (Mark 7. 21, 22.) And this evil eye consists in self love or selfishness, as opposed to benevolence and goodness. (See Matt. 20. 15, Deut. 15. 9, Prov. 23. 6, 28. 22.)

From all this put together, it appears that according to Scripture, self love is itself moral darkness; gives the mind a wrong taste; knows not what true happiness is; and therefore always seeks it in a wrong way, and in forbidden objects; consequently is in its nature opposed to universal benevolence; there being no more agreement between these opposite affections, than there is between light and darkness, good and evil.

IV. That self love is in its nature opposed to disinterested love or true holiness; and therefore is moral evil itself, seems to be evident, in that it appears to be the sum and source of every evil affection of the heart.

Pride is inseparable from self love; and I believe it is impossible to separate one from the other, they being the same affection; or at least the one involves the other, if there be any distinction; so that if one exists, the other exists also, and if one ceases to be exercised, the other must cease also. He who regards and loves himself only, does in this think too highly of himself; sets himself infinitely too high in his affections and feelings towards himself. Self love is the source of all the bitter envying and strife in the hearts of men; of all the contention and unrighteousness among men; and of all the opposition to God in heart and conduct. Where there is no self love, none of these things can possibly exist, nor anything that is morally wrong. This I endeavored to illustrate, and establish in the above mentioned inquiry, P. 28, 29. And I do not yet see how it can be proved not to be agreeable to the truth.

V. That self love is a wrong and sinful affection in the nature and in every degree of it, is evident, in that the holy Scripture never speaks in favor of it, but condemns it, and requires men to renounce it.

When St. Paul undertakes to give the worst character of men who should arise, he sets self love at the head; which no doubt includes all the rest: "In the last days perilous times shall come. For men shall be *lovers of their own selves,*" etc. (2 Tim. 3. 1, 2 etc.) If self love were a virtuous or an innocent affection, it would not be set at the head of a catalogue of the most odious and hurtful vices. Therefore the injunction is, "Let no man seek his own; but every man another's wealth." (1 Cor. 10. 24.) This does not forbid them to seek their own happiness, in any view and sense but directs them not to seek it *as their own* or in a selfish way, under the influence of self love, which seeks a person's own personal happiness, and nothing else. Therefore it is said that charity, or Christian love, "Seeketh not her own." Which is so far from including, that it excludes self love; for that seeketh her own and *nothing else;* and therefore cannot be included in Christian affection.

When Christ says, "If any man will come after me let him *deny himself,*" He asserts in the strongest terms, that self love must be crossed and renounced, in order to be a Christian; for it is impossible to tell what *self denial* is, if it do not consist in crossing selfishness, and giving up what self love seeks. That a man may deny himself in the exercise and gratification of self love, is an express contradiction; for this is gratifying and pleasing self.

The command, "Thou shalt love thy neighbor as thyself," has been supposed by some to approve of self love, and even to enjoin it, as a measure by which love to our neighbor is to be regulated. But this, I believe will appear to be a mistake, when carefully examined. He who desires and seeks the greatest possible happiness for himself, and for his neighbor, consistent with the honor of God, and the greatest general good, which he does who exercises universal benevolence, as has been shown, he, and he only, loves his neighbor as himself. He therefore has no need of the least degree of that self love which is distinct from universal benevolence, in order to obey this command. Perfect, universal disinterested benevolence is perfect obedience to it, and cannot possibly be otherwise. Therefore nothing but disinterested benevolence is here commanded, and no other kind of love is allowed or supposed; consequently self love is excluded by this precept. The least degree of that self love which seeks a man's own personal private interest and happiness exclusively, not having the least regard to his neighbor, will exclude and destroy that impartiality which is reasonable, and consists in loving his neighbor as himself. It necessarily renders him partial in his own favor, and seeks his own happiness exclusive of his neighbor's; consequently does necessarily oppose disinterested, impartial affection. This is particularly stated and considered in the abovementioned inquiry (Pages 24, 25, 26), which I have not seen confuted or answered, and I believe is unanswerable.

I have been the longer on this point (perhaps too long, and to little purpose) because it appears to me to have a close connection with the other, and if we were agreed in this, we should not long differ in judgment with respect to that to which I now turn my attention.

The question in dispute is: Whether it be the duty of any person to be willing to give up his eternal interest for the glory of God, and the general good? You say, Sir, "I do not find any such thing required in Divine law, or the Gospel; but it appears to me that the contrary is enjoined."

I wish to have the question decided by the law and the testimony. I appeal to these. And if the affirmative cannot be proved by the Scriptures, I am willing to give it up.

It is granted, "That persons are *required* to give up their temporal interest, and to lay down their lives, when the glory of God or the advancement of his kingdom in the world require it." If it be reasonable, and persons are required to give up their temporal interest, or ten degrees, or *one* degree of their interest, for the glory of God, and the general good, and it is contrary to the nature of universal, disinterested benevolence not to do this; then if it be equally necessary for the glory of God, etc., to give up *every degree* or the whole personal interest, it is equally reasonable to be willing to do this, and it must be *required*, and it is equally contrary to the nature of this benevolence not to do it. The glory of God and the greatest public good is an interest of infinitely more worth and importance, or an infinitely greater good, than the whole eternal interest of any individual person; and therefore when the latter interferes with the former, and consequently it is necessary that the latter should be given up to promote the former, universal benevolence will—it *must*—consent to it; and this is required, if it be required to give up any degree of personal interest, to promote the public good. This, I conceive, is as clear demonstration, as that three and two are more than two and two. This consequence cannot be avoided unless it be by denying that it ever is, or can be necessary for the glory of God, and the greatest good of his kingdom, that the whole eternal interest of any individual person should be given up and lost. But none will deny this, I presume, who believe, what is abundantly asserted in Scripture, that many of the human race will be miserable forever; for this could not take place, were it not necessary for the glory of God, and the greatest good of the whole.

It is said, this cannot be duty or required, since all are commanded to do that which is contrary to this, viz.: to repent and believe in Christ and be saved, to turn and live, etc. Answer: No repentance, believing and turning is required which is contrary to supreme love to God; and consequently seeking his glory above all things, and subordinating every other interest to this; but this love is implied and required in these commands. And if a willingness to give up a person's whole interest, if this be necessary for the glory of God, be not implied in this love, I will give up the point, and never plead for it again. A person must love himself more than God, and set his own personal interest above the interest and honor of God, and therefore not love God supremely and with all his heart, who is not willing to give up his whole interest, when necessary for the highest interest of God and his glory. And so long as he is of this disposition he will not repent, believe in Christ, or return to God.

If it be said, He knows it is not necessary for the glory of God, that his eternal interest should be given up, but the contrary; for God commands him to repent and come to Christ *for life;* and he turns and comes, that he may *live,* and not die.

Answer: His being commanded to repent, etc., is no evidence that he shall not live in impenitence, and perish, for many do so whom God commands to repent, to turn and live. And he knows not that he shall ever turn and come to Christ, until he *knows* he has actually turned and come, and therefore cannot know that he shall not be cast off, and that this is not necessary for the glory of God. Therefore in the *first act* in which he returns and comes to Christ, he comes, not knowing that he does come, for this can be known only by reflecting on what he does, or has done. He comes to a Sovereign God and Saviour, not knowing that it is not necessary that he should perish forever, for the glory of God, and casts himself at the foot of Christ, who *has mercy on whom he will have mercy, and whom he will he hardeneth;* and cordially submits to this Sovereign God and Saviour, and is willing to be in his hand, not knowing but it may be most for his glory to cast him off, and not desiring to be saved, if this cannot be consistent with the glory of God; and on this supposition gives up his whole interest. This is the disposition in which the sinner comes to Christ. And as most Christians are not soon, if ever, *assured* that they are such; and none perhaps have this *assurance* at all times; they thus submit to God, to dispose of them as he sees most for his glory. And as they increase in love to God, this submission is stronger, and more sensible; though they may not think this is a being willing to give up their whole interest for the glory of God; and not know, in this respect, what manner of spirit they are of; yet this is all I mean by being willing to be cast off, if most for the glory of God. And I think it impossible to love God, and to come to Christ for salvation, without such a disposition and a cordial submission to his will, who has mercy on whom *he will* and hardens whom *he will*, while he knows not what is his will concerning him.

And such a Christian, if he attain to know he loves God, and has this submission to him, will not by this lose this disposition; but it will increase as his love to God increases; and he will more and more sensibly feel, that were it not for the glory of God, and the greatest good of his kingdom, that he should be saved, he would have no desire, on the whole, to be saved, however desirable that be, in itself considered.

I observe it is said, "There is no direction or example in the Bible for praying for spiritual or eternal blessings with a willingness to be denied, on any consideration. But God allows his people to pray for them absolutely; and has absolutely promised to bestow them on all who are willing to accept of them on the terms of the Gospel, that is, in a way of free grace through the atonement. Ask, and ye shall receive, etc."

Answer: We are certainly directed to pray for spiritual and eternal blessings, with resignation to the will of God, be that what it may; which implies, and really is, a willingness to be denied, if what we pray for be contrary to the will of God to give, and not consistent with his glory, and the general good. We must *know* that we ask for things agreeable to his will. That is, we must know that it is his will to grant them before we can ask for them absolutely, and without any condition. For if we ask *absolutely* for *anything*, when we know not that it is the will of God to give it, we set up our own will, while we know not that it is agreeable to the will of God; which must be the highest arrogance, rebellion and stubbornness.

It will be said, We know it is the will of God to give Spiritual and eternal blessings to all who ask for them, because he has promised to do it. "Ask, and ye shall receive." Therefore we know, when we pray for those blessings, it is his will to give them; and consequently we may ask *absolutely*, not willing to be denied on any consideration; because we know that God is not willing to deny us.

Answer: All praying, and asking, is not asking in the sense of Scripture. We must *know* that we ask in truth, agreeable to the true import of direction and command, before we can know that it is the will of God to grant those blessings. But this we cannot know until we have first *asked*, if we do *then*. Therefore we must first ask before we can know it is the will of God to grant the blessings for which we ask; and therefore may not ask absolutely. And how few are there who absolutely know they have ever asked for spiritual blessings, so as to be entitled to the promise? None but assured Christians do know this. How few are they! Perhaps *not one,* at all times. From this view, I think it follows, that the prayer which entitles to saving blessings is never made absolutely, or without submission, not knowing whether it be the will of God to grant the things which are asked, or not; and that a person cannot know that it is the will of God to give him spiritual blessings, till he has thus submissively asked, and upon reflection knows that he has done it. And that, in this case, an unsubmissive asking is a wicked asking, which surely does not entitle to the promise. And that no person who does not know he has asked submissively, can know that he shall be saved, or ask saving blessings absolutely, without asking wickedly. And if he know that he has first asked submissively, and has obtained spiritual blessings, and so can *now* ask absolutely, knowing it is the will of God to save him; he can with truth say, "Lord, thou hast been pleased to give me saving blessings, and I know it is thy will, and for thy glory that I should be saved; but if this were not thy will, and for thy glory, but the contrary; salvation would not be desirable to me, in this view of it. I must say "Thy will be done." If this be not the feeling of his heart, his supposed assurance is nothing but delusion, and he has never yet asked so as to receive.

But there is a plausible, and in the view of some, an unanswerable objection to all this, as it implies that a person may and ought, for love to God, to be willing to be a sinner, and an enemy to God forever, if this be most for the glory of God, and the greatest happiness of his kingdom. This is thought to be contrary to the law, and all the commands of God, and in itself absurd and impossible.

If I am not much mistaken, most of the objections and arguments, if not all of them which I have seen offered against this, are founded on a mistake, or a supposition which is not true, viz. :—That to be willing to be a sinner, in this case, necessarily implies an inclination to sin, which is actually sinning, from love to God, and desire that he may be glorified, this being what God requires! If I could be convinced there were any truth in this, I should renounce the sentiment as false and dangerous. But I yet think directly the contrary to be true; and that a being willing to be a sinner, if this were necessary for the glory of God, is itself an exercise of love and obedience to God; and not to be willing, on this supposition, would be itself an act of sin and rebellion. If the dialogue which you mention be one that I have seen, I think this point is there proved by argument which cannot be confuted.

God has revealed that it is his will that some of our neighbors should be given up to sin and ruin forever, for his glory, and the greatest good of his kingdom. It is granted that we ought to acquiesce in this, and be willing that it should take place, in as many instances, and under those particular instances which God sees will best answer his ends; that such acquiescence is implied in love to God; and therefore implies no inclination to sin, or to think favorable of it; but the contrary; and that the least disposition to object, and oppose this known will of God, would be an act of sin, and rebellion against God. And if it be as necessary that we ourselves should be given up to endless sin and ruin, in order to answer the same end, as that our neighbor should be thus given up, we must consent, and be willing, on this supposition, that this should take place, if we love God with all our hearts, and our neighbor as ourselves. And so long as we continue of this disposition, we obey the Divine law, and are friends to God and holiness; and cannot fall into sin and ruin until we give up this disposition and imbibe the contrary, and become unwilling to suffer anything for the glory of God. In this view of the matter, I think, it appears that "It does not involve any absurdity, that a person ought to be willing to be fixed in a state of eternal enmity to God, from a principle of supreme love to him," on supposition that this be necessary for his glory. This is so far from being an absurdity, that a person must cease to love God supremely, in order not to be willing, on this supposition, and actually turn an enemy to him.

You think, Sir, "It may be the will of God to suffer events to take place with respect to us, which it would be sinful in us to be willing should take place, with respect to ourselves." If the will of God respecting such events be made known to us, it cannot be sinful in us to be willing they should take place; otherwise it would be a sin for us to say, "Thy will be done," without making any condition or reserve; which I believe none will assert. On the contrary, it is our indispensable duty to submit to the known will of God, with respect to every event, be it what it may. And not to be willing it should take place, as He has willed it should, is opposition to God, and therefore an act of rebellion.

The following instance is brought to illustrate this position. "It is the will of God to suffer the Saints, during their continuance in this life, to be imperfect in holiness. Yet it is their duty to be perfect; nor ought they to be willing to be unholy in any respect or degree; for that would be a willingness to transgress the divine law, and would be sinful." I am pleased with this instance, because I think it is suited to illustrate the point in view. I grant it is the duty of Saints to be perfect in holiness; but do not think it will follow from this, that they ought not to be willing to be unholy in any respect or degree, or that such willingness would be sinful; but the contrary. It is a holy will or choice, and not to be willing to be sinful, in this case, would be a transgression of the Divine law, and therefore sinful. It is, in itself considered, desirable to be perfectly holy in this life; and must be a duty, as their obligation to this cannot be made to cease. But it being the known will of God that they shall not be perfectly holy in this life; and therefore that it is, on the whole, wisest and best, most for his glory, and the general good, that they should be imperfect in this world; it is certainly their duty to acquiesce in this, and be willing it should be so, and say "Thy will be done." And this willingness to be imperfect and sinful, in this case, all things considered, is so far from being sinful, that it is a holy submission to the will of God; and the contrary would be opposition to the known will of God, to his glory and the general good, and therefore a transgression of the Divine law, and very sinful. It is, on the whole, all things considered, best, and most desirable that they should not be perfectly holy in this life; otherwise this would not be agreeable to the will of God. And not to be willing that should take place, which is on the whole best, most desirable, and agreeable to the will of God, is an unreasonable, wicked disposition, and directly opposed to God. And to be willing to be imperfect in this state of trial, is no part of that imperfection, nor has it any tendency to make them imperfect; but the contrary, as it is directly opposed to all sin, and is, as has been observed, a holy volition, a holy submission to the will of God.

The spirits of the just now made perfect, acquiesce in it, it is perfectly agreeable to their inclination and will, that they were imperfect in this life, and that all the redeemed should be so; and this acquiescence in the will of God, respecting this, is so far from being sinful, that it is part of their perfect holiness, and essential to it. And what reason can be given why this same disposition in the Saints in this life, is not a holy disposition? This is easily applied to the point in dispute; and I am mistaken if it do not serve to illustrate it, and obviate every objection made to a being willing to be sinful forever, on supposition this be the will of God, or most for his glory, and the greater happiness of his kingdom.

You say, Sir, "I believe that it is naturally impossible for any moral agent to be willing to be separated from all good, to all evil." I should believe this too, if I thought self love was essential to a moral Agent, and that it is right to exercise this to the highest possible degree, and wrong to suppress or counteract it in any instance. Yea, I should believe *more*, viz. :—that it is naturally im-possible for a moral agent to give up the *least degree* of personal good, or suffer *any evil*, for the sake of any public good, however great. But universal disin-terested benevolence will give up personal good; and be willing to suffer per-sonal evil for the sake of a greater public good, and for the same reason that it will give up one degree of private good, for a greater public good, it will be willing to be separated from all personal good, to all evil, if necessary to pro-mote a proportionable greater public good. And it appears to me, naturally impossible, or impossible in the nature of things, that it should do otherwise, unless it be defective, or counteracted by self love.

St. Paul's wish (Rom. 9. 3.) has been an eyesore to many. They have thought themselves sure that he could not mean what his words naturally impart; consequently have set their invention to work to find out some other meaning. Most of which invented, forced meanings are, I think, so low and flat as to be unbecoming an inspired Apostle, and really cast reproach on the sacred oracles. The most plausible of these, perhaps, is that of Mr. Glass, which is wholly built on the original word, translated, *I could wish*, not being in the optative mood; but in the past tense of the indicative. But Grotius, who was skilled in the Greek above most others, says it is common for the Greeks to use a word so, when it is to be understood in the optative sense, of which there is an instance it Acts 25. 22. And Glasse's sense is so low, that it appears to me to come to very little, and to be unworthy of the Apostle Paul; and exhorts the true spirit and force of expression. The words, taken in the most easy and natural sense, in which Calvin and others have taken them, do strongly express the feeling and exercise of true benevolence, which St. Paul ought to have had, and to express on such an occasion; and which he certainly did profess in a very high degree, who sought not his own profit, but the profit of many, that they might be saved.

Calvin, I suppose, is not cited as *an authority*, but only to show the propriety of their being called *Semi-Calvinists*, who do not agree with him in this sentiment.

Wishing we may each of us be led into all important in truth, I am, Dear Sir, with high esteem, and much affection, your obliged, humble servant,

S. HOPKINS.

Roger Sherman to Samuel Hopkins.

NEW HAVEN, OCTOBER, 1790.

DEAR SIR:—

I received your letter of the 2d August last, and am obliged to you for the observations it contains. I think there is no material difference of sentiment between us except on the last point. I am not convinced by what you have wrote on that subject that my former opinion was wrong; but I don't know that I can say much more to support it than I did before.

I believe we do not differ at all in opinion respecting that general benevolence wherein true virtue consists; which you admit includes a regard to our own greatest good and happiness, and that *regard* I call an exercise of love to ourselves. When I said that self love and love to others were distinct affections, I only meant that they were exercises of the same kind of affection towards different objects, viz., ourselves and others.

I do not fully understand the force of your observations on what I said respecting the ground or reason why self love in a being destitute of general benevolence is the source of moral evil, viz., "That this arises from the want of a good moral taste, or spiritual discernment, which *occasions* the person to place his happiness in wrong objects." You do not here distinguish between *occasion and positive cause* though you make a material distinction between them in your sermons on "Sin the *occasion* of great good." President Edwards I think has illustrated this point in his answer to Dr. Taylor on original sin, and in a sermon published with his life, on the enquiry, why natural men are enemies to God. He supposes original righteousness in man was a supernatural principle which was withdrawn on his first transgression, and his natural principles of agency remaining, were exercised wrong, and his affections set on wrong objects in consequence of such withdrawment. The will and affections are the powers of agency, and the exercises of them are holy or sinful, according to the objects chosen or beloved, or according as their exercises agree or disagree with the divine law. Moral good and evil consist in exercises and not in dormant principles; the heart is the seat not only of sin but of holiness according as it is differently affected. Your observations on self love in persons destitute of general benevolence are not opposed to anything I meant to express in my letter.

You say, "that love to being in general necessarily regards and wishes the greatest possible happiness to him who exercises this love; this is not indeed self love, which is a regard to one's self *as self,* and as distinguished from all others, and to no other being; but it is the same disinterested affection which wishes the highest happiness to every individual included in being in general and therefore to himself, as necessarily included in the whole, and one among others." There appears to me to be a little ambiguity in those words *as self* and what follows. I suppose that the good and happiness of *ourselves* and each individual *being* who is a proper object of happiness, is *individually* to be regarded, loved and sought as an ultimate end, or what is desirable for its own sake as a real good. "Man's chief end is to glorify God, and enjoy him forever." Therefore when a person seeks his own highest good and happiness in the enjoyment of God, and in connection with his glory, he answers the end of his creation. Those texts which you cited to prove that self love is sinful, I suppose are not to be taken absolutely to condemn all love to self, but such only as is opposed to, or unconnected with love to others, as appears from Phil. 2. 4. Look not every man on his own things but every man *also* on the the things of others. *No man ever yet hated his own flesh but nourisheth it and cherisheth it.* Our own temporal as well as spiritual good may be lawfully sought and enjoyed, and our sensitive appetites gratified, so that it be not done in a manner or degree prohibited by law. "Every creature of God is good and nothing to be refused if it be received with thanksgiving, etc."

I think you use the term *self love* in the narrower sense than it is used in general by others; and when pious persons find in themselves those desires and wishes of their own good and happiness, which I consider as inseparable from a moral agent, and which you admit are lawful as flowing from general benevolence, or as a part of it, when they find *self love* condemned by that general term, it creates in their minds groundless uneasiness and doubts as to their good estate. Though perhaps a critical attention to your definition and distinctions might prevent this.

As your observations on the other point have not removed my difficulties, I will make a few remarks on that subject.

1. The glory of God and his happiness do not depend on the will of his creatures. Acts 17. 25. *Neither is worshipped by men's hands as though he needed anything.* Job 35. 7. *If thou be righteous, what givest thou him, etc.* His goodness is his glory and that is displayed or manifested in his doing good. Exod. 33. 18, 19. *And he said I beseech thee, shew me thy glory. And he said, I will make my goodness pass before thee, etc.*

2. None of his rational creatures are miserable but for their own fault. He inflicts punishment, not in a way of mere sovereignty, but as a righteous Judge or Governor; and for the general good. *He gathers out of his Kingdom all things that offend and do iniquity.*

3. No person who has a holy love to God, can consistent with his *will* declared in the gospel, be finally miserable; and their self denial for his glory, and all their trials and afflictions in this life work together for their best good, and work out for them an eternal weight of glory.

4. The duties of self denial and suffering in the cause of God, are compatible only to this state of trial—and the precepts which require this, appear to me to be expressly limited to suffering in this life, and eternal life is promised as an encouragement to it; therefore I see no ground to extend them by reason or analagy to the point in question. Mat. 19. 29, John 12. 25, Luke 18. 25, etc., Mark 10. 29, 30.

5. No person who is to be a subject of everlasting misery is ever willing to endure it; but it is the providential will of God to suffer them to hate him and blaspheme his name because of their torment; therefore their willingness to suffer, is not necessary for the manifestation of his glory in their punishment. And it would involve an inconsistency to suppose any person to be willing to submit to the providential will of God, in all the circumstances of his dam-

nation, *unwillingness* to suffer and *enmity* to God on account of it, being material circumstances. You mention the third petition in the Lord's prayer, *"Thy will be done on earth as it is in heaven,"* as a proof that absolute submission to the will of God is a duty. I admit that God's perceptive will ought to be obeyed in all things, and his providential will submitted to as far as it is made known by revelation, or the event; but no particular person while in a state of probation can know that it is the providential will of God that he shall finally perish, but he knows that it is his perceptive will, that he shall turn and live. And for persons who doubt of their good estate, to put it to trial by supposing a case that never can happen if they have any degree of true love to God, or if they ever comply with the requirements of the gospel; and which it is certain their hearts never will be reconciled to, if it should happen, would only tend to fill their minds with greater perplexity and disquietude. True Christians are assured, that no temptation (or trial) shall happen to them but what they shall be enabled to bear; and that the grace of Christ shall be sufficient for them; but no such gracious promise of support is made to any who shall be the subjects of damnation, therefore a willingness to suffer this, is not a trial required of a true Christian. The angels in heaven do God's will, but we have no intimation that they are required to be willing to fall from their holy and happy state.

As to your observations on the Saints' imperfections in this life, I shall only remark, that I allow that they ought to approve whatever is ordered or permitted by God concerning them as most holy and wise; but not their own conduct in being unholy or sinful in any degree.

As to the submission of the awakened humbled sinner to the divine sovereignty, I admitted that a sinner ought to approve the law of God, as holy, just and good in the threatening endless misery to sinners; but this is consistent with their hoping in his mercy. The convinced publican prayed, *"God be merciful to me, a sinner."* I suppose that the divine sovereignty is the greatest encouragement that a convinced sinner has or can have, to hope for mercy. That a God of infinite goodness can (through the atonement) have mercy on whom he will, consistent with the honor of his law and government and of all his perfections, is a much better ground of hope, than if the sinner was left to his own will; but I don't see that this includes in it a willingness to be damned, though the convinced sinner has a sense of his just desert of damnation, yet he is invited and required to turn and live.

St. Paul's wish, Rom. 9. 3, taken literally (as translated) I think can't be vindicated.

1. Because it would have been opposite to the revealed will of God concerning him, he being a true Saint, could not be accursed from Christ.

2. It could have been of no use to his brethren—his damnation could not atone for their sins; and there was a sufficient atonement made by Jesus Christ. I think all that he intended was to express in strong terms his great affection and concern for that people and not that he did or could *really* wish damnation to himself for their sakes. Dr. Samuel Clark on the place says, "The expression is highly figurative and affectionate—But his intention was not to wish himself subject to the eternal wrath of God, which is absurd and impossible."

It still appears to me that no moral agent ever was or can be willing to be damned, and that no such thing is required by the divine law or the gospel. If a person could be willing to be forever abandoned to sin and misery, he must be so lost to any sense of good or happiness, as not to be capable of any regard to the glory of God, or the good and happiness of the moral system; for if he could take pleasure in these, he would not be wholly deprived of happiness.

The bad tendency of this doctrine if it be not well founded, will be:—

1. To give uneasiness to pious minds who may believe it upon the authority of those whom they think more knowing than themselves, but yet they can't find their hearts reconciled to it.

2. Pious orthodox Christians who think it an error will be prejudiced against the books that contain it, however orthodox and useful in other respects, and will scruple the lawfulness of keeping them in their houses, or any way encouraging the spread of such books, lest they should be guilty of propagating dangerous errors.

3. It will give the enemies of truth occasion to speak reproachfully of the authors of such books, and prejudice the minds of people against them, and so obstruct their usefulness. Therefore I wish you to cut off occasion, from those who may seek occasion.

I am, &c.

ROGER SHERMAN.

Letter to Simeon Baldwin, January 4, 1791
PHILADELPHIA

This and the next two letters from Sherman to his son-in-law address a range of ecclesiastical and political issues.

Dear Sir,

I received yours of the 23ᵈ of last month, I am sorry to hear that the Society have not made provision for the payment of Dr. Edwards salary for the current year. If he should leave us I expect it will terminate in a dissolution of the Society. Though the list is reduced by the causes which you mention the ability of the members to pay is not proportionably reduced. There are a number of able men in the Society who by proper exertion might relieve the difficulty, by contributing according to their ability, tho' beyond their proportion by such are, Deacon Austin, Jer. Atwater 1ˢᵗ & 2ᵈ, Abrm. Bradley, and Mr. Hugens— Elias Beers, and a number of others that might be named. I hope something will be yet agreed upon to make the necessary provision, [word cut out] provide for Dr. Edwards, how shall we support any other Minister. Enclosed is the last Gazette and a letter for Mrs. Sherman Senior.

Yours & etc.

Roger Sherman.

Source: Roger Sherman (1721–93) Collection (MS 447), box 1, folder 14, Manuscripts and Archives, Yale University Library.

Letter to Simeon Baldwin, January 21, 1791

PHILADELPHIA

Dear Sir

The enclosed, (Dunlap's) papers contain the whole of the report of the Attorney General on the judiciary. It is not expected that it will be considered this session. Tis probable something will be done respecting fees, Process and Execution. I think the Superiour Judges can acquire a knowledge of the rights of the people of these States much better by riding the circuit, than by staying at home and reading British and other foreign Laws.

I am respectfully yours

Roger Sherman

Source: Roger Sherman (1721–93) Collection (MS 447), box 1, folder 14, Manuscripts and Archives, Yale University Library.

Letter to Simeon Baldwin, November 26, 1791

PHILADELPHIA

Dear Sir,

I received your Letter of the 18th Instant enclosing your account which I carried to the Office and it is allowed—but the funds appropriated last session for those expences is exhausted. An appropriation Bill for the expences of another year is before the House and will be passed soon. When I shall get the money and transmit it in a N. York Bank bill.

There is a committee of [the] Senate to prepare a Bill providing compensation for the officers of the Judicial courts, to whom I have communicated what you wrote on that subject.

I wish the pacific disposition of the people of our Society may continue and increase. Their firm union among themselves will have the best tendency to incline others to join them and enable them to sustain their present burdens with greater facility and chearfulness.

I hope the Society will with a good degree of Unanimity agree to grant a sufficient tax to defray the Society expenses for the ensuing year. I shall chearfully pay my proportion of it. We have made a solemn contract with Doct. Edwards which we are under indispensable obligations to fulfill so long as he shall perform it on his part. What is expended for the support of religion is applied to advance the best interest of a people—and if they do it willingly it will have the most likely tendency to promote their temporal as well as spiritual good. I think we may rest assured of this if we believe a special Divine Providence, and that what was written aforetime in the holy scriptures was written for our learning, such as Prov. 3.9, 10. Haggai 1. 3 to 11. verses & chapter 2. 15 to 19 inclusive. Mal. 3.6 to 12. Rom. 15.4.

I have enclosed the two last papers, and two letters which I wish you to forward.

I remain respectfully yours,

Roger Sherman

Source: Roger Sherman (1721–93) Collection (MS 447), box 1, folder 14, Manuscripts and Archives, Yale University Library.

Letter to Nathan Williams, December 17, 1791

PHILADELPHIA

Nathan Williams (1735–1829) was pastor of the Congregational Church in Tolland, Connecticut, from 1760 to 1813. Rev. Williams was concerned about the extracts from Richard Baxter's Works *that Sherman attached as an appendix to his short sermon.*

Rev. Sir,

I received your letter of the 23^{d} of Sepr. last on the 17th of October, a few minutes before I set out on my journey to this place. Since my arrival here I have carefully attended to your remarks on the Extracts from Mr. Baxter, on the duties & priviledges resulting from Infant baptism. The subject is important and it is a melancholly consideration that so few of those who are favoured with the light of the gospel, attend the special Ordinances of it.

To remove the scruples of some, and to excite all to a due attention to their duty and interest in that case was my motive in publishing the Short Sermon to which those extracts are subjoined. That this was a judicious, and seasonable discovery I have had the opinions of Dr. Witherspoon, Dr. Stiles, Dr. Wales and several other Ministers, they said nothing concerning the extracts. You have not favoured me with your opinion on the Sermon.

I believe that Mr. Baxter's aim in what he wrote on that subject was to promote true religion, by exciting persons of every description to the profession and practice of it; and especially to caution them against resting in a form of Godliness, while destitute of the power of it. What he inculcates [*sic*] concerning those who were baptized in infancy, that it is their duty when they arrive at the age of discretion, solemnly and explicitly to renew their baptismal covenant, in order to their being admitted to the Lord's Supper and other priviledges of adult members of the church, is according to the general usage of the Congregational Churches in New England. A more full view of what he wrote than is contained in those extracts, would give a clearer idea of his

Source: Historical Society of Pennsylvania autograph collection, collection no. 0022A, Historical Society of Pennsylvania.

opinion, and of the proofs adduced in support of it. I do not think that his, or any other man's opinion is of any authority in the case, unless supported by the word of God.

When Mr. Baxter says in his answer 1ˢᵗ "Church membership is the same thing in infants as in the adults," I take his meaning to be, in respect of their spiritual union to Christ, the head of the church, whereby they become members of that body of which he is the head. According to 1 Cor. 12. 13, 27. For by one spirit are we all baptized into one body, whether we be Jews or Gentiles.—Now are ye the body of Christ, and members in particular. That Infants are capable subjects of this, appears from Mark 10. 14. Suffer the little children to come unto me and forbid them not: for of such is the kingdom of God.

If any particular church should receive as members unsanctified persons, would they be real members of the church of Christ? Whenever their true character is discovered, by scandalous sin or omission of duty, obstinately persisted in, are they not to be considered as heathen men &c. Matt. 18.17. 1 John 2.19. They went out from us, because they were not of us &c. And was not this the case under the Old Testament, Psa. 50. 5, 16 Gather my *saints* together unto me, who have made a covenant with me by sacrifice. But unto the wicked God saith, what hast thou to do to declare my statutes, or that thou shouldest take my covenant in thy mouth.

All mankind are divided into two classes, the righteous and the wicked.— Tares, are not wheat, tho' they may grow in the same field.—The owner of the field sowed it with good seed, but his enemy came and sowed tares among the wheat, *while men slept.* Does not this imply that vigilance might have prevented the sowing of tares? But if men may not discern the difference, will not the great head of the church, finally declare to all unsound professors, I know you not? He will know their persons, and their characters, but not recognize them as members of his church.

Does it not plainly appear from the following texts of Scripture, that a credible profession of real religion, was requisite for the admission of adult persons to baptism? Acts 8. 37. And Philip said if thou believest with all thy heart, thou mayest. And he answered and said, I believe that Jesus Christ is the son of God. 1 John 5. 1. Whosoever believeth that Jesus is the Christ *is born of God.* Rom. 10. 9, 10. That if thou shalt confess with thy mouth the Lord Jesus, and shall believe in thine heart that God hath raised him from the dead, thou shalt be saved: for with the heart man believeth unto righteousness; and with the mouth confession is made unto salvation.

You very justly enquire, "does not baptism succeed circumcision?" It doubtless does. What was signified by circumcision the Apostle tells us. Rom. 4. 11. And he received the sign of circumcision, a seal of the righteousness of the

Faith which he had being yet uncircumcised. The whole of that chapter treats upon the nature and use of circumcision. Rom. 3. 1, 2. What profit is there of circumcision? Much every way: chiefly, because that unto them were committed the Oracles of God. By divine institution the Infants of believing parents were to be circumcised under the Old Testament dispensation, Gen 17. 12, and are to baptized under the new, Acts 2. 38, 39. Rom. 4. 16. Gal. 3. 14, 16, 29.

In this transaction the parents in some sense become bound for the good behaviour of the child. Of Abraham God said, I know him that he will command his children &c. and they shall keep the way of the Lord. And Joshua said as for me and *my house* we will serve the Lord. And in the New Testament, parents are directed to bring up their children in the nurture & admonition of the Lord. This puts the child under the best advantages to learn his duty; and the most likely means for disposing him to do it. But all will allow that none can be entitled to spiritual or saving blessings on account of their infant baptism, or their relation to believing parents, unless when they arrive at the age of discretion, they exercise personal faith and holiness. And can they be entitled to the priviledges of adult members of the church, without a credible profession of these? See Rom. 2. 25, 28, 29. How can the church know that persons baptized in infancy, have, when adult, a knowledge or belief of the doctrines of the Gospel, or a disposition to comply with the terms of it, but by their express declaration of it? And is it not a plain dictate of reason and common sense, that the church should require, and the person be willing to give the best evidence of his qualifications for communion in special ordinances, that the nature of the case will admit of? This is what Mr. Baxter pleads for, and what is practiced by our church and by the christian churches in general.

He also inculcates the exercise of church discipline toward all whom he supposed to be the proper subjects of it; that is such who have personally covenanted to submit to the government & discipline of a particular church. But infants not having done this, he supposes they are not proper subjects of public censure, but should be considered as catechumens, preparing for adult membership, and as such should be taught their duty, and admonished to comply with it. And on their refusal or neglect to renew their Baptismal covenant, and make it their own act, after they come to ripe age, their relation to the church by virtue of their parents dedication of them will cease. You enquire whether if that be the case, the person must not be again baptized, if he should afterward join to the church. I suppose that when baptism has been once regularly administered, it ought not to be repeated in that case, any more than in case of an adult member being excommunicated and afterward restored.

We have a rule in the Heads of Agreement adopted by our churches that when a person not otherwise scandalous shall fully with draw from the communion of a church and can't be persuaded to return, the church *may* declare that they have no further watch & care over him. So that such a person is considered as having put himself out of the communion of the church without excommunication.

These general observations will shew how I understand Mr. Baxter's sentiments, and explain my view in making and publishing the Extracts.

I am Sir with much Esteem and Regard

Your friend and humble Servant,

R. S.

Copy of a letter to Doct. N. Williams[1]

---

1. The copy appears to be in Sherman's hand. —Ed.

Letter to Simeon Baldwin, December 22, 1791

PHILADELPHIA

Sherman's letter to his son-in-law addresses a variety of subjects.

Dear Sir,

I received your letter of the 15th instant. I am much pleased to hear that the Society have agreed so well in providing for the expenses of the next year. I hope that their union will promote an increase of members and wealth. I am sorry for the embarrassment respecting the new bridge, but hope the builders will be indemnified.

We hear that the wounded men at Fort Jefferson were not pursued by the Indians, but that they have been relieved & some of them have arrived at Fort Washington. The Congress have passed an appropriation bill which is sent to the President for approbation, so that I hope to transmit to you a bank bill in payment of your account by the next post.

Doctor Strong is here. He attends several lectures and is admitted a member of one of the Societies. His carriage and wheels are made, but the machinery is not begun. He has agreed with a workman to do it, but has not communicated the use of it to the workman or any other except Mr. Ellsworth and Mr. Wolcot and does not wish to have it talked of anywhere until it is done. The machinery will be small and enclosed in a case.

I wish John could find some steady business, it is difficult to introduce him into a public office as a clerk so many on the spot are applying. I shall speak with one or more of the heads of department.

I am respectfully yours,
Roger Sherman

Source: Typed manuscript, Roger Sherman (1721–93) Collection (MS 447), box 1, folder 14, Manuscripts and Archives, Yale University Library.

Letter to Jedidiah Morse, February 14, 1792

PHILADELPHIA

The Reverend Jedidiah Morse (1761–1826) is sometimes referred to as the "father of American geography." He requested that Sherman comment on parts of the first edition of his American Geography; Or, A View of the Present Situation of the United States of America *(Elizabethtown, N.J.: Shepard Kollock, 1789). Sherman responded with the following letter.*

Sir,

I received your letter of the 19ᵗʰ of December. There was 9 or 10 pages wanting, in the history that accompanied it, and it is but a few days since I could procure a book that contained the whole which is my only apology for not returning an answer sooner. I am not under so good advantage to obtain the necessary information as I should be at New Haven. I submit to your consideration the following remarks.

Page 213. Shetucket's River is formed by the junction of Willamantik and another river called in the north part of Windham.

214. The city of New Haven is not bounded east by the Mile River, but by the East River.

The same page. The longest and shortest day should be equal to 24 hours. Would it not be sufficient, and according to custom, to mention only the longest day?

216. The exports and shipping might (I suppose) now be accurately ascertained by the collectors of impost in the State.

217. I suppose the number of towns is now nearly 100, but I do not know the exact number.

Page 219. You say there are as many associations as counties. There are two in each of the counties of Hartford, New Haven, and Fairfield.

226. The college apparatus is much increased since you wrote before.

Source: Ferdinand Dreer autograph collection, collection no. 0175, Historical Society of Pennsylvania.

228 & 229. *Lieutenant* Governor is the present stile, the law enjoining an oath of fidelity is resealed.

230. The number of attorneys is considerably increased since your book was published.

239. The western territory, reserved by Connecticut, bounds east by Pennsylvania and extends west 120 miles, and extends from Latitude 41° to 42° 2′ and includes part of the waters of Lake Erie. And Kirby's Reports, have been published since you wrote—page 230.

Page 241. Last paragraph. Thursday should be inserted instead of Wednesday.

Your remark in page 239 respecting the ignorance of the Europeans, respecting the geography of America is in some degree just, so far as respected the interior parts of the country, but as early as 1635 when the Council of Plymouth resigned their Charter to the Crown, they said that the extent of it from the Atlantic to the South Sea was about 3000 miles, therefore could not be governed by the company while residing in England, and the Crown doubtless intended to strengthen its claim by intending its grants for colonization. As to the Indians' title, the best writers, such as Vattel, on the law of nature and nations, suppose that prime occupancy gives the best title to lands, and though some pretensions were made of title on the ground of prior discovery, they have been obliged to yield to prime occupancy. The earth was made for the use of mankind, to be tilled for subsistence. Therefore a few exotic people such as the natives of America—walking over the face of so large a portion of the Earth without bestowing any labour upon it, could not give them an exclusive right to it, though they doubtless have a common right with other nations.

It is best not to make remarks that will not bear examining. I suppose almost any lawyer could furnish you with Vattel on the laws of nations. I heard several gentlemen mention that you had wrote to them for information which I suppose they will give.

I am with much respect,
Your humble servant,
Roger Sherman

Letter to Simeon Baldwin, December 22, 1792

PHILADELPHIA

Sherman's letter to his son-in-law addresses a variety of topics, including how to best care for Sherman's son, John, who was struggling with alcoholism.

Sir,

Enclosed is the Paper of this day but it does not contain any news. It is long since we have heard from France. Important news is daily expected.

Enclosed is a letter for John Sherman which I wish to have Oliver send to him, and not leave it at his house. He writes to me that he wants five dollars to purchase corn & oats for his poultry which I wish you to supply him with out of my money in your hand, and if shall have occasion for more for the same purpose or to pay for his board, I wrote to him to apply to you for it. I would have you furnish more than you may judge necessary for those purposes, yet I don't wish to have him think that I have any distrust of his prudence in the expenditure unless it should appear to be necessary. He informs me that he totally abstains from spirituous liquors and determines to persevere.

I have been Informed by Deacon Austin that he was guilty of some improper conduct toward him, on occasion of his interference, between him & his family and that he had thoughts of having his wife apply for a separation at the next Superior Court. I have wrote to him, to suspend the matter till I return home as I think it would be attended with ruinous consequences and that I would undertake for his peaceable behavior in the meantime—but if a petition should be preferred, I wish you to have it continued till the next term, I do not think that there is legal foundation for a separation, for if there had been a breach of covenant (which he denies) yet cohabitation after it is known extinguishes the rights to take advantage of it. I am not without hope that all variances may be removed & perfect harmony restored, and a perpetual stigma on the family be prevented. I believe that a word of advice to Deacon Austin & my daughter from you may be of use.

Source: Typed manuscript, Roger Sherman (1721–93) Collection (MS 447), box 1, folder 15, Manuscripts and Archives, Yale University Library.

The Vice President has a majority of [eight?] votes, if none in the States of S. Carolina, Georgia or Kentucky, from whom we have not heard, should be in his favour. He has 70 of the votes returned, and we have heard of 3 Electors that did not attend and vote. So that the whole number given in cannot exceed 132.

I am sir with respect

yours &c.,

Roger Sherman

I don't wish to have this seen by any other person.

Letter to Simeon Baldwin, January 25, 1793

PHILADELPHIA

The following is a response to a letter from Sherman's grandchildren about their father and Sherman's son, John.

Sir,

Please to deliver the enclosed Letter to my grandchildren—they wrote to me and mention that their Father has taken some furniture that will incommode the family & that he talked of taking away some of the provisions and receiving the money that will be due from Boarders after the Vacancy, I hope he will consider himself as being equally obliged to provide for his children as their mother according to his ability and that he will not demand any thing from them (especially in my absence) which are the avails of their industry, in keeping boarders, or which may embarrass them in that business, and deprive them of the only means of livelihood. He will I hope take your advice. I cant at this distance point out what may be proper in every circumstance. I have kept an exact copy of what I have wrote to the children. I have said nothing that will affect any of their claims or occasion any dispute.

I am in health yours &c.

Roger Sherman

The children wrote nothing disrespectful of either of their parents.

Source: Roger Sherman (1721–93) Collection (MS 447), box 1, folder 16, Manuscripts and Archives, Yale University Library.

Letter from Simeon Baldwin to Roger Sherman,
January 28, 1793
NEW HAVEN

Sherman's daughters and younger sons led peaceful and productive lives, and many of his descendants were quite successful. For instance, his grandson Roger Sherman Baldwin grew up to have a distinguished career in state and national politics. He is perhaps best known for, along with John Quincy Adams, representing the slaves in the Amistad *case (1841).*

Mrs. Baldwin is getting well fast. We have taken the liberty to give the child the name Roger Sherman & I hope he will be no disgrace to the person whose name he bears.

    I am with much esteem

    your dutiful son

    Simeon Baldwin

Source: Roger Sherman (1721–93) Collection (MS 447), box 1, folder 16, Manuscripts and Archives, Yale University Library.

Inventory of Pamphlets and Books, 1793

The following inventory was apparently compiled by Sherman's heirs.

Inventory of Pamphlets belonging to the Estate of the late Roger Sherman Esq. Including bound Book[s]

- Well's Vindication 30 Pamphlets   £
- 112 Pamphlets written by a friend of College
- 65 ditto of the greatest Concern of the World an Enquiry
- 44 Scriptures[?] containing remarks
- 27 ditto on the Sacrament
- 14 ditto Animadversions by Mr. Beach
- 11 Old Pamphlets on various subjects of Divinity
- 25 ditto   ditto
- 5 ditto on Education by Dodrige
- 18 ditto Old Sermons N° 2
- 5 ditto History of Yale College
- 20 Old Pamphlets on [illegible] N° 3
- 3 of Doct Chauncey's Remarks
- 1 ditto Nile's Sermon's
- 1 Hutchiss's History of the Missispi   ⎱
- 2 Report of the Secretary of State respecting weights ⎰
- Measures of coins
- 1 Essay on Money
- 30 pamphlets on Miscellaneous Subjects
- 1 Address and recommendation's to yᵉ United States
- 1 ditto Commercial Conduct of yᵉ Province of N. York
- 20 Catalogues of Yale College   / History Dionysius
- 2 Addresses to Gen Washington respecting half pay
- 1 collection of Papers Relative to Half pay

Source: Roger Sherman Papers, Manuscript Division, Library of Congress.

- 2 True considerations respecting Great Britain & her Colonies
- 1 Appeal to the Impartial World as to the rights of America
- 1 Observations on the Nature of Civil Liberty
- 1 Memorial Addressed to the Sovereigns of America
- 1 on the American Revolution
- 1 Report of Commissioners for settling a Cartel
- 1 Sketches of the American Policy & 1 Case of the Sloop Active
- 1 Address to the Inhabitants of America
- 1 Debate respecting the Slave Trade
- 1 Memorial presented to the Congress respecting the Slave trade
- 1 Letter from London to his friend in America   ditto
- 1 Minutes of Debates in Council on the Banks of the Ottawa River
- 1 Serious Expostulation's with the house of Representatives
- 1 Major Andre tryal in the late War for a Spy ⎫
- 1 Oration delivered 24th Feb 1775 by David ⎬
  Rittenhouse Philadelphia all included in N° 4
- 1 Narrative of the Trial of John Peter Lenger
                    Printer of New York
- 1 Essay on the Constitutional Power of G Britain
- 1 Mr Adams on the American Revolution
- 2 Vindication of the Title of Contested Lands
- 1 Ethan Alling's on the proceeding of New York as to lands
- 4 respecting Susquehannah lands
- 1 Memorial of Nathaniel Sacket . Methods of Making Salt Petre
- 8 Pamphlets on Various Subjects 1 Sherman Sermons
- 19 ditto   ditto   • 1 Thatcher Sermons
- 1 Jeremy Belnap respecting Columbus 1 Stiles [sermons?]
- 1 Jenkin's Art of Writing and Principles of Trade   • 1 Case Sloop
  Active Bound Bound Books (a Letter on original Sin
- 1 Gov Hutchinson's History of the Massachusetts Bay   " 3 "
- 1 Winthrop's Journals   " 4 "
- 1 Edwards on Redemption   8 "
- 3 Volumns Adam's Defence of the Constitution of   15 "
  Governments
- 1 ditto of Scott on the book of Job   2 6
- 1 ditto on the American Constitution by Doc Franklin   1 6
- 1 Bailey's Dictionary   5 "
- 1 Edwards Against Chauncy   7 6
                                                            £4–3–6
- 1 Cheyne's Philosophical Principles   " 2 "

- 1 of Chauncey's View of Episcopacy   " 2 "
- 1 of Kelly's Astronomy   " 2 "
- 1 History of Cardinal Alberoni   " 1 "
- 1 Miscellany   " 3 "
- 1 Prynnes plea for the Lord's   " 1 "
- 1 Andersons remonstrance   " 3 "
- 1 Prynnes English Liberty   " 1 "
- 1 Coles on Sovereignty   " 1 6
- 1 Gadbury Ephemerides   " 1 "
- 1 Doc Sacheveral's Tryal   " 1 "
- 1 Prynnes Sovereign Power Parliament   " 1 "
- 2 Volumes of the lives of the Chancellors   " 2 "
- 1 Chauncey's Sermons   " 1 "
- 1 Dickersons Letters   " 1 "
- 1 Adam's Defence   " 2 "
- 1 Fishers Concordance   " 2 6
- 1 Swynock's Treatise   " 1 "
- 1 Sett of Cicero's Oratios in 3 Volumes   " 6 "
- 1 Wollaston's Religion of Nature   " 2 "
- 1 West on Moral Agency   " 1 6
- 1 Containing Sundry Sermons N° 8   " 2 "
- 1 Dickerson's Discourses   " " 4
- 1 Hopkin's Enquiry   " 1 6
- 1 of Turoll's Life of Coleman   " 1 "
- 1 of Burgess Vindication of ye Moral Law   " 1 "
- 1 Lambert's Deronde [?] on Spiritual Religion   " 1 6
- 1 containing 8 Sermons   " 1 6
- 1 Containing Hopkins Sermons etc.   " 1 6
- 1 of Lightfoote's Harmony   " 1 "
- 1 containing 4 Sermons   " 1 6
- 1 containing Sundry Sermons and Atonement   " 2 "

£6 16-10

- 1 Confession of Faith   " 2 "
- 1 Bradbury Sermons   " 1 6
- 1 containing 9 Sermons and   " 1 6
- 1 on Cases of Conscience by Pike Haywood   " 1 6
- 1 Constitution and discipline of the Primitive Church   " 1 "
- 1 Sundry Sermons of [Ross?]   " 1 6
- 1 15 Sermons of President Edwards   " 2 "
- 1 on the Religious Affections of Edwards   " 3 "

- 1 Whitfield Sermons   " " 9
- 1 Guthrie Sermons   [illegible]
- 1 Mr Knights Sermons on Faith   " 2 "
- 1 vol. Wilke's Work on North Britain   " 1 "
- 1 Forbes Works 2nd Vol   " 1 "
- 1 Watts discourses   " 2 "
- 1 Vol curse of Deism [?]   " 1 6
- 3 Vol American Preacher   " 12 "
- 1 Vol 1st Miller Agriculture   " 3 "
- 1 Watt's Psalms   " 1 "
- 1 Spring's disquisitions   " 1 "
- 1 Bellamy on true Religion   " 3 "
- 1 Manual Doctrine   " " 9
- 1 Perils of the times   " " 6
- 1 Shorter Catechism explain'd   " " 6
- 1 Sett Pools Anitations 2 vol. folio   1 4 "
- 6 Vol. Henry's Comments Folio 1 missing   2 14 "
- 1 Flavels Work's folio   " 12 "
- 1 Ridgley's body of Divinity folio   12 "
- 1 Townsend's Collections folio   2 "
- 1 Vol of John Milton Historical and Political Works   3 "
- 1 Gen Practice of Physick   3 "

14–8–7

Selected Bibliography

Many of the printed texts included in *Collected Works of Roger Sherman* are contained in the following primary source volumes. The secondary sources include every major biography of Sherman as well as works that consider his ideas and actions in the context of the American founding.

Primary Sources

The Documentary History of the First Federal Congress of the United States of America, 4 March 1789–3 March 1791. Vol. 4, *Legislative Histories: Amendments to the Constitution through Foreign Officers Bill [HR-1 16]*, edited by Charlene Bangs Bickford and Helen E. Veit. Baltimore: Johns Hopkins University Press, 1986 (cited as *DHFFC*, 4).

The Documentary History of the First Federal Congress of the United States of America, 4 March 1789–3 March 1791. Vol. 10, *Debates in the House of Representatives, First Session, April–May 1789*, edited by Charlene Bangs Bickford, Kenneth R. Bowling, and Helen E. Veit. Baltimore: Johns Hopkins University Press, 1992 (cited as *DHFFC*, 10).

The Documentary History of the First Federal Congress of the United States of America, 4 March 1789–3 March 1791. Vol. 11, *Debates in the House of Representatives, First Session, June–September, 1789*, edited by Charlene Bangs Bickford, Kenneth R. Bowling, and Helen E. Veit. Baltimore: Johns Hopkins University Press, 1992 (cited as *DHFFC*, 11).

The Documentary History of the First Federal Congress of the United States of America, 4 March 1789–3 March 1791. Vol. 12, *Debates in the House of Representatives, Second Session, January–March 1790*, edited by Helen E. Veit, Charlene Bangs Bickford, Kenneth R. Bowling, and William C. diGiacomantonio. Baltimore: Johns Hopkins University Press, 1995 (cited as *DHFFC*, 12).

The Documentary History of the First Federal Congress of the United States of America, 4 March 1789–3 March 1791. Vol. 13, *Debates in the House of Representatives, Second Session, April–August, 1790*, edited by Helen E. Veit, Charlene Bangs Bickford, Kenneth R. Bowling, and William C. diGiacomantonio. Baltimore: Johns Hopkins University Press, 1995 (cited as *DHFFC*, 13).

The Documentary History of the First Federal Congress of the United States of America, 4 March 1789–3 March 1791. Vol. 14, *Debates in the House of Representatives: Third Session,*

December 1790–March 1791, edited by William C. diGiacomantonio, Kenneth R. Bowling, Charlene Bangs Bickford, and Helen E. Veit. Baltimore: Johns Hopkins University Press, 1996 (cited as *DHFFC,* 14).

The Documentary History of the First Federal Congress of the United States of America, 4 March 1789–3 March 1791. Vol. 16, *Correspondence: First Session, June–August 1789,* edited by Charlene Bangs Bickford, Kenneth R. Bowling, Helen E. Veit, and William C. diGiacomantonio. Baltimore: Johns Hopkins University Press, 2004 (cited as *DHFFC,* 16).

The Documentary History of the First Federal Congress of the United States of America, 4 March 1789–3 March 1791. Vol. 17, *Correspondence: First Session, September–November 1789,* edited by Charlene Bangs Bickford, Kenneth R. Bowling, Helen E. Veit, and William C. diGiacomantonio. Baltimore: Johns Hopkins University Press, 2004 (cited as *DHFFC,* 17).

The Documentary History of the First Federal Congress of the United States of America, 4 March 1789–3 March 1791. Vol. 18, *Correspondence: Second Session, October 1789–14 March 1790,* edited by Charlene Bangs Bickford, Kenneth R. Bowling, Helen E. Veit, and William C. diGiacomantonio. Baltimore: Johns Hopkins University Press, 2012 (cited as *DHFFC,* 18).

The Documentary History of the First Federal Congress of the United States of America, 4 March 1789–3 March 1791. Vol. 19, *Correspondence: Second Session, 15 March–June 1790,* edited by Charlene Bangs Bickford, Kenneth R. Bowling, Helen E. Veit, and William C. diGiacomantonio. Baltimore: Johns Hopkins University Press, 2012 (cited as *DHFFC,* 19).

The Documentary History of the Ratification of the Constitution. Vol. 3, *Ratification of the Constitution by the States: Delaware, New Jersey, Georgia, Connecticut,* edited by Merrill Jensen. Madison: State Historical Society of Wisconsin, 1978.

Journals of the Continental Congress, 1774–1789. Vol. 1, *1774,* edited by Worthington C. Ford et al. Washington, D.C.: Government Printing Office, 1904 (cited as *JCC,* 1).

Journals of the Continental Congress, 1774–1789. Vol. 4, *January 1–June 4, 1776,* edited by Worthington C. Ford et al. Washington, D.C.: Government Printing Office, 1906 (cited as *JCC,* 4).

Journals of the Continental Congress, 1774–1789. Vol. 5, *June 5–October 8, 1776,* edited by Worthington C. Ford et al. Washington, D.C.: Government Printing Office, 1906 (cited as *JCC,* 5).

Journals of the Continental Congress, 1774–1789. Vol. 12, *September 2–December 31, 1778,* edited by Worthington C. Ford et al. Washington, D.C.: Government Printing Office, 1908 (cited as *JCC,* 12).

Journals of the Continental Congress, 1774–1789. Vol. 21, *July 23–December 31, 1781,* edited by Worthington C. Ford et al. Washington, D.C.: Government Printing Office, 1912 (cited as *JCC,* 21).

Letters of Delegates to Congress. Vol. 1, *August 1774–August 1775,* edited by Paul H. Smith et al. Washington, D.C.: Government Printing Office, 1976.

Letters of Delegates to Congress. Vol. 2, *September–December 1775,* edited by Paul H. Smith et al. Washington, D.C.: Government Printing Office, 1977.

Letters of Delegates to Congress. Vol. 3, *January 1–May 15, 1776,* edited by Paul H. Smith et al. Washington, D.C.: Government Printing Office, 1978.

Letters of Delegates to Congress. Vol. 5, *August 16–December 31, 1776,* edited by Paul H. Smith et al. Washington, D.C.: Government Printing Office, 1979.

Letters of Delegates to Congress. Vol. 6, *January 1–April 30, 1777,* edited by Paul H. Smith et al. Washington, D.C.: Government Printing Office, 1980.

Letters of Delegates to Congress. Vol. 7, *May 1–September 18, 1777,* edited by Paul H. Smith et al. Washington, D.C.: Government Printing Office, 1981.

Letters of Delegates to Congress. Vol. 11, *October 1, 1778–January 31, 1779,* edited by Paul H. Smith et al. Washington, D.C.: Government Printing Office, 1985.

Letters of Delegates to Congress. Vol. 15, *April 1–August 31, 1780,* edited by Paul H. Smith et al. Washington, D.C.: Government Printing Office, 1988.

Letters of Delegates to Congress. Vol. 17, *March 1–August 31, 1781,* edited by Paul H. Smith et al. Washington, D.C.: Government Printing Office, 1990.

Letters of Delegates to Congress. Vol. 18, *September 1, 1781–July 31, 1782,* edited by Paul H. Smith et al. Washington, D.C.: Government Printing Office, 1991.

Letters of Delegates to Congress. Vol. 21, *October 1, 1783–October 31, 1784,* edited by Paul H. Smith et al. Washington, D.C.: Government Printing Office, 1994.

The Records of the Federal Convention of 1787. Rev. ed. Edited by Max Farrand. 3 vols. New Haven, Conn.: Yale University Press, 1966.

The Sacred Rights of Conscience: Selected Readings on Religious Liberty and Church-State Relations in the American Founding. Edited by Daniel L. Dreisbach and Mark David Hall. Indianapolis, Ind.: Liberty Fund, 2009.

Secondary Sources

Boardman, Roger Sherman. *Roger Sherman: Signer and Statesman.* Philadelphia: University of Pennsylvania Press, 1938.

Boutell, Lewis H. *The Life of Roger Sherman.* Chicago: A. C. McClurg, 1896.

Collier, Christopher. *All Politics Is Local: Family, Friends, and Provincial Interests in the Creation of the Constitution.* Hanover, N.H.: University Press of New England, 2003.

———. *Roger Sherman's Connecticut: Yankee Politics and the American Revolution.* Middletown, Conn.: Wesleyan University Press, 1971.

Dougherty, Keith L., and Jac C. Heckelman. "A Pivotal Voter from a Pivotal State: Roger Sherman at the Constitutional Convention." *American Political Science Review* 100 (May 2006): 297–302.

Gerber, Scott. "Roger Sherman and the Bill of Rights." *Polity* 28 (Summer 1996): 521–40.

Hall, Mark David. *Roger Sherman and the Creation of the American Republic.* New York: Oxford University Press, 2013.

Robertson, David Brian. "Madison's Opponents and Constitutional Design." *American Political Science Review* 99 (May 2005): 225–43.

Rommel, John G. *Connecticut's Yankee Patriot: Roger Sherman.* Hartford: The American Revolution Bicentennial Commission of Connecticut, 1979.

Index

Page numbers followed by an italic *n* indicate a note; thus 157*n*2 guides the reader to note 2 on page 157.

Adams, John: Articles of Association signed by, 166; on Articles of Confederation, Sherman's proposal for, 244–45; as Board of War member, 244; Declaration of Independence signed by, 196; diary of, excerpts from, 152–53; in drafting of Declaration of Independence, 140–41, 193, 244; in drafting of Declaration and Resolves, 157*n*2; instructions for congressional commission to Canada by, 189–92; personal views on Sherman, xiv, xv, 152–53; Petition to the King signed by, 179; salary of, congressional debates on, 537–38; Sherman's correspondence with, on executive power, 678, 685–99; as vice president, election of, 525
Adams, John Quincy, 812
Adams, Samuel: Articles of Association signed by, 166; Declaration of Independence signed by, 196; in drafting of Articles of Confederation, 244; Petition to the King signed by, 179; Sherman's correspondence with, 208–10, 213–14
Address to the People of Great Britain (1774), 167–73
adultery, Connecticut legal code on, 77, 86
alcohol, imposts on, 605, 608, 612, 617, 619
almanacs by Sherman, 1, 3–38; from 1750, 3, 4–9; from 1751, 10–11; from 1752, 12–13; from 1753, 14–17; from 1754, 18–20; from 1755, 21–24; from 1756, 25–27; from 1757, 28–30; from 1758, 31–32; from 1760, 33–37; from 1761, 38; on bills of credit, 15–16; for Boston, 4–6, 11, 21–24, 33–38; content of, 1, 3; De Foreest's

(Henry) additions to, 3, 8–9; for New Haven, 25–32; for New London, 14–16, 19–20; for New York, 7, 10, 12–13, 17–18
Alsop, John, 166, 179
ambassadors, U.S.: to Britain, 521, 524; congressional debates on number of, 678, 702; to France, 521, 527, 549–51
Amelung, John F., 558
amendments, constitutional: Constitutional Convention debates on process for, 445, 450–53; Sherman's personal correspondence on, 507, 509; Sherman's "Observations on the Alterations Proposed as Amendments" on, 496–99. *See also* Bill of Rights, U.S.
American Geography (Morse), 807–8
American War for Independence. *See* War for Independence
Ames, Fisher: praise for Sherman by, xv; in U.S. Congress, 609–10, 624, 641, 668
Amistad case, 812
anti-Federalist essays, 470
Appeal to the Public, An (Trumbull), 738
appointment: of Continental army officers, Sherman's personal correspondence on, 181, 187–88, 201–2; to national judiciary, Constitutional Convention debates on, 352, 386–87
appointment power of executive, Constitutional Convention debates on, 418–19
Arabas, Jack, 132–34
Arabas v. Ivers, 132–34
arms, right to bear, in congressional debates: on Bill of Rights, 645, 660–62, 674; on Militia Bill of 1790, 710

arms supply, in congressional debates on
Militia Bill of 1790, 708
army, Continental. *See* Continental army
arson, Connecticut legal code on punishment
for, 91
Articles of Association (1774), xiii, 140, 162–66
Articles of Confederation (1777, 1778), 243–46;
attempted revision of, at Constitutional
Convention, 325, 326; debate and approval
in Continental Congress, 244–45; members
of committee drafting, 244; overview of,
243–46; representation in, approach to,
244–45, 252; Sherman's "Observations on
the New Federal Constitution" on defects
of, 478–79; Sherman's *Remarks on a Pamphlet* defending, 245–46, 296–322; Sherman's
role in drafting, xiii, xviii, 140, 251; state
ratification of, 245, 251, 260–61; text of,
251–58; Webster's (Pelatiah) *Dissertation*
attacking, 245, 275–95
assembly, right of, in Bill of Rights, 645, 671,
674
Austin, David: Sherman's letter to, 771–73; Sherman's letter to merchants signed by, 148–49

Babcock, Adam, 149
bail: in Bill of Rights, 644, 646, 674; in Connecticut legal code, 76
Baldwin, Abraham: at Constitutional Convention, 397, 409–10, 421; Constitution
signed by, 466
Baldwin, Roger Sherman, 507, 812
Baldwin, Simeon: family of, 507; Sherman's
correspondence with, 502, 507–8, 745, 769–
70, 799–801, 806, 809–11, 812
bank, national, congressional debates on, xviii,
561–63
bankruptcies, Constitutional Convention
debates on, 435
baptism, infant, 756–58, 802–5
Barbé-Marbois, François: Sherman's draft
letter to, 273–74; Sherman's notes on information sought by, 271–72
Bartlett, Josiah: Declaration of Independence
signed by, 196; in drafting of Articles of
Confederation, 244; Sherman's letter to,
269–70
Bassett, Richard, 465

Baxter, Richard. *See Practical Works of the Late
Reverend and Pious Mr. Richard Baxter*
Bedford, Gunning, Jr., 336, 382, 465
Bellamy, Joseph, Sherman's letter to, 727–29
Benson, Egbert, in U.S. Congress, 546, 662,
664–65, 714–15
bestiality, Connecticut legal code on punishment for, 91
bibles, Connecticut legal code on, 128
Biddle, Edward, 166, 179
Bill of Rights, Connecticut, 74, 75–76, 485
Bill of Rights, U.S.: Constitutional Convention debates on, 446; Sherman's "Letters
of a Countryman" on, 484–85; Sherman's
correspondence with Gibbs (Henry) on,
625–28; Sherman's role in drafting, xiii, 624;
text of, 673–75
Bill of Rights, U.S., congressional debates on,
624–77; call for day of prayer after, 676–77;
conference committee report and house
resolution in, 671–72; draft house committee
report in, 624, 643–44; excerpts from, 629–
42, 649–70; final house committee report
in, 645–47; Sherman's role in, xviii, 624
bills of credit: congressional debates on, 569–
70; Constitutional Convention debates on,
425–26; New Haven Convention on, 219–
20, 224; Sherman's "A Caveat Against
Injustice" on, 1–2, 39–49; Sherman's almanac on, 15–16; Sherman's personal correspondence on, 265
Bishop, Samuel, 139, 143
blacks, free, Connecticut legal code on travel
of, 119–22. *See also* slaves
Blair, John, 465
Bland, Richard, 166, 179
blasphemy, Connecticut legal code on punishment for, 92
Bloodworth, Timothy, 713–15
Blount, William, 465
Board of War and Ordinance, 140, 244
Boerum, Simon, 166, 179
Boston, Sherman's almanacs for, 4–6, 11,
21–24, 33–38
Boston Tea Party, 170–71
Boudinot, Elias, in U.S. Congress: call for day
of prayer by, 676–77; on Militia Bill of
1790, 713–14; on national power, 559–60

boycott of British goods, 140; Continental
Congress on, 155, 162–66; Sherman's letter
to merchants on, 148–49
Boyd, Julian P., 141
Braxton, Carter, 197
Brearley, David, 417, 465
bribery, in elections, Connecticut legal code
on, 89–90
Britain: Continental Congress's address to
people of, 167–73; Sherman's *Remarks on
a Pamphlet* on national debt of, 296–97;
Sherman's *Remarks on a Pamphlet* on power
of taxation in, 306–9; U.S. minister to, 521,
524
British Crown: Continental Congress's petition to, 174–80; Sherman on limits of
colonial obedience to, 50–51, 140, 147, 150–
51; Sherman's *Remarks on a Pamphlet* on
powers of, 306–9
British Parliament. *See* Parliament
Broom, Jacob, 384–85, 465
Burgoyne, John, 209, 211, 213, 215
Burke, Aedanus, 663, 676
Butler, Pierce: at Constitutional Convention,
330–31, 334, 353, 402–3; Constitution signed
by, 466
Butler, Zebulon, Sherman's letters to, 248–50

Caesar, Timothy, 137–38
Calvinist theological tradition, 723
Canada, instructions for congressional commissioners sent to, 189–92
capital, U.S.: congressional debates on establishing, 539–42, 544; New York as, 501, 502,
544; Philadelphia as, 502, 541–42, 544
capital offenses, Connecticut legal code on
rights of those on trial for, 93
Carroll, Charles, 196
Carroll, Daniel: at Constitutional Convention, 449; Constitution signed by, 465; in
U.S. Congress, 558–59, 658–59
Caswell, Richard, 166, 179
"Caveat Against Injustice, A" (Philoeunomos),
1–2, 39–49
census, Constitutional Convention debates
on, 376
chaplains, congressional, 529–31
Charles II (king of England), 53, 55, 65

Chase, Samuel, 166, 179, 196
children, Connecticut legal code on, 78–79
Christianity: baptism, infant, 756–58, 802–5;
Church of England, Sherman on, 31; Congregationalism, xvii, 1, 74, 723–24. *See also*
religious practice; theological writings of
Sherman
Church of England, Sherman on, 31
"Citizen of New Haven, A" (pseudonym),
470. *See also* "Observations on the Alterations Proposed as Amendments to the New
Federal Constitution"; "Observations on
the New Federal Constitution"
"Citizen of Philadelphia, A" (pseudonym). *See*
Webster, Pelatiah
citizenship, U.S.: congressional debates on,
556; Constitutional Convention debates on,
396–98
civil rights: Connecticut legal code on, 75–76;
Sherman's "Letters of a Countryman" on,
484–85, 486; Sherman's "Observations on
the New Federal Constitution" on, 479,
491–92; Sherman's personal correspondence
on, 474–75
Clark, Abraham, 197
Clymer, George: at Constitutional Convention, 428, 429–30; Constitution signed by,
465; Declaration of Independence signed
by, 197
colonial obedience to Crown, Sherman on
limits of, 50–51, 140, 147, 150–51
colonial rights, Continental Congress on, 140;
in Address to the People of Great Britain,
167–73; in Declaration and Resolves, 157–61
commerce, regulation of, Constitutional Convention debates on, 425–30, 449–50
Confederation Congress: Articles of Confederation on, 251–58; calls for prayer and
fasting by, 238; duration of Sherman's service in, xiii, 243; Treaty of Paris ratified by,
240
confession of faith, at White Haven Church,
731–35
Congregationalism, xvii, 1, 74, 723–24
Congress, Confederation. *See* Confederation
Congress
Congress, Continental. *See* Continental
Congress

Congress, U.S., Constitutional Convention debates on: age and citizenship qualifications for, 396–98; amendment process in, 445, 450–53; elections for, 332–34, 343–47, 349–51, 362–63, 392; eligibility for other offices in, 366–67, 435–36; enumeration of powers of, 334, 381–84, 401–4, 447–48, 467–68; New Jersey Plan on, 356–58; origination of paper money in, 352–53; records of proceedings of, 393–95; representation in, 349, 371, 375–80, 389–91, 449; salaries in, 364–65, 399; term lengths in, 350–51, 368–70; timing of meetings of, 388; treaties in, 442–44; two-branch structure of, 332, 360–62; veto power in, 339–40, 348, 382–84, 415–16; vice president as president of, 441–42

Congress, U.S., debates in first sessions of, 527–721; on Adams (John), 537–38; on Bill of Rights, 624–77; on congressional chaplains, 529–31; on executive power, 678–706; on imposts, 601–19; on Militia Bill of 1790, 707–21; on Morris (Gouverneur), 549–51; on national bank, 561–63; on national capital, 539–42, 544; on national debt, 565–99; on national power, 553–63; on newspapers, 543–47; on oaths, 533–35; Sherman's role in, xviii; on state debts, 558–59, 564–99; on western lands, 564, 621–23

Congress, U.S., powers of: congressional debates on, 557, 558; Constitutional Convention debates on, 334, 381–84, 401–4, 447–48, 467–68; Sherman's correspondence with Adams (John) on, 686–99; Sherman's "Letters of a Countryman" on, 485–90; Sherman's "Observations on the New Federal Constitution" on, 478–80, 491–93; Sherman's personal correspondence on, 471–72, 476–77

Congress, U.S., representation in. See representation

Congress, U.S., Sherman as member of, 501–721; in House of Representatives (1789–91), xiii, xviii, 501–2; letters written by, 503–27; overview of, 501–2; in Senate (1791–93), xiii, xviii, 502; sources of records on, 502, 527. See also Congress, U.S., debates in first sessions of

congressional elections: Constitutional Convention debates on, 332–34, 343–47, 349–51, 362–63, 392; first, 501; Sherman's "Letters of a Countryman" on, 489–90; Sherman's "Observations on the New Federal Constitution" on, 479–81, 491–92

Connecticut: Barbé-Marbois's (François) request for information on, 271–74; Bill of Rights of, 74, 75–76, 485; bills of credit in, 15–16, 39–49; Constitutional Convention delegates from, 325–26; constitution of, 53; Fundamental Orders of, 53; at New Haven Convention, 217; royal charter of, 53; Sherman in state and local government of, xiii, xvii–xviii, 54–55; Susquehannah controversy in, 55–56, 59–68

Connecticut, ratification of Constitution in: overview of, 469–70; Sherman's "Letters of a Countryman" on, 482–90; Sherman's letter to Huntington (Samuel) on, 469, 471–72; Sherman's role in, xviii, 469–70; state convention for, 469–70, 491

Connecticut Compromise, xviii, 233, 245

Connecticut Courant (newspaper): Sherman's "Observations on the New Federal Constitution" in, 491–95; on state ratification convention, 470

"Connecticut Farmer, A" (pseudonym), 245, 246. See also Remarks on a Pamphlet Entitled "A Dissertation on the Political Union and Constitution of the Thirteen United States"

Connecticut General Assembly: Constitutional Convention delegates from, 325–26; elections for, 53–54, 84, 87–90; judicial functions of, 53, 54; land grants by, Superior Court on, 135–36; leadership structure of, 54, 82; legal code on, 82–85, 87–90, 94, 107; in legal code revision of 1783, xviiin20, 56, 73, 74; lower and upper houses of, xvii, 53–54; oaths of fidelity in, 94, 107; origins of, 53; powers of, 82–83; in ratification of Constitution, 469–70; separation of powers in, 54; Sherman as member of, xiii, xvii, 54–55; on Stamp Act, 139, 143–44; in Susquehannah controversy, 56, 60–64, 66, 67, 248–50; U.S. senators selected by, 501

Connecticut General Court. See Connecticut General Assembly

Connecticut Journal, Sherman's article on Susquehannah controversy in, 56, 60–64
Connecticut legal code, 1783 revision of, xiii, 56, 69–129; on adultery, 77, 86; on blacks, free, 119–22; on children, 78–79; on civil rights, 75–76; on copyright, 74, 96–98; division of work on, xviii*n*20, 56, 70; on divorce, 86, 738; on education, 78–79, 114–18; on elections, 84, 87–90; on false witness, 91, 109; on felonies, punishment for, 91–93; final version of, 56, 57*n*9; on gaming, 95; on governors, 87–89, 106; on lieutenant governors, 87–89, 107; on militias, 99–100; on Native American servants, 119–20; on oaths, 94, 106–9; on observation of Sabbath, 110–13; on perjury, 108–9; on religious freedom, 74, 80–81, 92; on religious ministers, 101–5; on religious practice, promotion of, 128–29; review and approval by General Assembly, xviii*n*20, 56, 73, 74; scope of work, xviii, xviii*n*20, 56, 74; on servants, 119–22; Sherman's correspondence with Law (Richard) on, 56, 70–72; on slaves, 74, 119–22; on societies, regulation of, 123–26; on swearing and cursing, 127; on taxation, 80–81, 101–2; on teachers, 114–16; on vice, immorality, and profaneness, 128–29
Connecticut Superior Court, 132–38; dissenting opinions in, 57; functions and structure of, 54; judicial review by, 135–36; jurisdiction of, 84–85; on land grants by General Assembly, 135–36; oath for judges in, 107; reporting of decisions of, 57, 57*n*10; Sherman as judge in, xiii, xvii–xviii, 57–58, 132–38, 501; on slaves, 132–34, 137–38; state legal code on, 84–85, 107; text of selected opinions of, 132–38; types of cases in, 57–58
conscience, rights of, in Bill of Rights, 634, 638, 643, 645, 658–59
conscientious objectors, in Militia Bill of 1790, 716–17, 720
Constitution, U.S. (1787): Sherman's role in, xiii, xviii; text of, 454–66. *See also* amendments, constitutional; Constitutional Convention; ratification, of Constitution
Constitutional Convention (1787), 325–468; on address to the people, 449; on amendment process, 445, 450–53; on commerce, regula-

tion of, 425–30, 449–50; Connecticut Compromise in, 245; delegates not signing Constitution after, 453, 475; on federal vs. national government, 326, 330–31; on military forces, 404, 413–15, 438; on New Jersey Plan, 355–59; overview of, 325–27; on paper money, 352–53, 425; on prayer, need for, 372–73; on ratification process, 341, 432–34, 469; recognition of Sherman's role in, xvi, 326; Sherman's influence on, xiii, xviii, 325–27; Sherman's proposals in, 467–68; on slave trade, 389–91, 406–12, 420–22; start of, 326; synergy between Sherman and Madison in, xiii, xviii*n*15, 326; on treaties, 358, 384, 440, 442–44; on veto power, 339–40, 348, 382–84, 400, 415–16, 446; on vice presidency, 437, 441–42; Virginia Plan in, 325, 326
Constitutional Convention (1787), on national executive: election of, 336, 384–85, 417–18, 439–40; enumeration of powers of, 335–36, 418–19, 422–23; impeachment process for, 336, 386–87, 444; New Jersey Plan in, 357–58; removal of, 337; as single person, 335–36, 338–39, 384–85; term lengths of, 336, 384–85; veto power of, 339–40, 348, 400, 446
Constitutional Convention (1787), on national judiciary: appointment process for, 352, 386–87; in Council of Revision, 339; inferior tribunals under, 341–42; jurisdiction of, 341–42, 352, 425; New Jersey Plan in, 356–58; removal of judges, 423–24; veto power in, 339
Constitutional Convention (1787), on national legislature: age and citizenship qualifications for, 396–98; amendment process in, 445, 450–53; elections for, 332–34, 343–47, 349–51, 362–63, 392; eligibility for other offices in, 366–67, 435–36; enumeration of powers of, 334, 381–84, 401–4, 447–48, 467–68; New Jersey Plan on, 356–58; origination of paper money in, 352–53; records of proceedings of, 393–95; representation in, 349, 371, 375–80, 389–91, 449; salaries in, 364–65, 399; term lengths in, 350–51, 368–70; timing of meetings of, 388; treaties in, 442–44; two-branch structure of, 332, 360–62; veto power in, 339–40, 348, 382–84, 415–16; vice president as president of, 441–42

Continental army: appointment of officers in,
181, 187–88, 201–2; courts martial in, 212;
lashes given to soldiers in, 235–36; loss of
Fort Ticonderoga by, 208–9, 211; Sherman's
personal correspondence on, 181–88, 200–
202, 205–8, 211–16; slaves in, 132–34; supplies
for, 183–84, 264–66
Continental Association. *See* Articles of Association
Continental Congress: Address to the People
of Great Britain by, 167–73; Articles of
Association by, xiii, 140, 162–66; Articles of
Confederation approved by, 244–45; on
boycott of British goods, 155, 162–66; calls
for prayer and fasting by, 238–39; Declaration
and Resolves by, xiii, 157–61; Declaration of
the Causes and Necessity of Taking Up
Arms by, 140; establishment of committees
and rules for, 154; instructions for commissioners sent to Canada by, 189–92; negotiations with other countries, 267–68; on New
Haven Convention report, 217; Petition to
the King by, 174–80; on promotion of morals, 226–28; Sherman's appointment as
delegate to, 140; Sherman's personal correspondence on actions of, 154–56, 200–206,
231–32, 237, 260–61; Sherman's *Remarks on a
Pamphlet* on powers of, 302–22; Sherman's
service in, duration of, xiii, xviii, 243; Suffolk
Resolves and, 140, 154–55; in Susquehannah
controversy, 66. *See also* Declaration of
Independence
Cooke, Joshua, *A Pleasant Conceited Comedie,*
27*n*4
copyright, Connecticut legal code on, 74,
96–98
Cornwallis, Charles, 237
correspondence. *See* letters
corruption: in elections, Connecticut legal
code on, 89–90; in legislature, Constitutional Convention debates on, 366–67
Council of Revision, Constitutional Convention debates on, 339–40
Council of Safety, xiii
"Countryman" (pseudonym), 470. *See also*
"Letters of a Countryman"
courts martial, 207
Coxe, Tench, 470

Crane, Stephen, 166, 179
credit. *See* bills of credit; national debt; state
debts
criminal prosecutions, in Bill of Rights, 646,
671, 674. *See also* punishment
Crown. *See* British Crown
Crowne, John: "Charles the Eighth of France,"
29*n*3; *Juliana,* 27*n*3
cruel and unusual punishment, in Bill of
Rights, 644, 646, 674
currency. *See* bills of credit; hard money;
paper money
cursing, Connecticut legal code on, 127
Cushing, Thomas: Articles of Association
signed by, 166; New Haven Convention
report signed by, 225; Petition to the King
signed by, 179; Sherman's letter to, 150–51

Davenant, William: "The News from Plimouth,"
25*n*1; "Poems on Several Occasions," 28*n*
Dayton, Jonathan: at Constitutional Convention, 379, 414, 417; Constitution signed by,
465
Deane, Silas: Articles of Association signed
by, 166; in Continental Congress, 140, 154–
56; letter to Trumbull (Jonathan, Sr.), 154–
56; Petition to the King signed by, 179
debt. *See* bills of credit; foreign debt; national
debt; state debts
Declaration and Resolves (1774), xiii, 157–61
Declaration of Independence (1776), 193–97;
members of committee drafting, 140–41,
193, 244; Sherman's role in drafting, xiii,
xviii, 140–41, 193; text of, 193–97
Declaration of the Causes and Necessity of
Taking Up Arms, 140
Declaratory Act of 1766, 139–40
De Foreest, Henry, 3, 8–9
De Hart, John, 166, 179
deism, Connecticut legal code on punishment
for, 92
Denham, John: "Of Prudence," 32*n*3; "On
Justice," 25*n*2
depreciation, of bills of credit, 15–16, 39–49
despotism, Adams's (John) personal correspondence on, 686–88
Dickinson, John: Articles of Association
signed by, 166; in drafting of Articles of

Confederation, 244; in drafting of Petition of Congress to the King, 174–80
Dickinson, John, at Constitutional Convention: Constitution signed by, 465; on elections for national executive, 418–19; on elections for national legislature, 347; on national judiciary, 342; on removal of judges, 424; on slave trade, 410, 421; on taxation by states, 405
Dissertation concerning the Nature of True Virtue (Edwards), 776
Dissertation on the Political Union and Constitution of the Thirteen United States, A (Webster), 245; Sherman's *Remarks on a Pamphlet* in response to, 245–46, 296–322; text of, 275–95
divorce: Connecticut legal code on, 86, 738; legal reasons for granting, 57, 86, 738–39; Sherman's personal correspondence on, 738–40; by Sherman's sons, 725, 738, 809
Donne, John, "A Funeral Elegy," 23n
double jeopardy, in Bill of Rights, 645–46, 664–65
Dougherty, Keith L., xvin15
Douw, Volkert P., Sherman's letter to, 247
Duane, James, 166, 179, 244
due process, in Bill of Rights, 643, 646, 664
Dunbar, Samuel, 1
Dunmore, Lord, 156
duties. *See* imposts
Dwight, Timothy, xviii–xix
Dyer, Eliphalet: Articles of Association signed by, 166; as Connecticut Superior Court judge, 132–38; in Continental Congress, 140, 154–56; letter to Trumbull (Jonathan, Sr.), 154–56; oratorical skills of, xv; Petition to the King signed by, 179

ecclesiastical societies, 57, 80–81, 101–5
education: Connecticut legal code on funding for, 114–18; Connecticut legal code on responsibility for, 78–79; of Sherman, xvii, 1–2, 50
Edwards, Jonathan, Jr., 724, 725, 769–72
Edwards, Jonathan, Sr., 724, 724n8; *Dissertation concerning the Nature of True Virtue,* 776
elections, congressional: Constitutional Convention debates on, 332–34, 343–47, 349–51,

362–63, 392; first, 501; Sherman's "Letters of a Countryman" on, 489–90; Sherman's "Observations on the New Federal Constitution" on, 479–81, 491–92
elections, Connecticut state: of General Assembly members, 53–54, 84, 87–90; of governors and lieutenant governors, 87–89; state legal code on, 84, 87–90
elections, presidential: Constitutional Convention debates on, 336, 384–85, 417–18, 439–40; Sherman's personal correspondence on, 525; Sherman's "Observations on the New Federal Constitution" on, 479, 491–92
elections, vice presidential: Constitutional Convention debates on, 437; Sherman's "Observations on the New Federal Constitution" on, 491–92
Ellery, William: Declaration of Independence signed by, 196; Sherman's letter to, 514
Ellsworth, Oliver: at Connecticut ratification convention, 469–70; as Connecticut Superior Court judge, 135–38; "Letters of a Landholder," 470; letter to Huntington (Samuel), 469, 471–72; letter to Trumbull (Jonathan, Sr.), 260–61; in ratification debate, 469–70; in U.S. Senate, 501; Sherman as model for, xiv, 233; Sherman's letter to, 233–34
Ellsworth, Oliver, at Constitutional Convention, 325–26; on elections for national legislature, 350; on military forces, 413–14, 416; on powers of national legislature, 402, 404; on records of proceedings of national legislature, 394; on representation in national legislature, 380, 390; on salaries for national legislature, 364; on slave trade, 406, 409, 412
executive, national. *See* presidency
executive power: congressional debates on, 678–706; Constitutional Convention debates on, 335–36, 418–19, 422–23; number of ambassadors and, 678, 702; presidential line of succession and, 678, 704–6; removal of executive branch officials in, 678–84; Sherman's correspondence with Adams (John) on, 678, 685–99; Sherman's "Observations on the New Federal Constitution" on, 481, 492–94; treaty making as, 442–44,

executive power (*continued*)
497–98, 678, 703; veto power as, 339–40,
348, 400, 446

faith, confession of, at White Haven Church,
731–35
false witness, Connecticut legal code on, 91,
109
Farrand, Max, 467
fasting, Continental Congress's calls for,
238–39
federalism: congressional debates on, 553–63,
710, 717–18; Constitutional Convention
debates on, 326, 330–31. *See also* states,
rights and powers of
Federalist essays, 470
felonies, Connecticut legal code on punishment for, 91–93
Few, William, 466
fidelity, oaths of: Connecticut legal code on,
94, 106–7; Sherman's views on, 203–4
Fitzsimons, Thomas: Constitution signed by,
465; in U.S. Congress, 561, 577–78, 586–87,
714–15
Floyd, William: Articles of Association signed
by, 166; Declaration of Independence
signed by, 197; Petition to the King signed
by, 179; Sherman's letter to, 473
Folsom, Nathaniel, 166, 179
foreign debt: congressional debates on, 566–
68; financing of War for Independence
through, 214, 229, 267–68
founders, forgotten, xv–xvi
France, Morris (Gouverneur) as minister to,
521, 527, 549–51
Franklin, Benjamin: at Constitutional Convention, 332, 340, 371–72, 448, 454; Constitution
signed by, 465; Declaration of Independence
signed by, 197; in drafting of Declaration of
Independence, 140–41, 193, 244
freemen: Connecticut legal code on oath for,
106; criteria for status of, 54
free people, vs. slaves, Connecticut Superior
Court on, 137–38
Fundamental Orders of Connecticut, 53

Gadsden, Christopher, 166, 179
Galloway, Joseph, 166, 179

gaming, Connecticut legal code on, 95
Gates, Horatio Lloyd, Sherman's letter to,
211–12
General Assembly of Connecticut. *See* Connecticut General Assembly
General Court of Connecticut. *See* Connecticut General Assembly
Gerber, Scott, xvi
Gerry, Elbridge: anti-Federalist essays by,
470; Declaration of Independence signed
by, 196
Gerry, Elbridge, at Constitutional Convention: on admission of new states, 378; on
amendment process, 445, 451; on Council of
Revision, 339; on elections for national
executive, 439; on elections for national legislature, 332, 334, 343, 350–51; on military
forces, 413–14, 438; on national executive as
single person, 339; on paper money, 352; on
powers of national legislature, 402–3; on
reasons for not signing Constitution, 453;
on records of proceedings of national legislature, 394; on representation in national
legislature, 375; on slave trade, 410; on treaties, 443–44; on veto power of executive,
339–40; on vice presidency, 441
Gerry, Elbridge, in U.S. Congress: on Bill
of Rights, 652–53, 656, 658, 660–64; on
national power, 557; on newspapers,
545–46
Gibbs, Henry, Sherman's correspondence
with, 625–28
Giles, William B., 718
Gilman, Nicholas, 465
Gorham, Nathaniel, at Constitutional Convention: on appointment process for
national judiciary, 386; Constitution signed
by, 465; on elections for national executive,
417; on impeachment of national executive,
386–87; on paper money, 425; on powers of
national legislature, 447; on qualifications
for national legislature, 396; on records of
proceedings of national legislature, 393; on
representation in national legislature, 377,
390; on salaries for national legislature, 364;
on slave trade, 412, 421; on term lengths
for national legislature, 368; on vice presidency, 437

governors, Connecticut: election of, 87–89; oath for, 106. *See also specific governors*
Great Britain. *See* Britain
Griswold, Matthew, 145–46
Gwinnett, Button, 197, 244

Hall, Lyman: Declaration of Independence signed by, 197; Sherman's letter to, 240–41
Hamilton, Alexander, at Constitutional Convention: Constitution signed by, 465; on elections for national legislature, 363; on national government, 326; on need for prayer, 372–73; on New Jersey Plan, 359; on representation in national legislature, 349; on veto power of executive, 340
Hancock, John, 196, 470
Harding, Seth, 522
hard money, Sherman's support for, 217, 259
Harrison, Benjamin: Articles of Association signed by, 166; as Board of War member, 244; Declaration of Independence signed by, 197; Petition to the King signed by, 179
Hart, John, 197
Hartley, Thomas, 663–64
Hayward, Thomas, 32*n*2
Heckelman, Jac C., xvi*n*15
Henry, Patrick, xiv, 166, 179
Herkimer, Nicholas, 213, 213*n*
Hewes, Joseph: Articles of Association signed by, 166; Declaration of Independence signed by, 197; in drafting of Articles of Confederation, 244; Petition to the King signed by, 179
Heyward, Thomas, Jr., 197
Hillhouse, William, 217, 217*n*
Hinckley v. Willson, 137–38
homosexuality, Connecticut legal code on punishment for, 91
Hooper, William, 166, 179, 197
Hopkins, Samuel: *An Inquiry into the Nature of True Holiness*, 776, 778; Sherman's correspondence with, 725, 776–98, 776*n*
Hopkins, Stephen: Articles of Association signed by, 166; Declaration of Independence signed by, 196; in drafting of Articles of Confederation, 244; Petition to the King signed by, 179
Hopkinson, Francis, 197

House of Representatives, U.S.: elections for, 501; number of members of, 518–19, 524; Sherman as member of (1789–91), xiii, xviii, 501–2. *See also* Congress, U.S.
Houston, William, 335
Hovey, Joseph, 137
Howell, Thomas, 149
Humphreys, Charles, 166, 179
Huntington, Benjamin: on legal code revision of 1783, 73; letters to Trumbull (Jonathan, Sr.), 231–32, 267–68; at New Haven Convention, 217, 217*n*; in U.S. Congress, 554
Huntington, Samuel: as Connecticut Superior Court judge, 132–34; Declaration of Independence signed by, 196; Sherman and Ellsworth's letter to, 469, 471–72; Sherman's letters to, 504, 509–10, 512–13, 515, 518–25

immorality, suppression of: Connecticut legal code on, 128–29; Continental Congress on, 226–28
impeachment, of executive, Constitutional Convention debates on, 336, 386–87, 444; Sherman's "Observations on the Alterations Proposed as Amendments" on, 497
imports, price controls on, during War for Independence, 221–22, 224–25. *See also* boycott of British goods; imposts
imposts: congressional debates on, 572, 601–19; Sherman's personal correspondence on, 240–41, 505–6; Sherman's *Remarks on a Pamphlet* defending, 298–300, 310
imprisonment, Connecticut legal code on, 76. *See also* bail
Indians. *See* Native Americans
inferior tribunals, Constitutional Convention debates on, 341–42
inflation: Sherman's aversion to, 217, 259; during War for Independence, 217. *See also* prices
Ingersoll, Jared, 465
Inquiry into the Nature of True Holiness, An (Hopkins), 776, 778
Intolerable Acts, colonial responses to: Address to the People of Great Britain, 167–73; Articles of Association, 162–66; Declarations and Resolves, 157–61; Petition of Congress to the King, 174–80

Isaiah, book of, 51*n*, 147*n*

Ivers, Thomas, 132–34

Jackson, James, 589, 661

Jackson, William, 465

Jay, John: Address to the People of Great Britain drafted by, 167–73; Articles of Association signed by, 166; Petition to the King signed by, 179

Jefferson, Thomas: Declaration of Independence signed by, 197; in drafting of Declaration of Independence, 140–41, 193, 244; *Notes on Virginia*, 271; praise for Sherman by, xiv–xv; Stiles's (Ezra) introduction to, 323

Jenifer, Daniel of St. Thomas, 350, 465

Johnson, Thomas, Jr., 166, 179

Johnson, William Samuel: at Connecticut ratification convention, 469–70; as Connecticut Superior Court judge, 57*n*10; at Constitutional Convention, 325–26; Constitution signed by, 465; in legal education of Sherman, 2, 50; in U.S. Senate, xviii, 501, 502; Sherman's letters to, 50–51, 147

judges. *See* Connecticut Superior Court; Supreme Court, U.S.

judicial review, by Connecticut Superior Court, 135–36

judiciary, Connecticut. *See* Connecticut Superior Court

judiciary, national, Sherman's personal correspondence on establishment of, 510, 511. *See also* Supreme Court, U.S.

jurisdiction: of Connecticut Superior Court, 84–85; of U.S. Supreme Court, 341–42, 352, 425

jury, right of trial by, in Bill of Rights, 644, 646, 671, 674

justices of the peace: Connecticut legal code on oaths for, 107; Sherman as, 55

King, Rufus, at Constitutional Convention, 326; on amendment process, 445; Constitution signed by, 465; on Council of Revision, 339; on elections for national executive, 439; on legislators' eligibility for other offices, 367, 435; on military forces, 413; on powers of national legislature, 447; on ratification

process, 434; on regulation of commerce, 426, 428; on representation in national legislature, 376, 389; on salaries for national legislature, 365; on slave trade, 389, 410; on treaties, 443

King, Rufus, in U.S. Congress, 527

Kinsey, James, 166

Kirby, Ephraim, 137*n*; *Reports of Cases Adjudged in the Superior Court of the State of Connecticut*, 57, 57*n*, 808

land grants: by Connecticut General Assembly, Superior Court on, 135–36; Sherman's *Remarks on a Pamphlet* on, 304–5, 320–21. *See also* Susquehannah controversy

lands, western, congressional debates on, 564, 621–23

Langdon, John, at Constitutional Convention: on admission of new states, 430; Constitution signed by, 465; on elections for national executive, 417–18; on regulation of commerce, 450; on representation in national legislature, 449; on slave trade, 411

Laurance, John, in U.S. Congress, 561, 713–14, 720

Law, Richard: as Connecticut district judge, 511; as Connecticut Superior Court judge, 135–38; letter to Trumbull (Jonathan, Sr.), 237; in revision of Connecticut legal code, xiii, xviii, xviii*n*20, 56; Sherman's letters to, 70–72, 511. *See also* Connecticut legal code

Leavenworth, Jesse, 149

Lee, Francis Lightfoot, 197

Lee, Richard Bland, 562

Lee, Richard Henry: Articles of Association signed by, 166; Declaration of Independence signed by, 197; in drafting of Articles of Confederation, 244; in drafting of Declaration of Independence, 193; Petition to the King signed by, 179; praise for Sherman by, xiv; Sherman's letter to, 215–16

legislative power. *See* Congress, U.S., powers of

legislature, national. *See* Confederation Congress; Congress, U.S.; Continental Congress

legislatures, state. *See* state legislatures

letters from Sherman: to Adams (John), 695–

99; to Adams (Samuel), 208, 213–14; to
Austin (David), 771–73; to Baldwin (Simeon), 502, 507–8, 745, 769–70, 799–801, 806,
809–11; to Barbé-Marbois (François), 273–
74; to Bartlett (Josiah), 269–70; to Bellamy
(Joseph), 727–29; to Butler (Zebulon), 248–
50; to Cushing (Thomas), 150–51; to Douw
(Volkert P.), 247; to Ellery (William), 514;
to Ellsworth (Oliver), 233–34; to Floyd
(William), 473; to Gates (Horatio Lloyd),
211–12; to Gibbs (Henry), 626, 628; to Griswold (Matthew), 145–46; to Hall (Lyman),
240–41; to Hopkins (Samuel), 778–81, 794–
98; to Huntington (Samuel), 469, 471–72,
504, 509–10, 512–13, 515, 518–25; to Johnson
(William Samuel), 50–51, 147; to Law
(Richard), 70–72, 511; to Lee (Richard
Henry), 215–16; to merchants, 148–49; to
Morse (Jedidiah), 807–8; to Payne (Elisha),
262–63; to Sherman (Rebecca), 52, 741–42,
746, 774–75; to Stiles (Ezra), 323; to Trumbull (Benjamin), 229–30, 259; to Trumbull
(Jonathan, Jr.), 198–99; to Trumbull (Jonathan, Sr.), 154–56, 183–84, 200–206, 231–32,
237, 260–61, 264–68; to Trumbull (Joseph),
185–86; to Williams (Nathan), 802–5; to
Williams (William), 187–88, 516–17; to
Witherspoon (John), 738–39; to Wolcott
(Oliver), 207, 505–6; to Wooster (David),
181–82. See also specific topics
"Letters of a Countryman" (Sherman), xviii,
470, 482–90
"Letters of a Landholder" (Ellsworth), 470
letters to Sherman: from Adams (John), 678,
686–94; from Adams (Samuel), 209–10;
from Baldwin (Simeon), 812; from Hopkins
(Samuel), 781–94; from Huntington (Benjamin), 73; from Mitchell (Justus), 766–68;
from Sherman (Elizabeth), 743–44; from
Washington (George), 503, 526; from
Witherspoon (John), 740
Lewis, Francis, 197
Lexington, Battle of, 187
lieutenant governors, Connecticut: election of,
87–89; oath for, 107
Livermore, Samuel, in U.S. Congress, 656,
704–5, 714
Livingston, Philip, 166, 179, 197

Livingston, Robert: in drafting of Articles of
Confederation, 140, 244; in drafting of
Declaration of Independence, 140–41, 193,
244
Livingston, William, 166, 179, 465
loans, made by Congress, debates on, 558–60.
See also bills of credit; national debt; state
debts
Lovell, James, 244
Low, Isaac, 166, 179
luxury, Sherman on dangers of, 297
Lynch, Thomas, 166, 179

Macon, Nathanial, xv
Madison, James, at Constitutional Convention: on admission of new states, 430; on
amendment process, 451; on appointment
process for national judiciary, 352, 387;
Constitution signed by, 465; on elections
for national executive, 418; on elections for
national legislature, 333, 344–46, 350–51, 362;
on jurisdiction of national judiciary, 341–42,
352; on legislators' eligibility for other
offices, 366; on military forces, 413–15; on
paper money, 353; political synergy between
Sherman and, xiii, xvin15, 326; on powers of
national legislature, 334, 383, 402; on qualifications for national legislature, 396–97; on
ratification process, 341, 434; on records of
proceedings of national legislature, 394; on
regulation of commerce, 426–27, 450; on
representation in national legislature, 390;
on slave trade, 420–21; on taxation by
states, 405–6; on term lengths for national
legislature, 368–70; on treaties, 444; unofficial notes kept by, 327, 327n7; on vice
presidency, 437; Virginia Plan of, 325, 326
Madison, James, in U.S. Congress: on Bill
of Rights, 624, 630–41, 650–51, 654, 656,
659, 666–67, 669; on executive power, 678;
on imposts, 617; on Militia Bill of 1790,
715–16, 720; Sherman's note to, on national
bank, 563; on state and national debts,
587–89
Magna Carta, 484–85
marriage. See divorce
Martin, Luther, at Constitutional Convention, 383–84, 386, 406, 431

Maryland, Articles of Confederation ratified by, 245, 251

Mason, George: as forgotten founder, xvi*n*16; Henry's (Patrick) praise for, xiv

Mason, George, at Constitutional Convention: on admission of new states, 430; on amendment process, 450–52; on appointment process for national judiciary, 386; on Bill of Rights, 446; on elections for national legislature, 332–33, 344, 362–63; on legislators' eligibility for other offices, 366–67; on military forces, 415; on national government, 331; on powers of national legislature, 402, 404; on qualifications for national legislature, 397; on records of proceedings of national legislature, 394; on regulation of commerce, 426–27, 450; on slave trade, 408–9, 420–21; on term lengths for national executive, 336; on veto power of national executive, 446; on vice presidency, 441–42

Massachusetts Bay, bills of credit in, 15, 47

Mather, Cotton, 1

mayor of New Haven, Sherman as, xiii, 73

McClurg, James, 384–85

McHenry, James, 449, 465

McKean, Thomas: Articles of Association signed by, 166; Declaration of Independence signed by, 196; in drafting of Articles of Confederation, 244; Petition to the King signed by, 179

Mercer, John F., 394, 396, 398, 401

merchants, in boycott of British goods, 148–49

Middleton, Arthur, 197

Middleton, Henry, 166, 179, 180

Mifflin, Thomas, 166, 179, 465

military equipment and supplies: Connecticut legal code on destruction of, 91–92; Sherman's personal correspondence on, 183–84, 205, 264–66

Militia Bill of 1790, congressional debates on, 707–21; arms supply in, 708; exemptions in, 709–12, 716–21; federalism in, 710, 717–18; inspections in, 713–14; power of calling up forces in, 714–15; right to bear arms in, 710

militias and military forces: in Bill of Rights, 644, 645, 660–64, 674; Connecticut legal

code on, 99–100; Constitutional Convention debates on, 404, 413–15, 438. *See also* Continental army

Milton, John: *Areopagitica*, 17*n*; *Paradise Lost*, 38*n*2

ministers, religious: Connecticut legal code on, 101–5; Sherman's personal correspondence on removal and resignation of, 727–29

ministers of state, Sherman's *Remarks on a Pamphlet* on, 313–14. *See also* ambassadors

Mitchell, Justus, Sherman's correspondence with, 761–68

monarchies, Adams's (John) personal correspondence on, 686–90

money. *See* hard money; paper money

Montgomery, Joseph, call for prayer and fasting by, 238–39

morality, promotion of: Connecticut legal code on, 128–29; Continental Congress on, 226–28

Morris, Gouverneur, as minister to France, 521, 527, 549–51

Morris, Gouverneur, at Constitutional Convention: on admission of new states, 430–31; on amendment process, 451; on bankruptcies, 435; Constitution signed by, 465; on elections for national executive, 384–85, 419, 439; on elections for national legislature, 392; on impeachment of national executive, 387, 444; on legislators' eligibility for other offices, 436; on national vs. supreme government, 331; on powers of national legislature, 381–84, 447; on qualifications for national legislature, 396–97; on ratification process, 433; on records of proceedings of national legislature, 393; on regulation of commerce, 426–28; on removal of judges, 423; on representation in national legislature, 377, 390–91; on slave trade, 390–91, 411, 420; on treaties, 443; on veto power of executive, 400; on vice presidency, 441

Morris, Lewis, 197

Morris, Robert, 197, 465

Morse, Jedidiah: *American Geography*, 807–8; Sherman's letter to, 807–8

Morton, John, 166, 179, 197

Muhlenberg, Frederick Augustus, 675

Munson, Joseph, 149

national bank, congressional debates on, xviii, 561–63

national debt, American: congressional debates on, 565–99; Sherman's personal correspondence on, 214, 231, 267–68, 512, 525; Sherman's *Remarks on a Pamphlet* on, 297–300. *See also* War for Independence, financing of

national debt, British, Sherman's *Remarks on a Pamphlet* on, 296–97

national government, power of: congressional debates on, 553–63; Constitutional Convention debates on, 326, 330–31; Sherman's views on, 326, 554–63

Native Americans: as servants, Connecticut legal code on, 119–20; Sherman's personal correspondence on wars with, 524, 525; Sherman's *Remarks on a Pamphlet* on land of, 304–5, 320–21; as slaves, Connecticut Superior Court on, 137–38; and Susquehannah controversy, 55, 61, 65–66, 246, 304

Nelson, Thomas, Jr., 197, 244

New Hampshire, bills of credit issued by, 15–16, 39, 49

New Haven (Connecticut): Sherman as mayor of, xiii, 73; Sherman's almanacs for, 25–32

New Haven Convention (1778): delegates sent to, 217; report on, 217–25

New Haven Gazette (newspaper): Sherman's "Letters of a Countryman" in, xviii, 482–90; Sherman's "Observations on the Alterations Proposed as Amendments" in, 496–99; Sherman's "Observations on the New Federal Constitution" in, 491

New Jersey Plan, 355–59

New Light Congregationalism, 724, 727

New London (Connecticut), Sherman's almanacs for, 14–16, 19–20

newspapers: congressional debates on, 543–47; congressional proceedings in, 502; ratification debates in, 470. *See also specific publications*

New York (city): as national capital, 501, 502, 544; Sherman's almanacs for, 7, 10, 12–13, 17–18

New York Gazette (newspaper), 3, 9

New York Packet (newspaper), 624

Northwest Ordinance (1787), 244

Notes on Virginia (Jefferson), 271

oaths: congressional debates on, 533–35; Connecticut legal code on, 94, 106–9; Constitutional Convention debates on, 349, 432; Sherman's views on, 203–4

"Observations on the Alterations Proposed as Amendments to the New Federal Constitution" (Sherman), 496–99; Sherman's correspondence with Gibbs (Henry) on, 625–27

"Observations on the New Federal Constitution" (Sherman), 470; draft version of, 478–81; published version of, 491–95; revised version of, 678n3; Sherman's correspondence with Adams (John) on, 678, 685–99; Sherman's correspondence with Gibbs (Henry) on, 625–27

"one state, one vote," in Articles of Confederation, 244–45

oratorical skills, of Sherman, xv, 153, 331n

Paca, William, 166, 179, 196

Page, John, 557, 578, 587

Paine, Robert Treat: Articles of Association signed by, 166; Declaration of Independence signed by, 196; at New Haven Convention, 217, 217n; Petition to the King signed by, 179

paper money: Constitutional Convention debates on, 352–53, 425; New Haven Convention on, 217, 218, 224–25; Sherman's personal correspondence on, 200–201, 214, 215, 229–32, 265. *See also* bills of credit

pardons: Constitutional Convention debates on, 422–23; Sherman's "Observations on the Alterations Proposed as Amendments" on, 497

Paris, Treaty of (1783), 240

Parker, Josiah, 613

Parliament: in origins of War for Independence, 139–40; Sherman on limits of power of, 139–40, 147, 151, 152. *See also specific laws*

Paterson, William: at Constitutional Convention, 355–58; Constitution signed by, 465

Payne, Elisha, Sherman's letter to, 262–63
Peabody, Nathaniel, 217, 217*n*
Pendleton, Edmund, 166, 179
Penn, John, 197
Penn, Thomas, 55, 62
Pennsylvania, Susquehannah controversy in, 55–56, 59–68
perjury, Connecticut legal code on, 108–9
Petition of Congress to the King (1774), 174–80
Philadelphia, as national capital, 502, 541–42, 544
Philoeunomos (pseudonym), "A Caveat Against Injustice," 1–2, 39–49
Pickering, Timothy, xv
Pierce, William: at Constitutional Convention, 327*n*7, 332; on Sherman's oratorical skills, xv, 331*n*
Pinckney, Charles, at Constitutional Convention: on amendment process, 452–53; on appointment process for national judiciary, 352; Constitution signed by, 466; on elections for national legislature, 343; on impeachment of national executive, 444; on military forces, 415–16; on national government, 330; on oaths, 432; on paper money, 353; on powers of national executive, 335; on powers of national legislature, 402–3; on qualifications for national legislature, 397; on regulation of commerce, 429–30; on representation in national legislature, 378; on slave trade, 406–7, 409, 420; on term lengths for national executive, 336
Pinckney, Charles Cotesworth, at Constitutional Convention: Constitution signed by, 466; on legislators' eligibility for other offices, 366; on national government, 331; on paper money, 353; on powers of national legislature, 447; on regulation of commerce, 429; on slave trade, 409, 411; on term lengths for national legislature, 368
Pinckney, Thomas, 521, 524
Pitkin, William, as Connecticut Superior Court judge, 132–38
Pope, Alexander, *Essay on Man*, 12*n*, 14*n*, 15*n*
Practical Works of the Late Reverend and Pious Mr. Richard Baxter, The, 747, 756–60, 802–5
prayer: at Constitutional Convention, 372–73;

Continental Congress's calls for, 238–39; U.S. Congress's calls for, 676–77
Prescott, Rebecca. *See* Sherman, Rebecca Prescott
presidency, U.S.: line of succession for, 678, 704–6; Sherman's "Observations on the New Federal Constitution" on, 481, 492–94; of Washington (George), 525. *See also* executive power
presidency, U.S., Constitutional Convention debates on: election to, 336, 384–85, 417–18, 439–40; enumeration of powers of, 335–36, 418–19, 422–23; impeachment process for, 336, 386–87, 444; New Jersey Plan in, 357–58; removal of, 337; single person in, 335–36, 338–39, 384–85; term lengths of, 336, 384–85; veto power of, 339–40, 348, 400, 446
presidential elections: Constitutional Convention debates on, 336, 384–85, 417–18, 439–40; Sherman's personal correspondence on, 525; Sherman's "Observations on the New Federal Constitution" on, 479, 491–92
press, freedom of: in Bill of Rights, 644, 645, 671, 674; Constitutional Convention debates on, 448. *See also* newspapers
prices, during War for Independence: controls on, 217–25; fluctuations in, 200–201, 214
private property, compensation for seizure of, in Bill of Rights, 646, 664
profaneness, Connecticut legal code on suppression of, 128–29
pseudonyms: of Sherman, 39, 245, 246, 470; of Webster (Pelatiah), 245
public credit/debt. *See* national debt
punishment: of Continental soldiers, 235–36; cruel and unusual, in Bill of Rights, 644, 646, 674
punishment, in Connecticut legal code: for adultery, 77; for capital crimes, 91–93; for copyright infringement, 98; for gaming, 95; for not observing Sabbath, 110–13; for swearing and cursing, 127
Putnam, Israel, 181, 184, 187–88

Quakers: Connecticut legal code on oaths by, 108–9; Sherman's almanacs on meetings of, 7
Quarles, Francis, *Divine Fancies*, 22*n*4, 32*n*1

Quartering Act of 1766, 140
Quebec Act of 1774, 140

Rakove, Jack, 326, 467
Randolph, Edmund, at Constitutional Convention: on amendment process, 452; on elections for national executive, 419; on jurisdiction of national judiciary, 352; on national executive as single person, 338; on national vs. supreme government, 330; on powers of national legislature, 334, 382; on representation in national legislature, 376; on salaries for national legislature, 364; on slave trade, 411
Randolph, Peyton, 154
Randolph, Thomas: *The Muse's Looking Glass*, 21nn1–2; "Necessary Observations," 24n
ratification, of Articles of Confederation, 245, 251, 260–61
ratification, of Constitution, 469–99; Constitutional Convention debates on process for, 341, 432–34, 469; overview of, 469–70; Sherman's "Letters of a Countryman" on, xviii, 470, 482–90; Sherman's "Observations on the Alterations Proposed as Amendments" on, 496–99; Sherman's "Observations on the New Federal Constitution" on, 470, 478–81, 491–95; Sherman's personal correspondence on, 469, 471–77
Read, George: Articles of Association signed by, 166; at Constitutional Convention, 368, 404, 439; Constitution signed by, 465; Declaration of Independence signed by, 196; Petition to the King signed by, 179
Reformed (Calvinist) theological tradition, 723
religious freedom: in Bill of Rights, 643, 645, 658–59, 671, 674; in Connecticut legal code, 74, 80–81, 92
religious practice: Connecticut legal code on ministers in, 101–5; Connecticut legal code on observation of Sabbath, 110–13; Connecticut legal code on promotion of, 128–29; Continental Congress on promotion of, 226–28; Continental Congress's calls for prayer and fasting, 238–39; Reformed (Calvinist) tradition in, 723
religious tests: Constitutional Convention debates on, 432; Sherman's "Observations

on the Alterations Proposed as Amendments" on, 498. See also religious freedom
religious writings of Sherman. See theological writings of Sherman
Remarks on a Pamphlet Entitled "A Dissertation on the Political Union and Constitution of the Thirteen United States" (Sherman), 245–46, 296–322; attribution to Sherman, 245, 246; on Congress, powers of, 302–22; on land grants, 304–5, 320–21; on national debt, 296–300; on Susquehannah controversy, 246, 296, 304; text of, 296–322
representation: in Articles of Confederation, 244–45, 252; in Bill of Rights, 637–38, 643, 645, 655–57, 673; Constitutional Convention debates on, 349, 371, 375–80, 389–91, 449; Sherman's personal correspondence on, 474–76; Sherman's "Observations on the New Federal Constitution" on, 480, 493; slaves in population counts for, 216, 320, 357, 376–77, 389–91
republics, Sherman's correspondence with Adams (John) on, 686–90, 695–96
"Resolves of the General Consociation Convened at Guilford, November 24th, 1741," 724n4
Revolution, American. See War for Independence
Rhode Island, bills of credit issued by, 15–16, 39, 43–49
Ridgefield, Battle of, 181
rights. See Bill of Rights; civil rights; colonial rights; states, rights and powers of
Robertson, David Brian, xiii, 326
Rodney, Caesar, 166, 179, 196
Ross, George, 166, 179, 196
Rush, Benjamin, 197
Rutledge, Edward: Articles of Association signed by, 166; as Board of War member, 244; Declaration of Independence signed by, 197; in drafting of Articles of Confederation, 244; Petition to the King signed by, 179
Rutledge, John: Articles of Association signed by, 166; Petition to the King signed by, 179
Rutledge, John, at Constitutional Convention: on address to the people, 449; Constitution

Rutledge, John, at Constitutional Convention
(*continued*)
signed by, 466; on elections for national
executive, 417; on elections for national legislature, 350; on inferior tribunals, 341; on
legislators' eligibility for other offices, 366;
on military forces, 415; on national executive as single person, 335; on powers of
national executive, 335; on powers of
national legislature, 447; on qualifications
for national legislature, 396; on records of
proceedings of national legislature, 394; on
removal of judges, 423; on representation in
national legislature, 376; on slave trade, 406,
411; on treaties, 444

Sabbath, Connecticut legal code on observation of, 110–13
salaries: of judges, Sherman's personal correspondence on, 510, 511; of vice president,
congressional debates on, 538
salaries, in U.S. Congress: Bill of Rights on,
644, 673; Constitutional Convention
debates on, 364–65, 399; Sherman's personal
correspondence on, 507, 509–10
Saratoga, Battles of, 211
schools. *See* education
Schuyler, Philip, 181, 183, 184, 208, 209
Scott, Thomas, in U.S. Congress, 567–69
searches and seizures: in Bill of Rights, 674;
in Connecticut Superior Court cases, 58
securities, congressional debates on, 561–62;
Sherman's personal correspondence on,
512–13
Sedgwick, Theodore, in U.S. Congress, 577,
592, 641, 668
self-examination, Sherman's sermon on,
747–56
self-incrimination, in Bill of Rights, 646,
664
self-love, Sherman's correspondence with
Hopkins (Samuel) on, 778–79, 782–88,
793–96
Senate, U.S.: in removal of executive branch
officials, 678–84; secrecy of debates in, 502;
Sherman as member of (1791–93), xiii, xviii,
502; in treaty making, 440, 442–44, 497–98,
703. *See also* Congress, U.S.

Seney, Joshua, 578, 652, 713
separation of powers: in Bill of Rights, 644,
646–47, 666–68, 675; in Connecticut Gen-
eral Assembly, 54
servants, Connecticut legal code on, 119–22
Shakespeare, William, *Two Noble Kinsmen*,
27n3
Sherman, Elizabeth (wife), 2
Sherman, Elizabeth (daughter), letter to
Roger Sherman, 743–44
Sherman, John (son), 809, 811
Sherman, Josiah (brother), xvii; Sherman's
correspondence on sermon of, 761–68
Sherman, Mehetabel (mother), xvii
Sherman, Nathaniel (brother), xvii
Sherman, Rebecca (daughter), 507
Sherman, Rebecca Prescott (wife), xvii, 2;
Roger Sherman's letters to, 52, 741–42, 746,
774–75
Sherman, Roger: contemporaries on, xiii–xv,
xviii–xix; death of, xviii, 725; education of,
xvii, 1–2, 50; family of, xvii, 2, 725; inventory
of library of, 724, 724n8, 813–16; lack of schol-
arship on, xv–xvi, xvin16; life of, xvii–xix, 1;
oratorical skills of, xv, 153, 331n; pseudonyms used by, 39, 245, 246, 470; religious
beliefs of, xvii, 723–24; writings of, xiii, xvi–
xvii. *See also specific documents and writings*
Sherman, Roger, career of: in Confederation
Congress, xiii, 243; in Connecticut General
Assembly, xiii, xvii, 54–55; in Continental
Congress, xiii, xviii, 140; as judge, xiii, xvii–
xviii, 57–58, 132–38, 501; as mayor of New
Haven, xiii, 73; overview of, xiii, xvii–xviii,
1–2; in U.S. House of Representatives, xiii,
xviii, 501–2; in U.S. Senate, xiii, xviii, 502
Sherman, William (father), xvii
Sherman, William (son), 199, 741–45
"Short Sermon on the Duty of Self Examina-
tion, A" (Sherman), 747–60, 802
Silvester, Peter, 658, 676
slaves: in *Amistad* case, 812; Connecticut legal
code on, 74, 119–22; Connecticut Superior
Court on, 132–34, 137–38; emancipation of,
121–22, 132–34; fugitive, Constitutional
Convention debates on, 428, 430; Native
American, 137–38; in population counts,
Constitutional Convention debates on, 357,

376–77, 389–91; in population counts, Sherman's views on, 216, 320

slave trade: Articles of Association on, 163; congressional debates on imposts on, 613–14; Constitutional Convention debates on, 389–91, 406–12, 420–22

Smith, James, 197

Smith, Richard, 166, 179

Smith, William L., in U.S. Congress: on Bill of Rights, 652, 661; on executive power, 678, 704; on Militia Bill of 1790, 713–14; on national power, 557, 558; on newspapers, 546; on slavery, 613

societies: Connecticut legal code on regulation of, 123–26; ecclesiastical, 57, 80–81, 101–5

Spaight, Richard Dobbs, 351, 465

Spain, Continental Congress's negotiations with, 267–68

speech, freedom of, in Bill of Rights, 645, 671, 674

Stamp Act of 1765, 139, 143–44, 146

state debts, congressional debates on, 558–59, 564–99; Sherman's personal correspondence on, 512–13; Sherman's notes for speech in, 598–99; Sherman's role in, xviii

state debts, Constitutional Convention debates on, 404

state legislatures, Constitutional Convention debates on: role in elections for national legislature, 332–34, 343–44, 347; veto power of national legislature over, 382–84, 415–16. See also Connecticut General Assembly

state militias: congressional debates on, 710; Connecticut legal code on, 99–100; Constitutional Convention debates on, 404

state ratification. See ratification

states, admission of new, 378, 430–32

states, rights and powers of: in Bill of Rights, congressional debates on, 644, 647, 666–67, 675; Constitutional Convention debates on, 427–28, 449–50; in Militia Bill of 1790, congressional debates on, 710, 717–18; Sherman's "Observations on the New Federal Constitution" on, 478–79, 492; Sherman's Remarks on a Pamphlet on, 302–22

state taxation: Constitutional Convention debates on, 405–6; Sherman's Remarks on a Pamphlet on, 297–300

St. Clair, Arthur, 502, 520

Stiles, Ezra: Sherman's letter to, 323; on White Haven Church, 724

Stockton, Richard, 197

Stone, Michael J., 557, 662, 714

Stone, Thomas, 196, 244

Stout, Harry, 723

succession, presidential line of, 678, 704–6

Suffolk Resolves, 140, 154–55

Sullivan, John, 157n2; Articles of Association signed by, 166; in drafting of Declaration and Resolves, 157n2; letter to Washington (George), 235–36; Petition to the King signed by, 179

Sumter, Thomas, 663–64

Superior Court of Connecticut. See Connecticut Superior Court

Supreme Court, U.S.: Sherman's personal correspondence on, 476, 502; Sherman's "Observations on the New Federal Constitution" on, 494

Supreme Court, U.S., Constitutional Convention debates on: appointment process for, 352, 386–87; in Council of Revision, 339; inferior tribunals under, 341–42; jurisdiction of, 341–42, 352, 425; New Jersey Plan in, 356–58; removal of judges, 423–24; veto power in, 339

Susquehannah Company, 55–56, 61, 246, 304

Susquehannah controversy, 55–56, 59–68; Native Americans in, 55, 61, 65–66, 246, 304; origins of, 55; resolution of, 56; Sherman's Connecticut Journal article on, 56, 60–64; Sherman's legal brief on, 56, 65–68; Sherman's personal correspondence on, 248–50; Sherman's Remarks on a Pamphlet on, 246, 296, 304

swearing, Connecticut legal code on, 127

Symsbury Case, 135–36, 135n

taxation: in Bill of Rights, 670; of colonies by Britain, 139, 143–44, 146; Connecticut legal code on, 80–81, 101–2; Constitutional Convention debates on, 382, 401; funding for War for Independence through, 201, 214–16, 219–20, 229–31; Sherman's "Observations on the New Federal Constitution" on, 480, 493; Sherman's Remarks on a Pamphlet

taxation (*continued*)
on, 297–300, 307–10. *See also* imposts; state
taxation
Taylor, George, 196
tea, British, 163, 170–71
teachers, Connecticut legal code on, 114–16
term lengths, Constitutional Convention
debates on: for national executive, 336, 384–
85; for U.S. Congress, 350–51, 368–70
Thanksgiving Day Proclamation, 676
theological writings of Sherman, xiii, 723–816;
on Baxter's (Richard) *The Practical Works*,
747, 756–60, 802–5; in correspondence with
Bellamy (Joseph), 727–29; in correspondence
with Hopkins (Samuel), 725, 776–98; in
correspondence with Mitchell (Justus),
761–68; in correspondence with Williams
(Nathan), 802–5; on divorce, 738–39; on
infant baptism, 756–58, 802–5; on Josiah
Sherman's sermon, 761–65; on ministers,
removal and resignation of, 727–29; overview of, 723–25; on self-love, 778–79, 793–
96; "A Short Sermon on the Duty of Self
Examination," 747–60, 802; in White
Haven Church documents, 731–37
Thompson, Charles, 154
Thornton, Matthew, 197
three-fifths clause, 357, 376–77
Ticonderoga, Fort, 208–9, 211
Tilghman, Matthew, 166, 179
Townshend Acts of 1767, 140, 148
trade. *See* imports
treaties: congressional debates on, 678, 703;
Constitutional Convention debates on, 358,
384, 440, 442–44; president's role in, 442–
44, 497–98, 678, 703; U.S. Senate's role
in, 440, 442–44, 497–98, 703; Sherman's
"Observations on the Alterations Proposed
as Amendments" on, 497–98; as supreme
law of states, 358, 384
Trumbull, Benjamin: on divorce, 738–40;
Sherman's letters to, 229–30, 259
Trumbull, John, 154
Trumbull, Jonathan, Jr.: as governor of Connecticut, 154; as paymaster of New York,
188, 198; Sherman's letter to, 198–99
Trumbull, Jonathan, Sr.: as governor of
Connecticut, 154; Sherman's letters to, 154–

56, 183–84, 200–206, 231–32, 237, 260–61,
264–68
Trumbull, Joseph, Sherman's letter to, 185–86
Tucker, Thomas Tudor, in U.S. Congress,
656, 666–67, 670, 677

Varnum, James, call for prayer and fasting by,
238–39
Vermont, independence movement in, 262–
63, 269–70
veto power, Constitutional Convention
debates on: of executive, 339–40, 348, 400,
446; of national legislature over states, 382–
84, 415–16
vice, Connecticut legal code on suppression
of, 128–29
vice presidency, U.S.: of Adams (John), 525;
Constitutional Convention debates on, 437,
441–42; elections for, 437, 525; congressional debates on line of succession for,
678, 704–6
Vining, John, in U.S. Congress, 559–60, 652,
655, 662, 663
Virgil, *Georgics*, 38n1
Virginia Plan, 325, 326
voting. *See* elections

Wadsworth, Jeremiah, 326, 713–14
wage controls, during War for Independence,
217, 221
Walton, George, 197
War and Ordinance, Board of, 140, 244
Ward, Samuel, 166, 179
War for Independence, 139–241; origins of,
139–40; Treaty of Paris ending, 240. *See also*
Continental army; Continental Congress;
specific documents
War for Independence, financing of: foreign,
214, 229, 267–68; New Haven Convention
report on, 217–25; price controls and, 217–25;
Sherman's personal correspondence on,
200–201, 214–16, 229–32; through taxes, 201,
214–16, 219–20, 229–31. *See also* national
debt; state debts
war powers, Constitutional Convention
debates on, 402–3
Washington, George: Articles of Association
signed by, 166; Constitution signed by, 465;

in Continental Army, 181; election as president, 525; Petition to the King signed by, 179; Sherman's letter from, 503, 526; Sullivan's (John) letter to, on lashing of soldiers, 235–36; Thanksgiving Day Proclamation by, 676

Webster, Pelatiah, 275; pseudonym used by, 245; on Sherman as author of *Remarks on a Pamphlet*, 246. *See also* Dissertation on the Political Union and Constitution of the Thirteen United States

western lands, congressional debates on, 564, 621–23

Westmoreland (town), 56, 61–62, 66

Whipple, William, 196

White, Alexander, in U.S. Congress, 641–42, 704–5

White Haven Church, 731–37; confession of faith adopted by, 731, 734–35; confession of faith drafted by Sherman for, 731–33; covenant adopted by, 731, 737; covenant drafted by Sherman for, 731, 736; Sherman's personal correspondence on, 769–73; Sherman's membership in, 724, 731

Williams, Nathan, Sherman's letter to, 802–5

Williams, William: Declaration of Independence signed by, 197; praise for Sherman by, xiii–xiv; Sherman's letters to, 187–88, 516–17

Williamson, Hugh, at Constitutional Convention: on admission of new states, 430; Constitution signed by, 465; on impeachment of national executive, 444; on legislators' eligibility for other offices, 436; on salaries for national legislature, 364; on slave trade, 410, 421; on treaties, 443; on veto power of national executive, 446; on vice presidency, 441

Williamson, Hugh, in U.S. Congress, 561, 589–90, 705

Wilson, James: as Board of War member, 244; Declaration of Independence signed by, 196; Federalist essays by, 470; as forgotten founder, xviin16

Wilson, James, at Constitutional Convention: on amendment process, 445; on appointment process for national judiciary, 386; Constitution signed by, 465; on elections for national executive, 336, 417–19, 439–40; on elections for national legislature, 333, 343–44, 362; on jurisdiction of national judiciary, 342; on legislators' eligibility for other offices, 367; on military forces, 415; on national executive as single person, 335, 336, 338–39; on national government, 326; on paper money, 425; on powers of national executive, 336, 423; on powers of national legislature, 447; on qualifications for national legislature, 397; on ratification process, 432; on records of proceedings of national legislature, 394; on removal of judges, 423; on representation in national legislature, 349, 371, 375, 379; on slave trade, 410; on term lengths for national executive, 336; on treaties, 442–44; on veto power of executive, 339–40, 348

Wisner, Henry, 166, 179

Witherspoon, John: call for prayer and fasting by, 238–39; Declaration of Independence signed by, 197; Sherman's correspondence with, 738–40

Wolcott, Erastus, 325

Wolcott, Oliver: Declaration of Independence signed by, 197; Sherman's letters to, 207, 505–6

Wooster, David, Sherman's letter to, 181–82

Wyoming Valley. *See* Susquehannah controversy

Wythe, George: Declaration of Independence signed by, 197; instructions for congressional commission to Canada by, 189–92

Yorktown, surrender of Cornwallis at, 237

Young, Edward: *The Complaint*, 18n; "Night the Ninth and Last," 19n

The typeface used for the text of this book is Adobe Caslon, a 1990
interpretation by Carol Twombly of the classic face cut in the 1720s by
the English typographer William Caslon (1692–1766). Dutch typefaces
of the late seventeenth century served as Caslon's models for his
design, which became the first major English type to achieve wide
popularity. The modern version has smoothed out some of the
idiosyncrasies of the original cutting, while retaining much of the
warmth and straightforward honesty that have made the face a
favorite for almost three centuries.

Printed on paper that is acid-free and meets the requirements of the
American National Standard for Permanence of Paper for
Printed Library Materials, z39.48-1992. ♾

Book design by Erin Kirk New, Watkinsville, Georgia
Typography by Grapevine Publishing Services, Madison, Wisconsin
Printed and bound by Worzalla Publishing Company,
Stevens Point, Wisconsin